ST PETERSBURG BETWEEN
THE REVOLUTIONS

ST PETERSBURG BETWEEN THE REVOLUTIONS

Workers and Revolutionaries, June 1907–February 1917

Robert B. McKean

YALE UNIVERSITY PRESS
NEW HAVEN AND LONDON · 1990

In memory
of
my mother and father

Set in Linotron Bembo by Best-set Typesetter Ltd., Hong Kong and printed and bound by The Bath Press, Avon.

Library of Congress Cataloging-in-Publication Data

McKean, Robert B.
    St. Petersburg between the revolutions: workers and revolutionaries, June 1907–February 1917/Robert B. McKean.
        p.   cm.
Includes bibliographical references (p.
    ISBN 0-300-04791-6
    1. Leningrad (R.S.F.S.R.)—History—To 1917.   2. Labor movement—
Russian S.F.S.R.—Leningrad—History—20th century.
    3. Revolutionists—Russian S.F.S.R.—Leningrad—History—20th century.   I. Title.
    DK568.M35   1990
947′.453083—dc20
89-70734
                                        CIP

Maps on pages xvi and xvii reprinted from *1905 in St. Petersburg: Labor, Society, and Revolution* by Gerald D. Surh with the permission of the publishers, Stanford University Press, © 1989 by the Board of Trustees of the Leland Stanford Junior University.

CONTENTS

v

ACKNOWLEDGEMENTS

In the long gestation of this book the author has been indebted to many individuals and institutions for their help, which has been deeply appreciated. In the first place, the University of Stirling and the History Department granted several periods of study leave for research trips to Finland, the Netherlands and the Soviet Union and for writing up the materials gathered. The British Council and the British Academy both financed visits and exchanges to the USSR, Finland and the Netherlands. The services of the staff at the following institutions were of the greatest assistance: in Great Britain, the British Library, the Bodleian Library and St Antony's College Library, Oxford, the libraries of the universities of Aberdeen, Birmingham, Cambridge, Glasgow, Leeds and Stirling (in particular the invaluable aid of the inter-library loan desk); in the Netherlands, the International Institute of Social History in Amsterdam; in Finland, the Slavic Library of the University of Helsinki; in the USSR the library of the Academy of Sciences, the Saltykov-Shchedrin Public Library and the Central State Historical Archives in Leningrad, and the Lenin Library and the Central State Archives of the October Revolution in Moscow. Dr H. Shukman kindly granted me permission to consult his personal copies of the papers of Boris Nikolaevskii. A very great debt is also owed to four colleagues who read and commented in a most illuminating way on various parts of the manuscript; Roy Campbell (Emeritus Professor of History in the University of Stirling), Neil Tranter (Senior Lecturer in History at the University of Stirling), Geoff Swain (Lecturer in History at Bristol Polytechnic), and Robert Service (Senior Lecturer in History at the School of Slavonic and East European Studies, University of London). Important works by German scholars were made available to the author by his good friend John Lynch who translated them in exemplary fashion. Above all by far the greatest debt owed is to the two secretaries of the History Department at the University of Stirling, Margaret Hendry and Margaret Dickson, who transcribed innumerable drafts of a manuscript still written in longhand, if not quite by quill pen on vellum, on to the mysteries of the word processor. The most heartfelt thanks is extended to them.

ABBREVIATIONS, DATES AND TERMS

Abbreviations

The following abbreviations are used in the text.

AIT	Association of Industry and Trade.
GAU	Chief Artillery Administration (Ministry of War).
MVD	Ministry of Internal Affairs.
MTP	Ministry of Trade and Industry.
OK	Organisational Committee (Menshevik).
OSO	Special Council for Defence.
PK	Petersburg Committee (Bolshevik).
POZF	St Petersburg Society of Mill and Factory Owners.
PVO	Petrograd Military District.
ROK	Russian Organising Commission (of the Prague Conference, 1912).
RSDRP	Russian Social Democratic Workers' Party
SRs	Socialist Revolutionaries.
TsGAOR	Central State Archives of the October Revolution (in Moscow).
TsGIA	Central State Historical Archives (in Leningrad).
TsK	Central Committee (Bolshevik).
TsVPK	Central War-Industries Committee.

Dates

All dates are given in the Old Style. Until February 1918 the old (Julian) calendar remained in use in Russia. In the twentieth century it was thirteen days behind the new (Gregorian) calendar in use in the rest of Europe.

Terms

State Duma	the elected lower house of the Russian parliament created by the Fundamental Laws of April 1906.

fraction	the technical term for the parliamentary groups of the political parties.
guberniia	a province.
kassy	the elected sickness insurance funds established by the 1912 Law on Sickness Insurance.
meshchanstvo	one of the four estates or sosloviia into which the Russian population were officially classed; the term 'petty bourgeoisie' is a rough translation of this category.
nakaz	the mandate given by a group of electors to a candidate for elected office.
praktiki	practical workers; those Social Democrats and Socialist Revolutionaries working in the labour organisations legalised after the 1905 revolution.
pud	a measure of weight: 1 pud equalled 36.1 lb.
Stavka	the General Headquarters of the Russian army at the front during the First World War.
zemliachestvo	an association of peasants residing in a city or town; the members came from the same village or *volost'*.
zemstvos	the zemstvos (*zemstva*) were elected organs of local self government established in 1864 at provincial (*guberniia*) and district (*uezd*) level.

guberniia a province.

kassy the elected sickness insurance funds established by the 1912 Law on Sickness Insurance.

meshchanstvo one of the four estates or sosloviia into which the Russian population were officially classed; the term 'petty bourgeoisie' is a rough translation of this category.

nakaz the mandate given by a group of electors to a candidate for elected office.

praktiki practical workers; those Social Democrats and Socialist Revolutionaries working in the labour organisations legalised after the 1905 revolution.

pud a measure of weight: 1 pud equalled 36.1 lb.

Stavka the General Headquarters of the Russian army at the front during the First World War.

zemliachestvo an association of peasants residing in a city or town; the members came from the same village or *volost'*.

zemstvos the zemstvos (*zemstva*) were elected organs of local self government established in 1864 at provincial (*guberniia*) and district (*uezd*) level.

INTRODUCTION

No other event in the history of the twentieth century apart from the Nazi revolution has so captured the attention of historians as the Russian revolution of 1917 or aroused such partisan political passions. Until recently much of the historical writing on the revolution was at the level of general studies or monographs concerned with the high politics of the period or the role of revolutionary parties and their leaders. In the last decade or so, Western students of the revolution, influenced by the great advances made in the social history of European labour movements, have redirected the focus of concern both on to the masses, the peasants, workers and soldiers, and the history of the revolution in particular cities, such as Moscow, Petrograd and Saratov. Attention, too, has focused upon the first dress rehearsal for 1917 in 1905–7 with works devoted to the soldiers' experience, Moscow, St Petersburg, the Socialist Revolutionaries and the peasants in the south-west. The Duma politics of the new constitutional era after 1906, Stolypin's agrarian reforms and the impact of the First World War on industrial mobilisation have been explored in depth. Yet with the exception of two excellent monographs devoted to the legal labour movement in St Petersburg and Moscow between 1907 and 1914, no overall analysis in English of the history of labour in the capital between the revolutions of 1905 and 1917 has been attempted. The purpose of the present monograph is to fill this gap in Western historical literature.

In its definition of 'the St Petersburg labour movement' this study rests upon a broad understanding of the term. The history of the revolutionary parties and legal labour institutions cannot be divorced from their economic and social setting and the changes therein over the decade. Nor can the attitudes and actions of state authorities and employers be ignored, as these exerted a powerful influence upon the relationships between workers and socialist parties, as well as between them both and the state and factory owners.

The work, too, differs from other Western studies of the Russian labour movement and revolutionary parties in the early twentieth century in that the author was fortunate to gain extensive access to the wealth of archival sources in the Soviet Union pertaining to almost all aspects of the topic, thus supplementing the more limited range available of published primary material and of the more widespread contemporary labour and socialist press. The archives of the Tsarist secret police, the Okhrana, provided an invaluable corrective to the exaggerated reporting of revolutionary newspapers and periodicals, the selected reminiscences of socialist activists and the slanted collections of documents published in the USSR. At the same time the papers of the St Petersburg employers' association and the various Tsarist ministries allowed a more thorough examination of the vagaries of labour policy-making by bureaucrats, police officials, generals and industrialists.

The first central theme of this book is that the politicisation of the St Petersburg working class, which was limited to a distinct minority of skilled male workers, was less the product of the actions of revolutionary parties and legal labour institutions than the combined influences of the capital's economy, the social composition of the working class and the experience of operatives at work.

The economic and social structures of the capital both facilitated and furnished massive obstacles to labour mobilisation by the revolutionary opponents of the regime. The sectoral and occupational diversity of the labour force was a basic determining influence in labour history. Contrary to Soviet and most Western accounts, the dominance of commerce and the service sector (to 1914 at least) ensured that the largest component of the total labour force were commercial–industrial employees and servants who proved impervious to organisation or protest. Within a broadly based manufacturing setting, which embraced artisanal as well as factory forms of production, entire branches (animal and mineral products, food processing, textiles, woodworking) and types of labour (the semi-skilled and unskilled, women, peasant workers) lagged far behind in the strike struggles of 1912 to 1914 and 1915–16, in unionisation, participation in parliamentary and insurance elections and readership of the left-wing press. The dominant weight of peasant workers within the work-force, which became even more pronounced in the war years, acted as a further drag upon labour militancy. On the other hand, the greater size of the metalworking sector in St Petersburg, whose contribution to the urban economy grew disproportionately after 1914, ensured that its skilled, young male workers, together with their artisanal counterparts, who were in the main hereditary proletarians, urban-reared, better educated, more highly paid, comprised the guiding element in revolutionary and legal labour politics, as well as industrial unrest.

The economic history of St Petersburg was of equal importance in the evolution of labour and revolutionary politics. The three-year recession after 1907 allowed industrialists to undo the workers' conquests in the revolution of 1905 in a counter-offensive which itself nourished the very protest it sought to quench. Whilst the pre-war boom both created the conditions conducive to a revival of stoppages and subverted the employers' endeavours to apply unremitting repression, the wartime heated expansion of the economy permitted industrialists to buy off renewed unrest through high profitability, whilst contributing immeasurably to the incipient disintegration of the city's life by early 1917.

In similar fashion, the autocratic order in the factories, the conditions of work therein, as well as the St Petersburg employers' rejection of a West European style of industrial relations, acted as a major stimulant to workers' hostility to the propertied classes. On the part of the authorities, the inability of the bureaucracy to develop a clear-cut set of labour policies and its inconsistent wavering between reform, paternalism and repression, in conjunction with industrialists' antagonism to working-class representation, made highly problematic the evolution of labour politics in the capital along an evolutionary, peaceful path.

Another major theme of the book is that all the revolutionary parties, including the Bolsheviks, proved incapable of capitalising to a significant degree upon Petersburg workers' general estrangement from the regime. The importance attached by Bolsheviks to the underground and by the Mensheviks to legal labour organisations both proved misguided. Neither could act as a successful mechanism of mass mobilisation. Throughout the entire decade none of the revolutionary groups ever succeeded in establishing permanent, illegal all-city or district structures. All remained at the level of miniscule factory collectives in a very restricted range of industries and districts. None of the new legal labour institutions ever succeeded in establishing deep root among more than a minority of operatives. Trade unionism remained a sickly infant, lacking the healthy nourishment of regular finances or membership. The sickness insurance funds created under the 1912 legislation were restricted to their particular sphere of competence. The bulk of workers preferred sensationalist literature to the socialist press. During the war, the Labour Group of the Central War-Industries Committee lost support for most of 1916 by its non-revolutionary course.

A further leitmotiv is the divorce that runs through all the revolutionary parties between their nominal intellectual leaders in exile in Western Europe, riven by ideological schisms, and their predominantly working-class followers in the capital. None of the socialist luminaries in emigration, including Vladimir I. Lenin, exerted any meaningful influence over their parties or events. The unsung heroes of the Petersburg labour movement were the second-rank activists upon whose initiative rested the major policy decisions concerning the tactics and strategy of the local socialist groups. The revolutionary sub-élite was not afraid to reject the policy pronouncements and pretensions to leadership of exiled bosses. In two major areas, in their response to émigré factionalism and the outbreak of the First World War, they clashed head on with those living abroad. Local Bolsheviks in particular evinced an unquenchable thirst for the restoration of Social Democratic unity.

This study also seeks to counterbalance the distortions of official Soviet historiography which concentrates almost exclusively upon the Bolsheviks, falsely equates Bolshevism with Leninism, and ignores the contribution made by the other socialist factions. In fact Bolshevism, Menshevism and Socialist-Revolutionism all fragmented after the defeat of the 1905 revolution and then were further split by their respective responses to the First World War. Within the broader socialist movement, Social Democracy and even Bolshevism, Leninists were never in a majority. Even when Bolsheviks made limited headway against Mensheviks in 1913 and 1914, the real victors were independent-minded Bolsheviks who were far from being pliant tools in Lenin's hands. After 1914 the local Bolsheviks' distinctive stance upon the war scarcely enabled them to be described at all as Leninists. At different times Otzovists, Vperedists, the Bolshevik Conciliators and the Mezhraionka outnumbered the Leninists either on their own or in combination. Socialist Revolutionaries and Mensheviks, too, were not absent from the labour scene. Indeed practical collaboration amongst all socialist groups was a constant factor, given the paucity and feebleness of workshop cells.

The study highlights the extreme importance of industrial unrest between 1912 and 1917 as the chief vehicle for articulating working-class political and economic discontent in the absence of powerful revolutionary parties or professional organisations. Politically inspired strikes, the main form of labour factory protest, occurred above all in heavy industry, whose performance was vital to rearmament before and during the war. Many stoppages, too, were expressive of the opposition of mostly skilled workers to the autocratic factory order. On the other hand, the threat posed to the regime by labour disputes was less than it feared before the autumn of 1916. The geographic and sectoral basis of strikes was restricted for the most part to skilled operatives in medium-sized, privately owned plants in machine construction and electrical equipment industries in the Vyborg and Petersburg Side districts. The numerous frailties of the socialist factions and trade unions prevented them from offering effective leadership to labour protest, converting it into mass support for their goals or erecting permanent organisations upon it. The authorities and the employers, more by chance than conscious planning, proved successful in containing the strike waves by a combination of repression and concessions.

Indeed it may be argued that the regime might have been able to survive in its capital in the short run if it had not been for the economic and social impact of the war upon the working class, the middle classes and the soldiers of Petrograd by the last months of 1916 and the first weeks of 1917. The breakdown of the city's economy, together with changes in the composition of a bloated garrison and the impact of high politics all combined in a dangerous, explosive mixture which was to be ignited by the shortage of bread in late February 1917.

Map 1 St. Petersburg in 1905 (see key below)

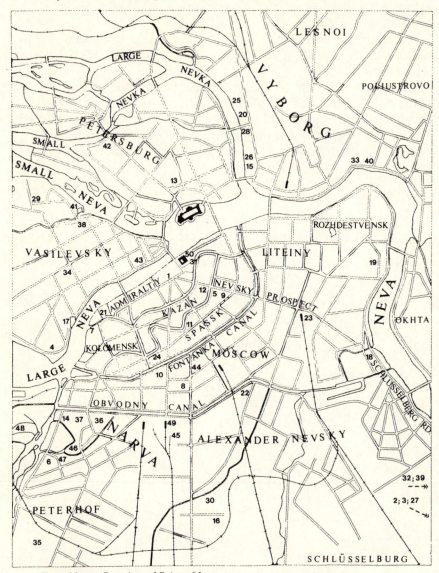

Key to Map 1: *Factories and Points of Interest*

1. Aleksandrovsk Garden
2. Aleksandrovsk Machine Works
3. Atlas Iron & Copper Foundry & Machine Plant
4. Baltic Shipyards
5. City Duma
6. Ekaterinhof Spinnery
7. Franco-Russian Machine Building Works
8. Free Economic Society
9. Gostinyi Dvor
10. Government Stationers
11. Haymarket (*Sennoi rynok*)
12. Kazan Cathedral and Square
13. Kirchner Bindery
14. L. L. König Spinnery
15. Lessner Machine Works
16. Mechanized Shoe Factory
17. Nail Plant
18. Nevsky Shipbuilding and Machine Works
19. Nevsky Spinnery
20. Nevsky Thread Factory ("Nevka")
21. New Admiralty Shipyards
22. New Spinnery
23. Nikolaev Railroad Station
24. Nikol'skii Market
25. Nikol'sk Weaving Factory

Map 2 City District and Subdistrict Boundaries

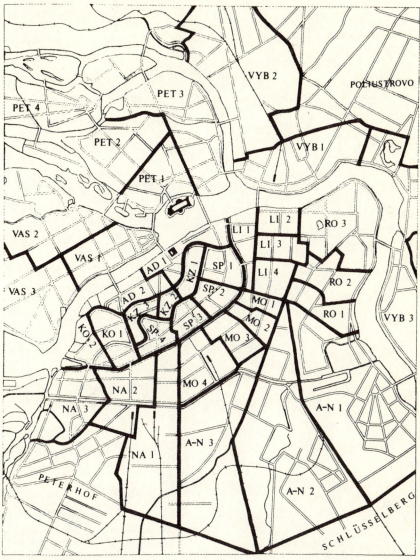

Key to Map 1 (continued)

26. Nobel' Plant
27. Obukhov Steel Mill
28. Old Sampson Spinning and Weaving Factory
29. Osipov Leather Works
30. Ozoling Machine Plant
31. Palace Square
32. Paul Factory
33. Phoenix Machine Construction Works
34. Possel' Horseshoe Works
35. Putilov Plant or Works
36. Russian-American Rubber Factory
37. Russian Spinnery
38. Siemens & Halske Electric Works

39. Spassk & Petrovsk Cotton Mills
40. St. Petersburg Metal Works
41. St. Petersburg Pipe Plant
42. St. Petersburg Rolling & Wire Mill
43. St. Petersburg University
44. Technological Institute
45. Train Car Construction Plant
46. Triumphal Arch (Narva Gates)
47. Triumphal Spinnery
48. Voronin, Liutsh & Cheshire Weaving Factory
49. Warsaw Railroad Station
50. Winter Palace

Chapter 1

ST PETERSBURG: URBAN ECONOMY AND WORKING CLASS

A foreign traveller visiting St Petersburg in the decade before the outbreak of the First World War, who trusted his guidebook and restricted his sightseeing to the recommended architectural masterpieces, art galleries and theatres, would scarcely have been aware that the Imperial capital was not only the seat of the court and the central government of the Empire but also a major industrial centre.[1] As befitted Peter the Great's vision of his northern foundation functioning as 'a window on the West', the city would have conveyed the impression to the less discerning visitor, at least in its external appearance, of a modern European metropolis. In the words of the English MP, Henry Norman, 'any quarter of it would be at home in Paris or Potsdam or Pesth'.[2] Although the capital lacked an overhead metropolitan railway (as in Berlin) or an underground (which London had pioneered), electric trams serviced its central streets; motor taxi-cabs were being introduced (328 by 1913) and the privileged possessed motor cars (2,585 in total by 1913). The telegraph and the railway connected the remote metropolis to all parts of Europe, the Empire and, via the Trans-Siberian, to China and the Far East. That vanished symbol of European bourgeois comfort and elegance in travel, International Wagons-Lits, had an office on the main thoroughfare. There were luxurious hotels such as the Astoria or the Evropeiskaia; fashionable restaurants, owned mainly by French or Germans; elegant shops on the Nevskii Prospekt, purveying consumer goods and foodstuffs from all over Russia and Europe; a Stock Exchange; electric street lighting; a rapidly expanding telephone service (56,185 subscribers by 1916). Modern mass forms of entertainment had arrived. At the close of 1911, there were 100 cinemas, 23 on the Nevskii alone; a large number of football clubs; even a nine-hole golf course. The former *Times* correspondent, Charles Dobson, noted in 1910 with some condescension that 'foreign crazes like bridge, diabolo and American jig-saw puzzles caught on fast enough . . .'. Public advertising, too, had made its appearance in the form of bill-posting.[3] Yet a more perceptive tourist would have noted in the course of a stroll along the Neva embankments the factory chimneys in the distance, and would have been somewhat alarmed by Karl Baedeker's injunction, printed in bold type, that 'unboiled water should on no account be drunk'.[4] A very adventurous sightseer, his or her curiosity aroused, perhaps, by the same guidebook's relegation of the 'unattractive' Vyborg district to a short paragraph, would have discovered, if he or she ventured thither, another and very different St Petersburg. The intrepid investigator would have encountered outlying working-class areas, whose urban environment far from deserved the epithets 'modern' and 'metropolitan'. These were districts without public transport, with ill-lit or unlit, unpaved streets, wooden houses, minimal or no piped water, a complete lack of sewerage, grossly overcrowded apartments, higher death rates and greater susceptibility to disease. Such industrial regions, with their urgent social problems, had represented a potential threat to the established order from the 1890s. Their working-class inhabitants had come together with members of the liberal professions, the intelligentsia and white-collar employees to force the monarchy in 1905 to grant the October Manifesto; the same coalition of social forces, with the crucial support of a revolt in a garrison swollen by wartime recruitment, overthrew the dynasty on 27 February 1917. In short, like its twin capital Moscow, St Petersburg was a 'dual' city of two different and sharply contrasting areas; the central part 'with the outward appearance of a modern and western city', and an outer ring of suburbs, woefully deficient in the attributes of modernity.[5] It was, also, a city with a dual economy and, consequently, a dual society and culture.

I

THE URBAN ECONOMY

Although industrialisation did not exert a great impact overall on Russian urbanisation in the nineteenth century and cities did not play a prominent role in the industrialising process, St Petersburg was a notable exception.[6] The city developed from the late 1860s as a centre of industrial and commercial might (see Table 1.i).

As distinct from Moscow which was at the centre of an industrialised province and which, consequently, did not occupy a dominating position in the local economy, St Petersburg exercised economic hegemony over its swampy, forested hinterland. According to the factory inspectorate, in December 1912 the city gave employment to

Table 1.i: *The Population of the City of St Petersburg (with suburbs), 1881–1914*[7]

	Total population	% increase	
15 Dec. 1881	928,000		
15 Dec. 1890	1,033,600	1881–90	11.3
15 Dec. 1900	1,439,613	1890–1900	39.3
15 Dec. 1910	1,905,589	1900–10	32.4
1 Jan. 1914	2,118,500	1910–14	11.2

188,983 industrial workers in its factories and mills, whereas the annual report of the governor of the province noted that a mere 34,221 individuals were similarly employed outside the city.[8]

It would be erroneous, however, to give the impression, as Soviet historians of the city have done, that the economy of the capital was overwhelmingly industrial. As the city census of 15 December 1910 revealed (see Table 1.ii), the urban economy rested upon a broad, heterogeneous base. It was distinguished by occupational and sectoral diversity.

Table 1.ii: *St Petersburg: Hired Labour Force, by Occupation, 15 December 1910*[9]

	Number	% of total
Catering	25,222	3.4
Factory manufacturing and construction	238,919	31.8
Individual artisans (*odinochki*)	58,000	7.7
Municipal enterprises and public utilities	41,000	5.5
Servants	260,000	34.6
Trade and insurance	76,403	10.2
Transport	51,623	6.9
TOTAL	751,167	100.1

The city's economy encompassed a bewildering variety of sources of employment, size of establishments, forms of ownership and sources of capital formation, which deny facile generalisations.

In the first place, following a pattern common to other European urban centres, the service industries (trade and insurance, catering, and domestic and occupational service) rather than factory manufacturing were responsible for the bulk of jobs. In 1910 361, 625, or 48 per cent, of wage earners found work in this sector, within which servants in private homes, factories and institutions comprised 260,000, or 35 per cent, of the total hired labour force. Because the revolutionary parties, for ideological reasons, regarded such workers as 'backward', 'unconscious' and 'dark' (*temnye*), they paid scant regard to them in this period as potential sources of support for their cause, with the exception to some extent of shop assistants and clerks. Moreover, in terms of the value of output, commerce occupied first place. Even at the start of the twentieth century, the general turnover of trade within the city reached 800 to 900 million roubles per annum, whereas according to the contemporary statistician D. P. Kandaurov the value of production of factory industry was 601 million roubles in 1913.[10] Within factory manufacturing the heavy goods sector (metalworking and machine construction) did not occupy quite such a dominating position as most investigators have suggested. It is true that in 1913, unlike Moscow where textiles constituted the most important industrial branch, metalworking and machines gave employment to over 40 per cent of the factory labour force and accounted for 35 per cent of the value of factory production. However, light industry (textiles and food), working for the mass consumer market, was responsible for 29 per cent of factory employees and contributed 31 per cent of the value of factory production.[11]

The deficiencies of official statistics have led in many historical accounts to a distorted picture of the balance between large-scale and small-scale, factory and artisanal forms of production in St Petersburg, as well as between modern and more ancient forms of retailing in the pre-war years.[12] Contrary to the widespread notion of the complete dominance of the factory form of production, a misconception fostered in part by the city censuses combining factory and artisanal groups into one undifferentiated whole, artisanal entrepreneurship flourished. Victoria Bonnell has calculated that in 1902 factory workers numbered 161,924 and in 1900 artisanal workers 150,709.[13] Whilst large-scale factory production predominated in textiles, metalworking and machine construction, small-scale, artisanal modes of manufacture (*remeslo*) were common in the food industry, widespread in printing and the treatment of animal products, as well as the construction industry. In addition the fabrication of clothing and shoes, woodworking, carriage-making, the fashioning of gold and silverware were all organised overwhemingly in small and dispersed workshops and firms.[14] In trade, too, the majority of the 16 to 20,000 commercial establishments were inconsiderable in size. The city had not witnessed to any large extent the retail revolution represented by the modern department store. Instead, its two most famous trading emporia, Gostinnyi Dvor and Passazh, both on the Nevskii, housed a multitude of petty trading outlets, 300 and 60 respectively. In 1913 there were 20 such markets. In addition some 14 to 18,000 street traders still hawked their wares in time-honoured fashion.[15] In short, St Petersburg possessed a dual economy – an economy of modern, large-scale, technically advanced, factories and mills, and an economy of a multiplicity of small-scale, technologically backward handicraft workshops, and older informal forms of retailing.

There were, also, different forms of ownership. The capital's manufacturing industry was noted for the presence of several plants of considerable size owned by the state. The Ministry of the Navy exercised responsibility for the Admiralty and Baltic Shipyards within the city, the Izhora arms-works at Kolpino and the Obukhov steel-works at Aleksandrovskoe Selo, both to the south-east of the capital. The Chief Artillery Administration (GAU) of the Ministry of War supervised the Arsenal, the Ordnance, Cartridge and Pipe works, Okhta Explosive and Okhta Gunpowder (all within the city limits) and the Sestroretsk small-arms works at the town of the same name (on the Gulf of Finland).[16] The balance of ownership between joint-stock companies, family firms and individuals varied widely between and within the different sectors of the economy. In 1913, out of 953 industrial enterprises counted by Kanduarov 151 belonged to joint-stock companies. While 23 of the 31 cotton mills were organised on a joint-stock basis, only 42 of the 284 metalworking and machine construction enterprises were joint-stock. Joint-stock forms of organisation also dominated the confectionery and tobacco industry. But in all other subdivisions of industry petty family firms or one-person businesses prevailed. Paper and printing trades, too, were characterised by the paucity of joint-stock companies (there were 17 such companies but 312 establishments), as were construction, clothing and retail trades (in which there were a mere 33 joint-stock ventures by 1913).[17] Although no overall estimate is possible, it would not be an unreasonable assumption that within the urban economy as a whole the joint-stock form of organisation was in a minority.

It is an axiomatic view of Soviet scholars, deriving ultimately from Vladimir I. Lenin's *Imperialism: The Highest Stage of Capitalism* and his writings in 1917, that, to quote P. V. Volobuev, 'the possibility and the inevitability of the socialist revolution in Russia . . . derived from the fact that there existed the hegemony of monopoly capital over the country's economy'. In the years before the First World War, A. L. Sidorov has argued, 'the high concentration of production facilitated the coalescence of the banks with industry and the formation of monopolies'; . . . The interests of industry and bank capital (Russian and foreign) and Tsardom became closely interwoven . . .'. The pre-war economy of St Petersburg is held to be the outstanding

5

paradigm of this process. Thus E. E. Kruze has written that 'there continued in 1909–1913 the process, begun earlier, of the fusing of bank and industrial capital and in consequence the formation of finance capital'.[18]

As far as heavy industry in the capital is concerned, there can be no doubt that the industrial revival after 1909, the attractiveness of investment in arms manufacture consequent upon naval and military rearmament and the expansion of companies' plants and new share issues (see later in this chapter, pp. 12–13) led to much greater involvement in investment in this sector on the part of the powerful St Petersburg joint-stock commercial banks. At the same time the inflow of foreign investors' monies into Russian banking rather than directly into industry after 1908, as well as the participation of foreign, mainly French and German, banks in placing Russian securities abroad, resulted in the greater reliance, direct and indirect, of St Petersburg heavy industry upon foreign capital.[19] In the case of Putilov, the largest joint-stock engineering company in the Empire, for example, the Russo-Asiatic bank came to regard investment in the firm as a highly attractive proposition after 1908 as the share of lucrative artillery orders from the state in its total output rose steadily, reaching 68 per cent of profits by 1911. Its chance came in 1912 when the firm sought to increase its capital from 16 to 25 million roubles in order to purchase the Neva Shipyards from the government and re-equip its factory. The bank, in conjunction with a syndicate of French banks headed by the Banque de l'Union Parisienne, bought the shares, thereby ending the dominant influence of the St Petersburg International within the company.[20] The same fate befell Baranovskii in the spring of 1914, with the two same French and Russian banks in this case displacing the St Petersburg Loan and Discount. The last-named bank, which had long financed G. A. Lessner, used the company as a bridgehead before the war for diversifying its activity into the arms industry, as the firm altered the balance of its output from steam engines and boilers into shells and mines.[21] As a new and technically advanced branch of industry, electrical manufacturing was particularly penetrated by foreign capital. Thus, Siemens and Halske and Siemens-Schukkert, the main manufacturers of dynamos, were directly controlled by the Berlin headquarters of the famous German company, whilst the Russian subsidiary of the Berlin Tiudor firm enjoyed a monopoly of the production of accumulators.[22] According to the calculations of E. E. Kruze, in 1913 25 of the 42 joint-stock companies involved in metalworking and machine construction were financed by St Petersburg banks, principally the Russo-Asiatic (eight firms) and the St Petersburg Loan and Discount (six).[23]

In the textile industry, in contrast, the role of bank capital was minimal. In 1913 a mere three of 23 joint-stock companies in this sector were dependent upon the banks and of these three, two were solely financed by external banks. Foreign influences were not absent, but took the form of ownership by non-Russian families or groups of investors. Given the early date of the emergence of textile manufacturing (in the 1830s and 1840s), which was overwhelmingly centred on cotton, much of this extraneous presence was British. The Neva Thread company, the largest of its kind in Russia, was completely dominated by J. and P. Coats of Paisley in Scotland. Petrovskaia and Spasskaia cotton were known to generations of mill hands as the 'Maxwells' as they were managed by David and James Maxwell for the British shareholders. Even some of the mills bore the names of their British owners, such as James Beck and James Thornton. The mill owners financed expansion from profits rather than through resort to the banks.[24]

This relative absence of bank capital in textiles was paralleled in other branches of factory industry. In 1913 a mere five of 25 joint-stock companies in food and tobacco were beholden in some way to the banks; one of the fourteen in chemicals; none of the seventeen in paper and polygraphy; three of the nine in leather; none of the eight such companies in the mechanical working of wood. In sum, out of 151 joint-stock companies involved in factory industry, 44 (or 29 per cent) were linked to bank capital; of the 44, 25 (or 57 per cent) were involved in heavy industry. Because she overlooked the failure of the official statistics to take into account the contribution of artisanal workshops to total manufacturing output, Kruze's suggestion that the 44 companies were responsible for 53 per cent 'of the entire output of Petersburg industry', overestimates their contribution.[25]

When the field of vision is broadened to encompass the entire urban economy, taking into account the service industries as well as manufacturing (factory and artisanal), the role of the commercial banks is further diminished. The overwhelming majority of commercial enterprises were small-scale and had not been penetrated by bank capital. Thus the theory of finance capital as applied to St Petersburg's economy, at least pre-war, requires substantial modification. It was heavy industry alone, not the economy as a whole, which felt the impact of bank capital between 1908 and 1914.

In the aftermath of the revolutionary upheaval of 1905 to 1907, St Petersburg's industrialists faced severe economic difficulties. Heavy industry, which had been plunged into a depression by the withdrawal of government contracts in 1901, had staged a short-lived, if limited, recovery during the Russo-Japanese War. The termination of hostilities and the labour disorders of 1905 and 1906 brought on a renewed recession, which lasted until 1910. The domestic private

market for capital goods afforded too narrow a basis for a permanent
revival. Although textiles had fared much better during the economic downturn after 1901 – peasant demand remained relatively
buoyant – towards the end of 1908 their pace also slackened. Printing
had experienced a boom during 'the days of freedom' due to the
relaxation in the laws of censorship, but the political reaction from
1907 onwards led to the closure of many firms. In addition to those
factors specific to particular branches of production, all employers
had to take into account the gains workers had secured in 1905 and
1906 largely as a result of strike action. Substantial pay rises and the
introduction of an eight- or nine-hour day and of overtime paid at
time-and-a-half rates, coupled with a chronic dearth of orders,
increased the pressure to reduce the wage bill in a city whose
manufacturing industry always had suffered from higher costs of
labour than elsewhere in the Empire, and promoted efforts to
increase labour productivity. The events of 1905, moreover, had
severely threatened the old autocratic factory order by resulting in
the abolition of fines and searches and the election of workers'
factory commissions or committees which granted operatives a
measure of influence over hiring and firing, hours of work and the
setting of rates. All of this was interpreted by factory administrations
as an unacceptable dilution of managerial authority.[26] In the years
after 1906, the capital's industrial community searched for policies
which would cut the costs of production in order to raise competitiveness, evade or abolish outright workers' new economic rewards
and restore the full prerogatives of management.

The first course of action pursued by factory owners amounted in
effect to a direct assault upon the benefits the labour force had secured
in the revolution. Mass dismissals affected all sectors in 1907 to 1909.
In engineering, by January 1908, 36 per cent of employees had
received the sack. St Petersburg Metals closed its shell shop; the
Neva Shipyards let go 300 in 1908 and a further 700 in 1909. As a
survey by the union of metalworkers revealed in 1908, the employers
used their financial plight as an opportunity to rid themselves of the
most skilled, highly paid, longest-serving metalworkers, who were
regarded with much justice as the most militant group within the
industry. They threw on to the streets the old, the sick and 'the
disturbers of internal order as well'. During 1908 lay-offs and
filtering of operatives spread to printing and textiles.[27] Reductions
in rates of pay of 30 per cent or higher assumed wide dimensions
throughout heavy and light industry in the years 1907 to 1911. In the
pressure-gauge shop of the Langenzippen metalworking and casting
plant wages were cut by half; in the boiler shop of the Baltic
Shipyards by 40 per cent.[28] Workers' factory commissions or committees were disbanded (as at Neva Shipyards); shop delegates

arrested or sacked (the Pipe works); meetings banned (St Petersburg Metals).[29] Fines and searches, which were thoroughly detested by workers, were swiftly reintroduced at many plants as early as 1907 and 1908 – among others at the Franco-Russian Society, Odner, Neva Shipyards, Pipe works, Obukhov, San Galli and St Petersburg Metals.[30] Less frequent was a direct and immediate assault upon the eight- or nine-hour day, operatives' most prized conquest of the revolution. It was not until 1909 that Aleksandrov Machines and the Franco-Russian Society increased the eight-hour day to eleven hours and St Petersburg Engineering from nine to ten hours. In the same year printshop owners lengthened the working day from nine hours to ten. A more usual practice was to resort to a covert extension of working hours through the adoption of overtime, which was no longer calculated at time and a half (a concession wrung from employers in 1905) but was paid once more at ordinary rates.[31]

The second set of policies adopted by factory administrations may be termed cost-reducing reorganisation.[32]

In the first place in the years of the depression, and even more so during the resurgence prior to the war, in heavy industry (where labour costs were crucial due to the capital-intensive nature of production) there occurred the modernisation of physical plant and an increase in mechanisation and labour-saving technology so as to reduce the high costs of production. The incidence of such technical improvements between and within individual shipyards, engineering and electrical factories was very uneven. The scope seems to have been particularly wide among state-owned plants which were made financially independent of the Treasury after 1905 and responsible for their own profits and losses. Thus at the Izhora small-arms works, new furnaces, machine tools and cranes were installed and an open hearth shop constructed; at Obukhov, electrification was introduced for machine tools and cranes; at the Pipe works, automatic machines appeared. In the private sector, the Franco-Russian Society took delivery of steam hammers, pneumatic drills and electrical lifting cranes; Langenzippen and United Cables purchased new machinery.[33] In general companies and plants in the capital goods sector (both state and private) continued to shun product specialisation, manufacturing as before a broad range of output, a fact which limited the adoption of mass production techniques. Plants combined both modernity and obsolescence. The process of re-equipment seems to have proceeded at a much slower pace in light industry. In carton and cigarette manufacturing, machine methods of production became more widespread, whilst electricity was applied to typesetting and electrically powered sewing and cutting machines became more common in the apparel trades.[34] In addition there may have been a greater use of technical and administrative personnel in order to implement innovations in factory organisation and production processes (as will be discussed later).[35]

In the second place women and adolescents began to replace male workers. In textiles the phenomenon reflected a trend which went back to the 1890s. As the factory inspectorate observed in 1912, the reason for this action was that 'the textile owners desire to lower the costs of production . . . by employing cheaper female labour'. In the capital's mills by the close of 1908 some 7,000 men had been replaced by women. By 1913 68 per cent of mill operatives were female as against 62 per cent in 1910 and 55 per cent in 1900.[36] The lower wages universally paid to female workers, as well as the (rather misplaced) belief in their 'docility' and lack of militancy, also made their employment an attractive proposition to engineering industrialists. The extent of the substitution of skilled male metalworkers by semi-skilled female and adolescent labour, however, should not be exaggerated. The installation of new machine tools at some plants in 1909 and 1910 allowed managers to replace older skilled workers with unskilled male apprentices, as at Langenzippen, the Pipe works and St Petersburg Engineering. Women first began to be employed in factories producing nails. Then in the years prior to the war they started to be hired for work as semi-skilled operatives, such as founders, borers and mortising machinists at Aivaz, the Pipe works, the Russian Society and United Cables.[37] Yet the total share of female labour in heavy industry rose at a very modest rate from 2.2 per cent to 2.7 per cent between 1910 and 1913. In 1913 adolescents constituted just 6 per cent of the total labour force in heavy industry.[38] Although dilution by unskilled or semi-skilled women and adolescent workers did not represent a quick or thorough threat to the dominance of the skilled metalworker before the war, the greater utilisation of new techniques was gradually altering the nature of the work he performed. Many tasks hitherto executed by hand and dependent on the experience and knowledge gained during a four-year apprenticeship were now taken over by machine tools, mastery of which required only a few months' training. Skilled metalworkers found themselves restricted more and more to fine metalwork in engineering and, as a consequence, many sought more satisfactory employment in the manufacture of instruments, optics and other such highly qualified branches.[39] The extent to which all these developments undermined the hitherto pre-eminent position of the skilled metalworker in heavy industry, and was perceived as such by him, is highly problematic. The minimal extent of dilution, the great boom of 1911 to 1914, and the consequent severe shortage of highly qualified labour (attested to by the numerous complaints by industrialists on this score) would suggest that the skilled metalworker still had a powerful role. The nature of the pre-war economic strikes in this sector (see Chapter 8) confirms the general impression that the threat to skill as such was not a cardinal factor behind the revived labour unrest.

A third and prominent feature of industrialists' strategy was wage reform in order to cut the wages bill, increase labour productivity and provide monetary incentives as a means to restore order in the workshops. Before 1905 pay generally had been calculated on a daily basis. But on 4 March 1908 the Engineering Section of the St Petersburg Society of Mill and Factory Owners (POZF), following the lead of the Baltic and Obukhov plants, resolved to replace daily wages by hourly rates of pay. By 1911 most enterprises (both state and private) in the capital goods sector had transferred to the new system. Many adopted what contemporaries described as the 'American method' of calculating pay, i.e. worksheets were introduced, on which the time of starting and finishing work and the labour of each hour were noted, thereby permitting a more exact accounting of work time by technical staff than had been the practice before 1905 and facilitating further cuts in rates of pay. In 1906 and 1907 the new system was introduced at Baltic Shipyards, N. Glebov, Obukhov, Pneumatic Machines, San Galli and Siemens and Halske.[40] Rates bureaux were established at, among others, Admiralty Shipyards, Lessner, Neva Shipyards, Nobel and Semenov, and wage incentive schemes introduced at many establishments, including the state-owned Baltic Shipyards, Obukhov and Sestroretsk small-arms works and private firms such as Phoenix, Pneumatic Machines, St Petersburg Engineering, San Galli and Semenov. In plants where central rating departments were introduced, the foremen's powers were consequently curtailed and workers lost their former right to bargain directly with foremen over rates of pay. Yet in many plants rate setting remained the prerogative of workshop foremen. The older custom of paying a full day's wage on Saturdays despite work ceasing at 2 o'clock in the afternoon was abolished.[41] It is not known whether these practices were adopted in other industrial sectors. Within heavy industry the changes did have the intended effect of lowering workers' earnings and intensifying the pace of work.

Fourthly, reorganisation involved a campaign to reduce inefficiencies in the utilisation of working time. The existing practice of allowing workers to arrive fifteen minutes late was abolished and some factories even introduced turnstiles and automatic clocks at the entrance to their premises, at which workers now had to time-stamp a card on entering or leaving, with the inevitable fine for lateness. The electrical industry in particular went over to this system. Some establishments, like the Neva Shipyards in 1912 and the Semenov machine construction company, introduced time and motion study.[42] These innovations, which constituted a further assault upon workshop customs and workers' limited discretion concerning the tempo as well as the pace of work, were unwelcome to the labour force.

In all the welter of new schemes, however, there was one surprising omission – the adoption of the new and fashionable principles of rationalising 'scientific management', propagated by the American Frederick Taylor. Although there was a marked increase of interest by managers and engineers (and socialist commentators including Lenin), in Taylorism – as Dr Hogan has shown – in practice the single St Petersburg factory to attempt to apply Taylor's precepts was that of Ivan Semenov, a populariser of scientific management.[43]

As trade-union leaders, socialist activists and ordinary workers were quick to perceive (the numerous articles and letters in the trade-union and socialist press testify to this), the cumulative effect of all the various strands of the employers' counter-offensive amounted to a sustained and successful onslaught on the 'conquests of 1905'. At least to 1911, wage rates were lowered and the gains of 1905 wiped out; many hands lost their jobs; the *ancien régime* in the factory was restored; the working day lengthened; the pace of labour intensified; shop customs were challenged; the tempo of the working day was altered. In their impact these changes proved to be a prime cause of the great upsurge of industrial unrest in the city on the eve of the First World War. In the economic stoppages of 1912 to 1914 basic workers' demands centred in effect on a return to the 'new order' in the factories so briefly established in 1905 and 1906 and an abrogation of all the hated 'counter reforms' of 1907 to 1911 (see Chapter 8). The employers had not eradicated the causes of labour militancy; they had merely and unwittingly nourished the roots of further discontent.

In the period 1910 to 1914 the fortunes of the city's capital goods industries experienced a remarkable change from recession to boom. As its assistant president, V. V. Zhukovskii, informed the Eighth Congress of the Association of Industry and Trade (AIT) in May 1914 'the revived prosperity of our engineering industry is based on the sudden increase in the amount of orders placed by the Ministries of War and the Navy'.[44] Between 1910 and 1914 government expenditure on armaments rose from 647 million roubles to 959 million. A significant proportion of this increase related to naval programmes – that of 19 May 1911 for the Black Sea Fleet and of 23 June 1912 for the Baltic Fleet.[45]

Many of the armaments contracts went to St Petersburg factories, both state and private, providing a further impetus to plant expansion and modernisation. From 1909 the state-owned Admiralty and Baltic Shipyards built Dreadnoughts. With defence orders worth 125 million roubles by 1913, Putilov spent 30 million roubles on construction work between 1912 and 1914, of which 4 million was devoted to building its own shipyard and 6 million on a new steel workshop. In 1913 the artillery department accounted for 83 per cent of the company's profits. The Russian Society began the erection of shells and mines plants in 1912. Ia. M. Aivaz secured orders worth 2 million roubles in 1913 from GAU and opened a new machine construction factory.[46]

In order to finance these refurbishments, firms had to augment their fixed capital by resort to the banks, thereby increasing their dependence upon the city's financial institutions. There were two ways of raising capital. Some hitherto family firms became joint-stock companies, such as Aivaz (1911), Baranovskii (1912), Langen-zippen (1911) and Nobel (1912). Some chose to resort to the banks: Baranovskii raised its capital from 3.5 to 8 million roubles; Phoenix, 6 to 11 million; Putilov, 12 to 25 million; St Petersburg Metals, 3.5 to 9 million.[47]

The pre-war revival in heavy industry also ensured a growth in profits and dividends. Baranovskii's net profit rose from 473,127 roubles in 1912–13 to 1,118,444 in 1913–14, and its dividend from 7 to 13 per cent. Lessner's net profit between 1913 and 1914 soared by 35 per cent and in 1913 its shareholders received a dividend of 15 per cent. The Russian Society's net profit went from 0.7 million roubles in 1913 to 1.1 million in 1914, when it paid a dividend of 9.5 per cent. The electrical industry, too, was highly profitable, with dividends ranging from 6 per cent at Tiudor in 1914 to 12.5 per cent at Diuflon in 1913–14.[48]

Other sectors of the industrial economy enjoyed mixed fortunes in the years immediately preceding the First World War. Chemicals benefited from the arms race, with a 70 per cent rise in output between 1908 and 1913. The great pre-war building boom in the capital brought spectacular expansion in the manufacture of glass, cement, bricks (their output soared by 83 per cent) and all forms of woodworking, with the formation of new companies such as Zhelezno-Tsement and the Petersburg Glass Industrial Society in 1911. After the setback of 1908 and 1909 and the bad harvest of 1911, textiles recovered well in 1913 and 1914, with an overall increase in output of 21 per cent, 1908 to 1913. Leather, rubber and printing experienced similar growth rates. Food and tobacco alone failed to expand to any considerable extent.[49]

The boom of 1910 to 1914, however, proved a mixed blessing for the organised industrial community of the capital. It entailed impor-tant and unforeseen consequences for the POZF's attempts to fashion a coherent labour strategy (see Chapter 9). The rapid expansion of the manufacturing labour force, in particular in heavy industry, meant that a chronic shortage of skilled labour ('there is a dearth of skilled workers' noted the factory inspectorate's report for 1912) was to undercut any co-ordinated anti-strike action among employers.[50] The growing dependence of the capital goods sector (which dominated the POZF) upon the state for orders ensured that the government's attitude towards labour disaffection and the penalties imposed by state contracts for failure to meet scheduled dates of delivery played a crucial role in the shaping of employers' policies. Rearmament, the product of Russia's declining international status, constituted a spur both to worker belligerence in its impact upon the internal life of the factories and to the efforts of the POZF and the authorities to find a workable solution to the epidemic of strikes that hit the city between 1912 and 1914. It also acted as a fundamental obstacle to the elaboration of a mutually acceptable and effective response. In this ironic fashion, the policies of workshop reorganisation, adopted in part as a response to a depression, were undercut by the long-awaited economic recovery.

II

THE MAKING OF A WORKING CLASS?

Due to the inadequacies of Imperial Russian statistical enquiries it is impossible to calculate the increment in the total hired labour force of St Petersburg between 1908 and 1913. At most there exist imperfect data concerning the expansion in the numbers of factory workers and their distribution between branches of production.

The data furnished by Tables 1.iii to 1.v conform to the general outline of the city's economy in this period sketched in the preceding section. The expansion of the factory labour force set in at the end of 1909 and 1910, when the annual percentage increase in the number of workers leapt to 8 per cent from 2 per cent for 1908–9. After maintaining an even rate of growth in 1910–12 of 11 per cent, a particularly quick tempo of recruitment occurred in 1912 and 1913

Table 1.iii: Number of Factory Workers, St Petersburg Guberniia, 1908–13[51]

	No. of workers		Annual % increase in no. of workers
1908	140,263	1908–09	1.6
1909	142,486	1909–10	8.1
1910	154,014	1910–11	10.6
1911	170,321	1911–12	10.9
1912	188,893	1912–13	15.5
1913	218,258	1908–13	55.6

Table 1.iv: *Occupational Distribution of the Factory Labour Force, St Petersburg City, 1908–13*[52]

	1908		1913	
Occupation	No.	% of total	No.	% of total
Animal products (leather, soap, tallow)	6,794	4.3	8,325	3.6
Chemicals	6,789	4.3	9,685	4.2
Food, drink, tobacco	18,284	11.6	20,406	9.0
Mechanical production of wood	4,569	2.9	7,146	3.1
Metals and machines	53,945	34.1	95,336	41.9
Paper and printing	19,038	12.0	24,507	10.8
Rubber	7,157	4.5	11,000	4.8
Silicates (cement, glass, brick-works)	7,604	4.8	8,556	3.7
Textiles	33,972	21.5	42,965	18.9
TOTAL	158,152	100.0	227,926	100.0

Table 1.v: *Percentage Increase in Size of the Factory Labour Force by Occupation, St Petersburg City, 1908–13* (see note 52)

Animal products	22.5
Chemicals	42.6
Food, drink, tobacco	11.6
Mechanical production of wood	56.5
Metals and machines	76.7
Paper and printing	28.7
Rubber	53.7
Silicates	12.5
Textiles	26.5
TOTAL	44.1

(15.5 per cent) as the rearmament programme's knock-on effect took hold. Among industrial occupations heavy industry revealed the most rapid progress with an augmentation of 76 per cent in its payroll between 1908 and 1913. Almost as fast rises in the number of employees took place in rubber manufacturing (54 per cent), the mechanical production of wood (57 per cent) and chemicals (43 per cent). The silicates sector increased more swiftly than Table 1.v would suggest as its plants, being located mostly in the province, were not included in the two statistical surveys of the city's factories.

Its work-force grew in fact by 49 per cent between 1910 and 1913.[53] The slowest rates of growth were recorded in paper and printing (29 per cent), textiles (27 per cent) and the food and drink sector (12 per cent). The varying pace of economic expansion within industries was reflected in the changes in the occupational distribution of the labour force between 1908 and 1913. The weight of factory employees in metallurgy and machine construction became even more pronounced, rising from 34 per cent to 42 per cent of the total. This stood in stark contrast to their 16.6 per cent share of the All-Russian factory labour force in 1913 or Moscow in 1912 where metalworkers accounted for a mere 16 per cent of factory hands but textile workers 35 per cent.[54] In the capital the proportion of mill hands fell between 1908 and 1913 from 22 per cent to 19 per cent of factory workers and of employees in the food, drink and tobacco industries from 12 per cent to 9 per cent. As a consequence light industry's share of factory wage earners dropped from 33 per cent in 1908 to 28 per cent in 1913. This image, however, of the dominant position held by metalworkers among the working population is a distorted one. When their numbers are set against the totality of the hired labour force, their percentage share declines precipitately. Although there exist no figures for wage earners in their entirety after 1910, the city census of that year reveals that heavy industry (62,440 operatives) was responsible for a mere 8 per cent of hired employees, whereas the service industries employed 48 per cent and domestic service 35 per cent.[55]

St Petersburg, like Moscow and most European cities, was a city of migrants (*prishli*). Both the general population and its working class grew not by net natural increase but by immigration (see Table 1.vi).

At no point in the period between 1881 and 1910 did the native-born inhabitants of the capital comprise more than 32 per cent of the population. As Table 1.vii reveals, the natural increase of the population in the 1900s never furnished more than 27 per cent of the annual growth in the number of residents. With lower birth rates than in peasant Russia (largely the consequence of lower marriage rates and later ages at marriage) and relatively high death rates, the growth of the city's population depended heavily on immigration. Between 1901 and 1905, the birth rate was 30.5 per 1,000 and the death rate

Table 1.vi: Birthplaces of St Petersburg Inhabitants, 1881–1910 (%)[56]

	St Petersburg	Outside St Petersburg	Total
1881	29.4	70.5	99.9
1900	31.7	68.3	100
1910	32.0	67.9	99.9

Table 1.vii: Natural Increase as % of Total Population Growth, St Petersburg, 1905–13 (see note 56)

1905	13.3
1906	16.3
1907	27.3
1908	24.5
1909	18.9
1910	17.8
1911	22.2
1912	11.9
1913	10.0

24.7; between 1906 and 1910, the figures were 30.9 and 26.3 respectively, although in the four years after 1911 there was a pronounced fall to 21.9 deaths per 1,000. An important constituent of the death rate was high infant mortality. Between 1887 and 1915, an average of 254 children per 1,000 died before the age of one. In 1909, 29 per cent of all deaths recorded were infants younger than one year.[57] There was a great surge in deaths in 1908 caused by the cholera epidemic.

The incidence of immigration, of course, varied considerably by social class, age and sex.[58] According to the 1910 census, 41 per cent of all gentry residents (7 per cent of the total population) and 57 per cent of the *meshchanstvo* or petty bourgeoisie (19 per cent of the population) had been born in St Petersburg. By contrast, only 24 per cent of all peasant inhabitants (69 per cent of the population), from which the vast bulk of the working class was drawn, were native to the city (compared with 22 per cent in 1900). Of all male and female peasant inhabitants below the age of 10, 65 per cent had been born in the capital. Above the age of 10 the proportion of native-born declined precipitately, to 11 per cent in the age group 16–30 and 6 per cent in the age group 31–40. Female peasants were more likely to be natives of the city than male peasants – 27 per cent as against 19 per cent respectively in 1910. The same was true for each age group. As in the Ruhr in the late nineteenth century, therefore, migrants were most likely to be young, unmarried male peasants.[59]

The majority of working-class immigrants to St Petersburg came from provinces in the North-Western and Central Industrial regions of the country, a pattern that antedated the development of the railways and was not altered by the Stolypin agrarian reforms. Within these regions, the contributions of individual provinces changed remarkably little over time.

As Table 1.viii reveals, St Petersburg province itself played a minor role as a source of wage earners, in part because of its low

Table 1.viii: Geographic Origins of Peasant Immigrants to St Petersburg, 1869–1910, by Province (numbers and % of total)[60]

	1869	% of total peasant population	1900	% of all peasant migrants	1910	% of all peasant migrants
Iaroslavl	45,180	21.8	92,188	12.8	105,960	12.8
Tver'	34,402	16.6	138,602	19.3	165,667	20.0
St Petersburg	27,012	13.0	55,888	7.8	59,355	7.2
Novgorod	18,254	8.8	58,812	8.2	69,540	8.4
Kostroma	12,530	6.0	30,215	4.2	31,197	3.7
Pskov	8,168	3.9	52,678	7.3	67,203	8.1
Riazan	7,361	3.5	34,300	4.8	39,948	4.8
Moscow	6,925	3.3	–	–	–	–
Smolensk	6,314	3.0	30,667	4.3	30,814	3.7
Vitebsk	5,476	2.6	30,625	4.3	36,895	4.5
TOTAL	207,307	60.7	718,400	73.0	828,237	86.0

Note: The remaining peasant migrants, whose places of origin have been excluded from the table, came in small numbers from a variety of other provinces. In the case of the 1869 census, there are no figures for the total number of peasant migrants, so the calculation has been based on the total peasant population.

population density and the location of many small manufacturing enterprises in its localities. The main provinces of origin were characterised by a lower soil fertility than average, a higher proportion of the population engaged in secondary industry, and consequently a lower ratio of involvement in traditional agricultural pursuits, a significant rate of out-migration and the greater literacy of their inhabitants.[61] This native Russian provenance of its labour supply meant that the capital's working class was homogeneous at least as regards racial composition (overwhelmingly Great Russian) and nominal religious affiliation (Russian Orthodox). Local ties also performed an important function in aiding incomers to locate jobs and in easing their transition into the urban and industrial environment. As the worker activist P. Timofeev remarked in his autobiography, '. . . everything is done by means of family connections'. In St Petersburg, as in Moscow, it was common for peasants from the same village or *volost'* to form associations called *zemliachestva*; the members (*zemliaki*) tended to work together and often even lived communally. At the Baltic Shipyards in 1903, for example, the ship workshop was filled with workers from two districts of Tver' province which provided the workshop's foremen, and before the war the day labourers of the city port were drawn exclusively from two provinces.[62]

Not only was there a ceaseless flow of peasants every year into the capital – deterred by neither depression nor revolutionary unrest (the population expanded by 367,600 between 1901 and 1909) – large numbers of them quit the city every year as well. As James Bater has shown, the transience of the population was a distinctive trend, just as it was in the cities of Imperial Germany. Between 1900 and 1910, 65 per cent of those migrants who, in 1900, had lived in the city for five years or less, had either abandoned residence in the city or died by 1910. The relative proportions for the peasant estate was 65 per cent and for the *meshchanstvo* 59 per cent.[63]

The overwhelming weight of the peasant element in the labouring population of St Petersburg exerted a decisive impact on the structure of its working class. The high proportion of immigrants was reflected in the distribution of the peasant estate and hired work-force by gender, age and family status.

Both among the city population in general and the peasant workers in particular men outnumbered women. According to the 1910 city census, in the former case 52 per cent were males and 48 per cent females; in the latter, 57 per cent and 43 per cent respectively. The imbalance was particularly marked among wage earners (of whom 80 per cent were men and 20 per cent women in 1910) and factory workers (of whom in St Petersburg province in 1912 71 per cent were male and 30 per cent female).[64] Because of the preponderant share of males without families in the work-force and among migrants to the city the share of women in the total labour force changed little between 1900 (19.2 per cent) and 1910 (20.3 per cent). For reasons outlined earlier in this chapter, however, the contribution of women to the factory labour force of St Petersburg province rose from 22 per cent in 1905 to 29 per cent in 1913. On the eve of the war, within manufacturing, women accounted for the largest portion of employees in textiles (68 per cent in 1913) and a high ratio in food and tobacco (47 per cent), chemicals (42 per cent), and a lower one in animal products (28 per cent) and printing (24 per cent). Yet, numerically, domestic service undoubtedly remained the largest single source of female employment. On the other hand, heavy industry, commerce, construction and transport were almost exclusively the preserve of male workers.[65]

Immigration also worked to imbalance the labour force in favour of young and young middle-aged groups. As the 1910 city census data relating to the distribution of the labour force by age were never published, figures for 1900 have to be utilised. At the turn of the century 10 per cent of factory workers were under 16 years old, 22 per cent were aged 16–20; 54 per cent 21–40, 13 per cent 41–60, and 0.8 per cent were over 60.[66] Thus the overwhelming majority of industrial wage earners fell into the age cohort 16–40 (76 per cent), and in some sectors the proportion was even higher – 80 per cent in machine construction, 78 per cent in textiles, 78 per cent in paper and printing. The low share of elderly operatives (i.e. over the age of 40) was due to the normal young age of migrants, low life expectancy and the early ageing of workers, as well as the propensity of older hands to return to their villages. A similar pattern was observable in commerce, where a 1908 survey discovered that a mere 5 per cent of commercial employees were older than 41 and that 42 per cent were aged between 18 and 30.[67] In St Petersburg factory industry before the war, moreover, less use was made of children and youths than elsewhere in the Empire. In 1912, a mere 1 per cent of the provincial factory work-force lay in the age band 12–14 and 7 per cent in the cohort 15–17, whereas the appropriate proportions for the Empire were 1 per cent and 9 per cent respectively. Considerable numbers of youths were employed in textiles, comprising 10 per cent of mill hands in the province in 1912 (most were girls, performing unskilled tasks such as piecers, twisters, bobbin tenders), and in paper and printing (12 per cent of wage earners in 1912, mostly boys). The highest ratio of adolescents, however, was to be found in the artisanal clothing trades where, in 1900, 23 per cent of all employees were younger than 17. In the pre-war years the masters resorted more frequently to the labour of young, often unpaid, apprentices as a substitute for privileged craftsmen.[68]

The effect of immigration was also reflected in the marital status of the capital's largely peasant, work-force. Whereas, in 1910, 57 per cent of the entire city population was single and 43 per cent married, the corresponding ratios for the peasant estate were 66 per cent and 34 per cent respectively. There was little difference overall between male and female peasant workers with regard to marital status; 58 per cent of men and 62 per cent of women were single, whilst the proportions married were 42 per cent and 38 per cent. There was, however, a distinct contrast between the sexes with regard to the age and rate of marriage. Just 3 per cent of male peasant workers aged between 16 and 20, and 32 per cent aged between 21 and 25, were married. Among female peasant workers the respective proportions were 12 per cent and 46 per cent.[69] More women married before the age of 25 than men, who went to the altar at a far later age in the capital than the countryside. As contemporary investigations by the union of metalworkers (1908) and S. N. Prokopovich (1909) revealed, the rate of marriage, the size and the settlement of workers' families in the capital were directly related to the age of the bread-winner and level of pay (and through the latter to skill). In the union of metalworkers' survey, for example, among 600 skilled engineering workers, 44 per cent of those earning 1 to 2.5 roubles a day were single, compared with 28 per cent of those earning 2–3 roubles and a mere 5 per cent of those paid more than 3 roubles a day. Three or more children were far more common among metalworkers in receipt of 2.5 roubles a day than among those with lesser incomes.[70]

At the turn of the century, indeed, the status of marriage had not been synonymous with the presence of the worker's family in the city. The 1897 All-Russian population census (the single statistical survey to touch directly on this issue) discovered that in St Petersburg a mere 19 per cent of married wage earners lived with their families (48 per cent in all-Russia). The highest ratios were in paper and printing (38 per cent), metallurgy and machine construction (31 per cent) and chemicals (29 per cent) – industrial sectors with a greater share of skilled workers who were better paid and had established more permanent ties to the city. The lowest percentages were in food (4 per cent) and the clothing trades (8 per cent), where wages were paltry and many employees lived on the premises, from which families were excluded.[71] The high cost of living in the capital, the lowly wages except for the skilled minority and the lack of cheap housing all acted both to delay the age of marriage (particularly for men) and to ensure that at this time the majority of married workers left their families behind in the village.

It is possible that by 1910 a greater number of industrially employed operatives were better placed financially to support a young family in the capital. Leopold Haimson has argued in favour of 'the strengthening of the working-class community', adducing the statistical evidence that the percentage of dependants in the totality of the industrial population (i.e. the number of children kept by their parents with them in the city) rose from 55 per cent to 71 per cent between 1900 and 1910. Such figures, however, present problems of interpretation. Firstly, they are restricted to the secondary sector and thus exclude the service industries where, as in the artisanal trades, employers provided accommodation from which workers' families were prohibited. Secondly, they refer to all employees in manufacturing industry, including managers and white-collar personnel, who enjoyed a greater ability to rear their children in an urban setting. This leads to an inflation of the proportion of dependants and a distorted perspective. To some extent, too, the figures may reflect the decline in infant death rates (from 27.4 per 100 in 1900 to 23.1 in 1913), which would also increase the numbers of children surviving.[72] The controversial nature of the evidence renders dangerous any dogmatic conclusion that there was a steep rise between 1900 and 1910 in the proportion of the total hired labour force capable of nurturing their children in the capital. The opinion may be hazarded that at least within certain branches of manufacturing industry, namely those employing a high proportion of skilled workers, the decade 1900 to 1910 marked an improvement, which cannot be accurately quantified, in operatives' family situation. Certainly in a year (1910) when the average annual wages of the St Petersburg industrial working class was calculated by the factory inspectorate to be 355 roubles, and contemporary researchers reckoned that a minimum income of 400 to 600 roubles per annum was required for the upkeep of a family in the city, the skilled and highly skilled alone could afford to lead a normal family existence.[73]

The weight of young peasant migrants in St Petersburg's working class exerted a detrimental influence on the overall extent of literacy (defined as the ability to read), with regard both to the city as a whole and to wage earners. In 1910, 75 per cent of all residents were literate; 85 per cent of men and 65 per cent of women, a rise of 7 or 8 per cent in all categories since 1900. The rate of literacy in the peasant estate had risen overall from 55 per cent to 62 per cent, 1900 to 1910, with 75 per cent of peasant men classed as literate in 1910 and 46 per cent of the women.[74] Sex, age, occupation and place of origin were all significant variables in the determination of working-class literacy. Thus workers of both sexes aged 6–20 were more literate than those between the ages of 21 and 40; men were always more literate than women, in particular after the age of 20 (see Table 1.ix).

Over the age of 20, the rate of literacy for peasants born in the capital (male and female) was higher than for immigrants. But levels of literacy for female (but not male) migrants fell sharply after their twentieth year, reflecting the reluctance of peasant fathers to educate their daughters (see Table 1.x).

Literacy levels fell sharply for both men and women over the age of 40. In general the high proportion of literates among the young (including migrants of both sexes) reflected the great strides in the provision of rural schooling from the 1890s. The differential rates of literacy within particular sectors of the economy were heavily influenced by the relative shares of men and women and the mix of

Table 1.ix: *Percentage of the Peasant Estate Aged 40 and below Literate, by Age Group: St Petersburg, 1910*[75]

Age group	Total	Male	Female
6–20	79.9	84.4	74.1
21–30	75.0	87.8	56.9
31–40	67.3	81.7	43.6

Table 1.x: Percentage of the Peasant Estate Aged 40 and below Literate, by Age Group and Place of Birth: St Petersburg 1910 (see note 75)

	Males		Females	
Age group	Native born	Non-native-born	Native-born	Non-native-born
6–20	76.2	73.5	88.0	75.0
21–30	95.5	91.4	86.8	52.5
31–40	98.1	84.6	81.9	34.8

skills within occupations. Thus in printing and heavy industry, employing for the most part highly skilled male operatives, 93 per cent and 73 per cent of the men respectively were literate in 1897. In textiles, with a preponderance of semi-skilled young women, a mere 21 per cent of female hands were literate (although 65 per cent of the men were). At the Aleksandro-Nevskaia mills of K. Ia. Pal' in 1914, for example, all 723 men were literate but only half the 1,210 women. In the clothing trades, however, in 1900 69 per cent of men and 75 per cent of women were literate, and the requirement of literacy was mandatory for employment in commerical establishments.[76]

It is an axiomatic view among Soviet scholars that, in the words of Z. V. Stepanov, 'the comparatively high literacy of the workers of Petrograd . . . was one of the conditions aiding the rapid revolutionising of the capital's proletariat . . .'.[77] Such an interpretation, however, begs the question both of the precise meaning contemporaries attached to the term 'literacy', and its quality. Thus it is not at all clear how literacy was defined by the compilers of the 1897 population census, and whether it included the ability to write as well as to read. The bulk of migrants to the city were educated in rural primary schools. Whether under the auspices of the church or the *zemstvo*, these provided only one or two years' schooling, and gave priority to reading and religious instruction. School-leavers apparently quickly forgot the ability to write. Moreover, in both urban and rural schools very many pupils never finished even these rudimentary studies. A survey of 11,000 St Petersburg textile workers in 1902 revealed that a mere 15 per cent had completed their schooling. In 1908, on a national scale, only 10 per cent stayed the course in rural and urban elementary schools, and in 1914 in the capital the ratio was 22 per cent. As Jeffrey Brooks has shown, this new urban, barely literate, readership comprised the audience for the burgeoning popular literature of serials, detective novels and cheap 'kopeck' newspapers (after 1908).[78]

A clear distinction, however, has to be drawn between the vast bulk of workers with their low level of educational attainments and the distinct minority of 'worker intellectuals' or the 'labour intelligentsia', the dimension of which expanded after 1905 with the influx of a larger number of young literate peasants and the emergence of working-class educational societies. These 'worker–intellectuals' were drawn overwhelmingly from the ranks of young (very often aged 16–20), better-paid, unmarried, skilled male operatives employed in both factory and artisanal establishments – by trade they were skilled engineering workers (machinists, turners, etc.), printers, joiners, tailors. They furnished the leadership of the new trade unions, co-operatives and educational societies after 1905 and the cadres of revolutionary activists. These were the workers who sought to broaden their intellectual horizons by attending Sunday schools, evening classes, the courses of the St Petersburg Society of Popular Universities and by taking out a reader's ticket in one of the city's eight public reading rooms.[79]

In addition to differences of age, gender and literacy within the labour force, the latter was also highly stratified according to skill and occupational specialisation.[80] Within each industry or trade, whether organised on factory or on artisanal lines, as well as in retailing and transport there existed distinct hierarchies.

Among both Soviet and Western investigators there is general agreement that a 'labour aristocracy' either did not exist at all in late Imperial Russia or else formed a miniscule stratum within the working class. Instead, at the top of the labour hierarchy stood the skilled workers (*masterovye*). In metalworking, for example, there were about 100 occupational categories. Machine construction in particular employed in 'cold' shops (pattern, machine, gun, gun-carriage) many highly skilled craftsmen, such as instrument-makers, millwrights, pattern-makers, milling-machine operators and less specialised tradesmen (fitters, turners, mortisers, etc.). Numerically, skilled workers constituted a majority in such plants. At the Baltic Shipyards in May 1901, for example, 4,377 out of a complement of 6,783 were designated skilled by the factory administration: at Aivaz in June 1914, 722 out of 1,024.[81] Moreover, there is some evidence that within particular workshops in metalworking establishments a significant minority of the best paid and most literate of craftsmen came not from the peasant estate but from the more settled and urbanised *meshchanstvo*. Thus, at the Baltic Shipyards in 1901, 50 per cent of skilled hands in the model shop and a third of tradesmen in the electro-technical and repair shop were from the *meshchanstvo*. At the Izhora arms-works in 1906 the electricians, pattern-makers, draughtsmen and coppersmiths likewise came disproportionately from this social group.[82]

Printing, too, was an occupation noted for its high ratio of skilled (and literate) wage earners and strict internal shop hierarchy, ranging from skilled lithographers, engravers, typesetters and draughtsmen at the top to bookbinders and unskilled machine operators at the bottom.

Mastery of a skill was a prerequisite for employment in the luxury branches of the artisanal trades. As in Paris after 1850, however, the spread of capitalism had given rise in artisanal production after 1900 to specialisation, division of labour, subcontracting and a decline in the level of skill. The majority of workers in craft industries were no longer fully-fledged, independent artisans but had become semi-craftspeople. They were dependent on suppliers, retail and wholesale firms and market traders. In the garment industry, for example, there existed a clear distinction between skilled tailors producing custom-made clothing in tailoring shops and specialised tailors, mostly women, producing only one part of an item and working in subcontracting shops producing readymade apparel. A similar distinction developed in shoemaking.[83] In the construction industry there existed a permanent core of highly qualified carpenters, electricians, joiners, masons, painters and plumbers.

Both the skilled factory worker and élite artisanal craftsman shared common attributes which distinguished them from the urban working masses. They were male; women were almost totally excluded from highly skilled trades. They were more likely to be fully assimilated to urban and industrial life and culture. Their level of technical expertise, acquired through training on the job or apprenticeship (of three years' duration in heavy industry but four or five years in artisanal occupations) fostered a sense of personal independence, pride in their craft and self-respect. Their higher general level of culture led at least some to take an interest in social and political issues and hence to be drawn into the revolutionary movement. The activists of the infant trade unions after 1905 and of the revolutionary parties, as well as the readership of labour publications permitted by the authorities came overwhelmingly from their ranks. Skilled operatives also evinced less sympathetic traits. Generally they were disdainful of the unskilled and new peasant migrants, and their attitude towards women was oppressive.[84] This feeling of superiority was an important cause of the relative neglect by labour leaders of women and the unskilled as potential sources of support.

Beneath the skilled came the semi-skilled, most of whom were women employed as machine operatives in the capital's mills. In textiles the minority of skilled jobs (overlookers, fabric printers, knitters, mechanics) were reserved for men. The numbers of the semi-skilled were also on the rise in machine construction before the war.

The bottom rung of the labour hierarchy was occupied by the

unskilled of both sexes, who were for the most part young immigrants of peasant origin. These were day workers and were not considered part of the regular labour force. In heavy industry they were employed to perform arduous and exhausting physical labour in the 'hot' shops of metallurgical and mixed enterprises – in foundries, rolling mills, crucible shops – and in the production of pipes, wire and nails, shells and fuses, as well as general portering duties. Chemicals, the factory manufacture of foodstuffs, tobacco and rubber production all employed mostly unskilled hands. The levels of literacy and cultural awareness of the unskilled were the lowest within the urban labour force.

The peasant origins of the majority of wage earners in the capital moulded their relationship to the countryside and the urban environment. Ever since the debates between Marxists and Narodniks in the 1890s, the issue of the creation of a hereditary proletariat in St Petersburg (as in Russia generally) before the revolution of 1917 has been the focus of political and ideological polemics as much as of dispassionate historical enquiry. Soviet investigators draw a distinction between 'cadre' workers – permanent urban proletarians, who have severed all bonds to village life, live solely by wage work and are 'class-conscious' – and 'peasant' workers, who still retain and cultivate their allotments. Thus E. E. Kruze has written that, on account of 'Petersburg workers' very weak links with the land ... the greater part of the Petersburg proletariat was already in the main cadre'. S. N. Semanov concurs with this view: '... at the start of the twentieth century the majority of workers had severed any connection with agriculture'.[85] Westen historians, however, have reached no consensus. S. A. Smith, for example, argues that 'a process of proletarianisation was taking place among the workers of St Petersburg'. G. D. Surh contends that the 'direct influence of the village on migrants to Petersburg' was weaker than elsewhere in Russia. On the other hand, Robert Johnson's study of Moscow has drawn attention to the symbiotic relationship between factory and village; the constant two-way movement between city and countryside ensured that Moscow wage earners were both semi-proletarians and semi-peasants.[86]

The absence of reliable statistical data and the paucity of contemporary academic investigations, as well as the tendency to exclude from the discussion all non-factory forms of urban employment, renders hazardous in the extreme any definitive conclusions as to the particular stage reached by the capital's operatives on the eve of the war in the transition between farm and factory.

On the one hand, there is evidence to suggest that at least a core of permanent factory workers was beginning to emerge in St Petersburg before 1914, with lengthy sojourn in the city, a fairly long record of factory work together with year-round employment and with minimal or no property relationships to their often far distant place of birth. Such characteristics distinguished skilled workpeople in particular.

According to the 1910 city census, the proportion of the peasant estate born in the capital or having lived there more than ten years was considerable – approximately 58 per cent (a rise of 7 per cent from 1900). And the proportion of male peasants born in the city had risen from 15 per cent to 19 per cent between 1900 and 1910, although the ratio for women peasants remained almost unchanged at around 25 per cent. There was a growing group of factory hands whose parents were workers. A survey between 1900 and 1902 of the mill labour force by V. Leontiev discovered that 16 per cent of the men and 21 per cent of the women were second-generation operatives. The single census to touch on this theme was the post-revolutionary industrial survey conducted in the autumn of 1918. It registered 18 per cent of the city's 1917 work-force as hereditary, with 20 per cent so classified in heavy industry and 25 per cent in textiles.[87]

Skilled workers, too, were noted for a considerable length of service in industry, often at the same manufactory. An enquiry at the Baltic Shipyards in 1906 found that 35 per cent of the labour force had toiled more than five years in the plant and the figure rose to 60 per cent among fitters and 59 per cent among machinists. Such prolonged periods of employment were especially common in large (over 1,000 workers) metalworking establishments. The 1908 investigation by the union of metalworkers, which covered 5,773 employees, calculated that in these plants 53 per cent of respondents had put in over five years' work. Unskilled workers and those employed in petty enterprises, however, on account of their low pay, constituted a highly unstable and mobile element.[88]

The same distinction between skilled and unskilled applies to the disruption of workers' ties with the land. As mechanised factory production required uninterrupted production and hence a stable labour force, annual departure for summer field work had ceased to be a phenomenon of great significance. In 1910, 130,733 'peasants' (or 10 per cent of the peasant estate) left for the countryside: the percentage of factory operatives among the departees is unknown.[89] But seasonal migration both out of and into the city was more common in some trades. Tailoring was a seasonal occupation; when orders fell off in the summer, many skilled tailors abandoned the capital for their villages. Conversely every summer some 200,000 unskilled peasants came to seek employment in construction and the port.[90] The proportion of the hired labour force both owning land and actually farming it is impossible to estimate as the data are so fragmentary. At the Baltic Shipyards in 1901, 46 per cent of 3,917 operatives of all categories possessed legal title to allotment land, but 42 per cent of these worker–landowners left their fields uncultivated. Leontiev's investigation of 10,285 textile hands in 1900–02 discovered that 65 per cent of the men retained their farms but not a single one of the women. The 1918 industrial census estimated that 17 per cent of those surveyed held land prior to October 1917, but only 11 per cent worked their plots. The ratio of workers owning land was related to the share of skilled wage earners in an industry; it was low in printing (10 per cent), higher in machine construction (24 per cent) and highest in cotton (34 per cent). In the light of the mass flight from the starving capital before the census of 1918 these figures cannot be taken as reliable indications of the extent of landholding. In general it may be concluded that women and skilled males preserved a less intimate property relationship with peasant society than the unskilled, and that many workers' ownership of allotment land was nominal rather than real.[91]

On the other hand, labour migration to the capital, prolonged residence in an urban milieu and year-round employment in manufacturing were not incompatible with the maintenance of diverse forms of ties to the countryside. As the researches of James Bater have revealed, many peasant migrants to St Petersburg did not remain there permanently. If the number of peasant-born residents grew by 401,700 between 1900 and 1910, 210,100 peasants either died or left the city between the same dates. It is probable that those leaving were mostly the young, unmarried, unskilled and semi-skilled rather than the more mature, skilled, married workers with firmer roots in the city. This phenomenon may be linked in turn to the unbalanced age structure of the labouring population, a mere 14 per cent of which was aged over 40 in 1900. In the absence of social security for the old, sick and infirm, return to the native village was an attractive, and often the sole, option, in particular for the poorly paid and unskilled.[92]

The earlier discussion in this chapter of the family situation of workers concluded that whilst it was possible that between 1900 and 1910 more skilled operatives were in a position to have their families with them in the capital, for the unskilled, a majority of the total hired labour force, this was less likely. This factor acted as a brake upon the assimilation of such wage earners to urban life and culture. At least at the start of the twentieth century it was a fairly common practice for married workers, whose womenfolk had joined them in the city, to dispatch pregnant wives to their native village to give birth and to rear their children to the age of 15 in the countryside. Leontiev's examination of 2,506 married male textile workers in 1900–02 noted that 27 per cent had done so. There is no information on the continuation or otherwise of this form of rural link prior to the First World War.[93]

The remittance of money by workers to relatives in the villages, either to pay taxes in order to retain title to allotment land or to contribute to the upkeep of their families or relatives, was not uncommon. A survey by the Russian Technical Society of 570 (mostly skilled) wage earners in 1908 discovered that 42 per cent of married and 67 per cent of single respondents devoted part of their earnings to this end. Another study in the same year, of 41 mill hands, noted that those who were married with their families still domiciled outside the capital spent 28 per cent of their income in monies dispatched home. It was also the general impression of the skilled worker P. Timofeev that the unskilled scrimped and saved to send money to their relations in the commune, whereas the skilled were more inclined to cease doing so 'if things aren't going well in the village'.[94]

In the light of the contradictory nature of the historical evidence it would be unwise to conclude either that a class of permanent, hereditary proletarians, totally divorced from the soil, had emerged in St Petersburg prior to the First World War or that, in the words of S. A. Smith, 'cadre workers ... were probably in a slight majority'.[95] There can be no doubt that a nucleus of urbanised workers, whose numbers cannot be accurately calculated, was in the process of formation. For the most part these were skilled factory hands with a relatively long record of service in industry and weakened links to peasant society, a relatively high proportion of whom had succeeded in establishing their families in the city. However, within the totality of the entire hired labour force, rather than within manufacturing industry alone, they were probably a minority. Above all they were constantly swamped by masses of new arrivals from rural areas: 69,774 workers were recruited to factory industry alone between 1908 and 1913. As in Moscow, there was a constant two-way process between the capital and the countryside; familial ties to native villages, if not direct continuation of the cultivation of farms, remained strong and were reinforced within the city by the *zemliachestva*. Thus the St Petersburg working class before 1914 was still at the transitory stage between agriculture and industry.

Chapter 2

ST PETERSBURG: THE WORKPLACE AND THE URBAN ENVIRONMENT

I

Experience at work and conditions within the workplace – its size, the arbitrariness of administrators, foremen and owners, poor standards of hygiene and safety, the length of the working day and the level of remuneration – both helped shape workers' attitudes to one another and constituted an important cause of and stimulus to the revival of labour unrest in St Petersburg prior to the First World War.

Following Marx, many scholars of the Russian labour movement have argued that the high degree of concentration of the workers in the capital, as in the Empire as a whole, facilitated labour organisation and working-class radicalism, as well as class solidarity and the development of class consciousness. This interpretation, however, rests upon flawed evidence.

In the first place, as the earlier discussion of the city's economy noted, the defects of official statistics have created a distorted picture of the prevalence of large industrial enterprises. It cannot be denied that within certain sectors of production concentration had proceeded apace (see Table 2.i).[1] In the cotton, other textile, chemical and metalworking industries the vast majority of the labour force, three quarters or more, was employed in establishments employing in excess of 500 workers. But these industries were exceptional. In food processing the proportion was just only over half; in paper and printing less than a quarter; in woodworking zero (Table 2.i). And bearing in mind the fact that the factory inspectorate inadequately registered small units of production, the proportion of workers employed in smaller establishments is almost certainly understated. In the artisanal trades the average place of business was of modest

30

Table 2.i: Distribution of Plant Size, by Industry: St Petersburg Province, December 1912, (%)

Industry	Number of workers per plant				
	Under 100	101–500	501–1000	Over 1000	Total
Chemicals	9.3	8.9	5.5	76.2	99.9
Cotton	0.6	8.0	27.0	64.4	100.0
Food processing	10.5	35.2	22.0	32.3	100.0
Metal, machines	9.2	17.6	21.5	51.6	99.9
Paper and printing	31.3	45.6	18.0	5.2	100.1
Textiles	3.0	12.8	25.7	58.5	100.0
Woodworking	48.1	51.8	–	–	99.9

dimensions – a mere five employees each in the clothing trade, and three to four per bakery. In the innumerable petty retail outlets, a handful of staff (up to twelve) was the norm.[2] By the nature of the profession in construction there was no fixed workplace at all. When the vast hordes of domestic servants are also taken into account, it can be argued that for a majority of the hired labour force the place of employment was in fact small-scale rather than large.

In the second place, as the history of the labour movement both in Moscow in 1905 and in the capital between 1907 and 1917 testifies, factory size alone was not enough to generate worker activism.[3] In St Petersburg textile operatives (mostly young, unmarried females) were to prove one of the least successful groups in forming independent legal labour organisations after 1906 or in furnishing recruits to the revolutionary parties.

Thirdly, the petty size of so many places of work proved no barrier to collective organisation – almost the reverse. Indeed in both Moscow and St Petersburg between 1906 and 1914 the trade unions with the broadest appeal were located in artisanal occupations characterised by their small-scale, intimate, nature of production. Even within heavy industry, massive plants were broken up into departments, in turn subdivided into a multitude of specialised workshops.[4] Thus it was no accident that the solitary, strong, industrial trade union in the capital was that of the metalworkers, whose factory nuclei rested upon individual shops with their core of skilled workers and feelings of comradeship and solidarity. In the mills, on the contrary, the departments and units were relatively large and solidarity less easy to attain.

In general it may be concluded that in St Petersburg the presence of relatively large numbers of skilled workers and a strong sense of trade identity rather than the large size of industrial establishments were the crucial determinants of militancy, labour organisation and revolutionary propensity. Because of their higher ratios of skilled, literate, more urbanised and settled male workers, metalworking, factory and artisanal, printing, tailoring and woodworking proved to be more fertile recruiting grounds for unrest and revolutionary activity than textiles, food processing, mineral production, domestic service and the retail trades with their greater proportions of unskilled female employees and workers with firmer rural ties. The Marxist belief in the revolutionary potential of gigantic industrial enterprises had unfortunate political consequences for St Petersburg revolutionaries, both intellectuals and skilled workers alike, as it induced a disdainful attitude towards employees in small plants, workshops and commercial establishments, who consequently suffered neglect as an 'unconscious' and 'backward' element.

Both before the revolution of 1905 and after the St Petersburg employers' successful counter-attack between 1907 and 1910 upon the workers' revolutionary gains, the *ancien régime* in the factory, in artisanal workshops and retailing was tantamount to managerial and personal autocracy. It was characterised by arbitrariness, lack of intervention by state authorities, intimidation and petty despotism. The power of the factory administration and the individual small-scale employer was effectively unlimited. With the exception of 1905 and 1906 the labour force in all sectors was denied the opportunity, whether through elected factory commissions or councils or trade unions, to participate in hiring or firing, the fixing of rates of pay or hours of work. Operatives in factories, however, for the most part rarely came into contact with the higher management. Instead the shop foreman, in the words of P. Timofeev, 'represents the lever of factory life which presses on the worker the hardest'. As authority in the factory was decentralised, foremen were directly responsible for calculating rates of pay, recruitments and dismissals, the distribution and execution of work and the imposition of fines, although in some metalworking plants after 1906 a new layer of technical and supervisory personnel took over many of the former duties of foremen. (see Chapter 1). Such omnipotence naturally bred abuses and a perpetual state of undeclared war between foremen and those enduring their tyranny. Women in particular suffered harassment at the hands of uncouth and insensitive overseers. There was also a covert element of racial tension as many foremen were of foreign extraction – frequently German in the electrical equipment industry or English and Scots in the mills.[5] Fines and searches, reintroduced after 1907, as well as medical inspection at times of engagement and the absence of 'polite address' (workers, like soldiers, were spoken to as 'thou' rather than 'you') were detested as assaults on workpeople's dignity. In the pre-war period most financial exactions were levied for poor workmanship. The vague definition of 'incorrect work' and 'negligence at work' in factories' tables of penalties left ample scope for capricious application.[6] In artisanal trades, such as baking and tailoring, and in retailing, with their confined and dense environment, the authority and presence of the owner was all-pervasive and particularly odious. Domestic servants were naturally worst off in this respect. Young female shop assistants, for example, were subject to sexual abuse from the bosses, who would hire only good-looking and well-dressed girls.[7] The pattern of economic strikes in St Petersburg both in 1905 to 1907 and in 1912 to 1914 testifies to the correctness of contemporary observations that for younger workers, both factory and artisanal, the old system of order in plants and workshops was becoming unendurable. In the words of L. Kleinbort 'workers wish to be considered as human beings.' A growing sense of self-respect and personal inviolability ensured that 'issues of dignity', protests against the wilful actions of foremen and managers and the misuse of fines and searches constituted an important segment of stoppages classed by the authorities as economic.[8]

The workplace in the capital was also characterised by generally unattractive working conditions, comparable to those in other European industrial societies. Standards of safety and hygiene were abysmal. A revealing insight into these is furnished by a remarkably thorough investigation conducted by St Petersburg trade unions in 1912 before the All-Russian Hygiene Exhibition. The most widespread defects uncovered were: the absence of ventilation, (in 42 per cent of metalworking establishments surveyed, 75 per cent of mills, 70 per cent of printshops); the presence of damp (in 44 per cent of metals plants, 59 per cent of mills, 56 per cent of printing plants); the non-dispersal of smoke, gas and steam due to the failure to install extractors (97 per cent of manufactories in heavy industry, 58 per cent of mills, 85 per cent of print shops). In woodworking, tailoring and printing, installations were often in basements and especially prone to damp; artificial light was the norm in daytime. In the mills temperatures were seldom below 22°C. Toilets and safe drinking water were often unavailable. As a consequence of this state of affairs, occupational illnesses were widespread. In metalworking, printing and woodworking lung diseases caused by various forms of dust were common. In the city as a whole in 1907, 305 deaths per 1,000 were ascribed to consumption. In textiles women were prone to deafness caused by the noise of the machinery; in retailing, rheumatism was a standard affliction. Tailors and bootmakers normally died before they reached their fortieth birthday.[9] Demands to improve hygienic facilities were a regular feature of economic strikes in the three years prior to the war.

The lack of elementary safety precautions, the intensification of labour in certain industries after 1907 on account of modernisation and the prolonged working day, all contributed towards a high rate of accidents in the capital's industries. With the onset of economic recovery from 1910, accidents in St Petersburg province rose from 7,865 in 1909 to 14,288 in 1913. Metalworking claimed a large share of the victims, in particular at state plants (there were 2,329 mishaps at the Izhora small-arms works alone in 1912). Deaths, however, were few – some 30 per annum on average.[10]

It is not easy to establish the average length of the real working day in St Petersburg's diverse economic sectors. Although formal hours of work (i.e. exclusive of overtime) witnessed a long-term downward trend from the 1880s to 1913, from twelve/fourteen hours to nine/ten hours, with a significant drop to eight or nine hours achieved in the period 1905–7, the widespread resort to overtime in the years after 1907 acted as a covert means of prolonging the period of labour. In St Petersburg province in 1914 nearly 30 per cent of the factory labour force was on overtime.[11] In general it may be said that, taking extra time into account, the shortest working day was experienced in heavy industry, printing and textiles. A survey of 11,488 printworkers early in 1913 discovered that the majority toiled officially for nine hours, but in fact laboured for ten due to one hour's overtime. In the mills ten or ten and a half hours were standard, with a lunch break in addition of one and a half hours. In machine construction, armaments and shipbuilding the pre-war boom led to the widespread resort to overtime of two or three hours, thereby lengthening the nine-hour day to eleven or twelve hours.[12] In the artisanal trades, food processing and retailing the period spent at work was atrociously long: over fifteen hours for carriage and boot workers; sixteen hours in the season for clothing employees; twelve to sixteen hours for shop assistants; fourteen hours or so in bakeries.[13] In most branches of industry plants stopped on Saturday afternoon at five o'clock until Monday morning. Apart from state enterprises under the aegis of GAU and the city's tramway personnel, holidays were rare or non-existent. On average in the province in 1910 operatives spent 283 days per annum at work and missed 11.3 days through truancy.[14]

Accurate measurement of workers' earnings in the capital suffers from the defects of the available statistical data. The general trend in aggregate money wages of factory employees is set out in Table 2.ii.

These figures reveal the upturn in money wages in 1906 and 1907 after a fall in 1905 occasioned by the strikes and plant closures of that revolutionary year. Rates of pay fell once more in 1908 and 1909 during the employers' counter-offensive but progressed steadily in 1910 and 1911 with the onset of industrial recovery and growing shortage of skilled labour. But they remained stable in 1912 and

Table 2.ii: Aggregate Money Wages of Factory Workers: St Petersburg Province, 1904–13 (roubles p.a.)[15]

1904	366	1908	374	1911	384
1905	295	1909	342	1912	375
1906	375	1910	355	1913	384
1907	381				

1913. In the twelve years from the turn of the century aggregate money earnings of factory hands in the city underwent an increase of 27 per cent. Although average annual wages in St Petersburg were the highest in the Empire (375 roubles per annum in 1912 as against 255 roubles), the cost of living was also the most expensive. When account is taken of the upward trend in the general index of retail prices in the capital from 119 in 1901 to 154 in 1913, a rise of 30 per cent, (1867 = 100), it becomes clear that real wages in effect stagnated. In this respect the experience of labour in the capital mirrored that of workers in Great Britain, France and Germany whose real incomes ceased to rise or even declined after 1905.[16]

Although the overall tendency of the movement of money and real wages is fairly clear, the general averages cited here are misleading, because the factory inspectorate excluded from its calculations state plants (with comparatively high levels of remuneration), artisanal trades and the entire tertiary sector (with below average rates of pay). Thus there exists no data from which estimates can be made of the aggregates of money and real earnings of the entire hired labour force in this period. Nevertheless certain general features of the structure of wages may be delineated.

In the first place, the major part of operatives' income came from cash wages: in 1913 a mere 6 per cent of workers' earnings in the province was derived from payment in kind. Secondly, piece rates predominated, covering 60 per cent of the labour force in heavy industry in 1909. Wages were formed of two elements – shop or day rates and piece rates. Earnings, therefore, oscillated wildly from week to week. Thirdly, rates varied greatly between industries. The highest annual earnings were to be found in metalworking, where, according to the factory inspectorate, in 1912 they amounted to 519 roubles. In the mechanical production of wood, printing and chemicals they approached the overall average of 375 roubles – at 420, 378 and 352 roubles respectively. All these were branches of production employing a sizeable proportion of skilled male adults. The lowest wages in manufacturing were paid in food processing and cotton, at 261 and 268 roubles per annum, industries with a high ratio of women and unskilled.[17] In artisanal trades, where the absence of pay books and rates tables was common, earnings were subject to fluctuation according to the seasonal nature of the work, ranging from 25 to 40 roubles a month. In retailing there were no contracts of hire and the mostly youthful shop assistants earned a miserly 12 to 17 roubles a month.[18] Fourthly, age, sex and skill all exerted an influence upon the level of incomes. In all occupations women were paid much less than men. In the cotton mills in 1908, for example, women's average annual income amounted to 261 roubles compared with 383 for men. Unskilled workers, paid by the day, and apprentices were at the bottom of the wages table. In 1908, when the top income for a skilled metalworker reached 2 roubles 60 kopecks a day, the unskilled were paid 1 rouble 5 kopecks and apprentices 85 kopecks. Even within the ranks of the skilled there were enormous variations both between and within plants. It is not known, however, whether the trend towards a reduction in the differences in income between skilled and unskilled workers, which H. Kaelble has detected in Western Europe before 1914, was repeated in St Petersburg.[19]

Outside the skilled elite in heavy industry and printing, therefore, real wages were falling. Researchers at the time estimated that wage earners required an annual income of 500 to 600 roubles to be able to raise a family in the city, yet the vast majority were paid well under 400 roubles a year. In the words of the contemporary investigator M. Davidovich, 'by the usual wage a male worker cannot support his family by his own forces.' Working-class families depended for survival upon the joint incomes of husband and wife.[20] Most workers earned at best enough only to subsist from day to day. The low and fluctuating level of wages, unemployment and under-employment, declining earning power in later life and the size and age of a worker's family all meant that insecurity and unpredictability remained the central facts of working-class life. It is not accidental that chronic poverty and the stagnation of real incomes were fundamental causes of economic strikes in the labour unrest of 1912 to 1914.

II

THE URBAN ENVIRONMENT

In no respect was the duality of St Petersburg more marked than in the disparity between its modern, metropolitan centre and its peripheral districts, to which such epithets could scarcely be applied. The ceaseless inflow of peasant migrants from the 1880s and unplanned growth of neighbourhoods had placed terrible pressure upon urban facilities. The consequent social problems of poor sanitation, disease, overcrowding and disgraceful standards of housing –

Table 2.iii: Social Composition of St Petersburg Districts, December 1910 (as % of total district population)[21]

	Gentry	'Bourgeoisie'	Peasants	Workers	Total %
Admiralty	11.0	19.7	63.5	13.0	94.2
Kazan	9.3	25.0	58.1	20.0	92.4
Kolomna	9.6	24.8	62.3	22.9	96.7
Liteinii	16.0	21.7	57.4	15.0	95.1
Moscow	9.0	23.3	64.4	25.2	96.7
Narva	4.7	19.1	73.2	30.3	97.0
Neva	1.7	14.6	81.6	36.8	97.9
Okhta	2.7	24.4	69.7	27.6	96.8
Petersburg Side	11.5	23.3	60.1	22.1	94.9
Rozhdestvo	9.3	21.5	65.6	25.2	96.4
Spasskaia	5.2	18.0	73.6	32.3	96.8
Vasil'evskii Island	8.4	20.5	66.6	24.6	95.5
Vyborg	4.1	16.8	72.3	29.0	93.2

Note: the 'workers' column has been calculated as a percentage of the total population of each district. As those included in this rubric were also included by the census enumerators under the categories 'bourgeoisie' and 'peasant', they are omitted from the estimation of total percentage.

the urban environment itself – contributed to the exacerbation of social unrest and class antagonisms.

As Table 2.iii reveals, the districts were not socially homogeneous.

The failure of the St Petersburg Duma, the elected municipality, to extend the tramway network (municipalised by 1902 and electrified after 1906) into the outskirts and the complete absence of a suburban railway system or an underground had checked the development of separate middle-class or working-class suburbs. In each district all social groups were intermingled. In that sense there were no purely working-class quarters. Even 'proletarian' Vyborg, for example, had 28 per cent of its population classed as non-peasant in 1910. And the central city districts of Admiralty, Kazan, Liteinii and Spasskaia, whilst they were high-class residential areas favoured by the gentry, bureaucrats and the professional middle classes, were also centres of entertainment, commerce (in particular petty trading) and artisanal occupations such as clothing, food processing, gold and silver and printing. Thus they contained not inconsiderable numbers of wage earners, as well as hordes of domestic servants. Nevertheless, within districts and between districts, there were perceptible trends towards residential and social segregation. Within the congested centre, working and tradespeople were consigned by high rents to basements or garrets. In Kazan district, the eastern first ward was distinctly upper class, whereas the western second and third wards sheltered a multiplicity of artisanal workshops. In Vasil'evskii Island the eastern-end first ward was home to nobles, merchants, officials and students (here were located the university and Stock Exchange) but at the western tip lay the Baltic Shipyards and in the north several machine and electrical construction plants, as well as cotton mills. Moreover certain, more outlying, areas did contain higher concentrations of purely industrial operatives – Narva to the south-west (dominated by the Russian-American Rubber Company), Neva to the south-east (with the Neva Shipyards, locomotive repair shops, Neva Stearine), Vyborg to the north-east (with machine construction and metal processing in the first place, followed by cotton), and beyond the official city boundaries Peterhof (the Putilov works) and Shlissel'burg (Obukhov steel). According to the forms of manufacturing and commerce present, the working class of each district – indeed of each ward – was characterised by different ratios of male to female, adult to juvenile, skilled to unskilled. These factors conditioned the contrasting response of the workers of individual neighbourhoods to events and the appeal of the revolutionary parties. Thus Vyborg came to the fore in this period because of its exceptionally high proportion of skilled, better educated, male workers with deeper roots in the city.[22] The close propinquity in which rich and poor lived in the central quarters, as well as the greater social and physical distance between privileged and underprivileged in the outskirts, contributed to the crystallisation of the class consciousness of at least a minority of skilled workers and to the inchoate, inarticulate, diffuse resentments of the unskilled.

In stark contrast to the electric street lighting and stone pavements of the city centre, the peripheral regions, if they were lit at all, were still illuminated by sparsely located kerosene lamps, as was the interior of most workers' dwellings. Lesnoi, Neva, Peterhof and Shlissel'burg all lacked pavements, making do with planked footways.[23] As to sanitation, the Governor General of St Petersburg himself felt compelled to warn the Tsar in his annual report for 1912 that 'the most serious sanitary deficiencies continue to remain in the capital.' The entire city lacked any underground system of sewage disposal; cesspools in backyards were the norm and rubbish was piled on the streets. Whilst in the aggregate by 1910 three-quarters of apartments had piped water and two-thirds water closets, working-class localities were least well off in this respect. In the second ward of Vyborg the proportion of dwellings with a piped water supply in 1900 was 48 per cent and in Peterhof and Shlissel'burg 7 per cent respectively. The proportion of one-room flats, the norm for workers, with such a facility was considerably less. Worse still the water, drawn from the grossly polluted Neva river, was heavily contaminated and spread contagious diseases unless boiled.[24] The St Petersburg Duma, elected by a mere eligible 12,000 citizens under the 1892 Municipal Statute and controlled by merchants, businessmen and home-owners reluctant to sanction more borrowing or higher taxes to pay for further urban improvements (the city's debts had reached 90 million roubles by 1910), finally consented in 1914 after years of obstruction to the construction of a pipeline to Lake Ladoga.[25]

The impure water supply was the direct cause of the capital's unenviable but sadly justified reputation for a high rate of infectious diseases. The cholera epidemic of July 1908 to October 1910 claimed some 8,800 lives. In 1907 67 deaths per 1,000 were from typhoid when the rate in Germany was 5 deaths, and in 1909 480 deaths per 1,000 were from infectious illnesses. There was a spatial dimension to the pattern of mortality, with densely populated, insalubrious wards experiencing death rates of 24.5 to 27.2 per 1,000 in 1909–12 as against 14.3 to 12.6 for better appointed neighbourhoods.[26]

Unlike the Central Industrial Region, the greater part of the St Petersburg labour force did not reside in accommodation provided by their employers. In 1897 a mere 10 per cent did so. A few manufacturing companies (Petrovskaia and Spasskaia Cotton, Koenig Sugar) and the brickworks still furnished barracks, as did the municipality for tramway staff until their abolition in 1911.[27] In artisanal trades (carriage-making, baking, tailoring) and in commerce it was commonplace for workers to live on the premises (often dirty and verminous) and to eat food supplied by the employers.[28] Most operatives, however, had to seek lodgings in the private sector.

Except for the wealthiest citizens, the capital's housing was marked out by its overcrowding. In this respect St Petersburg resembled the great industrial cities of the Ruhr.[29] Population density was at its worst in certain central wards with their four- and five-storey stone-built tenements (it reached over 70,000 per square kilometre in the second Kazan ward and third Spasskaia) and at its lowest in the outskirts with the predominance there of two-storey wooden houses (falling to 4 to 15,000 per square kilometre in Vyborg, for example). Nevertheless, contemporary investigations revealed the prevalence of dense living conditions throughout the city. A municipal sanitary commission inquiry in 1904 discovered *inter alia* that six people huddled together per room in the third ward of Neva district as well as in the second Vyborg ward.[30] In 1904, 51,732 individuals leased partitioned-off corners of rooms, sleeping on the floor, plank-beds or the stove. In 1910 another 63,089 resided in damp, frequently flooded basements. Innumerable workers (usually young single men) hired merely a bed or half a bed. The city's 37 doss-houses were home each night not to the rejects of society but to thousands of ordinary single male workers desperate for a place to sleep.[31]

The type of accommodation that workers could afford was related to marital status and level of wages (hence to skill). Workers had to be earning over 500 roubles per annum to be able to rent a room or a flat, i.e. the minority of skilled, married operatives. A survey in 1908 of 298 married, well-paid hands (mostly metalworkers) found that 140 resided in a flat (with rooms frequently sublet to lodgers) and that another 140 families rented a room. But single workers, those married with families still resident in the village, newly arrived migrants and the unskilled could afford at most a corner or a bed. They tended to form communal associations (artels) to share living costs.[32]

The acute housing shortage was the result of a number of factors. In the first place, there was the rapid growth of the peripheral regions. Between 1900 and 1910 the population of the Petersburg Side soared by 79 per cent; Okhta by 51 per cent; Vyborg, Neva, and Vasil'e vskii Island, between 45 per cent and 48 per cent. Secondly, in the words of the Governor General's annual report for 1912, 'the existing tramway system totally fails to meet the pressing needs of the capital's population for a complete, cheap, method of transport.' The paucity of the tram service to the outskirts, the failure to run early-morning trams for workers (operations began at 8 o'clock in the morning), the high-cost multi-stage system of tariffs, all compelled operatives to search for accommodation as close as possible to their place of work.[33] Thirdly, the St Petersburg Duma never regarded the provision of cheap working-class dwellings as falling within its remit. Fourthly, working-class housing was not profitable enough for speculative house-building. There existed several charitable or co-operative housing associations but their contribution to the alleviation of housing squalor was minimal.[34]

The consequence of what the municipality's own charity commission described as 'the complete insufficiency in our capital of the housing stock for workers', together with a new flood of migrants, was a steep increase in rents in the years prior to the war, a pattern similar to many West European cities. If the index of rent for a single room is taken as 100 in 1869, it had risen to 300 by 1905 and reached 460 by 1912. A study made in 1908 revealed that for workers earning average wages rent consumed 16 per cent of a single man's income; 9 per cent for a married man living without his family (they saved on accommodation in order to send money home); 12 to 19 per cent for a married man rearing his children in the city. The difficulties of finding a place to live, along with the inflation of rents, acted as another stimulus to economic strikes in 1912 to 1914.[35]

The few contemporary budget studies disclosed that for all categories of workers the purchase of food accounted for the largest part of expenditure. Workers' spending still went on necessities rather than new material aspirations. Single people devoted around 35 to 37 per cent of monthly income to this end, and married couples 50 to 60 per cent, the proportion declining as income rose. For all except the best-paid operatives, meat was a luxury. Diet was monotonous, consisting of bread (rye), cabbage soup, gruel and tea. The level of nutrition, therefore, remained low (itself a major cause of deficiency diseases), although workpeople who were single and earning high wages were able to enjoy more varied and healthy diets. The consumption of white bread and sugar increased throughout the 1900s. Fresh vegetables and fruit, milk or butter rarely appeared on working-class tables. Yet standards of nourishment in the city were certainly higher than in the native villages from which so many of its inhabitants had come.[36]

Cramped, damp living quarters, frequently excessive hours of toil, low levels of wages for many, unpleasant conditions of work in places of employment, were all among the factors impelling workers either to seek solace in drink or to augment paltry incomes by resort to prostitution or petty crime and worse.

The overwhelming majority of male workers drank. An 1909 investigation into the drinking habits of 1,750 skilled male operatives revealed that a mere 7 per cent were abstainers and 52 per cent had started to imbibe before their seventeenth birthday. On average the respondents devoted 13 per cent of monthly income to the purchase of alcohol, mostly vodka, with 48 per cent spending over 5 roubles a month. The lower the wage and the worse the form of accommodation the greater was the relative expenditure on spirits. Women, however, were far less inclined to drink. It would seem that after the defeat of the 1905 revolution the incidence of alcoholism increased.[37]

Prostitution, too, was a widespread social evil. In the years prior to the war there were about 50,000 registered and unregistered prostitutes and 500 brothels. Most whores were young (in 1910 44 per cent were aged 16 to 20) and from the lower social classes. Former domestic servants, grossly underpaid sales assistants and catering staff and, to a lesser extent, factory workers predominated among the street-walkers and inmates of the houses of ill repute. Single male operatives and married working men whose wives remained in the countryside were as much their customers as members of the upper classes. Owing to the defects of the police system of medical supervision (clients were never examined), venereal disease was widespread.[38]

Crime rates in St Petersburg are impossible to determine. The researches of Dr Neuburger suggest that what contemporaries described as 'hooliganism' (defined as incidents ranging from petty offences of public disturbance to serious crimes against property and person) underwent a resurgence after 1911 following on from a decline in 1908 to 1910. 1913 and 1914 in particular witnessed frequent assaults upon police constables, mass brawls ·and gang warfare in which workers were both participants and victims. Incidents became more violent. The revival of 'hooliganism' served to deepen the gulf between the classes. Middle-class opinion (if newspapers such as *Peterburgskii Listok* are any guide) showed scant sympathy for or understanding of the social causes of crime.[39]

<h1 style="text-align:center">III</h1>

The nature of the urban economy of St Petersurg, the characteristics of its labour force and the urban environment all interacted to exert a profound influence on the labour movement in the period between Stolypin's '*coup d'état*' and the outbreak of the First World War. The re-emergence of labour unrest between 1912 and 1914, its forms and demands, the ability of the new legal labour organisations born during the 'days of freedom' in 1905 and 1906 to strike deep roots and to become vehicles for non-violent opposition to Tsardom, the revolutionary parties' chances of success and the ability of employers and government to contain working-class protest were all conditioned in part by these factors.

On the one hand, circumstances at the place of employment and at home constituted a primary stimulus to endemic working-class discontent. As the economic stoppages of 1912 to 1914 clearly revealed, sanitary and unsafe living and working conditions, lengthy hours of work, the stagnation of real wages and the abuses perpetrated by foremen led directly to insistent demands for improvements in these areas. In addition the employers' reaction to the gains labour achieved in 1905 and 1906 – the restoration of the *ancien régime* in factories and plants and the policies of industrial and workshop reorganisation – further increased workers' resentment and acted as another spur to the explosion of protest prior to the First World War.

The forms of economic organisation in the city also facilitated labour organisation and revolutionary mobilisation. The overall predominance of small-scale units of production (and the division of larger plants into smaller-sized workshops), the pre-eminent role within manufacturing (both factory and artisanal) of skilled male wage earners and the relatively youthful profile of the labour force furnished bases for trade unions, educational societies and revolutionary cells. And the location of workers' dwellings – the peculiarly explosive combination of workers (particularly artisans and those employed in the service sector) living in close propinquity to the rich and powerful in the central districts with the evolution of more distinctively proletarian neighbourhoods in the outskirts – fostered social differences, distrust, envy and repulsion.

Changes, too, within the social structure of the working class acted to the advantage of the revolutionary opposition. There emerged a nucleus of hereditary, urbanised, settled operatives – skilled workers, educated rather than merely literate, with minimal ties to peasant society and their families living beside them in the city. These 'worker intellectuals' were the labour activists *par excellence*, the revolutionary sub-élite, the leaders of the nascent trade unions. They provided the revolutionary parties for the first time with a solid proletarian core. They were to prove far from pliant tools in the hands of *émigré* intellectuals – indeed the reverse was to be the case.

On the other hand, certain features of the city's economy and its labour force constituted formidable obstacles to the endeavours of both the revolutionary parties and the new legal labour institutions to make a broad appeal to the multiple strata within the working class. The internal stratification of the latter was decisive in this respect. The divisions (expressed in levels of income, place and quality of habitation, dress, links to the countryside, literacy) between skilled, semi-skilled and unskilled men and women, apprentices and adult workers, factory hands and service personnel, were impossible to overcome. Revolutionaries, prejudiced by class theory and being skilled males for the most part, wilfully chose to ignore the unskilled, women, domestic servants and commercial employees as sources of support, thereby fatally weakening the attraction of their cause. Moreover, the geographical dispersal of the work-force in the broadest sense throughout the city, together with the relatively backward transport system, rendered difficult labour mobilisation on an all-city scale and the building of strong, permanent links between the district and ward branches of trade unions and revolutionary groups. Vyborg may have emerged as the most distinctively 'proletarian' neighbourhood both in its social makeup and in the relative success there of labour institutions and socialist nuclei; it also remained relatively isolated in its 'advanced' position, a significant reason for the overall failure of the revolutionary parties (in particular the Bolsheviks) to secure broad working-class support.

In the case of the industrialist community, the distinctive features of heavy industry in St Petersburg and of the pre-war economic recovery – the growing dependence on state contracts and rearmament, the desperate shortage of skilled labour – complicated the evolution of a coherent labour strategy in general and of specific policies to counter the renewed outburst of industrial unrest after 1911. The strategies of industrial reorganisation, which in the short term had had apparently efficacious consequences from the POZF's point of view, were to be undercut by the boom beginning in 1910.

Chapter 3

THE LABOUR MOVEMENT IN THE YEARS
OF REACTION, 1907–1910

The years immediately after the '*coup d'état*' of 3 June 1907 by the president of the Council of Ministers, P. A. Stolypin, marked in many respects the nadir of the fortunes of the revolutionary parties and of the nascent legal labour movement in St Petersburg.[1] As Chapter 1 has shown, the capital's employers launched a thorough and effective campaign to rescind the workers' gains of the 1905 revolution. The mounting unemployment, the savage reductions in wages, the covert lengthening of working hours through the recourse to overtime, the abolition of workers' commissions and the re-establishment of the *ancien régime* in the factories caused widespread demoralisation and fear among workers, with a consequent pronounced apathy towards participation in illegal or legal forms of protest. The repressions directed by the Okhrana towards all revolutionary parties not only drove their intellectual leaders back into emigration to Western Europe, thereby rendering day-by-day control of their followers inside Russia well nigh impossible, but also so pulverised the underground in the capital that it proved quite incapable of furnishing leadership and direction to illegal and legal activists alike. Furthermore the ideological response of socialist intellectuals to the revolution's defeat in 1905 and to the opportunities opened up by the constitution of 1906 for new, legal forms of organisation potentially capable of securing a mass party base not only further exacerbated the divisions between Mensheviks and Bolsheviks but also split wide open both factions themselves. Bolshevism and Menshevism disintegrated into a series of mutually antagonistic groupuscules, further weakening their limited forces and diminishing their appeal to ordinary working people. The ever more bitter and fruitless internecine quarrels within Social Democracy also contributed to growing strains between fractions' *émigré* leaders and the second-rank socialist activists in the capital, who constituted a revolutionary sub-élite, determined to escape the control of the former and pursue their own policies. In both respects their wishes were to be fulfilled to a large extent in the entire period between 1907 and 1917. On the other hand, the 'renovated monarchy' did open up new perspectives for the revolutionary parties, which suggested to many Social Democratic literati (mainly Mensheviks) and labour activists that their party could tread the same evolutionary path as the German Social Democrats after the repeal of Bismarck's Anti-Socialist Laws in 1890. The Temporary Regulations of 4 March 1906 had permitted the emergence for the first time in Russian history of legal trade unions, educational societies and co-operatives. Under the electoral laws of 11 December 1905 and 3 June 1907 workers and their parties were represented in the new legislature, the State Duma. The relaxation of censorship restrictions allowed the publication of legal socialist journals and newspapers. In short the possibilities were apparently present for attracting to the socialist cause in an organised manner the great mass of the rank-and-file of the working class in all its forms, which hitherto had held aloof from the conspiratorial structures of the revolutionary parties. The seven years between Stolypin's 'coup' and the outbreak of war in July 1914, however, did little to validate the exaggerated hopes of the proponents of a legal labour movement. Menshevik dreams of a 'Europeanisation' of Russian Social Democracy proved to be an illusion.

I

After the 1905 revolution Bolshevism fragmented ideologically and organisationally both in the emigration and inside Russia. Acute differences of opinion arose over fundamental matters of philosophy, the correct response to the lessons of the revolutionary experience of 1905, the evaluation of the Duma monarchy and control over the faction's ill-gotten finances. Within the broader Bolshevik movement V. I. Lenin came to represent only one strand of thought. It would be quite erroneous, therefore, to regard Bolshevism and Leninism as identical in the entire period to 1917.

In Lenin's view the events of 1905–7 had proved the correctness of his previous analysis of the revolutionary process, namely, the inability of the counter-revolutionary bourgeoisie to make the Russian revolution, the vanguard role of the proletariat in the bourgeois–democratic revolution and the necessity of the revolutionary dictatorship of the proletariat and peasantry to secure the overthrow of the autocracy.[2] The Duma monarchy was sham constitutionalism. Under it 'the old feudal autocracy is evolving towards a bourgeois monarchy'. Stolypin pursued a Bonapartist policy of manoeuvring between Tsardom's allies, the Black Hundred landlords and the commercial–industrial *haute bourgeoisie*. In the countryside he implemented agrarian reforms on the Prussian Junker model of fostering a slow capitalist development through the agency of the landowners and rich peasants. The conclusion drawn from this analysis was that the bourgeois-democratic revolution had still to be completed in Russia. The party's goals remained, as in the past, the destruction of Tsardom, the convocation of a Constituent Assembly, the establishment of a democratic republic and the eight-hour day together with the confiscation of the gentry estates. A new revolutionary crisis would develop in time.[3] In organisational matters the party should emulate the example of the Social Democrats in Germany during the existence of the Anti-Socialist Laws (1878–90) by combining both illegal activities and work in the new legal labour institutions. Illegal party cells and committees would utilise the new organisations to maintain contact with the masses.[4] From late 1908 onwards Lenin claimed with increasing shrillness that the correct revolutionary tactics of Social Democracy, as outlined by him, were under threat from two directions – from Menshevik 'Liquidationism' on the right and Otzovism and Ultimatism on the left. (These tendencies will be discussed later.) He deliberately and falsely described all Mensheviks as seeking to liquidate the illegal structures of the party, to renounce immediate revolutionary aims, and to create an open, legal working-class party, a Stolypin 'labour' party. Those ideological revisionists represented the influence of fellow-travelling petty-bourgeois intellectuals.[5] With equal venom and disregard for the truth, Otzovism was condemned as 'Liquidationism' of the left, Menshevism turned inside out, an opportunist petty-bourgeois tendency. The essential task, he concluded, must be a fight on two flanks against both deviations.[6] As Dietrich Geyer has pointed out, Lenin's denunciations of the two 'heresies' was a carefully calculated strategy which played upon and deepened the undoubted differences within Menshevism, whilst blackening the reputation of his Bolshevik opponents through 'guilt by association'.[7]

The 'Left Bolsheviks' or the 'other Bolsheviks' as Robert C. Williams has described them, in their various guises of boycottists, Otzovists (Recallists), Ultimatists or Vperedists, offered different analyses and tactical prescriptions from Lenin of the changes taking place in Russia with the advent of constitutionalism in 1906–7.[8] The 'other Bolsheviks', whose views owed most to the philosopher A. A. Bogdanov, started from the premise that a bourgeois constitutional structure had not taken shape in Russia; the State Duma was a counter-revolutionary weapon which would merely strengthen the autocracy. The situation of the country continued to be fundamentally revolutionary. As a consequence the party must remain illegal and conspiratorial, committed to armed uprising, to the military-theoretical and practical preparations for this eventuality and the creation of a new élite of cadre workers to replace wavering intellectuals by means of a party school.[9] The 'other Bolsheviks' also adopted a negative stance towards the utilisation of the new 'legal opportunities' whilst the old order survived. At the faction's Tammerfors Conference in December 1905 and at the Fourth Party Congress in Stockholm in April 1906 the overwhelming majority of Bolsheviks, led by Bogdanov (Lenin excepted), supported a boycott of the new parliament, a view they continued to uphold after Stolypin's 'coup d'état' at the Second All-Russian Conference on 21–3 July 1907.[10] The boycottists and the Otzovists both regarded participation in the elections to and sessions of an anti-popular parliament as tantamount to collaboration with class enemies and sanctioning the 3 June electoral law. They explicitly denied Lenin's argument that the legislature could be utilised in the interests of revolutionary propaganda and agitation; the State Duma could not be turned into an organisation for revolution.[11] The boycotters' apprehensions seemed confirmed by the Social Democratic fraction's performance in the first session of the Third State Duma. Accusing the fraction of 'opportunist tactics' and ignoring party decisions, a movement began in the summer of 1908 among some erstwhile boycotters for the recall of the fraction from parliament (hence the name Recallists or Otzovists).[12] Some prominent boycottists, including Bogdanov and G. A. Aleksinskii, however, feared that Otzovism might split the Bolshevik faction. Hence they suggested an alternative course of presenting the parliamentary fraction with two ultimata: on unconditional subordination to the Central Committee and on pursuing revolutionary work outside the legislative chamber (hence the name Ultimatism).[13]

Profound philosophical differences also emerged between Lenin and the most prominent 'Left Bolsheviks', who, Robert Williams has averred, were drawn to relativism in science and syndicalism in politics. Lenin and Bogdanov came to blows over the thought of the Austrian Ernst Mach, whilst Lenin clashed bitterly with A. Lunacharskii and M. Gorkii over 'god-building', their pursuit of a new socialist religion of science.[14]

At the same time, behind the recondite debates in the realm of ideas lay a much more sordid materialistic quarrel over that element so crucial to any political party – finance. Lenin and his erstwhile colleagues fell out in 1908–9 over the fate of the 260,000 roubles stolen from the 'expropriation' of the State Bank in Tiflis by the legendary Kamo in June 1907. An even more bitter cause of discord within the faction, and between Bolsheviks and Mensheviks, was the fate of the Schmidt legacy. The Bolsheviks claimed that the wealthy young industrialist and party sympathiser, N. P. Schmidt, who died in jail early in 1907, had left his considerable fortune exclusively to them. Lenin used the liaison between his supporter V. Taratuta and the deceased's younger sister, as well as her fictitious marriage to another Bolshevik in 1908, to secure the bulk of the fortune for his own group within Bolshevism. In this way he laid his hands upon some 235,000 to 315,000 roubles.[15]

After the Bolshevik faction split apart at the expanded meeting of the editorial board of *Proletarii* in Paris in June 1909, the various strands in the Bolshevik opposition to Lenin coalesced around the Vpered (Forward) group founded in December 1909.[16] Containing such luminaries as Bogdanov, Gorkii and Lunacharskii, the Vperedists adhered to the principles of 'Left Bolshevism' described earlier in this chapter, namely the inevitability of a new revolutionary crisis, sparked off by an imminent European war, the centrality of the underground and preparations for an armed uprising as well as the spread of socialist ideas among conscious workers through a new type of workers' party school. The group in particular emphasised that consciousness was a sociocultural as well as a political phenomenon. Bolsheviks had to create within existing bourgeois society a proletarian culture.[17]

Even among those Bolsheviks who did not disagree with Lenin on strategic and theoretical questions, there emerged in the summer and winter of 1909–10 a coterie which parted company with their leader on one crucial issue. The Bolshevik Conciliators, whose most prominent representatives were the legal activists I. P. Gol'denberg-Meshkovskii and V. P. Nogin, as well as A. I. Rykov, were adamantly opposed to Lenin's desire to split the Bolshevik faction and the Social Democratic party. The leitmotiv of their activity over the next five years was the recreation of a united party. Thus by 1910, even within the Bolshevik emigration, let alone the party at large, Lenin was an isolated figure.[18]

In these years, too, a similar fate befell Menshevism. Like their rivals, the Mensheviks were racked by differences over their evaluation of the party's defeat in 1905, the prospects for the new constitutional regime and the utilisation of the restricted legal freedoms enacted by it.

Mensheviks were in agreement that the upheavals of 1905–7 had validated their earlier analysis of the revolutionary process in Russia. The revolution had been of a bourgeois character, in which the dominant role had been played by the urban middle classes. Events had proved the falsity of the Leninist concept of the worker–peasant alliance. Peasants had shown that they were capable only of chronic, atomised riots.[19] Although the Mensheviks agreed with Lenin that the Duma monarchy represented false constitutionalism, they proffered a different interpretation of its social base. The counter-revolution of 3 June 1907 had divided political power between the bureaucracy (hitherto independent of the gentry) and the class dictatorship of the noble landowners, driving the bourgeoisie into opposition. There existed a blatant contradiction between the bourgeois forms of the regime (its parliamentarism) and its anti-bourgeois character. Mensheviks, (like Lenin), concluded that the bourgeois-democratic revolution had not yet been completed in Russia.[20] They, however, could not agree among themselves on the future course of events. Martov and Dan argued that the bourgeoisie would not grow peacefully into the new order. Economic developments, 'the embourgeoisment of social relations' and the inherent contradictions of the regime would drive the middle classes into opposition, leading ultimately to a constitutional crisis. The more democratic strata of the rural and urban petty bourgeoisie, rather than the commercial–industrial middle class, would be the vanguard in a revived liberal movement. Whilst the St Petersburg intellectuals led by A. N. Potresov believed that this future crisis would be solved by further concessions from the monarchy rather than a new revolution, Martov and Dan kept an open mind as to the possible outcome.[21] In this situation the task of the working class and its political party was to act as an independent political force, compelling the bourgeois opposition to the left.[22]

The real source of strain within Menshevism after 1907 derived from conflicting attitudes towards utilisation of 'legal opportunities' and the balance between legal and illegal activities. At one extreme stood the Menshevik literati in the capital, represented by Potresov, Martov's younger brothers V. Ezhov and V. O. Levitskii, and E. Maevskii (pseudonym of V. A. Gukovskii). These started from Potresov's argument that the old Social Democratic party had ceased to exist as an organised entity. The revolutionary intelligentsia and professional revolutionaries had deserted en masse. At the same time the conditions in which the party had to operate had changed dramatically. Genuine legal political activity was now possible in Russia for the first time – in parliament, the press, trade unions and co-operatives. A new proletarian intelligentsia was being formed. The perspectives, they concluded, had opened up at last for the realisation of the Mensheviks' cardinal belief in the independent activity of workers themselves, liberated from the tutelage of intellectuals, and the reformation of the party as a solidly proletarian organisation drawing its strength from the activists in the legal labour institutions. In short the 'Europeanisation' of the Russian labour movement was at hand. The strength of this case within Menshevism derived from the fact that it articulated the opinions of

all those Social Democrats (*'praktiki'* or practical workers) working
in the emergent trade unions, workers' clubs and co-operatives.[23] At
the other extreme there was the veteran 'father of Russian Marxism',
G. V. Plekhanov. He and his small group of followers, the Party
Mensheviks, concurred with the Leninist diagnosis of the emergence
of a 'Liquidationist' tendency. Due to continued persecution by the
authorities the party had to remain illegal. He feared that workers'
self-activity, without Social Democratic leadership, might restrict
itself to the economic struggle alone. 'Liquidationism' bore the seeds
of revisionist opportunism. Plekhanov's break with his erstwhile
closest colleagues, together with his strong aversion to Bogdanov's
philosophy, opened the way, as Lenin had hoped, to a temporary
understanding between the two men.[24] The position of the
Menshevik *émigré* leaders grouped around the newspaper *Golos
sotsial-demokrata*, founded early in 1908, was far from enviable. As
Dietrich Geyer has noted, they had to strike a balance between the
contending points of view in an effort to prevent their faction being
split asunder like the Bolsheviks, driving Menshevik supporters of
the underground on to their opponents' side.[25] Thus Martov,
reflecting his long-stated distaste for the professional revolutionaries,
emphasised that the legal arena had now become the centre of
influence over the labour movement. On the other hand, he
defended the survival of forms of illegal organisation as necessary
adjuncts to the struggle for the open labour movement. He called
repeatedly for the formation of a broad party involving all conscious
elements working in both the legal and illegal spheres. He, too, like
Lenin, held up as his model the German Social Democratic party in
the years 1878 to 1890. Whereas Lenin had laid greater emphasis
upon the illegal side of the equation, Martov put more stress on the
open workers' organisations as the base for working-class political
mobilisation.[26]

A distinctive place in Russian Social Democratic politics was
occupied by Lev D. Trotskii. From exile in Vienna he adopted a
position independent of the factions and *émigré* squabbling, seeking
to influence events in the direction of party unity by his own
newspaper *Pravda*, financed by two wealthy supporters, A. Ioffe and
M. I. Skobelev, son of a Baku oil magnate. He had developed his
own distinctive theory of uninterrupted or permanent revolution in
his book *Itogi i perspektivy* in 1906. On the contentious issue of 'legal
opportunities' he argued that circumstances dictated an illegal form
for the party. Nevertheless, underground workers should participate
in open labour organisations. The party above all else had to be
revived on a strictly proletarian basis. To this end he endeavoured to
give his newspaper a popular style, thereby, he hoped, making it the
mouthpiece of the working-class activists inside Russia.[27]

Whatever their differences, the luminaries of the Russian Social Democratic party at least understood that the defeat of the revolution and the existence of the constitutional monarchy compelled them to re-evaluate their strategy and tactics. A similar sense of reality, however, eluded the official *émigré* leadership of the Socialist Revolutionary party. In the words of Manfred Hildermeier, 'political fossilisation' gripped the Socialist Revolutionaries (SRs) after 1907.[28] No fundamental revision of policy occurred at the sole two general meetings of the party after 1907: the First General Conference in August 1908 and the Fifth Party Council in May 1909. Party leaders – A. A. Argunov, V. M. Chernov, M. Natanson and N. I. Rakitnikov – adhered to the treasured maxims of the agrarian revolution, the dominant role of the peasantry, the conspiratorial character of the party, political terror and an immediate, general, popular, armed revolt. But the blind dogmatism of the party bosses did not go unchallenged. As within the Social Democratic party, a left and a right opposition slowly crystallised.

On the one hand, voices began to be heard from the left demanding a return to the model of Narodnaia Volia in the late 1870s, implying the dominant role of a revolutionary élite and extensive decentralisation of the party structure. These left critics, led by Ia. Iudelevskii and V. Agafonov, became organised as 'The Paris Group of SRs'. In contrast to the Bolshevik faction, the left within the SR party were few in number.[29]

On the other hand, the issue of the party's attitude towards the new 'legal opportunities' and the continued existence of conspiratorial structures served as the focus of division. The emergent right wing began its critique with the obvious fact that the circumstances in which the party was compelled to work in Russia had altered. The underground had disintegrated. The intellectuals had deserted en masse. Whereas illegal cells could not serve to attract the masses to the party, the new labour organisations did perform such a function. The party, therefore, must redirect its activity towards such bodies.[30] The extraordinary scandal surrounding the exposure of Evno Azef, the SRs' leading terrorist and chief of its Battle Organisation, as a provocateur lent great strength to the right's criticism of terror and conspiracy. Both at the Fifth Party Council and in the party press the right assailed the continued adherence to terrorist tactics as ill-conceived in the absence of that mass movement which was its essential base.[31] Among the right-wing critics A. Voronov (pseudonym of B. N. Lebedev) severely criticised party members in particular for neglecting the trade unions. He championed the reorganisation of the party structure in such a way as to rest the primary cells upon party members in trade unions.[32] In 1911–12 the right, led on this issue by N. D. Avksent'ev, also executed a volte-face in coming out against the party's boycott of the State Duma (see Chapter 6).

The party leadership, however, firmly rejected the propositions underlying the right's call for a revision of its strategy. Rakitnikov condemned the proponents of organisational change as 'the first swallow of a Liquidationist tendency'. As the party still retained a potential mass following, it merely had to renew its old underground formations in order to recover. The basis for a legalist approach was absent, intensive mobilisation of the proletariat was impossible and there existed no developed working-class political consciousness.[33]

Even the anarchist movement did not escape the disease of faction-al strife. The differences between anarcho-syndicalists and terrorists, which antedated 1907, grew more bitter among the miniscule exile communities. Anarcho-syndicalists, centred on *émigrés* in Paris, the hub of French syndicalism, supported the trade unions and called for greater organisation within a fiercely autonomous movement. The anarcho-communists, the descendants of the terrorists, still clung to the efficacy of terrorism.[34]

II

Stolypin's *'coup d'état'* of 3 June 1907 ushered in several years of remorseless decline in the Bolshevik underground in the capital.[35] Nominal membership of the Bolshevik party stood at 6,778 early in 1907. A year later this figure had been halved to 3,000. By the start of 1909, 1,000 individuals admitted to party membership. In the spring of 1910 the Okhrana estimated the total to be a minute 506.[36]

In the immediate aftermath of the dissolution of the Second State Duma the St Petersburg Okhrana took advantage of the govern-ment's triumph to launch a counter-offensive against the revolution-ary underground. At once there ensued mass arrests of members of the Bolsheviks' Petersburg Committee (henceforth PK), its military organisations and district activists in the Moscow, Petersburg Side, Second Town, Vasil'evskii Island and Vyborg party districts. By November 1907 V. I. Lenin and his wife N. Krupskaia, followed early in 1908 by his closest collaborators G. E. Zinoviev and L. B. Kamenev, had been forced to flee once more to Switzerland. Other leading members of the Bolshevik Centre, such as A. A. Bogdanov and L. B. Krasin, followed suit. *Proletarii*, the faction's press organ, was transferred to Geneva. In the first three months of 1908 the police struck again, concentrating in particular on party organisers in the Moscow, Petersburg Side and First Town Districts.[37] As the PK itself was compelled to admit in private, after the spring arrests 'work in the districts almost ceased ...'.[38] In the course of the summer some party districts, such as Narva, Neva, First and

Second Town, underwent a 'revival' with the formation of executive commissions or committees and the convocation of conferences. In the case of others, for example Moscow, Petersburg Side, Vasil'evskii Island and Vyborg, such recovery set in only in the last two months of 1908. The reports in the party press also mentioned the restoration of 'links' to some factories. The exact meaning of this word is hard to determine. The exiguous information available would suggest that it often signfied merely the rediscovery of a few Bolshevik sympathisers in a particular plant rather than the formation of enduring workshop cells, let alone factory committees. In any case, the numbers involved were extremely limited. At the close of 1908 the 'strongest' districts, First Town and Vasil'evskii Island, each laid claim to the allegiance of some 250 individuals.[39]

An acute shortage of cadres, a perpetual financial crisis and the flight of the intelligentsia from the party exerted a baleful influence in the fields of illegal publications and propaganda work. Although Lenin put particular emphasis on the political education of the working class, efforts in this direction had of necessity to be small-scale. The authorities regularly laid their hands upon underground presses and book depots. Apart from the Neva district which succeeded in publishing one issue of an illegal newspaper, *Bor'ba*, in July 1908, illegal press organs proved impossible to launch. A handful of leaflets only could be run off. The newspapers published abroad by the Bolsheviks reached the city most irregularly and in minute quantities. Although seven districts were able to set up propaganda and education circles (*kruzhki*) on the pre-1904 pattern, the membership of each never exceeded 20 individuals.[40]

After the break-up of the Military Organisation in July 1907 by the police, the PK refused to re-establish it. In the autumn of 1907 the party's Central Committee (TsK) on its own initiative took steps to reform it. Although the Soviet authors of the single study of this body assert that 'it attracted to revolutionary work the soldier masses', they themselves undermine their assertion by admitting that the Military Organisation suffered from a lack of finance, cadres and meeting places; as a consequence its work was of a 'chaotic character'. Whatever connections were established with units of the garrison were sundered for good by sweeping detentions in the spring of 1908. Meeting in October 1908, the PK acknowledged that the Military Organisation had ceased *de facto* to exist and all ties to the garrison had lapsed.[41]

The fragility of the illegal organisational base meant that the superstructure lacked firm foundation. The PK, elected at a city party conference in September 1907, lasted a mere two months before it was snuffed out. Its co-opted replacement in January 1908 fared better in that it survived to March 1909. But the state of affairs in the districts, described earlier, meant that its ties to the localities were tenuous or non-existent, in particular as the convocation of general city conferences became impossible.[42] Both PKs seem to have consisted almost exclusively of male Bolsheviks.

In contrast to the war years, the fact that Lenin and the Bolshevik Centre had returned to Geneva and then transferred their operations to Paris in December did not prevent a fairly regular correspondence between Lenin and Krupskaia and various collaborators in the capital. At the same time the *émigrés* sought to establish firmer organisational bonds with Russia. The August 1908 Plenum of the TsK set up in the capital a Russian Bureau of five members. However, neither written communications nor the new institution enabled Lenin to exercise daily control over the activities of Petersburg Bolsheviks. In his memoirs A. P. Golubkov, secretary of the Russian Bureau, admitted that this body 'naturally could not exert great influence'. Meetings were rare. The Bolshevik majority (I. P. Gol'denberg-Meshkovskii and I. F. Dubrovinskii) was uncertain, as the Bund representative at times took the side of the solitary Menshevik member, M. I. Broido. Factional strife also characterised the Bureau's activities.[43]

The causes of this precipitate decline in the Bolsheviks' illegal apparatus, which held good throughout the period to 1912, were various. The Okhrana was exceptionally well informed, since throughout 1908 and 1909 the secretary of the PK, Iu. D. Serova, was their agent. So was the other secretary of the PK from the summer of 1909, M. I. Khakharev, Serova's husband. Regular raids by the secret police decimated the ranks of the cadres. Fear of arrest and provocation, strengthened by the co-opted nature of the PK and the Azef scandal, greatly reinforced workers' existing suspicions of underground work. The new legal labour organisations seemed to offer a safer haven for activists and a more immediately fruitful source of party activity. The unemployment of the period and the employers' counter-offensive against labour's gains in the 1905 revolution induced widespread demoralisation and indifference to politics.

A final, and most important, factor was the alienation of the intelligentsia from the party. It is impossible to establish with any degree of accuracy the precise dimensions of this phenomenon but all the reports published abroad emphasised the increasing proletarianisation of the party in the capital, in particular at the district level. The PK included only four or five workers among its 22 members in September 1907; nine months later the ratio was reversed as a mere quarter of its sixteen members came from the intelligentsia. By summer 1908 twelve intellectuals alone were left in the city organisation.[44] The underground, therefore, lost many of its most experienced agitators, organisers and propagandists. The trend in St Petersburg, judging from Trotskii's national questionnaire on all-Russian party membership in 1910, reflected a national pattern that had set in in 1905.[45] This drastic change in the social composition of the party contributed much to a deepening of worker–activists' endemic distrust of intellectuals, in particular those living abroad, and their factionalist proclivities.

The disintegration of the Bolshevik underground continued in remorseless fashion throughout 1909. The limited recovery of several district organisations in the autumn of 1908 was aborted by widespread arrests before May Day 1909, leading to the collapse of all district apparatuses. A report published in *Sotsial-demokrat* in the summer observed bluntly that 'in all St Petersburg there are only tens of independent workers'.[46] Recovery from this débâcle was slow. Writing to Zinoviev in November 1909, V. M. Fedorov, a member of the PK, reported that no Bolshevik groups existed in the Moscow, Neva and Vyborg districts.[47] Whilst some nuclei re-emerged late in the year in the Narva and Second Town districts, firm organisational links to factories were lacking.[48]

The situation with regard to the PK was no better. At the start of March 1909 the Okhrana wiped out almost the entire central body. A Temporary Executive Commission of five replaced it until the summer when a new PK was chosen. However, as Fedorov confessed to Zinoviev late in the year 'we have not a single tie in the town'. District activists held aloof from the PK, rightly distrusting it as a nest of provocateurs. A survey published in *Proletarii* in December had the honesty to confess to 'the absence of a single leading centre, the lack of discipline and order, of connections between individual participants, of unity and planned work'. Local activists were forced to work independently of one another.[49]

The already gravely weakened ranks of Bolshevism in the capital were rendered even more impotent in 1908–9 by the ideological divisions within the Bolshevik Centre, outlined earlier in this chapter. In St Petersburg Otzovist views were first expressed in the spring and summer of 1908. Reflecting suspicions of work in legal organisations as a 'watering down' of class consciousness to the detriment of saving the illegal apparatus, Otzovists in the union of textile workers in the spring refused to provide information on the persecution of trade unions to the Social Democratic fraction in the Duma for their interpellation on this issue. The PK then went on to pass a resolution defending the slogan 'Down with the Third State Duma'.[50] Towards the close of the year a sceptical PK granted only a conditional approval to the attendance of a delegation at the First All-Russian Congress of Women, proposing that a walk-out occur at the first session after reading out a political declaration. At the same time the PK demanded only consultative voting rights for its representative to the St Petersburg Central Bureau of Trade Unions: his role was to be restricted to gathering information.[51] A year later it again suggested that the labour group at the First All-Russian Temperance Congress adopt tactics similar to those it had advanced for the Women's Congress.[52]

It is extremely difficult to establish with any degree of accuracy how widespread support was for such Otzovist prescriptions among the paltry coterie of Bolsheviks in the city. The official Leningrad party history denies that the local Otzovists commanded serious respect. Contemporary estimates by the Otzovists' opponents diverged wildly. A note in *Proletarii* asserted that 'Otzovist tendencies are strong', whereas V. O. Volosevich, a member of the PK, reassured the *émigrés* in a letter of September 1909 that 'there is in fact no Ultimatist trait here'.[53] Certainly from the middle of 1908 the Otzovists seem to have enjoyed a fluctuating majority on the PK and to have controlled its Executive Commission. In the districts, too, there were indefinite numbers of supporters, who embraced workers as much as professional revolutionaries. A communication in *Sotsialdemokrat* perhaps unintentionally furnished a reasonably accurate picture when it described the sectarian infighting among local Bolsheviks as 'discussions in narrow circles of the select.'[54]

Lenin's tenuous hold on the allegiance of Petersburg Bolsheviks, debilitated by the emergence of 'heresies' in the Bolshevik camp, received a near death-blow from the fact that his eager desire to split his own faction by the expulsion of the Otzovist and Ultimatist 'deviationists' met with fierce resistance from his ever-dwindling band of supporters in the city. Although the capital's Bolsheviks were represented officially at the expanded editorial board of *Proletarii* in June 1909 in Paris solely by M. I. Tomskii, a printer who had been chairman of the first printers' union in 1906, two other delegates present had experience of party life in the city – F. I. Goloshchekin (member of the PK in 1905–6) and I. P. Gol'denberg-Meshkovskii of the Russian Bureau. As so often in the years to come, Lenin discovered in Paris that St Petersburg Bolsheviks refused to be compliant tools in their leader's hands, but were prepared to pursue 'conciliatory' policies of their own devising. Thus in the debates on Otzovism and Ultimatism, both Gol'denberg-Meshkovskii and Tomskii vehemently and sensibly opposed a schism in the faction on this issue. Both abstained in the vote on the final resolution, which condemned the 'heresies' but failed to call for a split (presumably under the pressure of the opposition of the Bolsheviks from Russia).[55] On his return to the capital, Goloshchekin assiduously sought to convert his colleagues to his view that a split in the faction would be disastrous. His efforts struck a responsive chord as an inter-district conference rejected outright the Paris resolution on Otzovism, much to the anger of Lenin. Rykov, who visited the city after the Paris gathering, also warned the Bolshevik Centre that 'the lower ranks have a negative attitude towards "factional" discussions', a percipient comment which was to be validated by the entire history of the Petersburg Bolsheviks down to 1917.[56]

In many respects the year 1910 marked the absolute nadir of Bolshevik and particularly Lenin's fortunes within St Petersburg and abroad. From Lenin's point of view his complete isolation within the RSDRP in exile was exposed for all to see at the January 1910 Plenum of the Central Committee held in Paris. The composition of this gathering favoured consensus and efforts at a compromise in the factional squabbling. In order to hush up the scandals surrounding Bolshevik finances, Lenin was compelled to suppress the Bolshevik Centre and its press organ *Proletarii*, to recognise Trotskii's *Pravda* as an official party organ with a subsidy from the TsK and to hand over his funds to the new party executive. In addition his two-year-old strategy of a war on two fronts against 'Liquidationsim' and Otzovism was explicitly rejected in the resolution 'On the State of the Party'. Refusing to condemn the Menshevik 'heresy', this document called for the overcoming of the two 'deviations' by 'broadening and deepening Social Democratic work'. In addition the gathering endeavoured to meet Russian cadres' endemic distrust of foreign control by entrusting executive powers solely to a revived Russian Bureau of the TsK (of seven members).[57] As at the June 1909 meeting of the expanded editorial board of *Proletarii*, it seems that two of the St Petersburg Bolshevik Conciliators present at the Plenum – I. P. Gol'denberg-Meshkovskii, who had returned to the capital between the two assemblies, and I. F. Dubrovinskii – continued to mediate between Lenin and his diverse opponents.[58]

Within the capital the underground ceased to function in any meaningful way. Acting on information furnished by the provocateur, the Vperedist N. P. Bogdanov, (the PK met in his rooms), the Okhrana thrice wiped out the PK in the course of the year, on 7 January, 14 April, and in September. It did not revive thereafter. Even when it was in existence for a few brief weeks, it lacked ties to most district party workers who shunned it out of the justified apprehension of provocation at the top. As *Pravda* (Vienna) observed, 'an atmosphere of extreme distrust reigns in Petersburg party circles'. So poisonous were mutual suspicions that the PK even contemplated in August the *de facto* disbandment of the underground. Meeting infrequently, the body was paralysed as before by the differences between Otzovists and Leninists.[59]

The districts, too, were ravaged by the remorseless persecutions of the secret police, particularly in January, March and July. Even in the first half of the year only the feeblest signs of life were visible. In

Moscow a temporary district committee was finally formed in the spring, but party membership was reduced to 45 souls and no factory cells functioned. In Vasil'evskii Island the spring arrests led to paralysis. Whilst district committees were reformed in Vyborg and Petersburg Side some time in the New Year, they seldom met. After the July raids all district organisations ceased to exist. Their claims to do so were fictitious. Only at the end of the year did individual activists in five districts on their own initiative re-establish personal links.[60]

The formation of the Vpered group abroad in December 1909 represented another challenge to Lenin's vain hopes of retaining some sort of loyalty among Bolsheviks in the capital. It is evident that the foreign Vperedists made serious efforts to secure a following in the city. A. A. Bogdanov's letter 'To All Comrades' reached St Petersburg by February 1910 and was reprinted in 5,000 copies. In the summer large quantities of Vperedist literature, including the first issue of the journal, *Vpered*, arrived from abroad. Vperedists secured support in the Petersburg Side, First Town and Vasil'evskii Island districts. After the July detentions, however, these areas had no proper organisational structures. As the year advanced many Otzovists, who dominated the PK, metamorphised into Vperedists.[61] Although the Otzovists in 1909 do not seem to have been able to send a pupil to Bogdanov's school on the island of Capri, at least one student, if not more, did attend the Capri venture's successor in Bologna at the end of 1910.[62]

A further rival to Lenin was Trotskii. Although the latter never established any organisations of his own in St Petersburg, his newspaper, *Pravda*, became his instrument of influence. Printed in copies totalling 30–40,000 per issue in Vienna, anything from 500 to 1,000 copies of each number reached the capital at irregular intervals and were successfully distributed. Among committed Petersburg Social Democrats the newspaper seems to have been the most popular of the *émigré* publications. Even local Bolsheviks both sold and read it. One reason for this was the attested fact that Trotskii, unlike Lenin, refused to fill his newspaper with polemical, factional articles and ensured that it was written in a comprehensible, popular style, a point of difference with *Proletarii* which Bolsheviks in Russia repeatedly brought to Lenin's attention.[63]

After Stolypin's counter-attack against the Second State Duma in June 1907, the Menshevik underground in St Petersburg swiftly disintegrated. It was never revived over the course of the next three and a half years. As F. I. Dan bewailed in a letter to P. B. Aksel'rod at the end of 1907, 'Menshevism as an organisation bluntly no longer exists in Russia'. Within one month of Stolypin's 'coup', the Menshevik illegal apparatus in the capital had been destroyed. Dan, who returned to Russia with the express purpose of setting up a conspiratorial Menshevik centre, found no support for this enterprise among local Mensheviks. He and A. S. Martynov soon returned to join Martov and Aksel'rod in exile in Western Europe. The last surviving Menshevik member on the PK, Mark I. Broido, left it early in 1908 over the issue of Bolshevik expropriations. When a handful of Mensheviks in the Petersburg Side and Vasil'evskii Island districts endeavoured to elect representatives to the PK at the close of 1908, they were rebuffed. A report in the Menshevik central *émigré* organ in the middle of 1908 aptly characterised the state of the faction's underground in the capital as 'the silence of the tomb'. In the First Town District some Mensheviks alone conducted educational work.[64]

In addition to the general factors which explain the demise of the Menshevik illegal work – the withdrawal of many intellectuals, the attentions of the police, provocation and demoralisation – the Menshevik underground largely self-destructed. The overwhelming majority of Menshevik intellectuals and party workers in St Petersburg consciously abandoned conspiratorial structures as both too dangerous and outmoded. Henceforth they devoted their considerable energies to participation in and defence of the new legal organisations – parliament, trade unions, labour consumer co-operatives and educational societies.

Plekhanov's Party Menshevism seems to have commanded the loyalties of few Mensheviks in the city. By 1909 Party Menshevik groups, whose numbers cannot be ascertained, emerged in the Moscow, Neva, Petersburg Side and Vasil'evskii Island districts. It is possible that two Party Mensheviks may even have been elected to the PK. However, Lenin's expectations of reforming the party around an alliance between Bolsheviks and Party Mensheviks proved quite illusory as far as the capital was concerned. Apart from the Party Mensheviks' paucity of adherents, St Petersburg Otzovists firmly rejected the entire concept of an accommodation with them.[65]

As in the case of Lenin, the Menshevik exiled luminaries grouped around *Golos sotsial-demokrata* were in no position to exercise regular control over either their intellectual colleagues or the *praktiki* in the legal labour movement in the capital. The analysis earlier in this chapter of Menshevism as an ideology showed that profound differences developed between the foreign camp and those remaining inside Russia. These overt ideological tensions were deepened by the more covert dislike by the St Petersburgers of the *émigrés'* claim to predominance and leadership. The former attached no significance to political activity abroad.[66] The position of Martov and his friends was further weakened by the fact that, as in the years of the First World War, they could never push these differences to extremes or condemn the St Petersburgers outright for fear of splitting their faction and losing their sole potential conduit to the working class of the capital. Shortages of money, too, prohibited the convocation of a Menshevik conference at which a common point of view might have been hammered out.[67]

The strains within Menshevism exerted an especially damaging impact upon its position within the broader Russian Social Democratic movement after the January 1910 Plenum of the TsK. On their return to Russia the Bolsheviks, Nogin and Gol'denberg-Meshkovskii, genuinely sought an accommodation with the Menshevik legal activists. They, and those whose thought like them, comprised the Bolshevik Conciliators. They offered three places on the putative Russian Bureau to prominent Menshevik *praktiki*, K. M. Ermolaev, P. A. Garvi and I. A. Isuv, all members of the TsK selected at the London Congress in 1907. These gentlemen rejected the invitation because they, like the other St Petersburg Mensheviks, resented the compromises made by their exiled colleagues at the Plenum, in particular their assent to the Plenum's refusal to censure either the baiting of the 'Liquidators' by the Bolsheviks or expropriations. They were convinced, correctly, that the Paris accords were too lacking in substance to endure. Although they and the Bolshevik Conciliators agreed that the *émigré* Mensheviks at the Plenum should nominate other candidates for the Russian Bureau, Lenin and his supporters on the Foreign Bureau of the TsK blocked this. The Okhrana then settled the deadlock by arresting all the nominated members of the revived Russian Bureau.[68] The consequences of the débâcle were severe. Lenin used this 'sabotage' of the Russian Bureau by the 'Liquidators', as well as the endemic conflict on the reformed editorial board of *Sotsial-demokrat* and the Mensheviks' continued publication of their own *émigré* newspaper, to begin undermining the interlocking set of agreements made in Paris. Thus the mirage of party unity lasted at best a mere six months.

The Socialist Revolutionaries' underground in St Petersburg suffered as severe a fate as their Social Democratic rivals. The summer arrests of 1907 caught up the most experienced party workers and professional organisers. By the autumn of that year, party life had all but expired except in the Neva district.[69]

In 1908 in a fashion similar to the Bolsheviks the SR party organisation had become extremely decentralised. An unelected Petersburg Committee, founded by the *émigré* leaders of the party, had alienated party workers in the lower-level structures. As a consequence it lacked all authority over the local party and its decisions were ignored. Although district and some factory committees were revived in the Kolomna, Moscow, Narva, Neva, Town, Vasil'evskii Island and Vyborg quarters, their existence was really fictional. A chronic deficiency of finance, qualified activists and propagandists ensured that most circles never met and that party meetings were rare. As Andreev, the city's delegate to the party's Fifth Party Council in May 1909 pointed out, in an organisational sense the party had ceased to exist in the capital; isolated individuals alone were left.[70] Membership had shrunk at a rough estimate to 1,200.[71]

At one level 1909 marked some slight improvement. After a lengthy hiatus in illegal work over the winter and spring months of 1908–9, in the summer small groups re-emerged in several districts. A 'Central Group of SRs' was founded in place of the defunct and discredited PK. A college of propagandists covering eight districts also reappeared. On the other hand the dearth of party workers intensified. The military organisation, sadly depleted in personnel, was squashed by the police. The Azef scandal contributed much to a further collapse of morale, already shaken by Stolypin's agrarian reforms.[72]

Moreover, the fragmentary evidence available would suggest that the issues dividing the foreign leadership of the party, which had no visible control at all over their adherents in the capital, were replicated locally, further emasculating the metropolitan organisation. Although a city conference some time late in 1908 or early 1909 revealed a continued theoretical commitment to armed uprising, terror and expropriations, there were 'left' critics who, like the 'Paris Group of SRs', attacked centralised control by the party hierarchy. The 'Central Group of SRs', on the other hand, inclined towards Voronov's emphasis on the value of trade-union activity. This attitude, however, met with a firm rebuff at a meeting of district delegates in November 1909.[73]

In 1910 the SR party seems to have all but expired in the capital. A report early in 1910 in the party's central organ noted that interest in illegal work had fallen almost to nil. Towards the end of the year another police drag-net swept away 200 activists. At most there survived a 'United Group of SR Workers' and another coterie on Vasil'evskii Island.[74]

III

In view of the moribund state of the underground after 1907 and of the primacy accorded by St Petersburg Mensheviks to the legal organisations, most Social Democratic activists (Bolsheviks as well as Mensheviks) and some Socialist Revolutionaries devoted their energies overwhelmingly to work above ground – in the Third State Duma, trade unions, workers' educational societies, legal public congresses and from 1910 the legal press. In this way they hoped either to lay the foundations for a broadly based authentically working-class, legal Social Democratic party (the Mensheviks' aim) or to utilise the legal institutions both as a means of reaching out to the broad masses who shunned the underground and as a cover for conspiratorial activity (the Bolshevik view).[75] In both cases expectations were not fulfilled to any significant degree.

The dissolution of the Second State Duma and the promulgation of the new and more restrictive electoral law of 3 June 1907, reopened among Bolsheviks in St Petersburg all their previous divisions over the value of participation in parliament. At the party city conference early in July and at the Second All-Russian Conference, 21–3 July 1907, Lenin vehemently opposed a boycott of the elections. In the absence of a broad upsweep of the proletarian movement and in view of the bleak prospects for an armed uprising, he argued, a boycott of the elections to the Third State Duma made no sense. However, a majority of local Bolsheviks, led by Bogdanov and Kamenev, rejected Lenin's tactical prescriptions. Sitting in the new parliament was tantamount to sanctioning Stolypin's 'coup' and an anti-popular institution, the centre of a counter-revolution. At the Second All-Russian Conference Lenin's resolution in favour of taking part in the elections was carried against all other Bolshevik delegates on the votes of the Mensheviks, Poles and Bundists present.[76] The SRs, on the other hand, were not racked by doubts. Their Third Party Council, in July 1907, voted for a boycott both of the elections and of the legislature. The Third Duma was condemned in advance as a powerless, counter-revolutionary institution.[77]

In the elections in September 1907, the Bolshevik N. G. Poletaev, a metal turner, an experienced revolutionary activist since 1895 and a member of the executive committee of the Petersburg Soviet of Workers' Deputies in 1905, was elected as deputy from the capital's labour curia.[78] This victory, however, tells one little about the extent of support for Social Democracy or Bolshevism among St Petersburg workers at this time. In the first instance, the absence of the SRs from the polls made a crucial difference as they had garnered 36 per cent of the vote to the Bolsheviks' 15 per cent and the Mensheviks' 26 per cent in the ballot for the Second State Duma eighteen months before. In the second place, as a consequence of deliberate boycottism by more conscious workers (both Bolshevik and SR), of divisions within the Bolshevik leadership (the new PK voted on 3 September to boycott the elections) and widespread apathy by the broad mass of working-class voters, absenteeism was rife. Out of 59 factories entitled to cast ballots for delegates in the city proper, 28 witnessed a zero participation rate. Even in the 31 plants where voting did occur, a minute proportion of electors turned up to vote. Of 4,000 employees at Obukhov, for example, 796 did so. So impressed were Bolshevik boycottists by this apparent support for their line that at another city party conference they won endorsement for a boycott at the second stage, the choice of electors. However, the TsK overturned this resolution. Thirdly, the circumstances of the period prevented any meaningful election campaign. District committees were in a state of decay. Electoral meetings were banned by the authorities. Two electoral leaflets alone were printed. The Bolsheviks' own organ admitted that 'the electoral campaign in the city was extremely sluggish', despite efforts to set up a central electoral commission. Thus it would be erroneous to conclude that the majority of workers had revealed widespread sympathy for Bolshevism or Social Democracy. The broad masses remained quite indifferent to the elections. On the other hand, the distinct minority of politically conscious workers who took the trouble to cast their ballots clearly did so for Social Democrats, thus displaying strong party identification. The liberal and far-right parties could claim no working-class allegiance. As both 1907 and the early months of 1917 were to reveal, the presence of SR candidates would have made an appreciable difference to voting patterns.[79]

When the Third State Duma convened in the autumn of 1907 for its first session, nineteen Social Democrats took their seats, forming an independent parliamentary group (fraction). Contrary to the assertions of some Soviet historians that the group was split between Bolsheviks and Mensheviks, both factions remained at first in a minority of five apiece. The dominant bloc comprised those nine deputies who described themselves merely as unaffiliated Social Democrats, for whom factional allegiance was abhorrent. Among the Bolsheviks, too, at least two deputies (N. G. Poletaev and N. M. Egorov), as their later activities testified, shared profound conciliationist sympathies. Throughout the life of the Third State Duma the fraction asserted a rugged independence of control either by the émigrés of both factions or by local illegal activists.[80]

Bolsheviks and Mensheviks did adopt different attitudes towards parliamentary activity by Social Democrats. Lenin put forth the case that the national assembly should not be an instrument of legislative work on the part of the revolutionaries but of propaganda, agitation and organisation. The deputies were to explain that political liberty could be achieved only by revolution. They were to expose the counter-revolutionary essence of the two possible majorities in parliament, the Octobrist–Black Hundred and the Octobrist–Kadet. The fight in the Duma must not take priority over the proletariat's struggle outside the walls of the Tauride Palace, the seat of the legislature. The fraction was an auxiliary organ subordinate to the party's TsK.[81] His views formed the basis of appropriate resolutions at the Fifth Congress of the party, May 1907, and the Fifth All-

Russian Conference, December 1908.[82] In contrast, Mensheviks argued that parliament should become the centre of all-Russian labour agitation and the organisation of the proletariat. The fraction should support bourgeois liberals in their struggle to develop elements of genuine constitutionalism in the regime of 3 June.[83]

These theoretical divergences furnished one of the reasons for mounting Bolshevik criticism of the Duma fraction in the first session, 1907 to 1908. According to Lenin the deputies had committed 'serious errors'.[84] They failed to pursue a consistent line, departing from that set by the party. They mistakenly accorded priority to legislative measures. In its first declaration to parliament, the fraction, its critics charged, had made no mention of a Constituent Assembly or the party's programme minimum of 1903.[85] However, Lenin and Otzovists alike were not averse to blowing up out of proportion fairly minor incidents for their own factional ends.

The conditions in which the fraction had to operate rather than ideological perversity or insubordination to party diktats explain the Social Democratic deputies' cautious actions in 1907–8. As Dr Swain has remarked, fear of sharing the fate of their predecessor (the Second Duma fraction had been arrested on charges that included association with the illegal Social Democratic party) greatly influenced deputies' actions.[86] They also sought to emancipate themselves from the control of exiled leaders out of touch with events inside Russia, in particular a Bolshevik-dominated TsK. Hence on 22 November 1907 the fraction passed a resolution that 'it is an autonomous group . . .'.[87] The internal differences within the fraction, moreover, of necessity forced compromises upon its members, as their first declaration revealed.

Moreover, in late 1908 and early 1909 a rapprochement occurred between the parliamentary group and its would-be foreign controllers. The 'conciliator' Gol'denberg-Meshkovskii, entrusted with implementing the Fifth All-Russian Conference resolution on the fraction's subordination to the TsK, sought a genuine accommodation with the deputies. In December 1908 the fraction resolved to accept the primacy of the TsK, but also noted that it would fulfil only those resolutions of the TsK presented to it in the form of a veto. Even before this, at a gathering in October 1908 the fraction had decided to pay more attention to legal action outside the Tauride and to draft its own bills on social insurance and the freedom of trade unions.[88]

Yet it would be a mistake to conclude that these decisions signified the growth of Bolshevik influence in the fraction, as Zaichikov has argued.[89] Although personnel changes within the fraction (three deputies had left it) meant that the balance of forces had altered somewhat by the middle of 1909, no single tendency dominated. This compelled continual trade-offs. In their published report on the second session, for example, deputies lent their support to the Menshevik view concerning the 'move to the left' by the Kadets. They also openly discussed changes to the programme minimum. They asked the well-known Menshevik opponent of Lenin's theory of the nationalisation of the land, P. P. Maslov, to draft an agrarian bill.[90] In the light of the problems of communication with the *émigrés*, the collapse of the Russian Bureau by the middle of 1909 and the Bolsheviks' shortage of intellectual experts in the capital, both the exiled Bolshevik and Menshevik leaders could exert no day-to-day control over deputies' tactics and work.

Furthermore, although the Social Democratic deputies did begin from 1909 to attend public congresses, union and educational club meetings in the capital, one has to reject the contention of Soviet scholars that the fraction fulfilled the important task of the political education of the masses.[91] In the absence of legal labour newspapers before the foundation of *Zvezda* at the close of 1910, (see pp. 72–3) the deputies' speeches and notes of their parliamentary activities were published only in the bourgeois press, which most workers never bought. Not even the illegal socialist newspapers thought fit to print parliamentary debates. The fraction's annual reports were poorly distributed. Apart from trade-union activists and socialist intellectuals in the capital, the vast bulk of workers knew very little or nothing about their deputies' work. The latter were well aware of this fundamental flaw. At a fraction meeting in October 1908 reports revealed that the population was completely ignorant of their representatives' work. In the spring of 1910, they noted that 'our speeches meet with no response in the country'. Trotskii's admittedly very restricted questionnaire confirmed this sad verdict. His respondents revealed that, for the most part, they seldom encountered reports of the fraction's doings and were not interested in them.[92] Deputies, too, held aloof from the underground. And given their numerical insignificance in the legislature they stood no chance of securing positive legislative achievements as Mensheviks hoped. Indeed party dogma led them into voting against the sole significant piece of labour reform to emerge from the Third State Duma – the Social Insurance Laws of 1912.

IV

As contemporary commentators on the labour scene were quick to observe, the years immediately after 3 June 1907 marked a sharp turnaround in the fortunes of St Petersburg trade unions. In the summer of 1908 the bulletin of the Moscow Society of Factory Owners reported that 'our professional organisations are in the grip of a serious emergency'. A year later it wrote of the 'prolonged crisis' of the trade unions.[93] In July 1907 in the capital there were 61 trade unions with a nominal membership of 53,514, representing 22 per cent of the manufacturing labour force or 7 per cent of all hired workers. By 1910 the surviving unions commanded the allegiance of a mere 12,000 individuals, comprising 5 per cent of manufacturing workers or a miniscule 1.6 per cent of the total labour force.[94] Some unions underwent a spectacular decline. Membership of the union of metalworkers crashed from 9,338 on 1 January 1908 to 3,353 four years later; the union of textile workers fell from 2,000 to 653 early in 1911.[95] In two industries alone did unions put down some sort of roots. In printing, some 31 per cent of the labour force was organised in 1909 and in glazing, 41 per cent (due to the fact that one factory, Frank, dominated production).[96] In most other trades, however, the situation was abysmal. In January 1910, for example, the union of metalworkers secured the allegiance of a mere 5 per cent of those employed in heavy industry; in 1911, the union of bakers, 7 per cent and the union of tailors a derisory 0.7 per cent.

The causes of this precipitate downturn were uniform for all professional organisations. After June 1907 the secret police unleashed systematic repressions against trade unions and their organisers. In the autumn of 1907 it shut down the union of printers with 7,500 members; in spring 1908, the union of tailors; eight months later the union of office clerks and bookkeepers suffered a similar fate.[97] The prolonged economic recession brought in its wake high rates of unemployment. This factor, coupled with the employers' successful counter-offensive against the gains of 1905 and the defeat of the revolution, gave rise to widespread demoralisation among workers with the consequent avoidance of a dangerous labour activism which could lead easily to sacking or imprisonment.[98]

The unions of the capital found themselves ensnared in a vicious circle. Declining membership entailed a reduction in union budgets and hence the scope of services offered to members. The income of the union of metalworkers, for example, fell from 26,000 roubles in 1908 to 12,000 roubles three years later. Its outlay on grants to members for unemployment, judicial and medical aid had to be cut from 21,000 roubles in 1908 to a mere 1,700 roubles in 1910.[99] The smaller unions' incomes were generally derisory. The union of textile workers disposed only of 900 roubles in 1910 and the union of bakers 500 roubles.[100] Organisational requirements commanded a high and increasing proportion of union expenditure. The eight largest unions in the capital devoted 37 per cent of annual disbursements to this end in 1908 but 56 per cent two years later.[101] But the failure of unions to offer attractive benefits acted as a significant disincentive both to workers to join and to existing members to pay their dues regularly. The ratio of members up to date with their monthly dues varied between trade unions, from as low as 30 per cent in the union of woodworkers in 1908 to 57 per cent in the union of metalworkers in 1909, reaching, at its highest, 76 per cent in the union of textile workers.[102] The irregularity which marked the inflow of membership dues, the main source of all unions' incomes, compelled union executives to carry out periodic re-registrations of their nominal memberships. As a consequence laggards were expelled. Whilst 1,486 new members joined the union of metalworkers in 1910, for example, 1,268 left it, the majority having been excluded for the non-payment of dues. A re-registration drive in the union of woodworkers cut its nominal membership from 1,500 in 1908 to 400 within a year.[103] Thus, the expulsions completed the trap by making membership of professional organisations seem redundant to ordinary workers.

In the years after 1907 the minority to whom trade-union affiliation made some appeal comprised for the most part skilled, male workers. Artisanal trade unions, such as bakers, tailors, gold and silversmiths and workers in cardboard manufacture were by their nature skilled. A survey of the members of the union of metalworkers in 1908 disclosed that the union, too, recruited best in medium-sized firms (employing from 200 to 1,000 workers) in electro-mechanical, foundry engineering and machine construction enterprises, which required higher ratios of skilled, literate males. The union fared less well in large-sized establishments (over 1,000 workers), such as rolling plants, nail production, wagons and shipyards with their larger ratios of unskilled and semi-skilled. On the other hand, in numerical terms the union's greatest support came from the large-sized, locomotive, wagons and armaments plants and shipyards of the Neva and Vasil'evskii Island districts.[104] Moreover, these skilled workers both revealed longer experience in the industry (some 70 per cent of the membership was older than 24) and greater commitment to urban living (due to relatively high wages, 57 per cent were married). Almost all were literate.[105] Women and the unskilled by and large remained outside the union. In 1908 a mere 24 women had joined it, whilst only 16 per cent of the membership was unskilled.[106]

Indeed the relative absence of women and the unskilled is a characteristic of all trade unions in St Petersburg at this time, even in industries dominated by them. In the union of tailors, for example, 17 alone of 399 members in 1911 were women. A similar pattern prevailed in the union of textile workers where only a fifth of the 400 members were female.[107]

In the light of the general unattractiveness of union membership it was no accident that even paid-up members and elected officials showed less than zealous attention to union business. In the union of metalworkers, for example, twelve of the members elected to the board in February 1909 had resigned within three months and three district branches lacked all representation on it. A year later the secretary was discovered to have embezzled the funds, as did his counterpart in the union of bakers.[108]

The relationship between the socialist parties and the trade unions after 1907 was moulded by their different attitudes towards the balance between legal and illegal activities. The Mensheviks, in particular the 'Liquidationist' intellectuals and trade union organisers in the capital, argued that trade unions (indeed all legal labour organisations), in the words or M. L. Kheisin, a doctor and Menshevik publicist, were 'a school for the working class', providing workers with valuable experience in administering their own affairs, free of tutelage by intellectuals. The unions, observed P. N. Kolokol'nikov, a leading Menshevik trade-union organiser, 'are educating cadres of leaders'. For these reasons Mensheviks believed that trade unions should be 'non-party', 'neutral' in the matter of political allegiance. Party and unions should retain separate indentities.[109] Lenin, on the contrary, favoured 'party unions', the closest possible collaboration between trade unions and the party. The resolution of the Fifth Congress, May 1907, at which the Bolsheviks predominated, advised Social Democrats working in trade unions 'to promote trade union recognition of the ideological leadership of the Social Democratic Party and to establish organisational ties with the party . . .'. In February 1908 the TsK, again controlled by the Bolsheviks, elaborated on this last point by exhorting activists to 'form tightly knit groups in all such primary organisations in order to influence them systematically in the Social Democratic spirit under the guidance of the local party centres.' The PK had earlier endorsed this point of view in the summer of 1907.[110] In other words trade unions were to be subordinated to the (Bolshevik) underground and to be utilised for Bolshevik revolutionary goals. As Dr Rice has shown, the Socialist Revolutionaries never evolved a coherent policy towards trade unions. Not until 1907 did the Third Party Council adopt resolutions which, like the Mensheviks, sought an autonomous, 'neutral' role for trade unions. Party members should not found cells within unions. Most SRs in fact remained prejudiced against union work.[111]

There exists no reliable data on the party allegiance of union officials and rank-and-file members in the period 1907–10. The evidence is impressionistic. The SRs apparently enjoyed the least success. In 1908 the party still retained some influence among metalworkers, as the board of this union included nine SRs. As late as 1910–11 the vice-chairman of the union was the SR M. P. Zatonskii. The board of the union of marble and granite workers was also SR controlled. The SRs, too, enjoyed some support in several weak artisanal unions such as carton workers, confectionery workers, gold and silversmiths and commercial employees. But the party suffered from a lack of experienced and willing candidates for union office.[112] Contrary to the unsubstantiated argument of the Soviet researcher N. I. Kats, the Bolsheviks had not conquered a majority of trade unions by 1910.[113] Indeed the emergence of Otzovist views in St Petersburg meant that in 1908–10 many Bolshevik activists evinced overt hostility to participation in trade unions. The few eminent Bolshevik trade unionists, such as R. V. Malinovskii, secretary of the union of metalworkers in 1907–9 or S. I. Kanatchikov, secretary of the union of woodworkers in 1909, were the exceptions to the rule. The board of the union of textile workers was one of the few to fall under Bolshevik dominance. Mensheviks, on the contrary, were the most assiduous trade unionists. The unions of metalworkers and printers were their bastions in this period. Menshevik intellectuals dominated the illegal Central Bureau of Trade Unions until its demise in January 1910. These years did witness the emergence of an admittedly small coterie of genuinely proletarian leaders, worker–intellectuals, politically committed Social Democrats, nurtured for the most part by their activities in the trade unions and worker clubs. Furthermore, whilst this first generation of labour activists attached primary importance to legal activity and vehemently opposed control by the illegal party organisations, in the conditions of daily repressions by the authorities and employers they were not averse to some form of co-operation with the underground on their own terms. Thus at meetings, in the autumn of 1909, of Social Democratic trade unionists a motion to bury the underground was overwhelmingly rejected. On the other hand those present, while emphasising that the centre of gravity of party work should rest in the legal sphere, resolved to utilise illegal organisations formed of party members working in open labour institutions which would provide leadership to the political movement of the working class. Arrests of leading trade unionists in November 1909 and January 1910 aborted this plan.[114] The foundation of the St Petersburg Initiative Group early in 1911 realised these aspirations.[115] On the other hand some prominent unionists and those ordinary members who professed sympathy with the party normally described themselves merely as 'Social Democrats' without specifying factional allegiance. If sense of party identification was strong for many, factional loyalties were not. It is not without significance that the solitary contemporary enquiry into party support among rank-and-file unionists by the Central Bureau of Trade Unions recorded a third of members at the end of 1907 simply as revealing affinity with the

Social Democratic party as such; two years later, a half made such a claim.[116]

V

In addition to the State Duma fraction and trade unions, socialists utilised four other potential avenues of communciation to the broad mass of St Petersburg proletarians – workers' educational societies, the legal press, public congresses and the so-called 'petition campaign'.

One of the most novel features of working-class life after 1907 was a rapid mushrooming of labour educational societies and evening courses, testimony to some workers' eager desire for self-improvement. By 1909 fifteen such societies, each located in a specific district of the city and drawing upon inhabitants' loyalties to their own quarter, had come into existence, with around 5,000 participants. Membership of individual societies varied from as high as 700 at the Society of Education of the Vyborg District in 1911 to 264 at the Nekrasov Society of Education in the Petersburg Side.[117] Together with the trade unions, these cultural clubs and societies were a significant medium in the formation of a workers' intelligentisa and of proletarian cadres experienced in leadership and the conduct of their own affairs. All these institutions were run on similar lines with programmes of lectures, libraries, reading rooms, tearooms, excursions and musical evenings. They became local centres for mutual association and sociability.[118]

On the other hand, clubs, like trade unions, suffered from a variety of defects limiting their effectiveness either as means of socialist education or as conduits to the masses. The authorities placed innumerable obstacles in their way. From 1908 they effectively banned lectures on socioeconomic, legal and labour themes. Thus, for the most part, lecturers could discourse only on literature and the natural sciences. In 1910 the society 'Knowledge', for example, was debarred from offering talks on social insurance and illnesses at work. In its first two years of existence the society 'Enlightenment' was forced to cancel 21 lectures.[119] With a membership in constant flux – at the Society of Education of the Narva district during its first three years only 40 of 1,500 members were permanent – the educational societies failed to attract women or the unskilled. Participants were mostly skilled, young, single male workers from factories as well as artisanal workshops. At 'Enlightenment', a mere 75 of 371 members were women. Almost all those belonging to the society 'Source of Light and Knowledge' were under 40 years of age and half were single.[120] There was an interpenetration of membership, too, between trade unions and workers' clubs. At 'Knowledge' 88 of its 226 members belonged to professional organisations, 37 of them to the union of metalworkers, 25 the union of printers and 24 the union of textile workers.[121]

The factional allegiance of the boards of workers' cultural organisations is unclear. Certainly some local Bolsheviks, in particular female intellectuals such as P. F. Kudelli and K. N. Samoilova, played a prominent role in promoting workers' education, seeking in this work a more profitable outlet for their talents than fruitless and dangerous conspiratorial activity. At least one local society, 'Source of Light and Knowledge' in Vasil'evskii Island, was set up by local Bolsheviks at the close of 1907 as a rival to an established Menshevik-controlled club. There were illegal Bolshevik cells in other societies such as 'Enlightenment' and 'Science-Life'.[122] However, as was the case with the trade unions, the activists in charge of clubs tended to regard themselves as non-factional Social Democrats. Cultural associations did bring benefits for both Social Democratic factions as their premises were used as meeting places for underground committees, the PK and the Central Bureau of Trade Unions. Members of district committees also joined workers' societies and were elected to their boards. SRs, too, were involved in educational societies. They helped found the Narva district society 'Education' in 1910 and had an influence in several others.[123]

In sharp contrast both to the period 1905–7 and 1912–14, one of the severest handicaps faced by proponents of the open labour movement and underground activists alike in St Petersburg in the three years after 1907 was lack of access to legal publishing. The authorities maintained a rigid ban upon the publication of socialist daily newspapers, potentially the most effective means of communication with the masses. Although a few trade-union journals succeeded in publishing respectable print runs (*Edinstvo*, the organ of the union of metalworkers, in 1907 attained a circulation of 10,000 copies per issue and *Pechatnoe delo*, the journal of the union of printers, 4,000 copies), their contents were restricted to professional concerns and their distribution limited to union members.[124] It was not until 1910 that some change for the better occurred.

The Menshevik littérateurs were the first to seize the initiative. At the start of that year they launched a typical 'thick' monthly periodical, *Nasha zaria*. This became the mouthpiece of the leading 'Liquidationist' intellectuals, F. A. Cherevanin, P. A. Garvi, Iu. A. Isuv, V. O. Levitskii, E. Maevskii and A. N. Potresov. The journal, however, was in no sense a popular organ. In 1910 and 1911 its circulation was restricted to a minute 2,500 to 3,000 copies per issue and its content was given over to theoretical pieces. Its financial situation was chronically bad. Despite Potresov's hopes, the organ never became the mouthpiece of the State Duma fraction nor an affair of the Menshevik *praktiki*. Indeed its resolutely 'Liquidationist' line served as a cause of further strain between Menshevik *émigrés* and its editors.[125]

Potresov's plans were also frustrated by the fact that in December 1910 the Bolsheviks and Party Mensheviks stole a march upon their rivals by starting publication of a legal weekly daily newspaper, *Zvezda*, as the official organ of the Social Democratic Duma fraction. As with the history of the gestation of the Bolshevik daily *Pravda* in 1912, (see Chapter 6) the convoluted origins of *Zvezda* owed little to Lenin, who was to exercise minimal sway over its contents in its initial stages. The impetus came from the Duma fraction itself which had quickly grasped how their work in parliament was deprived of much of its significance without their own press organ to illuminate and explain their actions. The deputies' problem lay in their lack of financial means which reluctantly compelled them to seek external sources of funding from the Bolshevik Centre, the sole possible source of aid. Thus at the meeting of the expanded editorial board of *Proletarii* in Paris in June 1909, through the agency of Gol'denberg-Meshkovskii, the fraction sought a grant of 1,000 roubles. On the other hand, they endeavoured to avoid control of the new newspaper by Lenin and his minions by stipulating a composition of the future editorial board precluding Leninist dominance. From the outset Lenin himself was extremely lukewarm towards the project, precisely because he feared editorial authority would lie with the Bolshevik Conciliators, the deputy N. G. Poletaev and V. D. Bonch-Bruevich, the historian and ethnographer, two of the chief innovators of the project. In the end, however, he contributed 3,000 roubles towards the scheme.[126] The negotiations to set up the newspaper caused a rupture within the Menshevik wing of the Duma fraction. Two deputies opposed a joint venture with the Bolsheviks, viz. E. P. Gegechkori, a Georgian lawyer representing Kutais province and G. S. Kuznetsov, a railway worker who sat for Ekaterinoslav province. One deputy, I. P. Pokrovskii, a doctor elected from Kuban' and Terek regions, was a warm supporter. N. S. Chkheidze, endeavouring as always in these years to prevent a schism in the fraction, lent it tepid support. The fraction finally gave the plan its blessing by donating 2,000 roubles towards its expenses. The Menshevik exiles regarded this course of action as quite erroneous.[127] Thus Lenin did not control the political line of the new editorial board. Its first editors, V. D. Bonch-Bruevich and the Party Menshevik, N. Iordanskii, who also edited the monthly *Sovremennyi mir*, infuriated Lenin by failing to pursue a clear and consistent 'anti-Liquidationist' tack. By the summer of 1911 internal differences within the board, as well as Lenin's decision to break with the Party

Mensheviks who opposed his efforts to convoke a schismatic one-sided party conference, led to the newspaper's suspension. When it reappeared in the autumn, it had lost Iordanskii (replaced by Poletaev), had ceased to be the official organ of the parliamentary fraction and had become a more solidly Bolshevik (although not Leninist) undertaking.[128]

A noteworthy feature of the more pluralistic character of Russian society after the 1905 revolution was the convocation of a series of public congresses devoted to contemporary social issues. Both Bolshevik and Menshevik legal activists hoped to use attendance at these gatherings by workers' representatives for purposes of agitation and propaganda. In some respects they enjoyed comparative success. St Petersburg trade unions and workers' clubs managed to dispatch delegations to six congresses, where they presented reports and resolutions elaborating a class and socialist point of view on the issues under discussion. At the First All-Russian Women's Congress in December 1908, for example, they presented ten reviews upon themes as diverse as women in the factory, female artisans, women printers and commercial employees. The labour group persuaded the economic section to adopt their resolution calling for full freedom of union organisation and the democratisation of the state.[129] At the First All-Russian Temperance Congress at the close of 1909, twelve reports were delivered. The gathering supported the workers' resolution in favour of freedom of coalition.[130] Before both these congresses, moreover, the local unions in the capital had attempted to campaign among workers on the subjects to be raised at the gatherings. Thus in the autumn of 1908 the Menshevik legal organisers, led by Alexandra Kollontai, set up a commission of union representatives which arranged over 40 meetings, attracting some 600 women to discuss working women's lot: 13,000 copies of an appropriate leaflet were distributed. Materials for reports were gathered. A year later similar preparations occurred before the Temperance Congress with the dissemination of 12,000 copies of a questionnaire on workers' drinking and living habits.[131] On the other hand the claim of the Soviet historian N. I. Letunovskii, that the congresses strengthened party ties to the masses is exaggerated.[132] In the first instance, the authorities prevented any preparatory work before some congresses, as with the First All-Russian Co-operative Congress, April 1908, or arrested the delegates chosen, as on the eve of the Temperance Congress.[133] On other occasions the local activists themselves felt unable even to attempt preliminary meetings of workers, as before the First Congress of the Representatives of Popular Universities, January 1908 or the First All-Russian Congress on the Struggle against Prostitution, April 1910.[134] In view of the restricted nature of union membership and the absence of a daily legal labour press, it would be more accurate to describe Petersburg workers' overall attitude to such congresses as apathetic. Of equal significance in organisational terms was the fact that the labour groups formed at the congresses dispersed afterwards, leaving no permanent links behind them. Although the congresses undoubtedly contributed to the training and confidence of labour leaders attending them – the Bolsheviks such S. I. Kanatchikov, N. I. Lebedev, R. V. Malinovskii, N. A. Skrypnik and the Mensheviks K. A. Gvozdev and A. O. Iatsynevich – labour's participation therein left little other traces.

The closure of the union of printers in December 1910 and the temporary stoppage of the union of metalworkers in February 1911 led the leaders of these two bodies to propose collecting signatures among workers for protests to the State Duma against the persecution of the trade unions. This 'petition campaign' was soon broadened to include the demand for the freedom of coalition, which F. I. Dan had already raised in November 1910. He, Martov and the lawyer G. O. Baturskii (pseudonym of B. S. Tseitlin) all had exaggerated hopes that this first open political movement since 1907 might become the starting point for the organisation of an independent working-class party.[135] This Menshevik initiative divided the ranks of their Bolshevik opponents. Zinoviev, condemning it as the 'hothouse product of a dead Liquidationism', argued that the right of coalition could not be realised in Russia by peaceful means – only by revolution. This 'liberal' slogan separated a partial demand from the other revolutionary goals of the working class. A conference of St Petersburg Vperedists, Bolsheviks and Party Mensheviks in March 1911 anathematised the campaign as merely fostering constitutional illusions in a powerless and antipopular parliament.[136] However, the issue so split the editorial board of *Zvezda* that it kept silent for five months despite the protests of K. A. Gvozdev, chairman of the union of metalworkers, and the resolve of several unions to boycott it as a reprisal. It was not until the end of May 1911 that the newspaper finally expressed a hesitant opinion by publishing two articles by prominent Party Mensheviks, one cautiously in favour of the campaign and one hostile to it.[137] The success or otherwise of the 'petition campaign' is hard to gauge with reasonable accuracy. It understandably won the support of most unions and working men's clubs. The general meetings of the union of metalworkers in May and October 1911, for example, voted to support the demand for freedom of coalition. During the spring debates in the legislature on the insurance bills, N. S. Chkheidze read out the text of the petition for freedom of coalition. At the end of the year the Social Democratic fraction introduced a bill guaranteeing the right to strike. On the other hand collections of signatures proceeded only during par-

Table 3.i: Number of Strikes and Strikers in the Russian Empire and St Petersburg Province, 1907–10[139]

| | Strikes | | Strikers | |
	Empire	St Petersburg Province	Empire	St Petersburg Province
1907	3,573	1,023 (28.6)	740,074	279,881. (37.8)
1908	892	58 (6.5)	176,101	17,473 (9.9)
1909	340	9 (2.6)	64,166	4,119 (6.4)
1910	222	11 (5.0)	46,623	1,381 (3.0)

Note: Bracketed figures represent the number of St Petersburg strikes and strikers as a percentage of the Empire total.

liamentary sessions. By early 1912 some 14,000 individuals had signed copies of the petition. As the Mensheviks' oppenents never tired of emphasising, the Social Democratic bill stood no chance of success. Expectations of the campaign serving as the starting point of the regeneration of the party proved to be wildly optimistic. The broad mass of workers remained unaffected by the initiative.[138]

VI

No aspect of the St Petersburg labour movement after June 1907 was as drastically affected by the onset of political reaction, industrial depression, soaring unemployment and the employers' counter-offensive as the workers' strike struggle.

As Table 3.i. demonstrates, after 1907 (or more accurately after June 1907) the strike movement in the capital entered a precipitate decline, emitting the most feeble pulses of life. In sharp contrast to the years 1905–7, as well as the pre-war period of April 1912–July 1914, St Petersburg province ceased to play a vanguard role with regard to all-Russian stoppages.[140] As its share of the all-Empire total number of participants in strikes shrank from 10 per cent in 1908 to 3 per cent in 1910, the share of the Central Industrial Region (in which textile production predominated) rose from 16 per cent to 56 per cent of all strikers in the Empire.[141] Moreover, walk-outs of an economic character became the chief form of protest, whereas in 1905–7 as well as 1912–14, political actions occupied first place. The mass strikes on 22 November 1907 in opposition to the trial of the Social Democratic deputies of the Second Duma (72,000 downed tools) marked the end of the wave of politically inspired disturbances. In view of the unpropitious circumstances in 1908–10, as well as the moribund state of the underground, the local Bolsheviks were in no position to attempt to spark off mass strikes on the anniversary of 9 January 1905 ('Bloody Sunday') or May Day. On all of these occasions the Bolsheviks advised against striking, warnings heeded by workers.[142] Whereas metalworkers occupied the chief place in the strike movement in 1905–6 and 1912–14, they were responsible for a mere 6 per cent of strikers in the province in 1909 and 14 per cent the following year. In contrast textile workers comprised around 38 per cent of all strikers in 1907–8, peaking at 92 per cent in 1909. Only in 1910 did their share fall to around a quarter. Printers, too, proved to be as militant as metalworkers on occasions, forming 21 per cent of all strikers in 1907 and 38 per cent in 1910.[143] Again, in sharp distinction to the years immediately before the outbreak of the war, economic stoppages were overwhelmingly defensive in nature. The textile shutdowns of 1909, for example, were provoked by the employers' reductions in rates of pay and lengthening of the working day.[144] Two other characteristics mark the industrial action of 1908 to 1910; walk-outs were of short duration and a majority of strikers were defeated. This was the fate of the textile disputes and of a tramway strike in 1909.[145]

VII

The period between 3 June 1907 and 1911 was marked by the rapid decline of all revolutionary parties in St Petersburg, the evaporation of strikes, the break-up and decay of the underground, the fragmentation of both Bolshevism and Menshevism and the temporary triumph of employers and the authorities. In it can be discerned trends which were to characterise the labour and revolutionary movements of the capital between 1911 and February 1917.

In the first place, socialist ideologues in emigration, whether Lenin or Bogdanov, Martov and Dan, Plekhanov or Chernov were divorced from their overwhelmingly proletarian followers in the city. None of the exiled revolutionary leaders proved able to exercise effective daily control over their illegal party members or the new legal labour movement. Problems of distance and finance were compounded by the factional divisions and infighting of Bolshevism and Menshevism, which inflicted grave damage on their chances of success. In St Petersburg Leninists were never in a majority in this period, but jostled for hegemony within the Bolshevik faction between more numerous Otzovists, Vperedists and 'Conciliators'. The contentious issue of 'Liquidationism' permanently strained relations between the editors of *Golos sotsial-demokrata* and the Menshevik intellectuals in the capital. Instead, the crucial role in revolutionary and labour politics after 1907 was played by local working-class activists in illegal and legal spheres of action. There emerged a thin stratum of a workers' intelligentsia and trade-union leadership. These party and labour organisers disliked factionalism and distrusted the intellectual 'bosses' in the emigration. They fashioned and pursued their own policies. In no way were they mere executants of decisions taken outside Russia by *émigrés* often out of touch with events.

Secondly, the importance attached by Lenin, the Otzovists, Vperedists and Party Mensheviks to the underground as the mechanism of revolutionary mass mobilisation was not validated by the experience of these years. The assiduous attentions of the Okhrana, working-class disillusionment as well as fear of provocation all ensured that illegal structures were never resurrected in a permanent fashion. The Bolsheviks failed to establish a secure PK or district committees capable of furnishing leadership. These bodies never enjoyed more than intermittent or tenuous links to factory cells or circles. Lenin's famous depiction of the hierarchical, centralised and disciplined party, depicted in *What is to be done?* (1902), remained a mirage. Contrary to Dr Steffens' view, there is little evidence that the grassroots organisations in factories or artisanal workshops recovered by the end of this period.[146] The Bolshevik underground just survived, but only in the most extenuated, cellular form. The illegal organisations were bereft of finance, intellectual cadres, foreign literature and ties to the garrison.

In the third place, the Mensheviks' comforting and reasonable vision of a Russian labour movement treading the same path towards legality and mass, open organisations as its Western counterparts before it was equally flawed. Russia's new hybrid constitutional structure, like its Imperial German counterpart, proved to be a trap for unwary Social Democratic pragmatists. The appearance of legality belied the practice of the authorities and factory owners. Genuinely open, mass activity for labour and revolutionary activists was not possible. The severe restrictions and harassments of trade unions, workers' educational societies and co-operatives prevented them fulfilling their natural functions. As a consequence these institutions remained organisationally and financially feeble. The exerted little appeal to and did not attract the support of the broad masses. They could not and did not provide a broad popular basis either for the Mensheviks' plan of an open, genuinely mass proletarian Social Democratic party nor the Bolsheviks' more Machiavellian scheme of surrogates for the enfeebled underground. The State Duma Social Democratic fraction and public congresses, too, were weak instruments of revolutionary propaganda and political education of the masses. The layer of working-class intellectuals and labour leaders was pitifully minute, its ranks depleted by constant arrests and exiling. The attractiveness of the legal labour institutions was limited to a minority of mostly skilled, urbanised male workers in middle-sized plants in heavy industry and certain artisanal trades (baking, printing, tailoring in particular). Women, the unskilled, commercial employees, domestic servants and soldiers and sailors remained impervious to the revolutionary message.

Revolutionary and labour organisers might (and did) console themselves in these years with the thought that the precipitate decline of their movement was due solely to the fortuitous and short-lived combination of a strong president of the Council of Ministers (P. A. Stolypin), industrial recession with its attendant unemployment, and the natural disappointment of workers at the failure of the 1905 revolution. The 'crisis at the top' which set in even before Stolypin's murder in September 1911, economic recovery, the unexpected permission to found the Bolshevik legal daily newspaper *Pravda* in April 1912, the advent of the Fourth Duma elections in the autumn of the same year, the creation of new legal institutions – the sickness insurance funds – by the Insurance Laws of 1912, Lenin's success in convoking his own schismatic 'party' conference in Prague in January 1912, as well as the extraordinary eruption of working-class unrest in the form of mass strikes after the Lena goldfields massacre three months later, all seemed to presage the long-expected turning point in the fortunes of the revolutionary parties. The events of 1912 to 1914 were to show whether these expectations were indeed justified.

Chapter 4

THE REVOLUTIONARY PARTIES AND THE UNDERGROUND: 1911–1912

I

During 1911 Social Democrats, Socialist Revolutionaries and Anarchists still signally failed to recover from the years of repression and economic recession after the defeat of the 1905 revolution. Despite occasional reports in the foreign socialist press about a revival of illegal party organisations in the course of the year, the revolutionary parties remained fragmented into tiny, disconnected groups, woefully lacking in members, finance and inter-district ties.[1]

Within the Bolshevik wing of Russian Social Democracy, Lenin's faction continued to attract negligible support. Although the organ of the Central Committee, *Sotsial-demokrat*, claimed in the autumn that 'there is a great pull towards the party', their Vperedist opponents were nearer the truth in their observation that 'the Leninists remain isolated from all tendencies'.[2] There is no conclusive evidence that a Petersburg Committee (PK) existed in the last months of 1911. No leaflets under its signature appeared between 9 January 1910 and 1 May 1912.[3] Insignificant circles of Bolsheviks survived in isolation from one another in the Kolpino, Narva, Neva and Town districts and on Vasil'evskii Island, but their attitude towards Lenin's proposed conference reveals that these were Bolshevik Conciliators, i.e. Bolsheviks who sought the inclusion of all Social Democratic factions in a reunited party with the exception of the 'Liquidators'.

Lenin's antagonists within Bolshevism enjoyed slightly better fortunes. The Vperedists' 'strongholds' were located on Vasil'evskii Island and the Petersburg Side, where the police reported in the summer that they possessed 'well-structured' organisations. Bolshevik Conciliators were to be found in several districts. The real strength of the two groups derived from the fact that in the autumn of 1911 they combined to form 'The Central Group of Social

Democratic Workers of St Petersburg'. Leading roles in this illegal body were played by Bolshevik or Vperedist militants in the legal labour movement.[4] The group, the most active in the city at this time, succeeded in establishing links with all districts except Narva and in publishing four leaflets, as well as arranging town and district meetings. It also made contact with Trotskii in Vienna, sending his newspaper regular accounts of its activities.[5] The willingness of these two factions, whose high priests abroad were engaged in bitter doctrinal disputes, to co-operate amicably testifies to the local Bolsheviks' desire to heal the rifts within their own ranks and to the exiles' patent inability to command the obedience of their nominal followers.

St Petersburg Menshevism displayed less obvious fissiparous tendencies. After a secret conference of Menshevik activists in the legal labour movement in January 1911 had resolved that the former should take the initiative in restoring the shattered underground apparatus, an illegal St Petersburg or Central Initiative Group emerged, embracing in its membership both littérateurs and trade unionists prominent in legal institutions.[6] In the course of the year an indeterminate number of district initiative groups had been founded. In this way, notwithstanding the arid ideological polemics between Bolsheviks and Mensheviks over 'Liquidationism', in practice adherents of all Social Democratic factions in the city participated in both the legal and illegal spheres of action. Within the Initiative Group there existed concealed tensions between the intellectual 'Liquidators', desirous of creating a genuine, open, working–class party through the abandonment of the underground and participation in the new legal opportunities (the State Duma, trade unions, the press) and those same practical men, integral to their vision of the Europeanisation of the Russian labour movement. By 1911 the latter had concluded that effective utilisation of the limited arena of public activity, conquered in 1905–6, in the prevailing conditions of police repression, dictated the creation of illegal cells, whose primary function was regarded as preparations for the elections to the Fourth State Duma in the autumn of 1912. As much as their Bolshevik rivals in the city, they rejected the pretensions to dominance of any external central committee.[7]

There were also present individual Party Mensheviks, followers of G. V. Plekhanov, who defended the primacy of the illegal party and its cells and their hegemony over Social Democrats working in legal institutions. Some had co-operated with Vperedists and Bolshevik Conciliators in a short-lived 'General Municipal Group of Workers' earlier in 1911, whilst others joined the 'Central Group'.[8]

In addition to these coteries there were three other Social Democratic circles. The Group 'Unity', based on the Petersburg

Side, as its name suggests, supported the unity of all Social Democratic tendencies, including the 'Liquidators', and, like all the other above-mentioned sects, was intensely suspicious of the *émigrés*. It, too, seems to have been composed largely of legal activists who considered the underground a necessity, including N. M. Egorov, a Social Democratic deputy to the Third State Duma from Perm province. In the Narva district, there was a 'Group of Social Democratic Workers', which some time early in 1912 established links to the Central Initiative Group. Vyborg shielded a 'Group of Social Democratic Workers of St Petersburg'. There was also a Social Democratic student faction in St Petersburg University, but its members were arrested in February 1912.[9]

Although the Socialist Revolutionaries had secured a significant working-class following in St Petersburg in 1905–7, they were in a pitiable state at the start of 1912. Their PK and Oblast Area Committee had never been revived after their suppression in 1909. There were no district committees as such, merely small circles bearing titles such as 'The Labour Group of Socialist Revolutionaries' or 'The United Group of Socialist Revolutionary Workers', all cut off from one another. There were two groups in the university. A report published in the foreign organ of the party in the spring of 1912 correctly assessed the underground's condition as 'weak and insignificant'.[10]

There is even less information about anarchist activities in the capital. An Okhrana report of September 1911 mentions the spread of anarcho-syndicalism among tram workers, tailors and watchmakers, whilst early in 1912 leaflets of anarcho-communists began to appear occasionally in several districts.[11]

As all revolutionary coteries deliberately refrained from keeping proper lists of members and financial accounts for obvious reasons of conspiracy, it is quite impossible to paint an accurate picture of the size of the underground, its social composition or the state of its finances at the beginning of 1912. The total number of adherents was undoubtedly extremely minute and constantly changing due to frequent waves of arrests. The estimates claimed in the party press must be treated with the greatest caution, although even these testify to the paucity of supporters. Lenin's factional organ claimed some 300 in the summer of 1911, as did the 'Central Group of Social Democratic Workers' at the end of the year. At the Bolshevik's Prague Conference in January 1912 the St Petersburg delegate P. A. Zalutskii furnished the probably more accurate estimate of 109 supporters of Lenin.[12] The evidence adduced here suggests that within the Bolshevik faction the 'Central Group's' claim was the more accurate of the two. At the most, there must have been a mere 500 or so Social Democratic party members. In all districts and factories there can have existed only little groups of 10, 20 or 30 or so card-carrying members. These doleful figures must be set against the total labour force in St Petersburg of 783,000, of whom 240,000 were factory workers, at the time of the December 1910 city census.

Nor is it possible to prove or disprove the frequent contention of the foreign socialist press in 1911 that the membership of the illegal cells and committees was preponderantly proletarian with very few professional revolutionaries from the intelligentsia. Certainly all ten members of the PK in February 1912 were workers. The Central Initiative Group clearly comprised both elements, and the leader of the 'Central Group', N. P. Bogdanov, was a former student of St Petersburg University. Of twenty SRs arrested on 29 April 1912, ten were of middle-class origin (of whom at least four were students) and six came from the peasant *soslovie*, i.e. workers.[13] Nor were the committees exclusively the preserve of men. Seven of the above mentioned twenty SRs were in fact women, and a leading Vperedist in the city was M. V. Zhuraleva. All the known members of the Central Initiative Group, however, were male.

Whatever the true state of the finances of the various factions in the emigration, it may be surmised that very small, if any, amounts of money were transferred to the capital for the work of the underground. Most of the income of those living abroad was devoted to their publishing ventures, legal and illegal, either in their country of exile or in St Petersburg (see Chapter 6). Local reports from the city published in Trotskii's *Pravda* bewailed the lack of cash to pay for professional revolutionaries. Although the Bolsheviks had set up a network in 1908 for smuggling their foreign newspapers into Russia through the agency of I. A. Piatnitskii in Leipzig, little of this literature apparently reached the capital in 1911, as activists complained to *Rabochaia Gazeta* in the spring, in part because their transport manager inside Russia was a police agent. There were only twelve secret addresses in St Petersburg to which written matter could be dispatched. In the summer of 1911 revolutionaries in the city had received 300 copies of Menshevik and Trotskyist *émigré* publications and in the autumn a paltry twelve copies of the two Bolshevik organs. The various factions and cells themselves did not possess secure or permanent access to an illegal printing press. In the winter of 1911–12 the 'Central Group' alone published four leaflets and the Town district issued a hectographed appeal (in 2,500 copies) for organisation. The Socialist Revolutionaries also lacked regular supplies of central publications.[14]

The final and most debilitating weakness of the different socialist groups was the continuous absence of mechanisms to link up the isolated committees and factory cells and to provide all-city leadership, which could impart central direction to their activities, implement joint plans of action and act as conduits for instructions, advice and finance from the exiled leadership. The frequent arrests of activists, the strong fear of provocation and the suspicions engendered thereby, the mutual ignorance among committees of one another's existence, all constrained revolutionaries to shun the establishment of central city committees. The underground still remained at the end of 1911 but in an atomised, cellular form. The price of its survival was its impotence.

II

Contrary to Soviet historians 'The All-Russian Party Conference' convoked by Lenin in Prague in January 1912 did not mark an immediate turning point in the fortunes of the Bolsheviks in St Petersburg. The transparency of the Bolshevik leader's motives – his desire to equate the Bolshevik faction with the party – the blatantly manipulative character of the 'election' of the two delegates from the capital, and the dubious legality of the entire proceedings deepened divisions within Social Democracy.

Throughout 1910 and 1911 Lenin and his tiny cohort of followers in Western Europe had been cut off in personal and organisational terms from Russia. In an effort both to re-establish his ties to party members and to provide, indoctrinate and train convenors for his own factional conference, in the summer of 1911 Lenin had arranged his own party school at Longjumeau outside Paris. At least with regard to St Petersburg his endeavours proved less than successful. When three district committees condemned the school as a schismatic undertaking, the agent sent by Lenin to the capital merely selected three individuals. Due to the intervention of N. G. Poletaev, the Bolshevik deputy representing the city in the Third State Duma, only one of the three 'pupils' dispatched abroad was a Leninist (a woman rubber-worker) – the other two were a Vperedist (a metalworker) and a Bolshevik Conciliator, I. S. Belostotskii, a legal activist employed as a turner at Putilov. The memoirs of participants of this 'First Marxist University' reveal that the heavy schedule of lectures on Marxist theory, history, art, and philosophy induced apathy and discontent among the pupils, who had wanted practical training for their role inside Russia. Nor did the three students from the capital play an active part on their return in restoring party organisations or arranging the elections to the conference.[15] Thus Longjumeau failed to let Lenin gain control of the party machinery in the capital.

The contemporary report in the organ of the Central Committee that preparations in St Petersburg for the conference 'meet with great response among conscious workers' was a travesty of the truth.

Indeed the situation facing the agents Lenin sent to the city from Paris in the summer and autumn of 1911 – B. A. Breslav and I. S. Shvarts – was far from encouraging. There were almost no Leninist groups as such. The strongest body, the 'Central Group', opposed a factional conference as unrepresentative and dominated by the *émigrés*. It, together with the Vperedists, desired a gathering of all Social Democratic factions, with the exception of the 'Liquidators', convoked by the local organisations inside Russia with the foreign littérateurs restricted to a consultative vote. Even the small numbers of non-Vperedist Bolsheviks envinced little sympathy for Lenin's schismatic plan. At meetings in the summer in the Kolpino, Narva and Town districts and on Vasil'evskii Island they revealed their support for the Bolshevik Conciliators abroad by voting in favour of resolutions welcoming the formation of the Foreign Organising Commission at the close of May 1911 in Paris, dominated by the Conciliators, and by demanding a dominant role in arranging the conference for the militants inside Russia.[16] The very sparseness, however, of Leninist cells facilitated manipulation and fraud by his emissaries. There is evidence to suggest that these gentlemen disguised the true nature of Lenin's conference by claiming that it bore the imprimatur of the Foreign Organising Commission (the reverse was the case). The actual date of the 'elections' and the true numbers of participants remain shrouded in mystery. On 4 September 1911 thirteen Bolsheviks had selected a worker at Neva Shipyards to represent them at a gathering being arranged in Baku by Sergo Ordzhonikidze to set up a Russian Organising Commission (ROK), thereby supplanting the Bolshevik Conciliators' body in Paris. This delegate (who never arrived in Baku due to his arrest) was given a significant mandate to secure the transfer of the Central Committee to Russia 'as at present being abroad it is completely cut off from the local organisations of the empire', another indication of the distrust even Lenin's own adherents entertained towards foreign control. In August Breslav had pre-empted, either by design or accident, the future decisions of the non-existent ROK by orchestrating the election as delegates to the party conference of himself and three unidentified individuals. He was detained in Moscow two months later.[17] In November, after the creation of the ROK, S. S. Spandarian, an Armenian member, was dispatched to the city. He made contact with a tiny group of Bolsheviks at the giant Obukhov plant in the Neva district, one of whose number, E. P. Onufriev (a draughtsman), was elected a delegate at an assembly of fifteen district representatives. It is indicative of the dire straits to which Lenin's agents were reduced in their search for 'loyal' delegates that Onufriev had been inactive in party work since 1906, and that their second choice, P. A. Zalutskii, a metalworker at the

Franco-Russian plant, had arrived in the city only in 1911 after years in the Far East. The two men's pretensions to represent all Bolsheviks, let alone Social Democrats or 'the workers of St Petersburg' were utterly spurious. Even if one accepts the suspiciously accurate figure of 110 participants in the 'elections' given in the brochure *Vserossiiskaia konferentsiia RSDRP*, the number was very low and unrepresentative.[18]

Despite all Lenin's frantic endeavours to secure the dispatch of compliant and like-minded delegates, most of the fourteen 'representatives' from Russia gathered in Prague (6–17 January old style) – notwithstanding their fraudulent mandates and the illegal manner of their 'elections' – proved unwilling to act as obtuse executors of Lenin's designs. As the Bolshevik leader later conceded in private to M. Gorkii, the 'young workers in Russia' were 'furiously hostile to the *émigrés*'. At the conference, six Russian participants, including Onufriev and Zalutskii, as well as Lenin's trusted agent Ordzhonikidze, revealed their conciliatoriness and dislike of factionalism by issuing invitations to the conference, against Lenin's wishes, to the national Social Democratic parties and the editors of the party organs of the Vperedists, Trotskii, and the Party Mensheviks, all of whom refused to attend. At least four even wanted to invite the editors (Martov, Dan) of the Mensheviks' main newspaper *Golos sotsial-demokrata*. Their lack of interest in the paramount ideological issue dividing the exiles – 'Liquidationism' – and their objection to Lenin's resolve to exclude the 'Liquidators' formally from the party – resulted in a limited compromise resolution to the effect that the 'Liquidator' group around the St Petersburg periodicals *Nasha zaria* and *Delo zhizni* 'has once and for all placed itself outside the party', i.e. the 'Liquidators' were not expelled and no mention was made of Lenin's other Menshevik and Bolshevik opponents. In this debate the two nominees from the capital argued that 'among the workers one could not observe any Liquidators'. In addition, several delegates, including Onufriev, criticised *Sotsial-demokrat* for publishing articles unintelligible to ordinary workers. The underlying hostility on the part of those delegates working inside Russia towards the leaders in emigration burst forth in the demand, presented by Goloshchekin, Ordzhonikidze and Spandarian, that the Bolsheviks' *émigré* organisations should be dissolved.[19]

Other decisions of the conference, all the product of Lenin's pen, either met with a similar lack of enthusiasm on the part of his adherents in the capital or encountered real obstacles to their prompt implementation. The Bolshevik leader's prescriptions were based on his analysis that the first period of the counter-revolution was over and that a political revival had begun among broad democratic circles. The task remained 'the conquest of political power by the proletariat while carrying the peasantry with it'. Faithful to the views he had propagated since 1908, he emphasised 'the necessity of intensified work on restoring the illegal organisation of the RSDRP'. On the other hand, the illegal party cells should be 'surrounded by the broadest possible network of legal societies', which would serve 'as bases for their [i.e. cells'] activities among the masses'. Within legal institutions, party members should establish 'small Social Democratic cells closely bound up with the party, deciding on each matter in the spirit of the party's resolutions'.[20] In other words, as in the past, Lenin insisted on the vanguard role of the underground party in the economic and political struggles of the working class and the subordination to it (and its central institutions abroad) of Social Democratic legal activists.

It was perhaps symptomatic of the unimportance of the two St Petersburg delegates or of their previous support for conciliatory policies that neither was chosen for the new Central Committee (TsK) or the Russian Bureau of the former, elected at the close of the Prague proceedings. It is true that M. I. Kalinin appeared as a candidate member and after the conference I. S. Belostotskii was co-opted to the Central Committee, but they both played minor parts (if any) in the capital's organisations before and after the January assembly.

In the interval between the Prague Conference and the onset of the Lena events in the middle of April, there is little evidence that any of Lenin's plans of securing a sound base in St Petersburg had come to fruition. In contrast to 1911, a PK was resurrected some time in February 1912. Although all its ten members were skilled workers, (six of them employed at Putilov and nine of them in engineering) mostly in their mid-20s, with several years' revolutionary experience, not all were 'Leninists' – Belostotskii was a Bolshevik Conciliator and A. F. Kostiukov a Vperedist. This fact suggests, as I. Iurenev noted in his memoirs, that the PK lacked a united, authoritative leadership. Although Ordzhonikidze and Onufriev, who brought back several copies of the official report on the conference written by Zinoviev, managed to secure resolutions from the PK and cells on Vasil'evskii Island in favour of the Prague decisions, there are indications that neither had abandoned their conciliatory tendencies. Thus the PK resolution declared that 'true unity is possible only by means of joint work in the localities'. Onufriev boldly informed N. K. Krupskaia, Lenin's wife, on 7 March 'we are working with the Central Group', despite the fact that the latter had convoked a gathering which condemned Lenin's conference as a non-party assembly. In a letter written to an unknown recipient in the capital on 20 April, Krupskaia observed in alarm that 'a letter from St Petersburg informs us that the PK has spoken out in favour of the Liquidators' conference'. Moreover, the police, well informed of Lenin's intentions through their agent R. V. Malinovskii, who had won the former's trust, acted swiftly to thwart their implementation. Repeated arrests hit all socialist groups in February and March. The PK worked unsystematically, restricting itself to reports to party cells on the Prague conference. All factions still lacked solid ties to the districts, funds, an illegal press, propagandists; minute quantities of foreign literature reached the city. Lenin spoke the truth when he remarked in a letter of 28 March, apropos the capital, 'our affairs are bad there'. Apart from intermittent and frequently intercepted correspondence, he still lacked organisational ties to the city or any effective influence over his own followers.[21]

The first significant stimulus to the revival of activity by the illegal organisations came not from the Prague Conference but from the brutal suppression by local officials in faraway Siberia of a peaceful march by unarmed strikers at the Lena goldfields on 4 April 1912, with 172 dead and 372 wounded. This appalling tragedy, so reminiscent of the fate of Father Gapon's procession of supplicants to the Winter Palace seven years before, made a similarly profound impression on the capital's labour force, when the news reached the city two days after the shooting. As Colonel M. F. Von-Koten, the chief of the St Petersburg Okhrana, stressed in his report of 12 April to the Department of Police, 'the events at Lena have heightened the mood of the local revolutionary groups and of factory workers'. From 6 April onwards a series of meetings occurred in diverse factory and artisanal workshops all over the city to pass resolutions of protest, requesting the trial of the guilty, state compensation for the victims, as well as political demands for the freedom to strike and form trade unions, abolition of the death penalty and the electoral law of 3 June. Although such resolutions may have owed much in origin to local factory socialist activists (of whatever tendency), their widespread occurrence and the sums of money sent from a broad range of factories and artisanal trades to the 'Lena fund' set up by *Pravda* in its second issue of 24 April, as well as the wave of strikes in the middle of the month, all testify to the genuine sympathy of ordinary working people for the victims, repugnance at the methods resorted to by the authorities and disgust at the legal restrictions on trade unions.[22]

In attempting to respond to this widespread and unexpected outburst of working-class protest – unprecedented in its scope since 1905–6 – the diverse revolutionary groups found themselves handicapped by all the obstacles outlined earlier in this chapter. So fast did events unfold between 6 April and 1 May that none of the foreign leaders exerted any influence whatsover. Two members of the Russian Bureau, Ordzhonikidze and Stalin (the latter in flight from internal exile), were coincidentally present in the city but only for a very short time and both were soon arrested (the former on 10 April and the latter twelve days later). The police archives contain no evidence of any contribution by them. Despite the assertions of the Soviet scholar E. E. Kruze, the PK played a minimal role throughout the month, if it existed at all.[23] What is remarkable in the reaction of the sub-élites is the degree of co-operation achieved among the different, 'antagonistic' Social Democratic factions and between them and their rivals, the Socialist Revolutionaries. In view of the weaknesses of the underground cells, the initiative in fashioning a response to the Lena massacre was taken by both Social Democratic and SR students in the university. As early as 6 April they resolved to arrange street demonstrations in a protest embracing both students and operatives. Within a week a 'St Petersburg General Student Coalition Committee', involving both socialist parties and the Menshevik Duma deputy G. S. Kuznetsov, had issued an appeal, calling for demonstrations on Sunday 15 April on Nevskii Prospekt, the main thoroughfare bisecting the administrative and commercial heart of the city. Outside the academic milieu, local Social Democrates – Mensheviks as well as Bolsheviks – in the Narva and Moscow districts made similar proposals, although they apparently carried out little agitation for fear of arrest. None of these plans envisaged attempts to persuade the labour force to down tools. However, some militants (their factional allegiance is obscure) on Vasil'evskii Island adopted this tactic. At large meetings in the evening of 13 April at the Baltic Shipyards and at the nearby electrical engineering plant of United Cables, speakers called for a stoppage five days hence on May Day, new style. Even more extreme elements among the university students issued an appeal on the eleventh, urging their fellows to prepare for a general revolutionary uprising.[24] Despite the precautions of the authorities, including preventive arrests on the previous evening of student activists and a heavy police presence in the city centre, on the Sunday there occurred at least four separate attempts at demonstrations in or around the Nevskii, by crowds ranging in size from 300 to 1,000. However, these first street protests in the symbolic hub of the capital since 1905–6 were almost exclusively confined to students from the various higher educational institutions, as the students' leaflets had reached working-class quarters only in the evening of the fourteenth, a fact highlighted by the absence of disorders that day in these areas.[25] In the light of the evidence presented here, one can only conclude that the wave of strikes engulfing manufacturing industry from 14 to 22 April, involving some 140,000 operatives according to police estimates, marked an elemental response to the shootings at Lena; the walk-outs owed little to the underground.

The demonstrations and stoppages of the middle of April acted as a spur to local revolutionary leaders to mark 1 May by a repeat performance. In the words of a letter intercepted by the police, militants interpreted recent events as 'having had a great agitational significance . . . thereby raising the workers' spirits'. They were even more conscious of the necessity of co-ordinating and uniting all socialist forces. Some time in the latter part of April several students and young workers, members of a Marxist study circle at Putilov and Tenteleevskii chemicals, conceived of '1 May Committees' as the instrument to achieve these goals. Such bodies were established in the Moscow and Narva districts, the Petersburg Side and Vasil'evskii Island, but not in the Neva or Vyborg quarters. A 'Central Bureau of 1 May Committees' was also founded, embracing representatives from the 'Central Group', the group 'Unity', 'The Group of Social Democratic Workers of St Petersburg', the students at the polytechnic and 'A Group of Socialist Revolutionary Workers' (in the Neva district), i.e. a broad spectrum of the different factions (with the exception of the St Petersburg Initiative Group). The 'Bureau' succeeded in publishing and distributing in the factories 19,000 copies of its appeal, pleading with workers to withdraw their labour on May Day and to join demonstrations on the Nevskii. The political slogans proclaimed in the document were eclectic, embracing a Constituent Assembly, the democratic republic, an eight-hour day and confiscation of estates.[26] Most socialist organisers sensibly shunned futile suggestions of armed clashes with the police, emanating from anarchists. They had been alarmed at the fact that some youths had carried weapons on 15 April. Thus the appeal closed with the injunction 'Do not bring weapons'. Although a leaflet with similar advice appeared bearing the stamp of a 'PK', it must have been the product of individual Bolsheviks arrogating the title, as no such institution existed. The police noticed in alarm that 'the agitation for 1 May is very strong . . . in many working-class districts'. Social Democratic agents toured the factories. The day before May Day, in both the Moscow and Neva areas, at factory meetings speakers exhorted their listeners to heed the 'Central Bureau's' call. The scope and character of the demonstrations on 1 May, which set the pattern for such political manifestations in the next two years, were different from those of the previous fortnight. On this occasion working people rather than students comprised the majority of demonstrators, in part because the 'General Student Coalition Committee' held aloof. The extensive police precautions – the arrests, the searches, the confiscation of the pre-May Day issues of *Pravda*, the mounted and foot patrols of police and gendarmes throughout the city – proved relatively effective. The crowds reaching the city centre were less numerous (in groups of 100 to 400 or so) and quickly dispersed. All attempts by operatives to hold impromptu demonstrations on leaving their factories at the normal time for starting work were promptly prevented by the police, who succeeded in isolating the districts from one another. It is true that in comparison with the Lena walk-outs, there was much greater, more conscious and co-ordinated action by socialist militants to foment stoppages on May Day. Yet the relative paucity of illegal cells, the absence of '1 May committees' in two of the largest working-class districts (the very quarters where the withdrawal of labour was all-embracing) and the wide scope of the strikes (around 150,000 downed tools) suggests that the contribution of the activists to the unrest should not be exaggerated.[27]

The dramatic developments of April and early May seemed to open up for socialist militants new and exciting perspectives. In the week after May Day they arranged large meetings in various districts, with audiences from 500 to 6,000 at which speakers exhorted their listeners to participate in a campaign of strikes, involving political demands, and to estabilsh factory, district and municipal strike committees. Some hotheads apparently dreamed of launching a general stoppage on 3 June and propagated the reformation of a soviet of workers' deputies on the model of 1905 (the emergence of this proposal at the very outset of the revival of mass discontent testifies to the impact the St Petersburg Soviet had made upon activists and ordinary working people alike). More cautious voices warned against 'excesses' as merely provoking repression. Not for the last time in these years the second-rank leaders grossly overestimated their own strength and underestimated the determination of the authorities. The arrests carried out by the police on 15 May broke up the 'Central Bureau of 1 May Committees' and so disorganised the undergound that no illegal central or district Social Democratic committees existed from that date to early August.[28]

The first serious attempts to revive the underground Bolshevik apparatus occurred in the summer of 1912. The initiative came from within the city itself. A. M. Korelkov, a Vperedist (a former student at the university and an informer) set up circles in the Moscow, Narva and Town districts, but failed to revive cells or committees in the other areas of the capital. The strongest organisation existed in Narva, with seven to nine circles, embracing about 100 members at Putilov, Til'mans (engineering) and Tentelevskii (chemicals). A district committee was formed which published 1,000 copies of a leaflet with a call to establish illegal cells. This group, therefore, was not dominated by Leninists but Vperedists and Social Democratic supporters of party unity, such as I. Iurenev and N. M. Egorov.[29]

The second impulse was imparted from outside by Lenin. Despite his move from Paris to Cracow in June in order to be closer to Russia, the Bolshevik leader remained as isolated as he had been in effect from February from the sub-élites in St Petersburg (whatever his ties via correspondence with the intellectuals editing *Pravda*). As a result of police action in the spring Krupskaia had lost her secret addresses in the city for letters of a conspiratorial nature. Probably because of a lack of money, very little illegal literature was published abroad in the course of the year. The last and single number of *Rabochaia gazeta* in 1912 came out in August; *Sotsial-demokrat* appeared only in three issues (May, June and November) with the result that its expression of 'official' Bolshevik opinion on events was tardy. (Lenin published nine articles in the central organ in 1912 but 49 in *Pravda*). It is not known how many copies ever reached the capital, although it seems that the Bolshevik transport network into Russia declined considerably.[30] Given the importance Lenin attached to the Fourth State Duma election campaign and his designs to secure the return solely of Bolshevik deputies in the labour curia, in the summer he dispatched to St Petersburg his confidante Inessa Armand and G. Safarov, a young former polytechnic student, neither of whom were members of the Central Committee or the Russian Bureau, with instructions to revive the underground and a PK. The evidence suggests that on their arrival both agents were compelled to reach an accommodation with Korelkov's circles. Early in September they established a short-lived and shadowy 'Inter-District General Town Commission'. Before these fledgling groups could take effective steps to remedy what one activist accurately described in a letter as 'the great lack of co-ordination and organisational disorder', the police terminated their existence by detaining the ringleaders in the middle of September.[31] It is also extremely doubtful whether a PK was re-established.[32]

In addition to the above-mentioned coteries there also existed in the summer months weak, individual, isolated circles in Vyborg and the Petersburg Side, as well as an autonomous Neva grouping. Bogdanov's 'Central Group' survived in some form. There was also a 'Central Petersburg Group of Workers', comprising mainly union activists. Its members included Vperedists (I. P. Sesitskii, who attended the faction's Bologna school) and Social Democratic adherents of party unity (such as G. S. Lapchinskii, a trade-union lawyer).[33] None of these nuclei enjoyed organisational links to one another.

In view of the complete atrophy and disorder of the Bolshevik underground in the autumn of 1912, and the absence of any central co-ordinating agencies or functioning district committees, the contention of a Soviet investigator that 'in the last quarter of 1912 the St Petersburg Bolsheviks organised four mass political strikes' should be treated with great caution.

The first of these political stoppages occurred between 5 and 11 October in protest against the authorities' cassation of the elections of 30 workers' delegates in the elections to the Fourth State Duma; over 50,000 downed tools. The archives of the Okhrana contain no references at all to the intervention of Social Democratic groups in fomenting these walk-outs. The sole contemporary claim to the contrary was made by none other than Stalin, who fled to the city from exile some time in September. In the report on the elections sent by him to *Sotsial-demokrat*, he stated that a meeting of the executive commission of the PK decided on 4 October to call for a one-day strike in response to the government's assault on workers' electoral rights. Even if this report is accurate (and there exists no independent evidence in corroboration), the Bolsheviks, in the absence of an illegal press and district committees, possessed only small numbers of militants to spread the news.[34]

On 26 October the capital's newspapers conveyed the news of the death sentences pronounced two days before in Sevastopol on seventeen sailors of the Black Sea fleet found guilty of conspiring a mutiny. Soviet researchers have always argued that the ensuing stoppages (between 29 October and 1 November over 72,000 refused to work) 'were arranged by the Bolsheviks and proceeded under their leadership'. However, the report of Colonel Von-Koten, on 29 October, merely observes that 'the local Social Democratic organisations' (factions and groups unspecified) had considered agitation for such a strike as a token of disapprobation. As with the strikes earlier in the month, the party's institutional debility, the new detention of militants on 30 October and the lack of leaflets must have severely constrained the effectiveness of factory cells. In both sets of protests the socialist press (the newspapers of both tendencies) probably acted as a greater stimulus by publishing news of the first walk-outs and resolutions of protest passed at factory meetings.[35]

The third political strike, on the occasion of the opening of the Fourth State Duma on 15 November, involving some 36,000 hands, most definitely occurred against the wishes of the local Social Democratic sub-élites. Three new small coteries were involved: 'A St Petersburg Central Social Democratic Group of Trade Union Workers', yet another united Social Democratic grouping, founded by the lawyer Lapchinskii; a 'Group of Social Democrats', Bolsheviks involved in the educational society 'Source of Light and Knowledge' on Vasil'evskii Island; and non-factional intellectuals in 'A Group of Revolutionary Social Democrats'. These issued an appeal, condemning the State Duma as 'almost totally lacking in significance for the proletariat' and exhorting workers to down tools on 15 November and demonstrate outside the Tauride Palace, the seat of the State Duma. The non-factional character of the venture was reflected in the *mélange* of Bolshevik and Menshevik slogans in the document. The SRs declined an offer to participate for fear of repression. Both Leninists and their opponents, the St Petersburg Initiative Group, as well as the entire Social Democratic fraction in the State Duma, condemned the scheme in advance publicly in the socialist press. This first attempt at a demonstration in the city centre since May Day was a failure, the crowds never numbering more than 100 young workers and students.[36]

Towards the close of the year new life was breathed again into the Bolsheviks' underground apparatus. By December a PK finally came into existence. There were district committees in the Moscow, Narva and Neva areas but not elsewhere. Lapchinskii's group not only survived but began to expand. In this month for the first time in the entire year a genuine appeal was issued by the PK, calling on working people to support by a one-day stoppage of work the presentation to the State Duma on 14 December by the Social Democratic fraction of an interpellation concerning the authorities' persecution of new insurance institutions (the *kassy*). As the leaflet appeared only on the day of the strike, the role of the socialist press in highlighting the government's hostility towards the *kassy* and of activists in trade-union meetings held in the week prior to the interpellation was probably of greater significance. Over 55,000 walked out on the day.[37]

III

In contrast to the Bolsheviks' PK, which functioned intermittently at best in 1912, the Mensheviks' St Petersburg Central Initiative Group maintained a relatively unbroken existence throughout the year. As formerly, its fluctuating membership embraced intellectual 'Liquidators' (prominent were K. M. Ermolaev; V. Ezhov, the first secretary of the Menshevik legal daily newspaper *Luch*; Eva Broido, secretary of the Organisational Committee) and proletarian trade-union leaders (A. N. Smirnov; V. M. Abrosimov). At the close of 1912 the overall balance was six middle-class intellectuals and eight ordinary workers, seven of whom were employed in large heavy engineering plants and one in printing. Seven district Initiative Groups also sustained an almost continuous profile in the Moscow, Narva, Neva, Town and Vyborg areas, as well as in the Petersburg Side and Vasil'evskii Island. Total membership, however, remained exiguous – some 100 individuals. This state of affairs was accurately evaluated in a letter of F. I. Dan to P. B. Aksel'rod with the description 'this work meets with little enthusiasm on the part of broader labour circles'.[38]

Throughout 1912, as their private correspondence reveals, the Menshevik *émigré* leaders (Aksel'rod, Dan, Martov) – who took the view that an open Social Democratic party, basing itself on the new legal labour movement, must embrace of necessity in Russian conditions illegal forms of organisation – remained extremely anxious about the frailty of the underground in the capital. Martov, increasingly aware of the potential challenge posed to the Mensheviks' dominant position in open working-class institutions by the decisions of Lenin's Prague gathering, was insistent that Mensheviks revive their own distinct party. Tacitly supporting the practical legal activists in the St Petersburg Inititative Group, the foreign luminaries continually criticised the intellectual 'Liquidators' underestimation of the significance of the underground and the importance to the party of the mass of working people who remained outside the new legal framework.[39] Despite these strictures the Menshevik littérateurs abroad did nothing positive to help the illegal circles in the city. They allowed their foreign newspaper *Golos sotsial-demokrata* to cease publication at the end of 1911. They themselves admitted that its successor – *Listok golosa sotsial-demokrata* (three issues in February and March 1912) – was 'little read'. When A. S. Martynov proposed the printing of an illegal workers' newspaper or agitational leaflets, this sensible suggestion was ignored.[40]

The views and future role of the St Petersburg 'Liquidators' played an equally divisive part at the Mensheviks' 'August Conference of the Organisations of the RSDRP', convened by Trotskii in Vienna from 12 to 20 August 1912. When the Organisational Committee (OK), formed abroad in August 1911 by Lenin's opponents, decided in January 1912 to invite to its proposed conference representatives of Social Democratic groups working in the open labour movement, the *émigré* Polish Social Democrats, Bolshevik Conciliators and Party Mensheviks refused to attend. The invitation at first caused dissension within the Initiative Group itself, as the intellectual 'Liquidators' feared (correctly) that the conference would take steps to restore the underground. The methods by which the capital's delegates were elected remains far from clear. There were apparently attempts to involve other non-Leninist factions. A St Petersburg Regional Bureau was established, comprising representatives of the Initiative Group, the Bolshevik Conciliators, the group 'Unity' and non-factional Social Democrats. The 'Central Group' showed a willingness to participate. But the numerous arrests in the spring thwarted the plan to convoke a general all-city gathering of these circles to select emissaries. Contemporary reports in the Menshevik press claim that the Initiative Group alone nominated two of its members as delegates (Abrosimov, Smirnov) and that a series of district meetings involving over 250 legal activists confirmed this choice.[41] The elections, therefore, were only marginally more representative than those to Lenin's assembly.[42]

The proceedings of the August conference – which failed miserably to realise Trotskii's ambition of unifying the party or even the anti–Lenin forces – marked in certain respects a further defeat for St Petersburg's intellectual 'Liquidators', who comprised a distinct minority among the 33 delegates (the majority of whom were exiles). The Initiative Group had struggled in vain to ensure that the agenda was restricted to the Fourth State Duma elections. Trotsky and the Menshevik émigré littérateurs, however, succeeded in forcing through a compromise resolution on the organisational question, stating that 'even though its [the RSDRP's] organisation on the whole must remain underground', the latter should adapt itslef 'to the new forms and methods of the legal worker's movement'. This endorsement of their views were welcomed by the two emissaries from the capital. Delegates also warned 'comrades of the inadvisability and extreme danger of outbreaks in the army and navy . . .'. The re-elected OK was supposed henceforth to function in St Petersburg. Its ten members included four from the city – the worker Smirnov and three intellectuals: P. Garvi, arrested on his return in October; Eva Broido, who acted as the secretary until her detention in January 1913; and G. O. Baturskii (Tseitlin), a lawyer and contributor to Luch.[43] The OK proved to be as ineffective as the Leninist Central Committee in offering effective leadership to its nominal supporters.

It has proved extremely difficult to discover any concrete information about the actions of the Menshevik underground in 1912. As the Initiative Groups interpreted their chief function as providing covert support for legal activities, it may be that very little illegal work as such was carried on (perhaps one reason why the Okhrana left them relatively unmolested). As to the revived strike movement, Menshevik intellectuals, both at home and abroad, soon adopted a cautious attitude, in contrast to Lenin's enthusiastic endorsement of its potential. Within one month of the Lena stoppage, Baturskii, for example, was warning that concentration on the economic struggle at the expense of the creation of strong trade unions, alone capable of conducting labour disputes, was ill-advised. The August conference endorsed this view. Its resolution called upon trade unions to furnish the leadership of strikes and warned workers against thoughtless laying down of tools 'without taking into due account their own strength and that of their opponents . . .'. The series of autumn stoppages further alarmed the 'Liquidators'. In an unsigned editorial, which became notorious and provided the Leninists with a propaganda victory, Luch, in the middle of November, damned the current round of walk-outs as 'a dangerous illness' and 'a strike fever'. It is impossible to say whether individual Menshevik labour leaders and workers either endorsed or ignored such injunctions.[44]

Throughout 1912 the Socialist Revolutionary underground scarcely survived as an organisational entity. There was a total absence of mechanisms to co-ordinate the activities of small party groups. District committees were ephemeral. A gathering of five representatives in the spring sadly admitted that their circumstances precluded the establishment of a city-wide institution. By the autumn there existed four clusters – 'A St Petersburg Group of the Party of Socialist Revolutionaries', whose leaders were students at the Psycho-Neurological Institute, with tiny working-class circles in the factory quarters; 'A Labour Group', mainly of intellectuals, with branches in the Narva and Town districts; the 'University Faction'; and a group in the polytechnic. In the autumn the first two elected a temporary collective – 'The Secretariat of the Labour Group'. Occasional leaflets were issued. A 'Narva Group of Socialist Revolutionaries' issued one on 4 November, vainly inciting workers to down tools on the anniversary of Lev Tolstoi's death. There were also educational circles, but an acute shortage of propagandists placed severe limitations upon such work. A plan in the spring to publish an illegal *Izvestiia* came to naught. Although individual SRs participated in the events of April and May, the surviving cadres seem generally to have been hesitant about fomenting and participating in strikes and demonstrations out of fear of provoking police reprisals against their embryonic organisations. The extreme fragmentation of the party was frankly recognised by a meeting of propagandists in November 1912, which exhorted the scattered circles to unite and set up district committees. Contacts between the few activists within the city and the party's leaders in emigration were apparently infrequent. Unlike their Social Democratic opponents, the Socialist Revolutionaries made no attempt to convoke a party conference abroad in the pre-war years.[45] Nor is there any evidence as to the numbers of copies of *Znamia truda*, the foreign party organ, reaching the city.

Evidence concerning the activities of anarchists in 1912 is both tenuous and contradictory. One Okhrana report at the end of the year asserted that no firm anarchist groups survived in the city. Another, quoted by Dr Gooderham, refers to the existence of a pro-terrorist group which brought out a hectographed monthly, *Anarkhist*. It may be doubted whether such an organisation had established firm links with the anarchist *émigrés*. The new foreign anarcho-communist journal *Rabochii mir*, launched in Zurich in July 1912, contains no reports in its four issues for the year about anarchist bands in the city.[46]

Chapter 5

THE REVOLUTIONARY PARTIES AND THE UNDERGROUND: 1913–JUNE 1914

I

As the year 1912 drew to a close, Lenin in Cracow made a further attempt to establish more regular and effective communications with and control over illegal and legal activists alike inside Russia. In view of a scarcity of funds he was unable to convoke a party conference even on the model of Prague. Instead he arranged a gathering in the last week of December of several surviving Central Committee members, four of the new Bolshevik Duma deputies, and a few unrepresentative 'delegates' from Russia.[1] For the Bolshevik leader one of the chief designs of his schismatic tactics in the electoral campaign in the labour curia in the Fourth State Duma elections had been apparently realised with the arrival in the Tauride Palace of six of his 'own' Bolshevik Duma deputies (see Chapter 6). Lenin regarded the latter, all of whom came from genuinely working-class backgrounds, as a reliable conduit both to his supporters and to factory operatives as well as his personal instrument to ensure that the leaders of the underground and of the open labour movement both received and more importantly actually implemented his directives. The resolutions of the meeting, written by Lenin, summarised for his adherents in Russia his interpretation of the course of internal developments since Prague and his tactical prescriptions consequent upon this diagnosis. From the spring of 1912 he had understood the massive labour unrest, the street demonstrations, the discontent in the navy as proof that 'Russia has entered a period of revolutionary upswing', 'an era of open revolutionary struggle by the masses'. In this new 'nation-wide political crisis', Lenin ascribed a cardinal role to the strike movement. As early as 1910, in an analysis of the 1905 revolution, he had postulated a close connection between economic and political stoppages. Commenting on the events of April and

May 1912, he had argued that a national mass revolutionary movement could not succeed 'unless these forms of strikes [i.e. the
political and the economic] are closely interrelated'. Thus the Cracow resolution declared that 'mass revolutionary stoppages are of
exceptional importance'. It instructed party institutions to give
priority 'to the comprehensive support of mass revolutionary strikes'
and to inciting 'revolutionary street demonstrations'.[2] Cognisant of
the inadequacies of the underground, Lenin instructed militants to
concentrate on the establishment of illegal factory cells and above all
of city-wide co-ordinating organs. In this context the Bolshevik
leader assigned a pivotal role to the six Duma deputies, ordering
them to transfer the weight of their activity outside the walls of the
Tauride to the underground. The assembly also repeated Prague's
anathemas against the 'Liquidationists'.[3] In replenishing his TsK,
Lenin ignored once more any representation for his supporters in the
capital. The omission of Badaev, the St Petersburg deputy, is
perhaps an indication of Lenin's evaluation of his abilities. Instead he
chose Petrovskii (the deputy from Ekaterinsolav, who had pronounced conciliatory views) and I. M. Sverdlov, who fled from his
exile to the capital early in December.[4]

In the first half of 1913 the Bolshevik underground in St
Petersburg proved to be a less than satisfactory instrument of Lenin's
ambitious plans. At the very outset leader and followers adopted a
different tactic towards the anniversary of Bloody Sunday on 9
January. Lenin had written to Stalin on 6 December 1912 instructing
the party cells to arrange a one-day strike and demonstrations under
the three Bolshevik slogans (a democratic republic, the eight-hour
day, the confiscation of the gentry's estates). Although the capital's
activists shared their leader's diagnosis that 'a new revolution is
growing' (PK leaflet on 9 January), a meeting of the executive
commission of the PK on 23 December resolved to eschew stoppages
and demonstrations on 9 January, restricting actions to factory
meetings. The Bolshevik sub-élite wished to postpone both such
forms of protest to the tercentenary of the Romanov dynasty on 21
February. This point of view was also shared by all other socialist
groups in the city. The PK appeal may have proclaimed 'let the year
1913 mark the start of the second revolution', but it merely
suggested observing the anniversary by holding assemblies in places
of work and passing appropriate resolutions. Therefore the 71,000
hands who downed tools that day did so against the wishes of the
militants. There were also a few isolated efforts to form processions
in the city centre and factory quarters, quickly stopped by the
police.[5] The PK's inactivity on 9 January brought Lenin's wrath
down on its head. Writing to Sverdlov a month later he castigated it
because 'it does not know how to utter a word'.[6]

The Bolshevik leader's expectations received another setback with the tercentenary of the dynasty. For reasons that remain unclear, some time between its meeting on 18 January and early February, the PK abandoned its intention to foment strikes on 21 February. Instead it published a leaflet exhorting workers to hold 'revolutionary demonstrations' on that date. Copies at least reached the Neva district and Petersburg Side, and agitation was conducted among lower-ranking party members. The authorities, however, took effective precautions. Widespread arrests of revolutionaries occurred in the weeks before the twenty-first; the factory owners were persuaded at the last minute to observe that date as an official paid holiday. As a consequence the official festivities passed off without incident.[7]

In terms of organisation the underground experienced fluctuating fortunes. In the first six weeks of 1913, an entire city-wide network of district committees was created for the first time in several years – in Moscow, Narva, Town and Vyborg areas, as well as the Petersburg Side, Vasil'evskii Island and the Mining Institute. From Lenin's point of view these new groups seemed at last to be more compliant executors of his instructions. Perhaps under the influence of Sverdlov and Stalin, the PK approved the Cracow resolutions. It took steps to implement the latter's decision to secure 'unity from below' by persuading Party Mensheviks to join the Vasil'evskii Island and Narva circles. A leaflet urged workers to set up factory cells.[8] It would be erroneous, however, to conclude with Soviet scholars that henceforth the PK provided regular leadership. The sweeping arrests in the middle of February not only trapped Stalin and Sverdlov, but also destroyed all district committees. The PK's schemes to convoke a general town conference and publish an *Izvestiia* were frustrated. Recovery was a hesitant process. The PK, whose membership was constantly changing, suffered another liquidation on 18 April. In that month committees, benefiting from the amnesty of 21 February which permitted the return of many party workers, were reformed in the Neva and Vyborg quarters and in the following month, in Narva, Town and Vasil'evskii Island. But as the Okhrana noted in a report of 1 June, 'the PK has failed to forge close bonds with the districts'.[9] The composition of these groups was overwhelmingly working class. In contrast to 1912 there was a pronounced absence of sympathetic students.[10] Nor does there exist clearly substantiated evidence that Badaev or the other Bolshevik Duma deputies played the dominant role in the underground which Lenin so ardently desired. The Okhrana in early February observed curtly that 'there are no close ties between the PK and the Social Democratic fraction', whereas three months later it made the apparently contradictory claim that 'Malinovskii, Petrovskii and

Badaev act as the links between the PK and the district committees', making use of the labour delegates elected in the factories during the State Duma elections the previous autumn. It is possible that in the interval between these two documents these three adopted a more active profile. An eloquent witness against this conclusion is Lenin himself. At a meeting between the foreign members of his TsK and Malinovskii on 27 July 1913 the Bolshevik deputies were censured 'because they have failed to conduct intensively organisational party work'.[11]

This interpretation is further strengthened by the fact that after the arrest of Stalin and Sverdlov in February, Lenin seems to have lost independent organisational links to the underground. The correspondence of both Krupskaia and Lenin, as well as police reports in the spring of 1913, testify to Lenin's awareness that the party cells remained outside the orbit of the TsK's influence. In a letter dispatched in April to N. I. Podvoiskii in St Petersburg – the recipient acted as a channel for the Bolshevik leader's letters to the deputies and editors of *Pravda* – Lenin correctly remarked that 'the organisation of Social Democratic workers in most places is very weak and recent'. His endeavours to overcome this obstacle by the creation of regional bureaux bore no fruit as far as the capital was concerned. He also lacked the funds to dispatch his own trusted agents to the city, or to arrange the publication abroad and successful transport to Russia of substantial quantities of illegal literature. The central organ itself appeared in only two issues in the first half of 1913. The numbers of this, and of the four TsK leaflets published, reaching St Petersburg are unknown. Malinovskii's report to the Moscow Okhrana of 15 August came near the mark in its observation that 'the *émigrés* have no information on the localities and no opportunity to take into consideration present circumstances . . .'.[12]

Despite their organisational difficulties local Bolsheviks made determined efforts to implement the Cracow resolution concerning revolutionary mass strikes and demonstrations, as well as taking an independent initiative in a sphere of action which Lenin and the exiles had long ignored, namely policies to attract women workers to the party. In the latter case, some time early in the new year, a small group of Bolshevik female intellectuals, prominent among whom were P. F. Kudelli and K. N. Samoilova (both active in the Sampsonievskii educational society; Samoilova also acted as the secretary of the editorial board of *Pravda* from January 1913) decided to celebrate International Women's Day, adopted by the Second Conference of Socialist Women in 1910. In this undertaking they collaborated with the Mensheviks. The League for Women's Equality, the Society for Women's Mutual Aid (with some 500 members) and the union of textileworkers convoked a public meeting on 17 February. The two Social Democratic newspapers published special articles on the state of women. Various speakers from the different socialist factions delivered addresses on the economic and social position of women. Earlier plans to hold street demonstrations were abandoned. The event, however, remained an isolated phenomenon. Party intellectuals and activists soon relapsed into their previous indifference to women workers.[13]

The 1913 anniversary of the Lena tragedy stimulated both Social Democrats and Socialist Revolutionaries to renewed activity. The PK issued two leaflets some time in March, advising operatives to cease working on 4 April and to march to the city centre with 'revolutionary demands'. (Both documents curiously omitted all Bolshevik slogans.) The SRs were divided in their approach to the event, but one group put out an appeal similar in content to that of their rivals. The destruction of the entire network of Bolshevik district committees in the previous month, as well as the absence of such on the part of the SRs, would indicate that whatever agitation occurred was confined to individual factory cells. A more influential reminder of Lena – if the working population required any at all – was the publication in both Social Democratic legal organs the day prior to the anniversary of a Social Democratic bill to pay pensions to the victims of the shooting. In addition to the 78,000 who ceased working on 4 April, there occurred the first serious, if unsuccessful, attempts at demonstrations since May Day 1912. At noon, a crowd of 1,000 (both students and workers) gathered on Nevskii Prospekt but was promptly dispersed. More ominously, after lunch large numbers of workers endeavoured to cross the bridges from the three northern districts but the police blocked their passage.[14]

As in the previous year, all the different socialist groups resolved to observe May Day with appeals for stoppages and demonstrations. Both the Leninist TsK and the Menshevik OK published such proclamations, as did the PK. Even the Central Initiative Group adopted a militant posture, but its plan to issue an appeal proved abortive because of arrests. Some 20,000 copies of the various leaflets were distributed. A strike committee, uniting representatives of the PK and the SRs, was established. In contrast to the days prior to the Lena anniversary, the student's United Social Democratic Fraction called its colleagues to participate in the planned workers' protests. The police, however, acted ruthlessly to prohibit effective co-ordination by the revolutionaries. The members of the PK were detained on 18 April, and members of the strike committee five days later. The Bolsheviks succeeded in reviving only two district committees – in Nevskii and Vyborg. On the other hand, factory cells succeeded in holding brief meetings in many engineering factories in Vyborg on 30 April. Whatever the actual contribution of the socialist militants, the strikes on May Day reached a dimension unknown since the spring of 1912 – the police estimated 110,000 had downed tools; *Pravda*, some 250,000. This achievement was counterbalanced by the failure of the activists' project of large-scale demonstrations. The saturation of working-class quarters and the city centre by mounted and foot police detachments prevented large crowds of workers proceeding from their factories into the heart of the capital. There were only three occasions when small groups of 200 to 400 demonstrators penetrated the police cordons.[15]

The trial in St Petersburg in the middle of June of 52 sailors of the Baltic fleet accused of conspiracy to foment an uprising afforded local Bolsheviks a natural focus for arousing working-class sympathy and resistance. The revival of district committees in May may have helped agitation. Preventive detentions by the Okhrana, however, inhibited the PK from publishing a leaflet. Over the three days 17–9 June, around 36,000 walked out in a display of compassion and solidarity.[16]

In this same month the authorities made a determined effort to crush the legal socialist newspapers. As a protest against this policy, between 1 and 3 July some 30,000 operatives left their plants. The archives of the Okhrana contain no evidence that Bolshevik or other socialist militants had attempted to arouse this expression of opposition. The PK succeeded in issuing an appeal about the persecution of the labour press only in the middle of the month; this merely called for a strengthening of illegal cells. Nor did the actual closure of *Luch* and *Pravda* on 5 July evoke further action by the underground. As on previous occasions the role of the legal labour press itself may have been a more significant, if indirect, means of stimulating unrest. Both Social Democratic papers regularly published details of the confiscations, fines and arrests of staff inflicted upon them, and had recently made known the rejection by the State Duma on 21 June of an interpellation from the Social Democratic fraction concerning such repression.[17]

The rapid succession and significant dimensions of the four political stoppages from 4 April profoundly influenced the mood and strategy of the Bolshevik sub-élite in St Petersburg in the summer. Once more seriously overestimating their organisational vitality and convinced that 'we are approaching a new revolutionary upsurge, the decisive battle...' (PK leaflet in August), the militants impetuously took an ill-considered decision some time in July to launch a general political strike on an all-Russian scale in the autumn. They presumably hoped to repeat the success of October 1905. On 4 August they set up a strike committee to furnish planning and leadership. An indication of the seriousness of the intentions of the Bolshevik activists was the fact that the membership of this body also comprised representatives from the trade unions (through the illegal Central Bureau of Trade Unions) and from their rivals, the Socialist Revolutionaries. As in the past, the impatience and revolutionary enthusiasm of Lenin's followers proved to be their undoing. Their decision to bring forward the date of the putative general strike to 15 August and to set a three-day time span brought down on their heads the repressive apparatus of the state. Raids and arrests in the second week of the month prevented the immediate implementation of the Bolsheviks' over-ambitious scheme.[18]

The independent initiative of his adherents in the matter of the general political strike and their bellicosity also exerted a direct impact upon Lenin. In the last week of September 1913 he convened in the Galician village of Poronin another meeting of the foreign members of his TsK with five of the six Bolshevik parliamentary representatives. A lack of money and the regular collapse of illegal groups inside Russia had precluded the holding of even a restricted conference in the manner of Prague. Among the 22 individuals present, half of whom had attended the Cracow gathering, there was not a single elected delegate from local organisations. Although the Bolshevik leader had summoned the assembly with the purpose of forcing a final split in the hitherto united Social Democratic fraction in the State Duma (see Chapter 6) Badaev and Shotman, with the support of the Moscow representatives, evidently urged upon their listeners the adoption as official party policy of the new strategy of the Petersburg Bolsheviks. Influenced – indeed misled – by an erroneous report from Badaev, who gave a distorted impression of the true state of the underground in the capital, Lenin and the assembly decided that 'the movement has reached the point of considering a nation-wide political strike', centring as before on the three Bolshevik slogans, and fixed the date as 9 January 1914. Faithful to Lenin's theory of the dominant role of the proletariat in the bourgeois revolution, delegates envisaged no part for the liberal opposition in the general strike.[19]

In the capital, however, Bolshevik preparations for the general strike and work in other illegal spheres was severely hampered in the last half of 1913 by organisational debility. After the break-up of the PK by the police in July, the district committees atrophied. The revolutionaries also lacked access to an illegal press: no leaflets were published after August. There is no evidence that any committees existed between midsummer and the turn of the year. There was a constant search by activists for substitutes. Towards the end of September a meeting of party members in the union of metalworkers noted 'the lack in St Petersburg of strong party organisations, capable of leading a general strike' and resolved that they themselves would assume such a task. The legal sickness insurance fund boards (*kassy*) also seemed to offer an alluring prospect as surrogate co-ordinating organs. In October the revolutionaries adopted a scheme to establish a secret 'Insurance Centre' of *kassy* board delegates which would metamorphose into a Soviet of Workers' Deputies. Prompt retaliatory action by the Okhrana on 8 November put paid to this bold design. The collapse of their expectations constrained local Bolsheviks in the last month of 1913 to redirect their attention towards re-establishing the party underground. Committees were reformed in the Narva district, Petersburg Side and Vasil'evskii Island.[20]

The messianic dreams of the activists – 'they expect a repetition of 1905', the Okhrana observed in a report of 7 November – impelled them to take another independent initiative in the autumn. Although both the Cracow and Poronin gatherings had come to no decisions about socialist agitation among the armed forces and had never discussed the possibility of an armed uprising, some militants began to conceive of the latter. They decided to launch for the first time a campaign among the soldiers of the garrison and entertained hopes of fomenting stoppages and street demonstrations to coincide with the introduction by the government into the State Duma of a bill extending the length of military service. These plans never bore fruit due to the counter measures taken by the authorities.[21]

Nor did the remaining months of 1913 after the Poronin assembly witness a substantial improvement in Lenin's connections with his followers in the capital's underground. His design for another party school in the summer of 1913 on the model of Longjumeau in 1911 had been frustrated in part because the deputies Badaev, Petrovskii and Shagov had refused to participate in another factional venture. The extreme shortage of funds had meant that the Poronin resolution on the importance of increasing the output of illegal literature remained a dead letter. One issue alone of *Sotsial-demokrat* was published in the last half of 1913. Apart from the deputies, Lenin was unable to send his own agents to the city. And the former were absorbed by the factional struggle within the Social Democratic fraction. As late as the middle of December the TsK in Cracow had failed to secure the safe passage to the city of literature containing the resolutions of the Poronin meeting and correspondence was at best intermittent. No oblast' conferences were held.[22]

In view of the debility of the Bolshevik underground in the capital in the last five months of the year, the assertion of the Soviet investigator E. E. Kruze that 'the PK actively prepared and led a series of mass political strikes and demonstrations' must be treated with extreme caution. The complete absence of underground structures and an illegal press ensured that the revolutionaries' reaction to events was formulated only by *ad hoc* groups of Social Democrats.

The first of these occurrences arose in connection with the stoppages which erupted in Moscow between 23 and 25 September in protest against the closure of the new Bolshevik legal daily newspaper *Nash put'*. At the same time leaders of the Moscow tramway strike travelled to St Petersburg to seek support. On the evening of the twenty-fourth, Bolshevik members in the union of metalworkers, acting in a surrogate capacity, decided to call out the city's wage earners in a gesture of solidarity. Even before this, however, meetings had taken place in the engineering factories in the Vyborg district throughout the day. As on previous occasions the critical role was played by both Social Democratic journals which had given extensive coverage to developments in Moscow. Around 52,000 downed tools over the three days 25–27 September. No demonstrations were planned or took place.[23]

After the strike, presumably in the light of the Poronin resolutions, the activists altered their attitude towards such individual political protests. The Okhrana reported early in October that 'the local Bolsheviks now desire to cease individual stoppages in order to preserve their forces for a general strike'. As a consequence the anniversary of the October Manifesto of 1905 was ignored. Nevertheless 7,000 operatives walked out on 17 and 18 October.[24]

This policy of abstention did not last long. The prospective appearance in court on 6 November of four workers at the state-owned Obukhov armaments plant on a criminal charge of incitement to strike – the direct result of the Minister of the Interior's new policy of resort to criminal penalties as the instrument to break strikes (see Chapter 9) – represented a direct threat to labour's most effective means to defend its economic and political interests. From the middle of October the Bolsheviks began to plan walk-outs and demonstrations outside the court building. In the absence of an illegal press their agitation must have been oral rather than written. Indeed in this respect their Social Democratic rivals for once displayed more dynamism. For the Mensheviks the arraignment represented a challenge to their foremost political demand – the freedom of coalition. The Central Initiative Group issued and distributed in the factories an appeal to operatives to cease working on the day of the trial. On 6 November the Social Democratic fraction introduced into the State Duma a bill guaranteeing the freedom of strikes and trade unions. Many factory meetings were arranged in engineering, textile, printing and artisanal establishments; the resolutions passed included Bolshevik and Menshevik slogans (often in the same document). A combination of socialist agitation, widespread publicity about the charges and trial in the socialist press and the obvious threat to the weapon of the strike ensured a massive show of sympathy with the accused: between 70,000 and 84,000 left work in protest. The militants' vision of large-scale demonstrations was again unrealised. Heavy rain and police cordons reduced the attempts at manifestations outside the court to three isolated incidents involving a mere 50 to 500 people.[25]

According to the police there was no revolutionary involvement in the last political strike of 1913 when 2,000 to 3,000 downed tools on 3 and 4 December to express their opposition to a fine levied on Badaev for a speech at a cemetery three months before.[26]

The Leninist camp within the Bolshevik faction may have benefited throughout 1913 by the divisions within the broader grouping. In Paris in the first months of the year the literary group 'Vpered' split asunder, with the personal estrangement of its two chief luminaries, G. A. Aleksinskii and A. V. Lunacharskii, the latter withdrawing from the circle. Although the foreign Vperedists succeeded in publishing a May Day leaflet, it is not known whether any appreciable quantities reached the capital. There is no proof that Bogdanov's 'Central Group' or any other Vperedist organisation existed in the course of 1913. In the emigration, moreover, the bloc between the Bolshevik Conciliators and Party Mensheviks collapsed, with the former abandoning the editorial board of Plekhanov's organ, *Za partiiu* early in the new year. In St Petersburg the Conciliators never possessed their own separate groupings but pursued their aims from within the Leninist ranks. However, many prominent Leninist practical workers in the legal and illegal spheres adopted a conciliationist attitude towards party unity (see Chapter 6).[27]

II

In contrast to the previous year the Mensheviks' Central Initiative Group did not enjoy an uninterrupted existence in 1913. After its suppression by the Okhrana on 7 January, it was revived only in April. Its survival was very brief; new arrests extinguished it the following month. The Mensheviks did not succeed in restoring it until October. Again the police cut short its life on 7 November. As a consequence 'the Group's activity' in the laconic description of a police memorandum, 'was minimal'. Another difference with the past history of the Central Initiative Group concerned its membership. In its two transient incarnations the weight of intellectual adherents was less – a mere two of thirteen members in May (one was F. Dan, who returned from exile in January to act as editor of *Luch*) and three of eight in October (including Iu. A. Isuv, a contributor on the labour movement to *Nasha zaria*, and S. M. Shvarts, secretary of the Menshevik insurance journal, *Strakhovanie rabochikh*). Of the sixteen workers involved in the two coteries, there is information on the profession of eleven – nine were employed in heavy engineering (including four involved with the union of metalworkers), one in printing, and one in a consumers' co-operative.[28]

In the spring of 1913 there were also initiative groups in most districts. The strongest were located in Vasil'evskii Island and in the Expedition of State Papers, the government printers with a payroll of 4,700 in 1913. There were moves to set up circles among female workers. It is not clear whether such bodies survived the arrests of the summer. The Menshevik members of the Social Democratic fraction in the State Duma apparently adopted a very low profile towards illegal cells. The split in the fraction engineered by Lenin in October induced Menshevik activists, at the prompting of Dan and Martov (who came back to his native land in this month), to revive their underground organisations towards the end of the year.[29]

The Party Mensheviks, like the Bolshevik Conciliators, had no independent structures in St Petersburg. Nor did they pursue a consistent or united line of conduct. In the emigration, despite his earlier fulminations against the Prague Conference, Plekhanov made a temporary peace with Lenin and in the spring penned a series of fiercely polemical articles in *Pravda* against the 'Liquidators'. Imitating this rapprochement, some of his followers in the city joined the Vasil'evskii Island and Narva district Bolshevik circles.

In the autumn, however, other Party Mensheviks lent their enthusiastic support to a new grouping, the St Petersburg Inter-District Commission or Mezhraionka. The initiative in its foundation in October 1913 was taken by three individuals – K. K. Iurenev (a 25-year-old Bolshevik, active in the Dvinsk party in the 1905 revolution), N. M. Egorov (the working-class deputy representing Perm province in the Third State Duma and a member of the Social Democratic group 'Unity' in 1911–12), and A. M. Novoselov (a worker, member of the St Petersburg Bolsheviks from 1906 and prominent in the Vasil'evskii Island branch of the union of metal-workers). This body was designed to give expression to the strong desire for party unification still shared by many Social Democrats. Its platform called for the unity from below of all 'revolutionary Social Democrats', i.e. Bolsheviks and Party Mensheviks, as well as party agitation in the armed forces. The Mezhraionka soon began to fill the organisational vacuum left by the fragility of the other Social Democratic factions. By the end of the year it had created small circles in a majority of factories in Vasil'evskii Island, in particular at the state-owned St Petersburg Pipe works (with 5,500 hands), and by the spring of 1914 in most manufacturing establishments and printshops on the Petersburg Side. In the latter case membership totalled about 200 to 300 operatives, especially in the machine construction firm of St Petersburg Engineering (with a 1,000-strong labour force).[30]

Even more so than the Bolsheviks, the Mensheviks suffered from the absence of effective and permanent links between their intellectual leaders living abroad and the Initiative Groups in the capital. Although F. Dan at the start of the year and Iu. Martov in the autumn returned to the city, their attention was directed in large measure towards literary matters and factional squabbles, as was the correspondence between the exiles and the 'Liquidationist' legal luminaries. The OK was weakened by continual arrests and met only once in the year (in April) in St Petersburg. Indeed the 'August Bloc' fell apart in the spring on account of the quarrel between Trotskii and the Caucasian Social Democrats, on the one hand, and the editorial board of *Luch* over its 'Liquidationist' stance (see Chapter 6). Apart from the OK May Day leaflet there were no illegal Menshevik publications whatsoever. Nor did the Mensheviks succeed in holding another party conference, although in October the Menshevik Duma deputies, the Bund and the Latvian Social Democrats took a decision to convoke such a gathering.[31]

The Mensheviks' scepticism about strikes and revolutionary demonstrations as the means to force political and social concessions from, let alone overthrow, the monarchy grew deeper as 1913 advanced. An Okhrana report accurately summarised their attitude in the words; 'Mensheviks do not deny the educative value of stoppages and demonstrations, but only on the most important occasions.' In January, for example, both Dan and Martov privately endorsed *Luch*'s earlier attack on 'strike fever'. A month later, P. Garvi, writing in the theoretical journal *Nasha zaria*, condemned 'the elemental nature' of the strike movement which he ascribed in part to its 'proceeding for the most part apart from the existing trade unions'. Although the Central Initiative Group had proposed to distribute a May Day appeal, the June walk-outs alarmed it. Through the medium of *Luch*, it criticised them as 'chaotic, prematurely weakening the forces of the working class ...'. On the other hand, local Mensheviks participated in the preparations to mark by protests the trial of the Obukhov strikers on 6 November. In addition to the reasons outlined earlier for this course of action, the Mensheviks' dwindling control over the legal labour movement (see Chapters 6 and 7) may have induced them to regain workers' sympathy by temporarily softening their previous hostility to strikes.[32]

The first steps taken in 1913 by the surviving shadowy Socialist Revolutionary coteries in St Petersburg proved their undoing. The 'St Petersburg Group of the Party of Socialist Revolutionaries' and 'the Labour Group' both schemed to provoke stoppages and demonstrations on the tercentenary of the dynasty on 21 February. All members were captured in the middle of the month. Their place was taken by 'The St Petersburg Group of the Revolutionary Union'. It suffered a similar fate on 1 April when it published a leaflet exhorting walk-outs and street protests to mark the anniversary of the Lena massacre. A 'St Petersburg Collective of Socialist Revolutionaries' issued a similar appeal before May Day. By the spring there also existed small nuclei of party activists in all districts except Vasil'evskii Island.[33]

Moreover in May, under the impetus of the higher profile adopted by the party's militants in the strike movement in contrast to 1912, district representatives succeeded for the first time in convoking a city conference. This reconfirmed the party programme (the overthrow of the monarchy, a democratic republic, 'land and liberty' and a Constituent Assembly). It adopted an even more militant strategy than the Bolsheviks – rejection of the State Duma, a general strike, an armed uprising, acts of terror. Delegates elected the first Petersburg Committee of the party as a co-ordinating organ and a 'Council of Workers' Deputies' with members chosen by district circles. The assembly adopted a Leninist position on the relationship between illegal work and the open labour movement, according priority to the former and subordination of party legal activists to the underground committees.[34]

Like the Bolsheviks, in the summer local SRs were seized with the vision of an imminent revolutionary cataclysm. Assembling in secret on 2 July they, too, declared in favour of launching an all-Russian general strike in October and agreed to collaborate with the Social Democrats and trade unions in making secret preparations for this event. As an earnest of their intentions they dispatched a representative to the strike committee set up by the Bolsheviks on 4 August. A St Petersburg Military Organisation was also established.[35]

Owing to lacunae in the archival sources and the absence of reports in the foreign party press, the history of the party in the capital in the last half of 1913 cannot be traced. It is known that many members were detained in August, and there is no evidence that the ambitious organisational plans of the May conference were ever implemented. Little propaganda work was conducted and illegal literature was scarce.

There exists a little more information about the social composition of the various SR groupings in 1913. In contrast to the Bolsheviks, the former seem to have been dominated by intellectuals. The Okhrana archives yield a list of 40 prominent party militants detained by the police: of these, 33 came from middle-class and gentry backgrounds. At least nineteen of them were students, ten of them at the St Petersburg Psycho-Neurological Institute and three at the Institute of Mines. A mere six were workers, two of whom were employed in medium-sized engineering plants and one of whom had served in the 1905 Soviet of Workers' Deputies.

The least documentation available concerns the anarchists. Late in

1912 a small circle of anarcho-syndicalists emerged, all of whose members were former SRs. This group pursued the ludicrously over-ambitious scheme of uniting all the trade unions and co-operatives of the capital, Pskov, Olonets and Novgorod provinces into one overarching union, hoping thereby to gain control over the labour movement. Police intervention put paid to such fantasies. At the time of the textile lock-outs in St Petersburg at the start of 1913 (see Chapter 8), anarchists spread propaganda in favour of economic terror – to no effect. It remains doubtful whether the *émigré* anarchists managed to establish any ties to their followers in the city. In February 1913 the foreign journal *Rabochii mir* complained that such links scarcely existed and that very few copies of its issues had reached Russia. The periodical significantly published no reports from Russia throughout the year. Certainly the Russian anarchist movement in Western Europe remained fractured by the disputes between anarcho-communists and anarcho-syndicalists, with two rival conferences in the course of the year.[36]

III

The first two months of 1914 bore witness to a sustained, if short-lived, recovery of the Bolshevik underground. By February a PK had been reborn with delegates from new district committees in the First and Second Town, Moscow, Vyborg, Kolpino and Porokhovaia quarters and Petersburg Side, although the important working-class areas of Narva, Neva and Vasil'evskii Island were unrepresented. The restoration of links with the United Committee of St Petersburg Social Democratic Students, embracing seven higher-educational institutions, furnished the PK once more with a secret printing press after a lapse of six months. For the first time in several years a college of propagandists, relying on sympathetic students, came into being. As a consequence, small educational circles, numbering four to five workers each, sprang up. There was a secret insurance centre, and two party groups emerged among commercial employees. Plans were drawn up to secure broader working-class support by launching campaigns around the popular and topical issues of the eight-hour day and overtime. The new PK was apparently Leninist: it endorsed the Poronin resolutions and gave its approval to the convocation of a party congress. The scope of the party's revival, however, should not be exaggerated. An assembly of the PK early in February admitted that, Vyborg apart, the district organisations comprised miniscule groups of new, young and inexperienced members. The Social Democratic faction in the university embraced a mere eighteen individuals. The Okhrana's annual report observed that 'the PK's absence of ties to the localities deprived it of authority'.[37] Although the Leninist centre itself contained several older metalworkers with considerable experience in the underground and the union of metalworkers, it was in constant flux.[38] On 20 February the police seized many prominent Bolsheviks and extinguished the PK.

In the light of the origins of the Poronin decision to orchestrate an all-Russian general political strike on 9 January 1914 – a date carefully chosen to ensure the widest appeal of the venture – the local Bolshevik militants conducted as general an agitation as possible. Twelve thousand copies of a PK leaflet were distributed. Preaching the necessity of a new revolution, this document called upon working people to strike and demonstrate in the city centre. Although they were probably unaware of the Bolsheviks' ulterior motives, the Central Initiative Group, the Mezhraionka, the Vperedists in Paris and SRs made similar pleas. On the eve of the anniversary activists arranged factory meetings at the Aivaz, Baltic and Putilov engineering plants. The revolutionaries' hopes were fulfilled in part. The police estimated that around 110,000 walked out – the highest figure since 1 May 1913. The authorities, however, apprised of the Bolsheviks' true ambitions, had taken extensive precautions. Utilising for the first time in the pre-war years Cossacks and gendarmes as well as the police, they saturated the working-class areas with patrols and placed guards on all the bridges across the Neva. As a result the police successfully prevented mass demonstrations in the heart of the capital – there were only four minor occurrences, involving at most 200 to 300 people. In the industrial quarters there were around 50 attempts by workers on leaving their establishments in the morning to form demonstrative processions; these were promptly dispersed by mounted detachments. The response elsewhere in the Empire rendered nugatory the Bolsheviks' dreams of an all-Russian political stoppage; in Moscow a mere 9,000 downed tools.[39]

In stark contrast to the massive numbers of operatives of diverse trades attracted to the protests of 9 January, the revolutionaries' second attempt to celebrate International Women's Day met with little success. Although women socialist intellectuals (F. I. Drabkina, P. F. Kudelli, K. N. Samoilova and E. F. Rozmirovich, the secretary of the editorial board of *Put' pravdy*) established a special commission of labour organisations to arrange commemorative events and the PK issued an appropriate handbill, their endeavours were frustrated by a combination of the Bolsheviks' feud with the Mensheviks, which split the planning body, the Governor General's prohibition of all public meetings, with one exception, and the arrest of the principal Bolshevik female activists. Even the solitary legal assembly on 23 February ended in chaos when the chairman abruptly terminated the proceedings after the detention of three speakers.[40]

As an integral part of the Bolsheviks' plans to commemorate International Women's Day and as a means to attract women workers to the party, the above-mentioned female intellectuals launched the first issue of a new journal *Rabotnitsa* on 23 February with a print run of 12,000 copies. Altogether seven numbers appeared before the war, three of which suffered confiscation. It may be doubted whether it achieved its aim of 'meeting the needs of female operatives', in particular of the 'poorly conscious'. Rose Glickman has aptly noted that there was a noticeable divorce between the letters and reports sent in by ordinary wage earners and the theoretical articles by the editors, who ignored their correspondents' well-founded complaints about male hostility. Moreover those writing to the periodical, as their action reveals. represented the minute proportion of 'conscious' female workers – the same purchasers, probably, of the publication.[41]

The convulsions which shook the manufacturing districts of St Petersburg in March threw into sharp relief the strengths and weaknesses of the local Bolsheviks. The latter, on the one hand, attracted to their side radicalised factory youths by their militancy, their refusal to accommodate themselves in any way to the regime, their verbal and practical support for all labour disputes, their vision of an imminent revolution. The activists' responsiveness to the impatience of their new youthful supporters found effective expression in their continuing championship of a general political strike, the call for which was becoming more widely known outside party circles. On the other hand, as both Lenin and the Okhrana perceptively understood, the fragility of the underground precluded effective control by revolutionary cadres over the labour movement and left them in part at the mercy of the temper of their adherents.

The spontaneous outbreak of walk-outs between 6 and 12 March in protest at the authorities' repression of the labour press (some 20,000 were involved) placed the Leninists in a dilemma. Both the PK, reformed at the end of February, and the Bolshevik-dominated board of the union of metalworkers, opposed these stoppages as unsystematic and sporadic, as well as interfering with their scheme for a general strike on the anniversary of the Lena massacre on 4 April. Although the PK instructed its local activists to terminate the strikes, the paucity of its district and factory nuclei ensured that its order could not be enforced.[42]

Yet, on the very day these strikes died away, the local Bolsheviks suddenly altered their attitude. Perhaps out of a desire to take advantage of this new manifestation of labour unrest or in response to possible criticisms of faint-heartedness from their supporters, local leaders, meeting on 12 March, agreed to bring forward the general strike and demonstrations intended for 4 April to 13 March as a show of support for a Social Democratic Duma interpellation about the Lena massacre. An appropriate leaflet was hastily printed, but it made no mention of demonstrations. In view of the abruptness of the decision, the extent of agitation cannot have been impressive, a fact possibly reflected in the numbers responding to the call – around 55,000 failed to start work. As to street protests, the pattern of 9 January was repeated with only a single minor one in the city centre, and several, quickly suppressed, in factory districts.[43]

The Bolsheviks' ability to control events was dealt a further severe blow by the police, who detained many prominent militants in the middle of March. As in the autumn of 1913 the revolutionaries searched for substitutes, in the form of the boards of the union of metalworkers, and of the educational societies Sampsonievskoe (Vyborg District) and Nauka i zhizn' ('Science and Life', Moscow district), all of which were dominated by Bolsheviks. With the removal of possibly more level-headed leaders, these legal cadres, their fervour overcoming their judgement, once more set a date (19 March) for launching a general political strike. Some even dreamed of an armed uprising.

These designs, however, were overtaken by an outbreak of mass fainting fits among the female employees at the Russian-American Rubber Company's Treugol'nik plant and at the Bogdanov tobacco factory in the middle of the month and the natural outrage these evoked among ordinary workers in the capital, producing a wide series of stoppages in sympathy between 17 and 20 March involving around 84,000 hands. Contrary to the claim of the Soviet historian E. E. Kruze that the PK led this expression of anger, the police archives contain no evidence of widespread agitation by local revolutionary groups. The nature of the accident at the factory, the rumours of deliberate 'poisoning' by the employers, the widespread coverage in the socialist press, the visits to the plant by both Bolshevik and Menshevik deputies, and the Social Democratic interpellation in the Duma on 18 March, all explain the scope of the protest. In contrast to 9 January and 13 March there were only isolated and small-scale demonstrations in the factory quarters.[44]

The unexpected decision by sixteen engineering and electrical firms to counter the rash of March walk-outs by the declaration of a lock-out between 20 and 24 March (see Chapter 9) placed the Bolshevik militants in a quandary. The party intellectuals, now led by L. B. Kamenev, grouped around the editorial board of *Put' pravdy*, apparently urged caution; in an oblique editorial, the newspaper indirectly advised against responding by new political strikes, suggesting instead 'the force of unity and organisation' as the counterpoise to the lock-out. But at a meeting between the Bolshevik members of the board of the union of metalworkers and party delegates from the affected plants on 21 March, the latter demanded that their leaders launch a general political strike by way of riposte. In view of the recent emasculation of the district and factory cells and the uncertainty about the degree of sympathy such a call might evoke, the proposal was rejected by a majority of those present. In order to forestall any change of mind, the authorities now closed down the union of metalworkers, thereby depriving the Bolsheviks of their most signifiant legal *point d'appui*.[45]

The revolutionary sub-élites were aware that this second 'betrayal' of their own rhetoric could impair their reputation among their incautious followers. Hence at another gathering of metalworkers and party activists on 23 March, which reconstituted the PK, they offered compensation in the form of a suggestion to arrange street demonstrations on Good Friday. Some time after this decision they secured the support of Mensheviks and SRs. In the absence of district organisations, party agitators utilised meetings of the Sampsonievskoe and Nauka i zhizn' educational societies and both the PK and SRs distributed appeals in several large engineering plants the day before. Their efforts met with little reward, because of the festive nature of the occasion; a few minor processions took place.[46]

After the Okhrana's ruthless depredations of its networks in March, the Bolshevik underground in the city remained completely fragmented until the outbreak of the war. There is no evidence to suggest that PK or district committees were re-established.[47] Although the title 'PK' appeared on leaflets, no such continuously functioning body in fact existed. It ceased to play any positive role. The police reports for this period emphasise that 'illegal party work was to be observed occasionally only in the form of party cells in the factories and trade unions'. In place of the defunct formal party machinery, reliance had to be placed upon party groups in legal labour institutions. The board of the banned union of metalworkers continued to meet on occasion, and the premises and meetings of the Sampsonievskoe and Nauka i zhizn' educational societies provided useful platforms. Moreover, whatever their previous role, the Bolshevik Duma deputies – perhaps responding belatedly either to a TsK resolution of late December 1913 to transfer the weight of their activity outside the chambers of the Tauride Palace or to a renewed directive from Lenin to this effect late in April – began in the spring to play a more conspicuous part in the city's underground. In May and June they attended excursions by the above-mentioned societies into the woods surrounding the capital, where issues of the day were discussed. The scandal of Malinovskii's flight from Russia and exposure as a police agent in May, however, must have reduced the deputies' effectiveness. Neither this blow nor the debility of the underground induced a change in the strategy of militants, who remained as committed as ever to the launching of a national general political strike. Indeed by June there seems to have been a more accurate, if belated, assessment on their part of the serious difficulties of co-ordinating such simultaneous action over the vast expanses of the Empire, as the Okhrana reported that the St Petersburg Bolsheviks had begun to dispatch revolutionary literature into the provinces 'to raise the revolutionary mood there'.[48]

The argument of A. M. Volodarskaia that preparations for the Sixth Party Congress, set in train by a meeting of the TsK in Galicia on 2–4 April, 'assisted the further strengthening of party organisations in the localities' lacks substantiation, at least as far as St Petersburg is concerned. Although the TsK had ordered the establishment in the capital of an 'Organisational Section of the TsK', both to replace the defunct Russian Bureau and to supervise the PK, the Okhrana was convinced that this organ never came into existence. The same fate befell the decision of the TsK to establish a St Petersburg Oblast' Commission. The dilatoriness of the local Bolsheviks may have been due to the paucity of their forces and the extreme shortage of funds. It is also possible that Bolshevik Conciliators disliked the patently schismatic nature of Lenin's venture. Thus in the election of Social Democratic trade-union delegates to the International Socialist Congress in Vienna, who were also to attend the Sixth Party Congress, the illegal, Bolshevik-controlled board of the union of metalworkers deliberately split its mandates between both factions.[49]

The complete absence of formal Bolshevik illegal structures after March, the closure of the union of metalworkers and the numerical weaknesses of the other trade unions and educational societies render doubtful the assertion of G. A. Pochebut that 'all the large strikes began and ended on the appeals of the PK and district committees'.[50]

As part of the left's response to the arraignment by the government of the Menshevik Duma deputy N. S. Chkheidze for a speech in parliament, on 22 April Social Democratic and Trudovik deputies constantly interrupted the address of I. L. Goremykin, the president of the Council of Ministers. On the motion of the president of the Fourth State Duma, M. V. Rodzianko, they were expelled from the House for fifteen sessions.[51] In the evening of the same day, four Menshevik deputies, together with the Bolsheviks Malinovskii and E. Rozmi'rovich, the secretary of the latter's Duma fraction, instructed party representatives in the trade unions and educational societies (as surrogates for the destroyed underground apparatus) to arrange walk-outs in protest at the exclusion of the left-wing deputies. Both factions, therefore, co-operated throughout this episode. The Okhrana emphasised that the strikes occurring betwen 23 and 25

April (65,000 failed to report for work) were 'uncoordinated as the Social Democrats have lost their connections with the workers due to arrests . . .'. In the police files there is only one reference to the actual implementation of the deputies' instructions by legal activists – two meetings of the Sampsonievskoe educational society, attended by about 100 people. As in the past, the crucial role was played by both Social Democratic newspapers. Both had publicised the arraignment of Chkheidze and both had argued, with justification, that the Minister of the Interior, V. A. Maklakov, was endeavouring thereby to terminate criticism of governmental policies and take steps towards the restoration of a pre-October regime.[52]

The second lock-out by ten engineering and electrical firms from 24 April as a punitive response to the stoppages described here (see Chapter 9) once more faced activists with a difficult decision. The intellectuals, who ran *Put' pravdy*, repeated their earlier cautious advice. In an editorial in the issue for 27 April they proposed as the workers' riposte 'forms of action [unspecified] more lively, more versatile than the strike . . .'.[53] There is no evidence on the reaction of the working-class cadres. It may be surmised that the proximity of May Day induced them to postpone any agitation for further walk-outs directly intended as a protest against the lock-out.

As in the previous two years, all revolutionary factions sought to mark May Day by strikes and demonstrations, and all co-operated in their preparations. In addition to a leaflet bearing the PK's signature and the three Bolshevik slogans, the OK published a broadsheet with the political programme of the August Bloc (universal suffrage, freedom of coalition, etc.), as did the SRs and Mezhraionka. Both wings of the Social Democratic Duma fraction met to co-ordinate their plans. On 26 and 29 April the Bolsheviks succeeded in convoking meetings of factory workers (800 and 400 were present at the respective gatherings) addressed by the deputy M. K. Muranov. However, there were differences among the various groups about the purposes behind the 'official' celebration. Some Bolshevik activists aspired to turn the stoppages of 1 May into the long-desired general political strike. With the support of Lenin (whose views were transmitted via Petrovskii) and the SRs, they planned armed clashes with the police and attacks upon trams. The Mensheviks firmly rejected both proposals. The factions also differed over the location of the demonstrations – the Bolsheviks favoured the city centre; all others, the factory districts. As on 9 January, there was a disparity between the size of the stoppages (170,000 failed to report for work) and the failure of the revolutionaries to realise their more ambitious designs. A combination of wet weather and extensive precautions by the authorities (400 searches and 100 arrests pre-1 May; police patrols in working-class areas, and guards on the bridges and tramway depots) ensured the absence of large-scale demonstrations or battles with the police anywhere in the city.[54]

This pattern was repeated in the days before the second trial of the Obukhov strikers on 19 May. As in November 1913, all socialist groups were aware that the issue at stake was one with great attraction for workers. A pamphlet with the stamp of the PK exhorted wage earners to down tools on the day of the trial and to proceed to the court-house in the early afternoon. The lack of underground groups was compensated for by utilising the excursions of various educational societies into the forests, at which both Bolshevik and Menshevik deputies spoke in favour of a one-day walk-out. Whilst the former again defended armed clashes, the latter demurred. The publicity given to the trial by the socialist press must have made a contribution. Around 88,000 came out on strike. The broader aspirations of the Bolsheviks again met with failure. In the working-class districts there were only a few minor attempts at demonstrations as operatives downed tools and a mere 300 succeeded in reaching the court building.[55]

Between 9 and 11 June around 27,000 hands stopped work in protest at the concurrent trials of 25 St Petersburg lawyers for opposition to the infamous Mandel Beilis case and of a worker at St Petersburg Pipes for murdering his workshop chief. The police could discover no trace of socialist agitation behind either event, although both socialist newspapers had carried news of the affairs. As in March and April, the editors of the Bolshevik organ were more restrained in their approach to the continual interruptions of work. An editorial on 10 June drew readers' attention to the 'insufficiency of organisation and lack of preliminary preparation' behind the latest strikes.[56]

Throughout the first six months of 1914 the organisational connections between Lenin and the St Petersburg Bolsheviks remained extremely tenuous. The TsK met five times before the war, but apart from the gatherings of 2–4 April and in early July little is known about their composition or debates. Owing to arrests the Russian Bureau never functioned. There were lengthy intervals in correspondence between the Bolshevik leader and the Duma deputies – in February, March and June. Visitors to Cracow from the capital were rare – Petrovskii came in late April and early July (accompanied on this occasion by Kiselev). In no way, therefore, could or did Lenin exercise day-to-day control over his followers in the city. The formulation of Bolshevik policy in St Petersburg, in particular with regard to the events of March and April, lay directly with the activists themselves. As in 1913, the extreme lack of funds hampered all activities, precluding the dispatch of Lenin's own agents to the city (apart from L. B. Kamenev who returned in February 1914 to assume the editorship of *Pravda*) or the publication of any issues of *Sotsial-demokrat*.[57]

Lenin himself was acutely aware of the frailties of the party underground and the dangers these posed for his capacity to dominate events inside Russia. In April he gave an incisive and accurate analysis of his faction's problems to Petrovskii in Galicia. The nascent revolutionary mood lacked guidance 'due to the absence of underground organisations'. This factor, together with 'the lack of an authoritative party centre', 'strongly disorganises the growing labour movement which is escaping from Social Democratic influence', and, as a consequence, 'is moving in an anarchic, fragmented direction'.[58] For Lenin the crucial antidote to these perils was the convocation of a Sixth Party Congress in August, which, apart from legitimising his Prague *coup d'état*, would impart the requisite impetus to the revival of the illegal party apparatus and provide the desperately needed central machinery to co-ordinate action on a national scale (thereby making his leadership effective rather than nominal). And the summoning of a congress required the funds which he then lacked. It was absolutely characteristic of Lenin that he envisaged the secret negotiations which he conducted through the agency of the Bolshevik I. I. Skvortsov-Stepanov in the spring with the Moscow Progressists headed by the textile manufacturer A. I. Konovalov merely in terms of access to money. The Bolshevik leader short-sightedly refused to entertain seriously the plans of Konovalov for a *de facto* revival of the pre-1905 Union of Liberation, i.e. an extra-parliamentary coalition of liberals and revolutionaries which would countenance resort to 'active force'. For Lenin the national general political strike was to remain a purely proletarian enterprise.[59] As Ralph C. Elwood has shown, the Malinovskii affair and the decision of the International Socialist Bureau to summon a gathering of representatives of all the Russian factions in Brussels on 3–5 July threw Lenin off balance and led to the tacit postponement of the congress. Thus, before the war, he failed completely to overcome the defects of his party apparatus.[60]

IV

The underground of the St Peterburg Mensheviks was as sickly a plant as their rivals in the first half of 1914. After its suppression in November of the previous year the Central Initiative Group was reformed some time early in the New Year. It enjoyed a brief existence. No sooner was it again re-established in the first week of April than it was suppressed by the police. It does not seem to have been revived before the war. Meeting in the capital on 16 February, the

OK, perhaps reflecting the views of Dan and Martov who were now members, reaffirmed the importance of an illegal apparatus. In its annual survey the Okhrana noted that Menshevik activists had endeavoured to implement this decision. Cells were set up or renewed in educational societies and trade unions, but no district Initiative Groups re-emerged.[61]

By the start of 1914 the Menshevik leadership, both abroad and in the capital, had become thoroughly alarmed at the Bolsheviks' victories in the legal labour movement (see Chapters 6 and 7). At a private meeting of the new Menshevik Duma fraction on 31 January, A. I. Chkhenkeli (member of the State Duma for Kars and Batum) lamented that 'we have lost all our ties with the working class'. This opinion was endorsed by the OK in February: 'the Duma fraction', it observed, 'stands at a remote distance from the popular masses'. The remedies which the OK proposed, however, adhered closely to the path of legality: the sponsoring of popular legislative proposals in parliament (the freedom of coalition, democratisation of municipal government, abolition of the Pale of Settlement etc.); the concentration of political activity in political clubs; the organisation in insurance centres. A solitary deputy – Chkhenkeli – suggested that the deputies should abandon parliamentary activity in favour of illegal work. It was typical of the Mensheviks that at most a single of the OK's measures saw the light of day. The text of a bill on the freedom of coalition was published in the Menshevik newspaper early in April.[62] There is no evidence that deputies involved themselves with the underground.

Nor were the Mensheviks' renewed efforts to reach out to women workers any more impressive or long-lasting. Although an issue of *Severnaia rabochaia gazeta* was specifically devoted to women's problems on International Women's Day and at the suggestion of A. Kollontai a speical journal for women, *Golos rabotnitsy*, was launched at the same time, the latter lasted a mere two issues and the Menshevik press relapsed into its total indifference to the issue.[63]

In contrast to the Initiative committees, the Mezhraionka displayed more vitality. As well as its existing organisations on Vasil'evskii Island and the Petersburg Side, by the spring links had been established with the Moscow district, with cells in St Petersburg Wagons and the large Skorokhod shoe plant. The group had access to a press and printed leaflets devoted to 9 January, Lena and 1 May. Through the agency of the Menshevik deputy A. F. Burianov (Tauride province), who resigned from the fraction in January 1914 and declared his allegiance to Plekhanov, the Mezhraionka succeeded in forging ties to the leader of the Party Mensheviks, who now sought to launch his own legal anti-'Liquidationist' journal in the capital. In a marriage of convenience, the *émigrés* (with the collaboration of the Parisian Bolshevik Conciliators) furnished the funds and the Mezhraionka a distribution network among the workers. The first issue in 16,000 copies of *Edinstvo* appeared in May.[64]

The strength of the Mezhraionka should not be overestimated. It struck no roots in the southern working-class districts (Moscow excepted) or in Vyborg. There was no proper co-ordinating mechanism for the cells; the inter-district committee scarcely functioned. The organisers of *Edinstvo* soon came to blows over the pretensions of the exiled intellectuals to dictate the editorial content of the journal and the desire of its local supporters to include the Vperedists in the project. Even before the war broke out, the periodical failed to survive its fourth number.[65]

After his newspaper in Vienna ceased publication in the spring of 1912, Trotskii seems to have had little contract with workers' groups in St Petersburg until January 1914. There were no Trotskyist organisations as such – merely individual supporters. It may have been his continuing disagreements with the editors of *Luch* that induced Trotskii to found his own journal, *Bor'ba*, in the capital in February 1914. Although the new periodical claimed to be non-factional, its appearance deepened the rifts between its progenitor and his erstwhile Menshevik allies, in particular as it opened its pages to the Vperedist littérateur Lunacharskii. Its existence was always precarious, averaging at most 2,000 copies over its eight issues. Although Egorov of the Mezhraionka contributed an article to the sixth number, this body rejected the advances of the Trotskyists, who, like the Party Mensheviks, desperately required allies and distributors for their organ.[66]

The Mensheviks in the capital also remained as isolated as ever from other party groups elsewhere in the Empire and abroad. The OK (formed of rotating representatives from the Menshevik Duma fraction, G. O. Baturskii, Dan, Martov and Iulii Chatskii (Garvi)) met occasionally in the capital. The August Bloc fragmented further when the Congress of Latvian Marxists in January 1914 voted to withdraw its nominee. The decision in the autumn of 1913 to convoke an all-Russian Menshevik party conference proved impossible to implement owing to extreme shortage of funds and to the police's arrest of the agents dispatched to the provinces. Mensheviks also refused to recognise the validity of Lenin's proposed Sixth Congress, justly apprehensive that the Bolshevik leader would falsify the norms of attendance to secure his faction's predominance. The Mensheviks were rescued from Lenin's machinations and their own divisions by the intervention of the International Socialist Bureau, which convoked a 'unity conference' of all-Russian organisations in Brussels on 3–5 July. At it the OK, Vperedists and Party Mensheviks agreed to forget their differences and formed the '3 July Bloc'.[67]

Mensheviks also remained extremely ambivalent in their attitude towards strikes. In part their reservations derived from their different interpretation of the shape of a bourgeois revolution in Russian conditions and of the nature of the contemporary crisis. Although they believed that, in the words of a *Luch* editorial, 'reaction has entered its last phase', and that 'the regime has lost credit even among the capitalist bourgeoisie', they refused to predict, in Martov's phrase, 'the form in which there will be completed the historically inevitably process of the transfer of political power from the gentry to the bourgeoisie'. The perspectives involved either 'the path of "German-Austrian" evolution' (i.e. constitutional, non-revolutionary advance) or outside pressure applied by the proletariat and revolutionary parties upon the 'bourgeois' liberal opposition.[68] The unspoken fear of Menshevik intellectuals was that the apparently ceaseless and uncontrollable surge of labour unrest would frighten off potential 'bourgeois' allies. Thus the March stoppages encountered a cool reception. The Central Initiative Group, meeting on 8 March, condemned them as discrediting the political strike as a weapon of revolutionary struggle. In a comment in *Nasha zaria*, Dan correctly pointed to the 'territorial limitations' of the strike movement, confined as it was largely to the capital, as 'its chief source of weakness'. 'In the political struggle', he warned, 'the strike is not always the sole expedient means'. Such considerations dictated a negative attitude by Mensheviks towards a violent response by workers to the March and April lock-outs. Writing in the party newspaper on 28 March, Martov launched a frontal assault against 'the elemental development of the recent wave of political stoppages' which 'has led the workers into a dead end'. At a Menshevik Duma fraction meeting on 25 April, both Dan and Skobelev rejected the Bolshevik campaign for a general political strike. This point of view found a ready endorsement by the Mezhraionka. At the most Mensheviks would support strikes and peaceful demonstrations on 9 January, 4 April and 1 May.[69]

Although the Social Democrats expressed alarm in the first half of 1914 at what they described as 'a resurgence of left Narodnism', such a phenomenon did not occur, at least as far as the Socialist Revolutionary underground is concerned. There exists no evidence that their illegal networks were ever reformed from the summer of 1913. Isolated groups may have survived. Comprehensive arrests in the middle of April 1914 ensnared 64 militants. The Okhrana summarised the party's position in the first half of 1914 as 'complete disorganisation – Socialist Revolutionary activity has come to a total stop.' Activists sought substitutes in secret groups in two educational societies – the Sampsonievskoe (Vyborg district) and Znanie-Svet ('Knowledge-Light': Neva district). Nor did the party in the city establish firm links with the *émigrés*; the foreign organ, *Znamia truda*, published no news of the capital after its report on the May 1913 conference. The leadership living abroad was apparently anxious about their adherents' support for the Bolsheviks' extreme militance. An editorial in *Znamia truda* in April 1914 warned them 'that we are not in a position to give battle to the enemy. Premature, sporadic explosions . . . would be fateful'.[70]

Most unfortunately there is no source material about the condition of anarchism in St Petersburg in 1914. Although the exiles' journal *Rabochii mir* began to publish articles concerning internal developments in Russia, the previous silence about activities in the capital remained undisturbed. The editors entertained no illusions about their ability to influence events inside the Empire: 'with our paucity of numbers, of course,' one contributor observed, 'we cannot dream of any active role in the movement'. It is impossible to ascertain if any of the advice tendered by anarchists living abroad – the formation of anarchist factory groups and factory newspapers, the launching of a legal anarchist organ, the creation of propagandists – ever reached their comrades in the capital or was implemented. The attempt at least to unite the anarcho-communists in the emigration came to grief as the start of European hostilities precluded the congress planned for August.[71]

V

The material available does not permit a temporal analysis of revolutionary groups within individual St Petersburg factories and workshops in the years 1912 to June 1914 but a spatial and sectoral overview is possible.[72]

As Table 5.i illustrates, all revolutionary factions signally failed to establish on a broad basis factory or workshop cells in all branches of manufacturing in the two and a half years before the outbreak of the war – with the single exception of metal processing. The SRs were the least successful – with a mere five groups.[73] The Bolsheviks, unlike the Mensheviks, proved somewhat more adept at forming cells in non-metalworking manufactories (16 to 9 respectively), but their achievement was scarcely impressive.[74]

Even within metal processing, however, the spread of socialist nuclei was not comprehensive either geographically or within the subdivisions of this sector (see Tables 5.ii – 5.iv).

Of the nine districts with metal processing plants (see Table 5.ii), in Vyborg alone did the Social Democrats achieve a ratio of cells almost one-third of such establishments (29 per cent for the Bolsheviks and 23 per cent for the Mensheviks). In other areas the percentage was considerably less. In Vasil'evskii Island it fell to 14 per

Table 5.i: *Distribution of Revolutionary Groups by Industrial Sector, 1912 – June 1914*

Industry	No. of Menshevik groups	No. of Bolshevik groups	No. of SR groups
Chemicals	1	2	–
Food and drink	–	–	–
Glass and porcelain	–	1	–
Leather and rubber	–	3	–
Metalworking	30	33	5
Printing and paper	4	1	–
Textiles	2	2	–
Tobacco	1	–	–
Tramway depots	–	3	–
Wood	1	4	–
TOTAL	39	49	5

Table 5.ii *Metalworking: Distribution of Revolutionary Groups, by District, 1912 – June 1914*

District	No. of Menshevik groups	No. of Bolshevik groups	No. of SR groups
Kolomna (70)	1	–	–
Liteninii (10)	–	1	–
Moscow (15)	1	2	–
Narva/Peterhof (39)	6	5	2
Neva (33)	4	5	1
Okhta (7)	–	1	–
Petersburg Side (40)	4	4	1
Vasil'evskii Island (35)	4	5	–
Vyborg (35)	8	10	1
TOTAL	28	33	5

Note: The district location of two of the thirty Menshevik cells in metalworking could not be traced. Figures in brackets refer to the total number of metalworking plants within each district.

cent (Bolsheviks) and 11 per cent (Mensheviks); Neva, 15 per cent (Bolsheviks) and 12 per cent (Mensheviks); Petersburg Side, 10 per cent for both parties. Within the various branches of the metal working sector (see Table 5.iii), the Social Democratic factions

Table 5.iii *Metalworking: Distribution of Revolutionary Groups, by Sectoral Subdivision, 1912 – June 1914*

Subdivision	No. of Menshevik groups	No. of Bolshevik groups	No. of SR groups
Aviation	–	2	–
Electrical	4	5	1
Machine construction	12	12	3
Metal rolling	1	1	–
Mixed production	4	4	1
Optics	1	–	–
Ordnance/artillery, gunpowder	1	3	–
Railway workshops and rolling stock	2	4	–
Shipyards	1	–	–
Wire and nail	2	1	–
TOTAL	28	32	5

Note: Two of the Menshevik cells and one of the Bolsheviks could not be traced to any sectoral subdivision.

secured their greatest success in machine construction and to a lesser extent electrical manufacturing, and in installations employing 500 to 5,000 hands (see Table 5.iv). There was a direct relation between the two categories.[75] Both parties' relative organisational achievements in Vyborg derived in part from its higher than average proportion of machine construction and electrical goods firms. Four of the six mixed production establishments also witnessed the presence of Social Democratic cells.[76] All socialist parties were weakly represented in the artillery, gunpowder and ordnance subdivision; in shipyards; in wire and nail-making.[77] On the other hand, all districts contained important engineering factories in which no trace of socialist groups can be discovered between 1912 and 1914. In Neva, for example, such a list includes Westinghouse (electrical, 300 workers) or the Russian-American Cast Iron foundry (300); in Kolomna, the Admiralty Shipyards (2,000); on Petersburg Side, Langenzippen (machines, 1,000) or Tiudor (electrical, 200); on Vasil'evskii Island, Donets Iur'ev Metals (wire and nail, 2,800) or Northern Mechanical Boilers (900); in Vyborg, the New Arsenal (600) or St Petersburg Cartridge (2,000).

The absence or presence of socialist cells in a particular sector of industry or within a subdivision (such as machine construction) may

Table 5.iv: Metalworking: Distribution by Size of Establishment, 1912 – June 1914

Size	No. of Menshevik groups	No. of Bolshevik groups	No. of SR groups
0–100 workers	2	1	–
101–500 workers	6	7	1
501–1,000 workers	8	10	2
1,001–5,000 workers	7	10	1
over 5,000 workers	5	4	1
TOTAL	28	32	5

Note: Two of the Menshevik cells and one of the Bolshevik cells could not be traced.

have been linked to the ratios of skilled to unskilled, men to women, literate to illiterate. As Chapter 1 has indicated, chemicals, food and drink, leather and rubber, textiles and tobacco were all manufacturing processes employing large numbers of unskilled or semi-skilled women with lower than average literacy rates. They were also sectors with a very low proportion of trade-union membership (see Chapter 7). A similar diagnosis is applicable to engineering. Machine construction and electrical goods plants (which fell into the category of 500 to 5,000 operatives), proportionately employed far more skilled, young, literate males in 'cold shops' than gunpowder, metal rolling, mixed production, ordnance, shipyards and wire and nail, with their greater preponderance of less literate or illiterate unskilled and semi-skilled working in 'hot shops'. The relative paucity of socialist cells in printing remains an enigma, as this was a highly skilled trade with the greatest rates of literacy and its relatively successful trade union long remained a Menshevik bastion.

VI

The history of the revolutionary underground in St Petersburg in the two and a half years before the outbreak of the war was one of failure. Neither Lenin's high expectations of the role to be played by illegal organisations of revolutionaries nor the 'Liquidationist' intellectuals' fears about the dangers that such secret conspiratorial cliques posed to a truly workers' open party proved accurate. Due to the machinations of the secret police, with its carefully placed secret agents, all socialist factions failed to resurrect viable underground networks or to establish central (all-city) and district organs capable of furnishing leadership and direction to the labour and strike movements. The Leninists' PK existed in tenuous form for approximately ten in total of the thirty pre-war months; their district committees, around thirteen months. Whilst the Mensheviks' Central Initiative Group and district Initiative Groups seemed to enjoy a healthier existence (of seventeen and fifteen months respectively), the appearance belied the reality of minimal activity. No Soviet of Workers' Deputies ever re-emerged. All revolutionary parties exerted little attraction for women, the unskilled or semi-skilled, illiterates or semi-literates and members of the armed forces. For this reason entire branches of manufacturing remained almost totally devoid of socialist cells. Even within the one sector (engineering) in which Social Democrats (although not Socialist Revolutionaries) enjoyed at least some real measure of support, their influence was largely restricted to male skilled workers in machine construction and electrical goods production. The underground, therefore, did not act as an effective mechanism by which revolutionaries could reach out to the ranks of ordinary working people and establish a mass base. In the illegal sense, at least, all socialist factions, including the Leninists, remained as they had been in the years of reaction – miniscule sects. The Okhrana succeeded in keeping the illegal organisations mostly in a cellular or factory-based form.

None of the socialist intellectual leaders living abroad fashioned permanent personal and organisational links to their adherents in the capital. The *émigrés'* daily control of activists in St Petersburg was rendered impossible by problems of distance, interception of mail by the police, the arrests of agents dispatched to Russia, extreme shortage of funds, the infrequency of publication of foreign literature and its tardy or non-arrival in the city, the inability to establish or maintain effective all-Russian agencies of co-ordination abroad or inside the Empire and the barely concealed distaste of their followers for domination by foreign-based intellectuals. All these factors apply to the Bolshevik leader as much as to any other *émigré*. Throughout the pre-war years his leverage over his faction in St Petersburg, let alone all the other socialist groups who rejected his pretensions, was nominal and his ability to manipulate the underground in the city minimal.

Conversely, the crucial part within illegal organisations in the capital was played by second-rank activists, the majority of whom (at least in both Social Democratic parties) were skilled male operatives employed in the engineering industry with several years' experience in both the revolutionary and open labour movements. Throughout the pre-war period this sub-élite, whose membership was in constant flux, displayed a steely determination to fashion and implement its own policies independently of foreign bosses, not least in the realm of the restoration of Social Democratic party unity. In the matter of the response to the Lena massacre, for example, or in the formulation of the strategy of the general national political strike or in the attempts to provide some measure of leadership of political stoppages, local working-class militants repeatedly acted on their own initiative – indeed they scarcely had any other option in the absence of permanent ties to the exiles. The Social Democratic rank and file's dislike of the factional squabbling imported by intellectuals from abroad found expression in the frequent formation of united groups (such as the 'Central Group of Social Democratic Workers of St Petersburg' in 1911–12 or the Mezhraionka in 1913–14) and in the joint collaboration of all Social Democratic coteries among themselves and with the SRs in the preparations for particular strikes. This happened before ten of the twenty-six political walk-outs, April 1912 – June 1914 (in particular the anniversaries of Bloody Sunday 1905, Lena 1912, and May Day).

In view of the debilitated state of the revolutionary underground, none of the illegal socialist factions was able to exert consistent influence upon the course of the political strike movement. Out of the twenty-six instances of stoppages of a political nature analysed in Chapters 4 and 5, there were thirteen occasions for which there is no evidence of socialist agitation (by cells, district committees, illegal leaflets) in factories or workshops before the walk-outs, and thirteen in which there are traces of preparations by revolutionary groups beforehand. In all twenty-six political disputes the influence of the legal Social Democratic press (of both factions) was as or more important in furnishing widespread and detailed coverage of all strikes and in publicising Social Democratic deputies' speeches (written for them by Bolshevik and Menshevik intellectuals) and interpellations before 9 January, 4 April and May Day as well as concerning the police repressions of trade unions, *kassy* and labour newspapers. The militants signally failed, however, to implement their plans for massive working-class demonstrations in the city centre in conjunction with political protests (as they aspired to do on thirteen separate occasions). Owing to extensive preparations by the authorities, all such efforts came to naught – with the single exception of 9 January 1914. The difficulties of co-ordinating a general political strike on an all-Russian scale also proved insuperable, and labour unrest elsewhere in the Empire never reached the dimensions it did in St Petersburg.

In terms of illegal organisations, moreover, and of a vanguard role in political strikes, the Leninists never achieved a position of dominance in the capital, within either the Bolshevik grouping or the broader Social Democratic or socialist movement. The Bolshevik leader's audacious bid at the Prague Conference, January 1912, to equate his faction with the party came to naught, at least as far as the underground was concerned in St Petersburg. Although Leninists came to be the predominant organised group within the Bolshevik faction (in 1913 and 1914), the continued existence of individual Vperedists and Bolshevik Conciliators – let alone the various Menshevik and unitary Social Democratic coteries – testified to the obstacles in the way of his ambitions. It was an ironic comment on over two years of Lenin's schismatic scheming that the two comparatively 'successful' underground structures in the city in 1911–14 were both keen supporters of party unity and opponents of a party split, namely, the Vperedist 'Central Group', 1911–12, and the Mezhraionka, 1913–14.

In tacit recognition of the frailties of revolutionary illegal organisations in St Petersburg, in particular his own grouping's debility, the Bolshevik leader devoted much effort in the two and a half years before the war to securing Leninist control of all legal labour institutions – working-class representation in the State Duma, the legal press, trade unions, educational societies and the *kassy*. Thereby he sought both to deprive his Menshevik rivals of their one comparative advantage over his faction – their position of influence in such bodies – and to secure potentially more advantageous means of attracting mass support than the constantly suppressed and numerically small cells and committees. Although Lenin was to enjoy relative success in the former ambition, the price of victory was the imparting of factional strife to a new area of the labour movement, further enfeebling already imperfect instruments of working-class protest.

Chapter 6

THE REVOLUTIONARY PARTIES, DUMA REPRESENTATION AND THE LEGAL PRESS, 1912–JUNE 1914

At the Prague Conference, January 1912, Lenin had exhorted his followers not only to revive the underground apparatus but to devote as much attention to the implantation of secret cells in legal labour institutions (see Chapter 4). In this way he set the guidelines for a prolonged internecine struggle before the war between both factions of the Social Democratic party for domination of open lines of advance to potential mass working-class support. Thirty months after Prague, the Bolshevik leader came to the conclusion that his decision to split the labour movement had been vindicated. In a report submitted by him to the so-called 'unity conference' of the Russian Social Democratic Labour Party, convoked by the International Socialist Bureau of the Second International in Brussels in the middle of July 1914, he claimed that 'the specific feature of this period [i.e. from January 1912] is that a majority of four-fifths of class-conscious workers of Russia have rallied around the decisions and bodies created by the January Conference of 1912'.[1] Lenin based his startling assertion primarily upon events in St Petersburg in the years 1912 to 1914 when, he averred, his adherents had terminated the Mensheviks' hitherto pre-eminent position in all spheres of legal activity. Like all such statements by the Bolshevik leader, this both contained a modicum of truth and distorted the reality of pre-war developments. Whilst Menshevism did come to lose its hold on the legal activist minority in the capital, Bolsheviks, as distinct from and as much as Leninists, were the victors of the struggle. And their gains were in large part illusory. The trade unions, the social insurance institutions (the *kassy*), the legal press, the educational societies and representation in the State Duma, all proved incapable of providing Bolsheviks with a secure, permanent, mass base among the city's working population. Nor did Bolshevik legal activists prove any more amenable to direct control by their nominal chief in Cracow than their counterparts in the underground.

I

The first apparent triumph in Lenin's renewed onslaught upon the Mensheviks' legal bastions in the capital occurred in October 1912 in the labour curia during the elections to the Fourth State Duma, when the St Petersburg provincial electoral assembly chose the Bolshevik worker A. E. Badaev as the labour deputy.[2] Writing in *Pravda*, Stalin celebrated this victory as a demonstration that 'only the political line of *Pravda* met with the support of the St Petersburg proletariat'.[3] In fact analysis of the mechanics of Badaev's election must cast considerable doubt upon claims that it represented firm evidence of operatives' preferences for Leninist 'uncurtailed slogans' or a rallying of politically conscious workers to Social Democracy.

There did exist genuine differences of approach to the election campaign between Bolsheviks and Mensheviks. These, however, were deliberately exacerbated by the Bolsheviks' leader for his own sectarian purposes.

Both Lenin and Zinoviev, who contributed as much as Lenin to the fashioning of the Bolsheviks' electoral platform, believed that the electoral campaign provided revolutionaries with a rare opportunity for 'the political enlightenment of the masses' and 'socialist class propaganda and organisation of the working class', as well as the strengthening of the underground. Advancing the view that there were three contending forces in the elections – the Black Hundreds, the liberal monarchist bourgeoisie and the democrats – they argued that the party should pursue a 'left bloc' tactic of forcing the masses to choose between counter-revolutionary Kadets and the Marxists. In this case the correct electoral slogans were the revolutionary 'uncurtailed demands' of a democratic republic, eight-hour day and confiscation of the gentry estates.[4] But Lenin's most cherished goal was to break the unity of the Social Democratic parliamentary group, which in the Third State Duma had remained impervious to his efforts at control, and secure the return to the Tauride of his own Bolshevik deputies, who would utilise the tribune to disseminate his particular views and become a focus for open and secret working-class and revolutionary organisation. Thus both theoreticians attacked the Mensheviks' election platform as 'liquidationist' and 'unrevolutionary', and prohibited electoral agreements with 'Liquidationists', calling on workers to elect instead 'consistent Marxists' (i.e. Leninists). From the outset Lenin consciously split the party's electoral campaign.[5]

The Mensheviks' electoral strategy was shaped jointly by the émigrés and the 'Liquidationist' intellectuals. It rested on the Mensheviks' analysis of the class basis of the 3 June regime and the role of the bourgeoisie in the revolutionary process. The renovated monarchy was not bourgeois, they asserted, but a dictatorship of the serf-owning gentry. The industrial revival of 1910 and 1911 had deepened the social contradictions of contemporary Russia and fostered growing discontent on the part of industrial bourgeois circles. Propertied groups were abandoning Octobrism, and the Third State Duma was politically bankrupt. The break-up of the components of the 3 June counter-revolution had commenced.[6] 'The move to the left' by the bourgeois opposition, therefore, should dictate the Social Democrats' strategy. The goal of the elections must be the defeat of the landed and bureaucratic reaction in the State Duma (i.e. the Nationalist and Octobrist parties) and, correspondingly, the electoral victory of the Kadets as 'the most extreme bourgeois faction'.[7] The (unarticulated) conclusion was that the proletariat's tacit support for the liberal opposition required modification of the Social Democrats' minimum programme of 1903 as far as electoral tactics were concerned. Thus in contrast to the Bolsheviks' slogans, both Menshevik littérateurs (from the autumn of 1911) and the August conference (1912) advanced the 'partial demands' of universal suffrage, an all-powerful popular representation (i.e. a Constituent Assembly), the revision of the agrarian legislation of 1906 and an eight-hour day. The delegates to the Vienna gathering drew a clear distinction between long-term objectives (a democratic republic, the confiscation of gentry estates and the arming of the people), which could be achieved only by revolution, and short-term electoral considerations. The Mensheviks remained hostile to any schism in the party's election campaign and championed a common Social Democratic platform and candidates.[8]

The ranks of Bolshevism in St Petersburg evinced much sympathy for the Mensheviks' hostility to Lenin's schismatic tactics. At the start of 1912 the editorial board of the weekly *Zvezda* (N. N. Baturin, S. M. Zaks-Gladnev, S. M. Ol'minksii and the Duma deputy N. G. Poletaev), for example, published an article by the Bolshevik Conciliator, M. I. Frumkin, who demanded a single Social Democratic electoral platform and publicly accepted the Mensheviks' election slogans.[9] Lenin's strained relations from its foundation with the Bolshevik intellectuals in control of *Pravda* (see pp. 147–8) centred in part upon the latter's dislike of their leader's endeavours to split the party's electoral campaign. So profound was the editors' distaste for this design that they refused to publish a single article by Lenin or Zinoviev on issues of electoral strategy before the polls, ignoring all their pleas to the contrary. Their conduct brought down on their heads repeated charges by Lenin of being 'a sleepy old maid' and lacking 'a clear, firm, defined policy on the elections'. Not until 21 September 1912 (i.e. after the first stage of the elections) did the newspaper refer to a 'struggle of tendencies' in the labour curia.[10] The émigrés were forced to publish their polemics instead in the weekly *Nevskaia zvezda*, whose editor Baturin showed more sympathy for their case.

Bolshevik Conciliators, moreover, moved from words to deeds. At the beginning of July they, together with Party Mensheviks, agreed to invite representatives from the Central Initiative Group and the Menshevik weekly *Nevskii golos* to joint discussions of party platform and tactics. Such meetings indeed took place. But their initiators' hopes of establishing a campaign centre of all tendencies foundered on the intransigence of the Leninists. Nevertheless, early in September an assembly of delegates, embracing all shades of party opinion except the Pravdists, endorsed the election programme drawn up at the August conference.[11]

Contrary to the assertions of Soviet historians that 'Lenin led the entire election campaign' and that 'due to *Zvezda* and *Pravda*, the Bolsheviks conducted a wide electoral campaign', the notion of widespread Social Democratic electoral activity must be qualified.[12] Not only did Lenin not command the loyalty of most Bolshevik intellectuals in the capital, but he was deprived of the means of propagating his call for rival Social Democratic candidates and platforms by his exclusion from the pages of *Pravda* and by the complete absence of his own network of cells and committees (see Chapter 4). Indeed Safarov and Armand had been dispatched by him to the city to overcome these obstacles, but had failed. There may have existed a shadowy and illegal Bolshevik 'Central Electoral Committee', with branches in three districts (Narva, Neva and Vasil'evskii Island). The Central Initiative Group also set up a 'Labour Election Committee' with representatives of all party factions (except the Leninists) from all working-class quarters except the Petersburg Side and Vyborg. This body endorsed united lists of candidates and the August Bloc's electoral slogans. In view of the fragile nature of both factions' underground in the summer and autumn of 1912, considerable weight should be attached to the observations of the police that 'as the Social Democrats are widely scattered, they have no real influence' and to the conclusion of the Menshevik labour activist A. N. Smirnov that the 'Labour Election Committee' 'did not achieve much'.[13] By force of circumstance, campaigning had to be left in the hands of individual factory cells. The pressures of censorship made it almost impossible for the labour press to popularise the factions' respective electoral demands or to issue calls to form electoral committees or cells.[14] The Mensheviks were severely handicapped by the absence of their own legal daily newspaper until the middle of September 1912.

On the other hand both Social Democratic factions gained greatly by the Socialist Revolutionaries' quixotic decision to shun the elections. In the St Petersburg labour curia in the first stage of the elections to the Second State Duma in January 1907, the SRs had secured 36 per cent of the vote to the Bolsheviks' 15 per cent and the Mensheviks' 26 per cent, with 116, 78 and 78 delegates respectively.[15] After Stolypin's '*coup d'état*' of 3 June 1907, the Third Party Council had adopted the tactic of a boycott of the legislature. In 1911–12, however, a group of *émigrés*, led by N. D. Avksent'ev, campaigned for a repeal of this decision. Rejecting the party's commitment to political terror and armed rebellion, they argued that the 3 June regime was an accomplished fact. The party should utilise the 'new possibilities' of the elections and parliament's tribune to educate the masses politically, agitate for a new revolutionary upsurge and to dispel 'constitutional illusions' concerning the Duma.[16] However, majority opinion within the party, represented by the foreign organ *Znamia truda*, and in St Petersburg by *Zemlia i volia*, refused to abandon the existing ban on participation in a false legislature or in artificial and restrictive elections.[17] Although *Znamia truda* called upon party members to participate in the electoral campaign in order to propagate the concept of non-involvement in balloting, it later admitted that the 'apparent boycott [of the elections] proceeded almost without our participation'. In the capital Narodnik agitation seems to have been limited to two engineering factories (Koppel' and Neva Shipyards) and two textile mills (K. Ia. Pal' and Maxwell's).[18] The SRs' abstention from the elections both facilitated the Social Democrats' success and diminished the scale and significance of their victory.

Furthermore, the exclusion of entire categories of workers from the electoral rolls (women, men under 25 years of age and operatives in plants employing under 50 hands) as well as the low rates of voting by suitably qualified electors cast considerable doubt on the assumption that the results constituted a necessarily accurate reflection of the political opinions of the working population of the capital. Contemporaries estimated that around a fifth to one-third of qualified working-class voters cast ballots in the election of delegates on 16 September and 14 October 1912.[19] (The authorities cassated the results of the first round in 21 factories, but after the protest strikes of 5–11 October new elections were held in these plants on 14 October.) At the Izhora arms-works, for example, a mere 340 of 4,836 workers voted; at Okhta Gunpowder 462 of the 2,153 electors (the total labour force was 4,000); at St Petersburg Wagons, 500 of 1,400 workers; at the mills of K. Ia. Pal', 200 of 837 electors (2,000 employees); at Neva Paper, 108 of 304 electors (1,000 workers in total). Out of 185 factories included in the St Petersburg provincial electoral census (70 in the city and 102 in the province), there exists reliable data on participation rates in 20. In 11 engineering factories, the proportion of the total labour force who went to the polls varied from 7 per cent at the lowest (Izhora arms-works) to 44 per cent at the highest (Parviainen, 150 workers), with most in the range 20–30 per cent (Koppel', 700 employees, at 29 per cent, for example, or Okhta Gunpowder at 21 per cent). In the two porcelain establishments the rate was 20 per cent; the four textile mills were all under 5 per cent; the three paperworks in the 20–40 per cent range. The proportion voting was lowest in plants with large numbers of unskilled and semi-skilled peasant operatives and highest in those with more skilled, urbanised and proletarianised labour forces. Even in manufactories admitted to the electoral roll, managements often prohibited polling, as at the state-owned Obukhov (6,000 payroll) and Baltic Shipyards (7,500) or Siemens and Hal'ske (1,200) or Thornton cotton mills (1,700).[20] The statistics suggest not so much conscious boycottism, as the SRs claimed, as general indifference. As Lenin with rare candour admitted, 'the workers displayed little interest in the elections'.[21]

As in previous elections to the State Duma, among the distinct minority of labour voters party identification was strong. Of the 82 city delegates chosen in 70 factories in the city by 14 October, the overwhelming majority identified themselves as Social Democrats. The number with a 'non-party' label was around eleven.[22] No one stood or was elected as a Kadet, Octobrist or a 'Black Hundred'. As in 1906 and 1907, politically aware workers revealed their antagonism to liberal and right-wing parties.

An analysis of 56 delegates (from the capital and its environs) (see Tables 6.i and 6.ii) reveals that those selected (in particular Social Democrats) came in the main from large-scale engineering and machine construction plants, a partial reflection of the bias of the labour franchise towards such establishments. (Of the 70 factories on the capital's electoral rolls, 49 fell into this category; these accounted for 57 delegates.)

As Table 6.iii shows, the distribution of delegates among the districts was as uneven as by industrial sector, with a strong bias

Table 6.i: *Delegates, by Industrial Sector*

Metalworking	Textiles	Paper	Chemicals	Glass	Wood	Brickworks	Total
36 (19)	6 (5)	4 (4)	2 (2)	2 (2)	5 (5)	1 (1)	56

Note: Figures in brackets refer to the number of factories electing the delegates.

Table 6.ii: Delegates, by Size of Establishment

	Over 1,000 workers	*500–999*	*100–499*
All 56 delegated	33 (16)	6 (6)	17 (16)
44 Social Democrats	28 (10)	5 (5)	11 (11)
12 non-Social Democrats	5 (5)	1 (1)	6 (6)

Note: Figures in brackets refer to the number of factories electing the delegates.

towards the southern manufacturing areas (in particular Neva) and the environs (Kolpino and Sestroretsk), with few drawn from Petersburg Side, Vasil'evskii Island or Vyborg.

Eighteen of the 56 delegates came from five 'mixed' metal-processing establishments: Putilov (13,000 labour force) and Neva Shipyards (3,158), both privately owned; and the state-controlled Izhora arms-works (5,000), the Pipe works (5,000) and Sestroretsk arms-works, all of which employed many unskilled, newly arrived peasant workers. Five had been chosen in two state-owned explosives works: Okhta Gunpowder (over 4,000) and Okhta Explosives (1,000) and three in two state-controlled railway repair workshops. It had been precisely in these types of plants that the SRs had performed so well in January 1907.[24]

In terms of the electoral census (25 years of age), delegates were relatively young. Of the 25 whose age is known, twelve fell into the category, 25–30 (six were aged 25 and 26) and eleven in the category, 30–35; only two were over 40.

On the other hand, overt sectarian allegiance and firm sense of factional identity were weak. According to Stalin's contemporary account, 26 of the 82 city delegates declared themselves to be 'anti-Liquidationist', 15 'Liquidationist' but 41 as simply 'Social Democrats' or 'non-party', whereas a Menshevik commentator calculated 33 Mensheviks, 25 Bolsheviks, 11 'non-party' and 13 'Social Democrats'. This aversion to factional strife was also reflected in the passing of resolutions in eight metalworking plants and one paper and one textile mill in favour of Social Democratic unity in the election campaign.[25] Of the eighteen Bolsheviks whose biographies can be traced, nine came from the huge 'mixed' engineering works of Putilov, two Sestroretsk arms-works, one Neva Shipyards, one Izhora arms-works, whereas two were selected from the state-owned Nicolaev railway workshops, one Okhta Gunpowder and only one from the non-engineering sector (Pal' textiles). Nine of the eighteen had been or were then involved in revolutionary activity. The five Mensheviks, on whom personal details are available, were

Table 6.iii: *Delegates by City District and Environs*[23]

District	Brickworks	Chemicals	Glass	Engin.	Paper	Textiles	Wood	Total by district
Moscow	1			2				3
Narva		1		1				2
Neva		1		5		3	1	10
Okhta				2		1		3
Petersburg Side				1				1
Peterhof				1				1
Poliustrovo			1	1				2
Rozhdestvo							1	1
Staraia Derevnia							1	1
Vasil'evskii Island				1	1			2
City environs				4	2	1	2	9
Unlocatable			1	1		1		3
TOTAL BY INDUSTRY	1	2	2	19	3	6	5	38

chosen one each from Izhora arms-works, Kreiton shipyards, Neva Shipyards, Parviainen and St Petersburg Metals.

After the first election of delegates on 16 September 1912 the Bolsheviks around *Pravda* at last modified their previously hostile attitude towards a schism in the labour curia. They insisted that the theme of the second stage of the elections should be the struggle against the 'Liquidationists' and the election of 'consistent labour democrats' (i.e. Bolsheviks) as the six electors. The newspaper published lists of suitable candidates in its issues on the mornings of 5 and 17 October 1912. (As the elections of electors on 5 October were cassated by the authorities, they were held again twelve days later.) Even then, the Bolsheviks' own separate political platform or '*nakaz* (mandate) to the St Petersburg deputy', the work probably of Stalin's pen, was composed only some time after 5 October. In many respects this curious and contradictory document is far from being the 'anti-Liquidationist' product of Soviet historiography. Nowhere did it make mention of the 'Liquidationists'' alleged heresies; it referred in cryptic language to 'the full and uncurtailed demands of 1905', without specifying them; and it called 'upon the Social Democratic fraction of the Fourth Duma, in its work on the basis of the above slogans, to act in unity and with its ranks closed'. Contrary to E. D. Chermenskii, the *nakaz* was not 'unanimously accepted at factory meetings'. Knowledge of its existence was not widespread, as it remained unpublished by the socialist press and it appeared too late for dissemination at factory electoral meetings on 16 September. In fact there is evidence for its adoption at a mere two factory assemblies on 14 October – at Neva Shipyards and K. Ia. Pal' textiles. On the other hand from the middle of the month *Pravda* demanded that electors should be chosen according to the *nakazy* (mandates).[26]

The Bolsheviks' lack of consistency and clarity in their electoral strategy, their hesitations about an outright assault on their party opponents and their, fully justified, fears of Social Democratic activists' dislike of factional infighting all found clear expression in the electoral assemblies of 5 and 17 October. In contradiction of *Pravda*'s recent editorials, at the former they objected to a discussion of platforms and at the latter the Bolshevik chairman insisted with no success that balloting should proceed without any debate at all. At both gatherings the attitude of the few non-party and the majority of non-factional Social Democratic delegates was decisive. On each occasion representatives rejected the notion of choosing the six electors by factional lists or according to their support for particular platforms or *nakazy*, a course of action consistently propagated by *Luch* since its foundation. Those present cast their votes for candidates on their personal qualities. Thus, at the first meeting, four

Bolsheviks and two Mensheviks were elected; at the second, three of each. Moreover at the meeting on 17 October the confusion was compounded by the majority passing a resolution calling for Social Democratic unity in the second urban curia elections as well as the Bolshevik *nakaz*.[27]

The final irony of this tangled episode lay in the fact that at the St Petersburg provincial electoral assembly on 20 October the divisions within the Social Democratic camp allowed the Progressist and Octobrist landed and middle-class elements to select the workers' deputy. Before the ballot the Bolsheviks rejected a request to choose the candidate from the two Mensheviks (P. I. Sudakov and N. P. Petrov) who headed the poll on the seventeenth. As a result five of the six labour electors put their names forward. The motives for the assembly's choice of A. E. Badaev, the Bolshevik delegate and elector from the Nicolaev railway workshops, remain obscure. It may be that anti-Semitism played a part (Sudakov was Jewish) or, as the police reported, because Badaev was 'the only one without a past, with little education and raising few expectations concerning Duma oratory'. The new deputy indeed had passed through only primary education, had no record of active work in the party since he joined it in 1904 and was hitherto unknown to party activists.[28]

In contrast to the disagreements and chaos which marked the Social Democrats' election campaign in the labour curia, for the second urban curia elections on 25 October the two factions reached agreement on a single list of candidates (the lawyers N. N. Krestinskii and N. D. Sokolov together with N. S. Chkheidze, Menshevik member of the Third State Duma), all of whom supported party unity. In a far higher poll than the labour curia (48 per cent of the 70,824 voters), they were again defeated by the Kadet party leaders, P. Miliukov, F. Rodichev and A. Shingarev. However, compared to the autumn of 1907, the Social Democrats' share of the poll rose from 9 per cent to 20 per cent. The rise may have been due to the absence of the SRs, the decline in the Trudovik vote and the switch of support by part of the 20,000 commercial employee voters in the curia.[29]

The manner of Badaev's election was so ambiguous and chaotic that firm conclusions about working-class political sympathies in St Petersburg in the autumn of 1912 would be unwarranted. At most it can be stated that politically aware workers (a distinct minority) had shown a preference for Social Democrats – in the absence of the SRs. The same voters, as well as party activists and intellectuals of all tendencies including Bolsheviks, however, had revealed again a profound aversion to factionalism within their party. In that sense the elections marked a signal failure for Lenin. Nor had the electoral campaign fulfilled the higher expectations of the leaders of all socialist factions about a stimulus to party organisation and propaganda. Indeed the limited endeavours in the former sphere had merely led to renewed police suppression of revolutionary groups, while the scope of the latter was severely restricted. The elections and the Social Democrats' campaign, therefore, failed to capture the attention and sympathy of a majority of the working population in the capital.

II

In addition to Badaev, five other Bolshevik deputies were elected to the State Duma; all were from the working class. The leading personality among them was not Badaev but R. V. Malinovskii, the new labour representative from Moscow province and a police agent. Both Lenin and the director of the Department of Police, S. P. Beletskii, had supported his candidature with the identical aim of furthering the schism of the Social Democratic party.[30] However, in the first year of the Fourth Duma's existence, such expectations were not fulfilled. The six Bolshevik and seven Menshevik deputies, three of whom were workers, continued to form a united Social Democratic fraction under the chairmanship of the Georgian Menshevik N. S. Chkheidze.

In Soviet literature the Bolshevik representatives' conciliationism is attributed, in the words of S. M. Gribkova, to their 'inexperience and insufficient maturity in questions of intra-party struggle'.[31] Apart from the fact that four of the six had several years of familiarity with revolutionary and party work behind them, the true reason for their conduct, conveniently ignored by Soviet researchers, lay in the manner of their election. In the case of Malinovskii, M. K. Muranov (Khar'kov province) and G. I. Petrovskii (Ekaterinoslav province), the *nakazy* (mandates) with which they had stood at the polls explicitly called for the maintenance of the unity of the Duma fraction and their victories owed much to Menshevik votes.[32] In ignoring Lenin's wishes, the Bolsheviks at least kept faith with their electors.

The conciliatory attitude of the six Bolshevik parliamentarians assumed concrete form in several ways. They joined the Mensheviks in condemning the attempt of certain activists to launch a strike on the opening day of the State Duma (see Chapter 4). Four of them (excluding Malinovskii and Muranov) agreed with their Menshevik colleagues on 15 December 1912 to merge the two factional newspapers and to the reciprocal inclusion of deputies' names as collaborators of the respective editorial boards.[33] In the composition of the fraction's declaration, read out by Malinovskii on 7 December 1912, the deputies reached a compromise on drafts sent by Lenin and

Dan from abroad. Contrary to the claim of Soviet historians that the Bolsheviks forced the inclusion of their slogans, a close reading of the text reveals that the document omitted them, partly because the Mensheviks feared their incorporation would lead to criminal charges. Instead the document referred to a 'sovereign popular representation' and universal suffrage, but it did bow to Bolshevik demands by the exclusion of the Menshevik concerns for freedom of coalition and cultural–national autonomy.[34]

At the Cracow conference in December 1912, attended by four of the Bolshevik Duma representatives, including Malinovskii, Lenin endeavoured to end their 'conciliatory vacillation'. A resolution was passed declaring the Duma group subordinate to the party's central bodies (i.e. the Leninist Central Committee) and instructing the six to achieve equality with their seven Menshevik colleagues within the fraction. Although four of the deputies terminated their nominal collaboration with the editorial board of *Luch* at the close of January 1913 on the grounds of its 'anti-Liquidationist' character, neither Lenin nor Malinovskii were able to persuade the others to force a schism in the fraction. The two sides continued to collaborate throughout the first half of 1913. Thus a meeting of the Central Committee in Poronin on 27 July 1913, at which Malinovskii was the sole parliamentarian present, censured the six.[35]

Moreover, in this period the six deputies' stubborn refusal to implement the Cracow decision met with tacit support both from the Bolshevik intellectuals working for *Pravda*, and from Stalin, who lived secretly in the city from October 1912 to his arrest late in February 1913. In November 1912, for example, the party daily declared bluntly that 'the fraction must be united', whilst Stalin, writing in the paper in February 1913, exhorted workers to speak out against attempts to split the fraction 'from wherever they come'.[36]

During the Poronin gathering late in September 1913 the Bolshevik leader finally persuaded the five hesitant Duma representatives present to force a schism in the fraction. In the absence of concrete evidence, the reasons for their volte-face may only be conjectured. It is possible that the Bolsheviks' recent success in the elections to the board of the union of metalworkers (see Chapter 7) and the feverishly militant mood of local St Petersburg activists – as expressed in their adoption of the strategy of an all-Russian general political strike – emboldened the deputies to ignore the pressures for party unity. Their personal confrontation with Lenin no doubt played a role as well. On the flimsiest of pretexts, formulated by Lenin, which were mostly demonstrably false, the six Bolsheviks broke away in the last week of October 1913 to form an independent Russian Social Democratic Workers' Fraction.[37]

In the two months after the split both Bolsheviks and Mensheviks engaged in a campaign in the factories of the capital to secure signed resolutions to authenticate their respective claims to be the true representatives of working-class views. In his report to the International Socialist Bureau, written in June 1914, Lenin asserted that in St Petersburg 5,003 signatures had been collected in favour of his fraction and a mere 621 for his opponents: 'these objective data ... definitely proved ... that our Party line is correct'.[38] It would be dangerous to accept this conclusion or Lenin's statistics at face value. It is possible that activists falsified the returns made to the two factions' newspapers. An examination of the resolutions published in the socialist press reveals that frequently the numbers of signatures represented a minute proportion of workers at a plant (for example 58 out of the 12,000 at Putilov, or 42 of 6,000 at the Pipe works) or that entire factories were alleged to have voted for appropriate resolutions. As Martov percipiently observed at the time, such figures at most could possibly represent the opinions of the activist minority – they were and are not an indication of the feelings of the broad mass of factory and artisanal hands.[39] They may even be testimony merely to the better organisational skills of the Bolsheviks.

Whatever the difference the split made to the six deputies' role outside the Tauride Palace, it can be argued that inside parliament little changed in practice. Either as a united or a divided fraction, the Social Democrats were so few in number that they could make no positive contribution to legislative work or to the 'high politics' of the Duma opposition. Their efforts, as before, were directed in the main towards agitational parliamentary questions to ministers (interpellations), for the presentation of which they had to seek the collaboration of Trudoviks and Kadets. Moreover, both Social Democratic fractions soon endured further internal divisions.

The worst blow befell the Bolshevik Duma group with Malinovskii's sudden and apparently inexplicable resignation from the legislature on 8 May 1914, his immediate flight abroad and the spate of rumours that he was an *agent provocateur*, accusations assiduously propagated by the Mensheviks. The affair added renewed embitterment to intra-party relations, at least as far as intellectual leaders were concerned, discredited Lenin and distracted him from preparations for the Sixth Congress and events in the capital.[40]

The seven Menshevik deputies had suffered from the outset from lack of cohesion. A. F. Burianov (representing Tauride province, a factory worker) supported Plekhanov; M. I. Skobelev (the son of a Baku oil magnate, and elected by the Russian population in Transcaucasia) had collaborated with Trotskii on his Viennese *Pravda*; N. S. Chkheidze (Tiflis province, a journalist) and A. I. Chkhenkeli (Kars, Batum and Sukhumi, a lawyer) were Georgian

Mensheviks; I. N. Mankov (Irkutsk, an accountant) was politically to the right of his colleagues. Relations with the Organisational Committee (OK) were not always harmonious. Whatever their public stance, Menshevik leaders such as Aksel'rod, Dan, Martynov and perhaps Martov secretly welcomed the schism in the Duma group. The latter was weakened by the departure of Burianov, with Plekhanov's connivance, in January 1914, who entertained the quixotic hope that his action would hasten the reunification of the fraction. At the same time V. I. Khaustov (Ufa province, a metal turner), Skobelev and Chkhenkeli attacked the Menshevik organ as the vehicle for the personal views of Dan and Martov and proposed that the deputies establish their own newspaper. Shortage of funds and the opposition of Chkheidze ensured that the idea remained stillborn.[41] The Duma representatives and the OK also failed to reach agreement on their response to a perceived loss of working-class support.

Thus the Bolshevik leader's schismatic schemes concerning the Duma fraction took long to come to fruition, and even when achieved, his success was partial. As a coherent unit his own tiny parliamentary group lasted only a few brief months and was soon sundered by the Malinovskii scandal and the outbreak of the war. His Menshevik rivals, however, fared even worse. They were riven by personal and ideological feuds. Their refusal to participate in illegal work – out of fear of suffering the same fate as the Social Democratic deputies in the Second Duma in 1907 – reduced them to irrelevance.

III

If Bolshevik accomplishment in the elections to the Fourth State Duma and the extent of Lenin's control over the Social Democratic fraction in parliament should not be exaggerated, the Bolsheviks do seem to have proved far more successful than their rivals in the arena of legal publishing in the period 1912 to 1914. Not only did they manage to launch in St Petersburg the first Social Democratic daily newspaper, *Pravda*, on 22 April 1912 six months ahead of the Mensheviks, whose lawful organ *Luch* first appeared on 16 September of the same year, but the circulation of the former and the financial contributions sent to it by workers consistently outstripped the latter to the outbreak of war. 'These objective figures,' boasted Lenin in his 1914 report to the International Socialist Bureau, 'show that *Pravda* is a genuinely working-class newspaper'.[42] This statement, however, cannot be accepted at face value. The foundation of *Pravda* owed little to Lenin and much to the Okhrana. For its first year and a half its editorial board was far from being a pliant instrument in the hands of the Bolshevik leader and its collaborators sought to thwart his most cherished factional schemes. The outreach of the socialist press was relatively limited – its appeal lay with labour and party militants and with skilled male artisanal and factory workers rather than women, the unskilled and the poorly paid.

Contrary to the impression given in Soviet and Western literature on the topic, late in 1911 and early in 1912 there emerged two separate and mutually antagonistic attempts to found a cheap legal daily Social Democratic newspaper in the capital – one by the intellectuals responsible for the Bolshevik weekly *Zvezda* and the other by an 'Initiative Group' of metalworker activists.

In general terms the reasons behind both efforts were broadly similar. The existing trade-union journals, where were run by ordinary working-class trade unionists, confined their coverage to professional matters, enjoyed a limited distribution and were published irregularly. *Vestnykh portnykh*, the organ of the union of tailors, for example, appeared only once in 1911 and thrice in 1912. *Golos bulochnika i konditera*, the bakers' periodical, sold a mere 700 copies per number. The two current Social Democratic newspapers – *Zvezda* and the Menshevik *Zhivoe delo* – were weeklies, under the direction of intellectuals, and devoted much space to topics of socialist theory. All party luminaries were concerned to reach a wider audience in the imminent election campaign to the Fourth State Duma than the 29,000 and 23,000 readers respectively of these two publications.[43]

The initiative on the side of the Bolsheviks lay with the collaborators of *Zvezda* rather than Lenin or the Prague Conference. In the last two months of 1911 N. Baturin (pseudonym of N. Zamiatin), one of the paper's editors, and M. I. Germanov (pseudonym of M. I. Frumkin, an experienced legal activist in Baku and Moscow), both raised in public for the first time the notion of launching a legal daily Marxist newspaper, and in the New Year *Zvezda* opened a fund for workers' contributions. Although the delegates in Prague gave their unofficial approval to the venture, the Bolshevik leader's endorsement was half-hearted. At a meeting of the new Central Committee in Leipzig with the Duma deputies N. G. Poletaev and V. S. Shurkanov, the former agreed to assign 1,000 roubles to *Zvezda* but declared that it had no monies to underwrite the project. One reason for Lenin's conduct may have been his strained relations with the weekly's editorial board over his electoral tactics. Another possible factor was that the generally conciliatory views of the editors apparently influenced their attitude towards the future daily newspaper. Both Baturin and Germanov emphasised in their writings that the proposed organ should be controlled directly by workers and devoid of factional polemics, whilst Poletaev, the chief editor of *Zvezda* and one of the principal organisers of the new paper, refused to publish his leader's attacks upon *Zhivoe delo*. Lenin's lament at the end of March 1912 that 'we have no information, nor leadership, nor supervision over the paper' was an apt comment on his minimal contribution to *Pravda*'s birth.[44]

In contradiction to the legend propagated at the time by the Bolsheviks and subsequently in Soviet historiography, the financing of *Pravda* did not derive exclusively from a myriad workers' kopecks. Its promoters reckoned that its foundation would cost 10–12,000 roubles. By 22 April 1912, a mere 3,858 roubles had been sent to the editorial offices of the Bolshevik weekly (and a close scrutiny of the published lists reveals that several large amounts were in fact donated by a few nameless individuals). In addition the Central Committee furnished 3,000 roubles and the writer Maxim Gorkii 2,000. But the chief source of funds came from V. A. Tikhomirnov, the heir of a rich Kazan merchant and shipowner and friend of V. M. Molotov, who inherited 300,000 roubles and contributed a large sum to launch the newspaper.[45]

Contemporaneously a number of Menshevik legal working-class activists conceived the plan of establishing a labour publishing company which would create, *inter alia*, a Marxist daily newspaper for workers. The idea apparently originated in October 1911 with a circle of operatives who came to the capital from Baku. Either they or other hands or both (the evidence is very obscure on this point) set up in January 1912 an 'Initiative Group' to take charge of the project, which was announced through the pages of *Zhivoe delo* on the twenty-seventh of that same month. The nucleus comprised 'Liquidationist' metalworkers involved in trade-union affairs, although it also included a goldsmith and a 'Narodnik'.[46] The details of their scheme furnish testimony both to these militants' desire for party unity and to their suspicions of intellectuals. The progenitors emphasised that ordinary workers should control the boards of both the publishing company and the newspaper (whose projected title was *Rabochaia gazeta*), and that the new organ must be non-factional. At a meeting some time in March 1912, the 'Initiative Group' carried the suggestion that the existing two Social Democratic weeklies should amalgamate. Contrary to the later Menshevik assertions that 'the preparatory work assumed wide dimensions', the existence of the proposal remained unknown to most workers. Although the unions of architectural and construction workers, metalworkers and textile workers offered their assistance, a paltry 300 roubles was collected – in part because *Zvezda* refused to publish the group's appeal. Even the 'Liquidationist' intellectuals evinced little enthusiasm.[47]

Despite these setbacks, however, the campaign to establish an alternative workers' daily newspaper seemed to be crowned with success at a legal meeting convoked by several trade unions on 15 April 1912. The Bolshevik resolution condemning *Rabochaia gazeta* as a 'Liquidationist' enterprise won a mere 40 votes out of the 500–600 present. Instead the assembly endorsed the proposal to elect a commission of eight to draft the statutes of the projected publishing company. The future editorial board even chose the same date, 22 April, as its Bolshevik opponents to issue the first number of its paper. Thus, two rival Social Democratic dailies would have appeared simultaneously if the Okhrana, in furtherance of its policy of *divide et impera* towards the party, had not stepped in and shattered the Mensheviks' dreams by arresting all the collaborators of *Rabochaia gazeta* on 18 April 1912.[48]

The Mensheviks' inability to found their own daily organ for a further five months proved damaging to their cause. The successor to *Zhivoe delo*, shut down by the authorities in the first week of April, *Nevskii golos*, was a sickly offspring, with a mere nine issues before its closure at the end of August 1912, suffering from a chronic shortage of funds and readers. When *Luch* was finally launched on 16 September, it was very much the product of 'Liquidationist' intellectuals, in particular V. Ezhov and O. A. Ermanskii, with the backing of the new OK., rather than the genuine worker-controlled newspaper envisaged by the 'Initiative Group'.[49] The delay allowed *Pravda* to establish firmly its reputation as the working-class daily.

The continuing distaste of some union activists for the factional polemics conducted by the Social Democratic press and for the intellectuals' pretensions to dominate 'working-class' publishing found expression in the autumn of 1912 in a scheme to start a weekly central trade-union journal *Rabochii golos*, which would replace all existing professional journals and Social Democratic newspapers. The identity of the progenitors cannot be established, but succour for the project came from six artisanal trade unions (operatives in the carriage trade, baking, woodworking, gold and silver production, leather manufacture and tailoring) and a solitary industrial union (textile workers) which together raised 485 roubles for the venture. In contrast to the spring, the metalworkers proved hostile, as did printers and two unions of commercial–industrial employees, all of which possessed semi-successful trade periodicals. The enterprise split the Social Democrats as some Menshevik-dominated unions opposed the plan (the metalworkers and printers), whereas at least one Bolshevik-controlled one (the bakers) approved it. As in the spring of 1912, the police intervened to prevent the journal's launch in February 1913 by detaining all involved. The field of daily labour publishing, therefore, remained dominated by socialist intellectuals rather than workers and by partisan products, whose constant polemicising deepened the schism in the party.[50]

The standard Soviet account that '*Pravda* was led on a daily basis by the Central Committee under Lenin, which had solid ties with the newspaper' represents a distortion of the complex, strained and unharmonious relations between the Bolsheviks living abroad and the collaborators of the new daily for much of its existence.[51] The minor part played by Lenin in the foundation of *Pravda*, its editorial board's financial independence of the *émigrés* and its relative geographical isolation all facilitated the endeavours of the editors to secure and preserve a large degree of autonomy.

In its first year the editorial office comprised two State Duma deputies (N. G. Poletaev and I. P. Pokrovskii), intellectuals and littérateurs (N. N. Baturin, S. S. Danilov, S. M. Zaks-Gladnev and M. S. Ol'minskii), students (N. N. Lebedev, V. M. Molotov and F. M. Raskol'nikov), and the worker K. S. Eremeev.[52] Contrary to the supposition of G. V. Petriakov that the board committed 'mistakes' because it 'lacked experience', in fact most of its assistants had worked for *Zvezda*.[53] The editors, moreover, genuinely held different opinions from the exiles about the paper's line on the issues of party unity and electoral tactics, on which they displayed 'conciliatory tendencies'. In the very first issue, for example, Stalin wrote that 'we must show goodwill towards one another'. To Lenin's fury the organ's journalists shunned factional polemics with the 'Liquidators' and excised derogatory references from his articles (many of which they rejected outright).[54] Even more significantly they adamantly resisted for months his plans to split the electoral campaign. They tacitly santioned the unity of the new Social Democratic fraction in the Fourth State Duma and accepted the group's decision to amalgamate the two Social Democratic newspapers.

Despite his numerous irate letters, and his continual demands that 'a socialist organ must conduct polemics', distance and the absence in the capital of loyal agents ensured that Lenin's efforts to curb the independence of his fellow littérateurs were protracted and fraught with difficulties. Although Stalin, a member of the TsK, returned to St Petersburg in October 1912, he failed both to implement its resolution to reform the editorship and to ensure its strict subordination to the central party authority, and Lenin's injunction in December to transfer responsibility for the paper to Muranov. The evidence suggests that he shared the conciliatory attitudes of the editors. Thus the Cracow conference at the close of the year condemned the editorial board (and, implicitly, Stalin) as being 'insufficiently firm in party spirit' and instructed I. M. Sverdlov (who, escaping from exile, fled to the capital in this month) to reorganise the staff in his new role as *de facto* editor. Due to the covert opposition of Badaev,

Malinovskii and Petrovskii, it took Sverdlov several weeks before he forced the requisite changes.[55]

The arrest of both Stalin and Sverdlov in the course of February 1913 brought an abrupt halt to Lenin's success. Almost for want of better the Bolshevik Duma deputies had to be drafted, but none of them had previous knowledge of the publishing trade. This fact, perhaps, induced the Bolshevik leader to dispatch to Russia in May 1913, M. E. Chernomazov, who had been involved in the running of *Sotsial-demokrat* in Paris. The choice proved less than fortunate. Although the new editor gratified the exiles by accepting many more contentious pieces for inclusion in the paper, either before or after his return he became an Okhrana agent. Throughout his eight months' tenure of the post he implemented police directives to deepen the party schism and provide pretexts for the authorities to close down the newspaper or confiscate particular issues. He published letters from the Vperedist theoretician A. A. Bogdanov, for example, and from the Georgian Mensheviks. Even the resolutions of the Poronin conference were printed in number eight of *Za pravdu*. He acted in a dictatorial manner towards the other assistants.

The period of relatively more effective control by Lenin over the Bolshevik daily and of less troublesome relations between him and its staff commenced in February 1914. In that month, owing to Ol'minskii's evidence against him, Chernomazov was removed as editor. Evidently taking no chances, Lenin now persuaded L. B. Kamenev, his most trusted colleague apart from G. E. Zinoviev, to return to Russia from exile to rescue the paper's ailing fortunes. This 'cultured, knowledgeable editor' at last established the newspaper as a 'Leninist' organ. Yet even in these last months before the war Lenin's influence was far from complete. Correspondence was erratic. In March, the staff annoyed the *émigrés* by adopting a cautious attitude towards the lock-out in the St Petersburg engineering industry. They also entered into unsuccessful negotiations to include Party Mensheviks on the board.[56]

The world of Menshevik publishing was as lacking in comradely harmony as the Bolshevik. Thus during its brief existence the editorship of *Zhivoe delo* (the 'Liquidationist' intellectuals I. A. Astrov, V. Ezhov and E. Maevskii) was subject to a sustained critique both from Iu. Martov abroad and from other 'Liquidationists' living in exile in Pskov (F. A. Cherevanin, Iu. A. Isuv and V. O. Levitskii). Both attacked the paper's collaborators for failure to pursue a 'concrete goal and platform'.[57]

The disputes which racked *Luch* in 1913 almost wrecked the publication and contributed to the break-up of the August Bloc. Although the OK had sent T. Dan to assume the office of editor in January 1913, his basic difficulty lay in the fact that, irrespective of his or the *émigrés*' critical attitude towards the dogmas of 'Liquida-tionism', the latter's theoreticians comprised the sole Menshevik literary forces capable of producing a daily in the capital. The newspaper's critics – Trotskii, the Caucasian Mensheviks and the seven Menshevik Duma deputies – directed their assault at its cautious attitude towards the strike movement and in particular the appearance in January 1913 of an article by L. Sedov (pseudonym of B. A. Ginzburg) which condemned reviving sympathy for the underground as 'deplorable' and 'the psychology of irresponsibility'. A secret meeting of OK representatives in St Petersburg in April 1913 failed in its bid to force a 'non-Liquidationist' majority upon the board. Thereupon Trotskii and his representative on the executive, S. Iu. Semkovskii, ceased collaboration.[58] *Luch* and its successors continued to be controlled until the war principally by Dan and Martov after his return from exile in the autumn of 1913. Both endured and survived a renewed bout of hostility from several Menshevik parliamentary representatives early in 1914.

Due to the particularist outlook of Soviet historical literature, minimal information is available on legal Socialist Revolutionary publications in St Petersburg. A weekly newspaper, *Trudovoi golos*, appeared between February and July 1913. As it regularly printed articles by B. Vornov (Lebedev), a collaborator on *Pochin*, the foreign journal of the right wing of the party, it may have served as a vehicle for such revisionist views. It was succeeded by *Zhivaia mysl'* and other organs bearing variants on this title up until the outbreak of war.

With the fragmentary data to hand it is difficult to delineate with a reasonable degree of accuracy the extent and character of the read-ership of the socialist press in the capital in the period 1912 to 1914.

In comparative terms, at least, despite wide fluctuations in its circulation *Pravda* consistently outshone both its Menshevik and SR competitors. The fortunes of the new Bolshevik daily had been helped by the coincidence of its launch with the upsurge of labour unrest consequent upon the Lena massacre. Although its initial national distribution of 60,000 copies per issue could not be main-tained and fell to the range 32–40,000 by the summer and autumn of 1912, this compared favourably with *Luch*'s original modest total of 5–6,000. By January 1913 the figures were 31,000 and 9,000 respec-tively. However, the three short-lived successors to *Pravda* in the middle of 1913 suffered severely from confiscations and fines levied by the authorities, aided by the provocateur Chernomazov. As a result the numbers published per issue fell to 17–20,000, whereas their Menshevik rival's climbed to 14,000. The removal of Cherno-mazov, the return of Kamenev and the resurgent working-class protest all stimulated a revival in the Bolshevik daily's sales to 40,000 a day by June 1914. In that month, the Menshevik organ sold some 15–17,000 copies and the SR *Zhivaia mysl' truda*, 10–12,000.[59]

It is most unfortunate that there exist no separate statistics for the respective apportionment of readers between the three papers in St Petersburg, as distinct from an all-Russian scale. It is known that in April 1914 there were 2,800 subscribers to the Bolshevik daily in the city and 1,005 to its Menshevik opponent. But all three organs disposed of the vast bulk of each issue either by direct sale through newsvendors or distribution by means of sympathisers in factories and workshops or via tearooms, taverns and the libraries of educational societies and trade unions. Numbers available were also reduced by frequent confiscations. Of the 645 issues of *Pravda*, April 1912–July 1914, 155 suffered this fate.[60]

There is also the information provided by group collections in the capital for the two Social Democratic newspapers (see Tables 6.iv and 6.v).

This general impression is further confirmed by the fund-raising campaign in the spring of 1914 ('workers' press day', 22 April 1914),

Table 6.iv: St Petersburg: Group Collections for the Social Democratic Daily Press, Jan. 1912–July 1914[61]

	Bolsheviks	Mensheviks
1912	456	47
1913	1,617	256
1914 (to July)	2,181	259
TOTAL	4,254	562

Table 6.v: St Petersburg: Group Collections for the Social Democratic Daily Press, by Industry, July 1914

	Bolshevik		Menshevik	
	Metalworking	Printing	Metalworking	Printing
1912	126 (55)	–	–	–
1913	538 (90)	120	156 (46)	38
1914 (to July)	755 (127)	209	178 (43)	141
TOTAL	1,419	329	334	179

Note: Figures in brackets refer to the number of plants making group collections.

which ended with 11,680 roubles 96 kopecks gathered in the capital for Bolshevik publications and 4,446 roubles 13 kopecks for Menshevik.[62]

Such general figures, however, do not warrant either the assumption that 'workers and only workers support our newspaper' (an editorial in *Put' pravdy*) or that readership of the socialist press was other than a minority interest among the vast mass of workers.[63]

Leaving aside the imponderable question of the veracity of the statistics concerning contributions published in the socialist newspapers, there is evidence to suggest that both the Bolshevik and Menshevik press continued to receive donations from 'bourgeois' circles in the pre-war years, in addition to genuine monies from operatives and party members. At the start of 1913, for example, Lenin once more solicited funds from Gorkii, and in December of the same year the Bolshevik Central Committee instructed the editorial board of the party daily to appeal to wealthy sympathisers for aid. The Okhrana also discovered that A. I. Konovalov, the textile magnate and leader of the Progressist party, had assigned 2,000 roubles to Bolshevik legal publications in 1913 and a further 3,000 early in 1914. In the summer of 1913, *Luch* acknowledged a surprise gift of 6,000 roubles from an unknown well-wisher. And in a private letter early in 1915 Martov admitted that the wealthy Menshevik sympathiser, A. L. Popov, had provided much of the finance for the newspaper.[64] In the absence of the accounts of both Social Democratic newspapers it is impossible to ascertain the exact percentages of their finances deriving from 'bourgeois' and working-class supporters.[65]

A random survey of the lists of contributions from St Petersburg factories and workshops printed in the Social Democratic press suggests that readership was far from uniform among the working population.[66] Thus, the sample shows that *Pravda* and its successors were in receipt of donations from 55 engineering, machine construction, electrical plants and shipyards, 31 printshops, but only twelve food and drink manufactories, ten woodworking enterprises, six textile mills, six leather factories, three tobacco plants, three tramway depots, three bakeries and one each from groups of gold and silversmiths, tailors, telephonists and commercial–industrial employees. *Luch* and its descendants, on the contrary, were sent monies from eighteen metal-processing works, three printshops and a tailoring establishment. The general trend of these statistics, which is in line with the findings of V. T. Loginov and N. A. Kurashova cited earlier, also coincides with the collections of 'workers' press day' in St Petersburg in spring 1914 which revealed the dispatch of monies to *Put' pravdy* from 339 groups of donators in metalworking, 116 in woodworking enterprises, 113 in printing and 41 in textiles. *Severnaia rabochaia gazeta*'s funds came from 40 groups in metal-processing, 34 in printing, 27 artisanal outlets, 31 in commercial emporia and one each from textile mills, tobacco and shoe manufactories.[67]

A possible explanation for this uneven pattern of distribution lies in the ratios of skilled to unskilled, literate to illiterate and males to females in particular industries. The very low number of readers in textiles, for example, may be correlated with the high percentage of young women employed, who evinced little interest in politics. A contemporary investigation at Neva Thread, with 2,774 female and 500 male operatives, discovered that only around 40 of the employees read the labour press. Printing, on the other hand, was a highly skilled profession, requiring more than average literacy. A study of E. Tile printers, with 150 hands, revealed in March 1913 that 45 bought *Pravda* and 5 *Luch*. In metalworking, readership was widely rather than deeply diffused among all branches (engineering, machine construction, electrical goods, shipyards and 'mixed' production), in both state and private plants, in large and small (judging from the survey's list of 55 enterprises). It must be surmised, however, that readers were the minority of skilled, better-paid, young male workers. At the Pipe works, with 7,000 employees in spring 1913, 400 copies of the Bolshevik newspaper were sold a day, and 25 of its Menshevik rival; a year later, the figures were 700 and 210 respectively, with 200 for the SR *Stoikaia mysl'*.[68]

Further proof for the supposition that the bedrock of support for the socialist and labour press was furnished by the 'worker–intellectual' – the small stratum of skilled male operatives in both factory and artisanal establishments who sought to widen their mental horizons beyond the level of minimum literacy and popular fiction – may be found in the composition of the capital's twelve working-class educational societies.[69]

Membership of these institutions, which fluctuated in total from around 1,800 in December 1912 to 6,000 in July 1914, followed a pattern similar to the readership of labour publications. In the first place, males greatly outnumbered females. At 'Knowledge', 221 of 297 members in January 1914 were men, and 76 women; at 'Source of Light and Knowledge', the ratio was 291 to 41; whereas at 'Science-Life' it was 768 to 178. Secondly, most participants were both young and single. In 'Knowledge', 201 (145 men and 56 women) were aged 16–25 and 247 were single; 138 at 'Source of Life and Knowledge' fell into the category 16–20 years of age; and at 'Science-Life' 725 were single (603 men and 122 women) and 120 married (85 men and 35 women). Thirdly, the overwhelming majority of members were classed as skilled. A mere 20 in 'Knowledge' were unskilled, 30 at 'Source of Light and Knowledge'. This fact is reflected in the earnings of participants, which were above the general norm. At 'Knowledge' average pay was 40 roubles a month, and at 'Source of Light and Knowledge', 35 roubles. Furthermore the members' experience of schooling had been limited to two years, or even one, of primary instruction. Thus at 'Science-Life', 789 of 940 in January 1914 had not advanced beyond elementary level in their education. The 'worker–intellectuals', who availed themselves of the services of these societies, were often the backbone of the city's trade unions: 108 members of 'Knowledge' had joined trade unions; 505 in 'Science-Life'. The skilled oc-cupations from which membership of the societies was drawn were diverse and reflected the industrial profile of the districts in which these bodies were located. Thus 'Knowledge' (St Petersburg Side) embraced *inter alia* 97 metalworkers, 73 printers, 17 textilists, 17 joiners and 15 clerks. In contrast, 'Science-Life', based in the city centre around Ligovskaia street, was dominated by that area's artisanal trades – there were 225 printers, 112 tailors, 42 gold and silversmiths, 40 joiners and 85 metalworkers. Contrary to con-temporary Marxist arguments, the emergent working-class semi-intelligentsia was not confined to large-scale factory industrial instal-lations but was drawn as much from artisanal petty enterprises. It is perhaps instructive that the two least successful educational societies pre-war were located in the most solidly industrial suburbs – the Sampsonievskoe Society in Vyborg (220 members in 1913) and the Second Society of Education in Narva (222 members) – whilst the most successful (the above-mentioned three) all flourished in socially and manufacturing diverse areas.[70]

As distinct from the minority of 'worker–intellectuals', who did purchase socialist newspapers and participated in trade unions and educational societies, the overwhelming majority of rank-and-file workers in all occupations in St Petersburg preferred to read the new commercially produced popular fiction (short detective stories, adventure and women's novels) and the boulevard press.[71] The St Petersburg tabloid *Gazeta kopeika*, founded in 1908 by M. B. Gorodetskii, had by 1910 reached the unprecedented daily circulation of 250,000 copies. Its popularity owed much to its serialised fiction. The few contemporary studies of reading habits in individual St Petersburg factories all emphasise the attraction of *Gazeta kopeika* to operatives. At the Pipe works, for example, almost 2,000 copies of this newspaper were sold every day throughout 1913 and 1914, as well as 400 of its older rival *St Petersburgskii listok*. Other isolated investigations at New Cotton, and St Petersburg Engineering and Rozenkrants made similar discoveries.[72]

Even 'worker–intellectuals' preferred to relax in their leisure hours with novels (albeit *belles-lettres* rather than pulp fiction) far more than with sociopolitical literature. An examination of lending from the libraries of educational societies and trade unions confirms this observation. In 'Knowledge', for example, in 1912–13 215 readers borrowed in total 569 novels (mostly Tolstoy, Gorkii, Korolenko, Dostoevskii) but only 18 works on sociology and 27 on political economy. At 'Source of Light and Knowledge' in 1911, 1,587 of the 2,305 books taken out by 304 readers were *belles-lettres*. In the same year the members of the library of the union of metalworkers read 4,354 pieces of fiction, but a mere 310 writings devoted to social and political themes.[73]

If the outreach of legal labour publications was comparatively limited, all three socialist newspapers and trade-union journals play-ed an important part in shaping the perceptions of the 'worker–intellectuals' who both read and helped produce them.

As L. Kleinbort observed at the time, most trade-union journals in the capital after 1909 were edited by union activists themselves, workers whose educational attainments and aspirations marked them out as 'semi-intellectuals'. Whilst the editorial boards of all three socialist dailies and weeklies in 1912 to 1914 were dominated by intellectuals of non-proletarian origin, they depended greatly upon the services of 'worker–intellectuals' who were often simultaneously correspondents and distributors of the papers, members of trade-union executives and party cells. Both Social Democratic newspap-ers followed similar formats, with the first two pages devoted to theoretical articles by littérateurs and reports of the speeches by workers' deputies in the State Duma, but the last two centred on notices of industrial disputes, trade-union affairs, social insurance institutions and life in the factories. Coverage of all the latter aspects relied almost completely on activists dispatching relevant news and articles to the offices of the publications. Thus *Pravda* and its succes-sors in 1913–14 (to 21 April) received 7,874 pieces of correspondence from the St Petersburg region (4,043 concerned strikes).[74]

For the skilled, urbanised, youthful male workers, who formed the party and union militants before the war, the three newspapers provided, in the absence of propaganda circles or party schools or widespread illegal literature, their sole source of information on current events from a Marxist or SR perspective. The sections in the papers devoted to labour affairs rather than scholastic polemics (which were not popular with readers) strengthened activists' sense of class identity and solidarity and deepened their antagonism to-wards both Tsardom as a political system and capitalism. The party organs also spread revolutionary socialist ideas. They were of un-doubted significance in sustaining enthusiasm and fostering support in economic disputes by serving as a focus for workers' collections for strikers and their families (see Chapter 8). They contributed to political unrest by publishing Duma interpellations concerning malfeasance by the authorities and articles on the Lena tragedy, May Day and the anniversary of 'Bloody Sunday'.

Yet it would be erroneous to conclude that the two rival Social Democratic newspapers naturally promoted factional identification amongst their readers. Whilst the possession of *Pravda* and its broader readership provided the Bolsheviks with their most important (if limited) point of contact with more workers than any other legal or illegal means of communication, its editors consciously endeavoured to keep it a non-sectarian publication in 1912 and 1913. Much of the evidence provided in this and the two earlier chapters, on the contrary, testifies to militants' desire to eschew schismatic strife and maintain Social Democratic party unity. Operatives supported the labour press, it could be argued, as much because it alone defended labour's rights and interests as because of its factional colouring. *Pravda* certainly did not secure support as a specifically 'Leninist' organ, as it did not pass into Lenin's firm control until 1914 and did not propagate specifically 'Leninist' themes for much of this period.

IV

As with the history of the revolutionary underground in the years 1912 to 1914, the spheres of Duma representation and legal publishing proved to be a fertile ground for tensions between *émigrés* and intellectuals and activists alike inside St Petersburg. Far from the Bolshevik exiles dictating the course of the election campaign in the middle of 1912 or controlling the launch and conduct of *Pravda*, their sectarian schemes met with strong and initially successful resistance from their nominal followers. There was little that was 'anti-Liquidationist' or clearly 'Leninist' about the Bolsheviks' electoral strategy in the capital until the very eve of polling or about the day-to-day political line of the new daily. Neither the new Social Democratic group in parliament nor the editorial board of *Pravda* were pliant instruments in Lenin's hands until late 1913. His domination of both, therefore, took long to establish and was relatively short-lived. In both the Fourth Duma elections and in the realm of open publications Bolsheviks in the capital played the dominant role in fashioning policy independently of and consciously in opposition to their leader's designs. In each case local Bolshevik sub-élites, rather than being firm executants of Lenin's schismatic measures, endeavoured to preserve party unity, thereby revealing a more realistic grasp of their supporters' conciliatory aspirations.

The outcome of the Fourth Duma elections in the capital and the relative success of *Pravda* should not be interpreted as unqualified indications of comprehensive support for the Bolshevik cause or

Menshevism's decline. The low turnout at the polls in the autumn of 1912, the chaotic and tortured nature of the campaign, the striking absence of factional identification among delegates, all render hazardous general conclusions about working-class political sympathies. Both voters' choices as delegates and the circulation statistics for the Social Democratic press do indicate a clear preference for that party by a minority of the working population – in the absence of a strong SR presence. Skilled, young, male factory and artisanal workers, with their firmer roots in urban culture, revealed a growing commitment to Socialist Democracy, but equally they disliked factional infighting. Social Democracy's appeal to them lay in its militant defence of workers' concerns rather than in its polemics and theorising. But the overwhelming mass of ordinary operatives – in particular women, the unskilled, and the low-paid, as well as commercial–industrial employees and transport workers – evinced little interest in parliamentary politics or in the socialist press. As always they preferred to spend precious leisure time in the taverns or in reading about the latest sensational murder or robbery, or a pulp novel.

Neither the elections of 1912 nor Social Democratic representation in the legislature nor legal publications enabled revolutionary parties to secure a mass following. The sporadic electoral activities of isolated factory cells can scarcely be designated a 'campaign' as such and failed to involve the rank and file. In their first year as parliamentary representatives the six Bolshevik deputies played only a minor role in the underground and the seven Menshevik deputies remained effectively isolated to the war from their electors. Readership of the socialist dailies – and hence their putative influence – was numerically restricted.

On the other hand, the appearance for the first time in the history of the capital's labour movement of a daily Social Democratic press, which gave prominent and regular coverage to the parliamentary actions of the party's deputies, gave the party a distinct advantage over its SR opponents. Even if the Social Democratic dailies failed to capture the loyalty of the plebeian mass, their survival was one factor in securing the allegiance of the minority of militant 'worker–intellectuals', of young labour activists, to the Marxist banner.

Chapter 7

THE REVOLUTIONARY PARTIES, TRADE UNIONS AND SOCIAL INSURANCE, 1912 – JUNE 1914

In the memorandum written by Lenin for the 'unity conference' of the Russian Social Democratic Party, convoked in Brussels by the International Socialist Bureau in the summer of 1914, he adduced as the strongest corroboration of his claim of Bolshevik predominance within the Russian labour movement his faction's conquests of the trade unions and new social insurance institutions of the capital in 1913 and 1914. Unknown to the Bolshevik leader, the St Petersburg Okhrana endorsed his case. In its annual report, dated 3 December 1913, its head, Colonel M. F. von Koten, observed that 'in this year all party activity was directed towards the trade unions, in particular the union of metalworkers ...' and 'most St Petersburg factory workers came out for the Bolsheviks'. Soviet historians, too, have' naturally endorsed this view. The standard history of the Leningrad party organisation, for example, asserts that 'the Bolsheviks turned the unions into a strong base for work among the masses'. More recently Dr Victoria E. Bonnell has argued that by 1914 the capital's trade unions 'had again become vehicles not for accommodation but revolutionary struggle'.[1]

This interpretation, however, requires severe modification. In the first place it is inaccurate to describe the capital's professional organisations and educational societies as Menshevik bastions before 1913. Factional identification as distinct from party allegiance was not strongly developed. In the second place, whilst the Bolsheviks did succeed in taking over many union and club executives in 1913 and 1914 and in making an impressive showing in elections to central social insurance institutions early in 1914, their hegemony did not always result in significant changes in policies. Nor were these new Bolshevik trade-union and insurance officials, who were ordinary workers, mere executants of Lenin's will. In fact the Bolshevik exiles played a minimal part in the conduct of union affairs or the insurance campaign. As in the sphere of the labour press, Bolshevik legal activists in St Petersburg fashioned their own policies in an independent manner. Finally the Bolsheviks' victories were essentially hollow. The organisational, financial and legal weaknesses of trade unions, educational societies, consumer co-operatives. and social insurance organs vitiated their potential as mechanisms for attracting mass support. These legal labour associations were fragile and difficult instruments of revolutionary leadership. They failed to act as an effective substitute for a debilitated underground party.

I

Both the exact timing and the reasons for the sudden Bolshevik onslaught on the ruling bodies of open working-class institutions are difficult to ascertain with any degree of accuracy. The Prague Conference, January 1912, declared that the party should 'make broader use than before of every kind of legal opportunity' and that 'our illegal party organisations must use all existing legal workers' associations as bases for their activities among the masses'.[2] Maintaining the Bolsheviks' hostility to neutral or non-party trade unions, the assembly reconfirmed in effect the resolution of the Central Committee of February 1908, instructing members to establish party cells within legal labour organs as the instrumentalities of party control. Distrustful as ever of worker spontaneity, Lenin endeavoured to ensure that trade unions and legal activists remained firmly subordinated to central leadership. There exists no evidence, however, that his adherents in the capital hastened to implement this decision. One possible explanation for this delay was the even greater emphasis the Bolshevik leader himself placed at Prague and in his writings that year upon the revival of the underground apparatus. The launching of *Pravda* also absorbed much energy. Although from number 32, 6 June 1912, the new daily carried as a permanent feature a section entitled 'In the Societies and Trade Unions', the practice was not new: *Zvezda* had adopted a similar pattern. The sole trade-union executives to possess some Bolshevik members in the course of 1912 were the unions of architectural and construction workers and bakers.[3] Nor did the Cracow conference at the close of the year make any reference whatsoever to the trade unions. Instead delegates' attention had been focused on the supreme significance of mass revolutionary strikes, and once more, the reformation of illegal structures was accorded priority. Thus the local militants' attempt to wrest control of the revived union of metalworkers in the spring and summer of 1913 (see pp. 159–60), which marked the start of a successful, if tardy, campaign to implement the Prague resolution, represented an independent initiative, taken against the thrust of the Cracow proceedings.[4]

In the spring of 1913, moreover, as the struggle for hegemony over the trade unions began, it should not be thought that all nineteen functioning union executives were controlled exclusively by the Mensheviks or the Social Democrats (although the majority were). Two, bakers and architectural and construction workers, already possessed a Bolshevik majority on their boards. But five were run by coalitions involving the Socialist Revolutionaries: the two already mentioned, the unions of employees in the sale of textile goods and of employees in enterprises selling foodstuffs, and the leather-workers. The union of tailors was an SR preserve.[5] On the other hand, the SRs were in a minority position, as they had remained since 1906. Although the Second Party Council, October 1906, had made union membership and party cells therein mandatory, Narod-nik activists evinced little sympathy for such legal work and usually played a passive role in these organisations.[6] By 1912 it tended to be the emergent right wing within the party which emphasised trade unionism as one of the new arenas of public activity.[7] As these examples show, union members were on occasions prepared to countenance intra-party co-operation. Furthermore, Menshevik predominance within particular trade unions should not necessarily be interpreted as proof of factional alignment. To 1913 Mensheviks, Bolsheviks and SRs conducted elections to offices on a non-partisan basis; candidates were selected at district or factory meetings and won on their personal abilities irrespective of factional affiliation.

In the spring of 1913 the newly reopened union of metalworkers, which replaced two predecessors closed by the authorities in March and August 1912, became the arena for factional struggle and the Bolsheviks' breakthrough into prominence in the trade-union movement.

At the first general meeting on 21 April 1913, an interim executive was elected. The 700–800 present cast their votes in favour of a bare Bolshevik majority – thirteen Bolsheviks, five Mensheviks, one SR and seven non-party. Although the Bolshevik A. S. Kiselev became chairman, the Mensheviks V. M. Abrosimov and N. K. Morozov acted as secretary and treasurer respectively. The Mensheviks, confident of victory, had followed precedent with district meetings drawing up lists of candidates irrespective of their political views. Their opponents, however, sprang a surprise by breaking with past practice and publishing in *Pravda* beforehand a partisan slate of candidates. The fact that the assembly accepted the Mensheviks's plea to adhere to the previous method of election may explain the partial nature of the Bolsheviks' success. The editorial may explain the partial nature of the Bolsheviks' success. The editorial board of the union journal *Metallist* also became a coalition of two Bolsheviks

(A. S. Kiselev and A. A. Mitrevich) and two Mensheviks (G. O. Baturskii and S. M. Shvarts).[8]

The second general meeting, held on 25 August 1913, witnessed the firm consolidation of a solidly Bolshevik leadership. Of the thirty-one full and candidate members of the executive a mere three were Mensheviks. Before the poll both sides propagated in the press their respective opinions concerning the methods of election and their slates of candidates. In contrast to the previous assembly, the 1,800–3,000 members present (and only those in possession of valid membership cards were allowed into the hall by the police) rejected the Mensheviks' defence of a non-factional choice and opted to vote by lists, as *Severnaia pravda* had recommended on the eve of the ballot. Menshevik attacks on the alleged politically partisan conduct of the new board and the union organ and on the inexperience of the proposed candidates evoked merely hostility from the audience. No accurate count of the ballot papers was taken, but the Menshevik slate apparently secured a derisory 100–150 votes.[9] The Bolsheviks now monopolised the praesidium; I. P. Sesitskii (to September) and A. V. Gavrilenko (from September) as chairmen and A. S. Kiselev and P. I. Nikolaev as secretaries.[10]

Although the more general explanations for the Bolsheviks' pre-war ascendancy within legal labour institutions will be discussed later, two specific reasons for the Mensheviks' rout within the union of metalworkers may be advanced.

Writing early in 1914, the 'Liquidationist' legal activist, F. A. Bulkin (Semenov), a worker who had helped organise the first metalworkers' professional organisation, ascribed the unexpected turn-about in the union's controlling body to the influx into the factories and the union in the middle of 1913 of new, young and inexperienced workers; older trade unionists, on the other hand, had voted for the Menshevik slate.[11] It is difficult to prove or disprove this theory in the absence of a detailed breakdown of those attending the two general meetings. By 25 August the union numbered 5,667. In July, when 4,600 had registered, 3,416 had never participated before in a professional organisation, whilst 1,184 had belonged to one or other of the previous two unions. The proportions of old and new members present at the two electoral gatherings cannot be ascertained. But it would not be unwarranted to conclude that Bulkin's hypothesis is overdrawn and that the Bolshevik candidates secured votes from both groups of members.[12]

This viewpoint derives confirmation from the fact that the Menshevik leadership of the two earlier metallurgical trade unions had been subject to a continual barrage of criticism for its conduct of affairs over the period 1910 to 1913. The fundamental cause of this grassroots dissatisfaction rested on the union's declining membership in 1911 and 1912 despite the industrial revival (the respective figures on 1 January 1911 and 1912 were 3,895 and 3,353), its consequent financial difficulties and the cautious attitude this induced in Menshevik officers towards the strike movement. The Menshevik working-class activists in charge of the union attributed its debility to the Temporary Regulations of 4 March 1906, to operatives' lack of culture and to their apathy. Desirous of saving their organisation, they endorsed whole-heartedly the 'Liquidationist' intellectuals' scepticism concerning the renewed upsurge of strikes. They were of the opinion that the labour unrest was elemental in character and doomed to failure. Abrosimov, for example, bluntly informed a gathering in May 1912 that 'it was impossible for the union to respond in a lively fashion to the upsurge in economic disputes'.[13] Critics of the policies of the union's officials directed their fire on various fronts. The board, they argued, had failed to forge ties between itself and the rank and file; it ignored the daily life of workers. It had done little to disseminate the concept of professional organisation. In particular the charge was brought that those in power had eschewed militancy and refused to furnish direction to the economic struggles.[14] Different solutions were proposed to the apparent dead end in which the union now found itself: the formation of factory groups to agitate for the union and lead strikes; councils of factory elders; broader cultural–educational work; the development of mutual aid.[15] The union's officers, however, failed to refashion their strategy or implement any of the suggestions put forward by the dissentients (often for sound reasons).[16] Thus the timidity of the Menshevik activists in charge of the union in 1911–13 and the Bolsheviks' open and vigorous support for the strike movement ensured that old and new members alike of the revived union in the spring and summer of 1913 endorsed the election of a more responsive, bolder and more militant leadership.

The significance of the Bolsheviks' unprecedented victory in August 1913 and the fall of the Mensheviks' foremost legal fortress was not lost upon either side. Writing in *Novaia rabochaia gazeta*, F. Dan accurately described his faction's defeat as 'a radical, organised revolution'. An editorial in the rival daily jubilantly proclaimed that 3,000 had voted for Marxism.[17] Their achievement stimulated local Bolsheviks to further activity within trade unions. In this course of action they at last received encouragement from the *émigrés*. As in the matter of the general political strike, the independent initiative of his followers in the capital in taking over the union of metalworkers exerted an impact on Lenin. Thus at the Poronin convocation of the Central Committee in September 1913, he ensured the adoption of a resolution that '. . . it is especially important to intensify work in all legal workers' associations' and reconfirmed the necessity of setting up secret party groups within such bodies. His supporters were exhorted 'to seek the election of party adherents to all responsible posts etc.'.[18]

The tempo of Bolshevik takeovers of union boards increased markedly in the months after the Poronin gathering. In January 1914, two fell before their onslaught – the unions of sales employees in enterprises selling foodstuffs and household goods. The following month it was the union of employees in the tavern trade. In March three more succumbed – the unions of tailors, textile workers and woodworkers.[19]

The solitary stronghold of Menshevism left by the spring of 1914 was the union of workers in the printing industry, which clung to the procedure of plant nominations for candidates. At the general meeting of 10 November 1913, however, a significant indicator of printers' hitherto inarticulated discontent with Menshevik leadership had been their vote for the Bolsheviks' insurance slogan of a general municipal *kassa* and the abrogation of the union's earlier resolution in favour of a general *kassa* for all printers (see pp. 167–68). The Bolsheviks' breakthrough came six months later at the assembly held on 27 April 1914, when they pursued once more their tactic of voting by factional slates of candidates. The 600 present chose 17 Bolsheviks for the 30 seats on the executive. The last general assembly before the war, on 29 June 1914, confirmed the Bolshevik ascendancy.[20]

Due to the incomplete information on the factional affiliation of the 23 trade unions functioning in St Petersburg on the eve of the war, no accurate total of the number of unions which had fallen into Bolshevik hands is available. In his report to the International Socialist Bureau Lenin estimated sixteen and a half (the printers' executive) out of twenty professional organisations. A recalculation by the author reveals eleven and a half out of the fifteen whose factional allegiance could be ascertained. Three unions alone remained under Menshevik influence – accounting clerks in sales and sales manufacturing enterprises, pharmacy employees and draftsmen.

It is even more difficult to trace with any degree of accuracy the changing fortunes of both Social Democratic factions within the capital's educational societies. In February 1914 the Bolsheviks made a clean sweep of the board of 'Science-Life', ending SR control of the association from its inception in October of the previous year. The 'Sampsonievskoe' society also fell to them at this time, as did 'Source of Light and Knowledge' two months later. On the other hand as late as the spring of 1914, 'Education', 'Knowledge-Light' and the Second Society of Education in Narva were ruled by coalitions of Bolsheviks and Mensheviks.[21] There is unfortunately no information at all on the composition of the governing bodies of the consumer co-operatives.

This precipitate reversal of Menshevik fortunes in their traditional fastnesses owed almost everything to the Bolshevik sub-élite within St Petersburg and very little to the Bolshevik leader in exile. Apart from the fact that Lenin could not physically control the day-to-day activities of his faction's legal activists due to geographical distance, he displayed no interest whatsoever in trade-union affairs. A perusal of all his publications for 1912 to July 1914 reveals that he wrote absolutely nothing about the trade-union movement in St Petersburg, whilst his sole article to appear in a professional journal concerned 'Metalworkers' strikes in 1912' (*Metallist*, nos. 7, 8 and 10 (1913)).[22] If any correspondence passed between him and Bolshevik trade unionists in this period, it remains inaccessible in archives. This striking lack of interest in the one arena of activity in the capital where his party made equivocal gains is mute testimony to Lenin's lifelong disdain for trade unions as 'economist' organisations.

II

The Law on Sickness Insurance, 23 June 1912, apparently offered the revolutionary parties an alluring new arena of legal activity. It not only established sick benefit funds (*kassy*) to manage the disbursement of subventions to members who fell ill, but permitted direct workers' participation in the general assembly and executive boards of each *kassa*, in both of which elected operative delegates enjoyed a slim majority over the appointees of factory administrations.[23] Contrary to the argument of Dr G. Swain that the resulting Social Democratic insurance campaign compelled the St Petersburg working class 'to choose between two diametrically opposed strategies', all militant groups in the capital evinced a remarkable unanimity of opinion about the defects of the new legislation, the general use to be made of the new 'legal opportunities' and the fundamental desiderata of party propaganda.[24]

Choosing to ignore the significant advance marked by the reform, all three revolutionary parties condemned the statute on the grounds that it did not meet workers' needs. Its scope did not embrace workers employed in state or municipal undertakings, railway and postal staff, domestic servants, shop employees, artisans and agricultural labourers. The *kassy* fell under the supervision of the owners and the authorities. The employers alone were responsible for medical help. Three-fifths of the funds were derived from dues paid by working people. Benefits were too low. Two forms of insurance alone were covered.[25]

In their general response towards the law both wings of the Social Democratic party found themselves at one in their opposition to any boycott of the institutions created by it. Each endeavoured to convince labourers that non-participation would prevent them influencing the course of the legislation's implementation and merely strengthen thereby the owners' position within the *kassy*.[26]

Both factions, however, interpreted the value of the *kassy* according to their different and well-established concepts of the balance between legal and illegal activities. Thus the Prague and Cracow Bolshevik gatherings described the sick benefit funds as 'proletarian factory nuclei', which should be utilised to propagate Social Democratic ideas and develop class consciousness. The slogans of the party's insurance campaign should not be divorced from the ultimate goal of the overthrow of Tsardom. The Okhrana soon realised that the Bolsheviks hoped to take advantage of the legal protection afforded by *kassy* offices and meetings for revolutionary purposes.[27] The Mensheviks, on the other hand, looked upon the medical funds 'as a weapon of working-class organisation' and as a basis for strengthening independent and legal activity by workers. As the new institutions embraced the bulk of wage earners outside trade unions, they seemed to be a potentially far more effective vehicle of party influence.[28]

Local SRs proved to be as disunited in their attitude towards the social insurance funds as they had been to the elections for the Fourth State Duma. As on the previous occasion, the incipient right wing exhorted the party to refrain from any boycott. Voronov argued that workers could exploit the *kassy* for their own organisation. At first, however, the balance of opinion within Narodnik circles swung in favour of non-participation, with an appropriate proclamation printed in October 1912. By the close of the year, perhaps mindful of the damage wrought to their position by their absence from the State Duma elections, they changed their minds. The legal newspaper, *Trudovoi golos* and its successor, *Zavetnaia mysl'* both championed the new field of action.[29]

Whatever the discrepancies in emphasis about the importance of the *kassy*, all three groups devised a common series of general propagandistic demands which formed the basis of their agitation in 1912–14. These included state insurance against old age, unemployment, accident, disablement, illness, maternity, widowhood and orphanhood for all hired hands at the expense of the owners and state (by means of a progressive income tax) with wages paid in full; a single insurance organisation of a territorial type; workers' control of the *kassy* and the transfer of responsibility for medical help from the employers to the medical funds.[30]

Furthermore, in the matter of the more immediate tactics of insurance agitation, as the Bolshevik A. Enukidze noted in a letter to S. S. Shaumian in February 1913, 'there are no differences between the factions on this matter'.[31] Both Bolsheviks and Mensheviks, for example, supported the convocation of an All-Russian Labour Insurance Congress to give unity to the campaign and to fashion policies.[32] Each proposed the formation of factory insurance circles or commissions to acquaint operatives with the legislation, arrange factory meetings and nominate candidates for election to the various insurance organs.[33] When the Okhrana 'invited' (i.e. appointed) in November 1912 a few labour representatives to the highest central insurance institutions, the Insurance Council and the St Petersburg Capital Insurance Board, which were overwhelmingly bureaucratic in composition, all local Social Democrats demanded proper elections either through the agency of the proposed All-Russian Labour Insurance Congress or the trade unions and compelled the delegates chosen by the police to spurn their seats.[34] Each faction drafted almost identical model statutes for the *kassy* upon which employees were to insist in the meetings at which factory owners (by law) were to consult their labour forces on the rules for the medical funds. These blueprints recommended the highest allowances for the longest periods, full self-government for the workers in the sick benefit funds, the transfer of responsibility for medical aid to the *kassy* and complete security for members' families at the same level as participants. The single point of difference concerned the Bolsheviks' proposal for a general municipal medical fund (see p. 167).[35]

These identical approaches to the formulation of an insurance strategy bore fruit in attempts at collaboration among Social Democratic activists. In December 1912, 'the official representative of the St Petersburg Bolsheviks' (it is possible that the individual so designated was Stalin) proposed to the Menshevik littérateur V. Ezhov (pseudonym of S. O. Tsederbaum), then secretary of the editorial board of *Luch*, the formation of a joint insurance commission. Although the Mensheviks concurred, the police intervened to prevent its formation. In return the Mensheviks invited B. G. Danskii (pseudonym of the Pole K. A. Komarowski) and Malinovskii to join the board of their journal *Strakhovanie rabochikh*. They refused. On the other hand, *Pravda* refrained from critical comment on the journal and the Mensheviks' insurance policies before the spring of 1913. The general conduct of his adherents in the matter of the insurance campaign dissatisfied Lenin. Writing to N. I. Podvoiskii in April 1913, he castigated their inactivity in this field.[36]

Contrary to the opinion of Soviet historians that 'the Bolshevik party . . . stood at the head of the insurance campaign', the almost total identity of views between the two factions facilitated Menshevik domination of the first year of the party's insurance agitation.[37] There existed a Menshevik insurance commission, whose leading personalities were G. Baturskii (pseudonym of B. S. Tseitlin, a lawyer, and co-opted member of the Organisational

Committee) and S. Shvarts (pseudonym of S. Monoszon, who had a law degree and was a member of the St Petersburg Central Initiative Group in 1913). In December 1912 the group launched the first insurance journal, *Strakhovanie rabochikh*, of which Baturskii was editor and Shvarts secretary. In a series of articles in *Luch* in November and December 1912, V. Ezhov provided the initial draft of model statutes of the *kassy*, which B. G. Danskii later adopted in all essentials as the Bolshevik version. Iu. Chatskii, writing in *Nevskii golos* in June 1912, was the first Social Democratic activist to propound the concept of the All-Russian Labour Insurance Congress. When the first eight factories, which had been selected by the authorities as the vehicle for pilot schemes, set up in January 1913 a 'commission of eight', the initiative came from a Menshevik cell in the medium-sized Semenov machine construction plant. N. K. Morozov, a Menshevik worker in this establishment, who became the treasurer of the revived union of metalworkers in April 1913, was elected its secretary.[38]

This state of affairs changed drastically in the summer and autumn of 1913. As the Okhrana noted in its annual report dated 3 December 1913, 'after the Petersburg Committee was dissolved in July . . . all [Bolshevik] party work was devoted to the insurance campaign'.[39] The origins of this shift in direction lay with local militants rather than Lenin. Although the latter had written to N. I. Podvoiskii in April 1913 that insurance agitation was the most pressing task, his plea had been ignored and the Central Committee meeting of 27 July 1913 observed that 'the insurance movement at present had lost its acuteness'.[40] Yet in August and September St Petersburg Bolsheviks, without external prompting, launched a press attack on the insurance strategy of their rivals, accusing the Menshevik-dominated insurance commission of eight factories of lacking authority and failing to give direction to the insurance campaign or adopt militant slogans.[41] Thus the resolution of the Poronin session of the Central Committee at the end of September 1913, calling for intensified exertion in legal workers' associations, including, the *kassy*, the formation of party groups within these bodies and the 'election of party adherents to all responsible posts etc.' within medical funds, in effect endorsed an existing tendency within party work in the capital.[42]

In the absence of contemporary explanations from Bolshevik participants in the insurance movement, one has to hazard possible reasons for their sudden volte-face. As a field of revolutionary activity the *kassy* began to become an attractive prospect only in the summer and autumn of 1913 with the commencement of procedures to establish sickness benefit funds, first in the textile industry and secondly in the metal-processing sector. The allure of the *kassy* as possible conduits to the masses was probably all the greater with the destruction of the PK in July and the atrophied condition of district committees. The resounding victory of the Bolshevik faction in the balloting to the board of the union of metalworkers on 25 August may have encouraged militants to split a hitherto generally united insurance campaign.

In their search for a means to distinguish their insurance agitation from their opponents' and to project themselves as aggressive defenders of workers' interests, the Bolsheviks propagated assiduously from August 1913 onwards a slogan which B. G. Danskii and Ch. Gurskii had tentatively advanced in March 1913, namely a general municipal *kassa*. Placing great emphasis upon the militant nature of this goal, they argued that factory-based medical funds were deficient and that a general *kassa* of all enterprises of a given town alone could guarantee substantial benefits for wage earners.[43] In the light of the previous unanimity of opinion between the two factions concerning basic insurance issues, the lack of internal coherence to their argument and the insurmountable obstacles to its realisation, the Bolsheviks' abrupt highlighting of this proposition should be regarded as a schismatic device rather than a serious proposal.[44]

As it happened, the Mensheviks' position on this matter was ambiguous. Their theoreticians did support the notion of a general municipal *kassa* covering all operatives, but in practice they argued that such a scheme could never be implemented because of the lack of powerful trade unions and the atomised character of the working population. Instead they advanced the notion of general *kassy*, formed by the unification of several individual medical funds or those of an entire district or the same trade (a professional *kassa*).[45]

The Bolshevik faction's propaganda for a general municipal *kassa* was carried into the factories and trade unions in September and October 1913 in a concerted campaign by its followers. On 22 September a meeting of twelve engineering firms' *kassy* delegates adopted this objective. This pattern was soon repeated at area assemblies of engineering, machine construction and electrical plants in the Moscow, Petersburg Side, Town, Vasil'evskii Island and Vyborg districts. In total thirty-six metal-processing establishments, eight printing works, four textile mills, one leather and a tobacco manufactory supported the slogan.[46] At least two trade-union boards also welcomed it. The union of metalworkers, now under firm Bolshevik control, did so in September 1913. A more surprising coup occurred in the union of workers in the printing industry, whose Menshevik leadership had taken up a plan for a general professional *kassa* of all printers as early as December 1912, in the light of the financial weaknesses of the numerous petty print workshops. In the autumn of 1913 new Bolshevik members of the union executive attacked this decision. Despite opponents' valid objections to the concept of a general municipal *kassa* (both the St Petersburg Society of Mill and Factory Owners and the authorities were hostile to it), the majority of the 700 present at the general meeting on 10 November 1913 voted in favour of the scheme.[47] The predominance of engineering enterprises invalidates the argument of one Menshevik commentator that the notion secured the sympathy only of 'little conscious workers'.[48] In view of the vagueness of the Bolshevik project, the approval with which it was met would suggest that skilled workers and Social Democratic party sympathisers, in metal processing at least, sought hereby, as in the recent board elections in the union of metalworkers, to express their general dissatisfaction with the Mensheviks' perceived moderateness and lack of militancy.

From August 1913, Bolsheviks also endeavoured to take advantage of the near collapse of the insurance commission of eight factories in order to establish their own all-city organisation. *Severnaia pravda* called upon *kassy* delegates to elect an authoritative insurance centre. The ostensible motive was that the insurance campaign lacked leadership; such a body alone could ensure the convocation of the All-Russian Labour Insurance Congress and the formation of the general municipal *kassa*.[49] As the secret police soon discovered, there was a more dangerous explanation. The disappearance of the PK and district committees after July 1913 had deprived local Bolsheviks of a mechanism to conduct in the capital the proposed all-Russian general political strike. They hoped to convert the suggested municipal insurance centre into a Soviet of Workers' Deputies to furnish them with a measure of control over the mass walk-outs.[50] These plans did not remain solely on paper. By October Bolsheviks had succeeded in forming special groups of *kassy* delegates within factories (perhaps as many as 58) and uniting these in district insurance centres. It is unclear whether they managed to set up a central insurance institution. The Okhrana, in alarm, wiped them all out in mass arrests on 7 November. The district and all-city insurance groupings were never revived before the war.[51]

The culmination of the first phase of the Bolshevik onslaught upon the Mensheviks was the launching of their own weekly insurance journal, *Voprosy strakhovaniia* in October 1913, whose first numbers had print runs of 12–15,000 copies. The periodical was staffed by B. G. Danskii (who wrote on insurance matters for *Pravda*) and Dr A. N. Vinokurov, an old party revolutionary who ran a workers' hospital in the Neva district.[52] Although the Bolshevik press now castigated *Strakhovanie rabochikh* for its 'moderation' and espousal of 'partial demands', the insurance programme adopted by the new organ in its first issue was similar in all respects to its Menshevik rivals' with the exception of the demand for a general municipal *kassa*.[53] The unions of marble and granite workers, of gold and silversmiths, architectural and construction workers and woodworkers all endorsed the new publication, as did the educational societies 'Education' and 'Source of Light and Knowledge'. The Bolshevik executive of the union of metalworkers assigned it 100 roubles aid, yet continued as before to finance its Menshevik antagonist. The union of textile workers welcomed its appearance. Nevertheless it insisted 'upon unity of action in the insurance campaign'.[54]

The second stage of the Bolsheviks' bid for supremacy over the new insurance organisations commenced with the balloting to the official central insurance institutions. In many ways the saga of the elections in the labour curia to the Fourth State Duma repeated itself. Far from the 'brilliant victory' described by E. E. Kruze, the electoral campaigns and polls were characterised by ambiguity, confusion and, above all, the desire of party activists and workers' representatives to shun factional infighting and preserve party unity.[55]

In their efforts to gain a majority of labour places in the central insurance bodies the Bolsheviks combined two separate tactics – the use of the mandate (*nakaz*) to delegates (first adopted in the Fourth State Duma elections) and a factional list of candidates (the instrument of their victory in August 1913 in the union of metalworkers). Before the polls for the St Petersburg Capital and Provincial Insurance Boards on 22 December and the Insurance Council on 29 December 1913, the Bolshevik press exhorted electors to choose 'consistent worker democrats' (i.e. Pravdists) and published a *nakaz*. This document set out the normal insurance programme. Its two controversial points embraced the general municipal *kassa* and the demand (paragraph V) that those elected to the central insurance institutions keep their constituents informed through reports published solely in Bolshevik publications. The Mensheviks reiterated their adherence to the established trade-union practice of non-consideration of factional allegiance in the choice of candidates. In the light of the large measure of agreement between the two wings concerning the essentials of the insurance campaign (as outlined earlier), the Mensheviks considered the Bolshevik *nakaz* acceptable with the exception of the two deliberately schismatic paragraphs. Their mandate, drafted by G. Baturskii, differed from that of their opponents only in advancing the slogan of general *kassy* and its plea for the absence of partisan strife in the elections.[56] This case struck a responsive chord at a meeting of 23 representatives from *kassy* boards held on 18 December. Those present sensibly 'felt that there were no differences between the mandates' apart from paragraph V, which they rejected. They insisted on unbiased voting.[57] None of the three elections occurred, because the police had interrupted on 21 December a secret gathering of *kassy* nominees and revolutionaries arranged by the Bolsheviks. On both 22 and 29 December the assembled electors refused to proceed until the arrested were freed.[58]

Before the renewed elections to the Insurance Council on 2 March 1914, both factions reiterated their positions and republished their mandates. The Bolsheviks, however, revised paragraph V (now renumbered VI) to include as well the point that 'the representatives of the workers must in all activity follow the decisions of the organised Marxists'. The Mensheviks correctly interpreted this cryptic formula, dictated by the necessities of censorship, as meaning the delegates' subjection to the Leninist PK. They vehemently opposed it on the grounds that 'the *kassy* are not party organs'. For the first time the SRs also entered the fray. *Stoikaia mysl'* demanded the adoption of proportional representation in the balloting and advanced its own *nakaz* that the elected labour members should co-ordinate their actions with the resolutions of the (unspecified) insurance centre.[59]

On 2 March, 42 of the 55 *kassy* invited sent representatives, a total of 47, of whom 24 came from Putilov.[60] The outcome of the meeting was determined by two factors – the numerical weight and views of the Putilov delegates, who now represented a *kassa* board on which the Bolshevik Conciliator, A. S. Kiselev, secretary of the union of metalworkers, had formed an alliance with the 'Liquidators' at the recent executive elections; and the fact that most present, possessing no instructions from their factories, exercised independent judgement on the issues. As many speakers sensibly declared that no essential differences existed between the two mandates, the assembly voted for a united *nakaz*. Electors endorsed an amendment to paragraph VI of the Pravdist *nakaz* that reports by working-class members on the Insurance Council should be sent to all labour press organs. The St Petersburg Engineering factory nominee added an element of confusion by proposing a hitherto unannounced change to paragraph VI, namely that the labour delegates to the Insurance Council should be 'subordinated to the collective of the *kassy*', formed from the members of all *kassy* boards in the capital. This won only the support of some 12–20 individuals, and the original version of paragraph VI was carried instead by 35 votes. It is unclear whether the entire Pravdist *nakaz* was then balloted. Those present agreed on a united slate of candidates and by 43 votes the list published in *Put' pravdy* on the day of the elections was carried. A joint 'Liquidationist' – Narodnik ticket secured the sympathy only of 12 persons.[61] It seems that those drawing up the Pravdist list attempted to be conciliatory as they included two Mensheviks known to be opposed to schism in the elections.[62] All five members and seven of the ten alternates chosen for the Insurance Council were Bolshevik. Ten of the fifteen came from metal-processing plants (two St Petersburg

Metals, one each Erikson, Koppel', Lessner, Neva Shipyards, Puti-lov, The Russian Society, St Petersburg Engineering and St Peters-burg Nails); two from a chemical works (Neva Stearine); two from Russian–American Rubber; one from a textile mill.[63]

In the four-week interval before the polls for the St Petersburg Capital Insurance Board on 30 March 1914, the Mensheviks aban-doned their own *nakaz* and took up the new concept of the responsi-bility of those selected for the Board to the 'collective of *kassy*', which they hailed as a manifestation of independent working-class activity. The project struck a responsive chord among insurance activists anxious to avoid further infighting. At a gathering on 27 March, those sent by seventeen *kassy* boards endorsed both a mixed list of candidates irrespective of political loyalties and the SR call for proportional representation. They amended paragraph VI of the Pravdist *nakaz* to read 'subordinated to the collective of *kassy*'.[64]

This opposition to factionalism was strongly in evidence at the electoral assembly on 30 March, to which 53 *kassy* had sent del-egates – 37 described themselves as Pravdists, seven as Mensheviks, four Narodniks and five non-party.[65] Of the twelve representatives to whom their *kassy* boards had given directives, eleven (including Franco-Russian, Geisler, Neva Shipyards, Putilov and St Petersburg Engineering) brought instructions to vote for a non-schismatic list. V. D. Rubtsov (a non-factional Social Democrat, vice-chairman of the Geisler *kassa* board, a former secretary of the union of metalworkers in 1910 and now its treasurer) reported on the out-come of the meeting of 27 March. Under these influences, by a vote of 31 to 22, paragraph VI of the Pravdist *nakaz* was altered in the sense desired by the Mensheviks. But in a second, contradictory ballot, clarity was then sacrificed with the adoption of a second amendment by some 31 votes that 'the collective of *kassy* must be subordinated to the Marxist organisation'. When 28 individuals supported the suggestion of proportional representation, talks were held in which Rubtsov played a leading role. The breakdown of the negotiations, however, resulted in the passage of the slate published in *Put' pravdy*.[66]

The final elections – to the St Petersburg Provincial Insurance Board on 13 April – were almost a literal replay of those a fortnight earlier. Despite the Board's title, for reasons that remain obscure, the provincial *kassy* were excluded by the authorities, and the same capital factories' delegates, who had determined the outcome of the previous poll, did so a second time. Once more Rubtsov en-deavoured to reach an agreement – with more success. Not only was the same illogically amended *nakaz* passed but a united ticket of candidates was accepted.[67]

As with the elections in the labour curia to the Fourth State Duma

in the autumn of 1912, it would be incorrect to draw general conclusions from these three insurance ballots about the factional or
party sympathies (if any) of the mass of ordinary factory hands and
artisans in St Petersburg. State plants, commercial and shop employees and artisans all fell outside the law's purview. Private
electrical, engineering and machine construction plants (mostly of
medium size, in the range 1,000–3,000 workers) predominated at the
three insurance electoral assemblies, whilst all other sectors of production were weakly represented. Because the electors were apparently chosen by their *kassy* boards rather than at mass factory
meetings, they gave voice to the opinions of the activist minority. It
is evident that, as the Fourth State Duma elections had revealed,
party identification was strong among the voters – not a single
candidate chosen in all three contests was an SR; all were Social
Democrats. Yet it would be erroneous to conclude from these
polls, as one contemporary analyst of the results did, writing in the
Trotskyite journal *Bor'ba*, that 'the preponderance in St Petersburg
of the Pravdists is without doubt'.[68] The course of the elections
rather testifies, in a fashion similar to the Fourth Duma electoral
campaign, to the longing of Social Democrats, working in metal-
processing plants, for party unity and their distaste of factionalism,
sentiments shared by many Pravdists themselves, as their voting
patterns prove. It is obvious that even party militants sensed the
artifical nature of the Bolshevik-induced schism and correctly noted
the broad similarities between the two factions' insurance programmes. Thus even those who considered themselves Mensheviks could
vote in good conscience for the Bolshevik *nakaz*, in particular in its
amended form.

Moreover, this qualified Bolshevik success in the insurance sphere,
like their victory in the trade unions, was in all essentials the work of
second-rank leaders. Lenin displayed as little interest in the *kassy* as
he did in trade unions. Apart from the relevant resolutions drafted by
him for the Prague Conference and the Cracow and Poronin meetings of the Central Committee, not a single article flowed from his
pen on the tactics and strategy of the insurance campaign. The
solitary letter to Podvoiskii in April 1913 is the only item of his
published pre-war correspondence to refer to this issue.

III

The Bolsheviks' new-found ascendancy within trade unions and
central insurance organs constituted a flawed victory. Contrary to
the thesis of Victoria Bonnell that these bodies became the party's
'centres of struggle' against Tsardom, the trade unions in particular
failed to establish their legitimacy among the rank and file. As

possible avenues of influence for Social Democrats to the masses of manufacturing and service workers they suffered from a multiplicity of weaknesses which aborted the emergence of a sound and effective union movement on the eve of the war.

In the first place, the scope of union allegiance remained severely limited. Although some trade unions witnessed an influx of new members in 1913 and early 1914 (such as the metalworkers and the printers), it would be incorrect to speak of a 'revival'. The peak nominal membership of twenty trade unions is available for July 1914 – a paltry 28,629 (compared to 55,000 in 76 unions in 1906– 7).[69] In numerical terms the largest union was the metalworkers with 10,273 participants in March 1914, followed by the printers with 5,000 in December 1913; the bakers, 1,700 in February 1914; the employees in the sale of textile goods, 1,420 in June 1914.[70] Of the twenty, eleven had memberships of over 500 each, and nine under that figure. As percentages of the total labour force within their particular industries or individual establishments, the number of supporters was low. The highest ratio concerned printers, 22 per cent of whom were organised; for metals it was 8 per cent; leather, 10 per cent; in textiles, a derisory 2 per cent.

In the case of the union of metalworkers, for example, the allocation of its adherents between districts and specific plants was distinctly uneven (see Tables 7.i and 7.ii).

In general terms it may be observed that the union continued to fare best, as in the period 1907–10, in medium-sized firms (around

Table 7.i: *Distribution of Membership of the Union of Metalworkers, by District, Jan. 1914 (numbers and % of total)*[71]

	No. of members	% of total membership
Vyborg	2,833	27.6
Vasil'evskii Island	1,754	17.1
Petersburg Side	1,554	15.1
Moscow	1,031	10.0
Narva	700	6.8
Neva	665	6.5
1st Town	641	6.2
2nd Town	397	3.8
Kolpino	308	3.0
Sestroretsk	230	2.2
Porokhovaia	170	1.7
TOTAL	10,283	100.0

Table 7.ii: *Distribution of Membership of the Union of Metalworkers between Individual Plants, Jan. 1914*[72]

Plant	Type of production	Location of plant	Union membership	Total workforce in plant	Union membership as % of total workforce in plant
New Aivaz	machines, armaments	Vyborg	800	1,600	50.0
Nobel'	diesels, shells, mines	Vyborg	392	1,000	39.2
Erikson	telephones, telegraph	Vyborg	557	1,500	37.2
St Petersburg Metals	machines, shells, mines	Vyborg	1,125	4,000	28.1
St Petersburg Engineering	machines	Petersburg Side	200	1,000	20.0
Ordnance (state-owned)	ordnance	Liteinii	187	1,000	18.7
Baranovskii	fuses, shells	Vyborg	148	800	18.5
Odner	machines	Narva	50	270	18.5
Siemens-Schukkert	dynamos	Vasil'evskii Island	72	400	18.0
Pipe works (state-owned)	miscellaneous	Vasil'evskii Island	557	6,000	9.2
Phoenix	machines	Vyborg	36	450	8.0
Lessner	boilers, shells, mines	Vyborg	170	2,600	6.5
Franco-Russian (state-owned)	engines, boilers, turbines	2nd Town	80	2,200	3.6
Baltic Shipyards (state-owned)	ships	Vasil'evskii Island	192	6,650	2.9
Putilov	mixed	Narva	350	11,000	3.1
Admiralty Shipyards (state-owned)	ships	2nd Town	8	2,800	0.2

1,000 workers) specialising in the manufacture of different sorts of machines and electrical equipment mostly located in the Vyborg district (many of these were diversifying into arms production in 1912–14). It held out least attraction for operatives in large-sized, frequently state-owned, manufactories engaged in mixed production, metal rolling and shipbuilding. It is no coincidence that the former were noted for the employment of greater than average ratios of highly skilled, well-paid, literate male workers and the latter more poorly remunerated, unskilled and semi-skilled.[73] Unfortunately there are no similar data for the other trade unions.

Secondly, as in the past, the majority of the capital's trade unions were artisanal rather than industrial. In 1914 there were only three industrial professional organisations (in leather, metals and textiles) but thirteen craft unions and seven sales and clerical (four of which were founded in 1912 and 1913).

In all sectors of the city's economy, trade unions signally failed as before to capture the sympathies of the unskilled and women. Union membership embraced primarily a minority of male skilled artisanal workers (bakers, tailors, joiners and typesetters), employed in small-scale enterprises and workshops and, in factory industry, mainly the skilled in medium-sized, privately owned electrical, engineering and machine-building plants.

The unionisation of women bore no obvious relation to their representation within particular manufacturing sectors. In textiles, for example, in which by 1913 68 per cent of the labour force comprised unskilled or semi-skilled female machine operatives (mostly under 30 years of age), 277 of the 888 members of the union of textile workers in January 1914 were women (31 per cent). Although tailoring gave employment to as many women as men, a mere 20 seamstresses had joined the union of tailors in September 1913 (the other 618 participants were men). As to the union of bakers, a contemporary report at the close of 1912 calculated that 0.2 per cent of women employed in this trade had taken out union membership (41 as against 482 men). In metal processing, which witnessed a slow rise in the numbers of women employed in machine construction before the war (almost 3 per cent of the total payroll was female in 1914), a mere 123 women were attracted to the union of metalworkers – 85 came from the Vyborg district, mostly in New Aivaz, one of the few companies to hire women as machine operators in a significant quantity (in May 1914, 500 of its 1,600 hands were female). Despite the predominance of women employees as sales personnel, a miniscule proportion found union membership attractive – 30 adhered to the union of employees in the sale of textile goods (1,426 members in June 1914) and four the union of employees in the tavern trade (651 participants).[74]

This minimal female participation in the union movement stands in stark contrast to the readiness of many women workers to adhere to strike protests (see Chapters 8 and 14). Both the conditions of daily life and the attitudes of male operatives explain women's lack of enthusiasm for union membership. The traditional peasant belief in woman's subordination to the authority of the male was replicated in the factories and workshops. Female hands, for the most part un-skilled or semi-skilled, earning low wages, were continually at the mercy not only of factory managers and petty employers but also of foremen and fellow male workers. As a letter from one woman metalworker expressed it, 'every foreman, every journeyman and even the guard at the gate considers himself "our" boss'. The attitude of men towards women at work was one of disdain or even outright hostility to those they regarded as 'submissive'. In addition women, as everywhere in Europe, faced the double burden of long hours of work and domestic obligations. Whatever the nominal lip-service paid by male union activists towards the necessity of attracting women into the trade unions, the realities spoke otherwise. When two women were elected from the Vyborg district to the board of the revived union of metalworkers in April 1913, the male members loudly protested. Women, therefore, lacked both the time, the financial security, the self-confidence and the inclination to participate in an unfriendly male preserve, where, as one unionist openly admitted, 'males seldom look on women as comrades in the struggle for a better life'.[75]

The exact proportion of skilled to unskilled within particular unions is difficult to establish since only fragmentary data are avail-able. The membership of the artisanal trade unions was by its very nature skilled. Indeed within these organisations, the most special-ised and best paid were often to the fore. In the union of bakers, for example, the *baranochniki* (bakers of ring-shaped rolls) constituted one-half of the total. The men forming the majority in the union of textile workers occupied skilled jobs (with better wages) in the industry (such as engravers, fabric printers, mechanics and carpen-ters). The highly remunerated compositors contributed 929 out of the 1,550 participants in the recently reopened union of workers in the printing industry in the autumn of 1912, but the less well-off bookbinders and lithographers furnished 202 and 52 respectively. Unskilled workers also remained outside the ranks of the union of metalworkers. A survey of January 1914 revealed that 1,300 mem-bers earned less than 30 roubles a month; 6,937, from 30 to 50 roubles, whilst 2,000 took home more than 50 roubles. This finding correlates well with the evidence cited earlier relating to the profile of unionisation in large and medium-sized plants. Those who had flowed into the former in increasing numbers since 1910 were for the most part unskilled or semi-skilled male peasants earning considerably less than their skilled counterparts.[76]

Membership of trade unions, moreover, remained in a state of constant flux with a high proportion of adherents failing to pay their subscriptions regularly. Contemporary observers of the union movement were in agreement that patterns of union recruitment were directly related to the timing of industrial disputes. In the union of bakers, for example, a series of stoppages in the spring of 1912 lay behind a sudden surge in applications. Nevertheless, if 1,533 workers were attracted to the union in the course of 1912, 517 left it, most after the labour unrest had subsided. The union of gold and silversmiths witnessed a similar phenomenon in the summer of 1913 in conjunction with a series of stoppages involving bronze workers, as did the union of textile workers during lock-outs in this industry early in 1913. Eighty-seven per cent of members left the union of tailors in 1912 and 91 per cent the following year.[77]

The ratio of members paying their monthly dues varied over time and between trade unions. The lowest embraced the union of textile workers, with 20 per cent in September 1913, followed by the union of marble and granite workers at 32 per cent in October 1912. The highest was the union of gold and silversmiths with 89 per cent in May 1914. The average hovered around the 60 per cent level with the union of leather workers at 65 per cent and the printers at 63 per cent.[78] In the union of metalworkers 43 per cent had failed to settle their subscriptions at the start of 1914. In the Vyborg district this rate of default soared to 60 per cent and 68 per cent in Neva. At New Aivaz factory, 357 of 800 union members had sent in their contributions, 124 of 392 at Nobel' but a mere 23 of 174 at the Russian Society.[79]

This state of affairs constrained union executives to conduct regular re-registration of their nominal memberships with consequent expulsions. In 1913 such an exercise in the union of bakers resulted in 910 leaving the organisation. The unions of carriage and leather workers both forced out half their 500 adherents in this way in 1912 and 1913. The tailors excluded 403 in 1913–14.[80]

The low and constantly changing numerical complexion of trade unions, together with the far from even inflow of monies into their treasuries, ensured that all union executives had at their command a chronic insufficiency of funds. The annual pre-war incomes of thirteen unions could be traced. Two alone enjoyed revenues exceeding 5,000 roubles per annum: the printers (13,140 roubles in 1913) and the metalworkers (10,074 roubles, April 1913–January 1914); five had annual receipts in the range 1,000–5,000 roubles (including bakers and tailors); four, 500–1,000 roubles; one in the range 100–500 roubles and one under 100 roubles (architectural and construction workers).[81]

As union officers devoted a high ratio of annual expenditure to administrative expenses (the hiring of premises, salaries of full-time officials and postage) and cultural pursuits (subsidies to trade-union journals and libraries), little was spent on medical and juridical aid and unemployment and strike benefits, the very areas of support which would normally entice operatives into joining professional bodies. The union of marble and granite workers, for example, concentrated 86 per cent of its outgoings in 1911 (388 roubles) on organisational and cultural matters; the union of tailors was not far behind at 78 per cent of its 1912 outlay. The bakers, however, were more astute with 49 per cent of disbursements in 1913 focused upon such activities.[82] Even those trade-union executives permitted by their statutes to offer mutual aid to members could normally afford to pay out only small sums to recipients. In 1912 the union of tailors distributed a mere 11 roubles in sickness grants, despite the fact that 1,786 tailors attended the Hospital for Artisans in that year. The unemployment fund of the union of accounting clerks in sales and sales manufacturing enterprises had at its disposal 10 roubles in June 1913. Its fellow union of employees in the sale of textile goods laid out 207 roubles in grants in 1913 to 22 members out of work. The unions of bakers and tailors alone centred their resources on this field, dispensing 489 roubles to the unemployed in 1912 and 1,681 roubles in 1913 respectively.[83] The record of the seven unions with the legal right to offer benefits to members on strike was also uneven. The union of gold and silversmiths incurred 643 roubles in costs to this end in 1913, whilst the union of printers expended by far the largest amount – 6,297 roubles.[84]

One of the consequences of this ill-advised maldistribution of unions' expenditure was that both rank and file and union officials often still displayed a remarkable indifference to their organisations' affairs. The labour press was replete with constant complaints by militants on this score. Newly elected union officers frequently neglected their responsibilities. Some union treasurers, for example, absconded with the funds entrusted to them, as in the unions of bakers and textile workers. Of the 21 individuals selected to sit on the executive of the union of carriage workers in October 1913, ten never attended proceedings. In the union of printers two-thirds of office-bearers left the board in 1913 whilst executive meetings were frequently inquorate in the union of tailors.[85] Such dereliction of duty led to repeated elections for union officers with the result that most executive members were new to union matters and inexperienced (the union of metalworkers was an exception to this trend).

In addition to the specific factors cited here, more general explanations may be advanced for the conspicuous incapacity of trade unions to secure the sympathies of most of the city's labour force and to retain the loyalties of the minority of largely skilled workers who did join them.

The attitudes and policies of both employers and the authorities towards the union movement, described in detail in Chapter 9, contributed much to depriving trade unions of legitimacy in the eyes of their potential supporters. The Temporary Regulations of 4 March 1906 prohibited union intervention in strikes and collective bargaining. The St Petersburg Society of Mill and Factory Owners still refused to accord unions recognition. The St Petersburg Municipal Bureau for Union Affairs never ceased to exert a baleful influence on union statutes. At least four unions were not allowed to open district branches, including the bakers and printers; six were refused permission to establish councils of delegates (printers, tailors, textile workers). The union of tailors was disqualified from paying out strike benefits.[86] Arrests of union personnel, particularly Social Democrats, were frequent – one reason for the reluctance of officials to assume prominent roles. The union of metalworkers in the last four months of 1913 lost two presidents, and two secretaries of the union of tailors suffered a similar fate.[87] Such persistent persecution made it almost impossible for unions to perform their natural functions.

In the artisanal trades, whilst their particular conditions of work (especially the smallness of the establishments) in some respects facilitated unionisation, as Dr Bonnell has argued, they also acted as an impediment. Bakers, tailors and sales assistants frequently lived on the employers' premises, making them vulnerable to the threat of eviction in the event of involvement in union affairs or strikes. The excessively lengthy hours of work in many artisanal trades (a sixteen-hour day in baking, for example), as well as in retailing (twelve to sixteen hours) and restaurants (seventeen to eighteen hours), meant that few workers had the time or the energy for participation in professional organisations. Some sectors were also highly seasonal, such as the construction trade with a temporary mass influx of peasants for summer work, or tailoring with a trough in demand in the summer. Many activists also believed that the prevalence of piecework acted as a deterrent to a sense of collective identity. So profound was the dislike of this form of payment in the union of tailors that when in September 1913 the board resolved to lift a ban on the admission of pieceworkers to the union, a general meeting overwhelmingly rejected this decision.[88] A few unions also faced active competition from long-established societies of mutual aid. This was particularly so in the case of commercial employees, where the Society of Mutual Aid of Commercial Employees, established in 1869, had 900 members in 1912.[89]

The trade unions, therefore, conquered by the Bolsheviks from the Mensheviks in 1913 and 1914, offered unsteady foundations for the former's aspirations to convert them into mass bases of support for their faction, relying upon secret party cells within the unions.

There can be no doubt that election to trade-union boards provided a useful legal cover for illegal Bolshevik activities (although the Okhrana was always fully cognisant of them), but the extent of the interpenetration between the officials of union executives and the personnel of Bolshevik factory and district committees, as well as the actual numbers of party groups inside the trade unions, cannot be calculated. At best the data are impressionistic. Of the executive of the union of metalworkers in 1913 and 1914, at least eight Bolshevik members at one time or another also sat on the PK; the list includes A. S. Kiselev, the first chairman and subsequently secretary, and two police spies, P. I. Ignat'ev and V. I. Shurkanov. Even less is known about other union office-holders.

Nor could all the new Bolshevik officers of trade unions be described as 'Leninists'. Again, there is information only on the factional views of those elected to the board of the union of metal-workers. A. S. Kiselev, as his actions revealed, was a Bolshevik Conciliator; I. P. Sesitskii, a provocateur, had been a Vperedist, attending the Bologna school; P. N. Nikolaev, a former treasurer of the union, and its secretary after August 1913, supported the Mezhraionka.

Moreover, although the Bolsheviks had wrested control of the union of metalworkers in part by their critique of the Mensheviks' timid attitude towards strikes, the Bolshevik-dominated board soon found itself constrained by force of circumstance to attempt to assert some direction over the strike movement. Like their predecessors, Bolshevik officials swiftly discovered that they could exert little restraint over their members' propensity to down tools, or leverage over the conduct of disputes, in particular as union members constantly failed to consult the executive in advance of walking out (between 25 August 1913 and 18 January 1914 this happened in 29 of 41 clashes) and the POZF refused adamantly to recognise the union as an intermediary. The Okhrana accurately remarked that 'the union is merely a passive observer of strikes', a point of view echoed by Kiselev, when he warned the general meeting of 3 November 1913 that 'a majority of stoppages and conflicts proceed without any organisational influence on the part of the union'. In a vain attempt to exert some discipline over strikers the board and the general meeting of 25 August 1913 resolved that in future the union would pay out grants to members involved in strikes only if these had begun with the agreement of the union board and the latter led them. This approach was repeated in the strike instructions passed by the general meeting of 19 January 1914 with an additional restrictive clause that the eligibility for strike pay was one year's membership of the union. It is not clear how much of the union's expenditure was devoted to this cause: by 24 November 1913, the sum had reached 600 roubles out of a total disbursement of 7,600 roubles.[90]

After expressing his conviction to the general meeting of 3 November 1913 that 'any sharp corners between the two tendencies must be smoothed over', Kiselev endeavoured with some success to keep his promise. Thus at the general meeting on 19 January 1914 the board announced that in future the controversial and schismatic method of election by factional lists would be replaced by the former practice of nomination of candidates by the districts. Soon afterwards the prominent Menshevik legal activist and former vice-chairman of the union, A. N. Smirnov was re-elected to the executive together with the former secretary, the non-factional Social Democrat V. D. Rubtsov, who became treasurer.[91] In the elections, too, to the central insurance institutions in the spring of 1914, as has been pointed out earlier in this chapter, both Kiselev and Rubtsov played a pacificatory role.

The frailties of St Petersburg trade unions had important implications for both revolutionaries and workers. Illegal activists, whatever their party, aware of their inability to resurrect a city-wide underground apparatus or recreate a Soviet of Workers' Deputies, sought through the trade unions a broad outreach to the working class. For the manifold reasons cited earlier these expectations proved illusory. There were few attractive reasons why wage earners should have joined professional organisations in the capital before the war and they did not do so in any appreciable quantity. All those obstacles precluding the emergence of a broad-based trade unionism in the city before 1913 denied the Bolsheviks the potentiality of their new dominance within the unions. The latter were unable to provide the Bolsheviks with the mechanisms they so desperately required to make contact with more than a minority of skilled male factory and artisanal hands. But the unions also failed their own supporters and the broad mass of workers. Through little fault of their own, the trade unions were incapable of articulating effectively their members' grievances, defending their interests or securing material improvements. They could not act as a focus of leadership and inspiration during labour disputes. Thus in the great pre-war wave of economic strikes (see Chapter 8) the sole element of organisation was provided by factory-based organisations in the form of temporary strike committees rather than trade unions. For the brief period of each stoppage these were the bodies which won the allegiance of skilled and unskilled, male and female alike. But their transitory character ensured that they, too, could not act as permanent bases for the Bolshevik faction or its socialist opponents. Their revolutionary possibilities were equally deceptive.

IV

In the same way that the trade unions failed to act as efficacious channels to the broad mass of workers for the Bolsheviks, the *kassy* proved to be an equally doubtful asset. The implementation of the Sickness Insurance Law started late. By July 1914 only 64 medical funds, covering 87,888 wage earners, were functioning in St Petersburg province, whilst another 12, embracing 59,882, were in the process of formation.[92] Many sections of the capital's economy remained excluded from the legislation's purview – state plants, all establishments employing under 200 operatives, and commercial employees. The terms of reference of the *kassy* were strictly limited by their statutes, and the police, employers and authorities all ensured that they did not transgress the legal boundaries (see Chapter 9). So in general the sickness funds were infertile soil for sustained organisational efforts.

It is true that the Bolsheviks strove to secure the return of their followers to *kassy* boards from the autumn of 1913, but the extent of their success cannot be accurately quantified. Available data provide a list of sixteen metalworking firms, two textile mills, one chemical and one rubber manufactory in which Bolsheviks won election to *kassy* executives.[93] But Soviet historians' claim that 'the leading positions fell to the Bolsheviks' is exaggerated. In seven of the same twelve metal-processing companies, Mensheviks were also chosen by the electors and in at least two, SRs as well.[94] It is probably no accident that in all the factories concerned there existed at the time of the polls both Bolshevik and Menshevik cells; it was standard practice for these groups to nominate candidates beforehand. On the other hand, with rare exceptions such as the Bolsheviks Kiselev and N. M. Shvernik (a former Vperedist and head of the Vyborg branch of the union of metalworkers) or the Menshevik A. F. Iatsynevich (a former chairman of the same union in 1908–9), the majority of party adherents chosen to sit on *kassy* boards do not seem to have been activists of the first rank or to have belonged to district committees.[95] Thus interpenetration of memberships of Bolshevik committees and the sickness fund executives was not significant.

In the six months before the war the architects of the Bolshevik insurance campaign themselves certainly believed that their exertions had not borne fruit. Writing in *Prosveshchenie* in January 1914 B. G. Danskii lamented that 'the masses have ceased to pay any attention to insurance matters'. Four months later an editorial in *Voprosy strakhovaniia* noted that the balloting to the central insurance organs 'did not arouse any interest among the broad masses'.[96]

In some respects this jeremiad was overdrawn. There occurred, for example, little conscious boycottism of the new law. Among the first eight factories selected by the authorities at the end of 1912 to start the process of implementation there were instances of workers refusing to take part in the election of delegates to discuss the *kassy* statutes drafted by the owners. The board of the union of wood-workers voted to shun the legislation. At the gigantic Russian-American Rubber Company (13,000 hands), a meeting of 17 December 1912 resolved to refrain from participation in the polling. At the second factory of Neva Thread, Sampsonievskaia Thread, and the Leont'ev fabric printshops, operatives came to a similar decision. It was no accident that the majority of workers in these plants were women, who disliked the law's compulsory deductions from their meagre wages towards the costs of the *kassy*.[97] In contrast, the labour force at the engineering plants involved, Erikson, New Lessner, St Petersburg Metals and Semenov, went ahead with the ballot.[98]

Moreover, when in the winter of 1913 and 1914 the great mass of metal-processing factories, textile mills and printers came to choose representatives to review the employers' draft of the regulations of the medical funds or elect candidates to the *kassy* boards, attendance at the appropriate assemblies was astonishingly high in many establishments over all sectors. In metalworking, for example, 93 per cent (of 2,200 workers) voted at Franco-Russian, 77 per cent at Erikson (1,428) and 95 per cent at United Cables (1,178). At Neva Cotton the turn-out was 81 per cent (of 2,120 hands) and at the Petrovskaia mill 85 per cent (of 1,467). At Kibbel' printers, 480 of 540 employees (89 per cent) cast ballots.[99] Yet in the same random manner absentee-ism could be just as striking. At Diuflon (electrical), 36 per cent (of 280) voted; at the mills of K. Ia. Pal', 37 per cent (out of 2,116 hands) whilst a mere 1,600 of the 13,000 electors (12 per cent) turned up at the poll at Russian-American Rubber.[100] Nor were those elected to *kassy* executives as indifferent to their responsibilities as many union officers; a sample of attendance patterns culled from the insurance periodicals reveals normal ratios of 60 to 80 per cent of delegates turning up to meetings.

In the autumn of 1913, too, the Bolsheviks had attracted consider-able support for their slogan of a general town *kassa* and established insurance groups in at least 58 factories. The demand that *kassy* should take over from employers liability for medical aid began to win some acceptance. Before the war five sickness funds in engineer-ing, six in printing and one each in leather and textiles had expressed such a desire.[101] Yet, as Danskii ruefully admitted in his *Prosveshche-*

nie article, 'not one of the basic insurance demands has been achieved'.[102]

Responsibility for the relative ineffectiveness of the Bolsheviks' (and the Mensheviks') insurance campaign lay directly with the POZF and the MVD (see Chapter 9). Although *kassy* delegates presented amendments to the draft statutes, following the guidelines of the Menshevik-dominated insurance commission of eight factories, these were almost uniformly rejected by the employers, particularly in the metal-processing sector. Thus at Phoenix, San Galli, St Petersburg Engineering and St Petersburg Wagons, factory administrations threw out requests that the managing director unilaterally renounce his right to chair meetings of the *kassa* or appoint his nominees to general assemblies. At best minor changes to the regulations were accepted. Even on the rare occasions, as at the Shtuder sawmill, when an owner made genuine concessions (the right of members' families to receive grants), the factory inspector excised the offending articles.[103]

In similar vein revolutionaries' hopes for the convocation of an All-Russian Labour Insurance Congress were disappointed. Although the unions of leather, textile and woodworkers took up the idea in the autumn of 1912 and the union of textile workers petitioned the authorities at least for an insurance assembly of all St Petersburg factories, whilst the insurance commission of eight factories drew up a draft agenda, the MVD remained implacably hostile to the concept.[104]

The working-class representatives to the three central insurance organs formed labour insurance groups within each. In the short interval between their election and the war there was little time for them to realise the wish of one of the Bolshevik editors of *Voprosy strakhovaniia*, N. A. Skrypnik, that they become 'a centre, uniting the atomised activity of the *kassy*'. Their minority position within essentially bureaucratic institutions made implementation of their *nakaz* impossible. The delegates' request for a review of all existing *kassy* statutes was ignored. Indeed the St Petersburg Capital Insurance Board even prohibited the reading of a declaratory statement by its working-class members.[105] Nor did the labour groups succeed in forging firm links to their electors. *Kassy* boards showed concern only with the interests of their own plants, neglecting to send their central representatives materials. The latter in turn made no attempts to convoke city-wide meetings.[106]

The least effective of all the legal institutions as possible conduits of Bolshevik or Menshevik influence to the labour force of the capital were the educational and consumers' societies. Both were intensely local bodies, small-scale and restricted in their functions. Not a single cultural association possessed a membership exceeding one thousand; their participants were for the greater part young, single, skilled male workers. Consumers' organisations attracted even fewer recruits (at least three had under one hundred shareholders) and were limited to a few large plants (Neva Shipyards, Putilov, Obukhov) or districts. Contemporary press reports emphasise their inactivity and inertness.[107]

V

Whatever the qualifications which must be made about the degree and character of the Bolshevik ascendancy within the legal labour institutions of St Petersburg in the period between the spring of 1913 and June 1914, the Mensheviks had suffered an unprecedented set-back. The causes of their defeat much exercised the minds of Menshevik commentators at the time. They have also given rise in Western historiography to a lively debate within the last twenty years.[108]

The first possible explanation for the Bolshevik breakthrough may be described as sociological. It was initially advanced by G. Rakitin (pseudonym of V. O. Tsederbaum), writing in the Menshevik periodical *Nasha zaria* in the autumn of 1913. 'A significant influence in the character of the present working-class movement,' he argued, 'is one factor – the composition of the labour army'. Rakitin and other party analysts, such as Iu. Martov and F. Bulkin, contended that a continuous influx of peasants into the cities, driven hither by Stolypin's land policy, afforded a fertile soil for Bolshevism. This new stratum of the working class, retaining ties with the countryside, was uncultured, 'unconscious' (in the class sense) and inexperienced in the class struggle. Because their consciousness 'has been forged in the hearth of the daily struggle with proprietors', these peasant–workers retained a primitive, peasant world-view. They 'impart to it [the mass movement] a disorganising, impulsive and elemental character'. Rakitin also laid stress upon a second group within the pre-war labour movement – urban proletarian youths, who had grown up since 1905. Conscious and educated in class warfare, they formed the link between Bolshevik circles and operatives.[109]

The Menshevik critique, expounded earlier, clearly influenced Leopold Haimson in a famous article published in *Slavic Review* in 1964–5. His interpretation rested upon the influx into the labour force before the war both of a new generation of urban workers and 'the massive swell into the urban labour market of landless and land-poor peasants'. The new rural recruits 'had to be drawn from the almost purely agricultural, over-populated central provinces of European Russia', forced out by the Stolypin land reforms. They combined both resentment about their urban industrial experiences and rural grievances. They were led by young urban operatives, 'impatient, romantic, singularly responsive to maximalist appeals'.[110]

Bolshevik success, however, cannot be ascribed merely to the peasant outlook of wage earners. In the first place, whilst it is self-evidently the case that the pre-war increase in St Petersburg's working class came both from the children of urban proletarians and from rural districts, the absence of statistical data on the changes in the composition of the city's labour force between 1911 and 1914 renders impossible an exact accounting of the numerical contribution made by each source. As Chapter 1 showed, there was a long continuity of recruitment between 1869 and 1910 to the capital from the same provinces of the north-west and the non-black-earth central region. The bulk of migrants came, in decreasing order, from Tver', Iaroslavl', Novgorod, Pskov, St Petersburg and Riazan provinces. The pattern of immigration, therefore, long antedated Stolypin's agrarian policies. Moreover, Dr B. Anderson has revealed that these were areas with higher literacy rates than average, lower involvement in traditional agriculture, a high ratio of emigration, lower soil fertility and higher rate of involvement in secondary industry (see Chapter 1). It is possible, therefore, that the rural inhabitants who journeyed from these villages to seek employment in the capital were not necessarily illiterate or completely unfamiliar with an urban or factory milieu.

In the second place the minority who flocked into the trade unions and educational societies of St Petersburg in 1913 and 1914, who were elected to *kassy* and union executives and furnished the readership of the socialist press, were not callow, illiterate and unskilled peasant workers but skilled, highly paid, male, literate operatives, with several years' familiarity with and assimilation to urban living and the industrial workplace. The examination of the union of metalworkers in 1913 (see p. 160), of cultural clubs and of the legal labour press all testify to this point. Again the lack of precise statistics makes it impossible to quantify accurately the proportion of individuals concerned who had been born in the capital or in another urban setting, or the exact length of stay in the city by 1912–13, but the fragmentary biographical information about those Bolshevik proletarian activists in the fore of the legal labour movement before the war reveals that none were simple peasants recently arrived in the capital.

A second cause of the Mensheviks' failure has been held to be a generational conflict. V. V. Sher, the former president of the Moscow union of printworkers, argued in *Bor'ba* in 1914 that the Bolsheviks' victory was due to the fact that the strike wave had swept into the trade unions the young members of the temporary strike committees in the factories and workshops, who had clashed with the older trade unionists in a generational struggle. His analysis was endorsed by V. Torskii, who developed this theme by claiming that legal work could not satisfy youthful spirits who had borne witness to the upheavals of 1905 as children.[111] Leopold Haimson has incorporated this point into his synthesis.

An examination of the age profile of Bolshevik legal and illegal cadres reveals that Sher's argument is erroneous. Of the 54 members of the Bolshevik Petersburg Committee, 1912–14, there is information on the dates of birth of 17 individuals. Their average age in 1913 was 30 years. Not a single activist was under 21; five fell in the age cohort, 21–5; four, 26–30 years; five in the band 31–5 and three were over 35.[112] Unfortunately there exists only partial documentation on prominent Bolshevik trade unionists. In the union of metalworkers' executive in 1913 and 1914, the birthdays of seven Bolshevik office-holders could be traced; their median age in 1913 was 34 years whilst it was 29 years for three Menshevik board members, i.e. the new Bolshevik officials were actually older rather than younger than those they replaced. The sample involved, however, is so small that too great a weight should not be placed upon this rather impressionistic finding.

A third interpretation, and a highly controversial one at its publication, came from F. Bulkin, a genuine hereditary proletarian and worker–intellectual, a founder of the union of metalworkers in 1907 and a Menshevik activist of long standing. In an article in *Nasha zaria* in the spring of 1914, he ascribed Bolshevik predominance to the continued sway within the Social Democratic party of the intelligentsia with its narrow dogmatism and intolerance. 'Russia', he lamented, 'still has no independent workers' party'. Highlighting the long-established suspicion of many socialist operatives for non-working-class intellectuals, he blamed the latter for imparting factional strife into the open labour movement. The interests of the proletariat had become subordinated to partisan infighting.[113]

As Martov at the time and Victoria E. Bonnell more recently have pointed out, Bulkin's thesis lacked substance. Martov rightly observed that the revolt within the trade unions against established leaderships in 1913 and 1914 was directed precisely against 'Marxist-educated' trade-union officials impeccably proletarian in class origin – in fact against those best represented by Bulkin himself. In her study of the pre-war trade unions Dr Bonnell has emphasised that pro-Menshevik worker–leaders gave way to pro-Bolshevik ones in 1913 and early 1914.[114] An exploration of the biographies of Bolshevik militants, based on less than complete data, confirms the paucity of intellectuals in their ranks (with the exception of the editorial boards of legal labour publications). In the spring of 1913, for example, a mere two of the fourteen members of the PK were students – the rest were operatives. Of one hundred and five cadres working in district committees at this time, three alone were students. All Bolsheviks elected to the executive of the union of metal-workers and as representatives to the central insurance institutions in the spring of 1914 were proletarians.[115]

The contribution made by Bolshevik militants, both workers and intellectuals, has been accorded great weight in Soviet accounts and by Leopold Haimson. 'The Bolshevik Party cadres,' the latter has opined, 'were now able to play a significant catalytic role'. 'The greater revolutionary explosiveness' of Petersburg workers was due to their 'greater exposure to Bolshevik propaganda and agitation'.[116]

A cardinal theme of the present study is that a detailed investigation of the Bolsheviks' potential channels to the industrial masses in St Petersburg casts considerable doubt on the validity of this contention. As Chapters 4 and 5 have shown, the Bolsheviks signally failed before the war to resurrect viable city-wide and district organisations. The underground apparatus at best remained unstable and cellular, a woefully defective instrument of party influence. Propagandists and illegal party literature were remarkable by their absence. Contrary, moreover, to the view of Heather Hogan that the Bolsheviks succeeded in establishing more intimate ties to and contact with factory and artisanal workshops than their opponents, the analysis of Social Democratic factory cells carried out in Chapter 5 revealed that entire branches of manufacturing were almost devoid of socialist groups of both factions (such as food and drink, printing, textiles and tobacco).[117] The prospects of both wings of the party (not the Bolsheviks alone) were at their best in metal processing, in particular in machine construction and electrical goods manufactories (plants with 500 to 5,000 workers) in Vyborg, but far less so in other sub-sections of this sector in all other industrial quarters of the city. The strike committees which played such a significant role in economic disputes (see Chapter 8) were *ad hoc*, amorphous bodies, evaporating the moment a settlement had been reached. With regard to secret Bolshevik nuclei in open labour institutions, the trade unions, educational societies and *kassy* alike suffered from a multiplicity of weaknesses which deprived them of a mass base – their outreach was limited to largely skilled male workers, mostly in artisanal-type industrial production. No broad-based or effective trade-union movement emerged in the pre-war years. The Bolshevik Duma deputies, in St Petersburg at least, made an intermittent contribution to building up the underground and fostering trade unions and *kassy*. On the other hand, the Bolshevik daily newspapers did provide a continuous public platform over a period of twenty-seven months for venomous criticisms of Menshevik legalism and moderation and vigorous championing of workers' immediate economic interests. Even if their readership fell far behind the circulation of *Gazeta kopeika*, they were read by those very skilled operatives who deserted Menshevism.

The radicalisation of a minority of skilled male hands (both artisanal and factory) in the two and a half years before the First World War owed far more to their acquaintance with urban and industrial life than to their peasant roots, their 'youth', the sway of Social Democratic intellectuals or the indoctrination of Bolshevik cadres.

In the period 1910 to 1914 all workers, immigrants as well as those born in the city, had to endure what M. F. Hamm has described as the incipient breakdown of urban modernisation. The uninterrupted influx of newcomers to the factories and mills and workshops from 1910 put great pressure upon an already limited and malfunctioning stock of housing, water and fuel supplies, in particular in those residential quarters adjoining places of work. The environment consequently deteriorated, as Chapter 1 has demonstrated. The historically higher cost of living in the capital, together with a steep rise in rents before the war and greater overcrowding (all interlinked phenomena) acted as a critical stimulus to economic stoppages and wage disputes in the years 1911 to 1914 and were a fundamental cause of unrest on the part of unskilled and skilled, male and female workers alike.

At the same time labour found itself in an apparently most favourable opportunity to press home its economic demands with every chance of success. The pre-war industrial boom, particularly in the armament-related industries (see Chapter 1), with the severe shortage of skilled labour, seemed an ideal time for operatives to regain the higher wages, lower hours and the better conditions of service that they had wrung from the employers under the stress of revolution in 1905–6 but which they had lost in the subsequent reaction. Yet the St Petersburg Society of Mill and Factory Owners put up a stubborn and increasingly successful fight to defeat economic strikes (see Chapter 8).

In order to counter the growing and forceful resistance of the industrialists to their wage claims, both skilled and unskilled soon discovered that they lacked the institutional means to render effective the potential of the threat of the withdrawal of their labour. Whatever the vacillations and ambiguities of the labour policies of the government and the POZF (see Chapter 9), whatever the reasons for their failure to adopt truly punitive measures against stoppages, the authorities' ambivalent attitude towards trade unions and the POZF's outright hostility towards them rendered the unions feeble mechanisms to secure tangible improvements. For the skilled workers who joined them in 1913 and 1914 the unions soon lost their legitimacy, and the overwhelming majority of economic strikes were conducted by transitory strike committees. In the same fashion the worker–officials of the *kassy* and the labour group on the central insurance institutions quickly lost any illusions about achieving swift alterations in the provisions of the law in face of the determination of factory managers and bureaucrats to thwart any changes detrimental to their powers.

In their frustration and disappointment with their increasing reverses in the economic struggle, skilled operatives, the activist minority, began to lose their former faith in the Menshevik belief in the inherent value and possibilities of 'legal opportunities'. The Mensheviks' rationale for and defence of caution, moderation, of the legal, gradual path to reform seemed increasingly at odds with the reality of the militants' daily experience. As V. Torskii percipiently noted on the eve of the war, the Mensheviks' opposition to strikes – their attack on 'strike fever' – was particularly damaging to their cause.[118] Denigration of the solitary weapon workers had at their command to press for economic betterment, however valid the objections might have been, was politically inept. Thus the Bolshevik critique of contemporary society and Menshevism seemed to make sense. Bolshevik militance, revolutionism *à outrance*, their more apposite and forceful articulation of workers' interests and their defence and sponsorship of all and every stoppage became increasingly attractive to angry, disillusioned cadres.

Yet it would be mistaken to conclude that the new adherents to Bolshevism supported its factionalism. Another prominent motif of this study has been the aspiration of Social Democratic cadres to preserve the unity of their party and even to co-operate with the Socialist Revolutionaries. The history of the party's organisational efforts to furnish leadership to political strikes, of the Fourth State Duma elections, of the editorship of *Pravda*, of Bolshevik domination of the union of metalworkers, of the insurance campaign and the balloting to the central insurance organs all provide abundant evidence of the depth of the hostility of the rank and file to Leninist endeavours to split their party. The secondary Bolshevik leaders of both the illegal and the legal arenas were not Lenin's obedient instruments but had fashioned their own policies in the Fourth Duma elections, in the trade-union and insurance movements, in the matter of the general political strikes and had revealed a marked distaste for the *émigrés'* obsession with 'Liquidationism'. In general terms they can be said to have displayed marked conciliatory tendencies. Indeed many classed themselves as Bolshevik Conciliators or Vperedists, whilst others helped to form the Mezhraionka. When they took over trade unions or educational societies or *kassy*, their conduct of affairs often differed remarkably little in detail from that of their predecessors. The Mensheviks indeed lost much of their following among skilled workers in the open working-class institutions in 1913 and 1914, but the true victors were not Lenin and his tiny coterie in exile in Cracow (not the Leninists or Pravdists) but an independent-minded Bolshevik sub-élite which shared their antagonists' distaste for a party schism. The Bolsheviks' success came late (from the summer of 1913 to the spring of 1914), was shortlived (the events of July 1914 intervened) and limited, in that in all respects the faction had still failed to secure reliable conduits to the great mass of ordinary workers.

Chapter 8

THE REVIVAL OF INDUSTRIAL UNREST,
1911 – JUNE 1914

Throughout Europe the years immediately preceding the outbreak of the First World War witnessed unprecedented labour unrest after the industrial peace of the early 1900s. In France in 1906 approximately 400,000 workers downed tools to press for the introduction of the eight-hour day and in 1910 a national rail strike occurred. In Germany the Ruhr coalmines suffered massive work stoppages in 1905 and 1912. The United Kingdom was racked by a series of disputes between 1910 and 1914, including the first national railway shutdown in 1911 and the first national miners' strike in 1912.[1] Imperial Russia, and especially St Petersburg province, proved to be no exception (see Table 8.i).

In their efforts to understand the significance, trend and causes of the apparently sudden deterioration in labour relations, which followed upon the shooting of strikers at the Lena goldfields in Siberia in April 1912, contemporary observers were particularly struck by certain features of the ceaseless progression of stoppages in the two and a half years prior to the war. In the first place the increasing scope of protests inevitably evoked either fearful or hopeful parallels with the revolutionary upheavals of 1906 or even 1905. The annual report of the St Petersburg Society of Mill and Factory Owners (POZF), commenting on the upsurge of disputes in 1912, noted that 'their frequency and intensity can be compared only with those of 1905 and 1906'. This point of view was also endorsed at different ends of the political spectrum by the Bolshevik party conference in Cracow in December 1912 and the Kadet publicist A. Chuzhennikov.[3] Secondly, in the opinion of most commentators, the mounting strike movement was in form as much political as economic. Writing in the Bolshevik theoretical organ *Prosveshchenie* at the start of 1914, Grigorii Zinoviev emphasised that the mass political strike had become the dominant feature of working-class

Table 8.i: Number of Strikes and Strikers in the Russian Empire and St Petersburg Province, 1909–14[2]

Year	Strikes		Strikers	
	Empire	St Petersburg province	Empire	St Petersburg province
1909	340	9 (2.6)	64,166	4,119 (6.4)
1910	222	11 (5.0)	46,623	1,388 (3.0)
1911	466	22 (4.7)	105,110	10,937 (10.4)
1912	2,032	737 (36.3)	725,491	292,895 (40.4)
1913	2,404	755 (31.4)	887,096	355,662 (40.1)
1 Jan.–30 July 1914	4,098	1,632 (39.8)	1,448,684	679,578 (46.9)
1 Jan. 1912–30 July 1914	9,562	3,166 (33.1)	3,277,170	1,344,579 (41.0)

Note: Bracketed figures represent the number of St Petersburg strikes and strikers as a percentage of the Empire total. As the published factory inspectorate strike date for the period January to July 1914 omit the industrialised provinces of Warsaw and Petrokovskaia, the lacunae have been filled by utilisation of the original reports in the Ministry of Trade and Industry.

protest. Chuzhennikov concurred with this observation: 'the peculiar aspect of the movement in 1912,' he noted, 'was the great rise in the number of political stoppages'. At least one prominent representative of the industrial community did not dissent. Addressing the Eighth Congress of the Representatives of Industry and Trade in spring 1914, its assistant chairman, V. V. Zhukovskii, stated that 'the increase in the number of strikes is essentially an expression of genuine political protest'. Even high officials came to a similar conclusion. In a memorandum of 14 October 1913 N. A. Maklakov, the Minister of Internal Affairs, wrote that 'the development of the strike movement . . . unites the working class on a basis of hostility to the existing state structure.'[4] Thirdly, Lenin and his Bolshevik protégés, basing themselves on his 1910 analysis of the 1905 revolution which had drawn attention 'to the very close connection between the economic and the political strikes', argued consistently throughout the pre-war years that, in the words of Lev Kamenev, 'the political and economic stoppages are mutually reinforcing.' In the Bolsheviks' view, it was precisely the interweaving of the economic and the political struggle which imparted mass revolutionary character to the new strike movement.[5] Mensheviks, however, rejected such an interpretation. Their chief commentator on industrial relations, A. Mikhailov (pseudonym of Andrei Isuv), in his articles in *Nasha zaria*, always drew a clear distinction between walkouts of a political and an economic nature.[6] Fourthly, the upsurge gave rise to much controversy concerning the degree of spontaneity or organisation by revolutionary parties present in the conflicts. In public the Bolsheviks naturally attributed much of the responsibility for the industrial discontent to their illegal cells. The Mensheviks, on the contrary, disparaged this boast. In its annual review of the labour movement in 1913, their organ, *Novaia rabochaia gazeta*, remarked on 'the lack of leadership or preparation; the same disorganisation as before'. Bureaucrats and industrialists, however, were inclined to take Bolshevik claims at face value. The Engineering Section of the POZF pointed to what it considered to be the close connection between 'the protracted nature of the strikes of 1913 and the agitation and influence of the labour press, the Social Democrat deputies in the State Duma and working-class organisations'. The Council of Ministers itself echoed this sentiment. At their session of 24 October 1913 members agreed that 'the strikes are the result, in a majority of cases, of the illegal agitation of the revolutionary parties.'[7] Lastly, the Bolsheviks drew the conclusion from their analysis that the massive labour unrest signified a nationwide political crisis of a revolutionary character. Menshevik littérateurs, however, relying upon Lev Martov's premise that the form of the bourgeois revolution could not be foreseen, argued that the wave of strikes marked, in Mikhailov's words, 'only a political reawakening, but by no means a revolution'. Workers had joined the political struggle against the gentry–bureaucratic reaction for the first time since 1906. But the proletariat remained socially and politically isolated due to the refusal of the liberal opposition in parliament to support it and the complete passivity of the peasantry. The Mensheviks clung forlornly to the hope that the reviving labour movement would drive the bourgeoisie to the left.[8]

The general interpretation of the breakdown in industrial relations before the war advanced by contemporary Bolshevik intellectuals has been repeated, unsurprisingly, by Soviet historians. Scholars as far apart in time as M. S. Balabanov in the 1920s and G. A. Arutiunov fifty years later have postulated that in the years 1912 to 1914 'the mass revolutionary strikes and demonstrations became the main forms of the revolutionary struggle of the proletariat.'[9] The authors of the most recent general history of the Russian working class argue that 'at the basis of the proletarian movement of the years under consideration, in particular in 1912–1914, lay chiefly political factors' and that 'the political and economic motives of the workers' struggles were closely intertwined and mutually reinforced one another.' The focus of discontent was directed on to the Tsarist monarchy and capitalism.[10] Particular emphasis, too, is placed on the 'vanguard role' of the industrial disturbances in the capital. The wide dimension of the revived strike movement derived 'from the awakening to political life of new strata of workers' and the 'growth of the political consciousness of the proletariat.'[11]

I

As the data in Table 8.i indicate, the explosion of strikes, which swept both the Empire and St Petersburg in the spring of 1912 in the wake of the Lena goldfields massacre, did not take place in a setting of complete industrial calm. After an uninterrupted decline in the incidence of disputes from 1907, the year 1911 had witnessed a modest revival of strike activity in the country with a rise of 110 per cent in the number of strikes and 125 per cent in the number of strikers compared with 1910.[12] Even taking the factory inspectorate's estimates at face value, however, in 1911 the number of strikers constituted a mere 4.7 per cent of all workers who came within the purview of the factory inspectorate (compared with 2.2 per cent in 1910), figures which scarcely bear out Balabanov's assertion that 'the strike movement of the year [1911] had assumed the dimensions of a broad mass movement.'[13] The trend set in 1911 seemed likely to continue at a moderate pace early in 1912. In the Empire in the first three months of 1912 there was a rise of a quarter in the number of strikers compared with the same period of 1911 (from 11,859 to 14,789).[14] Contemporary observers were quick to note the connection between the obvious signs of industrial revival in 1911 and the re-emergence of tension in factories and workshops.[15] The stoppages, moreover, were almost exclusively of an economic character, with over 90 per cent of strikes and strikers falling into this category.

In this nascent phase of industrial action, St Petersburg province remained in the background (see Table 8.i). In 1911 its wage earners were responsible for only about 5 per cent of strikes and one in ten of strikers (according to the factory inspectorate).[16] The Moscow industrial region, in particular Moscow and Vladimir provinces, Tsarist Poland and the Baltic provinces, suffered far more from conflicts than the capital.[17]

In some respects, it is true, the strikes of 1910–11 in the capital were similar to those of the immediate pre-war period. The machine construction, printing and textile industries suffered from disputes which arose over issues of industrial discipline and authority in the workplace. The causes of these conflicts lay in the reorganisation of workshops by many employers after 1907, which altered established work procedures, threatened workshop customs and challenged workers' control over the pace of work (see Chapter 1). In the metalworking sector, for example, employees at Zigel' struck for five weeks in 1911 in protest against the introduction of overtime and the lengthening of the working day by four hours on a Saturday. At St Petersburg Engineering the turners rejected the imposition of hourly rates of pay, and 800 at Langenzippen walked out over a cut in the rates.[18] In the mills the source of bitter discontent lay in the employers' efforts to boost productivity by increasing the tempo of work. At J. Bek, Neva Cotton and Shtiglitz the sudden increase in the responsibility of female operatives from two to four machines provoked a withdrawal of labour, whilst at Mal'tsev two stoppages occurred over new shift systems. In the printing disputes employers' control was challenged by ultimata for the recognition of workers' representatives and hiring through the agency of the union of printers.[19] In this sense St Petersburg strikes in 1911 were mostly defensive. Another future pattern was presaged in 1911 – the manifest inability of strikers to make headway in their demands, despite propitious economic circumstances, as a consequence of the stiff resistance offered by the employers. In engineering all six strikes were lost by the workers and at least five of the eight stoppages in cotton suffered a similar fate. Printing workers alone secured some victories or at best compromises.

In other respects, however, the stoppages of 1910–11 in St Petersburg differed greatly from the later mighty wave of protests. The dimensions of the industrial unrest were still exceedingly modest; a mere 0.7 per cent of the factory labour force were involved in disputes. The metalworking and machine construction sectors accounted for 14 per cent of strikers in 1910 and 18 per cent in 1911, in sharp contrast to their later dominant role. On the other hand, cotton manufacturing furnished 70 per cent of strikers in 1911, a noticeable rise from its 23 per cent share of the total in 1910. These official data, however, present a rather distorted picture as they exclude the largest single group of strikers in the city in 1911 – the 13,000 dockers, who walked out at the height of the short shipping season in July to press for pay rises and a nine-hour day.[20] In engineering the six strikes of 1911 broke out in petty and medium-sized establishments rather than in plants employing over 1,000 hands. All disputes in St Petersburg, moreover, seem to have been of a wholly economic character, in this respect very different in nature from those of the immediate pre-war period.

The first three months of 1912 afforded little indication that the character of industrial relations either in the Empire or in its capital would assume a form radically different from that of the previous year. The events of the early spring in the Siberian mines of the Lena Goldfields Company, however, acted as the spark which ignited the hidden, smouldering discontent of St Petersburg workers. In the course of the strike which broke out in the goldmines at the end of February the strike committee was arrested on the night of 4 April. The following day soldiers opened fire on a crowd of 3,000 protesting strikers, killing from 170 to 270 and wounding 372.[21] The response of working people throughout the country, as well as in the capital, shattered the relative industrial calm of the 'years of reaction'. The massive walk-outs by wage earners in protest at the new 'Bloody Sunday', a chilling replay of the sanguinary reception of Father Gapon's peaceful petitioners before the Winter Palace on 9 January 1905, ushered in a new era of tension and unrest in factories and workshops through which workers' suppressed resentment at the reversal by employers of their gains in the 1905 revolution and cumulative reorganisations of work processes now found expression.

One of the most noticeable features of the revived strike wave within Russia between April 1912 and July 1914, compared with the previous cycle of popular urban unrest in 1905 to 1907, was the growing concentration of strike activity on the province of St Petersburg (see Table 8.ii). In 1905 and 1906 St Petersburg province contributed under a fifth of all strikers, whilst the Polish province of Petrokovskaia (Piotrkow), with the industrial centre of Lodz, was a greater focus of industrial disorder. In 1907 the capital was responsible for almost two-fifths of all strikers. By 1912–14 never

Table 8.ii: Distribution of Strikers, by Province: 1905–7 and 1912–30 July 1914 (% of total)

Provinces	1905	1906	1907	1912	1913	1914 (to 30 July)
St Petersburg	21.9	16.3	37.8	40.4 (56.3)	40.1 (67.8)	46.9 (60.3)
Other regions						
Lifland	9.4	8.3	2.8	11.0	13.6	13.2
Petrokovskaia	19.7	37.4	6.8	3.0	8.2	1.2
Warsaw	6.2	5.6	5.9	5.1	4.1	3.1
Moscow	9.7	4.8	4.9	11.1	10.6	10.5
Vladimir	5.4	4.6	11.5	5.4	1.5	1.4
Kostroma				–	0.5	4.0
Baku				0.9	2.9	3.5
TOTAL	72.3	77.0	69.7	76.9	81.5	83.8

Note: The calculations in this table are derived from the published annual reports of the factory inspectorate. The figures in brackets for St Petersburg in the period 1912–14 are based on the data of Table 8.vii.

less than 40 per cent of all strikers came from St Petersburg province. And the factory inspectorate's figures are themselves probably an underestimate. Revised estimates, based on data in Table 8.vii, suggest that the dimension of strike activity in St Petersburg province was even greater, rising to between 56 and 67 per cent between 1912 and 1914. All other regions of the country failed to match the strike propensity of the capital. The provinces of Lifland (which embraced Riga) and Moscow ranked a lowly second and third. Tsarist Poland, too, was far less afflicted by stoppages before the war than in the almost insurrectionary years of 1905 and 1906. Other industrial regions such as the Ukraine or the Urals scarcely counted at all. The hegemony of the capital stands out in even greater relief when a comparison is made of the intensity of strikes before the war within individual provinces. In St Petersburg the proportion of the factory labour force participating in strikes rose from 239 per cent in 1912 to 314 per cent in 1913. The first half of 1914 witnessed a further, if moderate, increase to 326 per cent (see Table 8.v). Lifland province alone approached this level. Here 137 per cent of industrial workers downed tools in 1913 and 228 per cent in 1914. In stark contrast no more than two-fifths of Moscow province's factory employees stopped work at any time in this period, whilst Warsaw and Petrokovskaia provinces never exceeded a ratio of 45 per cent.[22] The capital's dominating role proved paradoxically to be both the

Table 8.iii: St Petersburg Province: Strikes by Industry and by Three-monthly Periods, 1912–3 July 1914[23] (% of total)

Industry	1912				Total	no.
	Jan.–Mar.	Apr.–June	July–Sept.	Oct.–Dec.		
Animal products	–	60.0	5.0	35.0	100.0	20
Chemicals	–	80.0	–	20.0	100.0	10
Commercial–industrial*	–	20.0	60.0	20.0	100.0	5
Communications	–	56.3	–	43.7	100.0	16
Construction	–	50.0	35.7	14.3	100.0	28
Food/drink/tobacco	–	24.1	69.6	6.3	100.0	158
Gold/silver/bronze	–	63.6	9.1	27.3	100.0	22
Metals and machines	1.0	42.6	4.5	51.9	100.0	310
Mineral products	–	72.0	8.0	20.0	100.0	25
Miscellaneous	–	33.3	66.6	–	99.9	3
Paper and printing	0.7	37.1	14.3	47.9	100.0	140
Tailoring	–	50.0	10.9	39.1	100.0	64
Textiles	–	35.0	3.8	61.3	100.0	80
Woodworking	–	32.6	4.5	62.9	100.0	89
ALL INDUSTRIES	0.4	40.0	18.4	41.2	100.0	970

* It seems unlikely that there was a complete absence of strikes involving commercial–industrial employees in 1913 but no trace could be found in the sources.

Table 8.iii: (Continued)

Industry	1913				Total	no.
	Jan.–Mar.	Apr.–June	July–Sept.	Oct.–Dec.		
Animal products	6.0	59.7	19.4	14.9	100.0	67
Chemicals	30.0	60.0	–	10.0	100.0	10
Commercial–industrial	–	–	–	–	–	–
Communications	37.5	31.3	18.8	12.5	100.1	32
Construction	4.8	71.4	19.0	4.8	100.0	21
Food/drink/tobacco	9.4	67.5	9.4	13.8	100.1	160
Gold/silver/bronze	25.4	42.6	27.9	4.1	100.0	122
Metals and machines	15.8	47.3	23.7	13.2	100.0	569
Mineral products	37.5	43.8	12.5	6.3	100.1	16
Miscellaneous	–	–	83.3	16.6	99.9	6
Paper and printing	21.6	51.3	15.1	12.1	100.1	199
Tailoring	0.8	95.8	0.8	2.5	99.9	120
Textiles	16.8	54.5	11.9	16.8	100.0	101
Woodworking	17.2	30.5	36.7	15.6	100.0	128
ALL INDUSTRIES	15.8	52.7	19.6	11.9	100.0	1,551

Table 8.iii: (Continued)

| Industry | 1914 (to 3 July) | | | |
	Jan.–Mar.	Apr.–3 July	Total	no.
Animal products	38.7	61.3	100.0	31
Chemicals	17.6	82.4	100.0	17
Commercial–industrial	50.0	50.0	100.0	4
Communications	80.7	19.3	100.0	88
Construction	33.3	66.6	99.9	3
Food/drink/tobacco	38.3	61.7	100.0	154
Gold/silver/bronze	10.0	90.0	100.0	30
Metals and machines	39.2	60.8	100.0	655
Mineral products	–	100.0	100.0	7
Miscellaneous	12.5	87.5	100.0	8
Paper and printing	34.2	65.8	100.0	120
Tailoring	21.6	78.4	100.0	102
Textiles	39.6	60.4	100.0	101
Woodworking	23.9	76.1	100.0	71
ALL INDUSTRIES	38.0	62.0	100.0	1,391

major source of strength and weakness of the strike movement prior to the war as a form of opposition to the monarchy.

As Table 8.i shows, the aggregate number of strikes and strikers in St Petersburg between 1911 and 1912 rose by 431 per cent and 363 per cent respectively. The numbers of strikes and strikers in 1913 were only a modest 60 per cent and 46 per cent above 1912 levels. But the number of strikes and strikers rose by 31 per cent and 88 per cent respectively in the first six months of 1914 alone.

Tables 8.iii. and 8.iv. show the incidence of strikes in St Petersburg province between 1912 and July 1914 by three-monthly intervals. It is clear that the second quarter of 1912, with the massive protests against the Lena shootings and the unprecedented celebration by workers of May Day, imparted a significant impetus to the moderate strike revival of 1911. Much of the spring unrest proved only a temporary phenomenon. Between July and September the recorded numbers of strikes and strikers were 54 per cent and 95 per cent respectively below those from April to June. The last three months of the year, however, provided disturbing evidence that the earlier clashes presaged serious breakdown in industrial relations. Between October and December the number of strikes and strikers rose by 125 per cent and 200 per cent above July–September levels. Although

Industry	Jan.–Mar.	Apr.–June	July–Sept.	Oct.–Dec.	Total	no.
		1913				
Animal products	2.5	73.1	13.4	11.0	100.0	21,590
Chemicals	36.7	63.1	–	0.2	100.0	4,225
Commercial–industrial	–	–	–	–	–	–
Communications	35.1	39.3	20.1	5.4	99.9	4,612
Construction	33.0	13.7	53.3	–	100.0	182
Food/drink/tobacco	9.6	59.7	8.5	22.1	99.9	32,551
Gold/silver/bronze	12.7	70.0	10.9	6.3	99.9	4,194
Metals and machines	17.3	44.1	20.8	17.8	100.0	384,512
Mineral products	28.2	61.8	4.2	5.8	100.0	3,463
Miscellaneous	–	–	33.3	66.6	99.9	555
Paper and printing	15.8	59.0	10.9	14.3	100.0	24,720
Tailoring	2.1	94.5	1.4	2.1	100.1	1,693
Textiles	20.8	58.0	6.4	14.8	100.0	96,853
Woodworking	17.6	45.0	24.3	13.2	100.1	15,072
ALL INDUSTRIES	17.1	49.4	16.8	16.7	100.0	594,222

Table 8.iv: St Petersburg Province: Strikers by Industry and by Three-monthly Periods, 1912–3 July 1914 (% of total)

Industry	Jan.–Mar.	1912 Apr.–June	July–Sept.	Oct.–Dec.	Total	no.
Animal products	–	70.9	–	29.1	100.0	23,606
Chemicals	–	99.1	–	0.9	100.0	1,725
Commercial–industrial	–	1.4	97.9	0.7	100.0	517
Communications	–	41.7	1.1	57.2	100.0	15,642
Construction	–	49.0	37.7	13.3	100.0	1,314
Food/drink/tobacco	–	60.1	20.5	19.4	100.0	12,417
Gold/silver/bronze	–	93.9	1.5	4.6	100.0	1,339
Metals and machines	1.2	48.1	0.5	49.5	99.3	217,611
Mineral products	–	58.5	0.3	41.1	99.9	3,621
Miscellaneous	–	–	100.0	–	100.0	112
Paper and printing	0.2	43.9	11.7	44.2	100.0	22,326
Tailoring	–	55.3	8.1	36.5	99.9	739
Textiles	–	33.2	1.7	65.2	100.1	96,933
Woodworking	–	31.6	0.2	68.2	100.0	10,245
ALL INDUSTRIES	1.0	45.8	2.3	50.9	100.0	408,147

Table 8.iv: (Continued)

| Industry | Jan.–Mar. | 1914 (to 3 July) | | |
		Apr.–3 July	Total	no.
Animal products	75.0	25.0	100.0	44,050
Chemicals	1.4	98.6	100.0	5,022
Commercial–industrial	72.0	28.0	100.0	25
Communications	30.7	69.3	100.0	2,647
Construction	97.3	2.7	100.0	260
Food/drink/tobacco	47.3	52.7	100.0	74,360
Gold/silver/bronze	22.4	77.6	100.0	1,699
Metals and machines	45.2	54.8	100.0	475,330
Mineral products	–	100.0	100.0	1,538
Miscellaneous	50.7	49.3	100.0	986
Paper and printing	36.7	63.3	100.0	26,043
Tailoring	14.7	85.3	100.0	1,520
Textiles	38.2	61.8	100.0	98,173
Woodworking	20.4	79.6	100.0	12,344
ALL INDUSTRIES	45.0	55.0	100.0	743,997

significantly greater than in the comparable period of 1912, the number of strikes and strikers in the first three months of 1913 once more declined, by 39 per cent and 75 per cent respectively on the October–December 1912 levels. The spring of 1913, however, marked a significant turn for the worse in relations between employers and wage earners. Between April and June 1913 the incidence of strikes and strikers was far higher than it had been either in the spring of the previous year (by 11 per cent and 57 per cent respectively) or in the first three months of 1913 (by 234 per cent and 189 per cent respectively). As in the previous summer, the summer of 1913 witnessed a reduction in labour unrest, albeit at a higher plateau than twelve months earlier. On the other hand, in contrast to the winter of 1912, the incidence of striking continued to decline in the last quarter of 1913, to a level well below that of the previous winter. The trend proved only temporary. In the first six months of 1914 the numbers of strikes and strikers were 31 per cent and 88 per cent greater than in the first six months of 1913. Indeed the first and second quarters of 1914 surpassed all previous quarters in the incidence of labour unrest with the striking exception of the spring of 1913, which recorded the highest total of strikes (818) in the entire period. Although lower than in 1905, when 275 per cent of St Petersburg workers were on strike, the strike propensity of St

Table 8.v: St Petersburg Province: Total Number of Strikers Each Year as % of Total Labour Force, by Industry, 1912–3 July 1914

Industry	1912	1913	1914 (to 3 July)
Animal products	169.2	154.8	227.9
Chemicals	13.9	29.7	27.8
Commercial–Industrial*	0.003	–	0.0002
Communications	30.3	8.9	5.1
Construction**	0.007	0.0009	0.001
Food/drink/tobacco	74.2	183.0	364.4
Gold/silver/bronze*	19.1	59.9	24.3
Metals and machines	348.5	480.7	498.6
Mineral products	17.4	16.2	7.0
Miscellaneous*	0.003	0.1	0.2
Paper and Printing	117.4	118.7	106.3
Tailoring*	0.1	0.3	0.3
Textiles	241.2	224.4	203.2
Woodworking	141.2	210.2	138.9
as % of the factory labour force	239.6	314.5	326.4
as % of the total labour force	54.3	79.1	99.0

Note: With the undernoted exceptions the percentages have been calculated as a proportion of the previous year's labour force in each branch of industry and in factory manufacturing overall. In the case of construction (**) the estimate has been based on the seasonal summer labour force of approximately 200,000 rather than the small permanent core of around 20,000 workers. In the case of (*), in the absence of later data, computations have had to rely upon the city census of December 1910.

Petersburg factory workers between 1912 and 1914 (200 per cent) was distinctly and progressively higher than in 1906 and 1907, the last two years of the first Russian revolution (see Table 8.v).

As Tables 8.vi and 8.vii reveal, the incidence of stoppages was far from uniform among and within the different branches of the economy – a major source of weakness within the movement.

In the first place, the enormous numbers employed in the service sector remained almost totally unaffected by the discontent sweeping through manufacturing industry. No trace of disputes involving domestic servants could be found. Commercial–industrial employees, whether engaged in manufacturing, catering or retailing proved to

*Table 8.vi: St Petersburg Province: Strikes by Industry, 1912–3 July 1914
(number and % of total)*

Industry	1912		1913		Jan.–3 July 1914		Total: 1912–3 July 1914	
	no.	%	no.	%	no.	%	no.	%
Animal products	20	2.1	67	4.3	31	2.2	118	3.0
Chemicals	10	1.0	10	0.6	17	1.2	37	0.9
Commercial–industrial	5	0.5	–	–	4	0.3	9	0.2
Communications	16	1.6	32	2.1	88	6.3	136	3.5
Construction	28	2.9	21	1.4	3	0.2	52	1.3
Food/drink/tobacco	158	16.3	160	10.3	154	11.1	472	12.1
Gold/silver/bronze	22	2.3	122	7.9	30	2.2	174	4.4
Metals and machines	310	32.0	569	36.7	655	47.1	1,534	39.2
Mineral products	25	2.6	16	1.0	7	0.5	48	1.2
Miscellaneous*	3	0.3	6	0.4	8	0.6	17	0.4
Paper and printing	140	14.4	199	12.8	120	8.6	459	11.7
Tailoring	64	6.6	120	7.7	102	7.3	286	7.3
Textiles	80	8.2	101	6.5	101	7.3	282	7.2
Woodworking	89	9.2	128	8.3	71	5.2	288	7.4
TOTAL	970	100.0	1,551	100.2	1,391	100.1	3,912	99.8

* The category 'miscellaneous' refers mostly to public utilities owned by the St
Petersburg municipality.

be remarkably lacking in militancy. They never made up more than
1 per cent of all strikers during the period 1912 to 3 July 1914.
Railway workers, whose intervention in October 1905 tipped the
balance decisively against the regime, were extremely quiescent.[24]
Postal and telegraph employees never took industrial action. Thus
the pre-war crisis in relations between masters and wage earners
concerned only manufacturing industry, whilst the undoubted rise in
the intensity of strikes over the period was not a consequence of the
movement slowly drawing service personnel into its embrace.

Even within manufacturing industry, there were enormous differentials in strike incidence both between factory and artisanal
forms of production and between different branches of production.
All indices point to the unmistakable dominance within the new
labour protest of workers in the capital's metalworking and machine
construction establishments. Disputes in this sector accounted for an
increasing share of strikes, rising from 32 per cent of the total in 1912
to 47 per cent in the first half of 1914. Metalworkers constituted an
even higher proportion of all strikers, forming 53 per cent in 1912

Table 8.vii: St Petersburg Province: Strikers by Industry, 1912–3 July 1914 (number and % of total)

Industry	1912		1913		Jan.–3 July 1914		Total: 1912–3 July 1914	
	no.	%	no.	%	no.	%	no.	%
Animal products	23,606	5.8	21,590	3.6	44,050	5.9	89,246	5.0
Chemicals	1,725	0.4	4,225	0.7	5,022	0.6	10,972	0.6
Commercial–Industrial	517	0.1	–	–	25	–	542	0.03
Communications	15,642	3.8	4,612	0.8	2,647	0.4	22,901	1.0
Construction	1,314	0.3	182	0.03	260	0.03	1,756	0.1
Food/drink/tobacco	12,417	3.0	32,551	5.5	74,360	10.0	119,328	6.8
Gold/silver/bronze	1,339	0.3	4,194	0.7	1,699	0.2	7,232	0.4
Metals and machines	217,611	53.3	384,572	64.7	475,330	63.9	1,077,513	61.7
Mineral products	3,621	0.9	3,463	0.6	1,538	0.2	8,622	0.5
Miscellaneous	112	0.02	555	0.1	986	0.1	1,653	0.09
Paper and printing	22,326	5.5	24,720	4.2	26,043	3.5	73,089	4.2
Tailoring	739	0.2	1,693	0.3	1,520	0.2	3,952	0.2
Textiles	96,933	23.7	96,853	16.3	98,173	13.2	291,959	16.7
Woodworking	10,245	2.5	15,072	2.5	12,344	1.7	37,661	2.2
TOTAL	408,147	99.82	594,282	100.03	743,997	99.93	1,746,426	99.52

with an increase to 64 per cent the following year. In this respect the character of the strike upsurge in the city differed markedly both from the revolution of 1905–7 when metalworkers never contributed more than 28 per cent of all St Petersburg strikers and the post-revolutionary years of 1908–11 when their share of the total fell to below a fifth. In both these periods there existed a more even spread of strikers among industries. The pre-war pattern, however, did replicate the all-Russian distribution of strikers, of whom metalworkers accounted for slightly over half.[25] As Table 8.v. reveals, no other branch of manufacturing suffered from such an intensity of strikes. Even in 1912 the sum total of strikers in engineering exceeded the number of workers employed therein by three and a half times and in 1913 and early 1914 by approximately five times. Yet even in this sector there were exceptions. Seven of the large state-owned plants remained almost completely unafflicted by trouble, including the Arsenal, Izhora and Sestroretsk arms factories and the Cartridge and Pipe works.

Although the food-processing and printing industries each accounted for a larger proportion of strikes than textiles in the period 1912 to 3 July 1914, (12 per cent and 11.7 per cent of all stoppages compared with 7 per cent), the mills were responsible for a higher portion of strikers, furnishing 17 per cent of the total in contrast to food processing's share of 7 per cent and printing's 4 per cent. The textile industry's contribution to labour unrest, however, came not only a poor second to the metalworking sector (which contributed 62 per cent of all strikers), but it also diminished over time. Whilst 24 per cent of all strikers in 1912 were mill hands, the ratio fell to 16 per cent in 1913 and 13 per cent in the first half of 1914. This fall mirrored a national trend. Whereas the factory inspectorate calculated that 60 per cent of strikers in 1911 were textile workers, they returned an estimate of 28 per cent for 1912 and an even lower one of 21 per cent for 1914. There was a corresponding drop in the intensity of conflicts within the industry (see Table 8.v). Some of the largest mills, such as Ekaterinhof Cotton, Mala-Okhta, Russian Thread and Thornton, reported almost no strike activity at all.

The statistical evidence set out in Tables 8.vi. and 8.vii. also suggests that Haimson and Kruze's claim for a high ratio of strikes in industries other than metals and machines in the capital, and Balabanov and Ivanova's assertion that throughout the Empire other strata of the labour force besides metalworkers and textile workers were increasingly sucked into the strike movement in 1913 and 1914, requires considerable modification.[26] The intensity of strikes within chemicals, woodworking, food processing and the manufacture of articles of gold, silver and bronze was clearly greater in 1913 than in 1912 (Table 8.v). A similar pattern was observed in the first half of

1914 in the processing of animal products and in particular in the food and drink industry (with a rise of almost 130 per cent in the total of strikers). On the other hand, the first two quarters of 1914 were notable for a decline in the intensity of strikes in chemicals, the gold and silver trades, mineral products, paper and printing, tailoring and woodworking. The contribution, moreover, of all other branches of manufacturing together with construction workers and commercial–industrial employees remained small. Their share diminished over time, falling from 23 per cent of strikers in 1912 to 19 per cent in 1913 with a small rise to 22 per cent in the first six months of 1914.[27]

An analysis of disputes in individual manufacturing sectors (Tables 8.iii and 8.iv) reveals that the temporal pattern of strikes in particular industries tended to follow the general pattern for industry as a whole described earlier in this chapter. In metalworking, for example, the vast majority of strikes and strikers in 1912 were recorded in the second and last quarters of the year, which accounted for 48 and 50 per cent of strikers respectively. The spring of 1913 was the most disturbed quarter of that year in engineering, responsible for around 45 per cent of all strikes and strikers in the industry. Indeed the number of strikers in metalworking in the second quarter constituted an increase of approximately 60 per cent over the estimates both for the first quarter of 1913 and the second quarter of the previous year. Although the number of metalworkers on strike was 53 per cent lower in the summer of 1913 than in the spring, the numbers involved were 98 per cent greater than in the third quarter of 1912. In the first six months of 1914 another furious surge in unrest took place. The aggregates of strikes and strikers leapt by 83 per cent and 101 per cent respectively compared with the first half of 1913. A similar picture can be observed in textiles, in which the worst phases of unrest were recorded in the second and fourth quarters of 1912, the spring of 1913 and the spring of 1914. A broadly comparable trend can be observed in animal products, chemicals, food processing, the gold and silver trades, mineral products, paper and printing, tailoring and woodworking.

II

A fundamental determinant of the nature, scale and pace of stoppages, as well as of the hegemonic role played by the capital and its metalworkers, was the predominance of strikes of a political character.

Any analysis of the extent to which strikes were politically motivated is, of course, complicated by problems of definition. Political strikes were defined by the factory inspectorate, whose published annual reports furnished the raw data for contemporary commentators and subsequent scholars, simply as mass demonstrative strikes or protest strikes.[28] This definition overlooks the fact that some of the strikes the inspectorate categorised as 'economic' in motivation also included political or other non-economic motives. In engineering and shipbuilding, for example, after 1 May 1912 in ten disputes mostly at medium-sized plants the strikers included in a list of purely economic desiderata the annulment of fines levied by management for walk-outs on May Day, the pre-eminent political symbol of proletarian aspirations, and, on two occasions, the inclusion of May Day in the table of works holidays.[29] Some conflicts were precipitated by the arrest of workmates by the police, as at Baranovskii machine construction in November 1912 or St Petersburg Pipes in April 1914. The implementation of the Insurance Laws in autumn 1913 provided the occasion for industrial action in a few establishments such as the Geisler and Phoenix engineering plants.[30] Since, however, the number of economic strikes which also embraced non-economic motives amounted to only 4 per cent of all strikes classified as economic in aim, it seems reasonable to base the analysis summarised in Tables 8.viii–8.xiv on the criteria adopted by the factory inspectorate. (A list of all the mass demonstrative political

Table 8.viii: St Petersburg Province: Number of Political Strikes as % of All Strikes by Industry, 1912–3 July 1914

Industry	1912	1913	Jan.–3 July 1914	Total 1912–3 July 1914
Animal products	70.0	31.3	64.5	46.6
Chemicals	40.0	80.0	23.5	43.2
Commercial–industrial	–	–	–	–
Communications	31.3	31.3	4.5	14.0
Construction	–	14.3	–	5.8
Food/drink/tobacco	9.5	44.4	58.4	37.3
Gold/silver/bronze	50.0	34.4	86.6	45.4
Metals and machines	69.7	74.2	76.3	74.2
Mineral products	48.0	68.8	42.9	54.2
Miscellaneous	–	–	–	–
Paper and printing	51.4	75.9	70.0	66.9
Tailoring	78.1	50.0	71.6	64.0
Textiles	71.3	70.3	74.3	72.0
Woodworking	60.7	53.9	58.7	58.0
ALL INDUSTRIES	52.6	60.5	66.4	60.6

Table 8.ix: St Petersburg Province: Number of Political Strikers as % of all Strikers by Industry, 1912–3 July 1914

Industry	1912	1913	Jan.–3 July 1914	Total 1912–3 July 1914
Animal products	58.9	66.6	62.1	62.3
Chemicals	75.9	92.7	61.7	75.9
Commercial–industrial	–	–	–	–
Communications	30.9	28.0	24.2	29.5
Construction	–	46.7	–	48.4
Food/drink/tobacco	58.8	70.6	92.0	82.4
Gold/silver/bronze	90.1	80.5	76.8	81.4
Metals and machines	84.1	84.8	92.2	87.9
Mineral products	61.3	85.7	78.0	74.0
Miscellaneous	–	–	–	–
Paper and printing	64.6	86.2	81.4	77.9
Tailoring	81.2	47.3	82.8	67.3
Textiles	75.9	71.7	82.2	76.6
Woodworking	75.6	80.8	93.4	83.5
ALL INDUSTRIES	76.0	80.6	88.0	82.7

strikes in the capital between April 1912 and 3 July 1914 is contained in Appendix I).

The general pre-eminence of St Petersburg in the strike wave which swept over the Empire in the last two and a half years of peace derived in large part from its dominant position in nationwide political protest. Whereas during the upheavals of 1905 to 1907 political strikes were relatively unevenly distributed throughout the country, the capital and its province accounted for 56 per cent of all politically motivated strikes in 1912, a staggering 95 per cent in 1913 and 75 per cent in the first half of 1914.[31] As Tables 8. viii and 8.ix reveal, from half to two-thirds of all strikes and from three-quarters to nine-tenths of all strikers in St Petersburg province between 1912 and 1914 were associated with mass walk-outs over political issues. The overwhelming bulk of such shutdowns lasted only a day. In the absence of other legal or illegal means of protest or methods of effecting political change (a consequence of the frailties of the revolutionary parties and trade unions, the illegality of working-class parties and the ineffectiveness of a miniscule socialist representation in a conservative, gentry-dominated parliament), these one-day political stoppages suddenly became the main form of the labour movement in the capital, as observers such as Zinoviev and Chuzhennikov had noted at the time.[32] This development reflected a national trend. According to the factory inspectorate, 76 per cent of Russian strikers in 1912 were factory workers participating in political protests. Although the proportion fell to 57 per cent in 1913, it soared to 79 per cent in 1914.[33]

The dimensions and pace of the political upsurge were determined both by the timing and by the causes of individual outbursts. In particular a distinction may be drawn between two types of political stoppage. On the one hand there were those mass walk-outs which involved a generalised opposition to the Tsarist political system either by celebrating the international proletarian May Day holiday, commemorating the victims of its excessive use of force in the past (the anniversaries of 9 January and the Lena massacre) or by showing sympathy and solidarity with the repressed in the present. The latter occasions included among others the Lena tragedy in 1912, the court martial of Sevastopol naval mutineers in October 1912 and of Baltic Fleet sailors in June 1913. Numerically less significant were political stoppages occasioned by specific actions by the authorities to circumscribe workers' political freedoms gained in 1905 and 1906, among them being the cassation of elections from the workers' curiae to the Fourth State Duma elections, the persecution of the

Table 8.x: *St Petersburg Province: Number and % of Political Strikes by Industry (three-monthly periods) 1912–3 July 1914*

	1912			
Industry	Apr.–June	Oct.–Dec.	Total	no.
Animal products	57.1	42.8	99.9	14
Chemicals	100.0	–	100.0	4
Commercial–industrial	–	–	–	–
Communications	60.0	40.0	100.0	5
Construction	–	–	–	–
Food/drink/tobacco	73.3	26.7	100.0	15
Gold/silver/bronze	100.0	–	100.0	11
Metals and machines	36.1	63.9	100.0	216
Mineral products	58.3	41.9	100.2	12
Miscellaneous	–	–	–	–
Paper and printing	29.2	70.8	100.0	72
Tailoring	60.0	40.0	100.0	50
Textiles	38.6	61.4	100.0	57
Woodworking	18.5	81.5	100.0	54
ALL INDUSTRIES	40.2	59.8	100.0	510

Table 8.x: (Continued)

Industry	1913					
	Jan.–Mar.	Apr.–June	July–Sept.	Oct.–Dec.	Total	no.
Animal products	14.3	57.1	19.0	9.5	99.9	21
Chemicals	25.0	75.0	–	–	100.0	8
Commercial–industrial	–	–	–	–	–	–
Communications	–	50.0	30.0	20.0	100.0	10
Construction	–	66.6	33.3	–	99.9	3
Food/drink/tobacco	2.8	94.4	1.4	1.4	100.0	71
Gold/silver/bronze	2.4	83.3	4.8	9.5	100.0	42
Metals and machines	16.4	48.6	23.0	12.1	100.1	422
Mineral products	36.4	54.5	–	9.1	100.0	11
Miscellaneous	–	–	–	–	–	–
Paper and printing	21.2	50.3	17.9	10.6	100.0	151
Tailoring	–	100.0	–	–	100.0	60
Textiles	14.1	56.3	12.7	16.9	100.0	71
Woodworking	23.2	49.3	17.4	10.1	100.0	69
ALL INDUSTRIES	14.8	58.4	16.6	10.2	100.0	939

Table 8.x: (Continued)

| Industry | 1914 (to 3 July) | | | |
	Jan.–Mar.	Apr.–3 July	Total	no.
Animal products	35.0	65.0	100.0	20
Chemicals	25.0	75.0	100.0	4
Commercial–industrial	–	–	–	–
Communications	–	100.0	100.0	4
Construction	–	–	–	–
Food/drink/tobacco	45.6	54.4	100.0	90
Gold/silver/bronze	–	100.0	100.0	26
Metals and machines	43.6	56.4	100.0	500
Mineral products	–	100.0	–	3
Miscellaneous	–	–	–	–
Paper and printing	22.6	77.4	100.0	84
Tailoring	–	100.0	–	73
Textiles	42.7	57.3	100.0	75
Woodworking	15.9	86.1	102.0	44
ALL INDUSTRIES	35.2	64.8	100.0	923

socialist press in July and September 1913 and attacks on trade unions and the right to strike.

The revival of political strikes in St Petersburg was the direct consequence of the shootings thousands of miles away on the Lena goldfields in April 1912. As well as passing resolutions of protest at factory meetings and collecting money for the victims, workers gave vent to their disgust at the regime's brutality, and to their feelings of solidarity with the Lena strikers by withdrawing their labour in a series of walk-outs between 14 and 22 April. Approximately 72,000 to 140,000 downed tools.[34] The coincidence in time of May Day – the beacon of a millenarian socialist future so different from Tsarist reality – ensured that working people would seek to mark the occasion on a scale unknown since 1907. Whereas around 100,000 people had ceased working on that date in 1907, five years later a varying estimate of between 63,000 and 150,000 left their benches.[35]

Three-monthly aggregates of the numbers of political strikes and strikers are summarised in Tables 8.x and 8.xi. In 1912 the incidence of political strikes was greatest in the second quarter of the year, reflecting the aftermath of the Lena goldfield shootings and the May Day celebrations. The calm descending on the political front in the summer was shattered in the third and fourth quarters of the year when the incidence of political strikes once again rose dramatically as a result of events like the Sevastopol trial. 1913 offered the authorities no respite, the number of political strikes and strikers rising by 84 per cent and 54 per cent respectively over the levels of the previous year. The early months of the year brought another anniversary – that of Bloody Sunday 1905 before the Winter Palace. Seventy thousand took industrial action. In the spring months of 1913 the numbers of political strikes and strikers rose 167 per cent and 83 per cent above those of the previous spring. The strikes on the anniversary of the Lena massacre and on May Day encompassed far more workers than any other in the year. Some 77,000 people walked off the job on 4 April and almost double that figure a month later. This upsurge in political conflicts was the major factor behind the general growth in stoppages during the spring. Altogether 58 per cent of all political strikes (with 52 per cent of all political strikers) occurred in the months April to June. Whilst the summer months witnessed a decline of some 70 per cent in the number of strikes and strikers, they stood in stark contrast to the summer of the previous year with its absence of political unrest. They were also noteworthy in that the political disturbances occurred as a response to the relentless persecution of the Social Democratic newspapers in St Petersburg in July and Moscow in September. The last quarter of 1913 marked a further

Table 8.xi: St Petersburg Province: Number and % of Political Strikers by Industry (three-monthly periods) 1912–3 July 1914

| Industry | 1912 | | | |
	Apr.–June	Oct.–Dec.	Total	no.
Animal products	50.7	49.3	100.0	13,900
Chemicals	100.0	–	100.0	1,310
Commercial–industrial	–	–	–	–
Communications	91.7	8.3	100.0	4,830
Construction	–	–	–	–
Food/drink/tobacco	71.9	28.1	100.0	7,300
Gold/silver/bronze	100.0	–	100.0	1,207
Metals and machines	43.9	56.1	100.0	183,011
Mineral products	32.9	67.1	100.0	2,219
Miscellaneous	–	–.	–	–
Paper and printing	42.1	57.9	100.0	14,422
Tailoring	66.6	33.3	99.9	600
Textiles	36.9	63.1	100.0	73,580
Woodworking	26.5	73.5	100.0	7,750
ALL INDUSTRIES	42.6	57.4	100.0	310,129

Table 8.xi: (Continued)

| | | | 1913 | | | | |
Industry	Jan.–Mar.	Apr.–June	July–Sept.	Oct.–Dec.	Total	no.
Animal products	3.7	80.1	11.8	4.4	100.0	14,372
Chemicals	31.9	68.0	–	–	99.9	3,915
Commercial–industrial	–	–	–	–	–	–
Communications	–	65.9	21.7	12.4	100.0	1,291
Construction	–	29.4	70.6	–	100.0	85
Food/drink/tobacco	2.0	81.0	6.5	10.4	99.9	22,975
Gold/silver/bronze	2.4	82.9	7.1	7.6	100.0	3,376
Metals and machines	15.1	46.5	20.9	17.4	99.9	326,085
Mineral products	27.6	65.7	–	6.7	100.0	2,968
Miscellaneous	–	–	–	–	–	–
Paper and printing	16.5	59.1	11.9	12.5	100.0	21,307
Tailoring	–	100.0	–	–	100.0	800
Textiles	17.7	56.5	7.9	17.9	100.0	69,434
Woodworking	20.7	50.9	16.0	12.4	100.0	12,171
ALL INDUSTRIES	14.8	52.0	17.1	16.1	100.0	478,779

Table 8.xi: (Continued)

Industry	1914 (to 3 July) Jan.–Mar.	Apr.–3 July	Total	no.
Animal products	61.0	39.0	100.0	27,360
Chemicals	–	100.0	100.0	3,100
Commercial–industrial	–	–	–	–
Communications	–	100.0	100.0	640
Construction	–	–	–	–
Food/drink/tobacco	44.1	55.9	100.0	68,047
Gold/silver/bronze	–	100.0	100.0	1,304
Metals and machines	47.5	52.5	100.0	438,366
Mineral products	–	100.0	100.0	1,200
Miscellaneous	–	–	–	–
Paper and printing	27.3	72.7	100.0	21,197
Tailoring	–	100.0	100.0	1,258
Textiles	40.6	59.4	100.0	80,755
Woodworking	18.8	81.2	100.0	11,535
ALL INDUSTRIES	45.1	54.9	100.0	654,762

diminution in the total number of political strikes and strikers in comparison both with the same period in 1912 and with the third quarter of 1913. The explanation lay in the fact that it contained only one major sympathy stoppage – the trial of strikers at the Obukhov arms plant on 6 November.

The first half of 1914 witnessed a veritable epidemic of political disturbances. In comparison with the similar period of 1913 the aggregate of political strikes increased by a third, whilst the number of political strikers doubled. In both the first and second quarters of 1914 approximately 88 per cent of all strikers took part in walk-outs of a political nature. Thus on the eve of the war the clear deepening of labour unrest was fundamentally political in nature. Political disputes accounted for almost the entire rise in the overall figures of strikes and strikers between January and June 1914. One element in the swell of political strikes was a significant growth in the number of participants in strikes marking the anniversary of 9 January (a rise from 70,000 to 113,000) and May Day (135,000 to 170,000) as well as the second trial of Obukhov strikers on 19 May. Another was the particularly disturbed character of March, whose aggregate of political strikers (162,000) was the second highest of any month between April 1912 and June 1914. It was symptomatic of the times that it was soon exceeded in May 1914, when 236,000 employees participated in political stoppages.

Political conflicts involved an increasing proportion both of the factory labour force (a rise from 182 per cent in 1912 to 287 per cent in 1914), as well as of wage earners as a whole (from 41 per cent in 1912 to 87 per cent in 1914). But the incidence of political strikes, as was the case with stoppages in general, varied greatly among and within the various sectors of the urban economy.

As Tables 8.xii and 8.xiii reveal, commercial–industrial employees, domestic and institutional servants, postal and telegraph workers and the staff of municipal public utilities were conspicuous by their absence from political strikes. In the construction industry only three stoppages, involving a total of eighty-five participants, had political aims. A mere 1 per cent of all political strikes and strikers were accounted for by the labour force in communications.

In stark contrast the labour force in St Petersburg's metalworking and machine construction establishments played, in Lenin's words, 'a vanguard role' in political protest.[36] These workers dominated the strike movement in general because they constituted the largest single group involved in political unrest. The proportion of strikes in the metalworking and machine construction industries which can be

Table 8.xii: St Petersburg Province: Number and % of Political Strikes, by Industry, 1912–3 July 1914

Industry	1912		1913		Jan.–3 July 1914		Total: 1912–3 July 1914	
	no.	%	no.	%	no.	%	no.	%
Animal products	14	2.7	21	2.2	20	2.2	55	2.3
Chemicals	4	0.8	8	0.9	4	0.4	16	0.6
Commercial–industrial	–	–	–	–	–	–	–	–
Communications	5	0.9	10	1.1	4	0.4	19	0.8
Construction	–	–	3	0.3	–	–	3	0.1
Food/drink/tobacco	15	2.9	71	7.6	90	9.8	176	7.4
Gold/silver/bronze	11	2.2	42	4.5	26	2.8	79	3.3
Metals and machines	216	42.4	422	44.9	500	54.2	1,138	48.0
Mineral products	12	2.4	11	1.2	3	0.3	26	1.1
Miscellaneous	–	–	–	–	–	–	–	–
Paper and printing	72	14.1	151	16.1	84	9.1	307	12.9
Tailoring	50	9.8	60	6.4	73	7.9	183	7.7
Textiles	57	11.2	71	7.6	75	8.1	203	8.6
Woodworking	54	10.6	69	7.3	44	4.8	167	7.0
TOTAL	510	100.0	939	100.1	923	100.0	2,372	99.8

Table 8.xiii: St Petersburg Province: Number and % of Political Strikers, by Industry, 1912–3 July 1914

Industry	1912		1913		Jan.–3 July 1914		Total: 1912–3 July 1914	
	no.	%	no.	%	no.	%	no.	%
Animal products	13,900	4.5	14,372	3.0	27,360	4.2	55,632	3.9
Chemicals	1,310	0.4	3,915	0.8	3,100	0.5	8,325	0.6
Commercial–industrial	–	–	–	–	–	–	–	–
Communications	4,830	1.6	1,291	0.3	640	0.1	6,761	0.5
Construction	–	–	85	–	–	–	85	–
Food/drink/tobacco	7,300	2.4	22,975	4.8	68,047	10.4	98,322	6.8
Gold/silver/bronze	1,207	0.4	3,376	0.7	1,304	0.2	5,887	0.4
Metals and machines	183,011	59.0	326,085	68.1	438,366	67.0	947,462	65.6
Mineral products	2,219	0.7	2,968	0.6	1,200	0.2	6,387	0.4
Miscellaneous	–	–	–	–	–	–	–	–
Paper and printing	14,422	4.7	21,307	4.5	21,197	3.2	56,926	3.9
Tailoring	600	0.2	800	0.2	1,258	0.2	2,658	0.2
Textiles	73,580	23.7	69,434	14.5	80,755	12.3	223,769	15.5
Woodworking	7,750	2.5	12,171	2.5	11,535	1.8	31,456	2.2
TOTAL	310,129	100.1	478,779	100.0	654,762	100.1	1,443,670	100.0

classed as political rose from over 40 per cent in 1912 and 1913 to 54 per cent in the first six months of 1914. During the period 1912–July 1914 never less than 59 per cent of all striking workers in these industries pursued political objectives.

In their intensity, too, political disputes in the metalworking and machine construction industries surpassed the other manufacturing sectors, involving about 300 per cent of their employees in 1912 and 460 per cent in 1914 (see Table 8.xiv). The dominance and intensity of political strikes within heavy industry imparted the political colouring to the pre-war strike movement in the capital as a whole. At the very outset of the surge of political stoppages in 1912, workers in the metals and machine-building trades comprised almost two-thirds of participants in the Lena protests and May Day strikes. Thereafter in every quarter of the ensuing two years their share never fell below three-fifths. In contrast to other branches of manufacturing, metalworkers formed a slightly lower proportion of strikers in the mass commemorative or sympathetic stoppages (in the range of 50 to 60 per cent of the total) but a higher ratio in strikes concerning workers' political rights (in the range of 90 per cent of the total). Thus metalworkers constituted four-fifths of all participants in the protests against the repression of the labour press in July and Septem-

Table 8.xiv: *St Petersburg Province: Total Number of Political Strikers Each Year as % of Total Labour Force, by Industry, 1912–3 July 1914*

Industry	1912	1914	1914 (to 3 July)
Animal products	99.6	103.0	141.6
Chemicals	10.6	27.5	17.2
Commercial–industrial	–	–	–
Communications	9.4	2.5	1.2
Construction	–	–	–
Food/drink/tobacco	43.6	129.2	333.5
Gold/silver/bronze	17.2	48.2	18.6
Metals and machines	293.1	407.6	459.8
Mineral products	10.7	13.9	5.4
Miscellaneous	–	–	–
Paper and printing	75.8	102.3	86.5
Tailoring	1.1	1.4	2.3
Textiles	183.0	160.8	167.2
Woodworking	106.8	169.7	129.8
As % of the factory labour force	182.1	253.3	287.3
As % of total labour force	41.3	63.7	87.1

ber 1913, but only between 50 and 60 per cent of strikers involved in May Day stoppages in 1913. Such figures attest to a greater degree of political awareness on the part of workers in heavy industry and a readiness to move from a generalised discontent with the monarchy to a more active defence of the limited rights granted labour in the first Russian revolution. The data reinforce the evidence presented in earlier chapters that skilled metalworkers (in particular in machine construction and electrical engineering) displayed a higher level of political participation than other groups of wage earners, as is also exemplified by their membership of revolutionary cells and trade unions and readership of the socialist press. It may also be worth stressing that the propensity of metalworkers in the capital for political protest was significantly greater than that of those in the Empire as a whole who comprised 57 per cent of all strikers in 1912, 68 per cent in 1913 and 63 per cent in 1914.[37]

The second most important contributor to political conflicts comprised mill hands (Tables 8.xii and 8.xiii). The textile sector's share of the aggregate of political stoppages, however, was far less than heavy industry's. At its peak in 1912, it reached 11 per cent of all political strikes and 24 per cent of all political strikers. Although the absolute number of political strikes and strikers in textiles rose modestly in the next year and a half, the proportion contributed by the industry declined significantly to 8 per cent of political strikes and 15 per cent of strikers in 1913. Accordingly the intensity of strikes in textiles was both far less than in metalworking and declined over time, from 183 per cent of textile employees in 1912 to 167 per cent in 1914 (Table 8.xiv). The capital's textile workers followed the national trend for the industry. In 1912 mill hands contributed a quarter of political strikers nationally, but by 1914 their share had sunk to 15 per cent.[38] On the other hand, as Tables 8.viii. and 8.ix. reveal, those textile workers who did cease working did so over-whelmingly for political reasons. Approximately 70 per cent of all textile strikes and strikers were politically motivated. Tables 8.x and 8.xi demonstrate that in 1912 the peak involvement of textile work-ers in political strikes occurred in the last rather than in the second quarter of the year, a result of the two October political stoppages, when 27 to 31 per cent of political strikers were mill hands. In 1913, by contrast, the second quarter accounted for 56 per cent of the year's political stoppages among textile workers, the anniversary of the Lena tragedy and May Day attracting a broader sympathy than the July and September political strikes when only 6–9 per cent of political strikers were mill hands. This pattern was repeated in 1914 when the number of textile strikers in the two political strikes in May reached 14–21 per cent of the total.

The contribution made by all other branches of manufacturing to political unrest in St Petersburg was more modest, rising from 17 per cent in 1912 and 1913 to 22 per cent in the first half of 1914 – a level and trend very similar to that of the country as a whole.[39] As Tables 8.viii and 8.ix indicate, however, there were variations from industry to industry. Workers in chemicals, the fashioning of articles of gold, silver and bronze, mineral products and tailoring never comprised more than 2 per cent of participants in political strikes in each of the three years. On the other hand, animal products, food processing, paper and printing and woodworking were more affected by political discontent, accounting for 14 per cent of political strikers in 1912 and 1913 and for almost one-fifth in 1914. In 1912 and 1913, the intensity of political strikes rose markedly in food processing, the manufacture of gold and silver articles, paper and printing and woodworking, but only slightly in the animal product, mineral and tailoring industries (Table 8.xiv). In 1914, by contrast, the intensity of political strikes fell in chemicals, gold and silver, paper and printing and woodworking, whilst at the same time it underwent a rise in animal products and a major surge in food processing (Table 8.xiv). By 1914 the labour force in the food, drink and tobacco sector ranked second to metalworkers in the depth of its political disaffection. In the industries under consideration, moreover, a majority of workers withdrawing their labour did so for political reasons. As Table 8.ix shows, the proportion of strikers classed as political also varied considerably between industries, from a high of 90 per cent in food processing and woodworking in 1914 to a low of 47 per cent in tailoring in 1913. There was, too, a discernible tendency for the bulk of political strikes and strikers in the latter group of industries to be concentrated in stoppages of a commemorative or mass sympathy nature (Tables 8.x and 8.xi). In 1912 in tailoring for example, 60 per cent of all political strikes and strikers occurred in the second quarter of the year, coinciding with the Lena and May Day stoppages. In food processing, too, the corresponding figures were approximately 70 and 80 per cent. Only in the paper and printing industry was the distribution of political strikers more evenly distributed across the spectrum of protest. In 1914, for instance, just 2 per cent of 9 January and May Day strikers were printers compared with almost 8 per cent of those involved in the protests against the exclusion of left-wing deputies from the legislature on 22 April. This exceptional pattern reinforces statistically the impression gained from other evidence that the printers, like the metalworkers, possessed a relatively high degree of political consciousness.

Many variables moulded the differences in the incidence and intensity of political stoppages within the several branches of manufacturing industry. Levels of skill, degrees of literacy, size of plant, the ratio of the sexes, urban roots and village ties and length of service in industry all interacted to shape particular workers' responses to political developments prior to the war.

It has become an axiom among Soviet and many Western historians that the high concentration of workers in St Petersburg metal-working facilitated mass mobilisation in the industry, political education and communication.[40] Even within heavy industry, however, this explanation requires modification. Apart from the fact that in the large metals factories there were numerous small and specialised shops, an analysis of individual metal plants' involvement in pre-war political stoppages reveals that only four of the eleven giant establishments which employed over 2,000 workers apiece were affected by more than a quarter of the 26 mass stoppages of a political nature.[41] On the other hand, 23 plants whose labour forces ranged between 500 and 2,000 operatives were each hit by more than six political stoppages; fourteen of them by fifteen or more political strikes apiece.[42] More remarkably 43 factories with payrolls numbering 100 to 500 employees each endured seven or more politically inspired walk-outs; eleven of them, fifteen or more political strikes each.[43] The metalworking plants most prone to political disturbances were the medium-sized and smaller establishments in machine construction and electrical engineering rather than the gigantic mixed production plants or the ordnance manufactories or the shipyards. Concentration in large units of production was not the sole determinant of worker participation in political strikes, as is evident from an examination of other branches of manufacturing. Thus the textile industry was dominated by mills employing in excess of 1,000 hands, but came a poor second in militancy both in Moscow in September and October 1905 and to St Petersburg metalworkers in the years immediately before the war.[44] The prevalence of small-scale artisanal modes of production in food processing, printing, the treatment of animal products and woodworking proved no barrier to collective action in political protest or to unionisation (see Chapter 7).

Another assumption prevalent among historians is that industries like the treatment of animal products, chemicals, food processing, tailoring and textiles, with a high ratio of poorly paid, unskilled or semi-skilled young women and girls were far less politically active.[45] In these branches of manufacture female employees were mostly unmarried adolescents, less literate than their male counterparts, poorly paid with little sense of trade identity and, as the high rate of labour turnover attests, little commitment to their work. All these factors contributed to the relative passivity and lack of political consciousness among women workers. Yet this should not be exaggerated. The data analysed earlier in this chapter showed that in fact female unskilled or little skilled wage earners in animal products food processing (at least in 1913 and 1914) and textiles were increasingly drawn into the political strike movement or, more accurately, into the mass commemorative or sympathy strikes. More women were coming to share the revived and diffuse growing working-class discontent with the Tsarist political system. Contrary to Dr Mandel's view, therefore, women workers were not responsive merely to short-term economic goals.[46] But as the evidence analysed in earlier chapters relating to trade unionisation, readership of socialist newspapers, educational societies and membership of revolutionary groups revealed, female operatives seemed unable to sustain consistent participation in working-class politics outside the medium of the strike or give organisational focus to their grievances.

More significant variables in determining political strike militancy were skill levels and urban roots. The metals industry suffered far more than any other sector because its plants, especially in machine construction and electrical engineering, contained the highest ratios of skilled, well-paid, literate, younger males, men who for the most part had been born in the city, were fully absorbed into urban culture and possessed a greater commitment to their trade and place of work. The industry, too, contained a large share of worker-intellectuals. In some of the artisanal trades like printing and woodworking skill, in conjunction with literacy, was a factor favouring attraction into the political struggle. On the other hand, printing also illustrates the fact that very high levels of skill, trade identity and the presence of cadre workers did not necessarily translate into a corresponding degree of strike militancy.[47] In the total numbers of political strikers and in the political intensity of its strikes the paper and printing sector lagged well behind textiles with its very different social profile (Tables 8.ix and 8.xiv). No simple explanation exists for this difference. The prevalence of small units of production with their allegedly paternalistic relationships between owners and workers was not the determining factor.[48] Both food processing and woodworking, as well as animal products, displayed a greater propensity for participation in political strikes than printing (see Table 8.xiv). Yet those three industrires contained very many small units of production with notoriously harsh exploitation of their labour forces. As both David Mandel and Steve Smith have suggested, the print trade did possess a higher ratio of very highly paid, better educated and urban-born workers in the form of the typesetters. These 'labour aristocrats' enjoyed more direct contact with educated society in their work and tended to regard themselves as a cut above other workers.[49] Such factors may have attenuated the printers' commitment to the political strike as a form of protest, but they did not preclude a high degree of labour activism as such or opposition to Tsardom. In 1913 the printers were by far the most organised group of workers in the capital, with 22 per cent of the labour force represented in the union of printers, and the union's leadership had always been Social Democratic in its orientation.

In the case of commercial–industrial employees, the history of 1905 in Moscow and of Paris before the First World War both show that white-collar workers could be attracted to revolution and socialism.[50] Yet in the years prior to the war St Petersburg's white-collar workers displayed minimal signs of overt political disaffection. In the absence of detailed research by scholars on this social stratum in Imperial Russia, explanations must be conjectural. Although this category was as highly stratified as the working class, its intermediate social position and petty-bourgeois status and aspirations may have led, as in Imperial Germany, to a cultural and political segregation from the working class.[51] With regard to the railways, Henry Reichman has argued that the repression after 1905 and the *de facto* militarisation of the railroads crushed the potential for dissent.[52]

While the mighty swell of pre-war political stoppages can rightly be interpreted as an expression of working-class hostility towards the Tsarist monarchy, it would be erroneous to conclude, as Soviet historians do, that it was also directed against capitalism as such or that it signified the conversion of St Petersburg's masses to the Bolshevik cause.

As previous chapters have endeavoured to show, the debility of the revolutionary underground, the inherent frailties of the trade unions, educational societies and insurance funds, the vigilance of the police and the diversion of revolutionary energies into factional squabbling had interacted to deprive the Bolsheviks of firm conduits to the mass of ordinary factory people, artisans and white-collar workers. At best the Leninists had wrestled from their Menshevik rivals much of their following among skilled workers in the open labour institutions.

Soviet historians, however, would argue that, in the words of E. E. Kruze, 'the chief demands of workers in the mass political strikes were the general demands of the minimum programme of the Bolshevik party: a democratic republic, the confiscation of gentry lands, the eight-hour day.'[53] They emphatically reject the contemporary Menshevik claim that the political strike movement centred on their faction's slogan of 'freedom of coalition'.[54] A thorough examination of all resolutions passed at factory meetings in the course of the twenty-six mass political stoppages and published in the socialist press upholds neither of these assertions.[55] In at least seven of the twenty-six stoppages no resolutions seem to have been passed at all. Of the remaining nineteen mass political walk-outs, fourteen witnessed the adoption of resolutions, which merely expressed general sympathy for the victims of some arbitrary action by the authorities. This was particularly the case in commemorative strikes, such as the anniversary of 9 January 1905, the Lena massacre, and on May Day. There are only eight mass strikes in which specific political demands were put forward in factory resolutions. In three of these (1 May 1913, 6 November 1913 and 9 January 1914) some resolutions combined both Bolshevik and Menshevik slogans. Menshevik-inspired resolutions (forty-three in total) appear in five of the stoppages. A mere two resolutions containing the Bolsheviks' three political demands were to be found in two of the political strikes.[56]

Some general conclusions may be drawn from this evidence. In the first place, the presentation of specific political demands was a comparatively rare phenomenon, a fact not unrelated, perhaps, to the relative paucity of revolutionary cells in the factories and workshops (see Chapter 5). Secondly the resolutions do not reveal a significant degree of commitment to the political programmes of either Social Democratic party, least of all the Bolsheviks. This fact reinforces the finding in earlier chapters that the degree of party identification among the mass of workers (the skilled excepted) was low. Thirdly the complete absence in the resolutions of demands for the overthrow of capitalism is particularly striking. Whatever the criticisms of conditions in the factories and workshops and demands for improvements therein, the evidence suggests that until 1914 at least workers in the capital had come to accept the factory system, industrial society and the capitalist method of production. The Tsar's ministers and officials were correct in their anxiety that the pre-war strike movement revealed a deep antipathy to the regime among broad sections of the capital's work-force. But they should have drawn comfort from the fact that this discontent had not been translated into firm political commitment to any revolutionary party or into opposition to the existing economic structure. Their apprehensions, too, concerning the role of revolutionary activists in the political strike movement were rather misplaced. As the detailed analysis of the topic in Chapters 4 and 5 concluded, no socialist agitation occurred before thirteen of the mass political stoppages, and only limited preparations were initiated in thirteen others. All revolutionary plans for mass demonstrations in the city centre like-wise came to naught with the solitary exception of 9 January 1914. A more significant and dangerous role had been played by the Social Democratic daily newspapers. As in French strikes in the last quarter of the nineteenth century, strikes were also spread by the visits of crowds of strikers to neighbouring factories still at work.[57] In the political strikes wage earners gave vent to their opposition to the regime and to feelings of solidarity by leaving the factories en masse singing revolutionary songs and attempting to form local demonstrations on nearby streets. This happened during sixteen of the twenty-six political stoppages. Following a European-wide trend, violence was rare on these occasions.[58] It was limited to throwing stones or attempting to free comrades arrested by the police. A mere six such incidents could be located in the press and police archives.

III

As a comparison of numbers of strikes and strikers in Tables 8.viii and 8.ix with Tables 8.xix and 8.xx shows, political factors did not comprise the sole cause of disruption to the normal rhythms of industrial life in St Petersburg before the war. On the contrary, stoppages motivated by purely economic objectives were responsible for the bulk of working days lost in St Petersburg during the years immediately prior to the war.

The capital did not occupy such a pre-eminent position within the pre-war upsurge of economic disputes in the Russian Empire as it did in political protest. Although it accounted for approximately 55 per cent of all Empire-wide participants in economic strikes in 1912, its share of the total number of Russian economic strikers declined precipitately to 30–33 per cent in 1913 and the first six months of

Table 8.xv: *St Petersburg Province: Economic Strikes by Industry, 1912–3 July 1914 (% of all strikes in each industry)*

Industry	1912 %	1913 %	Jan.–3 July 1914 %	Total 1912–3 July 1914 %
Animal products	30.0	68.7	35.5	53.4
Chemicals	60.0	20.0	76.5	56.8
Commercial–industrial	100.0	–	100.0	100.0
Communications	68.7	68.7	95.5	86.0
Construction	100.0	85.7	100.0	94.2
Food/drink/tobacco	90.5	55.6	41.6	62.7
Gold/silver/bronze	50.0	65.6	13.4	54.6
Metals and machines	30.3	25.8	23.7	25.8
Mineral products	52.0	31.2	57.1	45.8
Miscellaneous	100.0	100.0	100.0	100.0
Paper and printing	48.6	24.1	30.0	33.1
Tailoring	21.9	50.0	28.4	36.0
Textiles	28.7	29.7	25.7	28.0
Woodworking	39.3	46.1	41.3	42.0
ALL INDUSTRIES	47.3	39.5	33.6	39.4

1914. This downturn reflected the growing predominance of political motives in labour disturbances in St Petersburg in 1913 and 1914.

Throughout the pre-war period the rate of growth of economic strikes in the capital lagged behind that of political stoppages. Whereas totals of political strikes and strikers rose by 84 per cent and 54 per cent in 1912 and 1913 respectively, the corresponding ratios fell from 33 per cent to 18 per cent. As Table 8.xv. demonstrates, the proportion of strikes classed as economic fell from 47 per cent of the total for the province in 1912 to 34 per cent early in 1914. The degree of participation in economic strikes, which was always at a level considerably below that for political strikes, likewise mirrored this trend. The number of strikers registered as economic decreased from 24 per cent of all strikers in 1912 to 17 per cent in 1914 (see Table 8.xvi). The intensity of economic strikes was also well below the level of that displayed in political disputes. A comparison between Tables 8.xxi and 8.xiv reveals that the intensity of economic stoppages (as measured by the number of strikers as a percentage of the total factory labour force) was three times less that of political strikes in 1912, four times less in 1913 and seven times less in 1914. The decline in all the above-mentioned indices strongly reinforces

Table 8.xvi: St Petersburg Province: Economic Strikers by Industry, 1912–3 July 1914 (% of all strikers in each industry)

Industry	1912 %	1913 %	Jan.–3 July 1914 %	Total 1912–3 July 1914 %
Animal products	41.1	33.4	37.9	37.7
Chemicals	24.1	8.3	38.3	24.1
Commercial–industrial	100.0	–	100.0	100.0
Communications	69.1	72.0	70.5	70.5
Construction	100.0	53.3	51.6	51.6
Food/drink/tobacco	41.2	29.4	17.6	17.6
Gold/silver/bronze	9.9	19.5	18.6	18.6
Metals and machines	15.9	15.2	12.1	12.1
Mineral products	38.7	14.3	26.0	26.0
Miscellaneous	100.0	100.0	100.0	100.0
Paper and printing	35.4	13.8	22.1	22.1
Tailoring	18.8	52.7	32.7	32.7
Textiles	24.1	28.3	23.4	23.4
Woodworking	24.4	19.2	16.5	16.5
ALL INDUSTRIES	24.0	19.4	17.3	17.3

the point that as 1913 and 1914 wore on, the strike energies of the capital's factory workers were increasingly being channelled into protests of a political nature. Nor did all economic conflicts necessarily involve the entire payroll of an establishment. In 1912, 32 per cent of economic strikes were in fact only partial walk-outs. Although this proportion underwent a diminution to 27 per cent the next year, it rose again to almost 40 per cent in 1914. On the other hand, economic disturbances inflicted far greater harm than one-day political walk-outs on the production process. According to the Soviet investigator Kruze, the capital's industrial community suffered 1.8 million lost working days in nine months in 1912 and 3 million both in the following year and the first seven months of 1914.[59] In this it reflected a national trend. According to the Department of Industry, in 1912 0.9 working days were lost for every one political striker and 10.6 working days for every one economic striker. By 1914 the corresponding figures had increased to 1.7 days and 14.3 days.[60]

Although the year 1911 and the first three months of 1912 had witnessed a modest upsurge in economic disputes in St Petersburg, the Lena shootings exerted as powerful a stimulus to economic unrest in the city as they did to expression of political discontent (see Tables 8.xvii and 8.xviii). Whereas the first quarter of 1912 accounted for a mere 0.8 per cent of the sum total of economic strikes in the year and 4.3 per cent of economic strikers, the second quarter was responsible for 40 per cent of economic stoppages and 52 per cent of economic strikers. In the spring months industrialists endured an explosion of long-restrained frustrations and unresolved grievances over changes in factory and workshop working conditions since 1907. Political protest acted as the spark to the combustible material of economic complaints. The scale of economic protest declined in the summer months. In the last quarter of the year, although the number of economic strikes was lower than in the spring and summer months, the number of strikers involved, while below that for April–June, rose substantially above summer levels. As in the spring, the politically inspired walk-outs of the autumn exerted a knock-on effect.

1913 saw no diminution in economic unrest. Unusually the first three months of 1913 saw the level of economic strike activity rise above that for the last quarter of 1912. As in the spring of the previous year, the mass political strikes of April to June 1913 acted as a spur to the unleashing of economic discontent. In comparison with the first quarter the aggregate of economic strikes soared by 104 per cent and of strikers by 45 per cent. For this reason the quarter accounted for 44 per cent of all economic strikes in the year and 39 per cent of strikers. The number of economic disputes in the spring (270) far exceeded those for the same period a year earlier (183),

Table 8.xvii: St Petersburg Province; Economic Strikes by Industry ('Three-monthly Periods) 1912–3 July 1914, (% of total)

Industry	1912				Total	no.
	Jan.–Mar.	Apr.–June	July–Sept.	Oct.–Dec.		
Animal products	–	66.6	16.6	16.6	99.8	6
Chemicals	–	66.6	–	33.3	99.9	6
Commercial–industrial	–	20.0	60.0	20.0	100.0	5
Communications	–	54.5	–	45.5	100.0	11
Construction	–	50.0	35.7	14.3	100.0	28
Food/drink/tobacco	–	18.9	76.9	4.2	100.0	143
Gold/silver/bronze	–	27.2	18.2	54.5	99.9	11
Metals and machines	3.2	57.4	14.9	24.5	100.0	94
Mineral products	–	84.6	15.4	–	100.0	13
Miscellaneous	–	33.3	66.6	–	99.9	3
Paper and printing	1.5	45.6	29.4	23.5	100.0	68
Tailoring	–	14.3	50.0	35.7	100.0	14
Textiles	–	26.1	13.0	60.9	100.0	23
Woodworking	–	54.3	11.4	34.3	100.0	35
ALL INDUSTRIES	0.8	39.8	38.7	20.7	100.0	460

Table 8.xvii: (Continued)

Industry	1913				Total	no.
	Jan.–Mar.	Apr.–June	July–Sept.	Oct.–Dec.		
Animal products	2.1	60.9	19.6	17.4	100.0	46
Chemicals	50.0	–	–	50.0	100.0	2
Commercial-industrial	–	–	–	–	–	–
Communications	54.5	22.7	13.6	9.1	99.9	22
Construction	5.6	72.2	16.6	5.6	100.0	18
Food/drink/tobacco	14.6	46.1	15.7	23.6	100.0	89
Gold/silver/bronze	37.5	21.3	40.0	1.2	100.0	80
Metals and machines	14.3	43.5	25.9	16.3	100.0	147
Mineral products	40.0	20.0	40.0	–	100.0	5
Miscellaneous	–	–	83.3	16.7	100.0	6
Paper and printing	22.9	54.2	6.2	16.7	100.0	48
Tailoring	1.6	91.7	1.6	5.0	99.9	60
Textiles	23.3	50.0	10.0	16.6	99.9	30
Woodworking	10.2	8.5	59.3	22.0	100.0	59
ALL INDUSTRIES	17.3	44.1	24.2	14.4	100.0	612

Table 8.xvii: (Continued)

| Industry | 1914 (to 3 July) | | | |
	Jan.–Mar.	Apr.–3 July	Total	no.
Animal products	45.5	54.5	100.0	11
Chemicals	15.4	84.6	100.0	13
Commercial–industrial	50.0	50.0	100.0	4
Communications	84.5	15.5	100.0	84
Construction	33.3	66.6	99.9	3
Food/drink/tobacco	28.1	71.9	100.0	64
Gold/silver/bronze	75.0	25.0	100.0	4
Metals and machines	25.2	74.8	100.0	155
Mineral products	–	100.0	100.0	4
Miscellaneous	12.5	87.5	100.0	8
Paper and printing	61.1	38.9	100.0	36
Tailoring	75.9	24.1	100.0	29
Textiles	30.8	69.2	100.0	26
Woodworking	37.0	63.0	100.0	27
ALL INDUSTRIES	43.6	56.4	100.0	468

although the total of participants fell by slightly over a tenth. In some respects the summer months of 1913 reflected the previous year's pattern with a marked decrease in economic stoppages, mirroring the similar trend in political actions. But the plateau reached was higher than a year earlier, with a doubling in the aggregate of participants from 9,000 to 18,000. Economic unrest in the autumn, like the political, followed a downard curve as regards the number of strikes. In contrast the total of strikers grew by a quarter. Overall in 1913 economic strikes were concentrated in the first six months.

In comparison with the first six months of 1913, the period January–June 1914 witnessed a rise in the number of economic strikes by 24 per cent and of strikers by 18 per cent. This acceleration in the tempo of economic stoppages mirrored the trend in political disputes, but at a lower level. In comparison with the last six months of 1913, however, the respective increases were of the order of 100 per cent.

The industry-by-industry analysis of economic stoppages, summarised in Tables 8.xix and 8.xx, shows both similarities and differences with that for politically motivated disputes.

In the first place, the service sector remained as indifferent to the swelling tide of economic discontent as it did to political protest. Domestic servants, commercial–industrial employees, postal and

Table 8.xviii: St Petersburg Province: Number of Strikers Involved in Economic Strikes, by Industry (Three-monthly Periods) 1912–3 July 1914 (% of total)

Industry	1912				Total	no.
	Jan.–Mar.	Apr.–June	July–Sept.	Oct.–Dec.		
Animal products	–	98.8	0.01	0.01	98.82	9,706
Chemicals	–	96.4	–	3.6	100.0	415
Commercial–industrial	–	1.4	97.9	0.7	100.0	517
Communications	–	19.4	1.6	79.0	100.0	10,812
Construction	–	49.0	37.7	13.3	100.0	1,314
Food/drink/tobacco	–	43.2	49.8	7.0	100.0	5,117
Gold/silver/bronze	–	37.9	15.1	47.0	100.0	132
Metals and machines	11.9	70.5	3.2	14.3	99.9	34,600
Mineral products	–	99.1	0.9	–	100.0	1,402
Miscellaneous*	–	–	100.0	–	100.0	112
Paper and printing	0.5	47.0	33.2	19.3	100.0	7,904
Tailoring	–	6.4	43.2	50.4	100.0	139
Textiles	–	21.4	6.9	71.7	100.0	23,353
Woodworking	–	47.3	1.0	51.7	100.0	2,495
ALL INDUSTRIES	4.3	51.8	9.5	34.4	100.0	98,018

Table 8.xviii: (Continued)

Industry	1913				Total	no.
	Jan.–Mar.	Apr.–June	July–Sept.	Oct.–Dec.		
Animal products	–	59.3	16.6	24.1	100.0	7,218
Chemicals	96.8	–	–	3.2	100.0	310
Commercial–industrial	–	–	–	–	–	–
Communications	48.8	28.9	19.6	2.7	100.0	3,321
Construction	61.9	–	38.1	–	100.0	97
Food/drink/tobacco	27.9	8.4	13.3	50.4	100.0	9,576
Gold/silver/bronze	55.5	17.2	26.7	0.6	100.0	818
Metals and machines	29.2	30.8	19.9	20.1	100.0	58,487
Mineral products	32.3	38.4	29.3	–	100.0	495
Miscellaneous*	–	–	33.3	66.6	99.9	555
Paper and printing	11.0	58.6	4.7	25.6	99.9	3,413
Tailoring	3.9	89.6	2.6	3.9	100.0	893
Textiles	28.6	61.6	2.5	7.2	99.9	27,419
Woodworking	4.4	20.2	58.8	16.5	99.9	2,901
ALL INDUSTRIES	26.6	38.7	15.5	19.2	100.0	115,503

Table 8.xviii: (Continued)

| Industry | 1914 (to 3 July) | | | |
	Jan.–Mar.	Apr.–3 July	Total	no.
Animal products	98.0	2.0	100.0	16,690
Chemicals	3.6	96.4	100.0	1,922
Commercial–industrial	72.0	28.0	100.0	25
Communications	40.5	59.5	100.0	2,007
Construction	97.3	2.7	100.0	260
Food/drink/tobacco	82.0	18.0	100.0	6,313
Gold/silver/bronze	96.2	3.8	100.0	395
Metals and machines	18.3	81.7	100.0	36,964
Mineral products	–	100.0	100.0	338
Miscellaneous*	50.7	49.3	100.0	986
Paper and printing	78.0	22.0	100.0	4,846
Tailoring	85.1	14.9	100.0	262
Textiles	26.7	73.3	100.0	17,418
Woodworking	43.4	56.6	100.0	809
ALL INDUSTRIES	44.1	55.9	100.0	89,235

* The discrepancy between the distribution of strikes and strikers in the miscellaneous category arises from the fact that the number of participants involved in the solitary strike in the second quarter of 1912 is unknown.

telegraph workers and the labour force in municipal public utilities constituted a derisory 0.5 per cent of participants in economic stoppages. The few disputes which occurred in the public utility sector in the autumn of 1913 involved only a handful of workers,[61] and only on the eve of the war did confrontation emerge in the commercial sector when, in the shops located in the city markets, a fairly widespread movement gathered apace among sales assistants to curtail the intolerably lengthy working day by forcibly closing premises at 7 o'clock in the evening.[62] Within St Petersburg manufacturing industry, however, economic conflicts were somewhat more evenly spread amongst the various branches of production than in the case of political disputes. Thus in the entire period from January 1912 to 3 July 1914 wage earners in the metalworking and textile industries formed 78 per cent of all strikers in political and economic disputes combined but 81 per cent of participants in political strikes alone. Together, these two branches contributed 60 per cent of all strikers in economic conflicts. Conversely, while all other sectors of production furnished only

Table 8.xix: *St Petersburg Province: Economic Strikes by Industry, 1912–3 July 1914 (% of total)*

Industry	1912 no.	1912 %	1913 no.	1913 %	Jan.–3 July 1914 no.	Jan.–3 July 1914 %	Total: 1912–3 July 1914 no.	Total: 1912–3 July 1914 %
Animal products	6	1.3	46	7.5	11	2.4	63	4.1
Chemicals	6	1.3	2	0.3	13	2.8	21	1.4
Commercial–industrial	5	1.1	–	–	4	0.8	9	0.6
Communications	11	2.4	22	3.4	84	17.9	117	7.6
Construction	28	6.1	18	2.9	3	0.6	49	3.2
Food/drink/tobacco	143	31.1	89	14.5	64	13.7	296	19.2
Gold/silver/bronze	11	2.4	80	13.1	4	0.8	95	6.2
Metals and machines	94	20.4	147	24.0	155	33.1	396	25.7
Mineral products	13	2.8	5	0.8	4	0.8	22	1.4
Miscellaneous	3	0.7	6	0.9	8	1.7	17	1.1
Paper and printing	68	14.8	48	7.8	36	7.8	152	9.9
Tailoring	14	3.0	60	9.8	29	6.2	103	6.7
Textiles	23	5.0	30	4.9	26	5.5	79	5.1
Woodworking	35	7.6	59	9.6	27	5.8	121	7.9
TOTAL	460	100.0	612	99.5	468	99.9	1,540	100.1

about one-fifth of participants in political stoppages, their share of economic strikers amounted to a third.

As in the case of strikes in general and political disputes in particular, metalworkers occupied the foremost place in economic stoppages. Over the timespan 1912–July 1914 they contributed a quarter of all economic strikes and slightly in excess of two-fifths of economic strikers (Tables 8.xix and 8.xx). The latter figure slightly exceeded metalworkers' contribution at the national level, where they furnished around a third of economic strikers.[63] On the other hand, the data outlined in the previous paragraph illustrate the fact that metalworkers were responsible for a far lower proportion of participants in economic clashes than in political strikes. Moreover, economic stoppages themselves accounted only for a fraction of strikers within heavy industry. Scarcely over a tenth of all strikers in metalworking participated in economic disputes (see Table 8.xvi). Further evidence for this tendency is provided by the fact that in engineering the intensity of economic strikes was far less than that of political stoppages (Table 8.xxi). Indeed a significant development occurred in this respect between 1913 and 1914. The first half of 1914 registered a decline of almost half in the intensity of the industry's

Table 8.xx: Number of Strikers Involved in Economic Strikes, by Industry, 1912–3 July 1914 (% of total)

Industry	1912		1913		Jan.–3 July 1914		Total: 1912–3 July 1914	
	no.	%	no.	%	no.	%	no.	%
Animal products	9,706	9.9	7,218	6.2	16,690	18.7	33,614	11.1
Chemicals	415	0.4	310	0.3	1,922	2.2	2,647	0.8
Commercial–industrial	517	0.5	—	—	25	–	542	0.002
Communications	10,812	11.0	3,321	2.9	2,007	2.2	16,140	5.3
Construction	1,314	1.3	97	0.008	260	0.3	1,671	0.6
Food/drink/tobacco	5,117	5.2	9,576	8.3	6,313	7.1	21,006	6.9
Gold/silver/bronze	132	0.1	818	0.7	395	0.4	1,345	0.4
Metals and machines	34,600	35.2	58,487	50.6	36,964	41.4	130,051	43.0
Mineral products	1,402	1.4	495	0.4	338	0.4	2,235	0.7
Miscellaneous	112	0.1	555	0.5	986	1.1	1,653	0.5
Paper and printing	7,904	8.1	3,413	3.0	4,846	5.4	16,163	5.3
Tailoring	139	0.1	893	0.8	262	0.3	1,294	0.4
Textiles	23,353	23.8	27,419	23.7	17,418	19.5	68,190	22.5
Woodworking	2,495	2.5	2,901	2.5	809	0.9	6,205	2.0
TOTAL	98,018	99.6	115,503	99.908	89,235	99.9	302,756	99.502

Table 8.xxi: *St Petersburg Province: Total Number of Economic Strikers Each Year as % of the Total Labour Force, by Industry, 1912–3 July 1914*

Industry	1912	1913	1914 (to 3 July)
Animal products	69.6	57.7	86.4
Chemicals	3.4	2.2	10.7
Commercial–industrial	0.003	–	–
Communications	20.9	6.4	3.9
Construction	0.007	0.0005	0.001
Food/drink/tobacco	30.6	53.8	30.9
Gold/silver/bronze	1.9	11.7	5.6
Metals and machines	55.4	73.1	38.8
Mineral products	6.8	2.3	1.5
Miscellaneous	0.003	1.4	2.4
Paper and printing	41.6	16.4	19.8
Tailoring	0.03	1.6	0.05
Textiles	58.1	63.5	36.1
Woodworking	34.4	40.5	9.1
As % of the factory labour force	57.5	61.1	39.2
As % of the total labour force	13.0	15.4	11.9

economic disputes, precisely as the numbers of metalworkers downing tools in politically inspired walk-outs surged dramatically. As will be argued later in this chapter, part of the explanation for this development lay in the accelerating tempo of defeats suffered by metalworkers in their economic conflicts. Within the industry, certain large plants with payrolls in excess of 1,000 operatives played an increasing role in strikes with economic aims. Between 1912 and 1914 the proportion of strikes in such establishments grew from 37 per cent to 50 per cent of the total. In 1912 large-scale enterprises also were responsible for over three-fifths of economic strikers in the industry. By 1914 their share had risen by another fifth. The Putilov plant alone, which employed over 10,000 workers, accounted for two-fifths to a quarter of this aggregate, suffering at least 62 economic disputes. On a lesser scale the Baltic Shipyards (7,000 workers) endured eight economic disputes and Neva Shipyards (4,000 workers) ten. In this respect there was a marked difference with political stoppages, where the weight of protest was carried far more by machine construction and electrical plants of medium and even small size rather than huge mixed production plants. The larger numbers of unskilled and semi-skilled in these latter establishments were more easily drawn into the economic than the political struggle. On the other hand other large-scale enterprises entirely escaped economic disturbances, including the state-owned Aleksandrovskii Locomotives, Arsenal, Ordnance and Sestroretsk arms-works.

Although the textile industry was responsible for a low proportion of economic strikes (hovering around 5 per cent), it occupied second place with respect to the number of participants in economic stoppages. In the intensity of its economic disputes it was roughly comparable with metalworking (Table 8.xxi). This pattern differed radically from that prevailing in political strikes. Furthermore the capital's textile workers contributed less to economic unrest than their counterparts in other provinces. Nationwide, textile workers constituted approximately two-fifths of economic strikers.[64] In 1912 the bulk of textile strikes occured in the fourth quarter but in 1913 in the spring months (Tables 8.xvii and 8.xviii). As in metalworking, mills with labour forces exceeding 1,000 hands carried the weight of unrest. Over the two and a half years these manufactories were responsible for three-fifths of textile economic strikes and almost nine-tenths of strikers. Finally, in 1914 mill operatives followed in a modest way the example of their more militant colleagues in metalworking in becoming more responsive to politically motivated industrial actions and less to economic considerations (Table 8.xxi).

Although the other branches of manufacturing in St Petersburg besides metalworking and textiles contributed more to the total of economic strikes than they did to political stoppages, it would be erroneous to conclude that the process was constant.

In 1912 two-fifths of all participants in St Petersburg economic strikes came from industries other than metalworking and textiles. In 1913 the ratio fell to a quarter before returning to two-fifths in the first six months of 1914. It follows that the contribution of St Petersburg's 'other' industries to economic stoppages was greater than their contribution to the capital's political strikes and greater than the contribution of 'other' industries to economic strikes in the Empire as a whole, where between 1912 and 1914 it hovered around a quarter.[65] Within the category 'other' industries, however, a distinction can be traced between two groups of industries. On the one hand, chemicals, the manufacture of gold and silver articles, minerals and tailoring contributed only between 2 and 3 per cent of all economic strikers, a contribution no greater than their share in political stoppages (Table 8.xx). On the other hand animal products, food processing, paper and printing and woodworking were far more affected by economic unrest, just as they were by political protests. These four branches accounted for approximately a quarter of all economic strikers in 1912 and 1914 and a fifth in 1913 (Table 8.xx). Although the four groups were responsible for a lower proportion of political strikers, nevertheless workers in these industries (except animal products) were increasingly driven by their mounting failure to force concessions from their employers into directing their focus of discontent along political channels. As Table 8.xxi demonstrates, in food processing and woodworking the intensity of economic strikes fell off sharply in 1914, whilst in printing the process occurred in 1913. In these three sectors, too, well over half the total of economic strikes over the entire period broke out in establishments whose labour forces numbered under 100 employees. In food processing, the proportion touched 86 per cent. Here most shutdowns affected bakeries rather than enterprises in brewing (3 strikes of a total of 229), confectionery or tobacco (13 strikes). On the other hand, the few plants with 1,000 and more employees of course contributed disproportionately to the aggregate of strikers. In animal products their share of the total reached 86 per cent, in food processing 59 per cent and in paper and printing 22 per cent.

A striking feature of economic stoppages in St Petersburg was the growing persistence and stubbornness with which they were pursued in 1912 and 1913. As Table 8.xxii makes clear, in the course of 1912 and 1913 the percentage of strikes lasting one day or between two and seven days declined from 15 per cent to a tenth and from 32 per cent to a quarter respectively. In stark contrast the proportion of disputes whose duration exceeded a month soared from 8 per cent to 32 per cent, an increase which came largely at the expense of the share of the total furnished by conflicts of intermediate length (8–30 days), which fell from 46 per cent to a third. 1914, however, ushered in a contrary trend, the proportion of strikes lasting longer than 30 days falling back to 14 per cent of the total and that of shorter term (2–7 days) and intermediate (8–30 days) stoppages rising to 39 per cent and 43 per cent respectively. It may be surmised that this reversal reflected both the great rise in the number of strikes lost by workers in 1913 and the linked phenomenon of the growing attractiveness of the political struggle.

The general pattern of changes in the length of economic strikes, however, was not uniform throughout all branches of manufacturing. Metalworking, certainly, followed the general tendency. Here there was an initial increase in the share of lengthy stoppages from 13 per cent in 1912 (8 strikes) to 43 per cent in 1913 (32 strikes). Under the influence of the factors outlined in the previous paragraph, the ratio slumped dramatically to 12 per cent in 1914. Establishments in heavy industry were affected by prolonged disputes irrespective of their size. Of the 46 strikes whose duration exceeded a month, 22 afflicted plants employing under a 1,000 wage earners. Some walkouts were of remarkable length. At the Siemens and Halske factories the entire work-force stayed out for 95 days in 1912. In 1913 the

Table 8.xxii: St Petersburg Province: Length of Economic Strikes, by Industry, 1912–3 July 1914*

Industry	1912					
	1 day	2–7 days	8–30 days	Over 30 days	Total	no.
Animal products	–	–	100.0	–	100.0	9,255
Chemicals	–	–	–	–	–	–
Commercial–industrial	–	–	100.0	–	100.0	500
Communications	41.9	42.3	3.1	12.6	99.9	9,715
Construction	19.0	81.0	–	–	100.0	790
Food/drink/tobacco	4.5	89.4	6.0	–	99.9	2,492
Gold/silver/bronze	38.7	30.6	30.6	–	99.9	62
Metals and machines	13.0	36.5	37.6	12.8	99.9	14,179
Mineral products	–	–	100.0	–	100.0	50
Miscellaneous	100.0	–	–	–	100.0	12
Paper and printing	11.6	12.7	40.2	35.5	100.0	5,202
Tailoring	31.9	33.3	8.7	26.1	100.0	69
Textiles	12.7	31.9	55.0	0.4	100.0	23,538
Woodworking	1.8	62.3	27.7	8.2	100.0	1,401
ALL INDUSTRIES	14.6	31.7	46.1	7.6	100.0	67,265

Table 8.xxii: (Continued)

Industry	1913				Total	no.
	1 day	2–7 days	8–30 days	Over 30 days		
Animal products	–	9.1	31.1	59.9	100.1	5,140
Chemicals	–	100.0	–	–	100.0	300
Commercial–industrial	–	–	–	–	–	–
Communications	46.7	30.8	19.0	2.5	99.0	3,151
Construction	–	100.0	–	–	100.0	82
Food/drink/tobacco	0.3	62.6	30.4	6.7	100.0	9,104
Gold/silver/bronze	–	–	98.8	1.2	100.0	805
Metals and machines	16.1	27.1	14.0	42.8	100.0	55,800
Mineral products	–	25.5	74.5	–	100.0	470
Miscellaneous	–	9.8	90.2	–	100.0	410
Paper and printing	15.1	8.9	8.7	67.4	100.1	3,410
Tailoring	8.2	81.6	10.2	–	100.0	49
Textiles	0.5	14.2	71.4	13.9	100.0	27,913
Woodworking	10.7	–	68.0	21.3	100.0	1,970
ALL INDUSTRIES	10.4	25.0	33.0	31.6	100.0	108,604

Industry	1914 (to 3 July)					
	1 day	2–7 days	8–30 days	Over 30 days	Total	no.
Animal products	–	67.2	32.6	0.2	100.0	14,875
Chemicals	–	1.0	99.0	–	100.0	1,705
Commercial–industrial	–	100.0	–	–	100.0	5
Communications	–	57.3	42.7	–	100.0	1,767
Construction	100.0	–	–	–	100.0	80
Food/drink/tobacco	–	48.7	51.3	–	100.0	5,792
Gold/silver/bronze	–	2.5	97.5	–	100.0	400
Metals and machines	7.7	39.4	41.1	11.8	100.0	29,308
Mineral products	–	–	–	100.0	100.0	100
Miscellaneous	–	100.0	–	–	100.0	26
Paper and printing	7.7	38.8	15.9	37.6	100.0	4,024
Tailoring	60.9	–	39.1	–	100.0	69
Textiles	–	8.4	55.6	36.0	100.0	15,425
Woodworking	37.6	35.8	26.6	–	100.0	534
ALL INDUSTRIES	3.9	38.5	43.3	14.4	100.0	74,110

* Percentages are based on the total number of strikers, where known.

Russian Society was shut down for 73 days, the Lessner plants for over 100 days, New Aivaz for 69 days and the Obuhnov arms-works for over four months in two separate conflicts. Beginning in 1913 the textile industry suffered a continuously escalating surge of very lengthy disputes despite an unceasingly high ratio of workers' defeats. In 1912 strikes lasting longer than 30 days formed only 0.4 per cent of the total. In 1913 the proportion had increased to 14 per cent. By 1914 it touched 36 per cent, a ratio three times as high as metalworking. In contrast, stoppages of less than seven days declined, from 44 per cent in 1912 to 8 per cent in 1914. While prolonged stoppages were rare in food-processing industries (only in 1913 did strikes longer than thirty days form 7 per cent of the total), the proportion of short strikes (under seven days) fell from 94 per cent of the total in 1912 to 49 per cent in 1914. In this industry, as in textiles, economic disputes became more stubborn on the eve of the war at the same time as its labour force became more responsive to political protest. In 1913 and 1914 small bakeries with less than 100 workers bore the brunt of strikes lasting longer than eight days rather than large tobacco plants. In the paper and printing and woodworking industries, too, there was an upward curve in the proportion of very lengthy strikes in 1912 and 1913, followed by steep decline in 1914.

Periods of economic upturn, such as St Petersburg industry experienced between 1911 and the outbreak of war, are normally conducive to labour's success in industrial disputes. Low unemployment, shortages of labour, particularly of skilled hands, high profits and pressing deadlines (especially in the case of armaments contracts won by the capital's heavy industry) all created circumstances favourable to wringing concessions from employers. This was certainly the case, for example, in nineteenth-century France.[66] But the quite remarkable feature about the outcome of economic stoppages in St Petersburg prior to the war (see Table 8.xxiii) is the extent to which the pattern of results differs from the norm. As early as 1912 workers won outright a mere 13 per cent of disputes. The following year their successes fell to just 7 per cent of the total and in 1914 to a miniscule 4 per cent. Conversely strikers lost 63 per cent of conflicts in 1912, 84 per cent in 1912 and 89 per cent in 1914. St Petersburg, moreover, was not an isolated case in this respect. It merely followed the national trend. According to the factory inspectorate in 1912, workers' successes comprised only 9 per cent of the aggregate of nationwide economic strikes. In the next two years this ratio sank further to 8 per cent and 6 per cent respectively. This stood in contrast to the revolutionary years of 1905 and 1906 when strikers' success rates reached 24 per cent and 35 per cent respectively.[67]

Table 8.xxiii: *St Petersburg Province: Outcome of Economic Strikes, 1912–3 July 1914**

Industry	W	1912 L	C	Total	no.
Animal products	–	100.0	–	100.0	9,535
Chemicals	–	–	–	–	–
Commercial–industrial	–	100.0	–	100.0	500
Communications	–	19.5	80.5	100.0	1,740
Construction	79.7	20.3	–	100.0	790
Food/drink/tobacco	29.1	47.1	23.8	100.0	3,871
Gold/silver/bronze	–	100.0	–	100.0	60
Metals and machines	15.2	59.9	24.9	100.0	28,202
Mineral products	31.8	–	68.2	100.0	440
Miscellaneous	100.0	–	–	100.0	12
Paper and printing	44.0	26.4	29.6	100.0	4,229
Tailoring	14.7	85.3	–	100.0	69
Textiles	2.8	68.2	29.0	100.0	21,770
Woodworking	23.3	15.3	61.4	100.0	1,401
ALL INDUSTRIES	12.5	62.8	24.7	100.0	72,619

Table 8.xxiii: *(Continued)*

Industry	W	1913 L	C	Total	no.
Animal products	–	91.6	8.4	100.0	6,024
Chemicals	–	–	100.0	100.0	300
Commercial–industrial	–	–	–	–	–
Communications	88.3	9.2	2.5	100.0	3,251
Construction	26.8	73.2	–	100.0	82
Food/drink/tobacco	12.2	84.1	3.7	100.0	5,690
Gold/silver/bronze	72.7	27.3	–	100.0	264
Metals and machines	5.8	88.5	5.7	100.0	47,931
Mineral products	–	–	100.0	100.0	120
Miscellaneous	–	–	–	–	410
Paper and printing	1.9	79.9	18.2	100.0	3,205
Tailoring	20.5	38.6	40.9	100.0	166
Textiles	0.1	87.3	12.6	100.0	24,510
Woodworking	0.6	56.3	43.1	100.0	1,854
ALL INDUSTRIES	7.2	84.2	8.6	100.0	93,807

Table 8.xxiii: (Continued)

Industry	1914 (to 3 July)				
	W	L	C	Total	no.
Animal products	0.3	99.7	–	100.0	16,387
Chemicals	1.4	98.6	–	100.0	1,232
Commercial–industrial	–	100.0	–	100.0	9
Communications	100.0	–	–	100.0	617
Construction	–	–	–	100.0	80
Food/drink/tobacco	1.1	84.7	14.2	100.0	5,644
Gold/silver/bronze	–	96.2	3.8	100.0	395
Metals and machines	3.5	90.0	6.5	100.0	28,182
Mineral products	–	–	–	–	–
Miscellaneous	–	63.8	36.1	99.9	72
Paper and printing	3.9	79.7	16.4	100.0	4,509
Tailoring	–	100.0	–	100.0	28
Textiles	8.6	84.4	7.0	100.0	11,819
Woodworking	–	30.2	69.8	100.0	368
ALL INDUSTRIES	4.2	89.1	6.7	100.0	69,342

*Percentages are based on total number of strikers, where known.
Symbols: W – all major demands secured by striking workers
L – all major demands rejected by employers: workers lost the strike
C – both strikers and factory owners made mutual concessions

In industrial relations in the capital compromise settlements were self-evidently unpalatable to both sides. They became even less so in 1913 and 1914.[68] On the other hand, at a national level there was a greater readiness to settle disputes by compromise. Such settlements constituted a third of the national total of economic stoppages both in 1912 and 1913, and even in 1914 reached a quarter. As both contemporary Bolshevik and Socialist Revolutionary commentators were quick to perceive, an important explanation both of the difference with regard to a willingness to be conciliatory and of the very high and increasing proportion of strikes lost by operatives in the capital lay in the ever fiercer opposition to workers' demands on the part of St Petersburg's industrial community, bolstered by its own organisation (POZF), the police and the Ministry of Internal Affairs.[69] This crucial aspect of the workers' strike losses is analysed separately in the following chapter.

Turning to an examination of the outcome of strikes in particular industrial sectors, metalworking followed very closely the trend outlined here. In 1912 three-fifths of strikes were lost by metalworkers. The following year and a half recorded defeats in nine-tenths of all conflicts. Contrary to the pattern discovered by Dr Perrot for French strikes in the 1870s and 1880s, length of dispute was no guarantee of success – the very reverse.[70] In the period 1912 to July 1914 all disputes in heavy industry exceeding a month in length and two-thirds of all those lasting 8–30 days were won by the employers. Workers were more successful in short strikes (under eight days) where they triumphed in 45 per cent of all conflicts. All of the strikes in the metalworking industries which resulted in victory for the workers occurred either in small enterprises or were partial strikes involving comparatively small numbers of employees. Stoppages were much more likely to fail in large and medium-sized plants. Compromise verdicts were also much more likely in smaller than in larger plants, though overall they were less common in the St Petersburg metal industries than they were nationally.[71]

In St Petersburg textile workers' victories were even rarer than in metalworking, never rising above 8 per cent of the total. Willingness to reach accommodations, too, was equally lacking and compromise settlements less common than at the national level, where they constituted a quarter to a third of the outcome of disputes. In food processing, paper and printing and woodworking, on the other hand, at least in 1912 strikers fared better, winning from a third to four-tenths of strikes. But in the following year and a half employers in these industries proved as determined as their counterparts in other sectors to break strikes. In food processing and printing the number of compromise settlements declined in step with a steep increase in outright victories by owners. Woodworking alone displayed some spirit of conciliation. The examples of food processing and printing demonstrate that strikes in small enterprises were as likely to be lost as in large plants. In the case of the former, 88 per cent of all strikes lost by workers throughout the pre-war period (96 of 109 disputes) occurred in enterprises whose payrolls were lower than 100 employees, whilst in printing the ratio was three-quarters.

The causes of the upsurge of economic strikes in St Petersburg were both specific to each individual stoppage and reflective of certain general, underlying factors. In Table 8.xxiv an attempt has been made to break down the multiplicity of strikes into four main categories of motive – disputes concerning wages, hours of work, working conditions (defined as sanitary and hygienic matters) and 'authority at work' (defined as management's control of all aspects of internal discipline).[72]

As Table 8.xxiv illustrates, the two main causes of economic stoppages were concerned with issues of authority at work and wages, the former increasing in relative frequency between 1912 and 1914 (from 31 per cent in 1912 to 34 per cent in 1913 and 41 per cent

*Table 8.xxiv: St Petersburg Province: Causes of Economic Strikes, by Industry, 1912–3 July 1914**

Industry	Authority strikes	1912 Hours	1912 Wages	Working conditions	Total	no.
Animal products	19.4	1.5	1.5	77.6	100.0	10,286
Chemicals	24.8	24.8	24.8	25.7	100.1	1,615
Commercial–industrial	1.3	49.2	0.6	48.9	100.0	2,140
Communications	9.4	10.9	29.9	49.8	100.0	14,612
Construction	20.3	3.5	–	76.2	100.0	1,724
Food/drink/tobacco	25.9	25.1	23.5	25.6	100.1	14,496
Gold/silver/bronze	7.6	36.3	13.4	42.7	100.0	262
Metals and machines	35.9	23.0	11.2	29.9	100.0	73,093
Mineral products	7.0	28.0	–	65.0	100.0	2,140
Miscellaneous	8.8	–	8.8	82.4	100.0	1,031
Paper and printing	35.5	21.7	9.3	33.5	100.0	10,410
Tailoring	16.0	24.6	19.7	39.7	100.0	325
Textiles	39.7	0.2	17.9	42.2	100.0	35,095
Woodworking	26.5	29.9	11.4	32.1	99.9	5,530
ALL INDUSTRIES	31.3	16.3	14.4	38.0	100.0	172,759

Table 8.xxiv: (Continued)

Industry	Authority strikes	1913			Total	no.
		Hours	Wages	Working conditions		
Animal products	34.6	22.8	11.1	31.6	100.1	17,114
Chemicals	–	96.8	–	3.2	100.0	310
Commercial–industrial	–	–	–	–	–	–
Communications	39.8	5.1	4.4	50.7	100.0	3,891
Construction	21.6	21.6	21.6	35.0	99.8	277
Food/drink/tobacco	31.6	23.9	18.3	26.2	100.0	16,181
Gold/silver/bronze	–	56.8	0.7	42.5	100.0	1,433
Metals and machines	34.1	24.8	8.6	32.5	100.0	127,028
Mineral products	16.2	3.4	16.2	64.2	100.0	770
Miscellaneous	9.4	28.6	24.0	38.0	100.0	1,540
Paper and printing	25.2	53.3	5.4	16.1	100.0	4,137
Tailoring	32.7	32.3	0.4	34.6	100.0	2,519
Textiles	38.5	13.3	9.9	38.3	100.0	29,452
Woodworking	23.8	9.1	11.2	55.9	100.0	5,649
ALL INDUSTRIES	33.7	23.1	9.6	33.6	100.0	210,301

Table 8.xxiv: (Continued)

Industry	Authority strikes	Hours	Wages	Working conditions	Total	no.
		1914 (to 3 July)				
Animal products	85.4	6.3	6.3	2.0	100.0	17,578
Chemicals	29.5	24.6	21.0	24.9	100.0	5,986
Commercial–industrial	32.0	32.0	18.0	18.0	100.0	50
Communications	21.9	20.7	–	57.3	99.9	3,327
Construction	80.0	–	–	20.0	100.0	100
Food/drink/tobacco	49.0	19.5	20.5	11.0	100.0	11,853
Gold/silver/bronze	36.0	36.5	1.9	25.6	100.0	1,055
Metals and machines	31.8	24.0	2.8	41.5	100.1	53,528
Mineral products	15.7	–	–	84.3	100.0	638
Miscellaneous	17.5	17.5	30.9	34.0	99.9	2,959
Paper and printing	43.6	19.5	2.5	34.3	99.9	8,603
Tailoring	36.3	5.5	7.1	51.1	100.0	888
Textiles	36.6	10.7	16.1	36.6	100.0	36,156
Woodworking	28.0	24.6	7.8	39.6	100.0	1,469
ALL INDUSTRIES	41.0	17.6	9.3	32.1	100.0	144,190

* Percentages are based on total number of strikers, where known.

in 1914), the latter declining in relative importance (from 38 per cent to 34 per cent and 32 per cent). Strikes involving disputes over working hours comprised 16 per cent of the total in 1912, 23 per cent in 1913 and 18 per cent in 1914. Disputes occasioned by sanitary and hygienic conditions were the least numerous, their share varying from 14 per cent in 1912 to less than 10 per cent in 1913 and 9 per cent in 1914.

Disputes concerning 'authority at work' and working conditions were far more common in the capital than nationally. Taken together, they comprised some 43 to 50 per cent of all economic stoppages in St Petersburg over this period. At the national level, however, disputes pertaining to the factory inspectorate's category 'order in enterprise', which equated directly with the combined classifications of 'authority at work' and 'working conditions', declined from 28 per cent of the economic total in 1912 to 15 per cent in 1913. Nationally, too, disputes in which wages formed the main focus of discontent constituted a far larger proportion of the total than in the capital, with an increase from 67 per cent of the total in 1912 to 81 per cent in 1913. In 1914 such strikes declined as a proportion of the total to 54 per cent. In addition, conflicts concerning hours were far less prominent on a national scale, contributing a paltry 5 per cent of the total in 1912 and 1913. In 1914, however, there occurred a dramatic leap in their share to a quarter.[73]

Throughout the period wages were the single most important issue for strikers in communications, the fashioning of articles of gold and silver, mineral products and textiles, where levels of remuneration were comparatively low.[74] In chemicals, metalworking, printing and woodworking, by contrast, where earnings were higher, disputes over wages were less frequent, though they did increase in 1914 as the process of inflation began to eat into the incomes of even the better-off operatives. Less than 4 per cent of all strikes over wages between 1912 and 1914 were a defensive reaction to wage cuts. The great bulk were offensive in character, seeking to increase wages over existing levels.[75] Only in the textile industry, where employers reacted to the continuing recession in the industry in 1912 and 1913 by the classic method of seeking to reduce their wage bills, was the proportion of strikes protesting at wage reductions relatively high. Almost all pre-war disputes arising over wage cuts were lost by strikers.[76]

The importance of working hours as a cause of economic strikes varied between industries. In food processing and metalworking, for example, strikes involving this issue constituted roughly a quarter of the total throughout the period. Among metalworkers a significant stimulus to disputes concerning the length of the working day was the widespread resort to overtime by employers in the pre-war boom (see Chapter 2). Workers reacted in several ways. In 42 strikes in this sector, strikers demanded either the outright abolition of overtime (on eight occasions) or, more frequently, that overtime should be genuinely voluntary and paid at time-and-a-half. No instance could be traced in which an employer conceded this claim, and only three where compromise settlements were reached. An equally common response was to demand that the working day should be cut to nine hours. This claim was put forward on twenty-three occasions, as against nine strikes in which workers requested an eight-hour day. The chance of either being met was equally negligible. On two occasions only did employers give way, whilst in eight cases some form of compromise was reached. Another common claim was to stop working on Saturdays and the eve of public holidays at two o'clock in the afternoon instead of the more normal time of five o'clock. This plea was made in thirty-one of the stoppages in the metal industry. Even this modest request was always rejected.

In textiles the number of conflicts in which hours of work were a source of unrest was lower than in metalworking and only became prominent in 1913 and 1914. In contrast to heavy industry, more-over, overtime scarcely featured at all as a focus of discontent, prob-ably because the continuing downturn in the industry to late 1913 rendered its use superfluous. Demands, too, for the introduction of a nine- or eight-hour day were almost as rare, occurring in only three disputes. In printing, hours of work became a major issue in the spring of 1913 on account of a prolonged series of strikes lasting two months in lithographic workshops in which the sole issue was the introduction of the 'English Saturday', where work stopped at 2 p.m. Fearing that a concession on this point would encourage a similar demand on the part of printers, the owners, encouraged by the POZF, broke the stoppages by means of a lock-out.[77] In other artisanal industries, such as food processing, the manufacture of articles of gold and silver and tailoring, as well as retailing, excessive-ly long hours of work ensured that demands for a curtailment of the working day were a frequent occurrence. In the summer of 1912, for example, many bakeries were hit by a rash of walk-outs, a cardinal demand in which was the restoration of the eleven-hour working day conceded by owners in the collective agreement of April, 1907. Most ended with a partial satisfaction of workers' demands.[78] Again, in February and March 1913 some thirty gold and silversmiths' workshops ground to a halt due to a series of disputes over the matter of pay for overtime and the introduction of a nine-hour day. Although the owners resolved on a lock-out, their disorganisation, coupled with a flood of orders associated with the tercentenary of the dynasty, forced many into meeting workers' demands.[79]

Although working conditions were uniformly unattractive throughout manufacturing industry (see Chapter 2), concern for their improvement occupied the lowest place in the demands pressed by strikers. In most cases proposals related to matters such as ventilation, the provision of hot water for washing and the making of tea, the installation of toilets and clocks and the supply of soap and towels. In food processing alone, where most bakery workers lived on the premises, did the quest for amelioration of working conditions occupy a consistently prominent place in stoppages. In the 1912 bakery disputes referred to earlier, strikers appealed to employers to improve sleeping accommodation by providing beds and bed linen and to provide better-quality food.

The most distinguishing feature of the pre-war upsurge in economic industrial unrest in St Petersburg was the dominant role played by disputes in which working people challenged in a variety of ways the all-pervasive authority of factory managers, foremen and petty workshop proprietors. In three industries – metalworking, paper and printing and textiles – authority issues appeared in a quarter to four-tenths of economic stoppages (see Table 8.xxv). Although this category was rather less significant in animal products, food processing, tailoring and woodworking, in the first three of these sectors, in 1913 and 1914 there was a distinct tendency for the number of such disputes to rise.

In Table 8.xxv an attempt has been made to break down authority disputes according to the motives for unrest. Strikes which were sparked off by the arrest of fellow workers by the police were comparatively rare, except in the case of printing in 1913, never forming more than 3–5 per cent of all authority disputes.[80] Also infrequent were strikes in which factory regulations were the overt cause of walk-outs, although in fact most conflicts touched upon some aspect or other of plants' internal rules of conduct. On the other hand, whereas demands for the sacking of foremen or other factory personnel scarcely featured at all in 1912, disputes involving their removal rose significantly thereafter, comprising 19 per cent of the aggregate of authority stoppages in 1913 and 21 per cent in 1914. Even these figures seriously underestimate the role of foremen and factory staff as agents of conflict, as disputes concerning fines, hiring and firing, courteous treatment and searches were almost always the direct consequence of actions taken by administrative personnel. In metalworking in particular, 1913 and above all the first months of 1914 witnessed a mounting dissatisfaction with supervisory staff and a growing willingness to challenge their authority. The most celebrated example of such a dispute occurred at the two machine construction plants of G. A. Lessner in 1913. On 23 April in the foundry there was discovered the body of a young Jewish worker,

Table 8.xxv: *St Petersburg Province: Authority Strikes by Type and by Industry, 1912–3 July 1914**

Industry	1912									
	A	FR	F	Fm	H&F	PA	R	S	Total	no.
Animal products	–	–	100.0	–	–	–	–	–	100.0	2,000
Chemicals	–	–	16.0	16.0	18.0	18.0	16.0	16.0	100.0	2,500
Commercial–industrial	–	–	–	–	98.7	1.3	–	–	100.0	520
Communications	–	6.1	31.3	–	–	31.3	31.3	–	100.0	3,375
Construction	–	–	–	–	5.9	79.4	14.7	–	100.0	340
Food/drink/tobacco	–	–	4.3	–	50.9	23.2	21.5	–	99.9	2,861
Gold/silver/bronze	–	–	–	–	80.0	20.0	–	–	100.0	150
Metals and machines	1.6	9.5	29.2	1.0	9.3	16.2	25.7	7.5	100.0	41,551
Mineral products	–	–	66.6	–	–	33.3	–	–	99.9	150
Miscellaneous	–	–	–	–	–	100.0	–	–	100.0	12
Paper and printing	1.1	1.3	5.5	1.9	31.4	22.7	31.4	4.7	100.0	4,669
Tailoring	–	–	–	–	11.2	88.8	–	–	100.0	63
Textiles	11.8	–	22.1	–	25.7	28.6	11.8	–	100.0	25,435
Woodworking	13.8	–	27.6	–	15.1	31.1	12.4	–	100.0	1,929
ALL INDUSTRIES	4.6	4.9	25.9	1.1	17.3	21.6	20.2	4.4	100.0	85,555

Table 8.xxv: (Continued)

Industry	1913									
	A	FR	F	Fm	H&F	PA	R	S	Total	no.
Animal products	–	7.8	28.1	21.7	10.1	26.8	5.4	–	99.9	13,800
Chemicals	–	–	–	–	–	–	–	–	–	–
Commercial–industrial	–	–	–	–	–	–	–	–	–	–
Communications	–	–	2.4	–	87.4	3.9	6.3	–	100.0	2,060
Construction	–	–	–	–	–	100.0	–	–	100.0	60
Food/drink/tobacco	–	74.2	–	10.6	1.4	7.9	6.0	–	100.1	5,124
Gold/silver/bronze	–	–	–	–	–	23.7	38.1	38.1	99.9	118
Metals and machines	5.0	8.5	14.5	17.5	26.2	21.4	6.4	0.4	99.9	76,341
Mineral products	–	–	–	–	–	100.0	–	–	100.0	125
Miscellaneous	–	–	–	51.3	20.5	7.7	20.5	–	100.0	195
Paper and printing	39.7	–	3.1	–	16.4	5.6	35.2	–	100.0	1,133
Tailoring	–	–	–	–	49.6	1.1	49.3	–	100.0	1,624
Textiles	–	–	32.6	26.2	11.2	21.3	8.7	–	100.0	24,018
Woodworking	–	1.1	9.6	9.6	32.1	25.9	21.7	–	100.0	1,565
ALL INDUSTRIES	3.4	9.0	18.3	18.6	21.8	20.9	7.8	0.3	100.0	126,163

Table 8.xxv: (Continued)

Industry	A	FR	F	1914 (to 3 July) Fm	H&F	PA	R	S	Total	no.
Animal products	–	–	29.9	2.6	6.2	30.3	31.1	–	100.0	2,608
Chemicals	–	–	–	12.4	17.6	14.4	55.5	–	99.9	1,800
Commercial–industrial	–	–	–	–	39.0	39.0	22.0	–	100.0	41
Communications	–	–	–	–	–	100.0	–	–	100.0	730
Construction	–	–	–	–	100.0	–	–	–	100.0	80
Food/drink/tobacco	–	–	15.0	–	22.4	23.3	17.1	22.1	99.9	9,488
Gold/silver/bronze	–	–	–	–	74.5	25.5	–	–	100.0	510
Metals and machines	11.5	5.4	10.5	38.9	25.7	3.5	3.7	0.7	99.9	20,139
Mineral products	–	–	–	–	100.0	–	–	–	100.0	100
Miscellaneous	–	–	–	–	100.0	–	–	–	100.0	20
Paper and printing	0.4	–	1.3	16.4	24.1	1.3	56.4	–	99.9	5,842
Tailoring	–	–	–	–	1.2	15.4	61.7	21.7	100.0	345
Textiles	–	–	17.1	20.4	15.6	26.9	5.7	14.3	100.0	20,949
Woodworking	–	–	29.0	16.1	40.3	6.0	8.5	–	99.9	414
ALL INDUSTRIES	3.7	1.7	12.8	21.3	21.0	16.9	14.2	8.4	100.0	63,066

*Percentages are based on total number of strikers, where known.

Symbols: A – arrests; FR – factory regulations; F – fines; Fm – the removal of foremen; H&F – hiring and firing of workers; PA – 'polite address': courteous treatment; R – some form of workers' representation; S – searches.

Iakov Strongin, who had hanged himself after being accused of the theft of nuts by the shop foreman, Laul. His workmates then struck for 102 days to secure the foreman's dismissal. They lost the dispute.[81] In textiles, too, apparently 'docile' female mill hands began to display a greater readiness in the eighteen months before the war to protest at foremen's abuses, although only one of eleven such disputes ended in complete victory for the strikers. Although working people resented as personally humiliating the practice of searches on leaving work in the evening and medical inspection at the time of initial hiring or rehiring after a strike, walk-outs over these aspects of factory life were comparatively rare. At their maximum extent in 1914 they never contributed more than 8 per cent of the aggregate of authority strikes.

The imposition of fines as punishment either for defective work or for striking was an important stimulus to unrest in 1912 and 1913 but less so on the eve of the war. In 1912 in metalworking, textiles and woodworking the major factor behind such stoppages was the levying of monetary penalties upon those workers who had downed tools on May Day. At the Siemens and Halske electrical plants the resulting protest lasted 95 days despite the sacking of the work-force and the arrest of 100 strikers.[82] In the 29 cases of strikes arising over fines in heavy industry, where the results are known, 24 were defeated by employers. In textiles 13 of 19 such stoppages were lost by the strikers.

Another area of managerial authority which came under increasing challenge in 1913 and 1914 was the complete and frequently arbitrary control exercised by administrative staff and foremen over the hiring and sacking of labour. In metals and machine construction in particular this issue assumed a growing inportance in the last year and a half of peace, where it arose in a quarter of all authority disputes. Many such conflicts took the form of a protest against the sacking of colleagues by management with a concomitant demand for their rehire. At the state-owned Obukhov arms-works, for example, the dismissal of 200 workers in the shell shop on 29 July 1913 for downing tools two days earlier sparked off a two-month-long stoppage by 5,000 of their workmates.[83] Employers as stubbornly defended their power in this area as in others. In heavy industry in the 24 stoppages arising over sackings, where the results are known, 20 were defeats for the strikers. In some artisanal industries – printing throughout the period, woodworking in 1913 and 1914, food processing in 1912 – hiring and firing was also an important cause of discontent.

Closely linked to hiring and firing were demands for some form of worker representation in order to give employees greater control of the situation at work. The importance accorded to this by strikers seems to have fluctuated. Whereas pleas for representation appeared in a fifth of all authority disputes in 1912, the next year a mere 7.8 per cent of such strikes included this demand. In 1914 the ratio doubled. By the term 'representation' workers meant different things. In 29 stoppages strikers demanded the institution of factory elders as allowed for in the permissive law of 1903, which St Petersburg owners had studiously ignored. In 56 strikes workers requested that managements recognise elected labour delegates who would conduct negotiations with factory boards. In 44 disputes strikers suggested that their respective trade unions should be granted recognition by factory administrations. Workers, however, had no concept of arbitration machinery, as only a single case could be discovered when strikers asked for it. Out of the sum total of 129 such strikes, there were at least 22 occasions when strikers specifically linked representation to consultation through elected workers' delegates on hiring and firing. Printers were by far the most insistent on being accorded some sort of voice in workshop affairs, above all in matters of dismissal. In 29 of their strikes they sought permission for elected representatives to be consulted by owners or foremen before operatives were sacked, and on 19 occasions they appealed for official recognition of their trade union. Printers were to the fore in this respect partly because they were better educated and partly because they had one of the few relatively strong trade unions, which in 1907 already had secured a collective agreement with the employers.[84] In 1912 many metalworkers, too, had displayed a comparative zeal for representation, although they pressed mostly for the implementation of the 1903 law on factory elders in the absence of their closed trade union. But in the next two years, perhaps due to the obvious futility of this request in the face of stiff employer resistance, they largely abandoned it. It would be erroneous to conclude, however, that such demands, either in metalworking or printing, amounted to workers' search for a 'constitutional factory order' (as Dr Hogan has suggested) or had radical implications.[85] Printing apart, the support for some form of representation was not as widespread throughout industry as it had been in 1905 and 1906; it fluctuated over time and contrasts sharply with the mass movement for factory committees in 1917. Many workers, it is true, wanted some kind of permanent mechanism to let them air their grievances and have them settled by negotiation rather than by the arbitrary diktat of foremen and supervisory staff. But such demands amounted to no more than a reform of management style; they did not constitute a challenge to ownership or management's overall responsibilities.

Throughout the pre-war period, contemporary commentators were struck by the more visible concern of workers, particularly younger workers, for their dignity, a growing feeling of self-worth and a readiness to defend it.[86] This was manifested in various ways. In strikes there was the frequent demand for 'polite address', or courteous treatment. Throughout the period approximately a fifth of all authority strikes contained such a request. On the eve of the war, however, in some industries, such as metalworking, printing and woodworking, appeals for humane consideration faded away, probably because they met with short shrift and contempt from employers and managers. The plea for 'polite address', which was never spelt out in detail in lists of desiderata during strikes, was really a symbol for underlying grievances. It represented a desire for respectful treatment in place of the arbitrary abuse of power by supervisory staff – the foul language, beatings, ill-treatment of women, fines, searches and medical inspection (see Chapter 2). In fact the two-word phrase neatly encapsulated the diverse forms of workers' challenge to authority in the workplace. The strikes, moreover, which arose in connection with the arbitrary sacking of workers, displayed a sense of solidarity with colleagues and a recognition of the interests workers held in common. In June 1913 the chief of the St Petersburg Okhrana noted in alarm that 'there is a significant growth in the class self-consciousness of workers'.[87] Certain strikes, for example, became *causes célèbres* for workers, assuming a symbolic importance. This was especially so in the case of the stoppages at Siemens and Halske and Lessner mentioned earlier. At an illegal meeting of the strikers at Siemens in July 1912 the chairman of the strike committee characterised it as a 'strike fought on the principle of opposition to the power of employers' organisations'.[88] And the Lessner stoppage was widely regarded as a fight for workers' dignity. Both attracted wide material support for the strikers: 10,000 roubles were collected in aid of the Siemens and Halske workers and 11,000 roubles for the Lessner strikers.[89]

In addition to the overt causes of economic strikes in St Petersburg in the years immediately before the war – issues of hours, wages, inflation, living and working conditions and the autocratic factory regime – there were at work deeper, more concealed factors.

In the first place, as has been mentioned earlier in this chapter, the industrial upsurge after 1910 offered apparently propitious circumstances for workers to remedy their grievances. Contemporaries of all political persuasions were quick to note this point. Indeed Menshevik and liberal commentators tended to seek the explanation of economic strikes solely in terms of the recovery in manufacturing industry.[90] In metalworking in particular, by 1913, there was a growing dearth of skilled specialists, the dread of unemployment receded and with it an important obstacle to striking. A police memorandum of the summer of 1913 emphasised that 'workers no longer fear being out of a job'.[91] A chronic dearth of skilled labour likewise helped undermine the effectiveness of the employers' weapons of mass lay-offs and blacklistings during and after disputes. The boom in heavy industry also led to a covert lengthening of the working day through resort to overtime, which played a prominent part in the outbreak of metalworkers' strikes.

Secondly, as both Lenin and the chief of the St Petersburg Okhrana percipiently grasped, the economic strike movement in the capital was in many respects the delayed, defensive response of workers to the onslaught of the employers in the years after 1907 upon the gains they had made during the 1905 revolution in respect of wages, hours of work and representation. Sometimes strikers made this point quite explicitly. An article devoted to the 1912 Siemens and Halske strike in the metalworkers' organ *Metallist* ascribed the root cause of the stoppage to the fact that workers had lost the benefits gained from the two-month strike at the plant in 1906, rates had subsequently been cut, the lunch break reduced to half an hour and foremen and engineers had become ruder.[92] During a walk-out by 300 mill hands at the weaving plant of Voronin, Liuts and Chesher in the spring of 1913 the strikers demanded restoration of the rates of pay in existence before 1910.[93] Although such explicit references by strikers are comparatively rare, it would not be unreasonable to assume that many workers regarded the pre-war boom as their apparent opportunity to make good the losses sustained during the years of reaction. The stagnation of real wages provided an additional incentive to do so.

Thirdly, in recent years the attention of labour historians in other European countries has become focused on a crisis of factory discipline in the late nineteenth and early twentieth centuries. In the case of France, for example, Michael P. Hanagan has argued that in the Stéphanois region south of Saint-Etienne the threat of technological change to skilled workers' control of the work process acted as a primary stimulus to labour unrest. And Lenard R. Berlanstein has noted a mounting challenge to managerial authority in Parisian factories in the 1890s and early 1900s due to the intensification of the work regime.[94] In her dissertation Heather Hogan has applied these insights to St Petersburg metalworkers. She has argued that their renewed strike militancy was a response to the 'industrial rationalisation' of 1907 to 1911, which had degraded the significance of skill and undermined metalworkers' control of their work environment.[95]

With respect to individual metalworkers' strikes between 1912 and 1914 there is validity in Dr Hogan's hypothesis. Specific connections can be traced between particular changes and the policies of cost-reducing reorganisation pursued at certain machine construction and electrical plants (see Chapter 1). At Ludwig Nobel, for example, much of the pre-war unrest in the factory can be linked to the fact that the response of the management to the approaching demise of the company's patent was a series of measures to cut the cost of production. These had included a wages bureau which centralised rates of pay in the hands of office staff rather than the foremen, and the introduction of overtime.[96] The 69-day stoppage at New Aivaz in the summer of 1913 provides a classic illustration. The dispute began on 9 July when a rude trainee time-work specialist was carted out of the factory in time-honoured fashion in a wheelbarrow. But behind this lay workers' discontent with changes in the work process – the introduction of time and motion study, the intensification of the pace of labour, the utilisation of women as machine operators, progressive reductions in piece rates and an attempt to be rid of the third shift.[97] The origins of the two lengthy disputes in 1913 at Obukhov also lay in workers' response to management reforms. The first stoppage was occasioned by the application of the 'American' system of pay with concomitant cuts in rates, the abolition of a bonus and the lengthening of the working day to twelve hours. The second was directly related to the introduction of automatic punch-clocks which lengthened the working day by fifteen minutes. Infringement of the new procedures entailed fines. When, on 12 November, 300 operatives in the lock shop refused to clock on they were sacked. The next day all other workshops stopped in protest.[98]

Yet it would be dangerous to assume that all metalworkers' disputes were provoked by 'scientific' plant reorganisations or that they represented skilled workers' resistance to deskilling. As the analysis of this topic in Chapter 1 attempted to show, the extent and forms of 'rationalisation' varied greatly within heavy industry. Seven metalworkers' stoppages alone could be linked directly to particular innovations at the place of work. In addition, the skilled metalworker was not yet facing large-scale dilution except in a few plants such as Aivaz. There is little direct evidence that skilled metalworkers perceived their status as craftsmen to be threatened. What, however, was resented rather was the increasing erosion of workshop customs (negotiations with the foremen on rates of pay, time for washing up and cleaning machines) and the more intensive work regime resulting from the assault upon workers' limited control over the pace of work. As Leopold Haimson has pointed out, younger metalworkers (urban-born, hereditary proletarians) especially found irksome the reimposition of managerial authority after the 'days of freedom' in the 1905 revolution.[99]

Both contemporary commentators and later historians have been much exercised about the role of organisation or spontaneity in the economic struggle. Most observers of the labour scene were agreed that, in the words of the Menshevik activist P. Garvi, 'the strike movement has proceeded for the most part apart from the existing trade unions'.[100] As the detailed analysis of the trade unions in Chapter 7 illustrated, these institutions were feeble instruments, quite incapable of providing leadership on a large scale to pre-war strikes. Systematic persecution by the police, the bitter hostility of most employers, the multiple prohibitions enshrined in the Temporary Regulations of 4 March 1906, insufficiency of funds and a chronic flux in membership rendered almost impossible consistent and effective guidance and aid to strikers. In addition throughout most of 1912 two major industries, metalworking and printing, lacked any trade unions and the textile workers' union was effectively moribund during the entire pre-war period. Indeed the sole unions capable of fulfilling their normal functions were certain artisanal professional organisations – printers and tailors in particular. Thus, in the spring of 1913 when tailors in four workshops downed tools, the union of tailors decided to support them by spreading the strike. It arranged for the election of shop delegates who met to work out a general list of demands which was then presented in many establishments. In the end some 800 tailors walked out in 55 workshops. It is instructive to note that the underlying cause of the stoppages was the threat of the Society of Owners of Tailoring Shops to introduce piece-rate systems, with a consequent reduction in hours and rates of pay.[101] In the above-mentioned lithographers' strikes in the spring of the same year, the union of printers paid out 3,000 roubles in strike benefits. But even in this dispute leadership apparently came from a special *ad hoc* group of lithographers independent of the union.[102] And there were many artisanal strikes in which the appropriate trade unions played no discernible role – in the stoppages in 30 gold and silver ateliers early in 1913, in those affecting 25 cobblers' establishments in May of the same year and in almost all bakery disputes.[103] The overwhelming majority of strikes began without the knowledge of union executives and were conducted without their assistance. Even the revived union of metalworkers fared no better in this respect (see Chapter 7).

If trade unions as official bodies played a mininal part in conducting strikes, revolutionary cells of whatever political hue were of even less significance. The Okhrana, which carefully monitored the course of major economic disputes, repeatedly emphasised this point in its internal memoranda. In a report of 27 June 1913, Colonel Von Koten, chief of the St Petersburg Okhrana, remarked that 'in the present stoppages the revolutionary organisations play a completely minor role'. Ten months later his successor repeated this conclusion.[104] The survey presented in Chapter 5 of the distribution of revolutionary cells within individual factories revealed that in almost all sectors of manufacturing party groups were non-existent on a permanent basis. The exception proved to be heavy industry – or more accurately machine construction and electrical plants employing between 500 and 5,000 operatives. It would be foolish to deny that individual revolutionary activists probably attempted to offer leadership once a stoppage began, but a survey of police files referred to the presence of such activists in just seven stoppages in the period between 1912 and July 1914.

The Okhrana itself continually noted that strike leaders were either unmarried youths aged 18–20 without family responsibilities and without a revolutionary past, or worker–intellectuals who had participated in socialist organisations during the 1905 revolution but were no longer members of the revolutionary underground.[105]

The manifest weakness of the trade unions and illegal revolutionary organisations, however, should not lead to the conclusion that strikes were completely elemental affairs, lacking all organisation. As some more perceptive commentators pointed out at the time, strikers sought surrogate forms of organisation.[106] The most significant of these were temporary strike committees and general meetings of strikers. In fact both in the socialist press and in police reports there are remarkably few references to strike committees as such. A significant exception was the Aivaz dispute in 1913, mentioned earlier, where a strike committee included at least one former member of the Bolsheviks' Petersburg Committee.[107] It is possible that socialist newspapers feared to draw the attention of the authorities to such bodies out of fear of provoking the arrest of members or that they were so widespread as to make comment superfluous. On the other hand, the practice of holding general meetings of strikers in order to provide information, and take collective decisions about the conduct of a dispute was relatively common and widely noted at the time. In the case of metalworking at least forty-one strikes in this period were conducted in this manner; in the case of printing, eighteen. Lengthy disputes in particular could not have been prosecuted without some such device. An excellent illustration of the role of meetings and the actions of strike leaders is furnished by the three-month stoppage at Siemens and Halske in 1912. General meetings were held weekly throughout the dispute. The very decision to launch the walk-out in protest at the May Day fine was taken at a gathering on 7 May which drew up a list of demands. The next day another assembly resolved to place all the jobs of strikers under a boycott (a common practice in protracted conflicts). Later meetings elected a finance commission, resolved to appeal to the workers of the German parent company to ban the fulfilment of contracts transferred there and to publish the names of strikebreakers in the union journal. Strikebreakers were also beaten up. Elected shop delegates distributed financial aid to some 700 strikers, many of whom sent their families to their home villages and pawned their possessions.[108] This pattern of activity was common in many metalworkers' disputes but much less so in textiles. Although strike committees, elected shop delegates and general meetings were comparatively effective forms of strike management helping to overcome differences among the many different grades of worker, they were temporary institutions. Indeed they helped strengthen workers' allegiance to their factory at the expense of the authority of trade unions and revolutionary parties. In this respect as others, factory autonomy acted as a barrier to broader, more permanent collective action.

The socialist press and trade-union journals played as significant a part in influencing the course of economic strikes as they did in political stoppages. Activists sent regular reports to both *Pravda* and *Luch*, as well as professional publications on the course of strikes, and used their columns to appeal for financial aid from other workers, to call for boycotts of strikers' jobs and to publish the names of strikebreakers. Collections were often channelled through the newspaper offices. In this way news of strikes and their causes spread throughout the city and the provinces, aiding a spirit of solidarity. The newspapers, too, helped maintain the morale of strikers, especially of labour activists.[109]

The material support of fellow workers was another element vital to the prosecution of stoppages of long duration. Funds primarily came from workmates in the same industry within St Petersburg, frequently from adjacent plants. During the 1912 stoppage at Erikson in the Vyborg district, for example, monies were collected from neighbouring machine construction enterprises such as Baranovskii, Lessner, Nobel and the Russian Society.[110] The total sums involved could be relatively large – 11,000 roubles were received and distributed during the famous Lessner dispute in 1913.[111] In general, however, individual contributions were small-scale.

IV

As Table 8.xxvi shows, the geographical incidence of strikes within St Petersburg city was distinctly uneven. Throughout the period certain districts were disproportionately affected by the breakdown in industrial relations. Two quarters stand out above all others – Vyborg and the Petersburg Side, each consistently accounting for nearly a fifth of all strikes. These were pre-eminently areas dominated by machine construction and electrical equipment enterprises of medium size (with labour forces of 500 to 2,000). They were also centres of textiles, whilst the Petersburg Side contained many printshops and woodworking establishments. Their prominent position stands in contrast to the revolutionary years of 1905 to 1907

Table 8.xxvi: St Petersburg City: All Strikes, by District, 1912–3 July 1914 (%
of total)

District	1912		1913		Jan.–3 July 1914		Total: 1912–3 July 1914	
	no.	%	no.	%	no.	%	no.	%
Admiralty	18	2.4	19	1.8	8	0.9	45	1.7
Kazan	20	2.7	20	1.9	4	0.4	44	1.6
Kolomna	13	1.7	24	2.2	23	2.5	60	2.2
Lesnoi	3	0.4	–	–	2	0.2	5	0.2
Liteinii	22	3.0	34	3.2	17	1.9	73	2.7
Moscow	96	12.9	144	13.4	88	9.7	328	12.0
Narva	51	6.8	68	6.3	69	7.6	188	6.9
Neva	77	13.4	132	12.3	116	12.8	325	11.9
Okhta	17	2.3	15	1.4	26	2.9	58	2.1
Peterhof	24	3.2	39	3.6	53	5.8	116	4.3
Petersburg Side	122	16.4	191	17.8	161	17.7	474	17.4
Poliustrovo	7	0.9	7	0.7	2	0.2	16	0.6
Rozhdestvo	15	2.0	26	2.4	25	2.8	66	2.4
Spasskaia	22	3.0	27	2.5	12	1.3	61	2.2
Vasil'evskii Island	67	9.0	127	11.8	108	11.9	302	11.1
Vyborg	147	19.8	186	17.3	182	20.0	515	18.9
Staraia and Novaia Derevnia	8	1.1	4	0.4	1	0.1	13	0.4
Environs	14	1.9	10	0.9	11	1.2	35	1.3
TOTAL	743	102.9	1073	99.9	908	99.9	2724	99.9

when the districts of Narva, Peterhof and Shlissel'burg were more
to the fore.[112] Below these two northern districts, three others each
contributed approximately 12 per cent of the aggregate of pre-war
stoppages. These were Moscow, Neva and Vasil'evskii Island. To
them should be added Narva plus Peterhof, which really constituted
a single industrial entity despite their administrative separation.
However, over the three years the contribution of each of these four
areas varied. Whilst the proportion of strikes furnished by the Neva
district remained roughly constant, the share attributed to Narva/
Peterhof rose from 10 per cent of the total in 1912 to 13 per cent in
1914, while that of Vasil'evskii Island rose from 9 per cent to 12 per
cent. On the other hand Moscow's contribution fell from 13 per cent
in 1912 to 10 per cent in 1914. Each of these four quarters had a
broader sectoral base than Vyborg and the Petersburg Side. Neva,
for example, was home to chemical plants, sawmills, paper mills and

silicates manufacturers as well as heavy industry and textiles. Narva and Moscow were also centres of artisanal production. In addition some of these districts contained very large general-production metals plants – Putilov in Peterhof, the Baltic Shipyards and St Petersburg Pipes in Vasil'evskii Island and Neva Shipyards in Neva. In sharp contrast, the central city wards – Admiralty, Kazan, Kolomna, Liteinii, Rozhdestvo and Spasskaia – were together responsible for a mere 12.8 per cent of all stoppages throughout the period. The outer peripheral districts – Lesnoi, Okhta, Poliustrovo, Staraia and Novaia Derevnia, together with small industrial centres such as Sestroretsk and Shlissel'burg in the environs – were of even less significance, their share totalling just 4–5 per cent of all strikes. In other words the pre-war labour unrest was focused throughout primarily on the two north/north-eastern districts of Vyborg and Petersburg Side, itself a factor of weakness. On the eve of the war there was little sign that the strike movement was progressively embracing both the central and outer areas of the city hitherto immune from its influence.

V

In the years immediately preceding the First World War the gravest danger to the Tsarist regime came not from the countryside, which was quiescent, or the armed forces, which remained loyal, or from the liberal opposition in the State Duma, which was paralysed by internal differences among and within the liberal parties over the methods of countering an increasingly reactionary domestic course, but from the industrial workers of St Petersburg. The challenge posed by the mass of operatives did not assume the guise of growing support for the revolutionary parties, in particular the Bolsheviks, or for the legal labour organisations, all of which were successfully contained by the authorities and failed to secure wide popular support. The threat to Tsardom in its capital lay in the strike movement beginning in April 1912. In the absence of effective socialist underground structures or powerful professional organisations, work stoppages became the main form of the labour movement.

The breakdown in industrial relations became dangerous for the monarchy due both to the increasing tempo and scale of disputes and the predominance of political stoppages, which were involving an increasing proportion of the factory labour force. In all these respects the last six months of peace assumed an even more menacing hue, with the number of strikers in the city exceeding the total for 1905. Labour unrest in St Petersburg was largely political in character. It gave vent to a diffuse and growing opposition on the part of more and more workers to the Tsarist political structure. It offered clear evidence that the granting of the new constitutional system and the State Duma had failed to allay workers' hostility to the monarchy, so forcefully expressed in the 1905 revolution. In that sense the political strikes were revolutionary in character. An especially alarming feature in ministers' views was the threat posed to the programme of rearmament by metalworkers' stoppages. Metalworkers were more skilled, more literate, more urban born, more politically aware and more politically disaffected than any other group of working people. Although other categories of labour were less drawn into the strike movement, those who did participate did so increasingly in politically inspired stoppages. Whilst most economic strikes did not bear an overtly political hue, the political unrest did act as a stimulus to the upsurge in economic conflicts. And the growing number of defeats suffered in economic stoppages drove workers more and more into political protest strikes. This was especially the case with metalworkers. Economic stoppages revealed the depth of workers' dislike of the managerial 'counter-revolution' of 1907 and 1911, with the consequent losses of workers' gains from the 1905 revolution and the attendant reorganisations of workshop practices. In heavy industry at least, unrest was not merely a by-product of economic recovery but was expressive of a genuine challenge to managerial authority. There were indications, too, that the younger, post-1905 generation of factory workers, urban-bred hereditary proletarians, above all in metalworking, was the group most alienated from the regime.

On the other hand, the strike movement as the main form of workers' opposition to the regime in the capital suffered from many weaknesses, which rendered far less effective its potentiality as a vehicle for forcing political change upon the monarchy, least of all for overthrowing it in the near future. In their opposition to Tsardom St Petersburg workers remained isolated from the provinces and other industrial and urban centres, which lagged far behind the capital in the political protest movement. In sharp contrast to the autumn of 1905, the liberals (a few isolated Left Kadets and Progressists excepted) refused to forge an extra-parliamentary alliance with labour as an instrument of pressure on the bureaucracy. Most liberals were too apprehensive of unleashing a *bunt*, an anarchic popular uprising which would sweep away cultural society as much as Tsardom. Furthermore, workers' general political discontent was not translated either into a widely received programme of concrete political demands or into a mass commitment to any of the revolutionary parties, including the Bolsheviks, or open labour organisations. Although both political and economic strikes were not as 'elemental' and 'spontaneous' as Mensheviks claimed, they were not led by the Social Democrats as bureaucrats and employers feared. Neither atrophied revolutionary cells and committees nor enfeebled trade unions nor temporary strike organisations could guide working-class opposition to the monarchy as expressed in the strikes into mass support for specific political goals nor furnish the permanent organisational structures requisite for such a task. Only a minority of skilled factory and artisanal operatives displayed a growing sense of party identification – with the Bolsheviks. Nor did the challenge to managerial authority translate into an outright rejection of private ownership or the general responsibilities of factory management. The strike movement failed to encompass all categories of workers or engulf the entire city. In both political and economic stoppages the service sector, communications, construction, chemicals, mineral products, tailoring and the manufacture of articles of gold and silver were little involved. Even in industries most afflicted, such as metalworking and textiles, there were plants which remained oases of calm. Strikes did not affect all quarters in an equal fashion. The Vyborg and Petersburg Side districts alone were the chief foci of industrial disputes. In the short run, too, both the authorities and the employers were able to contain the unrest. The former prevented mass demonstrations reaching the seat of government in the city centre. The latter, despite their inability to fashion a sensible and coherent labour policy (see the next chapter), defeated the majority of economic stoppages and short-sightedly preserved the autocratic factory order intact. For these reasons there was no revolutionary crisis in the capital on the eve of the war. The St Petersburg general strike, which broke out on 4 July 1914 and is analysed in Chapter 10, also reveals both the depth of working-class disaffection in the capital and the inability of revolutionary parties to capitalise on it.

Chapter 9

GOVERNMENT, EMPLOYERS AND LABOUR, 1912 – JUNE 1914

From the onset of the first significant industrial strikes in Russia in the middle of the 1880s until the collapse of the dynasty in February 1917, both the *ancien régime* and the business community failed to elaborate an effective, coherent strategy towards labour which might have retained the loyalty of the industrial workers to the monarchy and capitalism. In the sphere of labour relations policy-making remained confused, contradictory, highly ambiguous and ultimately sterile. The Imperial authorities and industrialists vacillated between repressive, paternalistic and liberal measures. Until 1905 the government had clung to the traditional, bureaucratic view that the state, as an independent agency above the interplay of conflicting estate or class interests, should remain the arbiter in all areas of social life. In the sphere of labour relations such an interventionist role on the part of officialdom impelled it towards two inconsistent policies: on the one hand, a radical restriction of the autonomy of factory operatives and complete support for the 'autocratic' factory order and, on the other hand, an occasional, reluctant and partial regulation of conditions at work. The shock of the 1905 revolution induced Tsardom to take the first hesitant steps towards a liberal labour or West European solution of the problem of workers' disaffection, i.e. the provision of legal means to enable the working class to pursue the legitimate satisfaction of its aspirations and to permit the peaceful resolution of industrial disputes, as well as the implementation of state-directed social reform to lessen the potential causes of revolt by industrial workers. These assumed the forms of the Temporary Regulations on Unions and Societies, 4 March 1906, authorising the formation of trade unions and educational societies, and the Social Insurance Laws, 23 June 1912, providing payments for sickness and accidents to industrial workers. But the highly ambiguous attitudes of the bureaucracy and factory owners towards labour reforms and inde-

269

pendent working-class organisations greatly lessened, perhaps even precluded, the possibility of the emergence of a legal labour movement pursuing an evolutionary rather than a revolutionary approach to securing a remedy for its grievances. The validity of these more general observations can be illustrated by an examination of the reaction of the government and industrialists to the labour movement in St Petersburg on the eve of the First World War when, as Chapters 4 to 8 have shown, the city had become the centre of labour and revolutionary unrest.

I

The capital's industrialists had first assumed an organisational identity in May 1897 with the formation of the St Petersburg Society for Assistance to the Improvement and Development of Factory Industry.[1] Under the impact of the great industrial strikes and revolutionary upheavals of 1905 this body was reformed in September 1906 as the St Petersburg Society of Mill and Factory Owners (abbreviated in the text to POZF) in order to defend managerial prerogatives and deal with economic conflicts. Membership of the POZF was open to factories and private firms employing a minimum of fifty hands and dues were fixed according to the number of employees, with a rate of 30 kopecks per worker. The total number of members fluctuated between 1907 and 1914 (see Table 9.i).

In the pre-revolutionary Society the dominant element had been the textile mills but after 1906, as Table 9.ii illustrates, the single most influential group were the engineering and electrical joint-stock companies.

Although the very large state-owned shipyards, steel and engineering plants held aloof from formal membership of the POZF until August 1913 when the representatives of the Ministries of War and the Navy joined the Engineering Section, privately owned large- and medium-sized enterprises were predominant within the associa-

Table 9.i: *Membership of the St Petersburg Society of Mill and Factory Owners, 1907–14*[2]

Year	Firms	Work-force	Engineering		Textile	
			Firms	Workers	Firms	Workers
1907	171	110,365	56	49,357	35	29,216
1909	160	95,937	45	25,339	33	37,335
1912	104	112,768	44	31,830	29	40,251
1914	176	154,296	50	52,495	28	45,380

Table 9.ii: Industrial Groups within the St Petersburg Society of Mill and Factory Owners, 1912[3]

Engineering	Electrical	Chemical	Textile
44 (31,830)	15 (5,091)	21 (12,716)	29 (40,251)

Paper	Wood	Tanning	Food
21 (6,602)	10 (1,572)	6 (4,994)	10 (–)

Note: The first figure refers to the number of firms in the group; figures in brackets refer to the total number of workers employed by these establishments.

tion. Of the 164 member firms in 1912, the size of the work-force in 115 can be traced. Analysis of this data reveals that 28 employed over 1,000 wage earners each; 25, 500 to 1,000; 48, 100 to 500; and a mere 15 under 100, i.e. almost half the total sample (53) possessed labour forces in excess of 500 operatives. Such figures meant that ascendancy within the POZF lay with firms which were tied to overseas capital (mainly French or German), either directly or indirectly through the St Petersburg joint-stock banks, whose directors and upper management were frequently foreign citizens, and which were increasingly dependent (in the case of heavy industry prior to the war) upon government contracts. Another consequence was that certain branches of manufacturing were poorly represented in the Society, namely printing, tanning, food, wood, chemicals. The many artisanal establishments remained aloof from membership, as did small businesses. The POZF, therefore, was not fully representative of the capital's manufacturers.

The governance of the POZF rested on the annual general meeting and the Council. In the AGM voting depended upon the size of the annual membership dues. Its function was restricted to electing the president and vice-president. Real power resided in the Council and in the two major sections, the engineering and the textile. The Council was composed of thirty-six members and five candidates. In 1913 and 1914, the only years for which exact figures could be located, thirty-four engineering and electrical firms belonged to the Engineering Section.[4] Companies were represented by directors or professional managers. An analysis of attendance at meetings of the Council and the Engineering Section, of contributions to debate and the private correspondence of the POZF for the period 1908 to 1917 reveals that effective control over the Society's policy-making was exercised by a very small group of about eleven individuals.[5] Almost all of these gentlemen were non-Russian by birth – they were of Swedish, German or French extraction. The foreign origins of so many directors and managers predominant within the POZF, the external sources of so much of their firms' finances, their growing dependence on a few major banks, their companies' close business links to the government, were all significant factors in the formulation of the labour policies of the POZF.

After the fiasco of the Progressive Economic Party in the First State Duma elections in 1906, the POZF was avowedly 'apolitical'. It abandoned the effort to secure sizeable representation for industry in a legislature dominated after 3 June 1907 by agrarian gentry indifferent, if not plainly hostile, to the concerns of business, and chose the path of pressure group politics. The Society set itself the task of influencing governmental legislation before it reached the legislative chambers, defending the interests of industry and shaping state economic policies. Despite its protestations, however, the POZF was a politically partisan institution which devoted itself to upholding the autocratic order both in politics and in the factories. Thus the convention signed on 15 March 1905 by 125 St Petersburg factories, the *de facto* charter of the Society, agreed to ban worker participation in the determination of wages or dismissals, and in internal factory order, not to pay strike money, nor to abolish fines or agree to a minimum wage.[6] The employers refused to accept trade unions, regarding them as revolutionary bodies, and rejected all forms of collective bargaining.

In addition to the POZF, there were at least four other employers' organisations in the capital, all in predominantly artisanal branches of manufacture. There was a St Petersburg Society of Printing Firm Owners and a Union of St Petersburg Owners of Typographical Firms, both founded in 1906. In the same year there was established a Society of Owners of Tailoring Shops, which had 142 members by 1913. In early 1913, in response to a wave of strikes which plagued bakeries in the summer of 1912, a Society of Bakery Owners was set up, embracing 250 firms with a 40,000 rouble strike fund.[7]

II

Soviet historians and contemporary socialist analysts of the labour movement have exaggerated the unity of the POZF and the effectiveness of its labour policies. In 1913, for example, *Metallist*, the organ of the union of metalworkers, referred to the Society as the 'strong organ of big capital'; 'the circle of its influence is extraordinarily variegated and wide'. In his 1927 study of the labour movement M. Balabanov entitled Chapter 8 the 'counter-attack of united capital'; described the POZF as 'the most active agents of the counter-revolution', and 'the first to adopt the European tactic of militant capital'. G. A. Arutiunov has argued more recently that 'in the struggle with the labour movement the bourgeoisie acted in a single front'.[8] Underlying these views is the unarticulated assumption that the employers had become fully class-conscious. The violent disagreements within the POZF concerning the formulation of labour policy in the years 1912 to 1914 and its failure to elaborate acceptable efficacious measures against strikes suggest very real limits to industrialists' awareness of their mutual interests. The different economic conditions affecting particular industrial sectors dictated contrasting and contradictory responses to renewed labour disturbances.

The harbinger of the pre-war crisis in industrial relations in St Petersburg proved to be the response of the capital's workers to the shooting of unarmed strikers on the Lena goldfields on 4 April 1912 (see Chapter 4). The POZF held an extraordinary general meeting on 17 April to decide its reaction to the unexpected outburst of walk-outs by employees. On 20 November 1907 the Society had introduced the imposition of fines by members upon workers participating in stoppages of a political character. It had exacted monetary penalties of 50 kopecks to one rouble on those who went on strike on 1 May 1908.[9] But the emergency gathering of 17 April concluded that it would be inappropriate to resort to sanctions on the grounds that the protests surrounding the Lena tragedy should be regarded as an exceptional occurrence, arising from events unconnected with normal factory life in the city. Although only a minority, led by the Society's president S. P. Glezmer, favoured the imposition of fines, the meeting reconfirmed the validity of the general system of fining and resolved not to pay wages for the lost workdays, in conformity with the resolution of the Engineering Section of 27 November 1907.[10] The unspoken supposition behind this decision was that any punishment of the strikers would merely strengthen discontent and promote further strikes.

In the light of the Lena protests, it became imperative for the Society to establish a common policy towards potentially massive disturbances on May Day. This proved to be a highly contentious issue among factory owners. In 1912 a mere 23 member firms (among whom were a few large metalworking plants) either included 1 May in the table of official holidays or celebrated it by custom.[11] At a united meeting of the Council, Engineering and Textile Sections on 26 April, a majority present (25) voted to uphold the Society's previous policy on monetary retribution for strikes on May Day.[12] There were four dissenters: Neva Shipyards, Nobel, K. Ia. Pal' and St Petersburg Metals. In the event a mere sixteen companies (i.e. a tenth of the membership) levied fines on their employees. The divisions ran across industrial sectors.[13] It cannot be accidental that many of the firms objecting to the imposition of financial penalties on their workers were experiencing rapid expansion and possessed full order books as a result of defence contracts. Moreover, several of the metalworking and electrical firms which penalised their work-force for stopping work on 1 May endured strikes after that date by their employees in protest at this punishment. These included Erikson, Koppel', San Galli, Siemens and Halske and Tiudor. The manifest divisions within the POZF over 1 May gave rise to a series of meetings in the first ten days of the month which devoted an exhaustive analysis to the advantages and disadvantages of fines as a system of deterrence against strikes. The proponents of fining, who were led by the vice-president M. I. Tripolitov and B. A. Efron, advanced several arguments. The unity of the factory owners alone prevented strikes. If owners gave way before force, they would no longer be masters in their own house. The workers had only struck on May Day because they had gone unpunished for the Lena protests. Their opponents could adduce more convincing evidence to bolster their case. The imposition of fines merely angered working people and embittered labour relations to no avail. The Lena disturbances had revealed to labour its power, which it would now use in the future. In a period of economic recovery there was a severe shortage of skilled craftsmen. Factory management could ill afford antagonising such men or losing them to rivals through impolitic fines or unnecessary strikes. There was also the problem of state penalties which the Ministry of the Navy had introduced early in 1912 for the non-fulfilment of contracts within the set time limits. The government refused to accept that stoppages which arose over fines or other such punishments or from factors over which managements exercised responsibility constituted bona fide causes for delays in delivery and accordingly imposed financial penalties on the defaulting contractors. The last two points seem to have been the primary factors behind the opposition to the utilisation of fines by those heavy industrial firms dependent on state defence orders. This was certainly so in the case of the five firms voting against resort to fines at the 26 April meeting. These genuine differences of opinion and interests produced a fluctuating voting pattern at the May meetings. On 2 May, 22 firms voted to retain financial penalties for May Day strikes, 12 were against, and 44 abstained. On 7 May, when the issue concerned fines for possible stoppages of work on the first monthly anniversary of Lena, 9 supported fines and 10 rejected them. The final resolution on 9 May papered over the cracks by leaving the decision to individual members.[14]

In view of the blatant flouting of the convention by a majority of members and the threat of the sixteen companies who had imposed fines for 1 May strikes to leave the Society, the Council embarked on a quest for guarantees that members would fulfil the convention of 15 March 1905. On 10 May a commission to review the convention was established under the chairmanship of B. A. Efron, a hardline supporter of employers' solidarity and repressive measures against strikers. The engineering group played the dominant role in this body. In its five sessions four contentious issues arose. The representative of Erikson suggested the shortening of the working day, but its competitors rebuffed this as producing a curtailment of output. V. V. Bari, director of Neva Shipyards, proposed the establishment of a minimum working day on the grounds that state plants worked a shorter day. The majority rejected such a scheme, concurring with Efron that workers would interpret this as a concession won by striking. A plan for minimum wages met a similar fate. Behind these recommendations lay the notion that industrialists might secure labour peace by timely partial concessions rather than unremitting repression. Such sensible ideas always met a frigid reception on the part of the majority within the POZF. The commission rehearsed again the arguments concerning fines but members remained as divided as ever.[15]

The convention of the POZF, 28 June 1912, reconfirmed all the clauses of its predecessor. It also strengthened it in certain respects. Article 1 prohibited any shortening of the working day. Articles 5 and 6 banned permanent representatives of the workers, including factory elders, and the intervention and mediation of trade unions in the internal affairs of the factories. Article 9 regulated blacklists. None of these points had been included in the previous convention. Stiff financial penalties were to be imposed on members who failed to comply with its provisions. The convention represented the owners' renewed determination to defend the old factory order and to repulse any compromise with workers' demands. Yet, with the exception of the clause concerning blacklists, the document was eloquently silent (not a mention was made of fines) on the means by which the POZF proposed to preserve the industrial status quo. It was a portent of future disunity that not until 1 March 1913 did a majority of members sign the new convention.[16]

Dr Hogan has argued that St Petersburg employers became increasingly alarmed at the ever-growing political nature of labour protest and that by 1914 they concluded that they faced a challenge not only to their economic interests but to their social and political prerogatives.[17] This contention requires some qualification. The POZF, it is true, became more and more concerned, as the annual reports of 1912 and 1913 reveal, about the role of 'external agents' in fostering discontent in the factories. It pointed specifically to the workers' press, 'some definite workers' centre', and the Social Democratic deputies in the Duma. But, as employers were aware, political strikes were short one-day stoppages. The real economic damage was wrought by economic disputes. It can be argued that it was as much this factor, as well as the apparently ever-increasing intensity of the strike movement, which impelled factory owners to adopt a wide range of measures to combat strikes.[18]

In contrast to the Association of Industry and Trade (henceforth AIT), the all-Russian organisation of industrialists, which advocated granting workers the genuine freedom to establish trade unions, from its foundation the POZF remained implacably opposed to all forms of labour organisations. In February 1908 it sent a circular to members prohibiting any dealings with trade unions. In the collective view of the Society trade unions were premature in Russian conditions. They were not institutions concerned with the pursuit of economic improvements for their members, but with 'politicking'. They were controlled by revolutionaries. Russian working people were not yet prepared to administer their own institutions as they were ill-educated and possessed an 'undeveloped character'.[19] A few solitary members of the POZF defended trade unions, such as M. P. Pankov (St Petersburg Metals) and S. P. Beliaev (a sawmill owner). Article 6 of the 1912 Convention, enshrining this view, was one that was indeed implemented by a majority of members. Out of 396 economic strikes in heavy industry in the capital, January 1912–3 July 1914, for which detailed information can be located, there was not a single one in which the employers agreed to negotiate with trade unions. In contrast print owners, most of whom did not belong to the POZF, showed a willingness to enter into negotiations with the union of printers.

In their determination to resist all demands threatening the prerogatives of factory management, the employers had long refused to implement the law on factory elders, 10 May 1903, which permitted the voluntary introduction of elected spokesmen for workers (designated factory elders). Before 1914 very few St Petersburg enterprises had accepted this institution; these were some state enterprises (Izhora arms-works, Obukhov, the State Expedition of Papers) and a few engineering plants (Franco-Russian, St Petersburg Metals). During the pre-war labour unrest, a fairly common request by strikers in all sectors of industry was for the recognition of elders by factory administrations. But the printing owners alone sometimes made such a concession. Moreover, when the POZF learnt of the plans of the Council of Ministers to introduce arbitration chambers to mediate in labour disputes, (see pp. 291–92) the Society's Council reacted negatively to the concept in the spring of 1914, concluding that these bodies would take decisions out of political considerations and would always be antagonistic to industrialists' interests. Yet in the summer of 1913 the newly formed Society of Bakery Owners proposed the formation of an arbitration court to settle labour disputes in its trade.[20]

The attitude of the POZF towards the implementation of the Law on Sickness Insurance of 1912 was at its best ambivalent. Whereas the leadership of the AIT had supported the introduction of this legislation, the Society had fought a long and relatively unsuccessful rearguard action against it in the various bureaucratic commissions and in the legislative chambers. It had raised particular objections on the grounds of cost to the clause compelling employers to provide medical aid and to the exemption of state plants from the law, thereby giving them, it was claimed, a competitive advantage.[21] The firms represented in the POZF were suspiciously dilatory in their implementation of the statute's provisions.[22] Although the latter allowed the voluntary renunciation by industrialists of certain of the rights bestowed upon them, very few chose to do so. Most insisted that they remain chairmen of the executive boards of the elected sickness funds (*kassy*) established to administer insurance against illness at work. Before the war a mere six firms (three were textile companies) had renounced the right to chair meetings of *kassy* boards. They rejected workers' amendments to the rules of the *kassy*, insisting on the model regulations drafted by the insurance commission of the POZF, under the chairmanship of M. P. Pankov. When this body proposed in June 1914 that the Society take upon itself the organisation of emergency medical help in the districts of the city in order to forestall worker's representatives claiming this right for the *kassy*, it was compelled to abandon the idea in the face of members' hostility. The leaders of the POZF were also most reluctant to permit general meetings of the factory workshops to discuss *kassy* statutes, fearing that 'these might instil in workers a belief in the admissibility of such meetings in general to discuss all questions affecting the life of the factory' (Council, 4 January 1913). It was typical of the Society's state of near permanent dissension that in practice most factory managements sanctioned general factory meetings devoted to insurance matters.[23]

The leaders of the Society also resisted firmly any requests by member firms to be exempted from the articles of the Convention prohibiting the shortening of the working day or permanent representation for workers. In September 1913 the Council, for example, condemned the engineering company, Ia. M. Aivaz, on the grounds that its concession of a special commission to oversee the hiring of workers 'created a dangerous precedent for other plants'. When the Erikson and Siemens and Halske electrical firms applied to the Council of the Engineering Section in March 1914 for permission to reduce the working day at their factories from ten hours to nine (in part because their principal competitor Geisler had already introduced shorter hours), their proposal was emphatically rejected because, in the words of Efron, 'shortening the working day would be interpreted as a concession to the labour movement and would create a demand for higher wages'. On the eve of the war the Council also threw out the project of the Moscow Society of Manufacturers to make May Day a legal holiday.[24]

In the great pre-war wave of strikes which swept over the city, factory owners resorted to what had long before become standard measures of repression. In all sectors of manufacturing as soon as labour stoppages occurred, managers closed the plants and sacked all the strikers. Many factory administrations sought strikebreakers, although this proved more and more difficult in 1913 and 1914 as workers' solidarity and hostility to scabs intensified. In lengthy disputes, attempts were made to transfer orders to other firms, but this tactic was often defeated by strikers securing the agreement of other operatives to blacklist such work. As a last resort recourse was had to the police to arrest strikers in an effort to intimidate their comrades. On occasions the POZF's officials even made formal approaches to the authorities. During the lengthy stoppage at the electrical firm Siemens and Halske, which began on 10 May 1912 as a protest against fines levied for a walk-out on 1 May and lasted 90 days, the strike's demise was hastened by a delegation from the Society on 28 July, at the request of the company's board, to the Minister of Internal Affairs. As much as the workers, the POZF recognised a principle at stake in the dispute: if the firm were compelled to make concessions, the strikers would claim a moral victory. After the visit the police made a series of arrests which broke the strike. With the institution of an Enquiry Office attached to the Society in December 1909, the circulation of blacklists of strikers compiled by the Office became the norm during labour conflicts. Lists were destroyed soon after disputes had ended. The fierce competition for skilled labour after 1910 ensured that private firms and state plants alike often ignored blacklists and hired workers on strike in their rivals' workshops. When the time came to readmit employees after the settlement of a dispute, filtering of the labour force was a widespread practice – 'agitators', 'ringleaders', 'troublemakers' were not rehired.[25]

Even if the POZF maintained a theoretically implacable hostility to concessions to workers' demands, it did seek greater uniformity and standardisation in the widely varying working conditions within the private heavy industrial sector and between it and state establishments, thereby, it was hoped, reducing labour turnover and strike activity. In August 1913 the Engineering Section revived its commission to compile a standard rates book and rules of internal order, which had functioned in 1907 and 1908. A representative of the Ministry of War joined it for the first time. But, at the very first session, this gentleman undercut the commission's rationale by rejecting out of hand identical terms of hire and rules of internal order between state and private enterprises. No substantive agreement could be reached on any issue. In a debate on uniform level of wages participants were driven to the reluctant conclusion that skilled labour shortages would and did induce employers to pay rates above any notional norms. The single achievement of the commission before the war was to draw up a set of model rules of internal order.[26]

As the previous chapter has shown, the various measures of repression applied by St Petersburg employers enabled them with increasing success to resist workers' claims and break strikes. But as the ever-rising curve of disputes revealed only too clearly, they signally failed to prevent their outbreak. In 1913 and 1914 the leaders of the POZF intensified their efforts to co-ordinate managerial response to labour unrest. Attention focused on three means – fines, a lock-out, and the Regulations on Industry.

Despite the questionable applicability of fines as a deterrent to strikes of a political nature and the clear divisions of opinion on the issue evident in the response of the Society to the stoppages of work in April and May 1912, much sterile debate took place in various meetings of the Council in the succeeding two years. The same arguments first advanced in the spring of 1912 were rehearsed again and again. After many months of discussion the futile and utopian conclusion to which the Society came, at a special conference on 24 April 1914, was that 'fines as a measure were possible only if all factories pursued united action in this matter'. Moreover at this gathering for the first time some industrialists at last raised, in their opinion, a central obstacle to the effectiveness of forfeits, namely their 'minimal' size. Article 145 of the Regulations on Industry, 3 June 1886, set this penalty at one rouble for workers paid at day rates and under that sum for pieceworkers. In view of the 'high' wages in heavy industry, the majority present voted in favour of a fine for pieceworkers of double the shop wage because the latter were the 'leaders of the strike movement'. A memorandum from the POZF to the Ministry of Trade and Industry on 10 June 1914 enclosed such a proposal.[27]

An analysis of the reaction of factory managements to politically inspired strikes in 1913 and 1914 reveals the different approaches between and within sectors of industry to the imposition of monetary punishments. When some 70,000 workers downed tools to commemorate Bloody Sunday on 9 January 1913, a single plant (the state-owned Obukhov) levied a fine on its work-force. Before the anniversary of the Lena shootings on 4 April 1913 (78,000 came out) the textile employers agreed to refrain from any disciplinary action. But in advance of 1 May 1913 (135,000 workers in all industries struck) six major mills issued warning notices that they would retaliate by fines for a walk-out on that date and were accordingly spared any disturbances. In the engineering sector Langenzippen alone resorted to a fine. After the one-day stoppage in protest against the trial of Obukhov workers on 6 November 1913, the same textile plants and the Skorokhod shoe company all made deductions from the workers' pay.[28] These firms likewise penalised their operatives for failure to come to work on 9 January 1914 (114,000 refused to enter their factories). On 24 April 1914 the Engineering Group resolved by nineteen votes to two to abstain from levying fines for stoppages on May Day (170,000 walked out).[29] In practice very few member companies in the POZF – the textile sector excepted – resorted to monetary penalties as a weapon in the struggle against strikes. It is possible that the greater willingness of some textile companies to utilise fines and to adopt lock-outs lay in their reluctance to see the incipient economic recovery in this sector, after the downturn of 1908–11, threatened by prolonged interruptions to production.

The manifest futility of fines as a deterrent compelled industrialists to consider the far harsher method of a lock-out in both political and economic disputes. In this field the pioneers were certain textile firms who made repeated use of this measure in an effort to break economic conflicts. When all 850 operatives struck for a pay rise in the Vyborg plant of Voronin, Liuts, Chesher on 4 June 1912, the factory administration closed down (i.e. locked out) all its other five mills which had continued to work. The second time this occurred was between 18 and 31 December 1912. In response to a strike by their workers in support of a Social Democratic interpellation in the Duma concerning the persecution of trade unions by the police, the management at Petrovskaia and Spasskaia mills (British owned) threw on to the streets 3,000 men and women.[30] On 22 January 1913 the directors of Russian Cotton (British controlled) reacted to a protest by 30 workers against a cut in rates by locking out all 1,200 operatives for a fortnight. A similar event took place at New Cotton (British owned) at the same time. After the labour force at Petrovskaia and Spasskaia refused to come to work on the anniversary of the Lena massacre on 4 April 1913, the factory was once more closed – for an entire month. The 3,000 hands at Nevskaia Cotton received similar treatment between 23 April and 3 May in reaction to a walk-out by 100 operatives in the carding department. And in the printing trade a series of strikes in the largest lithographic workshops in May provoked a joint, three-month-long, lock-out of the total work-force. In the course of a series of stoppages which plagued the numerous artisanal tailoring shops between April and June 1913, the Owners' Union considered but ultimately rejected a shutdown.[31] Yet until March 1914 the vast majority of the members of the POZF, including the heavy industrial sector, refused to give serious contemplation to the utilisation of this measure.

Although the president of the Society, S. P. Glezmer, had first suggested the adoption of a lock-out as official POZF policy on 5 May 1912, no more was heard of the idea until an extraordinary general meeting held on 10 January 1913 at which the representatives of Petrovskaia and Spasskaia mills and the Skorokhod shoe company recommended the benefits of this novel method of restoring calm to factory life from their own experience. Both gentlemen envisaged it as an instrument for crushing economic conflicts. They were supported by the hardliner B. A. Efron. All three remained in a distinct minority.[32] The first serious discussion of the concept, and an indication of a growing acceptance of the measure by heavy industry, took place in the Engineering Section's Commission on Measures of Struggle against Strikers on 14 June 1913 and in a meeting of the Section itself two months later. The Commission resolved to dispatch P. A. Bartmer, vice-president of the Section and a director of Nobel, to Germany to study the practical implications of a lock-out. One reason for the new interest in the notion was a deepening disappointment with the handling of labour unrest by the Ministry of Internal Affairs (henceforth MVD). The Ministry was accused of fearing to embitter industrial relations by recourse to repression. These initial debates also revealed two basic obstacles to a co-ordinated usage of closures by the POZF: firms dependent on defence contracts would refuse to participate; the state-owned plants would have to join the Society and adhere to a shutdown otherwise workers thrown out on to the streets would merely find employment in these factories. Although representatives of the Ministries of War and the Navy attended sessions of the Engineering Section from August 1913, they always felt unable to commit themselves on the issue. The wider membership of the Society, however, was far from convinced by the arguments in favour of a lock-out. On 12 November 1913 the Council concluded that 'no general agreement on a lock-out would be possible except in a time of mass revolutionary upheaval'.[33]

A significant shift of opinion in favour of closures came about in March 1914, at least among engineering industrialists. Several explanations may be offered for this development. There was the apparent prospect of a distinct worsening of industrial relations in the year ahead. At its February gathering the Council of the Engineering

Section had taken the gloomy view that 'they could expect a decisive strike movement in 1914'. Factory owners, Bartmer warned the Judicial Commission, were losing patience at the spiralling losses inflicted 'by the unending strikes'. There was the growing suspicion that, in the words of R. R. Liander (a director of United Cables), 'the government will not support us', and that the MVD's repressive measures against strikes 'have produced no tangible results' (memorandum of the Society, 10 June 1914).[34] Some engineering employers were undoubtedly thoroughly alarmed by the apparently ceaseless rise in politically inspired one-day stoppages. In particular the series of one-day strikes by a total of 20,000 workers which swept through the capital in protest at the repression of working-class newspapers and the union of metalworkers, culminating in a walk-out by 55,000 on 13 March in support of the Social Democratic Duma interpellation concerning the Lena events, was undoubtedly the immediate cause of the March shutdown. Other industrialists in the same sector, however, did not share this alarm. Emmanuel Nobel, for example, felt that St Petersburg's experience was exceptional as it was the centre of political life. L. I. Shpergaze (a director of Erikson) took the view that labour protest was directed against the government rather than employers.[35] Under the impact of these factors, the Council of the Engineering Section voted on 13 March in favour of the principle of a lock-out against political strikes without a specific instance in mind. When some 84,000 operatives left their benches on 19 March to express their sympathy with the female employees of the Russian-American Rubber Company's Treugol'nik plant, afflicted by an epidemic of fainting fits, the Council itself gave its general approval to the concept of a lock-out.[36] In fact the decision to launch the first co-ordinated closures in the engineering industry specifically against politically inspired stoppages was taken neither by the entire Council nor by the Engineering Section but on the private initiative of sixteen engineering and electrical firms on 19 March, most of whom employed around 1,500 hands. Between 20 and 24 March, these companies excluded their workers without pay. The state-owned Baltic and Obukhov factories followed suit. Of the 59 engineering and electrical companies represented in the POZF, 43 held aloof from the shutdown.

Delighted by the 'excellent results' of the closures, on 26 March a special meeting of the Engineering Section resolved to go over to the attack. It was agreed that all member firms would resort to this tactic against politically motivated disturbances in the weeks up to May Day. The new-found unanimity soon collapsed. At an extraordinary session of the Section on 19 April, the sixteen companies participating in the March exclusion proposed that this measure should be applied by the entire membership against anticipated political strikes on 22 April (the Bolshevik-inspired anniversary of the workers' press – no strikes occurred on that date) and on May Day. The representatives of Erikson, Neva Shipyards, St Petersburg Wagons, Siemens and Halske, argued against the proposition on the grounds that it was far too risky and that in the condition of boom in this sector dismissed workers could easily secure employment elsewhere. The proposal to impose a two-day lock-out for stoppages on 22 April was carried by a vote of twenty-three to ten. No decision was reached concerning May Day. When a section of the labour force went on strike on 23 and 24 April to protest the exclusion of the Social Democratic and Trudovik deputies from the Duma as a punishment for obstructing the address of the president of the Council of Ministers, Goremykin, a mere ten firms closed their plants. And ten of the companies which had shut out their labour force in March refrained from doing so on this occasion. An emergency meeting of the Section on 24 April decided by a vote of nineteen to two to abstain from all punishments (lock-out or fines) for 1 May walk-outs.[37]

Several explanations for such extraordinary vacillation are possible. There may have been successful lobbying by the opponents of the new tactic. (Attendance at the relevant gatherings embraced only a relatively small proportion of total membership.) There were openly expressed and justifiable fears for the loss of skilled workers to competitors and the imposition of penalties by the state for failure to meet contractual obligations on defence orders. There was the relative lack of participation by state-owned factories in the March and April closures. Doubts also existed about the legality of the lock-outs.

The manifest lack of co-ordination among engineering and electrical firms in the March and April partial closures imparted a palpable sense of urgency to the POZF's search for solutions to the apparent obstacles. Their attention focused on the threat of state fines for late delivery and the 'defects' of the Regulations on Industry.

Taking the view that 'further use of a lock-out is problematic if this problem is not settled', three May sessions of the Society were devoted to a discussion of the attitude of the authorities to failure to meet deadlines on defence contracts as a result of strikes. Encouraged by a reported shift in the attitude of the Ministry of the Navy, the POZF resolved to draft a memorandum to the relevant government departments. This document, presented by a delegation from the Society on 10 June, proposed *inter alia* that the authorities should no longer inflict financial punishment on any plant with a state contract (in any industrial sector) for late deliveries caused by industrial disputes.

Employers were also anxious about the legal validity of a lock-out and the threat of a challenge to it in the courts from workers. The problem arose from Article 98 of the Regulations on Industry, which defined the terms of the contract of hire. This declared that the statutory period of notice of dismissal was two weeks. Thus the March and April closures had been technically invalid. Moreover, factory administrations sacking workers without the requisite notification were obliged to pay two weeks' wages. For these reasons a special conference of the POZF held on 29 April 1914 concluded that 'a lock-out was impossible until the statutory time limit of notification was foreshortened'.[38] In the various meetings of the Society in the spring of 1914 which discussed the issue, the vice-president M. I. Tripolitov played the dominant role. In its suggestions for the reform of the Regulations, the POZF leadership was strongly influenced by the practices of German employer unions. The memorandum presented by a delegation from the Society on 10 June to the Ministers of Trade, War, the Navy and the State Comptroller embodied the fruits of lengthy discussions. Tbe desiderata embraced: the replacement of the fourteen days' notice of dismissal by a much shorter period in general strikes and three days' warning in partial stoppages; the right of the employer to write any conditions he chose into the contract of hire and to secure its observation by forfeits and deposits. The internal debates within the bureaucracy reveal that the industrialists stood little chance of securing the implementation of this programme (see p. 294).[39]

The impression that a majority within the POZF was emerging on the eve of the war in favour of a more militant position is reinforced by the fact that a special conference on 8 May seriously discussed Tripolitov's concept of an employers' anti-strike insurance fund to reimburse owners for losses suffered during conflicts. The meeting arrived at no firm conclusion. Moreover at sessions of the Council on 13 May and the Engineering Section on 22 May Tripolitov and N. S. Kalabin (the director of Neva Shipyards) advocated that lock-outs should be applied in economic as well as political strikes (on which discussion had primarily centred to that date), on the grounds that many contemporary strikes bore a mixed character. This point of view failed to secure general acceptance at the gathering of 22 May, which voted to shut factories for two weeks in the event of a future one-day political strike, and for one month if such a strike occurred a second time. The decision to increase the length of closure from the previous three or four days to a fortnight testified to the growing impatience of engineering employers, who had had to endure another one-day political strike on 19 May when 89,000 walked out in protest at the trial of Obukhov strikers.[40] The unprecedented labour disturbances which broke out in the capital after 3

July were to test almost to breaking point the new-found unity and resolution of the POZF (see Chapter 10).

III

The revival of the working-class movement after 1911 and the intensity of strikes which served both as an outlet for political discontent and as a means to remedy economic grievances constituted as great a challenge to Imperial authority as to employers. Throughout the pre-war years ministers and officials never forgot two fearful facts. In the words of the protocols of the session of the Council of Ministers on 5 July 1914, 'the employment in the capital of a tenth of the entire work-force of the Empire, in number equivalent to a sixth of the Imperial army, constitutes a serious threat to the safety of the state'. High bureaucrats were equally appalled by the knowledge that, 'half the labour force of the capital is composed of metalworkers, who form the most restless element, are the most prone to strike and participate in political demonstrations'. The problem for the government was compounded by their awareness that a significant proportion of employees in heavy industry were working on defence orders. The renascent labour movement apparently posed a threat not only to public order in the capital, indeed perhaps represented the most serious political danger for the regime since 1905, but also to the programme of rearmament regarded as crucial by officialdom to the revival of Russia's great power status. As the Minister of Internal Affairs, N. A. Maklakov, realised, 'the nonfunctioning of private factories engaged in fulfilling defence contracts would threaten the state's most vital interests in the present political conditions' (memorandum from Maklakov to Minister of Trade and Industry, 30 June 1913).[41] Ministers' concerns were all the greater because they were preparing a new programme of military and naval expansion, which was presented to the Duma in March 1914. Although the bureaucracy became more and more apprehensive about the character of the strike movement, like the employers, it signally failed to formulate a coherent, constructive response. As in the past, government labour policy remained highly confused, contradictory, inconsistent and ultimately self-defeating. The government never reached a consensus on how to tackle the problem of labour.

Before an examination of the factors peculiar to the period 1912 to 1914, several more general explanations may be advanced for the ambiguities of policy-making in this area.

In the first place there was the wider bureaucratic paralysis engendered by the institutional weaknesses of the Council of Ministers established in October 1905. In the absence of collective cabinet responsibility, ministers were able to pursue their own programmes without reference to their colleagues. V. N. Kokovtsov, president of the Council of Ministers from September 1911 to January 1914, and his successor I. L. Goremykin (January 1914 to January 1916) possessed neither the personal authority nor the political power (both were denied the Ministry of Internal Affairs at the Tsar's insistence) to impose unity upon ministers. The absence of a proper cabinet to co-ordinate imperial policy-making acted as a fundamental systemic constraint. This fact enabled the MVD and the Ministry of Trade and Industry (henceforth MTP) to pursue different and often antagonistic projects in the sphere of industrial relations.

Secondly there was the continued dependence of the upper ranks of certain central ministries upon recruitment from the hereditary gentry estate. This was particularly the case with regard to the pre-war Ministries of Internal Affairs and Justice, although not the MTP. Even if a majority of top bureaucrats in the MVD no longer possessed estates in the provinces (the proportion of landless high civil servants in all the central ministries grew from 63 per cent in 1881 to 78 per cent in 1914), their gentry connections, their Great Russian origins, the non-technical nature of their higher education (in 1914 51 per cent of MVD senior civil servants had attended university) meant that they showed little sympathy with or understanding of the problems of industry.[42]

It is also possible that the 'high politics' of 1912 to 1914 exerted a baleful influence on proposals to deal with industrial disturbances, although this must remain more a matter of conjecture than documented fact. Before the outbreak of war neither the reactionary elements in the Council of Ministers, two of whose most vigorous champions were P. A. Stolypin's successors as Ministers of Internal Affairs (A. A. Makarov, September 1911 to December 1912 and N. A. Maklakov, December 1912 to June 1915), who sought a return to pure absolutism, nor those supporters of the new political status quo established after October 1905 (led by Kokovtsov) were in a position to push through à outrance their respective designs. All aspects of public policy became caught up in the increasingly bitter struggle for dominant control of the governmental apparatus and influence with Nicholas II. The consequence was a growing paralysis of decision-taking in the highest spheres even before the infamous (and exaggerated) 'ministerial leapfrogging' of 1915 and 1916. It may be surmised that policy-making in the sphere of labour relations was no exception. The views and programmes of the Minister of Internal Affairs, Maklakov, and the Minister of Trade and Industry, S. I. Timashev (who held the post from December 1909 to February 1915), concerning the labour question were in part a reflection of their wider political sympathies.

THE MINISTRY OF INTERNAL AFFAIRS AND THE LABOUR PROBLEM

The attitudes of the higher officials of the Ministry of Internal Affairs towards renewed industrial conflict were moulded by several contradictory considerations. On the one hand, there remained the deeply ingrained bureaucratic distrust of all, including working-class, spontaneity and self-activity. By the middle of 1913 the Ministry's civil servants and the police were becoming alarmed that strikes were no longer restricted to economic issues. This view was shared by the Council of Ministers which observed on 24 October 1913 that 'the strike movement is assuming all the more a political colouring'. Their conclusion derived from their belief that 'stoppages are very often the product of illegal agitation by the revolutionary parties and . serve as a clear manifestation of the development of the revolutionary movement'. This overestimation of the role of socialist groups in fomenting labour unrest in the factories rendered all the stronger ministerial concern, shared by Maklakov, about delays in the programme of rearmament through unnecessary disputes. On the other hand, there survived in the pre-war MVD the *dirigiste* tradition of intervention in the internal affairs of factory life to remove the economic and social causes of working-class discontent. As Dr Bonnell has pointed out, there was the more recent and unwelcome realisation by the Ministry that the introduction of an elected legislature, inclusive of Social Democratic and Trudovik deputies, made it imperative to pay some attention to public opinion. These incompatible strands of repression and moderation inevitably produced an MVD labour policy permeated by vacillation and general uncertainty.[43]

In the sphere of trade-union activity, the MVD had always been haunted by the fear that workers' legal organisations would 'provide a base for the propaganda of [Social Democratic] ideas among the masses and their gradual [conversion to] revolution' (MVD secret circular, October 1912).[44] From 1906 it had recourse to a variety of measures in order to prevent unions falling under the sway of 'revolutionary agitators' and intervening in industrial conflicts, as well as to weaken their potential as instruments of working-class leadership.

In the first place, the MVD took advantage of the fact that the legal existence of all trade unions was dependent on the submission of their charters to the St Petersburg Municipal Bureau for Union Affairs for registration. This bureaucratic body, which included the director of the Department of Police, twice refused to register a proposed union of metalworkers, in October 1912 and January 1913. On the latter occasion the Bureau objected to a long list of articles in the charter, including the right to open a library and a tearoom, memberhip for the unemployed, the formation of branches in the workshops and a council of delegates. It banned the registration of a union of carton workers in September 1912 and one of flour workers in March 1914.[45] The authorities also ordered revisions of existing union charters. In September 1912 the Governor General of St Petersburg demanded re-examination of the charter of the union of tailors with a view to the excision of the article permitting a council of delegates. A similar event befell the union of bakers in November 1913. In March 1914 the Governor General commanded the union of metalworkers to hand over its accounts and books. In the last two cases these actions presaged the closure of the unions.[46] The Municipal Bureau exerted much ingenuity in excising from the charters of unions, which it did consent to register, all clauses possibly strengthening them as genuine agents of collective action. The union of printing workers, registered in August 1912, was prohibited from paying unemployment or strike benefits, conducting an inquiry into working conditions or setting up an unemployment bureau. The police entertained a special animus against union councils of district delegates, regarding them as an important means of promoting ties between union executives and the rank and file. In the case of at least four unions their statutes expressly forbade such an institution.[47]

Since the majority of trade unions sought to remove these debilitating restrictions on their activities, the MVD fell back on more repressive action. The police frequently took advantage of the legal requirement of the Temporary Regulations of 4 March 1906 that they attend every general meeting of a union in order to prohibit gatherings in advance or close sessions for discussing topics considered to be *ultra vires* in respect of the union's charter or the agenda of the meeting. At the general meeting of the union of textile workers, for example, on 28 April 1913, the officer present refused to permit reports from district branches or a discussion concerning publication of a union journal. The police terminated a gathering of the union of printers on 16 March 1914 when it began to examine the strikes in the trade.[48] In the two and a half years before the outbreak of the First World War, some twenty union general meetings were so prohibited or closed. There were frequent arrests of the officers of trade-union executives, in particular of those with connections to the socialist parties. Such repressive measures were facilitated by the detailed knowledge of union affairs made available to the Okhrana by the successful penetration of union executives by its agents. In the last resort unions were closed down if their activities were considered to have contravened their registered charters. This happened on nine occasions from 1912 to 1914.

As if such persecution was insufficient, an inter-ministerial conference presented to the Council of Ministers in May 1914 a bill to revise the Temporary Regulations in an even more restrictive sense. The proposed amendments included the attendance of the police at all union meetings (including executive ones); a ban on union membership by unemployed workers or those employed in a factory for under a year; an age eligibility for election to union offices (a minimum of 25 years); a restriction of union organisation of strikes to plants with no social or government significance or under peaceful conditions.[49] The war shelved the project.

Even without the passage of the proposed new trade-union legislation, which would have rendered them totally harmless, the MVD's punitive reprisals, as Chapter 7 has shown, emasculated the trade unions on the eve of the war. Their memberships involved a minute fraction of the work-force in their industries. They played a minimal role in the strike movement, unable to offer leadership or adequate finance to strikers.

The rights granted to workers by the Law on Sickness Insurance, 23 June 1912, aroused great suspicions in the MVD. In a confidential circular sent to provincial governors on 7 September 1912 the Minister of Internal Affairs, Makarov, expressed the fear that 'by creating strong working-class organisations which will have at their disposal large sums of money, the Insurance Law will heighten workers' consciousness of their own interests'. He was also rightly concerned that the sick benefit funds (*kassy*), like the trade unions, would be infiltrated by socialist activists 'as our working population is easily swayed by the persistent propaganda of the revolutionary parties'. The Ministry and its surrogates intervened in the application of the new law to ensure that 'the activities of the new workers' organisations must not exceed the limits prescribed by the law'.[50]

The Department of Police, which was represented on the Insurance Council by three persons including its director, S. P. Beletskii, endeavoured to ensure the return of 'suitable' workers' delegates to the highest insurance institutions (the Insurance Council and provincial insurance boards). As the law stipulated that elections of labour representatives to these organs could not take place before a minimum of eight *kassy* had been instituted in the capital, the MVD decided to 'invite' (i.e. appoint) certain workers to serve on these bodies in an interim capacity. In the autumn of 1912 the Okhrana drew up a list of thirty-eight potential worker members, eighteen of whom were Social Democrats (all delegates in the St Petersburg labour curia in the Fourth Duma elections). It suggested that the seven interim delegates should be drawn from right-wing parties or non-party workers. The police rejected all the socialists on the list with two exceptions, particularly those who were young and single.[51]

In general, the MVD intervened less in the implementation of the Insurance Law than it did in the sphere of union affairs. It possessed dependable allies in the employers and the Insurance Council, both of which struggled with much success to prevent any considerable departure from the strict letter of the law by the workers' representatives on the executive boards of the *kassy*. Yet in the last resort the authorities were prepared to arrest delegates to general meetings and elected board members. By the summer of 1914 in the capital some 50 workers connected with insurance had been detained by the Okhrana.[52]

As well as acts of repression against individual trade unions and *kassy*, in the summer of 1913 Maklakov was constrained by his anxieties concerning the potential damage inflicted upon the programme of rearmament by apparently unending stoppages of work to consider broader punitive measures to crush the strike movement. After a conference in his Ministry, he set out his proposals in a memorandum of 30 June 1913 to Timashev.

In the first place he advocated a greater exploitation of their administrative powers by the authorities. But he drew a careful distinction between the application of administrative penalties (under the 1881 Statute of Reinforced Protection) against strikers (which he favoured) and against workers desisting from striking (he advised against punishing them on the grounds that it merely exacerbated public opinion and gave rise to interpellations in the Duma). He also suggested that factory administrations should dismiss all workers considered to be 'harmful'. In a circular of 28 July to provincial governors, he ordered the police to keep a close supervision over sacked workers 'who, as they are without work, constitute a most dangerous element'. In August 1913, the Statute of Reinforced Protection was renewed in the capital for another year.[53]

The response by the government to strikes of a political character was regarded purely as a problem of criminal law. The composition of the Council of Ministers and 'high politics' ensured that the notion of political concessions in the face of labour unrest was never once considered. Both reactionaries and moderates regarded them as inadmissible. Debate, therefore, centred on what ministers believed to be the defects of the criminal law in the area of industrial relations. After the *ukaz* of 2 December 1905 had abrogated criminal penalties for strikes as such, unaccompanied by the use of force or attacks on property (but prohibited strikes in 'enterprises of state or social significance'), Articles 1359^3–1359^8 of the Criminal Code limited criminal liability to incitement or coercion of workers to stop work, deliberate damage to owners' property by strikers and participation in a strike association. In his memorandum of 30 June 1913, Maklakov made use of a Senatorial comment on the aforesaid articles to propose that all leaders and instigators of political strikes in plants fulfilling defence contracts should be liable to criminal prosecution. 'Criminal penalties,' he noted, 'are the real means of struggle against strikers.' His circular to provincial governors instructed them to implement this advice. Major General Drachevskii, the St Petersburg Governor General, at once posted the requisite warning notice in all factories. The Minister of Internal Affairs also hastened to remove the deficiencies of the criminal law. In a memorandum to the Council of Ministers, 14 October 1913, which it approved at its session of 24 October, he recommended a bill to establish criminal liability for those who incited or defended strikes which put forward political or revolutionary demands. Both the MVD and the Council ruled out any restoration of criminal penalties in economic strikes, 'as previous practice had revealed that it was of no practical use'.[54] The report of an inter-ministerial conference under Timashev on 9 July 1914 upheld these conclusions. On the other hand it unexpectedly shifted the scope of the legal argument by its suggestion that incitement to a political strike should be categorised as a 'state crime', as defined by Articles 129 to 131 of the Penal Code, thereby permitting preliminary detention and a higher penalty of three years' imprisonment.[55] There seems to have been no instance of the use of the Criminal Code against participants in political strikes before the war.

The MVD and the police, however, were unwilling to abandon their long tradition of direct pressure on factory owners to improve the economic conditions of their work-force. Their experience and agents' reports convinced them that the widely varying conditions of labour within and among factories constituted a prime cause of bad industrial relations. In a letter to Maklakov on 27 June 1913, Colonel M. F. Von-Koten, chief of the St Petersburg Okhrana, suggested that the strike movement might be weakened if employers increased pay and could standardise conditions of labour, in particular the working day and overtime. The MVD accepted these recommendations and repeated them in a circular to provincial governors on 28 July 1913. There is no evidence that the police applied them in St Petersburg.

A more novel suggestion came from S. P. Beletskii, director of the Department of Police. In a memorandum to the MVD of 31 August 1913 he advocated the institution of arbitration chambers to resolve industrial disputes. Maklakov hastened to place a draft for 'conciliation courts' before the Council of Ministers in a memorandum of 14 October. The aims of the proposed institution would include 'disarming revolutionary circles' and 'obviating recourse on occasions to administrative repressions'. In the desire to ensure that, unlike the trade unions and *kassy*, the courts, confined at first to Moscow and St Petersburg, would not fall under the sway of 'revolutionary agitators', elected representatives of both employers and workers were to be excluded. He seemed oblivious to the obvious fact that their bureaucratic composition (the provincial governor, the senior factory inspector, a member of the regional court) would vitiate the courts' potentiality as instruments of industrial conciliation.[56]

THE MINISTRY OF TRADE AND INDUSTRY AND THE LABOUR PROBLEM

A rational, co-ordinated approach by the government to labour was severely hampered by the bifurcation of responsibility between the MVD and MTP. The latter ministry, established in 1905, ranked low in terms of finance, bureaucratic prestige and political influence. Its incumbent, S. I. Timashev, was well experienced in economic and labour affairs, having been chief of the Department of Industry of the Ministry of Finance before 1905 and manager of the State Bank. His different career pattern from Makarov and Maklakov ensured that he took a more relaxed view of the pre-war labour unrest. In his judgement, and that of his officials, the upsurge in industrial disputes was a natural phenomenon of a period of economic recovery. Writing to Maklakov on 26 July 1913, he remarked that 'workers normally use such times of revival in economic life, as at present, to increase their demands upon employers'. The fact that heavy industry was particularly affected by a deterioration in labour relations, an internal MTP memorandum accurately noted on 28 June 1914, was to be explained in part by the acute shortage of (skilled) labour in plants working on defence contracts, which was naturally exploited by the workers and their organisations to press economic demands. In a letter to Kokovtsov, Timashev also pointed out that strikes in engineering were of short duration, particularly those of a political nature. These arguments led the minister to the comforting conclusion that 'he did not observe any extraordinarily disturbing signs in the present strike movement'.[57]

The single institutional instrument at the command of the MTP as a means of directly influencing factory life was the factory inspectorate. The province and city of St Petersburg were covered by one senior factory inspector and twelve district inspectors. The factory inspectorate was a relatively feeble instrument of labour policy. All state-owned plants and artisanal establishments were excluded from its purview, as were the distributive trades after 1910. Its remit was restricted to the observation and violation by employers of the various pieces of labour legislation passed since the 1880s. It was debarred from direct intervention on its own initiative to improve conditions in the workshops. The workers regarded it with suspicion as an agent of the employers.

During the turbulent pre-war years the first instance when Timashev's more 'West European' attitude towards labour was displayed occurred in the reaction of the Council of Ministers to the events of April and May 1912. 'In view of the disturbed times' ministers resolved to refrain from punishing by fines workers at state-owned plants who reacted to the Lena shootings by walking out in protest. As to the issue of financial penalties for striking on May Day, the Council left the decision to the respective departments. The Ministry of the Navy refused to impose fines or pay wages, whereas the Ministry of War decided to arrest all who struck. The Minister of Trade and Industry advocated prudent conduct in relation to the strikes of 1 May. He upbraided a delegation from the POZF in early May for stimulating the strike movement by levying fines, as well as imploring the employers in vain to rescind them. 'As economic stoppages always end with partial concessions to the workers,' he advised the industrialists, 'it would be better if they could improve labour's conditions, thereby forestalling strikes.'[58]

Timashev's awareness of the comparative futility of repression also brought him into direct collision with the MVD in its attempts to impede the proper functioning of the sick benefit funds. (The implementation of the Insurance Laws came within the competence of the MTP.) The minister was of the opinion that 'the activity of the insurance funds constitutes a significant instrument for improving the welfare of the masses', and 'the introduction of the law will undoubtedly weaken the influence of the socialist parties'. He objected to police prohibitions of electoral meetings and the arrest of kassy delegates. In a letter of 15 February 1913 to Maklakov, he implored the latter 'to be more cautious in your actions . . . which can only hinder the proper functioning of the kassy'. The plea was ignored.[59] The MTP also suspected the St Petersburg industrial community of deliberately impeding the prompt formation of kassy. In a meeting with a delegation from the POZF in March 1913, V. P. Litvinov-Falinskii, chief of the Department of Industry, upbraided the employers' inaction. He thought it reasonable that factory managers should accept workers' amendments to kassy regulations.[60]

In the light of his characterisation of labour conflict as an inevitable phenomenon, the Minister of Trade and Industry adopted a cautious response to the various measures proposed by the MVD in the middle of 1913. In his reply to Maklakov of 26 July 1913, Timashev advised the greatest circumspection in recourse to mass dismissals and the criminal law. In both cases he rightly feared that the remedy would merely exacerbate the disease, provoking further stoppages of work. Although the Council of Ministers and the inter-ministerial conference in its report of 9 July 1914 shared this point of view as regards economic disputes, it is evident from the recommendations of the commission concerning the Penal Code that its chairman had been overruled by the other members.[61]

Timashev's more enlightened attitude towards independent workers' organisations evidently influenced the response of the Council of Ministers to Maklakov's scheme of conciliation chambers. In their guidelines of 24 October 1913 to the inter-ministerial commission, ministers observed that a purely bureaucratic composition for the proposed bodies would not secure workers' or employers' confidence. Both groups should be permitted to elect representatives to sit on the chambers. The commission's report, 9 July 1914, duly repeated this recommendation. But in its rather desperate search for a method of choosing five workers' delegates to the courts of conciliation which would hinder the election of party activists, the commission encountered almost insurmountable obstacles, all of which were the consequence of the authorities' own labour policies. The West European practice of collective agreements, it noted, was impractical in Russia 'as our trade unions in their present state cannot guarantee their observation'. Factory elders were too few to be able to act as workers' representatives. Their widespread introduction into the factories might lead to the creation of special strike committees. Although 'this procedure is seriously defective', the report suggested that the executive boards of the sick benefit funds elect workers' delegates to the courts.[62]

On his own initiative, the Minister of Trade and Industry endeavoured without great success to strengthen the employers' legal position vis-à-vis strikers. The internal documents of the Ministry show that it shared the POZF's doubts concerning the legality of dismissals and the defects of the Regulations on Industry. The remit of the inter-ministerial commission, established by the Council of Ministers on 24 October 1913, was broadened at Timashev's insistence to include a review of the terms of the contract of hire. Despite the observation in its report that 'the correct arrangement of the laws governing contractual relations would be the most effective means of regulating the strike movement', the proposals of the commission ignored the demands of the POZF memorandum of 10 June 1914. The report rejected the Society's requests to increase the size of fines or to reduce the two weeks' notice of dismissal. It failed to revive the ministry's own draft bill of 1909 which had shortened the period of warning to seven days.[63]

By the summer of 1914 the Ministry's Department of Industry had come to the same conclusion as a section of the employers that lock-outs were the most effective measure against strikes. This view naturally brought civil servants to accept the POZF case for the waiver of financial penalties for late delivery caused by stoppages. A memorandum from the Department to the Council of Ministers, 28 June 1914 (in response to the POZF delegation on 10 June), emphasised that 'this rule has placed factories in an extremely difficult position in the struggle against the contemporary manifestations of the strike movement'. It advocated the abolition of the practice and extensions to delivery schedules in the event of labour disputes. Although the Ministry of the Navy was prepared to revise its policy, the Ministry of War was reluctant to do so.[64]

The contradictions, vacillations and bankruptcy of the government's labour politics found eloquent expression in a session of the Council of Ministers on 5 July 1914. After an alarming analysis of the situation in the capital, ministers reached the impractical conclusion that the single most effective solution would be to curtail the growth of industry in the city by a variety of measures, including prohibition of the building of new factories, a transfer of state orders to other industrial districts, raising customs and railway tariffs on imports and exports to the city (in particular on English coal), thereby increasing the costs of production to unacceptable levels. 'The question of the removal of industry has become utterly vital.'[65]

IV

In the years prior to the war no single approach to the problem of labour conflict commanded the unequivocal support of either the authorities or the employers of St Petersburg. Neither formed united ranks behind policies of complete repression or thorough paternalistic measures or liberal labour reforms. The possibility of the Imperial government adopting and honestly implementing a genuine West European system of labour relations was remote in view of the obstacles (political and ideological) from within the bureaucracy, the near paralysis of decision-taking in the highest bureaucratic circles on the eve of the war and the hostility of the capital's industrialists. On the other hand a co-ordinated, coherent programme of unremitting repression, utilising to the full all the powers of the law, proved just as elusive to formulate and implement on the part of both officials and factory owners. The constant and fruitless search for a labour policy acceptable to a majority of its members by the leaders of the POZF foundered in the last resort upon economic conditions and the rock of pre-war rearmament, the very source of renewed industrial prosperity. The shortage of skilled labour in heavy industry engendered by the pace of expansion and firms' dependence on state contracts with stiff penalties for late delivery undercut all efforts to fashion an unbending response. The intense competition among engineering and electrical companies for skilled workers and state orders made factory directors and managers in these sectors reluctant to adopt truly punitive measures out of fear of conferring advantages on their competitors. In textiles, on the other hand, different market forces – an incipient, fragile recovery from a lengthy recession – impelled some companies to look favourably upon a harsh response to work stoppages. In summary, the POZF vacillated in its choice of different retributive solutions to labour disputes without ever implementing any in a consistently united manner. Even the bureaucratic world was unable to come to a unanimous and favourable verdict about recourse to unrestrained repression, regarding it as likely to inflame labour and educated society, which now possessed wider sources of influence and protest in a legislature and comparatively free press. The paternalistic course was also discovered to be defective. As in the past the administration never felt itself in a position to compel reluctant employers to improve conditions of work. In any case the scarcity of labour militated against standardisation of wage rates, hours of work, etc., as the POZF discovered. The abysmal and complete failure of the *ancien régime* and the unenlightened business community of St Petersburg to formulate a sensible, logical, consistent and mutually acceptable strategy of industrial relations rendered doubtful the possibility of a legal labour movement taking root in the capital before 1917. The uncertainties and contradictions of labour policy (both official and private) made a significant contribution to pre-war industrial unrest.

Chapter 10

THE ST PETERSBURG GENERAL STRIKE, JULY 1914

I

The apparently ceaseless surge of economic and political stoppages from the spring of 1912, as well as the endeavours of the Bolshevik underground to capitalise on labour unrest by launching a national political general strike, reached a peak in St Petersburg in the fortnight before the outbreak of the First World War. The mass walk-outs, the demonstrations, the clashes between strikers and police and Cossacks, the erection of barricades, which occurred between 3 and 15 July 1914, all unprecedented in scope since the revolution of 1905, posed acute problems for revolutionaries, industrialists and Imperial authorities alike. For socialist activists Lenin's diagnosis in the spring of that year that the workers' movement was escaping the party's control proved close to the mark. In the absence of all city or district co-ordinating mechanisms, the sub-élites of all tendencies could not furnish effective leadership or direct the explosion of discontent towards clearly defined goals. Yet again notions of utilising events in the capital – the theory of the vanguard role of the Petersburg proletariat – to set off an all-Russian political stoppage turned out to be illusory. The Bolsheviks' contempt for the bourgeoisie as a potential ally, in addition to most liberals' dread of a new revolution and dislike of a left alliance, ensured that the workers' grievances failed to evoke the sympathetic support of the Duma opposition, in stark contrast to the 'Days of Freedom' in the autumn of 1905. The unusual length and scope of the walk-outs after 3 July also represented a severe challenge to the programme of rearmament at a time of heightened international tension and a potential embarrassment to Franco-Russian relations with the simultaneous state visit of President Poincaré. Government ministries, the police and the POZF were compelled with some urgency to confront their debilitating internal divisions and the

297

confusion and contradictions in their labour policies. Former doubts and hesitations about a strategy of firm repression were cast aside. Unlike February 1917, the *ancien régime* in state and industry still retained sufficient cohesion and confidence in itself and the armed forces' loyalty to act decisively and brutally. The militants' complete lack of preparations for an armed uprising, the atrophy of the Bolsheviks' illegal apparatus, the absence of succour from the liberal parties, the feeble response to developments in the capital elsewhere in the Empire, and ministers' successful resort to measures of suppression all ensured that the general strike remained an isolated phenomenon rather than a prelude to the overthrow of the monarchy.

II

The July events in St Petersburg had their immediate origins in the reaction of the local Bolsheviks and a minority of mostly engineering workers to the Baku oil strike.[1] The chief of the Okhrana, Colonel P. K. Popov, informed his superiors that the underground in the capital sought to take advantage of the situation in Baku for agitational purposes, but it did not believe that 'the occasion is propitious for a lengthy stoppage'. In a leaflet printed towards the end of June party militants exhorted wage earners to display solidarity by stopping work one hour earlier than normal and contributing a day's wages to a fund for the homeless in Baku. 'We do not,' the document emphasised, 'resort for the present to the Baku method of struggle.'[2] Contrary to the claim of E. E. Kruze that 'all over town' gatherings were held 'in all large factories', the labour force replied with little enthusiasm to the Bolsheviks' entreaty. On 1 July some 1,069 operatives left work an hour before the hooter according to the police (*Trudovaia pravda* estimated 5,349) and on the following day 1,731 (4,700), mostly in twenty private metalworking plants in Petersburg Side and Vyborg, five woodworking establishments and six printshops.[3]

As part of the Bolshevik campaign of meetings in the factories to discuss resolutions of protest against the treatment of the Baku strikers, an assembly was arranged for the evening of Thursday the third at Putilov. An accurate picture of what happened on that occasion is difficult to paint as the sources of information offer such conflicting details. An hour or so before the termination of the day shift at six o'clock, the workers of various departments walked off the job. The secret police maintains that most of the total labour force of 12,000 then went home peacefully, leaving only 1,000 behind on the premises. All contemporary newspaper accounts, however, both bourgeois and socialist, agree that the entire complement of operatives, 12,000, congregated in the factory yard. Two speakers called for a one-day strike as a display of sympathy for comrades in Baku; an appropriate resolution was passed.[4] The authorities evidently had been concerned about an escalation of unrest. Forewarned of the convocation, the police and the factory inspectorate had held several conferences, in the words of a report in the Kadet organ *Rech'*, 'about measures to nip any movement in the bud'. A detachment of mounted and foot police (the exact number of which is unknown) was stationed outside the plant from four in the afternoon.[5] Before the business had been finished, the police erupted into the factory grounds. The captain in charge requested those assembled to disperse, but this proved impossible as the police had shut the gates after their entry.

From this point onwards accounts directly contradict one another. The official version, given by the local district police officer to Colonel Popov and transmitted by him to the Assistant Minister of Internal Affairs, General V. F. Dzhunkovskii, was that the police had had recourse only to their whips and that no one had been hurt. The chief of the Okhrana apparently had reason to doubt his subordinate's version as he informed Dzhunkovskii late on the evening of the occurrence that 'secret information' (presumably agents' reports) indicated that a few policemen had fired several shots in the air. This version was furnished to the press by the Governor General's office, and repeated the next day in a majority of newspapers. Unfortunately for the authorities, as soon as the incident took place, the Putilov workers had sent for their Duma deputy, the Bolshevik A. E. Badaev. The former claimed that the police had fired two volleys of live shot directly into the unarmed crowd. Badaev ensured that this account appeared the next morning in all three socialist newspapers. Further confusion concerned the number of casualties. The editorial on the front page of *Trudovaia pravda* on 4 July stated baldly that two had been killed and fifty wounded, yet Badaev's article 'On the spot' in the following issue noted, with more honesty perhaps, 'there are in fact as yet no definite figures'. Some sixty people were arrested.[6]

It is impossible to establish the truth of the incident beyond doubt, in the welter of contradictory evidence. The contention of the official historians of the Putilov factory that 'the Tsarist government had prepared a grandiose provocation' and hoped in this way 'to drown in blood the growing revolution' cannot be sustained.[7] The nation-wide response to 'Bloody Sunday', 1905 and Lena, 1912, had shown how provocative and self-defeating was the calculated shooting of defenceless, peaceful civilians. On the other hand, it is quite possible that the commanding officer on the spot had used his own initiative in giving an order to fire, a decision taken either in a calm fashion or in a panic. It is clear that Colonel Popov entertained suspicions about the true course of action taken by his underling. The authorities and the directors of the company had subsequently every reason to deny the true course of events at the factory. It is also rather unlikely that the Putilov workers would lie to Badaev. There is one non-partisan witness who corroborates the participants' version. The correspondent of *Rech'*, suspicious of the official communiqué, made his own enquiries the day afterwards among members of the Putilov board. They informed him that as the crowd rushed at a small wicket gate to escape the police charge, the latter fired their Mausers; they confirmed that they had seen bullet holes in the factory wall, proving the police had resorted to live ammunition.[8] On balance it is probable that, as at Lena, the police had recourse to firearms. But there is no firm testimony concerning the total of dead, if any, or wounded.

III

The news of some sinister occurrence at Putilov spread rapidly to all working-class districts by the morning of 4 July. The means of communication were various. There was the telephone. All three socialist dailies carried their version of the event, with its explicit denial of the official communiqué, although the police made strenuous efforts to confiscate all copies, including searches of street newsvendors. A PK leaflet may hav been distributed (see pp. 304–5).

Whatever the source of information, the reaction of the labouring masses was immediate, spontaneous and explosive. The workers' deep resentment and revulsion at a government which again permitted such an atrocity – and it is instructive of popular suspicion of the authorities that no one accepted the official denials of casualties – and their instinctive sympathy for the victims and solidarity with the Putilov work-force found expression from the morning of the fourth in an ever-widening circle of stoppages (see Tables 10.i–10.iii).

According to police estimates, after the first mass walk-outs on 4 July, a dip occurred the following day with 22,487 (or 32 per cent) returning to their benches. After the normal period of rest on Sunday the sixth, the numbers downing tools on 7 July greatly exceeded those of three days before (an increase of 39,063). There may have been a partial resumption of work on 8 July (the police version) or a further rise in the total out in protests (according to newspaper accounts). It is indisputable that the four days from 9 to 12 July represented the peak of the movement. Although the aggregate of between 130 and 140,000 strikers on 10 to 12 July had been surpassed in individual political strikes in the months since April 1912 (e.g. 150,000 on 1 May 1912 or 250,000 on 1 May 1913), there had not been such a continuous run of labour unrest in the capital since September–December 1905. However, a more detailed examination

Table 10.i: *St Petersburg General Strike, 4–15 July 1914: Number of Strikers on a Daily Basis*[9]

	Police reports	Press reports	
4 July	70,937	89,744	(*Trudovaia pravda*)
5 July	48,450	68,131	(*Trudovaia pravda*)
6 July (Sunday)	–	–	
7 July	110,000	109,160	(*Trudovaia pravda*)
8 July	78,595	140,000	(*Rech'*)
9 July	117,000	120,000	(*Rech'*)
10 July	110,000	135,000	(*Rech'*)
11 July	110,000	133,000	(*Rech'*)
12 July	–	130,500	(*Rech'*)
13 July (Sunday)	–	–	
14 July	–	76,000	(*Rech'*) (locked out)
15 July	–	55,000	(*Rech'*) (locked out)

Table 10.ii: *St Petersburg General Strike, 4–12 July 1914: Number of Strikers as % of the Manufacturing Work-force*

	%
4 July	17.8
5 July	13.5
7 July	21.6
8 July	27.7
9 July	23.8
10 July	26.7
11 July	26.4
12 July	25.9

Note: Since there is no exact comparable figure available thereafter, the table is based on the December 1910 city census, which estimated 504,000 employed in the manufacturing sector. As the aggregate must have been greater by 1914, the percentages would be less.

of the statistics throws doubt on the aptness of the epithet 'general' as applied to the stoppages.

The material does not permit a comprehensive and accurate allocation of strikers among the various sectors subsumed under the heading 'manufacturing'. Hence it is impossible to calculate the proportion of those exclusively employed in factory industry

Table 10.iii: St Petersburg General Strike, 4–7 July 1914: Number and % of Strikers, by Industry[10]

	Metal processing		Textiles		Printing		Woodworking	
	no.	%	no.	%	no.	%	no.	%
4 July	62,106	79.8	6,200	14.1	4,608	19.8	3,307	11.0
5 July	53,595	68.9	1,250	2.8	2,223	9.6	1,067	3.5
7 July	61,345	78.8	21,200	48.0	5,168	22.2	2,569	8.6

Note: Percentages are calculated from the aggregate of the labour force in each sector in 1913.

participating in the July strikes on a daily basis. But estimates can be made for various branches of production for the period 4–7 July.

The pattern of participation was uneven. As on previous occasions in 1912 to 1914, operatives in metal-processing plants were in the forefront of the struggle from the outset, whereas mill hands were slower to respond and the numbers involved never rose above half of the textile work-force. Whilst all leather manufactories were swept up into the protests, as were some 45 per cent of bakers, the ratios were far less in printing and woodworking. Moreover, whole areas of employment held aloof. With the exception of part of 8 July and the entire following day, tram drivers and conductors continued to report for duty. The railways remained unaffected until the late afternoon of 9 July when the workers of the Baltic and Warsaw lines walked out and the Nikolaev Railway depot joined them the following morning. Commercial–industrial employees in all branches, post and telegraph workers, the majority of shop and restaurant staff, domestic servants and all engaged in the professions were conspicuous by their aloofness from the display of solidarity with the Putilov victims – in marked contrast to the autumn of 1905 and February 1917.

Furthermore the propensity to strike varied according to the size of plant. In metalworking, for example, in the period under consideration, over 70 per cent of establishments employing more than 1,000 hands suffered disruption to production, whereas only 18 to 30 per cent of workshops with under a complement of 100 joined the movement. Repeating the pattern of the last two years, large and medium-sized private electrical, engineering and machine construction firms were to the fore, such as Aivaz (1,500), Baranovskii (900), Erikson (1,500), Koppel' (1,000), Langenzippen (1,000), New Lessner (1,800), Neva Shipyards (5,000), Nobel' (1,000), Rozenkrants (3,000), San Galli (1,500), Siemens and Halske (1,200), Siemens-Schukkert (2,500 in both factories), St Petersburg Engineering (1,500), St Petersburg Metals (4,000) and United Cables (1,300). The commitment displayed by workers in state-owned plants in this sector was less whole-hearted. Several held aloof throughout; the Arsenal (2,200), Ordnance (2,000) and the Sestroretsk arms-works. Some walked out only on 7 July (Baltic Shipyards with 6,650 workers) and others on 9 July, as, for example, Admiralty Shipyards (2,800) and Obukhov (6,000). In textiles, 11 of 17 mills with over 1,000 hands participated from 7 July, but none of the 57 manufactories with under 200 operatives showed a willingness to express sympathy. Of printshops, around a third of those hiring over 100 workers came out, whereas the proportion of very small concerns (under a payroll of 100) afflicted by disruption rose from 13 per cent on 4 July to 38 per cent three days later.

This statistical analysis, therefore, would suggest that the description of the stoppages of 4 to 12 July as a 'general strike' requires careful qualification. The term is almost accurate only with reference to the metalworking sector and leather production, far less so for other branches of factory output. When manufacturing in the aggregate and non-productive sources of employment are also taken into consideration, the phrase is far too broad to be applied to the events of July.

The series of walk-outs between 3 and 15 July are also normally described in the literature as 'political' in motivation. Whilst it is possible to regard the natural outpouring of working-class anger at the treatment meted out to the Putilov labour force both as an expression of instinctive solidarity and in the broadest sense as a condemnation of the political system perpetrating the outrage, a perusal of the resolutions passed at factory meetings and printed in the socialist press (up to its suppression on 8 July) reveals that very few actually put forward specific political claims. It is possible that documents overtly containing the three Bolshevik slogans could not be published for reasons of censorship, yet more straightforward demands for freedom of trade unions, meetings and strike (the political issue in a sense at the core of the occurrence at Putilov) were seldom advanced.

IV

The 'new Lena', as the skirmish at Putilov was swiftly characterised by activists, opened up for the revolutionaries perspectives both alluring and fraught with peril.[11] The foremost handicap faced by all socialist militants was the non-existence of all-city and district organisations through which they could offer coherent and firm leadership to the elemental outburst of indignation and direct it towards specific goals determined by the sub-élites. By the summer of 1914 the Socialist Revolutionaries completely lacked general and district branches, and possessed only a few factory cells. The Mensheviks were in a similar plight, although their factory nuclei were somewhat more numerous. After their suppression in March 1914 the Bolsheviks' PK and district committees had not been revived. Within manufacturing, moreover, the factory groups of the Bolsheviks and Mensheviks were very unevenly spread; their highest concentration was in machine construction and electrical equipment plants in Vyborg and to a lesser extent in Neva, Petersburg Side and Vasil'evskii Island. In the absence of overarching institutional mechanisms these factory-based collectives, where they existed, were the sole means the second-rank leaders had at their disposal to channel and control the emergent movement.

Furthermore, in fashioning their response to the Putilov shooting, the local socialist working-class activists remained bereft of advice and guidance from the *émigrés*. The suddenness of the crisis and the rapidity of its development prohibited foreign consultations. Although A. S. Kiselev, the Bolshevik secretary of the defunct union of metalworkers, returned to the capital on 5 July after a fortnight's sojourn with Lenin in Poronin, he had left Galicia before the incident at Putilov. The conversations with Lenin, Zinoviev and the Duma deputy G. I. Petrovskii, who joined them, centred on the forthcoming party congress, the imminent meeting of the International Socialist Bureau in Brussels devoted to the party schism, and the work of the Duma fraction.[12] Indeed so absorbed was the Bolshevik leader in the proceedings in the Belgian capital that his published correspondence for the first fortnight of July contains no references at all to events in St Petersburg.

The first to seize their opportunity were certain Bolshevik militants meeting on the evening of the third. Arrogating to themselves the title 'PK', they adopted the suggestion of A. M. Ionov to call wage earners out on a three-day strike and to orchestrate street demonstrations throughout the city on Monday 7 July.[13] The leaflet they drafted affords significant clues as to the intentions behind this decision. It is evident from the document's plea for tram drivers, shop assistants and commercial–industrial employees to display solidarity by joining the protest stoppages that the local Bolshevik élite regarded the Putilov mishap as an appropriate psychological moment to realise their long-cherished and hitherto elusive goal, set in the summer of 1913, of launching a national political general strike. The police's hamfistedness at Putilov might be the sufficient spark to an all-Russian conflagration. On the other hand, those present at the Bolshevik council of war were equally well aware of the risks they faced in trying to circumscribe the popular passions being unleashed. Conscious of their complete failure hitherto to subvert the garrison, they bluntly warned hot heads that 'as the time has not yet come for armed uprising, we beg comrades to refrain from excesses'. The police also thought that the Bolsheviks deliberately had chosen the Monday (7 July) as the date for mass demonstrations in view of the fact that the forces of law and order would be diverted on that day to protect the arrival of President Poincaré of France on a state visit.[14] In addition to the appeal, which was distributed on 4 July in unknown quantities in working-class quarters, *Trudovaia pravda* devoted front-page and extensive coverage to the shooting, Badaev's visits to the police and MVD, the official denials of police recourse to firearms, the resolutions passed at factory meetings, the stoppages, the demonstrations and clashes. Its editorial of the fifth revealed that its intellectual editors approved the militants' strategy.

The Mensheviks, however, do not seem to have been so prompt or as united as their rivals in their reactions. Thus the editors of the Menshevik daily relegated news of the happenings at Putilov to a small item on an inside page. Even on the fifth, when the scope of the protests had become clearer, an editorial merely asserted that 'the task of the proletariat lies in planned organised struggle by the masses to secure freedom of association'. Yet other Mensheviks willingly adopted the Bolsheviks' course of action, supporting strikes and demonstrations whilst likewise exhorting workers to avoid clashes with the police. Such was the resolution of Menshevik factory representatives in Vasil'evskii Island on 5 July. SRs made identical pleas.[15]

This broadly similar response and the adoption of a common strategy, as well as the painful knowledge of their organisational weaknesses, dictated, as in the past, a considerable degree of co-operation among all the socialist tendencies. Ten year later the Bolshevik V. Kaiurov recalled that in factory collectives Bolsheviks, Mensheviks and Narodniks jointly discussed the forms in which the workers' dissatisfaction should express itself. The rivals co-operated in practical efforts to make good the defects in their illegal structures. In Vasil'evskii Island a strike committee, containing representatives of all party factions (including the Mezhraionka) and the Narodniks was established, as was an identical body in Vyborg. The above-mentioned strike committee of Vasil'evskii Island plant delegates also came to the logical conclusion that a council of workers' deputies (a soviet) was desperately required as a central instrument of co-ordination. It never came into being.[16]

At first, the growing dimensions of the walk-outs after the fourth and the scale of demonstrations more than met revolutionaries' expectations. But the manifest reluctance of strikers to heed militants' pleas to return to work after the seventh, the embittered mood of their supporters, the escalation in ill-advised, one-sided and fruitless battles with the police and troops between 8 and 10 July, the emergence of a 'Left oppostion' within Bolshevik ranks all bore eloquent testimony to the limits of socialist influence on the working masses in general and to the Bolsheviks' control over their new adherents in particular.

On the first day of the stike, 4 July, in the morning some 42,000 hands in 87 plants turned up at the normal starting time. Instead of proceeding to work, they assembled outside factory gates, passed resolutions of protest and sympathy and for the most part dispersed peacefully home. After lunch around 28,000 in another 65 establishments emulated their example. The police successfully broke up several large demonstrations on the streets in Narva, Petersburg Side and Vyborg, whilst blocking access to the centre across all the bridges. There were two instances of police recourse to firearms: in Narva district, they shot at a large crowd of engineering and electrical workers surrounding the Skorokhod shoe company in an attempt to force out its female employees, and, again outside Putilov, at a large assemblage of local workers who had come to express their condolences.[17]

The next day, Saturday 5 July, not only did the number of strikers diminish but a deceptive atmosphere of calm descended on working-class quarters. No street manifestations or encounters with the police occurred. The Okhrana counted six instances of 'disorder', but these merely encompassed random arrests of operatives for singing revolutionary songs on leaving their benches in the morning. Sunday, 6 July, was likewise tranquil.[18]

At one level Monday, 7 July, vindicated militants' preparations and judgement. Not only did the aggregate of strikers mark a significant rise over 5 July (109,000 against 68,000 according to press reports), but the movement now encompassed hitherto relatively unaffected categories such as bakers and textile operatives. An effective testimony to the desire of activists and ordinary workers to maintain discipline was the compulsory closure by roving bands of all wine shops and taverns in Vyborg and on Ligovskaia street in Neva district. The revolutionaries' hopes concerning demonstrations suffered disappointment. The city centre remained free of disorder. The police closed all bridges across the Neva. There were only three minor attempts at demonstrations on or near Nevskii Prospekt. The largest manifestations, which now included many female operatives, took place in Vyborg, in particular by a 20,000-strong crowd on the main thoroughfare in the morning, but all were broken up without undue severity by the police. Indeed the latter opened fire only once in the course of the day – in Neva district. From the socialists' point of view, however, there were already inauspicious signs that workers' bitterness would lead them to ignore warnings against physical violence. In Liteinii, Moscow, Petersburg Side, Town and Vyborg districts there were repeated, successful endeavours to halt tramcars, wreck their interiors and steal the drivers' keys. As the daily police account remarked 'the mood of the workers is greatly heightened'.[19]

The dramatic events of the succeeding three days afforded proof of the relative impotence of all socialist factions to restrain their followers or bridle the passions they had helped unleash. Not only did the strikers completely ignore the fact that the protest was supposed to have ended on the seventh, as well as later Bolshevik and Menshevik appeals to return to work, but the movement's momentum gathered further pace, rising to 140,000 strikers on 8 July. Violence became more widespread with the erection of the first barricades and engagements with police and Cossacks, dispatched to the city on the evening of the seventh.

Developments on 8 July, the day President Poincaré paid an official call on the city authorities, bore out the observation of *Rech*'s reporter that 'the strike is assuming a more menacing character'. Vyborg, where the stoppage was now almost total, was the epicentre of the disorders. On four separate occasions crowds of 1–2,000 strikers stopped and overturned trams. By the evening around 200 tramcars in the city had suffered damage. In the morning the workers of Baranovskii, Lessner and Russian Society (about 5,000 in all) attempted to march from Vyborg into the city centre but were cleared from the streets by Cossacks. In this district there occurred three instances of the building of flimsy barricades of telegraph poles and beer barrels, two in the north-western sector (one at Ekval engineering plant) and one in the centre. In Petersburg Side a barricade was set up near St Petersburg Engineering, and on Vasil'evskii Island on Bol'shoi Prospekt. All these obstacles, in addition to demonstrations, were quickly broken up by the police and Cossacks who now regularly had recourse to firearms to restore 'order' in face of the showers of stones thrown at them. On the other hand the heart of the capital remained quiet.[20]

The worst encounters happened on 9 July, once more in Vyborg, which, in the police's words, 'was especially explosive'. Throughout the city the tram service ceased to function, as drivers refused to take out their wagons without police protection. The employees of the Central Electricity Station walked out. In Petersburg Side, Vasil'evskii Island and Vyborg crowds again closed all wine and vodka outlets. Throughout the day in Vyborg demonstrations continued without interruption despite repeated charges by mounted police and Cossacks. Assaults on representatives of authority increased. At nine in the morning on Finliandskaia street a policeman was beaten unconscious; two hours later on Arsenal Prospekt a police convoy with arrested workers was attacked; crowds endeavoured to destroy the Sampsonievskii bridge and pumping station. At ten in the morning on the Sestroretsk railway telegraph poles were cut down and placed across the track; two trains were obliged to return to the city before Cossacks were dispatched to guard the line. In the evening the district, which was without street lighting, witnessed many collisions between workers, police and Cossacks. Barricades of gas-lamp standards, telegraph and telephone poles were constructed in several areas, in the north-west, along the main thoroughfare and in the eastern part. The worst skirmish occurred about ten o'clock in the evening on Bol'shoi Sampsonievskii Prospekt between a Cossack patrol and several thousands manning a barricade; stones were flung and even pistol shots were directed at the troops who opened fire, killing five and wounding eighteen. In other districts, however, there was a marked absence of barricades or battles, with the exception of police shooting into a crowd on Pushkarskaia Street on Petersburg Side.[21]

Although 135,000 still stayed away from work on 10 July, there were the first signs of a possible diminution in unrest. After the urgent entreaties of the capital's mayor, Count Tolstoi, the Governor General (General Major D. V. Drachevskii) ordered police protection for tram drivers so that services were resumed. Attacks on trams ceased with the solitary exception of an isolated incident in the morning on Vasil'evskii Island. Moreover, the dispatch of large numbers of Cossacks and police detachments into Vyborg, putting it in effect under military occupation, began to exert a calming influence. Demonstrations ceased by noon and there was only a single attempt to erect barricades. Indeed demonstrations and skirmishes with troops were more frequent elsewhere in the city; there were two such incidents in the morning in Narva and two in Neva.[22]

By 11 July the peak of violent conflict had been passed. Most strikers reported for work as normal in the morning to discover that they had been locked out by their employers, although state plants reopened their doors. 'The extremely agitated mood of the working class,' Colonel Popov opined, 'visibly declined today'. Throughout the entire city only two clashes occurred (both in Moscow district), and few workers were to be observed on the streets, which were patrolled by regular detachments of police and Cossacks. The tramway service now functioned without interruption. Despite the continuation of the lock-out on 12 July, calm finally descended on the working-class quarters.[23]

The continuation of the stoppages on 8 July, the attacks on trams and the construction of barricades evidently caught revolutionary leaders unawares. Thus in its editorial of 8 July *Trudovaia pravda* described the demonstrations of the previous day as 'the culmination of the movement of protest'; 'our future task,' the writer concluded, 'lies in giving organisational form to the solidarity revealed by the working class'. On the same day, through the pages of their party organ, the Mensheviks' Organisational Committee stated curtly that 'the strike movement has ended'.[24] Nor did the local Bolshevik sub-élite instruct its followers to erect barricades or fight the police. Recalling these events ten years later, Kiselev remarked that 'it happened in an elemental fashion'. On the other hand, it is possible that, as other Bolshevik memoirists were to claim, more impetuous militants in factory cells, cut off from one another and lacking central directives, acted independently and exhorted workers to more aggressive forms of opposition or, less plausibly, that there were present Moscow metalworkers who had participated in the uprising of December 1905.[25]

The weakness of the revolutionary underground had been compounded by massive arrests after 4 July, the failure to set up a soviet of workers' deputies as a strike centre and, above all, by the closure on the evening of 8 July of all three legal socialist newspapers and the surviving trade unions. The Okhrana, on the evening of 9 July, summarised the situation of the socialist groups as 'completely confused. They are aware that they are powerless and cannot provide the movement with leadership due to the frailty of the present functioning party organisations.' Both Social Democrats and SRs, it concluded, 'have decided to liquidate the strike'.

Probably on the evening of the ninth, a meeting of prominent Bolsheviks who had escaped arrest was convened at Shuvalovo outside the city to analyse the party's perilous position. The gathering rejected the contention of I. Grachev that the street disorders represented an incipient mass revolt. Instead those present took the view that 'the movement would quickly die out', and drafted a leaflet, distributed the next day, admonishing strikers 'to halt temporarily the protest movement in the same organised manner in which it began'. The contents of the appeal, the memoirs of Kiselev and Popov's memoranda all reveal that the Bolshevik sub-élite had made a realistic assessment of their vulnerability. The participants at Shuvalovo were in agreement that, in Popov's words, 'the local underground lacks exact ties to the masses', and 'it is unable to convert the present strikes into an armed uprising due to a lack of weapons'. The Bolsheviks had failed so far to penetrate the garrison and had made no preparations for armed revolt. The crowds threw only stones; there was the very occasional use of revolvers. The militants were perhaps mindful of the disastrous course of the premature Moscow uprising of December 1905. They were also aware of the weak response of other industrial centres to events in the capital, leaving it isolated and exposed to the severest repressions.

For these reasons a second Bolshevik leaflet, dated 11 July, desperately pled with workers 'to refrain from extreme measures'.[26]

As the drama of 9 to 11 July had highlighted, Bolshevik cells 'do not have sufficient strength or authority over the working class to terminate the strike' (Okhrana report, 11 July). Nor could they exercise restraint on their more recent converts. The decision to call a halt to the movement encountered fierce resistance on the part of what might be termed an emergent 'Left Opposition'. These 'revolutionary-minded labour youths' disregarded the harsh facts of life facing the party. Instead, embittered, millenarial in their expectations, they insisted on interpreting the street disorders as 'the prelude to the last excesses of an armed uprising'. The leadership of this rebellion was provided by Bolsheviks elected earlier in the year on a Pravdist list to the executive of the educational society 'Science-Life' (based in the city centre, with a membership drawn largely from local artisanal trades). Meeting there on 9 July, seven oppositionists resolved to issue a call for an armed uprising. They also proposed the spreading of the strike to embrace railway and postal workers, the destruction of railway bridges, the seizure of the Arsenal and the murder of policemen. At a second gathering in the same premises two days later, the line of the 'PK' was condemned and the earlier resolution reconfirmed. However the appeal printed by these party rebels on 12 July merely exhorted in a vague manner 'Comrades, prepare for everything. Prepare for struggle against the government and the capitalists.' A more serious step was the convocation in the evening of the same day of factory delegates in the building housing 'Science-Life' to discuss the proposal for an uprising. Well informed of these plans, Popov ordered a raid and detained all the ringleaders, thereby causing the scheme's abortion.[27]

Thus, as in the weeks immediately preceding the *coup d'état* of October 1917, the Bolshevik leadership's failure to follow through at once on their erstwhile militant slogans very rapidly lost them the support of their newest recruits, formerly attracted to the party by its stance of uncompromising hostility to the regime. The Bolshevik lawyer N. N. Krestinskii admitted that in consequence 'the leadership of the struggle passed in some places to anarchists and extremists from working-class youth'.[28]

V

In his analysis of the St Petersburg general strike Leopold Haimson has depicted the stoppages as 'driving the frightened autocracy to its knees'.[29] Whilst it is true that the MVD and ministers had shown much concern in the previous two years about the threat posed to order and the rearmament programme by the existence of the capital's working class and had become alarmed at the role of the revolutionaries within an increasingly politicised strike movement, there is no evidence that they felt the regime was in any serious danger throughout the general strike. The Austro-Hungarian ambassador, Count F. von Szapary, emphasised to his government on 10 July, that the Tsar's ministers did not regard the disorders 'as the start of any general movement'.[30] Indeed previous bitter dissension within the bureaucracy concerning the fashioning of labour strategy was temporarily forgotten in a common conviction that the appropriate response to the renewed outburst of unrest should be confined to pitiless police measures. In stark contrast to the disastrous division of authority in the capital with a consequent incoherence of policy-making in the monarchy's ultimate crisis in the last days of February 1917, the MVD and its police were left in sole charge of crushing the stoppages and demonstrations by force. It is probable, too, that the state visit of President Poincaré of France rendered the authorities all the more determined to present to their guest a picture of orderly calm, at least in the city centre. For reasons of international politics the Imperial government could not afford to give their distinguished visitor the impression that the dynasty was unable to cope with working-class disturbances.

In the days immediately after the Putilov incident, therefore, the Minister of Internal Affairs, N. A. Maklakov, who took a personal interest in the handling of the unrest, resorted to a panoply of repressive actions. By 5 July squadrons of mounted and foot police were dispatched to all working-class quarters and strengthened the following day. Important factories were physically occupied by police. Apprised of the revolutionaries' plans through its secret agents, the Okhrana carried out a series of raids on the editorial offices of the legal socialist press and the premises of unions, educational societies and sick-benefit funds. The culmination came on 8 July with the closure of the three legal socialist newspapers and the trade unions. On 6 July the Governor General, aware that the reception by the Municipal Duma for President Poincaré two days hence would place severe strain upon the police (216 constables were assigned to guard his route) with a serious impairment to its ability to patrol the suburbs, requested that the chief of staff of the Imperial Guard dispatch Cossack regiments. These arrived on the evening of the seventh, at the same time as the Governor General and police chiefs drew up a plan of action. From 8 July there was no hesitation in ordering forces to open fire in cases of necessity. In order to prevent any contact between the potentially more volatile sailors of the Baltic Fleet and demonstrators, the former were confined to barracks. When the city's electricity supply was threatened by a walk-out at the Central Electricity Station, naval stokers were summoned to maintain supplies. During this week of ferment the Council of Ministers first met on 11 July. Accepting Colonel Popov's interpretation that 'the gradual liquidation of the strike movement has commenced', it decided to refrain from declaring a state of emergency. It ordered the MVD to take all requisite steps to crush the protests. These included, at the urgent insistence of the Okhrana, the summoning of three Guards regiments to the capital. Indeed by the eleventh, high officials evinced more alarm about the obduracy of the employers as the remaining obstacle to the restoration of social tranquillity.[31]

In contrast to the government the industrialists displayed less unanimity in elaborating their reaction to the general strike. The POZF had been rent for the previous two years over its course of action towards the labour problem, although by the early summer of 1914 a majority had been emerging in favour of a more militant position. From the outset firms had adopted different attitudes towards the Putilov shootings and the surge of sympathy strikes. The board of Ia. M. Aivaz, for example, chose not to regard the protests as serious, whereas as early as 5 July the Russian Society proposed a lock-out. By the eighth greater alarm was being expressed. A. A. Bachmanov, director of G. A. Lessner, placed a political construction upon events, arguing that 'the dimensions of the strike movement are reminiscent of similar events in 1905'. The gravest concern was felt by metal-processing companies, particularly in Vyborg, which hitherto had borne the brunt of the stoppages. An unusually well-attended meeting of the Engineering Section of the POZF on 8 July, therefore, considered the desirability of implementing their previous decision of 22 May to close down plants for a fortnight in the event of a future one-day political strike. Past discord regarding the difficulties of such a tactic promptly resurfaced. The representative of United Cables feared delays (and consequent fines), caused by a lengthy closure, in the fulfilment of Treasury orders. The director of Siemens-Schukkert, on the contrary, argued that a lock-out would be effective only if it lasted two months and involved Moscow factory owners. Ten firms supported Bachmanov's proposal for an indefinite lock-out, eight of whom (all located in Vyborg) at once shut down their plants for fourteen days. Nine voted conditional approval and fourteen rejected the suggestion.[32] Thus a majority of metalworking plants failed to endorse the ultimate sanction the employers' organisation possessed. By the next day many had changed their minds. A general assembly of the POZF, to which over two-thirds of members sent delegates, voted to close establishments to 14 July, i.e. for a duration within the legal seven days' period of notice and far short of the length of time advocated by hardline Vyborg engineering companies. By 14 July some 76,000 operatives had been refused admission in 75 manufactories.[33]

At first this firmer stance met with the approval of both the MVD and the MTP. S. I. Timashev, who had closely followed the unfolding drama through the reports he had ordered from the factory inspectorate, had evidently altered his former scepticism concerning the efficacy of a lock-out. He informed A. A. Bachmanov, vice-president of the Engineering Section of the POZF, that ministers would not exact financial penalties from firms for tardiness in meeting contractual deadlines due to the present dispute. Indeed he was critical of industrialists' lack of solidarity. On 10 July Maklakov likewise had expressed his sympathy for the employers' forceful response. Yet to the consternation of the POZF at two in the afternoon of the eleventh the senior factory inspector, I. A. Fedorov, telephoned Bachmanov with the request of the MVD that all factories should reopen their gates by 14 July.[34]

The motives for this volte-face have given rise to controversy among historians. The most obvious explanation is Maklakov's surmise, based on the reports submitted by Colonel Popov to the Council of Ministers at its session in the morning of 11 July, that thousands of workers now wished to return to work and that the tide of protest was beginning to ebb with the successful destruction of all legal and illegal revolutionary organisations. The minister and his colleagues, therefore, were apprehensive lest the lock-out rekindle the embers of disorder. As the chief of the St Petersburg Okhrana warned his superiors 'the inability of workers to resume their occupations, their extreme state of want (shops deny them credit) deepens their discontent and could lead to further undesirable excesses'.[35]

Soviet scholars, however, advance the view that a connection exists between the alarm of high officials and the deepening international crisis in the Balkans. E. E. Kruze, for example, has argued in melodramatic vein that 'the government, preparing to enter the world war, wanted to be left free to act and to drown the revolutionary capital in the blood of the workers'. In a more restrained manner M. S. Balabanov has observed that the regime could not take energetic measures for war if the armaments plants were at a standstill due to a lock-out.[36] The chronology of the July crisis does not bear out either contention. It is true that, at its session on the morning of 11 July, the Council of Ministers resolved to petition the Sovereign to authorise the mobilisation of four military districts and the fleet 'if events subsequently dictated it', i.e. the decision referred merely to a hypothetical contingency. Indeed the Minister of Foreign Affairs, S. D. Sazonov, both opposed immediate mobilisation and pursued a conciliatory policy towards Austria–Hungary until 15 July. Bureaucrats and the Tsar naively regarded the threat of partial mobilisation as a diplomatic weapon against Austria–Hungary alone and had no intention at this stage of becoming involved in a war with Germany. The German ambassador, Count F. Pourtalés, reported to the Wilhelmstrasse that at the Council of 11 July the ministers, having discussed the domestic situation, had reached the conclusion that neither did the disturbances presage a revolution nor would the outbreak of war, if it come, produce domestic upheaval. Soviet scholars, lastly, pass over in silence the awkward fact that for reasons that remain mysterious the Minister of Internal Affairs changed his mind a second time on 12 July, when he telephoned Bachmanov to withdraw his request of the previous day.[37]

The industrialists, having nerved themselves to act decisively, were in no mood to listen to Maklakov's entreaties. As Bachmanov pointed out to another general meeting of the POZF shortly after noon on 12 July, the value of the lock-out in industrial disputes would be discredited if the owners now rescinded their decision. Perhaps fortified by the unexpected support for its stance from the MTP, the POZF rebuffed the government. The eight Vyborg plants independently resolved to stay closed until 22 July.[38] At another assembly of the Engineering Section of the POZF two days later unamimity collapsed. Unfortunately the archives provide no information as to possible behind-the-scenes pressure on employers on the part of officials or the police. On 14 July Colonel Popov indeed again advised 'that all measures must be taken to renew pressure upon the owners to reopen their establishments at once'. It may be surmised that the persistent stubbornness of the POZF further alarmed ministers who, fearful of a renewal of unrest in conse-quence, had declared a state of emergency after all on 13 July. Fears of an impending war with Austria–Hungary certainly exerted an impact on some manufacturers, although the convocation on 14 July took place the day before the Habsburg monarchy declared war upon Serbia. The directors of United Cables and Rozenkrants, for exam-ple, urged on their audience a retreat from the resolution of 22 May due to 'international complications'. They also shared the authorities' opinion that the prolongation of the dispute merely risked further embittering industrial relations. Although the eight Vyborg en-gineering companies held fast, five of those represented announced their resolve to readmit their labour force the next day and nine by the seventeenth. Between 15 and 17 July, with the exception of the eight impenitent members, the lock-out disintegrated. The numbers shut out declined from 76,000 on 14 July to 55,000 the following day to 5,000 by 19 July. 43,000 returned on 17 July alone.[39]

VI

Many commentators have interpreted the July general strike in St Petersburg as the harbinger of revolution. E. E. Kruze refers to the 'revolutionary capital'; G. A. Arutiunov to 'the revolutionary proletariat'; L. Haimson to the 'revolutionary explosiveness' of the strike. The events of July, M. S. Balabanov contends, 'spoke not only of a general revolutionary situation, but also of a ripening of the revolutionary process . . .'. The validity of this thesis is open to doubt.[40] In fact the first fortnight of July 1914 was not analagous to the period 23–6 February 1917 or the first sixteen days of October 1905. In contrast to both these latter times the working-class and revolutionary movements of July 1914 in the capital suffered from a series of weaknesses which inhibited them from presenting a serious threat to the dynasty.

In the first place the epithet 'general' is an inaccurate description of the strikes of 4 to 15 July in St Petersburg. One of the failings of the stoppages, unlike October 1905 or February 1917, was precisely the inability of the protesters to secure the support of all sections of the labour force or of other social strata. Although the walk-outs of early July embraced more workpeople than at any time since the revival of labour unrest in the spring of 1912, certain categories of manufacturing and service manpower held aloof – port and shipping employees, constructions trades, commercial–industrial employees, postal and telegraph workers, most shop and restaurant staff, and particularly railwaymen (whose withdrawal of labour had been the decisive factor in forcing the autocracy momentarily to its knees in October 1905). Even among factory wage earners, operatives in small plants and in state-owned establishments, mill hands, printers and woodworkers, were less than whole-hearted in offering assistance. The opposition to the Putilov 'massacre' was at its strongest in private metal-processing plants with a payroll of over 1,000.

Secondly, whereas in 1905 educated society through the Union of Unions, the central organ of the nascent professional organisations, or on 27 February 1917 the State Duma had displayed understanding for the workers' cause and by its participation lent decisive weight to the opposition to the regime, the professional classes and the liberal parties failed to express any concern or solidarity. Several coincidences partly explain this lack of co-operation. Duma deputies, students and many professional people were on holiday and as was normal had fled the heat of the capital for their dachas or estates.[41] In the press, reports of the visit of President Poincaré and subsequently of the Austro-Serbian crisis were accorded pre-eminence. In any case the strike of the printers prevented the publication of a majority of newspapers between 9 and 11 July. At a more profound level the indifference of the parliamentary opposition accurately reflected the aversion most liberals felt since their experiences in 1905–6 for a revolutionary strategy and their consequent adherence to the legal, reformist path of change. The left Kadets and some Progressists, such as A. I. Konovalov, alone saw the validity of a broad 'left' alliance of liberals and socialists and the necessity for extra-parliamentary pressure on the government.

In the third place, the fuse of the general strike in St Petersburg failed to light the tinder of the national general strike, to which the local Bolsheviks had been committed since the summer of 1913. Demonstrations and stoppages occurred elsewhere in the Empire but none matched the scale or violence of those in the capital. In Moscow, for example, the local revolutionaries proved quite incapable of furnishing leadership. Colonel Martynov, the chief of the Okhrana, aborted any concerted action by arresting all activists on 6 July. The proportion of Moscow operatives withdrawing their labour was minute – no more than 2–3 per cent of the manufacturing labour force or 7–10 per cent of factory hands. The strikers came mainly from the metalworking and printing sectors whereas the city's most prominent industry, textiles, remained unaffected. There were no street demonstrations or clashes with the police. In Riga, on the other hand, some 40,000 participated in a three-day walk-out between 8 and 10 July. In the Ukraine, too, there were small-scale sporadic expressions of sympathy: 6,717 struck in Khar'kov on 7 July; 1,023 in Kiev on 13 July; the shipyards in Nikolaev on 10 July. All such refusals to work were widely scattered, uncoordinated, and easily contained by the local authorities.[42]

The fourth, and perhaps most important, deficiency of the general strike was the atrophy of the revolutionary organisations. Although all three socialist tendencies endeavoured to utilise the Putilov incident to revolutionise further the working class through a three-day political stoppage, none – some hotheads apart – considered the time propitious for launching the final assault on the regime, for making the 'second Russian revolution'. The course of events validated their apprehensions concerning their capability to control the protests or to channel them towards limited, if ill-defined, goals. In the absence of central mechanisms of co-ordination, either of a soviet or all-city or district committees or of a widespread network of factory cells, Social Democrats and SRs could not restrain either the irate operatives or their own impetuous followers. The revolutionary sub-élites, wiser after the Moscow fiasco of 1905, neither desired nor had made preparations for an armed rebellion; stones, telephone poles, and beer barrels were workers' improvised weapons rather than rifles or machine guns.

Moreover, the Imperial bureaucracy and industrialists alike displayed steady nerves, resilience, faith in themselves and determination to defend their interests at whatever cost. The uncertainty and vacillation, so characteristic of officials' response to disorder in 1905 or February 1917, were not present in the summer of 1914. The government was never in danger of losing its hold on the capital; the revolutionaries had not penetrated the garrison, the troops of which displayed no hesitation in obeying orders to open fire. The violence and barricades were largely confined to a single district, Vyborg, which could be and was rapidly and effectively isolated and suppressed. Working-class crowds completely failed to reach the administrative heart of the city. Indeed it was the over-reaction of metal-processing firms which alarmed ministers most and threatened the prolongation of the disturbances after 11 July.

The St Petersburg general strike, therefore, remained an isolated phenomenon. Although it bore witness to a widespread sense of working-class distaste for the regime's methods of dealing with labour unrest and the frustration of skilled metalworkers in particular at their growing inability to achieve tangible economic improvements, the general sense of opposition to the regime remained diffuse and unfocused. As the preceding chapters have attempted to show, the vast majority of ordinary workers in the capital remained outside the ambit of all revolutionary parties and uninfluenced by their ideologies. A minority of skilled workers, factory and artisanal, alone expressed an interest in revolutionary politics in the pre-war years and some awareness of socialist dogmas. Their frustrations and impatience for instant economic and political change led them to forsake Menshevik legality for Bolshevik militance. But the frailty of the Bolsheviks' legal and illegal organisations, of the underground and the trade unions, rendered them unable to direct this discontent towards their chosen political targets. As Lenin had foreseen, the elements of anarchy and spontaneity within the working-class movement had proved in the last resort uncontrollable by his or another party. In the short run, on the eve of the First World War, the monarchy remained safe in its capital so long as and because its opponents, liberals and socialists, remained politically divided between and among themselves; the revolutionary parties lacked a mass base and the mechanisms to reach out to more than a fraction of the city's work-force; the armed forces remained impeccably loyal; the Okhrana's network of secret agents and repression continued to function well. The vicissitudes of three years' hostilities dictated that all these preconditions of survival, these blocks to revolution, would be undermined.

317

Chapter 11

THE IMPACT OF THE WAR UPON PETROGRAD'S WORKING CLASS, JULY 1914–FEBRUARY 1917[1]

Within two days of its relatively bloodless defeat of the first 'general' strike in the capital since 1905, the Romanov monarchy took the step that ultimately sealed its fate; on 19 July 1914 Nicholas II declared war against Germany. If there had been any secret apprehensions among the Tsar's ministers that the outbreak of hostilities might spark off a renewed revolutionary outburst, the early months of the war must have seemed highly reassuring in this respect at least. The mobilisations of the summer passed without serious protest; the city's workers apparently enlisted with the same patriotic fervour sweeping the upper classes; the wave of strikes receded to vanishing point; the revolutionary underground remained completely pulverised; the destruction of the trade unions and the labour and socialist press had deprived revolutionary activists of their sole legal means of influence. Such impressions were dangerous illusions. Although none of the revolutionary parties succeeded in re-establishing permanent or deep-rooted legal or illegal organisations in Petrograd during the war or in reaching out to the broad mass of workers (the war indeed further exacerbated intellectual divisiveness and revolutionary infighting), the social and economic repercussions of the war in the capital ultimately proved fatal for the regime. The wartime expansion of the urban economy, the rapid growth of the labour force, the deterioration in living and working conditions intensified popular discontent to breaking point. Even more so than in the years immediately prior to the war, however, the expression of working-class grievances in the form of work stoppages, which re-emerged in the summer of 1915, owed little to relatively impotent socialist groups and much more to workers' desperation in the face of declining real incomes and erratic food supplies. The dynasty might have been able to cope with Petrograd labour's resentment, as it had between 1912 and 1914, if the national economy had not begun to disintegrate by 1916, thereby rendering almost insoluble the problems of supplying the city's inhabitants with eatables and fuel. Its chances of survival were reduced to nil by the war's most invisible and insidious effect – the slow undermining of the loyalty of Petrograd's bloated garrison.

I

THE WAR AND THE URBAN ECONOMY

The initial months after Russia's declaration of war on the Central Powers quickly threw into relief both the problems and opportunities which hostilities presented to Petrograd's industrial community and the variegated impact of the war upon the different sectors of the urban economy.

The mobilisations of 18 July and 1 August removed some 138,000 adult males of all occupations and social classes from their place of work. A mere 9,166 were granted exemptions on grounds of illness, of whom 5,450 were employed in state or private plants with armament contracts.[2] The military authorities also requisitioned stocks of raw materials and horses.[3] The commencement of operations was accompanied by a suspension of the Stock Exchange, a moratorium on debts, the curtailment of foreign commerce and a reduction in internal trade. The German navy's blockade of the Baltic at once cut off the capital's imports of English coal. There was a marked discrepancy in the influence of these factors on the different industrial sectors. Despite the anxieties occasioned by their minimal stocks of coal, the heavy goods industries which had been awarded defence contracts before the war fared best. Thus the ring of Petrograd arms manufacturers, financed by the Russian-Asiatic Bank, formed a group to purchase abroad scarce raw materials. Although the cotton mills and papermaking and printing plants possessed satisfactory coal stocks, they lacked the necessary quantities of raw materials. The shortage constrained several of them to curtail or stop production. The mills introduced a four-day week and over half the employees in printing were made redundant. Artisanal trades such as gold and silvermaking suffered. The introduction of prohibition hit hard at the spirits trade. The authorities calculated that 13,486 factory workers in the city were unemployed by November 1914.[4]

One of the most intractable impediments to the efforts of manufacturers to ensure uninterrupted output and to raise productivity from the autumn of 1914 onwards was the shortage of labour, in particular of skilled workers. In its autumn 1915 survey of Russia's industrial regions *Promyshlennost' i torgovlia*, the organ of the AIT, observed that 'metalworking plants at present are experiencing a dearth of hands'. A year later the periodical could see no improvement: 'the market remains barren of qualified labour'.[5] In the absence of reliable statistics it is difficult to provide accurate quantifiable data in confirmation or qualification of such contemporary impressions.

It is known that from 18 July 1914 to 1 March 1917 the military authorities issued call-up papers on nineteen separate occasions.[6] The male groups liable to conscription comprised the age cohort 20–40 years at the outbreak of war and those young men of 17–19 years who celebrated their twentieth birthday during the war. The Soviet historians I. P. Leiberov and O. I. Shkaratan calculated that the number of factory workers coming under the rubric was 116,200 and that up to 1 October 1916 164,000 men in the capital received exemption, of whom 115,000 were employed in industry. They conclude that between 1914 and 1916 around 40,000 of the pre-war industrial labour force were taken from their benches by the army. They contend that the majority of operatives in defence plants were permitted postponement of military service on account of their possession of scarce skills.[7] The authors' purview unfortunately has excluded both artisanal and service workers. There are no data on the numbers of these groups summoned to serve with the colours or receiving postponement of service. It would not be unreasonable to assume that their rate of deferment was much lower than for skilled factory hands.

In general terms, too, demand for labour exceeded supply in Petrograd throughout the war years. From the day it opened its doors on 29 January 1915 to 31 January 1917 the new Petrograd Labour Exchange recorded 351,098 vacancies whilst 234,197 workers signed on.[8] The incidence, however, of this general crisis varied over time and among different strata of the city's labour force. The deficit in the supply of labour rose sharply in August to October 1915. Between January and April 1916 the shortages of fuel and raw materials induced a fall in the demand for labour. From the spring demand underwent a strong revival until October.[9] The shortfall of skilled operatives was especially severe throughout 1915 in the metalworking and machine construction industries. Even when the engineering market weakened in the first half of 1916, managements still found it impossible to hire boilermakers, founders, hammermen and riveters. The employers' quest for unskilled labour was as much in vain as for skilled. In 1915 a mere 21 per cent of vacant posts notified to the Labour Exchange in the former area were filled, and 16 per cent in the latter case.[10] The single exception to this shortage of labour lay in the domestic service sector which displayed a general surplus of supply over demand in 1915.

The shortcomings of the labour market constrained Petrograd

employers to adopt a diversity of solutions to the impediment of the scarcity of labour: among them a more satisfactory system of defer-ments of national service and the demobilisation of skilled workers from the active army; substitutes for lost wage earners; regulation of the labour market and the raising of wages.

As the POZF, like the majority of contemporaries, had not envisaged at first a lengthy period of hostilities, it had not raised any very cogent objections to the initial mobilisations. By December 1914, however, its Engineering Section had become alarmed about the capacity of firms to keep to delivery schedules. It resolved to petition the military authorities for the liberation of office and factory personnel from military duty in the future. By March 1915 521 plants in the city had forwarded the names of 144,881 individuals to the Society for exemption from conscription. Two months later the POZF demanded a ratio of 40 per cent deferments in engineering as against the Mobilisation Department's figure of 25 per cent.[11]

If the POZF and the Central War-Industries Committee (TsVPK) (the origins of which are discussed in Chapter 15) enjoyed some measure of success in the pressure they were able to exert upon the War Department in the matter of deferments, both suffered repeated setbacks in the numerous attempts to persuade General Headquarters (Stavka) to release and return specialist workers and technical staff taken in the initial mobilisations. Both the First and Second Congres-ses of War-Industries Committees passed resolutions to this effect. Neither a delegation from the First Congress to *Stavka*, petitions from the TsVPK in January and July 1916 nor two votes in the Special Council for Defence (OSO) in favour of the proposal met with a warm response from the generals. By 1 January 1917 the total allowed back from the trenches to Petrograd had reached a paltry 1,143.[12]

In their efforts to utilise more intensely the services of women and juveniles, employers faced the obstacle of various protective factory acts. At the First Congress of War-Industries Committees in late July 1915, a resolution was passed in favour of the abrogation of all restrictions for the duration of the war on the employment of female and juvenile labour 'however detrimental this may be to their health'. A few days later the TsVPK dispatched an appropriate memorandum to the Department of Industry, whose officials gave it warm support. The Council of Ministers accordingly sanctioned the requisite permissive derogations from the law.[13] The industrialists placed so high a value on this 'victory' that, when at the Second Congress of War-Industries Committees in the last four days of February 1916 the Menshevik-dominated Labour Group proposed the restoration of the relevant articles of the laws prohibiting the use of women and children in certain industries and at night, they were brusquely informed by P. P. Kozakevich, chairman of the Labour Department of the TsVPK, that 'some of these measures are necessary'. In time-honoured fashion the awkward suggestion of the Labour Group was neatly shelved by the decision of the Congress to remit it to the TsVPK for further consideration. The issue never surfaced again.[14]

In addition to deferments and the greater hiring of women and children, the capital's employers' hopes were also placed upon the services of prisoners of war and the 'yellow races' (Chinese, Japanese and Korean citizens), whose labour was widely exploited elsewhere in the Empire. The military authorities, however, demurred at the presence of enemy aliens in defence factories. Although the Council of Ministers permitted the import of Chinese workers for hire in the coalmines and engineering plants of European Russia in the summer of 1915, the high costs of transporting them to Petrograd and the fear of antagonising the native labour force ensured that the first, unspecified (probably miniscule) number arrived in the capital only in late 1916.[15] On the other hand, expectations about the suitability of evacuees and refugees for factory work proved somewhat less illusory.

The insatiable demand for labour found partial satisfaction from another source – the enticement of workers (in particular those with highly prized scarce skills) from other factories through the blandishment of paying higher wages than competitors. The TsVPK survey of the labour market in 1916 noted that 'plants are now resorting to suborning specialists from one another'. In 1915 the factory inspectorate had remarked that the practice had already become commonplace in Petrograd heavy industry. When the Petrograd Factory Conference insistently recommended to the POZF in September 1916 that factory managements reach an agreement to refrain from such 'poaching', the Society's Council refused to intervene.[16] One example may suffice to illustrate this trend. The high wages, as well as exemption from conscription, enticed qualified workers from other Petrograd and provincial factories to the state-owned Obukhov works.[17]

But the contribution, however limited, made by the Petrograd Labour Exchange to the regulation of the labour market owed nothing to the employers. Its creation in January 1915 had not depended upon them. The initiative came from three disparate groups – the Imperial Free Economic Society; the municipal guardianships of the poor, and the municipal Commission for the Collection and Distribution of Donations for the War.[18] The capital's employers may have had frequent recourse to the services of the new institution, but they wished to bear no responsibility for its management. When the Council of the POZF received an invitation to send its representative to the executive committee of the Exchange in January 1916, it declined.[19]

A second severe obstacle to the uninterrupted running of production lines lay in the irregular deliveries to Petrograd of the requisite quantities of fuel and raw materials. In this respect all manufacturers found themselves at the mercy of factors beyond their control, dependent on supplies thousands of miles distant, a poorly developed, badly managed railway network, and a state economic regulatory apparatus excluding all representation by the city's industrial community. The Special Council for Fuel, established in August 1915, and its regional organ, the Petrograd Regional Conference on Fuel, established a priority system of supply according high value to ensuring continuity of output by state and private armaments plants, but treated all other manufacturing sectors, as well as civilian requirements, as a residual.[20]

After the initial dislocations caused by the commencement of hostilities in the summer and autumn of 1914, the monthly total number of wagons of coal from the city's new source of supply in the Donbass declined drastically between November 1914 (9,226 wagons) and January 1915 (4,500), with a recovery of sorts only in the spring (8,132 wagons in April). The output of the Donbass mines dropped alarmingly after July 1914 owing to loss of manpower while much of even the available production was reserved for the army. Increased imports of wood could in no way compensate for the shortfall in coal, as by the spring of 1915 the railway goods yards were overflowing with unloaded wagons of wood, as well as of coal, due to shortages of stevedores and carters. The Donbass coal, too, was significantly higher in price than pre-war imported coal. The conversion of the capital's factories to oil burning offered a difficult and costly solution only in the long term.[21] After some improvement in the summer months, another marked deterioration set in. Between September and December 1915 a mere twenty-nine wagons of Donbass coal reached the city. The state-owned plants received almost their total complement, at the expense of private firms. By the middle of December factory reserves of coal were close to exhaustion, whilst 16,000 coal wagons lay unloaded in the freight yards. The 1886 Electricity Company, which supplied power to all defence establishments, was constrained to curtail the supply of electricity. Putilov had been compelled to shut down many workshops.[22]

In the first three months of 1916 the shortfall in the imports of fuel and raw materials grew worse. Some factories stopped work completely. The Petrograd regional commissioner for fuel informed his colleagues at a conference late in March 1916 that 'there is an extreme shortage of fuel in the capital'. In his report to the Tsar on 15

June 1916, General M. V. Alekseev, the chief of staff, observed that 'Petrograd's private defence factories . . . are receiving at best some 50 to 60 per cent of the necessary materials'. In that month the railways delivered 197 of 360 wagons of coal required. By December 1916 79 plants were at a standstill, although few factory administrations had been compelled to close down their operations completely. Many defence establishments, such as Franco-Russian, Langenzippen, Northern Pipes and San Galli were compelled to suspend production for periods of a week or longer.[23]

Despite the initial shock caused by the start of fighting and the chronic difficulties posed by the intermittent flow of labour, fuel and raw materials, those industrial companies fortunate enough to secure military contracts from the authorities and the voluntary organisations, above all in heavy industry, were soon plunged into feverish expansion on a scale even greater than in the boom prior to hostilities.

In the autumn of 1914 the Chief Artillery Administration (GAU) included among the recipients of its first domestic contracts the members of the pre-war group of Petrograd armaments firms financed by the Russo-Asiatic Bank (Baranovskii, Neva Shipyards, Putilov, the Russian Society), as well as a second group comprising Petrograd Engineering, Petrograd Metals, Phoenix and Westinghouse.[24] When GAU began in the spring of 1915 to tilt the balance of its sources of munitions supply from its earlier reliance upon state armaments plants to domestic 'mobilised' industry, Petrograd firms found special favour in the highest reaches of the military bureaucracy. On 6 June 1915, for example, the newly established Special Council for Defence awarded Putilov a contract worth 113 million roubles for the manufacture of 3 million three-inch high explosive shells and 700 field guns. With the support of the banks the company brought together a group of nine companies (including Baranovskii and the Russian Society) to execute this order with the technical assistance of Schneider-Creusot of France. Large orders for shrapnel and explosives were placed with Lessner at the close of 1915, and for telephones and telegraph apparatus in February 1916 with the main electrical equipment manufacturers. V. A. Lebedev and Diuflon manufactured aircraft engines.[25]

In the light of the cornucopia of contracts available to the capital goods sector, the high prices which firms could charge GAU and the slump in civil engineering demand, factory managements were enticed into spending enormous sums of money in 1915 and 1916 in expanding, re-equipping and modernising their plants. In general terms private industry restricted itself to the production of machine tools and shells (the latter were relatively unsophisticated munitions), whereas the state armament works concentrated on the manufacture of more sophisticated items such as heavy artillery and small arms. In the state sector, for example, Obukhov's shell and artillery departments were re-equipped to turn out heavy ordnance, the factory supplying 16.5 per cent of the total Russian output of ordnance between 1915 and 1917.[26] Private engineering, electrical and machine construction companies pursued product specialisation in armaments. This allowed special components producers to reap economies of scale, introduce continuous flow methods, two- or three-shift working and mass production techniques. In short, pre-war industrial reorganisation was taken a stage further. The state-owned Petrograd Pipe works, which concentrated on the manufacture of time fuses, percussion tubes and explosive charges, introduced three-shift working without holidays. Russian Renault and the Russian Society of Optical and Engineering Products, which specialised in the production of fuses, went over to mass production and scientific management. The Putilov and Neva Shipyards were re-equipped a second time to make hand grenades and detonators in place of the absent orders for battleships. The state's Sestroretsk small-arms works applied continuous flow methods.[27]

The finance for this programme of factory enlargement and conversion was derived from heterogeneous sources – subventions from GAU (often up to one-third the value of an order), credits from the banks, flotation of new capital, the inflated prices for munitions. By October 1915 Putilov had been granted 40 million roubles in economic aid from the Treasury and 11 million from the State Bank. From the summer of 1915 advances from the Special Council for Defence and GAU to firms awarded War Department contracts became standard practice. In August 1915, for example, Reks (electrical accumulators) received a subsidy of 464,000 roubles. One month later the Russian-American Rubber Company was granted an advance on an order for kite balloons and Russian Renault for car engines. Other firms raised their fixed capital: Baranovskii from 13 to 22 million roubles in 1916; Siemens and Halske from 5 to 10 million in the same year.[28]

In contrast to the heavy goods manufacturers the war exerted a more variegated impact on other industrial sectors. As the Petrograd factory inspectorate's annual report for 1915 noted, the woollen, leather, linen, hemp, chemicals and food industries were all experiencing boom conditions. The Russian-American Rubber Company enjoyed a monopoly of the production of rubber shoes, rubber clothing, Bickford fuses and tyres. The fortunes of the cotton mills, however, were subject to fluctuation. Throughout the war cotton textiles suffered from the chronic shortage and high prices of raw cotton. After a severe drop from August 1914, output underwent a recovery in the spring of 1915, with many mills returning to normal from a three- or four-day week and one-shift working. But in January 1916 another period of interruptions in supply led to severe reductions in production and the number of working days. Because of prohibition the breweries and vodka distilleries remained closed. The great scarcity of paper in the second half of 1915 was accompanied by cuts in output and the labour force in printing. Woodmills, furniture making, the construction industry all endured contraction. In general, small establishments, the artisanal trades and all businesses without war contracts suffered most from the erratic supplies of raw materials, fuel and labour; they were ranked low in the table of priorities by the state regulatory agencies.[29]

Despite all the difficulties they experienced with the ready availability of raw materials, fuel and labour, the majority of Petrograd companies succeeded in expanding both their gross output and their profits. The net profits of 21 of the largest companies in the city rose from 12.5 million roubles in 1913 to 54 million in 1916. As a percentage of fixed capital the net profits of six large metalworking and electrical firms grew from 10.4 in 1913 to 79.5 in 1916. Thus the Russian Society increased its net profits from 1.1 million roubles in 1914 to 7.5 million in 1916 (and its dividend from 9.5 to 18 roubles a share); Baranovskii from 1.9 million roubles profit in 1914 to 5.3 million in 1916 (its dividend from 14 to 28 roubles a share).[30] New companies were formed. The year 1915 witnessed the incorporation of V. T. Fefelov (shells), the Russian Electricity Company 'Dynamo' (detonators), Russian Renault (fuses) and Vlokh (engineering). In 1916 there occurred a wave of speculation in the share of armaments firms and several speculative takeovers. Thus Petrograd Metals bought out the Swedish-owned machine firm, Ekval'.[31]

In the opinion of Soviet scholars wartime developments strengthened the coalescence of bank and industrial capital.[32] In the case of Petrograd heavy industry, already deeply penetrated by the capital's banks before the war, their argument has some validity. But the forms of this relationship changed. In contrast to direct lending to firms to finance expansion, as in the boom of 1911 to 1914, the banks concentrated more on the handling of industrial shares. The state, in the form of the Special Council for Defence, assumed much responsibility for industrial modernisation through its advances.[33] It is far from evident, however, that the number of companies coming under some degree of bank control in metalworking, machine construction and electrical equipment concerns grew between 1914 and 1917, and there is no evidence that the banks attempted to penetrate sectors hitherto relatively immune from their influence such as textiles, woodworking, food processing or printing. A comparison of the list of Petrograd companies drawn up by I. F. Gindin and L. E. Shepelev, which they claim were dominated by the banks in 1917, with a similar calculation made by E. E. Kruze for 1913 (see Chapter 1) reveals surprisingly little change.[34] On the eve of the February revolution, as in 1913, the theory of finance capital has relevance to the capital goods sector, but does not reflect an accurate picture of the city's economy as a whole.

The consequences of the feverish and artificial expansion of Petrograd's industry during the war were to be far-reaching for both factory owners and their employees. In Petrograd province the size of the factory labour force grew from 218,258 in 1913 (the factory inspectorate's underestimate) to 419,108 on 1 January 1917 (according to the Economic Commission of the Provisional Government), 134,464 of whom were employed in state-owned armaments plants – an increase of 92 per cent. The capital proper witnessed a growth of 58 per cent in its number of factory operatives – from 242,600 on 1 January 1914 to 382,628 on 1 January 1917. By the latter date the city's manufactories gave employment to almost 12 per cent of the Empire's industrial workers.[35] The vast bulk of establishments were engaged in production for the war effort. Estimates vary as to the exact proportion of factory hands so employed, from around 75 per cent up to 94 per cent (and touching 98 per cent in metalworking).[36] The livelihoods of both industrialists and factory workers had become bound up to an extreme and unhealthy degree with the Moloch of war. This crucial factor dominated the attitudes of employers to the broad range of labour problems engendered by the war. It also entailed significant repercussions for the composition of the working class and its living standards.

II

THE WAR AND THE SOCIAL COMPOSITION OF THE WORKING CLASS

Table 11.i confirms the general outline, described earlier in the chapter, of the war's impact on the different branches of industrial production. The fastest growth was recorded in metalworking (136 per cent) and chemicals (85 per cent). Within the former, massive rises in their labour forces were recorded at state munitions plants – 194 per cent at the Izhora arms-works (3,025 to 8,902 employees); 186 per cent at the Petrograd Pipe works (6,650 to 19,046); 77 per cent at Obukhov (6,000 to 10,600). Some private firms, too, experienced similar unchecked expansion – 278 per cent at Lessner's 'new' factory (1,722 to 6,511 hands) and 92 per cent at Petrograd Metals (3,500 to 6,704). Although the numbers involved were far less, growth was proportionately great in leather and shoes (58 per cent) and mineral processing (77 per cent). The greatest decline in employment occurred in food processing (−30 per cent), mainly in the drinks trade where, for example, the Bavaria brewery lost 82

Table 11.i: Growth and Distribution of the Factory Labour Force of Petrograd City, 1 Jan. 1914–1 Jan. 1917[37]

Industry	No. of workers 1914	1917	% of total factory labour force 1914	1917	% increase or decrease 1914–17
Animal products	8,000	12,600	3.3	3.2	+57.5
Chemicals	21,600	40,100	8.9	10.2	+85.6
Food processing	22,700	15,800	9.4	4.0	−30.4
Metalworking	100,600	237,400	41.5	60.4	+136.0
Mineral products	2,200	3,900	0.9	1.0	+77.3
Miscellaneous	14,900	5,700	6.1	1.5	−61.7
Paper, printing	27,500	26,500	11.3	6.7	−3.6
Textiles	40,100	44,100	16.5	11.2	+10.0
Woodworking	5,000	6,700	2.1	1.7	+34.0
TOTAL	242,600	392,800	100.0	99.9	+62.0

per cent of its payroll (970 to 176). In textiles, some firms underwent contraction – Sampsonievskaia Cotton's complement shrank by half (from 3,200 to 1,592), whilst others enjoyed very modest expansion.[38]

Within manufacturing the weight of particular sectors was altered significantly after 1914. Whereas heavy industry employed 42 per cent of factory wage earners in 1914, it accounted for 60 per cent in 1917. On the other hand the share of light industry (textiles and food) declined from 26 per cent to 15 per cent. Both these developments marked intensifications of trends well under way before the First World War. It is extremely unfortunate that, owing to the absence of social investigations during the war, there exist no data concerning the totality of the hired labour force on the eve of the February revolution. It is impossible, therefore, to assess the war's impact on the numbers employed in the artisanal trades and the service industries. At best it may be postulated that, as with the pre-war years, the traditional view of the dominant position occupied by metalworkers among the entire working population requires modification. There can be no doubt that the significance of metalworkers increased between 1914 and 1917, but their percentage share of the total hired labour force was not of the order of 60 per cent.

During the war years, as before, immigration remained the cardinal determinant of the enlargement both of the number of factory workers which grew by over 150,000 between 1914 and 1917 and of the city population as a whole, which rose from 2,118,500 in January 1914 to 2,420,000 three years later.[39] Indeed immigration assumed an even greater significance as the period 1914 to 1917 witnessed a net natural decrease of urban inhabitants with a decline in the numbers of births from 55,460 to 38,700 and a rise in deaths from 47,587 to 61,000.[40] No statistical estimates were made at the time either of the annual influx or outflow of peasants nor of their distribution between factory manufacturing, artisanal occupations or the service sector. The Soviet scholar I. P. Leiberov has suggested (without adducing sources for his calculation) that half to three-quarters of newcomers to factory industry were migratory peasants.[41] The impact of the war on peasant agriculture and in particular rural handicrafts drove youths (under 18 years of age), women and older males (over 40 years) into the cities in search of work. The pattern of this immigration, moreover, remained remarkably similar to the past, being drawn from the same provinces in the North-Western and Central Industrial regions. In 1917, 15 per cent of the capital's workers had been born in Tver' province; 9 per cent in Petrograd province; another 9 per cent in Pskov; 7 per cent in Vitebsk; 6 per cent in Novgorod; and a further 6 per cent in Smolensk.[42]

The insatiable demand for labour was also met from other sources. The loss of the breadwinner, with the mobilisation of workers, compelled the wives and young children of many Petrograd factory hands and artisans to seek employment. From the summer of 1915, the army's misconceived and disastrous 'scorched earth' policy during its retreat from Poland led to a flood of refugees. By January 1916 there were some 60,000 to 84,000 displaced persons in Petrograd.[43] Most were peasants rather than skilled workers and the anti-Semitic authorities quickly dispersed Jewish deportees to other regions.[44] In addition in July and August 1915 150 plants, together with their skilled work-force, were evacuated from Riga. Twenty-five of them, together with a further twenty-five from Lithuania, were relocated in Petrograd.[45] This influx of non-Russians altered to some extent the hitherto racially homogeneous nature of the capital's labour force. According to the highly unreliable 1918 industrial census, which covered 107,262 wage earners, 16 per cent of working people were of non-Russian extraction – 6 per cent were Poles, 2 per cent Latvians, 1.8 per cent Estonians, and 2.3 per cent Finns.[46] Another social group from which the wartime working class was drawn was the rural and urban petty bourgeoisie, members of which sought factory jobs either in the face of the sharp rise in the cost of living or to seek exemption from military service. Leiberov estimates (again without providing the requisite documentary evidence) that some 25–30,000 recruits to industry came from these strata.[47] There were also worker soldiers, i.e. wage earners who were called up but performed their military service by remaining at their work-benches (and still subject to military discipline). Contemporary estimates reckoned their number as 11,129 in GAU munitions plants and 27,426 in POZF establishments. In addition by 1 January 1917 a paltry 1,143 soldiers (specialist workers) had been allowed back from the trenches by *Stavka* (the General Headquarters of the army at the front).[48]

It is integral to Soviet historians' understanding of the revival of the revolutionary movement in Petrograd in 1915 and 1916 and in particular of the Bolsheviks' ultimate victory in October 1917 that the wartime replenishment of the industrial work-force from many different social strata, in conjunction with the relatively small proportion of factory workers conscripted, did not alter the balance between the 'majority' 'cadre' and the 'minority' 'peasant' elements in the capital's labour force to the detriment of the former. Thus Z. V. Stepanov contends that 'the capital's working class in large measure preserved its cadre composition'. I. P. Leiberov concurs: 'the basic mass of the pre-war worker cadres remained'. Cadre workers, he claims, constituted 50–52 per cent of the Petrograd proletariat in 1917.[49] Some Western historians do not dissent from such an interpretation. David Mandel, for example, argues that 'despite very significant changes in the social composition of the Petrograd working class, it managed to retain a strong urbanised core . . .'.[50] But as Dr S. A. Smith has correctly pointed out, Leiberov's calculation rests on the unwarranted and patently false assumption that 'by 1917 all those workers who had been working in industry in 1914 were "cadres"'.[51] As the analysis in Chapter 1 of the pre-war working class of St Petersburg attempted to show, a nucleus of urbanised workers was in the process of formation, but that within the totality of the hired labour force, rather than within manufacturing alone, they were probably a minority. It would be reasonable to conclude that the wartime influx of newcomers (who were, in the main, peasants) led to a further dilution of the 'cadre' group among both factory operatives and all hired working people. In the absence of solid and reliable statistical data the exact proportions of both 'cadres' and 'peasants' cannot be established.

Soviet scholars also seek to relate particular political developments in the wartime labour movement in the capital to the changes in the social composition of its working class. Thus both Stepanov and Leiberov, basing their hypothesis on Lenin's *Imperialism: The Highest Stage of Capitalism*, advance the view that the emergence after 1914 of a tiny stratum of highly paid 'labour aristocrats' in certain munitions plants (Izhora arms-works, Neva Shipyards, Obukhov, Putilov), in chemicals and in printing explained the espousal of defensist views on the war among Mensheviks and Socialist Revolutionaries.[52] Leaving aside the fact that an economic definition of a 'labour aristocracy' has been severely criticised at least with reference to the Victorian labour movement in Great Britain, there is available no data at all on the social composition of those workers who supported the different strands of socialist opinion on the war. In any case operatives' views on the war may have been moulded by factors other than class or social origins (see Chapter 12).

A more detailed examination of the social structure of the working class during the war – the balance between the sexes, age cohorts, incidence of marriage and literacy and the ratios of skilled to semi-skilled and unskilled – reveals that in its overall impact the war did not fundamentally alter the social profile of the labour force. It reinforced pre-war trends rather than introducing new ones.

The war did, of course, alter the balance of men, women and youths (aged 15–17) in the industrial labour force (see Table 11.ii). Between 1913 and 1917 the rate of increase in the employment of

Table 11.ii: *Sex and Age Composition of the Petrograd Factory Labour Force, 1913–17*[53]

Industry	Year	Men	Women	Youths	Total	% increase of women and youths 1913–17
Animal products	1913	71.1	20.5	8.4	100.0	
	1917	46.3	42.8	10.9	100.0	24.8
Chemicals	1913	56.1	41.6	2.3	100.0	
	1917	46.8	46.7	6.5	100.0	9.3
Food processing	1913	51.8	40.7	7.5	100.0	
	1917	22.2	66.0	11.8	100.0	29.6
Metalworking	1913	91.2	2.7	6.1	100.0	
	1917	73.1	20.3	6.6	100.0	18.1
Mineral products	1913	76.2	16.7	7.1	100.0	
	1917	59.0	20.6	20.4	100.0	17.2
Textiles and sewing	1913	32.0	57.0	11.0	100.0	
	1917	18.7	68.6	12.7	100.0	13.3
Woodworking	1913	96.9	1.1	2.0	100.0	
	1917	71.8	20.7	7.5	100.0	25.1
All industries	1913	66.2	25.7	8.1	100.0	
	1917	58.5	33.3	8.2	100.0	7.7

adult women in factory industry (111 per cent) was faster than for men (46 per cent) and youths (39 per cent). The proportion of adult women, however, employed in the factory labour force rose only modestly from a quarter to a third of the total, and, once more, was merely the continuation of a pre-war trend. The most obvious changes in the balance of the sexes occurred in woodworking and in metalworking where by 1917 adult women (some 45,000) constituted 20 per cent of employees. Indeed in many munitions plants the figures were much higher than the overall average: 31 per cent at Aivaz (as against 2 per cent in 1914); 48 per cent at United Cables; 27 per cent at Siemens-Schukkert (3.1 per cent in 1914). The other male bastion to fall to women was woodworking, where by 1917 1,191 (on a payroll of 5,724) were females. In textiles the significant development was the marked decline in the proportion of male workers from 32 per cent to 19 per cent as skilled men of draft age sought jobs in heavy industry in order to qualify for deferments. At the James Beck mills, for example, men constituted 37 per cent of wage earners in 1913 but only a fifth in 1917. Russian Cotton experienced an even greater decline, from 42 per cent to 19 per cent.[54] A similar phenomenon for identical reasons could be observed in food and tobacco, leather and shoes and mineral processing. In all these branches of production, women were favoured by employers, as in the past, because they were cheaper to hire and, in the words of the annual report of the Petrograd factory inspectorate for 1915, 'they were more docile and less insistent in their demands and pretensions'.[55] The employment of youths and of juveniles (aged 12–15 years) grew most rapidly in industries not requiring skills and paying badly – in food and tobacco, leather and shoes, chemicals, mineral processing. In 1917 the largest single group of young workers was to be found in the metal industries (13,590), but in textiles young single women played proportionately a more significant part. At the second factory of the Neva Thread Company in 1916, 1,070 of the complement of 1,955 employees were girls aged 15, and 755 were adult women.[56] In the absence of censuses of the entire city population and all gainfully employed persons during the war and the revolution, it is unfortunately impossible to estimate changes in the balance of the sexes within the totality of the hired labour force. It is probable, as before 1914, that more women in 1917 were employed in the service industries than in factory manufacturing (129,800).[57]

The age balance within the labour force was also affected by the rapid wartime industrial expansion, in particular by the removal of young men to serve with the colours and the influx of males aged over 40 to take their place. The statistical evidence relating to changes within the age profile of the working class is unreliable; at best a tentative hypothesis can be advanced.[58] Whereas 76 per cent of working people surveyed in 1900 fell into the age cohort 16–39, 65 per cent did so in 1918; the proportion of over-40s rose from 14 per cent to 31 per cent. In 1918 there was a noticeable difference in the age structure between the sexes surveyed – 54 per cent of males were aged 16–39, but 79 per cent of women workers, reflecting the losses of young men through conscription (41 per cent of males were over 40 years old, but 18 per cent of females) and the relatively high proportion of young women aged 16–20 employed in industries such as textiles (26 per cent of women fell into this age band but only 13 per cent of men).[59]

There exist only fragmentary and oblique data pertaining to the rate of marriage among Petrograd workers by 1917. There are no overall statistics which would permit a firm judgement to be made about variations in the pattern of marriage among workers between the 1910 city census (see Chapter 1) and the revolutions of 1917. A survey of the 12,000 members of the union of metalworkers in January 1918 revealed that 37 per cent of the men and 54 per cent of the women were single. But as metalworkers were among the highest-paid proletarians in 1917, marriage was a more feasible proposition than for those more lowly paid. The investigation confirmed the findings of studies prior to the war that marriage took place at a later age in the capital than the countryside and that skilled operatives could afford larger families than semi-skilled or unskilled. Among women workers the most visible and tragic impact of the war was expressed in the high percentage of widows recorded among female metalworkers – 28 per cent of those in the age cohort 31–40 and 49 per cent of those aged 41–50. Young women textile workers in their twenties also found it more difficult to enter into marriage during the war.[60]

It is possible that between the 1910 city census and 1917 the notable advance in literacy already made among workers continued. If the 1910 census recorded 75 per cent of male and 46 per cent of female peasants as literate, the 1918 industrial census estimated the corresponding percentages in its sample as 89 and 65. Contemporary surveys, too, upheld the conclusions of earlier investigators that men were always more literate than women (the January 1918 enquiry among metalworkers discovered literacy percentages of 92 and 70 respectively) and that rates of literacy declined steeply among older females. Moreover, there seems to have been little improvement in the quality of working-class literacy. It would appear that most operatives had experienced no more than two years' primary schooling. An investigation of 724 skilled metalworkers at Putilov in the second half of 1918 found that 71 per cent had attended school for at most one or two years.[61] As before the outbreak of the First World War, however, 'worker–intellectuals' remained a distinct and crucial phenomenon.

The fate of the skilled worker during the war is a subject of historical controversy and almost no solid research. C. Goodey, for example, posits the hypothesis that wartime dilution was a contributory factor to revolutionary unrest. Dr S. A. Smith, on the contrary, finds striking 'the absence of any militant opposition from the *masterovye*' (the skilled workers) to de-skilling.[62] The introduction in heavy industry of continuous flow methods, mass production techniques and automatic machines, together with the sharp rise in the employment of women and the early mobilisation of young factory operatives would, on the face of it, seem to imply a sustained assault on the privileged role of the skilled metalworker. Yet there is evidence to cast doubt upon such an interpretation. The continual difficulties that metalworking employers encountered in recruiting skilled operatives, described earlier in this chapter, and the ceaseless steep rise in wages they were forced to pay such men would suggest that they retained a powerful bargaining position vis-à-vis factory managements; the course of wartime economic stoppages in the capital goods sector corroborates this viewpoint (see Chapter 14). Furthermore, women tended to be employed as semi-skilled operators on automatic machines in assembly lines turning out standard items such as cartridges, shells and shrapnel. Such was the case of the 685 female employees in Petrograd Engineering (with a complement of 2,907 in 1917).[63] The pre-war patterns of skilled, semi-skilled and unskilled between and within particular industrial branches (discussed in Chapter 1) seem to have survived the war. Thus the 1918 industrial census calculated that within metalworking and machine building half of the labour force was skilled, 13 per cent semi-skilled and 36 per cent minimally skilled or unskilled. Within textiles the proportions were 6 per cent, 53 per cent and 39 per cent respectively, and within printing 42 per cent, 30 per cent and 18 per cent respectively. These statistics cannot be accepted as accurate calculations with reference to 1917 in view of the demobilisation of war industries consequent upon the signing of the Treaty of Brest-Litovsk. But the general picture may be accepted. The census also confirms the impression from the few pre-war enquiries that skilled workers were more likely to display more lengthy terms of service in industry. It noted that 66 per cent of skilled workers surveyed in plants employing over 500 workers had entered industry in 1907 or earlier, but only 41 per cent of the semi-skilled and 27 per cent of the completely unskilled. As a consequence skilled operatives in all manufacturing sectors tended to be middle-aged, whilst the semi-skilled and unskilled fell more into the younger age groups.[64]

III

THE WORKPLACE DURING THE WAR

The war brought no changes for the better in the conditions of work for a majority of the labour force – indeed the reverse. The working day was lengthened; days of rest disappeared; rates of industrial accidents and illnesses soared; inflation ate away the rapid upswing in nominal wages.

In certain branches of factory manufacturing wartime expansion imparted a significant impetus to the concentration of production well under way in the 1900s. In general terms the number of industrial enterprises employing over 500 workers escalated from 64 per cent of the total in 1914 (St Petersburg province) to 78 per cent in 1917 (the city and its suburbs), and from 49 per cent to 68 per cent for plants with over 1,000 employees.[65] Thirty-eight factories had payrolls in excess of 2,000 operatives. As before the war, huge works predominated in chemicals, metalworking and textiles. By January 1917 in chemicals, for example, Okhta Explosives had a work-force of 10,200 and Okhta Gunpowder, 5,725: in metalworking, Izhora arms-works, 8,902; Obukhov, 10,600; Petrograd Cartridges, 8,292; the Pipe works, 19,046; Putilov, 24,449.[66] Establishments of gigantic size (over 5,000 employees) were for the most part state-owned munitions plants. In machine construction, electrical goods, wagons and textiles the labour force tended to average 1–2,000 per manufactory. Yet, as with the city's industrial structure prior to hostilities, the vagaries of official statistics distorted, in all probability, the degree of concentration. As far as can be ascertained from fragmentary data (in the absence of comprehensive investigations by the bureaucracy), places of work in all other manufacturing sectors, in artisanal trades and in the service industries remained small-scale. An exact accounting of the total hired labour force, however, by size of workplace is impossible.

The arbitrary powers of factory managers and individual employers remained unchecked throughout the war. The suppression of most trade unions in July 1914 removed even this feeble instrument for the protection of workers' interests. Foremen continued to act as petty tyrants, their actions often provoking strikes in protest. Thus at Aivaz engineering in October 1915 operatives complained that the Latvian foreman Straupe wrongly sacked workers, hired only his fellow countryman and established incorrect levels of pay.[67] At least in the mills the incidence of fines rose during the war. At Neva Thread in 1915 the penalty for the infringement of factory rules was increased from 20 to 50 kopecks.[68]

The capital's already dismal record in the matter of occupational illnesses and accidents grew markedly worse after 1914. The continuation of insanitary working conditions was compounded by a growing malnourishment caused by the decline in real wages for most workers and interruptions in the arrival of food supplies. The Erikson medical fund, like many others, experienced a steep rise in grants to sick members – from a total expenditure of 500 roubles per month early in 1915 to 3,600 roubles in June and 6,767 roubles in July of the same year. The sudden influx of refugees to Petrograd in the autumn of 1915 also heightened the probability of infectious diseases among all classes of citizens. In the second half of 1915 there were almost 60,000 cases of infectious diseases – typhus, scarlet fever, dysentery, diptheria.[69] The intensification of labour, the increase in overtime and the length of the working day, the greater utilisation of women and children and of machinery all contributed to the growth of industrial accidents. At Putilov, 4,000 out of a labour force of 22,000 suffered injuries at work between January and September 1915. Mishaps were most common in metalworking and most frequent on Mondays, as the introduction of prohibition in August 1914 had failed to curb the practice of hard drinking on Sundays.[70] Some impression of the scale of wartime sickness and industrial injuries among factory hands can be gleaned from the reports of the factory medical funds for 1916. At Petrograd Metals the 8,136 members of the *kassa* recorded 1,698 accidents and 7,395 cases of illness; at United Cables, (2,511 members), 336 and 2,454; at Lessner (7,716 members), 1,972 and 9,082 respectively.[71]

The war brought a distinct lengthening of the working day. As early as the autumn of 1914 the Petrograd Bureau for Factory Affairs was inundated with petitions from the chief arms manufacturers to permit the introduction of obligatory overtime. By 1915 the practice had become standard among factories with defence contracts. In heavy industry, on the eve of the February revolution, overtime amounted to 19 hours per worker a week. Sunday working, from seven in the morning to two in the afternoon, became common and compulsory. The removal of legal restrictions upon night work for women and children on 9 October 1915 facilitated continuous shift working. In metalworking 11–12 hours a day became the norm, and 12–13 in textiles. The working week increased from 54 to 60 or even 70 hours.[72]

One of the most ominous consequences of the war for the daily lives of Petrograd working people lay in the rise of the cost of living. In the absence of a comprehensive price index for Petrograd, patchy data must be utilised.

The general trends depicted in Tables 11.iii and 11.iv can be supplemented by Strumilin's study of the monthly prices of individual foodstuffs. It would seem that the first surge in food prices came in January to March 1915 when the cost of one and a half *funts*

Table 11.iii: *Prices of Foodstuffs in Petrograd Consumers' Co-operatives, July 1914–September 1916*[73] (kopecks)

	1 July 1914	1 Dec. 1915	1 Sept. 1916
potatoes (1 *pud*)	41	–	110
flour (1 *pud*)	250	402	472
bread (1 *pud*)	266	420	460
salt (1 *pud*)	29	101	113
butter (1 lb.)	52	101	187
sugar (1 lb.)	13	20	24
eggs	31	46	60

Table 11.iv: *Cost of the Daily Food Intake of an Unskilled Worker in Petrograd, January 1914–February 1917*[74] *(kopecks)*

	1914	1915	1916	1917
Jan.	26.0	25.3	33.5	52.8
Apr.	25.7	30.4	34.6	(Feb.) 64.2
July	26.3	30.6	36.4	
Oct.	24.6	32.7	47.7	
Dec.	25.2	35.6	49.5	
Yearly average	25.7	30.5	38.6	

(1 *funt* = 0.90 lb or 409.4 gm) of black bread went from 4.5 to 5.2 kopecks and of half a *funt* of meat from 10.7 to 12.2 kopecks. Thereafter prices stabilised until late summer, when the cost of black bread increased from 5.2 to 6 kopecks between July and September and potatoes from 2.4 to 4 kopecks for one and a half *funts*. A period of relative price equilibrium ensued until the spring of 1916. Then the price of black bread accelerated from 6.0 to 7.5 kopecks and meat from 10 to 11 kopecks. From the autumn of 1916, however, all food product prices entered an inexorable upward path. Black bread soared from 7.5 kopecks in November 1916 to 9.0 in January 1917; meat, from 11.5 kopecks in July 1916 to 16.0 kopecks in October 1916, at which level it stayed to February 1917 when it rose to 24.0; potatoes rose from 5.6 kopecks in September 1916 to 13.0 in February 1917.[75]

The impact of this wartime inflation on workers' earnings varied enormously between and within industries (see Table 11.v).

The money wages of industrial operatives underwent unprecedented growth throughout the war, advancing from an annual

Table 11.v: *Money and Real Annual Wages of Workers in 175 Petrograd Plants,* 1913–16[76] (roubles)

Industry	1913		1914		1915		1916	
	Money	*Real*	*Money*	*Real*	*Money*	*Real*	*Money*	*Real*
Animal products	434	434	416	412	566	435	759	368
Chemicals	356	356	502	497	492	379	835	405
Food processing	339	339	311	308	340	262	605	294
Metalworking	506	506	603	597	842	648	1,262	612
Mineral products	369	369	362	358	420	323	594	288
Printing	677	677	649	643	734	565	937	455
Textiles	311	311	337	333	418	321	613	297
Woodworking	492	492	550	545	582	448	774	376

average of 405 roubles in 1913 to 809 roubles in 1916. Due to the dominance of highly paid defence industries within its industrial structure, real wages in Petrograd industry in aggregate also experienced an uninterrupted increase until the autumn of 1916, when the new and vicious surge in the inflationary spiral produced a sharp fall in real incomes. A closer examination of individual branches of production reveals a more complex pattern. In fact in metals and chemicals alone did real wages escalate over the period 1913 to autumn 1916 – by 21 per cent and 13 per cent respectively. All other sectors of manufacturing endured a precipitate and continuous decline in real incomes between 1914 and 1916. Printers, the highest paid group of operatives prior to the war, suffered an especially severe contraction in real earnings (of the order of 33 per cent). As before hostilities, age, sex and skill continued to act as powerful determinants of levels of remuneration. The gap between the pay of men and women widened further. At the end of 1916 skilled male metalworkers earned 5–6 roubles a day but women 1.5–2 roubles. At the Tule cotton mills early in 1916 the men were paid 1.2 roubles a day but the women a mere 60 kopecks. Even within metalworking and chemicals the highly skilled and skilled alone benefited from the war. Wage differentials between these groups and the semi-skilled and unskilled apparently became even greater. A study of 3,160 members of the closed union of metalworkers in December 1916 discovered that only 20 per cent of turners and 14 per cent of skilled metalworkers (*slesari*) took home between 150 and 200 roubles a month at a time when the monthly wage in heavy industry was reckoned to be 114.2 to 127.5 roubles; 33 per cent and 40 per cent respectively had a monthly income of under 100 roubles.[77] The available materials refer solely to industrial operatives' earnings. As there exists no information on changes in the patterns of remuneration of artisans and employees of the service industries, no definite conclusion can be drawn as to the aggregate incomes of all hired workers. But the undoubted decline in real wages for most working people constituted the single most important factor behind the re-emergence of the strike movement from the summer of 1915 and was a cardinal underlying cause of popular discontent.

The widely differing forms and gamut of wartime remuneration between and within individual manufacturing sectors, the competitive increments to entice specialists away from rival firms and the unwelcome recrudescence of industrial disputes, overwhelmingly concerned with improving incomes, impelled the organised industrial community from the summer of 1915 to renew its earlier search for a uniform approach by employers to wage levels – with the same fruitless results.

Manufacturers' growing disquiet at 'the workers' irresponsible wage demands', which according to A. A. Bachmanov, 'had rendered this issue critical', constrained a joint gathering of the Sections of the POZF on 9 October 1915 to revive the commission to compile a standard rate book and rules of internal order. Although this body endeavoured over the next year to categorise all wage earners by group and to ascertain their exact remuneration (through the distribution of questionnaires to factories), the POZF signally failed in utilising such data to draw up, let alone implement, uniform rates of pay for all the myriad categories of the labour force. Indeed the exercise had lost much of its validity at the outset as at its first session the commission adopted the suggestion of General M. Z. Shemanov, the managing director of the state-owned Obukhov works, to exclude from the scope of the enquiry operatives employed in the manufacture of shells and grenades 'as their inclusion would exaggerate the general level of wages'.[78] The exigencies of the war and the deficiencies of the labour market dictated that the Society's endeavours to establish notional norms of wages were self-defeating. In their desperate desire to attract workers employers, including the state-owned plants, ceaselessly outbid one another by offering higher rates than competitors. Manufacturers' half-hearted endeavours, therefore, made no impact on wage differentials.

IV

LIVING CONDITIONS

The massive rise in Petrograd's population by 301,500 between the outbreak of war and the February revolution (as against 212,911 in the period December 1910 to January 1914) placed an already inadequate housing stock under the severest strain (see Table 11.vi).

Table 11.vi: *Growth in Population of the Districts of Petrograd, December 1910–November 1915–April 1917*[79]

District	Dec. 1910	Nov. 1915	Apr. 1917	% increase 1910–17	% increase 1900–10
Admiralty, Kazan, Spasskaia	206,630	–	311,590	50.8	−1.4
Kolomna	85,024	–	96,000	12.9	19.0
Liteinii	123,883	–	224,600	81.3	7.2
Moscow	173,704	–	194,000	11.7	12.3
Narva	191,988	222,537	–	15.9*	40.1
Neva	172,558	–	190,000	10.1	47.7
Okhta	40,098	–	60,789	51.6	51.6
Petersburg Side	212,647	291,990	360,000	69.3	79.4
Rozhdestvo	135,676	–	166,000	22.3	30.6
Vasil'evskii Island	190,788	226,455	268,000	40.5	45.5
Vyborg	97,547	132,554	150,465	54.2	48.0
TOTAL	1,905,589	2,300,000	2,420,000	27.0	32.4

* 1910–15

Although no statistics are available on the enlargement of population of the districts between the 1910 census and the eve of the First World War, the general trend between 1910 and 1917 is reasonably clear. The most distinctive feature is that the population of the more identifiably industrial districts did not grow particularly rapidly (see Table 11.vi). Indeed these areas experienced rates of population growth between 1910 and 1917 no greater than in the ten years after the turn of the century. Whilst the Vyborg district's population grew by 48 per cent between 1900 and 1910, it rose by 54 per cent in the seven years after 1910; Moscow district by 12 per cent and 11.7 per cent respectively; Vasil'evskii Island by 45 per cent and 40 per cent respectively. Furthermore one industrial district, Neva located in the south-east, experienced a far faster rate of population growth in the first decade of the century (48 per cent) than in the period 1910 to 1917 (10 per cent). The highest percentage upswings surprisingly were recorded in the central wards rather than in the outlying manufacturing regions. Thus Admiralty, Kazan and Spasskaia combined, which had suffered an actual decline in population of 1.4 per cent between 1900 and 1910, recorded a leap of 51 per cent in the seven years before the February revolution. Almost all this growth occurred after the outbreak of the war. A similar pattern is revealed with respect to the Liteinii district. In the case of the latter the figures partly reflect the enormous wartime expansion of reserve soldiers in the capital's garrison, four major barracks of which were located in this district close to the Tauride Palace, the seat of the State Duma, whilst the former three districts may have experienced over the period an advance in the number of artisans, traders, commercial employees and service personnel. Indeed even the industrial quarters included barracks, so that their growth must have embraced soldiers as well as workers.

The war did not alter significantly the general distribution of industrial operatives by district (see Table 11.vii). On the eve of the monarchy's overthrow, as before the war, the more outlying areas contained the highest concentrations of purely industrial operatives, with Vyborg continuing to occupy first place in this respect, followed by the Neva, Vasil'evskii Island and Narva districts. It is extremely unfortunate, however, that, in contrast to 1910, there are no separate data for all hired workers by district in January 1917. It is evident that the percentages of hired workers by district would be considerably higher than for factory hands alone. In this way it is impossible to ascertain how the war, with its varied and hitherto unexplored impact on artisanal trades and the service sector, altered the social profile of the entire hired labour force in each district. This lacuna in the evidence is especially regrettable as the concentration of Soviet scholars on industrial workers has given a rather distorted picture of the composition of the working class of each district both before and during the First World War and the revolutions. In particular it has led to an overemphasis on the centrality of metal-workers in the labour movement. Thus the figures in the last column of Table 11.vii would be considerably lower if they could be recalculated for 1917, on the basis of the same information available for 1910, as a percentage of all hired workers in each district.

The suppression of the capital's labour and socialist press early in July 1914 and the influx of many professional people into the army and the voluntary organisations meant that almost no social investigations were undertaken of living conditions between 1914 and 1917. It can be surmised with considerable justification that they deteriorated badly in the absence of any measures whatsoever by the state or the Municipal Duma to improve housing standards and to tackle the deep-seated urban problems outlined in Chapter 2. Rents, according to the Soviet scholar Stepanov, rose by 200 to 300 per cent. A survey taken early in 1915 of the 3,161 members of the medical fund at the Franco-Russian engineering works discovered that 32 per cent lived in a corner of a room; 43 per cent in a single room; and only 25 per cent could afford to rent a flat. The 1920 city census showed that a mere 15 per cent of houses in the Neva dis-

Table 11.vii: Distribution of Workers, Industrial Workers and Metalworkers, by District, December 1910–January 1917[80] (%)

District	1910 Workers as % of district population	1917 Industrial workers as % of district population	Metalworkers as % of districts' industrial workers
Admiralty, Kazan, Spasskaia	25.2	1.8	32.9
Kolomna	22.9	10.9	88.1
Liteinii	15.0	–	–
Moscow	25.2	10.8	52.3
Narva	30.3	18.6	16.9
Neva	36.8	20.1	69.7
Okhta	27.6	7.0	72.8
Petersburg Side	22.1	10.5	93.4
Rozhdestvo	25.2	6.2	20.2
Vasil'evskii Island	24.6	19.4	72.3
Vyborg	29.0	45.8	84.1

Note: The discrepancies between the columns for 1910 and 1917 are explained by the fact that 'workers' in 1910 refers to all hired working people not just industrial operatives. There are no separate figures for the distribution of 'workers' in general by district in 1917.

trict and 17 per cent in Moscow district enjoyed piped water and sewerage.[81] These findings reveal no amelioration at all in urban facilities in working-class neighbourhoods.

A new and unexpected strain was placed on workers' daily existence during the war by the increasingly irregular availability of foodstuffs.

The supply mechanism in Petrograd suffered from the existence of several competing authorities. Until the spring of 1915 the city's provisioning remained dependent upon the pre-war networks of private commerce, when the deteriorating condition of the urban market constrained the Petrograd Duma to intervene directly in purchasing provisions. Its Municipal Food Supply Commission concentrated its attention on securing adequate deliveries of meat, the daily demand for which soared from 18,000 *puds* in January 1915 to 26,000 a year later. As the city lacked refrigerated meat stores, it always depended on the daily importation of 1,000 head of live cattle to its stockyards. Before the war two-fifths of its meat requirements had been met from Siberia, which was cut off by rail for the first nine months of hostilities. From the spring the Commission dispatched delegates to buy cattle in the Volga region, and from June stocks of grain. By the summer the Commission had become the sole purveyor of meat to the population through a network of 45 municipal butchers' shops. It also controlled ten bakers' shops and, from the autumn of 1916, a bakehouse. The municipality also had endeavoured to regulate retail prices from the close of 1914 by the introduction of statutory prices for all viands sold in the city.[82]

In the summer of 1915 overall responsibility for the provisioning of the capital, as for other urban areas, was assumed by the Special Council for Food Supply, established on 17 August. A month later it set up a Petrograd Regional Conference for Food Supply, as a consultative organ to General Major Prince A. N. Obolenskii, the Governor General of the capital, who was appointed Petrograd Regional Commissioner for Food Supply. The Petrograd Duma was made subordinate to him but, as the Governor General's Office did not possess the requisite administrative apparatus to implement its new responsibilities, the Food Supply Commission remained the chief vehicle for the distribution of foodstuffs.[83]

The efforts of the new state apparatus of regulation and the Petrograd municipality, as well as of industrialists and consumers' co-operatives, foundered upon innumerable rocks: uncontrolled inflation; speculation; the priority accorded to the army in the scheduling of the shipment of food products; the continuous influx of people into the capital; the disorganisation of the railways and the disruption of the natural economic ties between the country's regions of food production and consumption. It was most unfortunate that the single most effective and equitable administrative measure that could have been implemented in the capital, a system of rationing, was discussed and rejected by the Special Council for Food on 28 December 1915 on the grounds that the inevitable failure of such a method, due to technical problems, 'would be very dangerous in its consequences for the structure of government itself'. Instead the Council proposed a reduction in the city's population, but this decision was never implemented.[84] Another disastrous error was made in the calculation by the Special Council of the number of railway wagons of food-stuffs required to arrive daily in the capital: fixed at 405 on 12 December 1915, the total was based on the peacetime requirement of the civilian population and ignored the increase in the size of the garrison and the labour force.[85]

Even the distributive network for such provisions as were avail-able proved grievously defective. The financial resources of the municipality were too inadequate to permit it to enter the market on the requisite scale. As its expenditures spiralled (in particular the provision of pecuniary aid to the families of reservists and the programme of municipal outlets), inflation curtailed its income; its reserves became exhausted; and by March 1916 the city was unable to raise new loans.[86] Municipal shops were poorly organised, the low salaries attracting drunken managers who indulged in swindl-ing. The statutory prices were determined in an arbitrary manner and were widely flouted. Large traders sold the worst-quality mer-chandise at the fixed rates and falsified their price lists. The quality of bread in particular declined.[87]

The precedence afforded military traffic on the railways ensured that an erratic proportion of all purchases of comestibles reached the capital. On 12 December 1915, the Special Council for Food Supply estimated that a monthly total of over 12,000 wagon-loads of food supplies would be needed to meet the basic food needs of the city. In fact as the figures for actual arrivals show (Table 11.viii), in only two months (September and October 1916) was this figure exceeded, whereas in December 1916 and January 1917 severe shortfalls were experienced. The most chronic deficit concerned the raw materials for baking bread; at no time were the targets met, in particular of rye for black bread, the staple ingredient of working-class diet. The schedules for the delivery of meat products, butter and eggs stood a more reasonable chance of fulfilment, but tea and salt were always in deficit.

The result of all the obstacles described above in the provisioning of the capital was a wild fluctuation in the availability of foodstuffs in the shops for all inhabitants. Early in 1915 reserves of butter and oats were exhausted. In the autumn of 1915, owing to particularly severe delays on the railways, food shops opened their doors only twice or

Table 11.viii: *Number of Railway Wagons of Foodstuffs Arriving at Petrograd, July 1916–January 1917 (by month and product)*[88]

	Estimated average monthly needs	Actual arrivals			1916 Oct.	Nov.	Dec.	1917 Jan.
		July	Aug.	Sept.				
Wheat	–	72	82	239	71	29	45	55
Wheat flour	1,500	1,433	484	552	807	1,248	719	1,131
Rye	900	496	1,096	891	262	278	141	121
Rye flour	1,200	1,013	709	210	–	449	417	112
Potatoes and cabbages	600	293	298	866	2,330	1,052	434	349
Cattle	3,000	1,477	3,437	4,086	2,364	3,282	2,594	1,625
Fowl	300	345	406	607	238	223	636	410
Fish	300	110	241	790	1,026	1,092	342	–
Eggs	300	819	465	628	631	210	55	48
Butter	150	190	227	137	289	230	196	257
Sugar	600	343	233	296	740	620	589	358
Tea and salt	150	1	62	88	134	81	116	119
TOTAL	12,150	8,297	11,594	12,639	14,168	11,332	8,654	6,556

Note: The figures for total monthly arrivals are greater than the addition of individual items, as certain products have been excluded from the table.

thrice a week; queues of 2–3,000 purchasers became common. In January 1916, sugar reserves fell to four days' supply. Two months later the working-class districts suffered from the complete absence of bread for days at a time.[89] The twelve weeks before the February revolution witnessed a disastrous turn for the worse with regard not only to the transfer of food supplies to the city, but to the state of its reserves and inflation. The total stocks of rye flour, estimated to be 1,383,923 *puds* on 15 January 1917 had fallen to 664,000 *puds* exactly one month later – barely enough to last twenty days. There were no reserves at all of tea, fish, potatoes, meat or eggs. In working-class neighbourhoods, bread supplies again became extremely scarce, many bakeries being forced to shut down. Meat, ham and sausages had vanished from the markets, as had boots, galoshes, soap and fabrics. The existence of the black market, speculation and the conspicuous consumption of the rich and wartime profiteers in the midst of the starvation of the majority further deepened workers' resentment, kindled by the acute shortage of food and the decline in real wages.[90]

The endeavours of both blue- and white-collar employees to cope with the food crisis by founding or joining consumers' co-operatives achieved very little. The war indeed witnessed a revival in the sickly co-operative movement in Petrograd. November 1915 saw the formation of the co-operative 'Unity' in Vasil'evskii Island, which drew its 3,000 members from 15 factories, and the society 'Moscow Gates', with 2,000 shareholders. A month earlier a 'Consumers' Society of Commercial–Industrial Employees' came into being. By February 1917 there were 23 consumers' co-operatives with around 50,000 members.[91] Whilst the co-operatives were aided by the decision of the municipal guardianships of the poor to open their own shops, they found themselves compelled to charge higher prices than private traders, thereby removing one incentive to membership. Dues, moreover, tended to be set too high for most operatives. Some, such as the Vyborg Workers' Co-operative, ran into financial difficulties. Like all other retail outlets, co-operative trading establishments were crippled by the irregular shipments of provisions to the capital.[92]

The POZF, too, fared no better than the municipality or the workers' co-operatives in its intervention in the issue of food supply. Its first step occurred on 9 October 1915 when it set up a Food Council. Factory managers, aware that continued increments in pay could not properly compensate for the shortages and inflated prices in the market place, were anxious to help in a practical manner. The new institution acted in effect as a middleman: it did not open its own retail outlets. Throughout 1916 it distributed stocks from the reserves in the Governor General's warehouses to consumers' societies, shops and smaller plants. However, the Food Council's allocation from the monthly total of wagons of provisions arriving in the capital was miniscule.[93] As a result its direct contribution to the amelioration of the food crisis was slight.

In addition to these measures, individual companies founded their own factory-controlled co-operatives. In November 1915, after a meeting of engineering employers of the Vasil'evskii Island, organisations of this type were founded at Possel', Siemens and Halske and Siemens-Schukkert. At the same time the administrations at Erikson, Lessner and Phoenix established the Consumers' Society of the Vyborg District and furnished it with a loan of 100,000 roubles. Several textile mills, as well as the Skorokhod shoe company, also set up co-operatives or opened factory shops.[94]

Another and later approach adopted by factory managers was the establishment of factory canteens, which had been hitherto a rare phenomenon. In October 1916 canteens were opened at Atlas-Petrograd, Aivaz, Erikson, the Russian Society, Siemens and Halske and Siemens-Schukkert. The Petrograd Duma also assigned 450,000 roubles to the municipal guardianships of the poor, five of the twenty of which had set up canteens in their districts by the close of the year, serving manual and white-collar workers.[95]

V

For industrialists and workers alike the war brought benefits as well as losses. The increasing reliance placed by the state upon Petrograd's manufacturers for armaments, clothing and footwear for the armed forces ensured that after a temporary hiatus the pre-war boom not only continued but also deepened. The fact that the Imperial army at the front was better clothed, shod and equipped by 1916 than it had been in 1915 and that it recovered from its shortfalls of material in the spring and summer of 1915 owed much to the capital's industries.[96] In this respect the Tsarist war economy worked relatively well. A ceaseless flow of profitable state contracts from the summer of 1915 nourished the rapid expansion of heavy industry, despite the difficulties managements experienced in the face of the shortages of skilled labour, fuel and raw materials. Industrialists were not the sole group, moreover, to profit from this feverish progress. In metal processing and chemicals skilled male operatives experienced an unprecedented advance in real incomes until the autumn of 1916. They also escaped the fate of being drafted into the army which was the lot of unskilled and skilled workers in non-priority branches of manufacturing.

But, both at the national macroeconomic level and at the micro-scale of the Petrograd economy, the priority afforded the army and war-related industries by the state regulatory apparatus established in the summer of 1915 with respect to shipments on the railways and the provision of fuel was at the expense of all other sectors of the economy and was itself an important cause of the incipient break-down of the economy by 1916. In this respect Petrograd, far removed from its sources of supply, was at a particular disadvantage. Despite the strenuous efforts of the capital's municipality and the state authorities to establish by the autumn of 1915 a planned system of deliveries of essential commodities, the gathering disorganisation of the railways and the military's stubborn refusal to consider civilian needs as of equal importance defeated all such schemes. Thus in 1915 and 1916 all the city's inhabitants, except the very rich, suffered the ravages of inflation and periodic shortages of fuel and food. The fact that the urban middle classes, as well as working people, had to endure such miseries goes far to explaining their ultimate support on the 27 and 28 February 1917 for the revolution in contrast to their indifference to the pre-war labour unrest.

For most workers, then, the war brought no amelioration in their living and working conditions. The working day and week grew longer; accidents at work soared; the incidence of illness increased; the *ancien régime* in the factories pressed ever harder and became even more intolerable; and unskilled, women, skilled operatives in non-defence industries and apprentices all experienced a drop in their real incomes; the desperate search for scarce supplies of fuel and comestibles at soaring prices became an insufferable feature of everyday life and rents tripled as the pressure grew on a woefully defective housing stock due to the wartime influx of migrants, refugees and evacuees.

Whilst the slow breakdown of the city's economic and social fabric immeasurably strengthened the tempo of working-class alienation from the regime and deepened tensions among all social groups, the revolutionary parties proved unable to benefit from this propitious turn of events. One of the reasons of their failure (which is explored in Chapters 12 and 13) was the changing social structure of the working class during the war. The weight of the crucial segment within labour of hereditary, urbanised, skilled operatives (the 'worker–intellectuals' and labour activists *par excellence*) was reduced by conscription, the immigration of new peasant workers and the increased hiring of women (in particular on assembly lines in shell manufacture). Industrial expansion aggravated the internal stratification of the work-force by widening the gap in earnings between skilled and unskilled, men and women, adults and youths. The socialist groups had been unable to overcome this fundamental obstacle to labour organisation and revolutionary mobilisation before 1914; the war rendered their task even more formidable. The same failing remained with respect to the geographical dispersal of hired labour throughout the city, which the war did nothing to reduce.

Chapter 12

THE REVOLUTIONARY PARTIES AND THE LABOUR MOVEMENT: I. JULY 1914 – JULY 1915

Russia's declaration of war on Germany on 19 July 1914 came at an unfortunate time for the revolutionary parties in Petrograd. From the spring of the year all factions lacked both city-wide and district illegal organisations and a broad range of cells in factories and artisanal workshops. The Bolsheviks' conquest of the trade unions, educational societies and the sick benefit funds had likewise failed to secure them a mass base due to the manifold weaknesses of these institutions. During the July days the authorities had suppressed the legal labour press and most trade unions. The failure of the 'general strike' in the capital had left the working class and the revolutionary activists exhausted and demoralised. The July events had illustrated the inability of the socialist sub-élite to provide effective leadership or direct workers' discontent towards clearly defined political goals. At one level the war created new opportunities for the revolutionary opposition. The great boom in war-related industries and the near doubling in size of the factory labour force (from 218,258 to 419,108), in particular in metalworking, as well as the predominance of gigantic plants in munitions and chemicals, seemed to widen the potential pool of recruitment. The continuous defeats from the spring of 1915, the sharp deterioration in working and living conditions, the less than effective conduct of the war, the revival of liberal opposition in the State Duma in the summer of 1915 and the scandals surrounding the throne in the person of Rasputin all increased popular discontent to fever pitch by the last months of 1916. On the other hand, the war intensified all the existing difficulties the revolutionary parties experienced in attempting to establish permanent links to the broad mass of wage earners and to furnish guidance to the labour movement. The outbreak of hostilities imparted a renewed impetus to embittered factionalism as a consequence of theoretical differences over the correct attitude to be adopted towards the catastrophe and the collapse of the Second International. The state of wartime communications rendered control by *émigré* leaders over their followers in the capital almost impossible. Even more than in the years before the war socialist sub-élites pursued their own policies. The almost total destruction of the legal labour press, trade unions and educational societies, as well as the arrest of the five Bolshevik State Duma deputies in November 1914, deprived activists of their imperfect legal channels to working people. Illegal activity alone was left to them, but the constant repressions of the secret police rendered this a feeble instrument. At a deeper level, the changes within the working class erected even more formidable obstacles to mass revolutionary mobilisation. The proportion of 'cadre' workers – hereditary, urbanised, skilled male operatives – was lowered because of mobilisations into the army and the influx of peasants, women, refugees and petty bourgeois elements. The expansion of industry further aggravated internal stratification within the working class.

I

The rapidity with which events developed in the summer of 1914 – the outbreak of war at the close of July, its pan-European character, the shock of the German Social Democratic Party's support for the 'defence of the fatherland' and its vote for war credits in the Reichstag, the entry of French and Belgian socialists into bourgeois governments – meant that the foreign leaders of the Russian revolutionary parties took time to fashion their ideological response. By September three distinct general positions on the war began to emerge which cut across all previous factional lines and held out the possibility of a radical realignment of tendencies. The theories fashioned by the intellectuals abroad were in part to influence their followers' responses in Petrograd. But revolutionary activists in the capital also modified these intellectual constructs and even rejected parts of them.

At one extreme stood the defensists, represented by Georgii Plekhanov, the 'father' of Russian Marxism, G. Aleksinskii, a Vperedist, and prominent right-wing SRs such as N. Avksent'ev, I. Bunakov and B. Voronov, all of whom co-operated from autumn 1915 on the Parisian newspaper *Prizyv*. Starting from the distinction between aggressive and defensive wars, the proponents of defencism argued that the war was the product of German imperialist aggression, whereas France and Belgium waged a war of national defence. For this reason the German Social Democrats were to be castigated for supporting such a war and succumbing to chauvinist passions, whereas the French and Belgian socialists were fully justified in joining governments of national unity. A German victory in Western Europe would signify the triumph of militarism and reactionary Prussian Junkerdom over democracy and culture. As for Russia, the country's very existence was at stake. Victory over Germany was the precondition of Russia's political and economic emancipation. The defeat of Russia would set back her economic and social development by turning her into a German colony and would lead to the restoration of total autocracy. As Russia was fighting a defensive and popular war, democracy (i.e. the socialists) must participate in the war effort.[1] Defensists, however, were split on the crucial issue of whether the war should entail a suspension of the revolutionary struggle against the autocracy. Plekhanov was at least consistent both in arguing that the outbreak of revolution might impair the war effort and in urging the Menshevik fraction in parliament not to vote against war credits.[2] He drew the conclusion from these premises that the socialists should aid the liberal opposition seize power.[3] By the autumn of 1915, however, his SR allies, who dominated the editorship of *Prizyv*, revised their earlier view, under the impact of the Imperial government's inauspicious conduct of the war, that the attainment of victory must take precedence over revolution. Avksent'ev and Bunakov now urged the readoption of the revolutionary tactic and a joint struggle with the bourgeoisie.[4]

At the other extreme was the defeatism of V. I. Lenin, who developed his theories in his 'Seven Theses', written at the end of August 1914, and in 'The War and Russian Social Democracy', published in issue 33 of a revived *Sotsial-demokrat* on 1 November. His views assumed a programmatic form in the resolutions he drafted for a conference of Bolshevik *émigrés* held at Berne early in March 1915.[5] The starting point for his analysis was that the war was a bourgeois, imperialist war, the product of the contradictions of capitalism at its highest stage (imperialism). He denied the defensists' distinction between aggressive and defensive wars. Defence of the fatherland had been permissible in the 'progressive' wars of the nineteenth century as these promoted national unification in the interests of capitalist development. But support of war and the defence of the fatherland were impermissible in the imperialist age when all capitalist countries had been guilty of the war's outbreak. In Lenin's opinion the war had brought to a head the crisis both of European capitalism and of the socialist movement. The Second International had completely collapsed both ideologically and politically because the socialist leaders of France and Germany (the social chauvinists) had betrayed their internationalist beliefs. Equating the social chauvinists with the opportunists in the pre-war International, Lenin castigated them for abandoning the class struggle, renouncing revolutionary methods and accepting the *Burgfrieden* (or class truce) at the start of the war. The Bolshevik leader came to explain the growth of opportunism and social chauvinism by the emergence in the decades before 1914 of a labour aristocracy and socialist party bureaucracy, a stratum of privileged workers who became bourgeoisified due to the crumbs thrown their way from the super-profits of imperialist expansion. Such groups had become agents of the bourgeoisie within the proletarian movement. According to Lenin the war could be terminated only if it was turned into a civil war of the classes. 'The correct slogan is the conversion of the present imperialist war into a civil war', meaning the socialist revolution in Western Europe and the bourgeois revolution in Russia. The defeat of one's own government was the lesser evil. As the first steps towards the civil war he urged the ending of the class truce, the formation of illegal organisations, fraternisation at the front and mass revolutionary action. He envisaged the creation of a new, Third, International of independent revolutionary Marxist parties as the means to convert the imperialist war into a civil war. His policy entailed a schism within existing socialist parties and a complete break from the social opportunists and chauvinists. Even within Lenin's own faction, however, his views did not meet with whole-hearted support. At the Berne conference, V. N. Kasparov and G. L. Shklovskii attacked his slogan for a United States of Europe. N. Bukharin, N. V. Krylenko and E. F. Rozmirovich objected to his labelling Russia's defeat a 'lesser evil' and his extremely narrow definition of the prospective Third International. Later on in 1915 Bukharin and his friends clashed with their leader over his adoption of the slogan of national self-determination.[6]

Between the two extremes lay a variety of attitudes to the war which may be classed as 'internationalist'. Amongst Mensheviks this position was represented by the Foreign Secretariat of the Organisational Committee, namely I. S. Astrov, P. B. Aksel'rod, L. Martov and S. I. Semkovskii. Prominent Bolshevik internationalists included the Vperedists A. V. Lunacharskii and D. Z. Manuilskii, the Bolshevik Conciliators A. Lozovskii and V. A. Antonov-Ovseenko. These four co-operated with Martov and L. Trotskii on the Paris newspapers *Golos* and its successor, *Nashe slovo*. The SR leader V. Chernov was the chief ideologue of internationalism in his party. Internationalists shared certain basic assumptions. The war was imperialist in nature, the result of the contradictions inherent in capitalism. Both the Entente and the Triple Alliance were pursuing predatory designs; neither was waging a war of national liberation. Russia pursued dynastic rather than national goals. The victory of either side would be dangerous for social peace and political progress. Internationalists, therefore, condemned defencism, the class truce and support by socialists for the war effort, including Russia's.[7]

They were equally adamant in their opposition to Lenin's defeatism. Chernov argued that Germany's victory would signify the triumph of a government hostile to Russian democracy. Trotskii rejected the notion that Russian socialists should pin their hopes on the revolutionising effects of defeat; the exhaustion consequent upon loss of the war could be so great as to depress the revolutionary will.[8] But internationalists differed among themselves as to the causes of the collapse of the Second International and their prescriptions for how socialists should respond to that disaster. Aksel'rod, for example, approved of the conduct of the French and Belgian socialists as they were defending democratic regimes from attack by a semi-absolutist Germany. Martov refused to accuse the French and German socialist leaders of treachery; they were in fact truly in tune with the masses who had fallen under the spell of patriotism. Chernov, on the other hand, came closer to Lenin's explanation; industrial socialism had degenerated before the war because it had linked its fate to the growth of capitalism and in this way its revolutionary character had been sterilised.[9] The members of the Menshevik Foreign Secretariat regarded the means of organising a socialist peace movement as the reformation of the existing Second International. They vehemently opposed Lenin's call to purge the 'treacherous' social chauvinists from the International as this would split and weaken the international movement. They insisted, however, that the official leaderships of the socialist parties renounce their support for the war effort and cease policies of class collaboration.[10] Chernov called for the establishment of a revolutionary International by a conference of socialists opposing the war as a third force of the toiling masses of all countries. Trotskii, the editorial board of *Nashe slovo* and Lunacharskii, who revived the Vpered faction's journal in August 1915, all urged the creation of a new Third International consisting exclusively of revolutionary socialists.[11] It was not until the summer and autumn of 1915 that the *émigré* Menshevik leaders, under the impact of the formation of the Progressive Bloc in the State Duma and the revival of labour unrest, began to consider the possibility that a bourgeois revolution in Russia might act as a stimulus to the peace movement in other European countries. Arguing that Russia's military defeat marked the downfall of the 3rd June political system, Martov advanced the case that the liberal opposition, led by the commercial–industrial bourgeoisie, had launched a bid for power. This could be the starting point for a mighty social movement which might become revolutionary. Martov and Aksel'rod put forward the slogan of the All-Russian Constituent Assembly for peace and the liquidation of Tsardom.[12] Their prescription was logically contradictory, as the liberal parties sought political change in order to continue the war more effectively. In the first year or so of the war, Chernov refused to advocate a struggle against the war by revolutionary means; active opposition to the war in Russia should be conditional upon a similar movement in Germany. Later he took the view that a revolution in Russia would be complemented by and act as a spur to upheavals in Germany and Austria-Hungary.[13] Developing the thesis he had enunciated in his *Itogi i perspektivy* (published in 1906), Trotskii posited the notion that the movement of the Russian proletariat should be linked not to the movement of the urban bourgeoisie and peasantry but to international proletarian militancy. The revolutionary struggle of the Russian working class would itself impart a great impetus to the revolutionary offensive of the European proletariat.[14]

II

The reception of the war by revolutionary intellectuals, rank and file party members and the mass of wage earners in Petrograd has been a subject of bitter dispute ever since the event. Most contemporary educated Russians were immensely impressed by the apparent cessation of domestic strife in the first weeks of hostilities and the formation of a patriotic union (*union sacrée*) between Tsar and people.[15] This interpretation was subscribed to by the secret police. In a memorandum of 24 August 1914 the chief of the Petrograd Okhrana, Colonel K. P. Popov, remarked that, 'the workers, under the influence of the patriotic mood, have foresworn the revolutionary struggle against the government and accepted the necessity of internal unity.'[16] On the other hand, the Bolshevik Duma deputy, G. I. Petrovskii, writing to a comrade in Moscow at the start of September, emphatically asserted that 'there was no such [patriotic] mood, and there could not be'.[17] Soviet historians have laboured since the 1920s to demonstrate that, even in the absence of instructions from Lenin, cut off in Galicia and then Switzerland, and before the reception of his 'Seven Theses' in Russia in the autumn of 1914, both local Bolshevik leaders and at least 'conscious' proletarians alone remained unaffected by the wave of chauvinist patriotism, immune to all defensist notions and resolutely hostile to the war from the outset. Writing in the 1920s, M. G. Fleer argued that the 'silence' with which the declaration of war was received by the proletariat 'was in itself a firm protest against the war, if, however, a passive protest'.[18] Fifty years later, academician Mints contended that 'the party committees of the Bolsheviks in Russia acted decisively against the imperialist war'.[19] The conclusion reached by Soviet investigators is that the position taken by the Bolsheviks inside Russia in the first weeks of the war anticipated the tactical line set out later by Lenin in his 'Seven Theses' and the

Central Committee Manifesto.[20] In contrast, the American scholar Tsuyoshi Hasegawa believes that 'patriotic fever seized the workers as well'.[21] The fundamental problem facing the historian is that, in the absence of any contemporary mechanism of ascertaining public attitudes such as opinion polls, it is in fact impossible to come to firm and reliable conclusions about the reaction to and views of revolutionary activists and workers on the war. The evidence available is exiguous, tendentious, contradictory and capable of different interpretations. At best, tentative impressions may be drawn from it.

Russia's declaration of war on Germany on 19 July 1914 caught the revolutionary parties in a state of organisational paralysis. Neither the Bolsheviks nor Mensheviks nor SRs then possessed central city or district committees. Over a thousand party and union members had just been arrested for participation in the July general strike. The first mobilisations removed many more from party work.[22] Therefore, the response to the war could be fashioned only by small, isolated and decimated groups of activists. As fragmentary evidence indicates, some Petrograd Bolsheviks were aware of the anti-war resolution of the Stuttgart Congress of the Second International in 1907 (readopted at the Copenhagen Congress in 1910 and the Basle Congress in 1912), which called on the working class and its representatives in national parliaments to prevent the outbreak of a threatening war 'by means they consider the most effective'.[23] Certain activists attempted to implement the precepts of these documents. As early as 16 July unknown Vyborg revolutionaries drew up a leaflet which put forth the slogan 'war upon war'. Some time before 19 July, A. Shliapnikov drafted an apparently unprinted leaflet in the name of the defunct Petersburg Committee. (The revolutionary parties refused to accept the capital's change of name and referred throughout the war to 'Petersburg'.) This document followed closely the International's analysis of the causes of international tensions, with the emphasis upon militarism and armaments, and described Tsardom's war aim as a thirst for new lands. It exhorted workers to heed the International's call to protest against the war.[24] On the day war was declared, the secret police noted that militant revolutionary youths were arranging factory meetings, at which they exhorted all socialist tendencies to oppose the war and the soldiers to turn their weapons against the internal enemy, the autocracy. The extent and scope of such gatherings is unknown. There were also sporadic attempts by Bolsheviks, at least in the central Town district, to arrange demonstrations against the war.[25] The militants also put great trust in the anticipated anti-war actions of the West European socialist parties, in particular the German Social Democratic Party.[26] The Stuttgart resolution of the International, however, furnished a far from clear guide to action. As the document had been a compromise between the German socialists, who opposed the adoption of the general strike as the tactic ·to prevent war, and the French and Russian parties, which urged precisely this course of action, it had left unspecified the actual means to be adopted.[27] The Okhrana correctly noted that neither the two appeals cited here nor the Bolshevik orators at meetings were able to specify any concrete measures of opposition to the war, such as a general strike or street demonstrations. Apart from the Bolsheviks, the Mezhraionka, at a meeting on 20 July, also adopted the slogan 'war upon war'.[28] There is unfortunately no evidence on the reaction of Menshevik and SR militants. However, as Shliapnikov admits in his memoirs, 'events developed so rapidly that organised workers were caught off guard'.[29] The volte-face in the position of the German Social Democratic leadership, which voted for war credits in the Reichstag on 4 August n.s. (22 July o.s.) came as a tremendous shock to Petrograd revolutionaries. An unsigned article in *Sotsial-demokrat* (written by Shliapnikov) observed that it 'exerted at first a depressing effect upon the general mood', whilst Iurenev was aware of a 'feeling of perplexity' among activists.[30] The German comrades' failure to uphold internationalist principles seriously weakened the hotheads' case for mass protest action. Furthermore a more dispassionate analysis of the revolutionaries' situation in the middle of July – the exhaustion and demoralisation of workers after the July strike, the successful implementation by the military authorities of mobilisation, the imposition of martial law in the capital on 18 July and the pulverisation of the underground by the police – ensured that surviving leaders in fact refrained from concrete calls for anti-military action.

The information available on the immediate response of the capital's labour force to the war is extremely limited and confusing. The very few published memoirs are those of working-class socialist activists rather than of apolitical plebeians, and perhaps bear the imprint of the interpretation of the party's role current at the time of their appearance in the early 1920s. 'Healthy proletarian instinct' saved the working class, Shliapnikov averred, from the intoxication of patriotic feelings. These reminiscences always claim that only 'backward' workers, artisans, commercial–industrial employees, and the *lumpenproletariat* participated in patriotic manifestations.[31] On the other hand, some memoirists present a completely different picture. A. I. Mashirov, an organiser in the First Town district in the last half of 1914, recalled that on his return to the capital he encountered workers heading patriotic demonstrations. I. S. Gavrilov, an employee of the Rozenkrants plant in Vyborg, remarked that in the autumn the workers of the district insulted and hurled stones at German prisoners of war.[32] Apart from a single instance on 19 July, when workers left the New Lessner and Erikson factories shouting 'Down with the war', the Okhrana reported no other anti-war demonstrations in working-class quarters.[33] Whether labouring people participated on a large scale in the patriotic processions of polite society must remain an open question. The reports in the capital's middle-class press described crowds as being formed for the most part of officers, students, society ladies and members of the professions, with a sprinkling of artisans, shopkeepers and shop assistants. One may conclude that at the very least there was no large-scale, overt opposition to the war among the mass of factory and artisanal hands. This inference is strengthened by the almost complete absence of strikes (only some 11,000 struck on 19–20 July) and the prompt reporting for military service of male workers called up in the middle of July. There was certainly passive acceptance of the war. Many operatives evidently regarded hostilities as a chance to improve their economic lot as there was a rush into jobs at defence plants in anticipation of higher wages.[34]

The true attitude of the revolutionary intellectuals and the three socialist parliamentary groups towards the war is even more difficult to disentangle from the welter of politically inspired memoirs and the imperative necessity of Soviet historical literature to assert the Bolshevik claim to be the sole consistent socialist opponent of the war. It is the misfortune of Soviet investigators that at the session of the State Duma convened on 26 July the Bolsheviks consented to a joint Social Democratic declaration on the war with their Menshevik rivals, read out by the Menshevik deputy, V. I. Khaustov; that this document contained a defensist statement that 'the proletariat ... will at all times defend the cultural wealth of the nation against any attack from whatever quarter'; that all three fractions' deputies refrained from voting for war credits and walked out of the chamber. Since the middle of the 1920s various inconsistent reminiscences and Soviet scholars have sought to get around this problem by claiming that the Mensheviks had insisted on inserting the offending clause for fear of losing their influence upon the working masses and that the document was essentially of Bolshevik provenance.[35] As an excellent piece of detective work by Dr D. Longley has revealed, the Bolshevik claim to a unique stance is further weakened by the fact that since the 1920s Soviet investigators have relied on a corrupt version of the declaration which appeared in a Tula socialist leaflet in the autumn of 1914 and which imparted a more clearly internationalist hue to the document.[36] The original and genuine version was an altogether milder affair. Whilst it blamed the war on 'a policy of conquest' and 'the ruling circles of all belligerent countries' and implied that Russian workers had sympathised with the German proletariat's earlier protest against the war, it made no reference to the pre-war decisions of the Second International or the Russian government's role in the war's outbreak or the continuation of the revolutionary struggle against Tsardom.[37] In sharp contrast the Trudovik leader A. F. Kerenskii, whilst he adopted the patriotic cause in his statement that Russian democracy 'will rebuff the aggressors and defend the homeland and cultural heritage', displayed sharp antagonism to the government and openly and boldly called for revolution once the war was over. Furthermore, unlike the Bolsheviks, the Menshevik and Trudovik deputies, together with the Left Kadets, attempted to make the legislature's support for the emergent patriotic union conditional upon the government's assent to political reforms. The majority of Kadets, led by P. N. Miliukov, and other parties rejected this proposal.[38] A tentative conclusion may be that the Social Democratic declaration reflected the hesitant efforts of both Bolshevik and Menshevik deputies, alike isolated from foreign centres, to reconcile the irreconcilable pressures of genuine distaste for the war, disorientation in the light of the news of the German Social Democrats' abandonment of internationalism and the patriotic fervour of educated society and perhaps of sections of the working class.

In the weeks after the 26 July session of the State Duma two developments compelled the Bolshevik leadership in Petrograd to attempt to define more coherently their attitude to the war. Some time in August the Duma fraction received a telegram from the Belgian socialist Emile Vandervelde, president of the International Socialist Bureau, who had entered the cabinet as Minister of State, in effect asking his Russian colleagues to follow the Belgium example. And in September the Bolshevik Duma deputy, F. N. Samoilov, who had been recuperating in a Swiss sanatorium at the start of the war, brought to Russia a copy of Lenin's 'Seven Theses'.[39] Both the content of the final Bolshevik reply to Vandervelde, which was settled at a conference of four of the Duma deputies with L. Kamenev, editor-in-chief of the defunct *Pravda* and several representatives of the party underground at the close of September, and the manner of its composition pose as many problems for Soviet historians as does the declaration of 26 July.[40] Despite the presence of Samoilov and knowledge of Lenin's new ideas, the reply signally failed to reflect any of Lenin's key arguments, in particular his espousal of defeatism. Although it marked an advance in that it openly opposed defencism and the class truce and urged a continuation of the revolutionary struggle against Tsardom, a course of action specifically recommended in the event of war in the Stuttgart resolution of 1907, it was marked by sympathy for the Entente countries. In particular it left the distinct impression that once Tsardom had been removed the war would become one of defence for the new bourgeois democratic Russia.[41] In many ways, the response came close to the views of the Menshevik A. N. Potresov and anticipated the revolutionary defencism of the Majority Socialists and Bolsheviks such as Kamenev himself and Stalin in the spring of 1917. Soviet historians have sought to get around these embarrassing facts either by falsifying what transpired at the conference (I. P. Leiberov claims that the gathering approved Lenin's 'Theses') or by completely failing to subject the document to textual criticism (as in Mints) or by ascribing a dominant role in the fashioning of the reply to Kamenev (as in Dazhina and Tiutiukin).[42] It is indeed evident from several sources that Kamenev entertained the severest doubts about Lenin's 'Theses', especially the propagation of defeatism. Most spectacularly at his trial in February 1915 he publicly repudiated all Lenin's theories on the war and called in his defence the 'social chauvinist' Iordanskii. That this was not merely a device to secure a lighter sentence is confirmed by the fact that when the police raided another conference of the Bolshevik deputies with party workers on 4 November they discovered in Petrovskii's possession notes dictated to him by Kamenev amending the 'Seven Theses' and above all sidestepping the call for defeatism.[43] Kamenev's objection to the slogan of Russia's defeat was apparently widely shared amongst Bolsheviks. In his memoirs Shliapnikov admits that 'the question of "defeatism" did cause perplexity'. In his unsigned article for no. 33 of *Sotsial-demokrat*, he also acknowledged that there was widespread sympathy among workers, one that it is known he personally shared, for the plight of the Entente countries and a desire for their victory. In a letter dated 1 September Petrovskii informed his correspondent that the Duma declaration would form the basis of the party's response to Vandervelde, whilst at his trial he proclaimed his adherence to the views expressed in the declaration rather than his leader's pronouncements. Furthermore it is apparent that neither the Duma deputies, nor Kamenev or Shliapnikov shared Lenin's thesis on the collapse of the Second International.[44] It seems that an early draft of the reply written by the Bolshevik lawyer N. Krestinskii, Petrovskii and the veteran Latvian socialist lawyer P. I. Stuchka circulated widely among socialist groups in various towns. At least some of the respondents, from Saratov and Moscow amongst others, argued both for the necessity of Germany's defeat as removing a prime obstacle to the long-term success of Russian democracy and for the continuation of the domestic struggle against the autocracy.[45] Thus, up until the detention of the five Bolshevik deputies early in November 1914, Lenin's principal lieutenants in Petrograd once again found themselves at loggerheads with his extremist stance. Their position on the war could not be described as Leninist; rather it combined both pre-war internationalism and covert revolutionary defencism. They were in a far better position than an *émigré* to understand the dangers and difficulties of propagating the concept of their country's defeat at a time of heightened patriotic feelings, Germany's initial victory at Tannenberg, the near total collapse of all party organisations and the semi-defensist opinions of many party adherents.

Even after somewhat more regular ties to Lenin were established with Shliapnikov's departure for Stockholm in October 1914 and the appearance of copies of *Sotsial-demokrat* in the following two years, setting out at length Lenin's theories, his followers in Petrograd continued to adopt a highly selective approach to their use of his prescriptions. A textual analysis of forty-seven leaflets and appeals published illegally by Bolshevik militants between January 1915 and 22 February 1917 is most illuminating. Not a single leaflet mentioned the essential Leninist slogan of the defeat of Russia being the lesser evil or his call to promote fraternisation at the front. Thus local activists continued throughout the war to shun themes likely to be highly unpopular, for the reasons outlined earlier, with the masses. Ten leaflets made reference in the form of short phrases to the necessity of turning the imperialist war into a civil war and nine to the formation of a Third International. In all cases no explanation was provided for the significance of these concepts. With two exceptions, a Petersburg Committee memorandum of 7 April 1915 and a lengthy leaflet of the Russian Bureau in January 1917, no attempts were made to reproduce Lenin's analyses of the causes of the Second International's collapse. Perhaps reflecting the continuation of the deep conciliatory tendencies within Bolshevik ranks before the war, there was no continuous endeavour to denounce and slander the opinions of those Mensheviks and SRs whom Lenin castigated as 'social patriots', with the exception of the short period of the elections of Labour Groups to the War-Indutries Committees in the autumn of 1915 (see Chapter 13). In one aspect alone did Petrograd Bolsheviks come close to their leader's analysis, that is in the interpretation of the economic causes of the war, but even here the phrase 'an imperialist war' was striking by its absence. For the most part the party's illegal literature concentrated, as before the war, on attacking the government's policies towards the working class and setting out in harrowing detail the war's consequences for the masses. Almost all documents called for the continuation of the revolutionary struggle against the autocracy as the means to terminate the war and ended with the old Bolshevik slogans of a democratic republic, the eight-hour day and confiscation of the gentry estates. There is a sharp contrast between the central focus of Lenin's theoretical constructions and activity in the war, which concentrated almost exclusively upon the collapse of the Second International and creation of the Third International as the vehicle of the civil war, and the concerns of his followers in Petrograd, for whom European socialist developments were peripheral. This is further confirmed by the complete silence in illegal literature about the anti-war conferences of 'Internationalist', anti-defensist socialists held in Zimmerwald in September 1915 and at Kienthal in April 1916.[46]

The telegram from Emile Vandervelde also acted as a stimulus to the Mensheviks to fashion a more comprehensive response to the war. Although there were apparently several earlier versions, including one by E. Maevskii, the former secretary of *Luch*, the final draft was largely the product of the pen of A. N. Potresov, the distinguished Marxist littérateur, who had been absent from the capital at the time of the composition of the Social Democratic statement to the Duma.[47] Like its Bolshevik counterpart this document, compiled in the lack of knowledge of the opinions of the Menshevik exiles, revealed understanding for the Belgian and French cause, as one of self-defence of democratic liberties against 'the aggressive policy of Prussian Junkerdom'. The choice, however, facing Russian socialists was more complex, as reactionary Russia had entered the war as an ally of the Anglo-French Entente. For that reason socialist democracy in Russia could not 'accept responsibility for the actions of the Russian government . . . by taking active part in the war'. On the other hand, reflecting awareness of and attempting to strike a balance between the unacceptability of defeatism and the nationalist enthusiasm, the response ended by promising 'that in our activity in Russia we are not opposing the war'.[48]

Following Lenin's contemporary splenetic animadversions against his Menshevik rivals, Soviet works insist on classing all Mensheviks as 'social chauvinists', i.e. the latter allegedly preached a class truce for the duration of hostilities, complete support for the government and the war effort and the rejection of the revolutionary struggle.[49] Such a blanket condemnation conveniently ignores the many different and complex shades of opinion among the Mensheviks in the capital.

In the first place, a paltry number of Menshevik intellectuals in Petrograd replicated Plekhanov's outright capitulation to nationalism. His few adherents included A. Iu. Finn-Enotaevskii and N. Iordanskii, Party Menshevik and editor of the monthly periodical *Sovremennyi mir* (which reprinted many of Plekhanov's articles). An Okhrana survey of socialist attitudes to the war in January 1916 noted that the Russian supporters of Plekhanov 'exerted minimal influence upon the public mood'.[50]

In the second place, the intellectuals grouped around the literary journal, *Nasha zaria*, A. N. Potresov, E. Maevskii, F. A. Cherevanin and P. P. Maslov, developed in time a distinctive version of defencism, which rested on the notion that internationalism and self-defence were not mutually exclusive but interconnected. The proponents of self-defence, like Plekhanov, began with the distinction between aggressive and defensive wars. The victory of Germany would amount to a disastrous encouragement to the status quo of semi-absolutism in Europe. For Russia it would mean her political and economic enslavement as a German colony. In contradiction to Lenin, they contended that Russia's defeat would not provoke another revolutionary outburst on the model of 1905.[51] Their rejection of defeatism, however, did not mean, contrary to Soviet historians' assertions, that they lent their support to the existing regime or had abandoned the revolutionary cause. Throughout the war, in sharp contrast to Plekhanov, they advised the Menshevik fraction in parliament to vote against military credits.[52] They repeatedly emphasised that the outbreak of fighting did not signify that socialists had abandoned the liberation movement.[53] On the other hand, genuinely and correctly fearful of the consequences of a German victory in the east, they did give a whole-hearted endorsement to the concept of the country's self-defence. By 1916 indeed they envisaged the overthrow of the monarchy as removing the most formidable obstacle to the successful mobilisation of society against the invader. Their view was neatly summarised in the phrase: 'Without Russia's rebirth there can be no defence; but without her defence there can be no rebirth.'[54] Adhering to a major tenet of Menshevik doctrine, the group envisaged a broad coalition of progressive social forces, embracing both the bourgeois liberal opposition in the State Duma and the proletariat, as the mechanism of revolution.[55] Like the Menshevik internationalists abroad, they remained adamantly hostile to annexationism and regarded the revival of the Second International as the vehicle for peace making.[56]

It would also be erroneous to describe the miniscule Menshevik Duma fraction as a whole as either defensist or social chauvinist. As Ermanskii, an advisor to the deputies, pointed out in his memoirs, the fraction was subjected to contradictory pressures from both Menshevik defensists and internationalists and could not formulate a collective stance on the war, owing to internal dissensions.[57] A. F. Burianov, who had formally left the group early in 1914, accepted Plekhanov's premises and cast his ballot for military appropriations. The Irkutsk deputy, I. N. Mankov, followed his lead in January 1915 and was excluded from the fraction for his pains.[58] A. I. Chkhenkeli, perhaps influenced by the Georgian leader N. Zhordania's unconditional support for the war, inclined towards defencism and refused to recognise all the decisions of the Zimmerwald Conference.[59] The Ufa respresentative, V. I. Khaustov, felt himself in sympathy with the self-defence nostrums of the *Nasha zaria* group.[60] On the other hand, the remaining three members, N. S. Chkheidze, M. I. Skobelev and I. N. Tuliakov, came much closer to Martov's particular internationalist outlook. In their view, the war was imperialist in origin and the proletariat could not tie its interests to the defeat or victory of either coalition of belligerents. Russian socialists must reject the patriotic union. They advocated an immediate campaign for a non-annexationist, democratic peace and subscribed to the resolutions of the Zimmerwald Conference. They supported the reconstitution of the old International. Moreover, the emergence of the Progressive Bloc and the renewal of strife between the State Duma and Goremykin's cabinet in the summer of 1915 induced these three parliamentary representatives, like Martov, to envisage the replacement of the 3 June regime by a genuinely democratic republic as a potent stimulus to the European peace movement.[61] However, at least Skobelev of the three harboured revolutionary defensist notions. In July 1915 he informed Moscow party colleagues that socialists could not participate in self-defence because of the untrustworthy nature of the government. In the event that the system was democratised, socialists could then afford support to a defensive war effort.[62] On either account, the three deputies remained firmly committed to the achievement of their party's political goals and the continuation of the internal battle against the monarchy. Chkheidze, the parliamentary group's leader, desperate to prevent further haemorrhages of support from his fraction, refused to break openly in public with his more defensist-inclined colleagues, leaving an unfavourable impression of irresolution.[63]

The left wing of Menshevism during the war in the capital was represented by the Central Initiative Group, which evolved as early as August 1914 a radical internationalist stance against the war. Subscribing to the thesis that the war was the product of advanced capitalist competition, the left internationalists rejected as unacceptable both a German victory, which would signal the defeat of European democracy, and an Entente triumph which could serve as the cause of future wars by inflicting a punitive peace treaty upon the vanquished. They spurned both Lenin's defeatism and Potresov's concept of self-defence. They also followed Martov in linking the struggle for peace (their slogan was 'peace at all costs') to the internal campaign to liberate the country from the Tsarist yoke. And like Martov they opposed the creation of a new or Third International. In sharp contrast to most Mensheviks, however, they adamantly refused to accept the 'reactionary' and 'anti-popular' bourgeoisie as the ally of the working class.[64]

A distinctive and eclectic position on the war was put forward by the Mezhraionka. This seems to have been the work of I. Iurenev (K. K. Kortovskii), who was influenced by both Lenin and Trotskii. The war, he wrote in an unpublished manuscript, was the consequence of capitalism at the highest stage of development; the internationalisation of economic life sought to break the barriers of the national state. Drawing upon Lenin's distinction between nationalist wars of the nineteenth century and the imperialist world war, Iurenev and his supporters rejected all defensist justifications for the civil peace and took over Lenin's slogan of the conversion of the imperialist war into a civil war. On the other hand, like the Petrograd Bolsheviks, the members of the Mezhraionka were very wary of Lenin's concept of defeat. They also shared the left internationalists' hostility to the reactionary, anti-democratic and predatory bourgeoisie and denounced the concept of a bourgeois–proletarian alliance against the monarchy.[65]

It has proved extremely difficult to gather primary material on the various strands of opinion among Petrograd SRs. An indeterminate number were defensists. Towards the close of 1915, for example, there appeared a single issue of a legal periodical, *Narodnaia mysl'*, whose editorial displayed an acceptance of the notions of Avksent'ev and Bunakov outlined earlier in this chapter. It may be, as Dr Melancon has argued, that SR proletarian activists were internationalists almost from the start of the war.[66] On the other hand Kerenskii's position seems to have won much popularity among party intellectuals. Thus, at a conference in his flat on 16 and 17 July 1915, representatives of local Socialist Revolutionary groups, Popular Socialists and Trudoviks adhered to his double-edged policy. They adopted a resolution which both exhorted workers to participate in defence against external aggression and demanded an immediate peace without annexations. Moreover, like the Menshevik defensists, those present looked favourably upon a prompt seizure of power which would lead to the convocation of a Constitutent Assembly as the vehicle to secure both peace and victory over the enemy.[67]

In conclusion, it is impossible to say with any measure of certainty which of the multifarious strands of opinion on the war found widest acceptance among revolutionary party members, whether they were intellectuals or proletarians. On the basis of the evidence outlined in this section, it can be stated with some conviction that the extremes, Lenin's defeatism and Plekhanov's defensism *à outrance*, found little sympathy and much hostility in the capital's socialist circles. As police reports continually emphasised, internationalist positions secured broadest acceptance.[68] But it is not possible to pinpoint which of the particular internationalist outlooks commanded the greatest backing. On the other hand, from the authorities' point of view, there was one extremely disquieting common feature amongst all the different theoretical reactions to the war, namely the refusal to consider abandoning the revolutionary struggle against the regime. The outbreak of war may have brought the government a respite in its relentless battle with its opponents in Petrograd, but the lull was deceptive and extremely short-lived. The accumulative and deleterious economic and social impact of the war upon the capital's labouring masses completed their alienation from the monarchy and provided a potentially more fertile soil than ever before for the revolutionary parties to secure a permanent mass following. Their failure to capitalise on this opportunity is the cardinal theme of the rest of this and the succeeding chapter.

III

If, in the far more propitious circumstances of peacetime and despite dwelling close to the Russian border in Austrian-controlled Poland, Lenin had found it extremely difficult to exercise effective dominance over his adherents in St Petersburg, the disruption caused by the war rendered such a task quite impracticable. After July 1914 all communications between Russia and the West had to be conducted across the far northern Swedish–Finnish frontier. After his release from a fortnight's incarceration in an Austrian goal in August 1914, Lenin and Krupskaia took up abode in the Swiss city of Berne, in which his closest collaborator Zinoviev also lived. Although Samoilov returned to Russia some time in September, it was not until Shliapnikov reached Stockholm in the middle of October 1914 that the first tentative link was established between the Bolshevik leader and the Petrograd organisations. Shliapnikov had been chosen because he possessed a legally valid French passport as a result of his pre-war residence in that country.[69] His arrival and sojourn in the Swedish capital until the spring of 1915 brought Lenin little comfort and at best a minimal increase in his ability to fashion events in the capital. From fragmentary evidence, it can be inferred that Lenin was far from satisfied with his followers' attitude to the war. Publicly and privately he kept silent about the Duma declaration and, in as yet unpublished correspondence, criticised the Bolsheviks' reply to Vandervelde.[70] A fundamental problem in establishing illegal means of transport of agents and literature into Russia was a chronic shortage of funds to pay the costs both of publication and of the requisite services of smugglers and guides across the remote and inhospitable far northern terrain. Whatever his sources of income, Lenin was in no position to subvent Shliapnikov's smuggling operations, let alone dispatch funds to Petrograd. After the arrest of the five Bolshevik Duma deputies in November 1914, ties to Petrograd became even more fragile. In his memoirs Shliapnikov admits that he 'sent back news only occasionally' and that 'there were no permanent properly established links with Russia'. After he abandoned Stockholm in spring 1915, transport to Petrograd came to a complete halt. Nor did the Petrograd Bolsheviks take any initiative themselves to re-establish connections with Lenin after the autumn of 1914.[71] In these conditions Lenin's sole instrument for influencing the conduct of his followers was the revived central organ, *Sotsial-demokrat*, a two-page monthly newspaper devoted for the most part to theoretical articles written by Lenin and Zinoviev. It is not possible to establish with any accuracy the number of copies published per issue or reaching Russia. It is known that the earliest editions were printed in Geneva in runs of 2,000 copies, and that a small quantity of these was dispatched and received in Petrograd. After Shliapnikov abandoned Stockholm, even this trickle dried up completely.[72] As the analysis earlier in this chapter disclosed, reception of *Sotsial-demokrat* was no guarantee that all its progenitor's ideas would meet with broad acceptance by his supporters. Thus Lenin, increasingly isolated in neutral Switzerland, starved of news of developments inside Russia (as his frequent complaints in his letters testify), chronically short of cash and prevented on this account from moving to Stockholm, could exert no appreciable control over the party or developments in Petrograd. Throughout the war the making of policy and its execution in the capital lay almost exclusively in the hands of the Bolshevik sub-élite.

Moreover, during the first year of hostilities, even within Bolshevik ranks in Petrograd there existed no continuously functioning central party institutions to provide overall direction and leadership. Following a statement in Badaev's earliest memoirs, Soviet historians aver that at the outset of the war the five Bolshevik deputies reconstituted along with Kamenev the Russian Bureau of the Central Committee.[73] The author, however, could discover no corroboration of this assertion in the relevant Okhrana files. Even if such a body was established, the almost total atrophy of the local underground in the autumn would suggest that it displayed little activity in the capital. A similar discrepancy concerns the Petersburg Committee, defunct since March 1914. Both M. G. Fleer and I. P. Leiberov assert that the Duma deputies took steps to resurrect this body at the start of August 1914. However, two Okhrana reports, dated 5 and 24 August, categorically state that the PK had not yet been reformed.[74] On the other hand, some sort of shadowy PK had been set up by early November. This group failed to make firm connections to scattered party members in the districts before it was liquidated on 8 January 1915.[75] Although a PK was set up again within a week, it survived a mere fortnight. Revived at the close of March, this time it lasted a month. On neither occasion was it capable of refashioning district institutions in the brief time available to it.[76] In fact it was only in June and July, some sixteen months after its last solid reincarnation, that the all-city organ was placed on a more solid footing. Even then it succeeded in forging links to activists only in the First Town, Petrograd Side and Vyborg collectives.[77]

In the absence of effective leadership from abroad or from the PK, revolutionary strategy and tactics were at the discretion of rank and file socialist militants throughout the first year of the war. Their position was unenviable. The destruction of almost all legal labour organisations inflicted a severe blow. Bolshevik revolutinaries, prevented from re-establishing a legal daily newspaper or trade unions and deprived of their representation in parliament after November 1914, were left solely with the underground as their potential conduit to the capital's workers. The party's intellectuals, formerly grouped around *Pravda* and subsequently in 1915 the legal insurance journal *Voprosy strakhovaniia*, were very cautious about non-legal publishing ventures, where their skills would have been at a premium. Those factory operatives who had been granted deferments from military service were deterred from participation in illegal activity out of a fear of being dispatched to the trenches as a penalty.[78] The continual arrests and call-ups removed many experienced activists. It is possible, furthermore, that, at least in the first months of the war, the local Bolsheviks' failure to adopt an overt patriotic stance acted as a stumbling-block. The Okhrana naturally favoured this comforting perspective, reporting on 11 December 1914 that 'the Leninist position on the war has lost them the sympathy of broad strata of the working class'.[79] There exist some impressionistic data which would suggest that the secret police's observations were not quite groundless. Isolated attempts in August 1914 to distribute anti-war leaflets met with a hostile reception. At the advanced Petrograd Metals plant, one memoirist recalled, the workers exhibited indifference in the first year of the war to the Bolsheviks' anti-war case. At other cardinal defence enterprises such as Erikson and Putilov operatives voluntarily surrendered as much as a fifth of their weekly wage in order to provide support to the families whose breadwinners had been summoned to military duty.[80] Work stoppages remained extremely rare occurrences until the summer of 1915 (see Chapter 14). Bolshevik leaders themselves privately, if indirectly, admitted the existence of this impediment. In the spring of 1915, for example, they acknowledged their 'inability to attract the masses to the socialist camp by demonstrations against the war'.[81]

In the face of these formidable obstacles militants found it impossible to reconstruct continuously functioning party district organisations on a broad scale in the first year of the war. The solitary area to witness almost uninterrupted activity was the First Town, which covered the central city wards and the Moscow industrial quarter.

Due to the efforts in particular of the turner T. K. Kondrat'ev and A. I. Mashirov (who was involved with workers' evening classes at the Ligovskii Dom), some ten small workers' groups existed by October 1914, with almost 120 members. These embraced artisans (bakers, joiners, printers and tailors), metalworkers, railwaymen and tram drivers. A district executive committee was set up. In the summer of 1914 these activists published an anti-war leaflet (based upon the Stuttgart resolution) and a single issue of a newspaper *Rabochii golos*. Mass detentions in the spring of 1915, however, dealt a severe blow.[82] No other party district could match this qualified success. In supposedly 'red' Vyborg, to quote one worker's reminiscences, 'in the factories . . . in the first year of the war the mood was not particularly revolutionary'. Activists clustered about the newly established branch of the workers' Lutugin university. The few groups in existence by the middle of 1915 limited their efforts to the collection of monies in aid of political exiles. (The same was the case in the Narva suburb.) Although cells were located in engineering establishments such as Phoenix, New Lessner and Aivaz, other major enterprises were completely devoid of formal party collectives, as at Rozenkrants or Petrograd Metals.[83] On the Petrograd Side party work did not revive until June 1915 when a district committee was resurrected.[84] No evidence exists that committees were revived or significant groups functioned in the other working-class quarters of the city. Amongst students, tiny coteries of Bolshevik sympathisers emerged toward the close of 1914 in several institutions, including the polytechnic and the university. A United Social Democratic Committee of the Higher Educational Institutions was formed, but was soon liquidated by the security forces. The revolutionaries, also, encountered a widespread mood of patriotism among the students.[85] Contrary to Leiberov's claim that the party organisation had been reborn by the spring of 1915, there had sprung up only occasional miniscule factory and artisanal nuclei, usually resting on personal acquaintanceships. At most the party's membership did not exceed 500.[86] In the almost complete absence of all city or even district networks, consistent planned activity or the formulation of an agreed strategy proved a chimera. Agitational work could take place only on the most restricted scale. In all the constraining circumstances the outreach of the twenty-five or so anti-war leaflets published to the summer of 1915 and the unknown copies of *Sotsial-demokrat* reaching the city was likely to have been inconsiderable. The analysis earlier in this chapter of Bolshevik leaflets also refutes the Soviet argument that local Bolsheviks launched a stiff campaign against the 'social chauvinists'.[87]

The atomised nature of the underground, the crucial absence of a legal newspaper and trade unions, the apprehensions of worker-reservists and the slow fading of the workers' neutral (perhaps patriotic) attitude to the war ensured that the endeavours of the Bolshevik sub-élite to respond to political developments met with resounding failure.

The arrest of the five Bolshevik Duma deputies on 5 November 1914 and their trial on 10 February the following year surprisingly evoked no open expression of protest whatsoever among working people. As the chief of the Petrograd Okhrana reported complacently to his superiors, apropos the former event, 'workers reacted inertly, even coldly'. A meeting of delegates of the banned union of metalworkers refused to organise factory protest meetings. Although both the PK and the Students' United Social Democratic Committee rushed out proclamations exhorting their constituents to strike on 12 November, work and studies proceeded as normal, with the exception of a half-day walk-out at the Psycho-Neurological Institute.[88] A similar fiasco occurred on the day the court opened proceedings against the parliamentary representatives. Although militants came out in favour of a strike and street demonstrations on 10 February, their pleas met with hostility even among party adherents in the factories, including Vyborg. The police noted that worker-reservists were especially antagonistic to this plan. No stoppages occurred either in industrial or educational establishments.[89] On both these occasions the highly limited geographical scope of the illegal apparatus prohibited widespread agitation.

Whereas in the last years of peace the anniversaries of Bloody Sunday and the Lena massacre, as well as May Day, had served as the occasions for work stoppages on an ever-larger scale, the first four months of 1915 could not have stood out in sharper relief. Although the Petrograd Committee issued a leaflet appealing to wage earners to down tools on 9 January, the almost total lack of factory cells and committees precluded any meaningful preparations. Activists themselves were compelled to acknowledge their extreme weakness and to reject any consideration of provoking demonstrations. Around 2,000 operatives alone stayed away from their benches.[90] For the same reasons local leaders refused to contemplate any reaction to the Lena commemoration on 4 April, to the disgust of more extreme members.[91] Sweeping police raids and detentions towards the end of April put paid effectively to revolutionaries' plans for 1 May. 'The work of local Leninists,' the police reported at the time, 'is at present completely disorganised'. Although the remnants of the PK succeeded in publishing a leaflet on the very eve of the workers' 'holiday', the small number of copies remained undistributed for the most part. A mere 600 workers refused to report for work on that day.[92]

If the health of the Bolsheviks' underground was sickly, it at least showed some signs of feeble life. In stark contrast the Mensheviks' illegal network, destroyed in spring 1914, remained as extinct as the proverbial dodo. The intellectual 'Liquidators', long hostile to clandestine activity, saw no need to revive the underground in the more dangerous and unpropitious circumstances of the war. The feeling was widespread among Petrograd Mensheviks that revolutionary work should be postponed until the termination of fighting.[93] The Organisational Committee and the Central Initiative Group betrayed no sign of existence in this period. The endeavours of the Duma deputy Khaustov to convoke a secret all-Russian conference of Mensheviks came to naught.[94] The sole sphere in which Mensheviks displayed any initiative was publishing. As A. N. Potresov's literary group had espoused some form of defensist views, the authorities allowed them to commence publication at the start of 1915 both of a new 'thick' journal, *Nashe delo* (a replacement for the defunct *Nasha zaria*), and weekly newspaper *Severnyi golos*. However, neither lasted long, the former being suppressed after six issues and the latter after three months.[95] Both the Mensheviks' dearth of organisations and the 'Liquidationist' intellectuals' aversion to strikes as a form of labour protest resulted in their complete indifference to the possibility of utilising the political anniversaries. Moreover, when intermittent communications were restored between Martov and other *émigré* leaders, in Paris and Switzerland, and prominent Menshevik intellectuals in Petrograd by the close of the year 1914, the latter's evolution towards 'self-defencism' placed the severest strains on relationships. Matters were made worse by the refusal of the editors of *Nasha zaria* and *Nashe delo* to publish letters or articles by their foreign colleagues explaining their radically different stance on the war.[96] The Menshevik exiles, therefore, like Lenin, remained powerless to influence their followers or events inside Russia.

In one respect alone did Mensheviks reveal a boldness of vision. In the middle of July 1915 the All-Russian Union of Towns convoked a national economic conference to discuss the problems posed by inflation. The Kadet leader of the union sent out invitations to thirty-six trade unions and factory medical funds, ten of them in Petrograd. The Bolsheviks, faithful to their policies of rejecting collaboration with an 'imperialist' bourgeoisie, refused to attend. As a consequence five of the medical funds in the capital which they controlled (including Lessner, Putilov and Russian-American Rubber) ignored the event. The Mensheviks, on the other hand, succeeded in sending five *kassy* representatives.[97] At the conference the thirty-six working-class delegates (half of whom came from Moscow) constituted an independent Labour Group, which was advised by a team of socialist luminaries, including among others

Khaustov, Skobelev, Kerenskii, P. P. Maslov, Cherevanin and the Moscow Bolshevik Conciliators. Despite the various strands of opinion concerning the war, the Group not only passed on a majority vote an internationalist resolution on the war, which rejected the patriotic union, but it also adopted a political declaration which demanded a Constituent Assembly, universal suffrage and the complete democratisation of the country. The Group also voted against the official conference final statement because it was both defensist in tone and advanced the Kadets' moderate slogan of a 'government of confidence'. Thus the proceedings revealed that both the Menshevik and SR intellectuals and workers present at this assembly remained irrevocably committed to the struggle against the regime and to a radical political programme.[98]

The SRs' illegal apparatus also emitted only the faintest signals of life in the first year of the war. Neither a PK nor district committees were reconstructed. Part of the local leadership adopted the Menshevik line of postponing political action among the masses until peace was restored. Miniscule coteries survived. In autumn 1914 there existed an autonomous Narva group and in the central wards nuclei among various artisanal trades. One or two issues of *Rabochaia mysl'* were published in October. There was apparently a distinct SR Internationalist group, 'The Organising Commission of the PSR'.[99] The complete lack of formal party organisations and the constant liquidation of their illegal press constrained local activists from any consideration of launching campaigns in connection with 9 January, 4 April and 1 May 1915.[100] In these debilitating circumstances and in the absence of any ties to the nominal leadership in emigration, A. F. Kerenskii endeavoured to fill the void. In the first place, at a meeting convoked by him late in August 1914, it was resolved to merge the monthlies *Russkoe bogatstvo* (the Popular Socialist organ) and *Zavety*. The police promptly shut them down. He then fell back on his idiosyncratic 'non-party' course by establishing a so-called 'Information Bureau' inside the Imperial Free Economic Society.[101] The military defeats in the spring and early summer and the first stirrings of a revival of political discontent among Kadets and Progressists impelled Kerenskii to renew his typically over-ambitious efforts not only to revive the SR organisation on a national scale but to reunite the three strands of Narodnik thought. After he had toured the Volga and southern Russian provinces and V. V. Vodovozov the north, he convoked the July conference referred to earlier in this chapter. The list of those present would suggest that the gathering was heavily weighted towards Popular Socialist intellectuals, Trudoviks and partisans of Kerenskii rather than a broad representation of local SR rank and file working-class activists. This factor helps to explain the meeting's adoption of a resolution corresponding to Kerenskii's position on the war. But this document, like the resolution proposed by the Labour Group at the contemporaneous conference in Moscow, serves to emphasise how irreconcilably hostile even moderate Narodniks now were to the monarchy and how prepared they were to envisage revolution in wartime. The delegates elected a central bureau of populist organisations.[102] However, there is not the slightest evidence that by July 1915 Kerenskii had succeeded in reviving solid illegal networks in the capital itself.

There is available only the most fragmentary data about the anarchists in Petrograd. Although a minority of anarchists abroad led by the veteran P. Kropotkin came out in favour of the war against Germany, most Russian anarchists condemned the war. They followed the lead of the Geneva journal *Nabat* which predictably blamed the war's cause upon the existence of the state, which rested on militarism. Anarchists, therefore, remained committed to the destruction of all states through armed uprisings. Early in 1915 there emerged in the capital a group of anarcho-communists which published 500 copies of a leaflet entitled 'Anarchy no. 1', calling for a resort to terror and expropriations and a general strike on 9 January. There was also a nucleus in the Putilov plant. Links with the West seem to have been severed.[103]

In the first six months after the outbreak of hostilities the most 'successful' of the revolutionary factions was the Mezhraionka. In Vasil'evskii Island an inter-party strike committee survived after the July 1914 disturbances. Some time in the autumn it set up an illegal Social Democratic district committee which adhered to the Mezhraionka platform. Cells functioned in eleven enterprises, including the Pipes works and Siemens-Schukkert. In October in the Town district a group emerged, as did circles in several plants on Petersburg Side, among which were Petrograd Engineering and Langenzippen. In Narva, where the Mezhraionka had put down no roots before the war, Bolsheviks and Party Mensheviks created a committee which won some 130 adherents, mostly in Putilov workshops. In November this autonomous organisation voted to join the Mezhraionka. The latter also possessed a press which printed five leaflets and one edition of the illegal newspaper *Vpered*.[104] As in the past, however, the Mezhraionka signally failed to penetrate the Neva or Vyborg quarters. In view of the crucial importance the Mezhraionka ascribed to the army as the key to a successful revolution, it set up a military propaganda group which managed to issue a leaflet to the soldiers. But it possessed no cells in individual Petrograd military units.[105] By the close of the year the Mezhraionka had attracted over 300 followers.[106] Judging from the membership of the Mezhraionka committee itself, the leadership derived from three groups at this time – students, skilled metal workers and, in particular, printers. The organisation's expansion soon attracted retribution from the security forces. Early in February 1915, widespread arrests almost completely wiped it out, paralysing its activity for months thereafter. By the summer its adherents did not even reach a hundred.[107] The Mezhraionka's initiative at the start of the year in dispatching two of its number abroad in order to re-establish links, including the rich intellectual sympathiser A. L. Popov, who did the rounds of all the various factional *émigré* leading lights, likewise came to naught.[108]

Chapter 13

THE REVOLUTIONARY PARTIES AND THE LABOUR MOVEMENT: II. AUGUST 1915–22 FEBRUARY 1917

I

The dramatic events of the summer of 1915 greatly raised the expectations of the regime's socialist opponents in Petrograd and seemed to offer their best opportunity since July 1914 to utilise emergent mass working-class discontent. The artificial domestic calm induced by the outbreak of the war was shattered. The military defeat suffered in Galicia in the spring, the subsequent German invasion of Poland, the spy mania triggered by the Miasoedov affair and the nationalist pogrom in Moscow coincided with the first sharp upswing in inflation, the erratic availability of consumer products and the consequent re-emergence of labour unrest. The Tsar's replacement of his most reactionary ministers in June 1915 and the reconvocation of the State Duma the following month were interpreted by militants as a weakening of the government. The Okhrana noted in alarm in the middle of August that the parliamentary speeches of the Menshevik and Trudovik deputies (reported in the liberal press), attacking the 'irresponsible government' and demanding the complete democratisation of Russia's political and social structure, evoked a warm response among workers.[1] As in the previous two years, revolutionary hotheads leapt to the unrealistic conclusion that, in the words of a police report, 'the present marks the start of the second Russian revolution'. For the first time since the July general strike of the previous year, the Bolshevik underground placed at the top of its agenda the launching of a general political strike against both the war and the monarchy. Aware of the lack of viable conspiratorial structures to provide effective leadership for the desired mass stoppages and street demonstrations, the Leninists once more put forward the concept of a Soviet of Workers' Deputies to co-ordinate actions. Some militants even began to dream of an armed uprising.[2] The Bolsheviks, however, were not alone in basing overly optimistic plans upon a mistaken estimation of the

375

government's vulnerability. A. F. Kerenskii, the local SRs as well as the Trudovik and Menshevik parliamentary fractions all shared such illusions and similar prescriptions. The secret service noted that Kerenskii and Chkheidze had convoked meetings with groups of wage earners at which they recommended the establishment of factory collectives as nuclei of a future soviet in a struggle for a Constitutent Assembly.[3] The political protest strikes which erupted in Petrograd in the middle of August and early September 1915, together with the Central War-Industries Committee's decision to seek working-class representation in the war-industries committees, seemed to offer socialist parties a renewed chance to secure mass support and instruments of pressure against the government.

As on previous occasions in the past, the shooting of strikers by police elsewhere in Russia, at the textile centre of Ivanovo-Voznesensk on 10 August 1915, served as the occasion for political protest in the capital. Between 17 and 20 August, 16,000 operatives downed tools in 23 factories. Compared with the reaction to the Lena massacre the dimensions of the response were exceedingly modest. A perusal of the list of factories affected reveals that the protest was limited to the more medium-sized engineering and defence establishments in Vyborg and Petrograd Side. The Okhrana could find no trace of agitation for the strike by any revolutionary group.[4]

The revolutionary activists were quicker in their reaction to the next outburst of unrest. In the course of the summer the secret police had become aware that Social Democratic militants had sought to escape surveillance by accepting posts as employees of the Putilov sickness fund. At the end of August 33 of these people were arrested. The situation in the mammoth plant was already tense as rates of pay had fallen behind price rises (in particular for the unskilled and semi-skilled), while the board had refused to follow the example of other companies in granting a special 'war supplement' to wages. To make matters worse at this moment the Tsar prorogued the State Duma, whose proceedings had aroused widespread expectations of political change. These three factors together ensured a stormy reception of the news of the detentions. On the evening of 1 September 6,000 assembled Putilov operatives voted in favour of a three-day stoppage. Their action secured the endorsement of some 79,000 fellow workers over the next four days.[5] On 2 September local Bolsheviks and other militants (SRs, Menshevik Internationalists and members of the Mezhraionka) created an all-city strike committee and resolved to issue an appeal calling for the organisation of a Soviet of Workers' Deputies. It is possible that at Putilov and some Vyborg factories elections of delegates were held.[6]

It would be erroneous, however, to accept Lenin's contemporary view, repeated by Soviet writers, that the events of early September amounted to a 'revolutionary crisis' or to describe the stoppages as a 'general city strike'.[7] Whilst the total on strike stood comparison with many of the political walk-outs of the pre-war years, it represented only a fifth to a quarter of all factory workers. As in the previous month the movement embraced mainly privately owned, medium-sized defence plants in the northern industrial district.[8] Nor did the revolutionaries attempt to foment clashes with the police or lead mass demonstrations towards the city centre. In the light of the debilitated state of the conspiratorial structures described in the previous chapter, they were not in a position to do so. The fear of conscription still acted as a powerful disincentive to mass prolonged stoppages. Thus, when General A. P. Frolov, commander of the Petrograd Military District, acceded to employers' pleas and threatened on 4 September both to close all plants and summon all worker-reservists to the colours, the strikes ceased overnight. It was these factors which presumably induced the SRs and members of the Mezhraionka to urge the calling off of the stoppages.[9] Moreover, it is not clear whether or what particular political demands were put forward by the strikers at individual plants. The solitary political resolution recorded in police files is that passed at the Putilov meeting mentioned earlier. As well as reflecting economic discontent (a 15 per cent increase in wages was requested), it also bore traces of the contemporary political programme of the Menshevik and Trudovik fractions, namely a responsible ministry and a protest against the prorogation of the Duma.[10] The liberals' meek acceptance of the interruption to the Duma's debates, the Progressive Bloc's adherence to an extremely moderate programme of a 'government of confidence' and its abhorrence of mass, extra-parliamentary means of struggle, as well as the absence of unrest in the garrison, all testify to the fact that September 1915 was not a dress rehearsal for the February revolution. Furthermore Richard Abraham's contention that Kerenskii 'came close to precipitating a revolution of the masses around "bourgeois" leadership' must be discounted.[11] Although Kerenskii personally shared the belief, widespread among the revolutionaries, that the walk-outs signified the beginning of the long-anticipated revolution, the Trudovik and Menshevik deputies feared that the stoppages came at an inappropriate time. Thus the Trudovik fraction resolved on 4 September to call on workers to return to work, while Skobelev and Tuliakov visited Aivaz, Erikson and Putilov factories to this end.[12] Kerenskii's organisational efforts before the eruption of the September stoppages, moreover, comprised only a part of a broader activity by different socialist groupings and had not borne fruit in the formation of district SR or other revolutionary structures. The Okhrana, which had overestimated his influence in the summer, was more accurate in its report of 4 September when it declared that there was no proof that Kerenskii or the Menshevik deputies had engineered the strikes.[13]

The general strategy developed by the Bolshevik sub-élite in the summer and autumn of 1915 was worked out quite independently of Lenin, who was particularly isolated at this time. Although the secret police reported that Shliapnikov, on his return to the capital in late October 1915, brought a letter from the Bolshevik leader approving the PK's course of action, there is evidence to indicate that in fact differences existed between them.[14] In private correspondence with Shliapnikov before his departure from Sweden and in his article 'Several Theses' (published in no. 47 of the central organ), Lenin bluntly rejected his supporters' adoption of the call for a Workers' Soviet. Displaying his ambivalent attitude towards independent working-class organisations, he argued that the soviets were of value only in a revolution. He also dismissed the slogan of a Constituent Assembly, which Petrograd Bolsheviks advanced intermittently in their literature along with their socialist rivals.[15] Nor did Shliapnikov's presence in Petrograd apparently improve matters to a great extent. It is evident from his letters that Lenin had envisaged at most a short trip to the capital by his lieutenant in order to create groups of 'old, experienced, sensible Pravdist workers who have fully mastered the question of the war' (a hint of Lenin's dissatisfaction with his followers' ambivalent attitude to his defeatism) and restore conspiratorial contacts with abroad.[16] Reading between the lines of the tortured account given in Shliapnikov's memoirs, it is evident that relations between the members of the PK and Lenin's emissary were extremely strained. The PK sought to usurp Shliapnikov's functions as a member of the Central Committee (to which Lenin had co-opted him) by demanding that it alone control the means of communication with the provinces and abroad. Lenin's doubts about the total loyalty of his followers found expression in Shliapnikov's orders to re-establish the Russian Bureau of the Central Committee independently of the PK. It may be surmised that Petrograd Bolsheviks' less than whole-hearted enthusiasm for their leader's theories on the war lay behind both Lenin's proposal and the PK's rejection of it. The PK demanded that the Russian Bureau should be selected from among its own members and refused even to convoke a plenum which Shliapnikov could attend.[17] As a consequence it took Lenin's agent until January 1916 to set up the Russian Bureau. It lasted at most a month before it was broken up by arrests, and it achieved nothing.[18]

Although the failure of the September strikes did not persuade the Bolsheviks to rethink their general strategy, they did reconsider their tactics. Admitting in private that they lacked the institutional mechanisms for direct revolutionary agitation on a broad scale or sufficient intellectual forces for widespread socialist education via workers' circles, the sub-élite decided in opportunistic yet realistic fashion to make use of the growing popular discontent caused by inflation and food shortages. In the first half of October they began to set up illegal 'food commissions' in factories in the Moscow, Narva, Petrograd Side and Vyborg districts. It was also hoped that these would be able to provide leadership to economic strikes.[19] But the militants' new-found sense of caution and realism soon gave way once more to enthusiasm for direct revolutionary action. On 19 October, 2,000 employees at Phoenix Engineering abandoned work to demand the sacking of a foreman. Four hundred and thirty workers who had received deferments from military service were at once called to the colours. A meeting of representatives of the largest Vyborg plants in the presence of a delegate from the PK resolved to utilise the occasion to launch a general protest strike and mass demonstrations 'which might serve as the prelude to the second great Russian revolution'. Although factory gatherings were held in various Vyborg plants, it is evident that wiser counsels soon prevailed. And the Mensheviks and SRs both opposed such a venture as foolhardy. On 28 October, therefore, the local leadership formally abandoned its too ambitious plans.[20]

Despite the depletion of their forces by the arrest of a majority of the PK early in November, the Leninists soon returned to their revised tactics, now formally expressed in 'Instructions to Party Workers' drawn up by S. Ia. Bogdatian-Bogdat'ev, an old party activist who had returned to revolutionary work in that autumn. They sought to use economic agitation for higher wages and a shorter working day as the springboard to the desired general political strike. They converted existing secret food commissions into strike committees and created a 'General City Strike Committee' which they hoped to turn into a soviet. In this work local Bolsheviks and SR-internationalists again co-operated, another step on the road to their historic collaboration in the autumn of 1917. The October scenario was repeated exactly a month later when 5,000 employees at New Lessner downed tools on receipt of the news that eight sacked worker reservists had been summoned to military service. The PK again mistakenly regarded this event as a favourable pretext to launch a general stoppage. As the Lessner conflict lasted a single day, nothing happened.[21]

In the autumn of 1915, for the first time since the summer of 1912, Social Democratic organisations arose in the Baltic Fleet. As the naval mutinies of 1905 had revealed, the navy was potentially fertile ground for revolutionary activity. The mechanisation of naval warfare had meant that a large proportion of ratings were drawn from youthful, educated urban working-class elements. The arbitrary, stringent discipline imposed by a mainly aristocratic officer corps, the monotonous inactivity of winter months in ships frozen into the ice and the poor pay were all permanent sources of grievance.[22] In the ships moored off Kronstadt Bolshevik-inclined NCOs established collectives independently of orders from the PK, to which they secured links only in December 1915. It is significant that the authorities' reports all emphasise that these agitators eschewed the propagation of party slogans. Instead they opportunistically utilised the anti-German mood among ordinary sailors, who blamed Russia's defeats on treason by officers of German origin.[23] There were also SR cells. Moreover, these putative revolutionaries had no immediate plans of action. The indictment at their trial accused them of preparations 'for a general rising of the Baltic Fleet at the end of the war to coincide with demobilisation'.[24] Even the PK, when links were finally established with it, warned the sailors against any collective action on 9 January 1916.[25] The naval revolutionaries were very small in number (some 20–30 individuals), had few ties to sailors at Helsingfors or Reval and were wiped out by arrests at the close of the year.[26] The solitary disturbance in the fleet, on the battleship *Gangut* in October, had nothing to do with the illegal collectives. Like the celebrated *Potemkin* mutiny of 1905, it was occasioned by bad food which the sailors blamed upon officers of Baltic German origin.[27]

II

In the early autumn of 1915 the revolutionary parties were suddenly presented with an unexpected opportunity to recoup their political fortunes. The tiny coterie of liberal politicians led by A. I. Guchkov and A. I. Konovalov, which dominated the Central War-Industries Committee (TsVPK), managed to persuade the emergent liberal majority in the Council of Ministers to accede to their request to permit both working-class representation in the committees and genuinely free elections held in the absence of the police.[28] As the latter was quick to perceive, both the election campaign, which was scheduled to last a fortnight, and the new working-class representatives furnished the underground once more with the legal means to seek mass support. On the other hand, these new 'legal opportunities' not only reopened the sterile Liquidationist controversy but also, more significantly, in the words of General Globachev, chief of the Petrograd Okhrana, 'the issue of participation or non-participation in the committees raised in an acute form the socialists' attitude to the war'.[29] Because the TsVPK and its industrialist backers were committed to the war and were overt supporters of imperialist war aims, no united revolutionary front could be established. Instead the elections and the subsequent formation of the Labour Group of the TsVPK deepened factional differences and further embittered intra-socialist relations.

All those left-wingers who had taken a negative stance on the war were fiercely antagonistic to the war-industries committees. The Bolsheviks' PK, meeting in late August, resolved to participate in the election campaign for purposes of agitation, but at the general meeting of electors their delegates would refrain from casting their ballots. The strikes of the first week of September emboldened local militants to revise their strategy in a much more daring manner. Another session of the PK adopted Zalezhskii's proposal that the general convocation of electors should declare itself a Soviet of Workers' Deputies, which would launch both a general political strike and an armed uprising. These recommendations were given written form by Bogdatian-Bogdat'ev in a 'Nakaz of the Petrograd Proletariat'.[30] Although this document proclaimed workers' opposition to the war, the war-industries committees and the bourgeoisie, as well as advancing the slogan of civil war, neither it nor any other local Bolshevik literary production at this time mentioned Lenin's key concepts of defeatism, the Third International or social chauvinism. It is debatable whether all local Bolsheviks shared these adventurist notions. There is in existence a resolution of the Russian Bureau, supposedly dated September 1915, which, recommending a boycott of the war-industries committees, is silent on the prescriptions of the nakaz. As Shliapnikov, however, had not returned at this time to Petrograd, the dating of the document must be erroneous. It may refer to the second round of elections at the end of November.[31] In this matter, as others, the formulation of local Bolsheviks' strategy rested solely upon their own initiative, although it won the retrospective approval of Lenin.[32] The Mezhraionka, too, exhorted workers to shun the war-industries committees as bourgeois institutions.[33]

The issue of workers' membership of the war-industries committees found the Mensheviks in greater disarray than the Bolsheviks. The outright defensists both abroad and in the capital warmly welcomed the TsVPK's invitation as allowing workers the chance to organise legally in defence of both the country and their own interests. They also argued that participation would facilitate the process of revolutionising the bourgeoisie.[34] The Menshevik littérateurs and theorists of self-defence and the praktiki trade unionists (who were to constitute the future Labour Group of the TsVPK) argued that workers could not hold aloof from the mobilising process of the bourgeoisie at such at critical juncture in the war's fortunes. They had to join the war-industries committees in order to protect wage earners against attacks by the employers and the government. As committed supporters of legal methods of struggle, these 'Liquidationists' thought it was unwise to ignore the new opportunity for open organisation. Indeed they sought to capitalise on this unexpected turn of events by proposing that an All-Russian Congress of Labour should be convoked to take the final decision on participation.[35] Among the Menshevik Duma deputies, Khaustov and Tuliakov adopted a similar position, whilst Chkheidże favoured joining as a means of agitating for peace and achieving collaboration between the bourgeoisie and the proletariat. His point of view was also shared by Menshevik leaders exiled in Siberia, the so-called Siberian Zimmerwaldists, and the Petrograd Initiative Group. On the other hand, the Menshevik diaspora in the West, represented by the Foreign Secretariat of the Organisational Committee, vehemently rejected the notion of workers' inclusion in the war-industries committees.[36] Their negative opinion, however, evoked little sympathy among local Mensheviks.

As for the SRs, the internationalists among them opposed participation, whilst Right SRs supported them. Like the Bolsheviks and Mezhraionka, SR-internationalists campaigned for the election of delegates hostile to the war-industries committees.[37]

The elections covered all Petrograd plants with defence contracts and labour forces in excess of 500 employees. In total 219,036 workers, who were older than 25 years of age, in 101 factories were entitled to vote.[38] The majority of establishments involved were in the metalworking, machine construction and electrical industries, although some textile mills, leather-working manufactories and printers fell within the scope of the elections. It is far from clear how widespread was electoral campaigning by the revolutionary factions in the capital in the two weeks before voting for electors took place on 21 September 1915. Two leading Bolshevik participants have emphasised in their memoirs the formidable constraints preventing the development of effective agitation on a large scale. The paucity of Bolshevik and other revolutionary parties' activists, the absence of cells in many leading plants and the atrophied state of district committees described in the previous chapter all combined to ensure that in many factories no meetings were held and that no Bolshevik candidate came forward for election. The Bolsheviks, and one would surmise the other revolutionary groups, concentrated their efforts on certain crucial engineering plants.[39] A close reading of all the available sources could locate only 21 enterprises where electoral meetings were held at which the rival factions set forth their points of view on the war and the war-industries committees. It was symptomatic of some workers' desire for permanent factory organisations that these gatherings demanded that the temporary electoral commissions established by them should become enduring institutions.[40]

Legal propaganda via newspapers was unavailable to any sect.[41] The Petrograd Initiative Group, the OK and the Menshevik Duma fraction published no documents setting out their case. On the other hand, very limited numbers of copies of both the Bolsheviks' and Mensheviks' *nakazy* (mandates) were published in secret and distributed in the factories.[42] It has been impossible to ascertain the percentage of eligible voters who actually cast their ballots on 21 September. Conscious boycottism was rare, occurring at five plants.[43] It would be extremely injudicious to draw all-embracing conclusions from the results of the voting either about employees' attitudes to the war or the war-industries' committees or about the relative strengths of the respective revolutionary factions among workers. According to the police, there were some 60 to 70 Bolshevik electors, about 80 Menshevik and SR electors and the rest (some 60–80) classed themselves as non-party. Even more confusing was the fact that five of the sixteen factories which had voted for the Bolshevik *nakaz* proceeded to select Mensheviks as their delegates. The reverse also took place. The differences among the socialists clearly confused workers. As always the parties chose as their candidates known labour activists (electors to the Fourth State Duma, trade unionists, *kassy* representatives) whom workers selected irrespective of their party label or views. The most honest comment on the results was made by Shliapnikov in an unpublished letter to Lenin on 30 November: 'the attitude of the workers is not easy to make out'.[44]

The obscurity of the election results was not properly clarified by the assembly of delegates on 27 September. One hundred and ninety electors turned up. After a prolonged debate lasting over twelve hours, the final vote came down in favour of the Bolshevik stance by 95 to 81. The reasons for the Bolsheviks' unexpected victory and its exact meaning have been a subject of bitter controversy ever since the event. On the one hand, the Mensheviks present made a series of tactical errors. Led by K. Gvozdev, who was elected chairman, they were so confident of success that they gave the Bolsheviks the posts of assistant chairman and secretary. They did not present their own resolution until almost the end of the meeting. They allowed the vote to be taken on the principled issue of participation before any decision was taken on the question of elections. The latter was an unfortunate error of judgement as many Menshevik electors favoured temporary elections in the interim before an All-Russian Labour Congress settled the issue once and for all. The Bolsheviks, on the contrary, were better prepared. They smuggled in two of their leaders, Bogdatian-Bogdat'ev and Zalezhskii, using the mandates of two Putilov delegates without their permission; they distributed their *nakaz* in advance to electors; they went over at once to the attack in their speeches. It is evident that their militant stand made a distinct impression on the SRs and part of the non–party delegates who came over to their side. It is possible that many of the SRs present were in fact opponents of participation.[45] The highly charged atmosphere deriving from the September stoppages and the prorogation of the State Duma, as well as workers' innate distrust of employers' organisations, also help explain the outcome. Yet it would be rash to accept at face value the claim of Soviet historians that, in the words of Mints, 'the Bolsheviks' victory testified to their real influence among the workers'.[46] In the light of the fact that the voting excluded whole categories of wage earners (those under 25, workers in plants employing less than 500 operatives, artisans, commercial–industrial employees), that rates of turn–out varied drastically and that a significantly higher percentage of voters had supported Menshevik and SR candidates than Bolshevik ones, the latter's success tells one little about the extent of their support or workers' views on the war.[47] The Bolshevik leaders themselves were evidently unsure about the reliability of their new–found adherents as they refrained from putting to the meeting after the vote their plans for the proclamation of a soviet, a general strike and an armed uprising.[48]

The discovery by Gvozdev of the chicanery resorted to by the Bolsheviks at the assembly on 27 September was utilised by him to petition the TsVPK to arrange a second electoral meeting. He also secured the backing of most Putilov electors, who felt particularly aggrieved as one of their impersonated delegates had been arrested.[49] At the second assembly on 29 November, 176 electors attended.[50] In the interval between the two gatherings the Bolshevik position had been strengthened by a proclamation issued by local SRs, which called upon workers to refrain from joining the war–industries committees before the convocation of an All–Russian Labour Congress to resolve the matter.[51] Having concerted their tactics in advance, the Bolshevik and SR electors read out statements condemning the assembly as 'a falsification of the will of the Petrograd proletariat' by a 'group of usurpers and traitors', following this with their prompt departure from the hall. The 109 left behind proceeded to elect ten representatives to the TsVPK (all were Mensheviks) and six to the Petrograd War–Industries Committee (three Mensheviks and three SRs).[52] If the Bolsheviks' triumph on 27 September had quickly turned to dust in their hands, the Mensheviks' victory two months later was to prove in the short run to be a pyrrhic one. Their ability to reverse their earlier defeat clearly owed not a little to the Bolshevik and SR walk-out (itself an indication of these factions' doubts concerning their chance of success at a second ballot) as well as to the Bolsheviks' successive failure in the preceding weeks to launch a general political stoppage, which rendered more attractive the Mensheviks' more moderate, less hazardous course of action. The argument that the Menshviks' Labour Group drew its strength from 'labour aristocrats' and new workers from petty-bourgeois strata is unverifiable.[53] Although it is true that seven of the eleven Mensheviks chosen at the assembly represented very large 'mixed' plants (the Baltic Shipyards, the Pipes works, Putilov and Obukhov), employing proportionately more semi-skilled and un-skilled than skilled, six worked at more specialised engineering works (Aivaz, Erikson, Lessner and Promet). The pattern of voting by particular categories of operatives is impossible to ascertain.

III

Buoyed up by their partial success in the elections to the war-industries committees in the capital, local Bolsheviks resolved to repeat their strategy at the close of 1913 by utilising the anniversary of Bloody Sunday on 9 January 1916 to ignite a general political strike. Some militants even envisaged the event as a pretext for armed insurrection. They hoped that planned demonstrations in the city centre would provoke the police to open fire, thereby leading to the construction of barricades. Their exaggerated expectations were nourished by rumours that the soldiers of the garrison would revolt and come over to the workers' side.[54] SRs lent their backing to their rivals' scheme. The extent of agitation by the local underground is difficult to gauge. The food commissions and strike committees established in the autumn served as a conduit to the masses. The Petrograd Metals strike committee decided to constitute itself as an armed detachment. At some plants, such as Old Lessner, illegally acquired weapons were concealed. The PK managed to publish and distribute fairly widely a leaflet exhorting workers to leave their benches on the appointed day. This document, however, curiously made no mention of the war. The SRs, too, printed a proclamation calling for the start of revolutionary action on 9 January.[55] On the other hand, the Mensheviks' OK, the Central Initiative Group, the Menshevik Duma fraction and the new Labour Group of the TsVPK all opposed the Bolsheviks' and SRs' call for a stoppage. A series of sweeps by the Okhrana in the last fortnight of December 1915 carried off the entire PK, leading SRs and the Bolsheviks' technical group and college of organisers.[56] The number of strikers on 9 January 1916 (60,000 in 68 factories) was almost the same as the total in the September stoppages of the previous year, but only half the figure reached in January two years before. The argument, however, of the Soviet historian Fleer that the strikes of 9 January 1916 ᵣepresented 'a turning point in the history of the labour movement' cannot be substantiated.[57] In the first place, as in August and September of the previous year, the walk-outs afflicted for the most part small and medium-sized defence plants, together with a minority of textile mills and printworks, with Vyborg playing a predominant role. Secondly, there were only a few demonstrations, confined to seven plants, whereas the city centre remained peaceful. Thirdly, whilst a few hundred soldiers joined in a workers' demonstration in Vyborg the following evening, this remained an isolated, premature incident. It did not, as Fleer asserts, 'mark the start of the unity of the workers and soldiers of Petrograd'.[58]

Less than a month after the January stoppages the gigantic Putilov works seemed about to replay the role of spark to the labour movement as it had done in the summer of 1914. Events there unfolded at a favourable conjuncture for the revolutionary parties. The imminent reopening of the State Duma had heightened political tension in the capital with widespread expectation of a renewed political clash between a discredited regime and the Progressive Bloc. A pointed reminder of the monarchy's arbitrariness was the coincidental anniversary of the trial of the five Bolshevik parliamentary representatives. The government's draft legislation on the militarisation of defence plants (discussed in Chapter 15) was a particular cause of unease among wage earners who understandably interpreted the measure as a form of reinserfment. All the revolutionary tendencies organised factory meetings in protest at the bill.[59] Putilov itself furnished fertile soil for unrest. Rates of pay were lower than at other plants of comparable size and had only been raised twice since the start of hostilities.[60]

The first Putilov stoppage arose out of economic considerations and caught local revolutionaries unawares. It began on 4 February in the electrical workshop when 230 struck for a 70 per cent pay rise. As the chief of the Petrograd Okhrana noted in anger, the over-hasty and disproportionate response of the head of the factory, General Meller, turned a minor economic dispute into 'an ideological struggle'. On the morning of 5 February, Meller persuaded the commander of the Petrograd Military District, General Prince Tumanov, to summon the reservists among the strikers to the colours. After lunch, various departments came to a halt as workers left their benches in a show of sympathy and solidarity with their threatened workmates. At a mass gathering in the evening, representatives of all revolutionary groups (excluding the Bolsheviks) had little difficulty in persuading workers to support an all-factory strike.[61] The Bolsheviks in the plant, who numbered a mere eighty, entertained a more grandiose vision. Meeting the following morning, they dispatched emissaries to other districts to gauge the extent of support for an all-city stoppage. It seems that they met with scant sympathy, as Putilov worked on 9 January. Their prospects of success were shattered both by the secret police, which carried out a massive purge of the underground to pre-empt the implementation of the PK's decision to launch the general strike on 10 Feburary, and the administration, which cowed the labour force by closing the factory. Within four days work resumed.[62]

Scarcely had the plant recommenced operations than trouble erupted once more. Spurred on by the partial concession regarding wages granted to the employees of the electrical workshop, various other departments came out on strike in the days after 17 February to press for pay increases. These disputes owed nothing to the revolutionaries whose cells had not recovered from the recent liquidation. The initially successful mediatory efforts of the local factory inspector were again undercut by the unwise reaction of the factory administration. At its request, on 23 February General Prince Tumanov ordered the plant shut and the call-up of worker reservists.[63] Meeting two days later, the Bolsheviks' PK resolved to launch a general city-wide strike in four days' time. Their leaflet and agitation sensibly focused on workers' resentment at the treatment of the reservists and their fears concerning the mobilisation of the factories. The district committees arranged for the election of plant strike committees which would include delegates from all socialist groups. The SRs' Petersburg Committee backed the Bolshevik stance.[64] The coincidental sequestration of the Putilov firm by the Special Council for Defence inadvertently imparted a considerable stimulus to the incipient wave of protests. Between 29 February and 4 March some 50,000 operatives ceased working. As in the previous September and on 9 January unrest lay disproportionately among private defence establishments in the northern manufacturing districts, above all Vyborg.

In his study of the February revolution of 1917 the late George Katkov made the astounding claim that the renegade socialist, Alexander Helphand-Parvus, and through him his paymasters the German Foreign Office, 'controlled and supported' the strike movement in Russia in 1916. He rested his case essentially on the January–February stoppages in the capital.[65] His evidence was in fact minimal. As he himself was compelled to admit, the Germans ceased to promote subversion in Russia from February 1916. The biographers of Parvus also showed that the latter failed to establish his own network inside the country and that it is not known what happened to the profits of his front exporting agency.[66] The Okhrana evidently had its suspicions and mounted an investigation. Its most secret report, dated 29 July 1916, concluded firmly that the Germans and Parvus were not acting as bankers to the revolution. The police correctly observed that the local socialists were in fact starved of funds, being unable to finance the dispatch of emissaries to their colleagues abroad or pay the costs of legal printing of materials.[67]

The period of frenetic efforts by local Bolshevik militants, which had begun in September 1915, to ignite a general political strike and armed uprising came to an abrupt end with the two Putilov stoppages. A lengthy stagnation in illegal Bolshevik activity set in, lasting until the autumn of 1916. The sweeping arrests of activists in February and at regular intervals thereafter pulverised the underground, depriving it of continuously functioning leadership either from the PK or from district committees. As so often in the past, the party survived in an atomised, cellular form. The PK was wiped out towards the close of April. Although reformed two weeks later, it was twice broken up over the succeeding three months.[68] The largest factory organisation in the city, numbering 150 members at New Lessner, was completely destroyed after a strike there in March. Thereafter the entire membership of the party in the Vyborg district oscillated between 100 and 200. In the spring the Latvian section numbered 114; the Estonian a miserly 15; Petersburg Side 60; Moscow 90. Important plants, such as Erikson and Petrograd Metals, were devoid of cells. Party activity at Putilov never recovered properly in 1916 with miniscule groups (totalling six to ten individuals) in the workshops.[69] The Okhrana also noted that for the first time the party found it difficult to attract new recruits. It ascribed the phenomenon to repeated mobilisations removing the keenest activists.[70] A good indication of the frailty of the Bolsheviks' conspiratorial nuclei was the fact that they made no attempt whatsoever to provoke stoppages and demonstrations on the anniversary of the Lena massacre and May Day (which fell on a Sunday), both of which passed without significant interruption to industrial production.[71] In the police archives there is almost no evidence of concrete activity by the Bolsheviks' organisations throughout the spring and summer, apart from the publication to coincide with May Day of the third issue of the illegal newspaper *Proletarskii golos*.[72] The revolutionary enthusiasm and chiliastic visions of Bolshevik militants, however, remained untempered by the harsh reality of their powerlessness. In the middle of May, a meeting of activists, who had sought refuge from the police as *kassy* employees, reconfirmed their previous strategy. Interpreting the labour movement 'as merging into an armed uprising', they gave their approval to acts of terrorism, expropriations and the distribution of arms. Their verbal extremism, however, was not matched by their deeds.[73]

Throughout the first nine months of 1916 the Bolsheviks in Petrograd conducted their own affairs. Lenin had the most minimal contact with the city after Shliapnikov left it in February to return to the West. Whatever little monies the Bolshevik leader possessed were spent upon publishing *Sotsial-demokrat*, a mere six issues of which appeared that year. He did not have funds to spare to repair the illegal transport routes for literature into Russia, which collapsed some time in the spring or to dispatch a replacement for Shliapnikov.[74] Moreover, the latter became sucked into the personal and ideological dispute between Lenin and the Piatakov/Bukharin circle over the fate of the journal *Kommunist*. This embittered relations between the Bolshevik leader and his lieutenant, who, partly as a result, sailed for the United States to raise money.[75] Lenin, too, seems to have been remarkably uninterested in affairs inside Russia. He devoted most of his time to his researches on imperialism, the state and national self-determination, in the libraries in Zurich, to which he had moved from Berne in February. And he and Krupskaia spent most of July and August completely cut off at a retreat in the mountains.[76]

The political events of the summer and autumn of 1915 shook Petrograd Mensheviks from their previous languid inactivity. The Duma deputies together with their Trudovik colleagues hoped to utilise the formation of the Progressive Bloc to remove the legislative obstruction to a more liberal trade-union law. They convoked public meetings and set up a committee to act as a pressure group.[77] They also participated with the Left Kadets in the latter's scheme to establish inhabitants' committees as a link to working people. Nothing came of any of these plans, owing to police intervention.[78]

The differences within Menshevism, deriving originally from the war, burst forth anew in a more bitter and damaging fashion in the spring and summer of 1916. The first cause was the request in March from Martov for a mandate for the forthcoming second conference of internationalist socialists at Kienthal in Switzerland. Whilst the internationalist-inclined Central Initiative Group favoured Martov's plea, the divisions within the Duma fraction over the war led it to adopt a negative stance.[79] The Menshevik internationalists felt themselves in a stronger position, having succeeded at the close of 1915 in launching a legal monthly journal, *Letopis'*.[80] The second cause was the conduct of the Labour Group of the TsVPK, which is discussed in the next section. From the spring onwards the Central Initiative Group became more and more dissatisfied with the Labour Group's cautious activities and alleged 'defencism'. In late June it demanded that the Labour Group adopt the resolutions of the Zimmerwald Conference or resign from the TsVPK. The Central Initiative Group's discontent drove it to set up the first Menshevik wartime cells in large factories and to distribute the Zimmerwald Manifesto. Aware of the dangers of weakening the party even further, the Menshevik Duma fraction endeavoured in vain to reconcile the anatagonists. For the same reason the otherwise inert OK procrastinated on the Central Initiative Group's proposal for the convocation of an all-Russian Menshevik conference.[81]

The available information on the Socialist Revolutionaries is unfortunately exiguous. The SR-internationalists had assumed organisational shape by the close of 1915 as the 'Petrograd Group of SRs' led by the student A. Sadikov. A city conference in December 1915 also elected a PK. A month later another gathering adopted the Zimmerwald resolutions. By the start of 1916 they had succeeded in establishing some thirty-five cells, particularly in the large state-owned 'mixed' defence plants, such as the Baltic Shipyards, Neva Shipyards, Obukhov, the Pipes works and Putilov. Their total membership may have been 600, i.e. at least on a par with the Bolsheviks. After comprehensive arrests in April and July, the local SRs were left in complete organisational disarray.[82] Nor could the SRs benefit from Kerenskii's dynamic personality, both because he had to absent himself involuntarily from politics from February to August due to an operation to remove a diseased kidney and because the SR-internationalists rejected his internationalist stance as insincere.[83]

After the severe police repression in the spring and summer of 1915, the Mezhraionka committee had been refounded by September. Its chief organisers were L. M. Karakhan, a former student at the university and N. Egorov, ex-deputy from Perm province in the Third Duma. Through the organisational efforts of Karakhan and the funds of the wealthy supporter A. L. Popov, the faction succeeded in publishing at the end of 1915 both the legal trade-union journal *Tekstil'shchik* and the illegal newspaper *Vpered*. But these enjoyed the briefest of existences, the former lasting only two issues and the latter one. The group's bid to purchase Sukhanov's monthly, *Sovremennik*, fell through.[84] In the first half of 1916 the increase in factional infighting arising over the war-industries committees and the arrests of their opponents made the Mezhraionka a more attractive organisation for activists. It also benefited from a revival of interest in revolutionary work among student youth. Committees were reformed in the Petrograd Side, Town and Vasil'evskii Island districts, with cells in factories such as the Baltic Shipyards, Franco-Russian, Nails and the Pipes works. In the autumn new committees were established in the Narva and Neva quarters. There were ties to regiments in Krasnoe Selo and Oranienbaum. In August the Mezhraionka succeeded in publishing a legal weekly newspaper, *Rabochie vedomosty*, the first edition of which was printed in 6,000 copies.[85] The extent of the Mezhraionka's revival, however, should not be exaggerated. Most factory cells were miniscule. The Vyborg and Moscow districts remained devoid of the group's presence in any significant way. Estimates of total membership vary from 500 to 150. The editorial board of the new organ was riven by ideological disharmony. The police closed it down after its second issue.[86]

IV

The formation of the Labour Group of the TsVPK, comprising the ten workers' representatives elected at the meeting of 29 November 1915, appeared to offer Mensheviks an unparalleled opportunity to restore their influence among Petrograd's workers. The new Group was not devoid of experienced labour activists. Its chairman, Kuzma Govzdev, a railwayman by trade, had served a revolutionary apprenticeship in Saratov in 1905–9, first as an SR, then as a Social Democrat. Transferring to the capital in 1910, he had swiftly risen to the position of chairman of the union of metalworkers and had been a founder member of the Central Initiative Group. Three other members of the Labour Group had also served in that organisation before the war. One of them was the provocateur, Vladimir Abrosimov, who had fulfilled the function of secretary of the union of metalworkers in 1912 and 1913. Both he and Gvozdev were leading *praktiki*, that is proponents of the utilisation of 'legal opportunities' in preference to the underground.

Precisely because the Labour Group seemed to herald the revival of Menshevism, it was immediately subjected at the time (and ever since by Soviet writers) to a virulent campaign of misrepresentation and obloquy by Bolsheviks. It has been accused of 'social opportunism', of betraying working-class interests, of supporting social peace and class collaboration and acting as strikebreakers.[87] An examination of the speeches of its leaders and resolutions passed at its meetings reveals the baselessness of such charges.[88]

In its attitude to the war and its practical programme for the working class the Labour Group was deeply influenced by the theory of self-defence advocated by the *Nasha zaria* littérateurs. Indeed two of the latter became intimately associated with the Group. Boris Bogdanov, a member of the OK, acted as its secretary and E. Maevskii as an assistant secretary.[89] Condemning the war as a struggle for markets, the Labour Group favoured a peace without annexations or indemnities. It believed the way to terminate the sanguinary hostilities was through the revival of the Second International. On the other hand, accepting the distinction between aggressive and defensive wars, it admitted that the working class had an interest in Russia's salvation from defeat by Germany. This fact, however, did not signify the acceptance by workers, it argued, of social peace or class collaboration. The class struggle was an integral feature of contemporary society and the economic interests of industrialists and their employees were antagonistic. Like the proponents of self-defence, the Labour Group argued that the country's safety required the immediate conquest of political power by the bourgeoisie in a political alliance with the working class. The political programme of the Group was far from moderate. It embraced a Constituent Assembly, the freedom of the press and association, the eight-hour day, land to peasants and the democratisation of local self-government.

The new Labour Group's initial problem was its lack of legitimacy in the eyes of its constituents. The disputed nature of its election and the continual vilification of its intentions by the Bolsheviks, SRs and Mezhraionka meant that it could not take for granted its acceptance by workers as the natural defender of their interests. For these reasons the Labour Group at once launched itself into a frenzy of activity both to demonstrate the advantages of its chosen course of action and to prove the falsity of the accusations that it was the mere lackey of the bourgeoisie. Thus, at the very first meeting of the TsVPK which it attended on 3 December 1915, it refused to accept responsibility for the activities of the committee and turned down the proferred post of assistant chairmanship. At no time in its existence did a member of the Group participate in the work of the TsVPK departments concerned with the distribution of military contracts. It allowed three of its number to attend the Bureau of the TsVPK only with a consultative vote.[90] Within the first two months after its election, it had drawn up a programme of labour reforms – a minimum wage, the implementation of the 1903 law on factory elders, arbitration chambers, labour exchanges, the restoration of trade unions and the labour co-operatives and the democratisation of local self-government.[91] In particular it posited as its most pressing task the convocation of the proposed All-Russian Congress of Labour. It envisaged this body as not only bestowing upon the Labour Group the legitimacy it so earnestly desired, but as a forum to organise the working class on a national scale. The leaders of the Group, as well as A. I. Konovalov, the vice-chairman of the TsVPK, had other, more covert, motives as well. They envisioned the Congress of Labour as establishing an all-Russian union of workers which would act as a workers' soviet, thereby bringing to bear effectively the pressure of the working-class movement on Tsardom.[92] The Labour Group quickly attached to itself ten commissions, including those for food supply, trade unions, statistics, labour co-operatives, the protection of labour and social legislation.[93] It also demanded the revival of legal labour organisations, the payment of unemployment benefit by the state, the Group's representation on the Petrograd Labour Exchange and the holding of factory meetings in the absence of the police.[94] These endeavours seemed to bear fruit remarkably quickly. The Second All-Russian Congress of War-Industries Committees, meeting at the close of February 1916, lent its sanction to the Labour Group's reform programme.[95]

The high expectations with which the Labour Group and its Menshevik sponsors had begun its operations were soon dashed. As Lewis Siegelbaum has astutely pointed out, the Labour Group found itself in a dilemma.[96] Its initial strategy of legalism relied upon the good faith of the progressive industrialists who dominated the TsVPK. But the Labour Group and the latter both grossly over-estimated their ability to persuade the majority of manufacturers or the authorities to implement the designated labour reforms. By the summer of 1916 the organised industrial communities of Moscow and Petrograd had wrecked the plans for arbitration chambers and factory elders, whilst the government had resolutely banned the Labour Congress.[97] At this time, too, the Labour Group eschewed reversion to the underground both because it was averse to it in principle and because it would provide the police with the excuse to do away with the Group altogether.

Furthermore, as was the case with the Mensheviks in 1913 and 1914, the Labour Group's ambivalent attitude towards strikes cost it much potential support. Whilst it accepted in principle the strike as the most legal weapon of the labour movement, it considered the circumstances unfavourable to strikers' success. The Group was apprehensive lest Petrograd workers ran ahead of the labour move-ment elsewhere in Russia as in the spring and summer of 1914. It also feared that stoppages in defence industries only served to alienate the liberal opposition from its working-class 'ally'. Thus the Labour Group had issued an appeal exhorting workers to refrain from participating in the protest stoppages of 29 February–4 March.[98] The Group expected that the introduction of arbitration chambers would provide an institutional mechanism to resolve disputes. Until this happened, the Group was not averse to mediating in strikes both in the capital and elsewhere in the Empire at the request of the workers involved. The fact that most of its conciliatory attempts came to naught (they succeeded in only three of nine such incidents in Petrograd) was scarcely the fault of the Group. Despite the support of the leaders of the TsVPK in these occasions, both came up against the intransigence of the POZF and the military authorities. Unfortu-nately for the Labour Group, however, its controversial profile made it the most convenient scapegoat for others' failings.

By the summer of 1916 there were ominous signs that the Labour Group's uncertain hold on the loyalties of workers and even fellow Mensheviks was being further eroded. There was the increasingly embittered dispute with the Central Initiative Group described earlier, which drove the Labour Group to emancipate itself from external supervision. This found concrete expression in the launching in October 1916 of its own periodical *Put'*, edited by Bogdanov and Maevskii. When the Labour Group managed to convene in July a meeting of mostly Vyborg factory representatives in order to elicit support against the criticisms of the Central Initiative Group, it found to its dismay that most speakers condemned its actions and demanded its recall from the TsVPK. Even members of the Labour Group itself began to lose heart, becoming indifferent to their duties and contributing less and less to debates in the TsVPK Bureau.[99]

V

The five months after September 1916 marked a profound intensification of popular discontent in Petrograd and mounting, overt hostility towards a thoroughly discredited regime. The same leitmotiv began to appear in the Okhrana's reports with a regular monotony. In the words of one memorandum: 'there is to be observed an exceptionally nervous and highly charged mood among the workers'.[100] The most basic cause was the marked deterioration in living conditions for all social strata. From October 1916 there occurred a steep and unbroken decline in the delivery of scheduled supplies of essential foodstuffs and fuel to the city. Bread became scarce in working-class districts and entire categories of goods unobtainable in the shops. Early in the New Year there was a mass closure of petty retail outlets whilst shops still functioning curtailed their hours of business. The hitherto erratic rise in prices henceforth accelerated without interruption. Its impact was worst on the unskilled, semi-skilled, women and all workers in non-defence industries, whose real wages had declined unceasingly since 1914. But even the formerly privileged male skilled workers in heavy industry and chemicals, whose real incomes had grown, suddenly discovered that they were no longer exempt from the ravages of inflation. This was a fundamental factor in the growth of labour unrest. The city's population blamed the sharp deterioration in its living standards upon the government's inept handling of the economy.[101] At the same time the drama of high politics also exerted a powerful and fatal impact on an urban populace, apprehensive of the spectre of catastrophic food shortages and imminent starvation. Popular suspicions of treachery in high places, the influence of Rasputin, the alleged pro-German proclivities of the Tsarina and the president of the Council of Ministers, Boris Stürmer, and their supposed manoeuvrings for a separate peace found their apparent confirmation in the Kadet leader's sensational oration with its insinuation of treason at the first session of the reconvened legislature

on 1 November. His censored speech, together with equally denun-
ciatory addresses by the Menshevik and Trudovik deputies, was
widely circulated in secretly printed copies. The Okhrana reported in
alarm that the charges 'had electrified the masses'. After Miliukov's
philippic the Tsar personally became tainted in the popular mind
with treachery.[102] Workers' anger with the constant queuing for
frequently unavailable and highly priced foodstuffs and hostility
towards an inept and apparently treasonable government and dynasty suddenly erupted in two mass stoppages of work in October 1916.

Although the Bolsheviks had just launched a campaign to exploit
the food crisis in the interests of revolutionising workers, with a
few factory meetings in Vyborg and the printing of 4,000 copies
of an appropriate leaflet, the stoppages which began in that district on 17 October caught them unawares.[103] Between 17 and 21
October, some 90,000 operatives walked off the job. It would be
mistaken, however, to describe this industrial action, as Soviet
works do, as 'a general all-city political strike'.[104] In the first place,
the plants disproportionately affected were, once more, medium-
sized, privately owned engineering and electrical establishments in
the three northern districts of the city. The southern quarters
(Moscow apart to some extent), the gigantic state-owned defence
establishments and all other branches of manufacturing were scarcely
affected. Moreover, not only had the local Bolsheviks not initiated
the strikes but the PK actually issued an appeal exhorting workers to
return to their benches.[105] Whilst the stoppages can reasonably be
interpreted as expressing a general dissatisfaction with the political
system, no specific political slogans were advanced by the strikers. A
contemporary report in the bulletin of the Labour Group ascribed a
mixture of motives to the protesters: discontent with food shortages
and the war, commemoration of the October Manifesto, solidarity
with a rumoured insurgency in Moscow.[106] On the other hand, the
strikes were accompanied by disquieting signs for the authorities.
There were food riots in Novaia Derevnia as well as much window
smashing and attempts at demonstrations in Vyborg. Even more
ominous was an incident involving the 181st Infantry Regiment.
When police attempted to disperse demonstrators outside the barracks, the soldiers rushed out to attack them with sticks and
bricks.[107]

The last-named event served in part as the occasion for the next
October explosion of unrest. The PK resolved to utilise the arrest
and court martial of 120 soldiers of the 181st Infantry Regiment,
together with the imminent trial of the Baltic Fleet sailors detained at
the close of the previous year, to launch a mass wave of sympathy
walk-outs lasting three days. The extent of Bolshevik agitation is
uncertain, but cannot have been very widespread as the PK took its
decision two days in advance of the trial and succeeded in print-

ing only 2,500 copies of its leaflet.[108] Between 26 and 28 October, 88,000 downed tools. The stoppages affected the same types of establishment and area as a week previously. The blunders of the authorities, however, needlessly inflamed and prolonged the dispute. On 28 October the commander of the Petrograd Military District, General S. S. Khabalov, ordered the closure of eleven Vyborg defence establishments (employing 32,000 operatives in total) and called up the 1,750 reservists working therein. The PK at once advised the strikers to stay out until the military's order was rescinded. In fact they returned to work within the next two days, before Khabalov revoked his order on 1 November.[109]

The events of the autumn facilitated the revival of all the revolutionary parties' organisations. In the case of the Bolsheviks they succeeded in reforming district committees in all quarters of the city, as well as drawing into their orbit local Estonian, Latvian and Lithuanian socialist groups, which found their support in industrial workers evacuated to the capital from these regions in 1915.[110] As James D. White has shown in a fascinating piece of research, the revived Vyborg committee at this time derived its strength from the Sormovo–Nikolaev *zemliachestvo*, formed of some fifty experienced working-class party activists (all of them skilled metalworkers) who had participated in the underground at the Sormovo works at Nizhnii Novgorod and the Naval' shipyards in Nikolaev. These militants, however, were also to be a source of discord within party ranks, as they were fierce proponents of workers' independence and freedom from control by perfidious intellectuals.[111] On his return to the city in late October 1916 Shliapnikov re-established the Russian Bureau. Perhaps as a result of his previous tense relationship with the PK, the composition of the Bureau was not drawn from the former body. Its members were Shliapnikov himself, P. A. Zalutskii (who had attended the Prague Conference of 1912 as a St Petersburg delegate) and V. M. Molotov (former secretary of *Pravda*'s editorial board).[112]

But the extent of the revival of Bolshevik influence should not be exaggerated. On the eve of Tsardom's fall their total membership in Petrograd may have been between 1,500 and 3,000.[113] This represented a miniscule fraction of a factory labour force numbering 392,800 by 1917. Moreover, two districts alone accounted for over half the total – Vyborg (600) and Narva (800). Other areas were almost devoid of Bolsheviks – 50 members in Neva district, 130 each in Petrograd Side and the city centre; 15 in Sestroretsk; 30 in the students' organisation. Yet in 1917 the population of the Neva quarter stood at 190,000 and of Petrograd Side at 360,000. The membership of the 84 factory cells, claimed to have existed by Leiberov, was extraordinarily thinly spread. At Putilov (24,000 workers in 1917), for example, there were 100 party members, whilst at New Lessner (6,511) there were 75 members, at the Russian Society (7,300) 45, and at Ordnance (5,000) 2.[114] The Russian Bureau and the PK lacked funds, personnel and literary resources to develop their activities widely. The Bureau disposed of a mere 1,000 roubles for party work. Although a fourth edition of *Proletarskii golos* was prepared, the police seized all copies before distribution. The most irregular ties to Lenin were re-established only in December. Relations, moreover, remained strained. The Russian Bureau favoured co-operation with Lenin's Bolshevik ideological opponents and even considered publication of *Sotsial-demokrat* inside Russia.[115]

The appeal of the other revolutionary parties to workers was even more limited than the Bolsheviks. In the Menshevik camp the frigid relations between the Central Initiative Group and the Labour Group turned into outright warfare in August with the publication of a leaflet by the former excoriating the latter for 'pursuing an anti-labour policy'. A campaign was launched to recall the Group from the TsVPK with highly critical articles published in *Letopis'*. By the end of 1916 the Central Initiative Group claimed around 400 adherents in 25 to 30 factory cells.[116] The SR-internationalists never succeeded in reforming their organisations after the severe repressions in the middle of 1916. Led by Petr A. Aleksandrovich, who returned to Russia at some uncertain date in the latter half of the year as V. Chernov's emissary, they may have numbered 200 to 300. No formal PK could be resurrected, although Aleksandrovich and some worker SRs may have fulfilled some of its functions. There is no evidence that district committees were restored. By finally nailing his colours to the mast of defencism Kerenskii, on the other hand, had begun that drift away from the SRs which proved so fatal to his political prospects as premier in 1917.[117] There existed scattered anarcho-communist cells at Diuflon, Petrograd Metals, the Pipe works and Putilov.[118] The Mezhraionka was something of an exception to this dismal pattern. In the first weeks of 1917 the Okhrana's agents reported a noticeable rise in the group's popularity among both workers and students, at the Bolsheviks' expense. Four committees functioned, in Narva, Neva, Vasil'evskii Island and Vyborg. Mezhraionka supporters began to infiltrate Bolshevik committees in the hope of taking them over from below.[119]

The emergent revolutionary crisis, as well as their mutual weakness and hostility to the 'defensist' Labour Group, at last compelled all socialist tendencies sharing an internationalist perspective on the war to explore more formal mechanisms of collaboration than their hitherto *ad hoc* co-operation. On 7 November 1916 a joint meeting of local Bolsheviks, Menshevik- and SR-internationalists discussed the creation of an inter-party information bureau. In a separate move the

Mezhraionka suggested the convocation of a conference embracing itself, the PK and the Central Initiative Group, which would elect a single central Social-Democratic centre. By early February 1917 the Mezhraionka's pressure began to pay dividends as many Bolshevik cells in Vyborg factories passed resolutions in favour of re-establishing party unity.[120] The Bolshevik leadership also came under repeated pressure from Chkheidze, Kerenskii and Aleksandrovich to reach an accord on joint revolutionary actions. None of these efforts bore organisational fruit, as ideological differences ran too deep to be overcome. The Bolsheviks in particular remained adamantly hostile to Menshevik and Trudovik policies of endeavouring to 'revolutionise' the liberal parliamentary opposition by popular pressure from outside the Duma.[121]

The political and economic events of the autumn exerted a profound influence on the strategy of the Labour Group of the TsVPK. By then the Labour Group's moderate course had run into a dead end. Its policy of restraint during the two October stoppages merely served to underline its lack of a hold upon working-class sympathies. The continuation of its former orientation threatened it with political bankruptcy and Menshevism with final schism. At the same time the renewed aggressiveness of the Progressive Bloc in the November session of parliament seemed to justify its faith in the political force of the bourgeoisie. Under these conflicting pressures the Labour Group and its Menshevik supporters made a drastic alteration to their course. Throwing their former caution to the winds, at a meeting in early November they resolved to launch the final offensive to overthrow the regime and to secure the establishment of a 'Government of National Salvation'. As the resolutions of a conference of Labour Groups in the middle of December testify, the Labour Group, faithful to Menshevik principles, placed the State Duma at the centre of an oppositional movement embracing all classes of society. The purpose of working-class pressure was to enmesh the moderate politicians in mass political actions against the government in order to secure its replacement by a 'provisional revolutionary government'.[122] Just as startling a volte-face was the Group's simultaneous decision to abandon partially its legal path in favour of setting up illegal factory 'assistance groups', whose function would be to provide the Group with permanent ties to workers, counter their critics and act as vehicles of extra-parliamentary influence on the liberal parties. The Labour Group's new, aggressive stance significantly evoked a warm response among working people, in part because the State Duma had suddenly acquired an unaccustomed aura of authority and popularity among workers after the session of 1 November.[123] At many of the major defence establishments 'assistance groups' did come into being.

Moreover, when the majority of the State Duma voted to suspend the Menshevik and Trudovik deputies from the House for barracking the new president of the Council of Ministers, A. F. Trepov, at the sitting of 19 November, not only did the new factory commissions pass resolutions of protest, embodying the Labour Group's revised political programme, but four sent delegates to the president of the Fourth Duma, M. V. Rodzianko, to press their case.[124] The Labour Group's rapid recovery of popularity emphasises the fact that at this time workers would respond to any party or group irrespective of its political stance so long as it articulated their resentments against the political system.

Despite their ideological divisions all the revolutionary parties worked together to promote a one-day strike on 9 January 1917, albeit for different reasons. At the end of 1916 the Bolsheviks' Russian Bureau and PK reached a consensus that the time was again propitious for launching the long-desired general political strike. But their vision was even more ambitious. They also planned to spark off street demonstrations involving all social strata, which would compel the authorities to call in the army. Anticipating the actual course of events six weeks later, they expected the resulting mass shootings to serve as a stimulus to the garrison's mutiny. The first attempt at implementing this scheme was to occur on 9 January. Apprised of this strategy, the police struck hard in the days before the anniversary of Bloody Sunday. Mass arrests occurred on at least six occasions. As the PK's later report to the Russian Bureau was compelled to admit, the destruction of party organisations inflicted severe damage on the party's preparations. The PK was unable even to print a leaflet. The sole groups to succeed in publishing limited copies of appeals were the Mezhraionka and the Central Initiative Group. While the SRs favoured a strike, Aleksandrovich and working-class party members opposed Bolshevik plans for demonstrations and an armed uprising as premature.[125] The Labour Group, too, lent its imprimatur for the first time to a general political strike. 'It endeavours,' the Okhrana reported, 'to play a leading role in the labour movement in order to increase its popularity'. The Group alone succeeded in convoking factory meetings (at the Arsenal, Petrograd Engineering and Obukhov among others) both before and on the day of the stoppage at which its speakers expounded its programme.[126] The number of workers downing tools on 9 January was the highest in the war so far – 142,000 or 36 per cent of the factory labour force. Such a figure had been surpassed only once before since 1911 – on May Day 1914 when 170,000 had walked out. For the first time in the war almost all the gigantic mixed production defence plants participated in the protest, including Franco-Russian, Neva Shipyards, Petrograd Metals, Obukhov and Putilov. In all districts, indeed, the day witnessed a near total shutdown in heavy industry. On the other hand, most other manufacturing sectors remained relatively strike free. The Bolsheviks' sanguinary expectations, furthermore, remained unfulfilled. Massive demonstrations did not occur.

The relative success of the walk-outs on 9 January, the forthcoming session of the State Duma and the recovery of the Labour Group's nerve and credibility emboldened the latter to take more drastic steps. At a meeting on 16 January the Group adopted Bogdanov's proposal to launch a general strike on 14 Feburary (the day parliament reconvened) and to organise demonstrations outside the Tauride Palace in order to pressure the Progressive Bloc into seizing power and setting up a Provisional Government. A corresponding appeal was printed. Members of the Labour Group toured the factories to seek support for their plan, and a 'propaganda college' was established. Despite the arrest of eleven adherents of the Group on 27 January, the three left at liberty together with working-class supporters continued the campaign.[127] The local Bolsheviks were well aware that the Labour Group's plan represented a serious challenge both to their overblown claim to 'hegemony' in the labour movement and to their dismissal of the State Duma as an irrelevant factor in power politics. Their response, however, was singularly inept. The Russian Bureau and the PK fell out over the correct tactics to adopt. In a leaflet issued about 6 or 7 February the PK mistakenly chose the religious holiday of Shrove Tuesday (10 February) as the date for a pre-emptive open-ended general strike since this marked the second anniversary of the trial of the Bolshevik Duma deputies. The Russian Bureau, more alert to religious susceptibilities, selected 13 February as the appropriate time for a one-day stoppage and even, in propitious circumstances, demonstrations. The confusion was compounded by the fact that the Central Initiative Group and the Mezhraionka issued leaflets hostile to the Labour Group's enterprise. They, the Bolsheviks and the SR–internationalists all opposed the creation of a liberal government committed to the war.[128] Both the PK and the Russian Bureau pressed ahead with their own schemes. The predictable result was disastrous from their point of view. On 10 February only five enterprises among the few still working on the holiday came out on strike, and none three days later. On the other hand, despite the strictures of the internationalist socialists, the proclamation of General Khabalov warning that troops would open fire on demonstrators and the appeal of the Kadet leader Miliukov to workers to refrain from participation in the strike and demonstration, 85,000 employees failed to report for work on 14 February – testimony both to the workers' indifference to doctrinal factional squabbles and their responsiveness to any opportunity to express antipathy to the regime. As before, the defence plants disproportionately bore the brunt of unrest. There were attempts at demonstrations in the Narva and Neva districts, but massive police precautions, not workers' indifference to the State Duma, prevented all except around 400 demonstrators reaching the Tauride Palace. For the first time in the war, too, student groups attempted to lend their weight to the protests. SR and Social Democratic students at the Polytechnical Institute led a procession to the Nevskii Prospekt, whilst at the Forestry, Psycho-Neurological and Medical Institutes meetings approved a one-day stoppage.[129]

VI

In stark contrast to the years of peace, the revolutionary parties found the most minimal opportunities for legal activities during the war years. The authorities preserved a permanent prohibition on the publication of daily labour newspapers. The surviving 'thick' journals were compelled by the exigencies of censorship to conduct their ideological debates in the most Aesopian language, intelligible only to the initiated socialist intellectual. Their circulation was in any case miniscule. The solitary trade union to survive unscathed was the obscure union of pharmaceutical employees. When the Labour Group of the TsVPK succeeded in June 1916 in reviving a Menshevik-dominated union of metalworkers, a potentially influential source of support, it was shut down by the authorities after two months' existence. Its proposed journal never saw the light of day. The reborn union of printers lasted just over a month in the middle of 1916. A similar fate befell the Labour Group's endeavours to launch three new educational societies in the autumn of 1916. According to the Soviet scholar I. P. Leiberov there were also eleven illegal unions in existence by the start of 1917. But their total membership did not even reach 10,000.[130]

The sickness benefit funds or *kassy* alone still held out the prospect of a legal avenue of approach to workers. By December 1915 84 *kassy* functioned in the city, embracing 108,000 members, and another 97 were in the process of formation.[131] At the start of 1915 the two main insurance monthlies, the Bolsheviks' *Voprosy strakhovaniia* and the Mensheviks' *Strakhovanie rabochikh*, resumed publication after a six months' hiatus.[132] On the other hand police depredations reduced working-class representation on the Insurance Council from fifteen to three, on the Petrograd Capital Insurance Board from six to two and on the Petrograd Provincial Insurance Board to nil. In an eloquent comment on the complete indifference of ordinary workers and socialist insurance activists to this sad state of affairs, throughout 1915 neither the surviving labour delegates nor any *kassy* either complained to or petitioned the appropriate ministries for new elections. The authorities finally consented to permit supplementary ballots to the Insurance Council in January 1916 only under pressure from the Menshevik fraction and the Duma budget commission.[133]

The new elections were in most respects a repeat of those held two years previously. Both the Bolsheviks and the Mensheviks advanced exactly the same, almost identical *nakazy* (mandates), whilst the Mensheviks formed an electoral bloc with the Populists.[134] There was the same pressure from below for party unity in the elections. At the only two pre-electoral meetings, both organised by the Menshevik-controlled Erikson *kassa*, most present condemned factionalism. At the electoral assembly, however, the 71 electors, representing mostly the *kassy* of private firms in heavy industry, voted in its entirety the Bolshevik slate with the addition of two Mensheviks. On the other hand, the Menshevik *nakaz* was carried.[135]

At the electoral assembly to the Petrograd Capital Insurance Board on 10 October 1916, despite a narrow majority in favour of unity, those present selected four Bolsheviks (one was the police informer Sesitskii) and a single SR.[136] A fortnight later three Bolsheviks and two Mensheviks were chosen as delegates to the Petrograd Provincial Insurance Board.[137]

As the earlier discussion in Chapter 7 emphasised, the *kassy* were defective instruments of outreach by revolutionaries to the mass of operatives. The Law on Sickness Insurance excluded from its purview workers in state-owned enterprises, artisans and commercial employees. Employers and the police continued to ensure that the activities of the *kassy* remained strictly confined to insurance matters. The *kassy* could not and did not replace the defunct trade unions in the war, as S. Milligan has suggested.[138] Throughout 1915 the remnants of the Labour Groups remained completely inactive. Four of the nine Bolshevik replacements elected on 30 January 1916 were detained within the week. Although *Voprosy strakhovaniia* did attempt to broaden its coverage to embrace topical, political and economic issues, such articles were heavily censored, were infrequent (thirteen in all were published in two years) and none touched on the cardinal issue of war or peace. As R. Arskii admitted in his memoirs, the conditions of wartime publishing made it very difficult for the journal to follow any open political line.[139] The Menshevik periodical attempted even less in this respect. Moreover, for at least the first half of 1916, the Bolsheviks' insurance ranks were rent by discord. Almost certainly at the instigation of the Okhrana, their agent Chernomazov, now the secretary of the Lessner *kassa* board, with the support of the PK as well as other Bolshevik fund secretaries, launched a schismatic attack on the editorial board of the party's insurance organ for its 'opportunism'. A resolution of the PK condemned the journal for departing from the political line set by the PK.[140] On the other hand, the *kassy* came to provide the Bolsheviks with one inestimable service in the war. Bolshevik party workers sought a legal covering by becoming *kassy* chairmen, secretaries and white-collar staff. Between 1914 and the February revolution, eighteen members of the PK trod this path. Their term in office or employment, however, was relatively brief, as the Okhrana, well aware of their motives, soon arrested them. *Kassy* offices were also used to store party literature or as meeting places for factory cells and district committees.[141]

VII

The war opened up alluring prospects for the revolutionary parties in Petrograd. There was the enormous expansion of the factory labour force, the drastic and cumulative deterioration in living and working conditions, the series of military disasters in the spring and summer of 1915, the inept conduct of the war, the dynasty's fatal loss of prestige and suspicions of Germanophile treachery in high places and the re-emergence of liberal opposition in parliament. Moreover, with the exception of a handful of die-hard Menshevik and SR defensists, all local socialist factions, including the mainstream of Menshevism, rejected the concept of social peace and class collaboration during the war and remained committed to the revolutionary struggle to overthrow the monarchy. Nevetheless, it proved impossible to overcome the obstacles to the revolutionaries' endeavours to utilise the rapidly changing domestic situation in the interests of creating an organised socialist opposition movement resting on firm institutional links to the labouring population. On the eve of the February revolution, as in April 1912 or July 1914, none of the socialist groups had succeeded in establishing permanent organisations with mass support or in providing effective leadership to a diffuse, if profound, popular dissatisfaction with the regime. Nor had the severe handicap of factional infighting been overcome.

In the first place, the war had deepened ideological divisiveness. The socialists' ideological response fractured existing groupings in Petrograd and produced new alignments primarily between internationalists of various hues and revolutionary defensists. The war was the occasion for a further divorce between Lenin and his followers in the capital. Indeed, the description 'Leninist' is scarcely accurate to describe Petrograd Bolsheviks during the war, as they abjured cardinal elements of their leader's wartime ideology. In particular they renounced Lenin's defeatism, realising the psychological impossibility of propagating such a doctrine in Russia's wartime circumstances. Lenin, in turn, came to reject in 1915 local Bolsheviks' adoption of the slogans of a Soviet of Workers' Deputies and a Constituent Assembly. These ideological differences, as much as the difficulties of wartime communications or finance, ensured that Lenin's influence over Petrograd's labour movement remained minimal throughout the war. Even more so than in the years of peace, therefore, the sub-élites fashioned their own strategy and tactics. Although, moreover, the ideological realignments began to assume a shadowy organisational form by late 1916, with the coming together of Bolshevik, Menshevik and SR-internationalists, the continuing factional discord, in particular over attitudes to the State Duma and collaboration with the liberal bourgeoisie, precluded concrete agreements.

Secondly, in the almost total absence of legal labour organisations, the revolutionaries were thrown back upon the underground as their sole means of influence on the working class. It proved an even more defective instrument than in the years immediately preceding the war. None of the socialist factions, mercilessly persecuted by the Okhrana, possessed the institutional mechanisms capable of furnishing effective leadership. The Mensheviks obtusely abandoned the illegal path altogether until the middle of 1916. SR district groupings existed for the briefest of time, for a few months late in 1915 and early 1916. The Bolsheviks signally failed to establish a continuously functioning PK or district committees. Their ambitious plans to recreate a Soviet of Workers' Deputies in the autumn of 1915 never bore fruit. A proper Russian Bureau survived only for a month or so early in 1916 and on the eve of the revolution; its relations with the PK were less than comradely. Thus, Bolshevik organisation was reduced to the lowest level of the illegal factory cells. But these nuclei remained as unevenly distributed as in the 1912–14 period. The information available on thirty-five Bolshevik factory groups reveals that a mere six existed in branches of manufacturing other than heavy industry. With the latter the geographical scope was just as limited; ten were located in Vyborg plants, six on the Petrograd Side and four in Vasil'evskii Island. The fluctuating membership of the party was always miniscule throughout the war. Furthermore, with the exception of the Baltic Fleet in the autumn of 1915, none of the revolutionary parties succeeded in penetrating the armed forces.

As a consequence of these defects, from the summer of 1915 the Bolsheviks were unable to realise their plans for a general political strike and mass street demonstrations. On the five occasions in the first year of the war when local militants sought to spark off political stoppages, they evoked no response at all from workers. In the second year and a half, there were no Bolshevik preparations before three of the eight mass political strikes; in the case of the other five their and other revolutionary groups' efforts were severely hampered by the secret police. Moreover, none of the eight stoppages were of a genuinely 'mass' character as they were confined to privately owned heavy industrial defence establishments in the three northern manufacturing quarters. Five of the political walk-outs witnessed no street demonstrations and three were accompanied only by small-scale protests.

As before the war, the Bolsheviks still failed to predominate within the Social Democratic or broader socialist and labour movements. As the elections to the War-Industries Committees and the Insurance Council revealed, there was no clear-cut swing towards the Bolsheviks among party activists, let alone the broad masses. The political sympathies of the minority of socialist militants still encompassed a bewildering spectrum of views. Indeed as the war progressed, there came to the surface again the temporarily submerged longing for Social Democratic unity.

Furthermore the doctrinal hostility of the Bolsheviks, the Central Initiative Group, the Mezhraionka and the SR-internationalists to the TsVPK and its Labour Group proved to be a costly error. Although the Labour Group's initial, loyalist strategy of seeking to secure labour reforms through collaboration with the industrial bourgeoisie misconceived the reality of power politics, its adoption late in 1916 of an overtly revolutionary and illegal course of action evoked a warm response from workers. At the time of its arrest, the Labour Group, together with the Mezhraionka, had emerged as formidable challengers to the Bolsheviks.

Lastly, the rapid expansion of industry after 1914 created another impediment to revolutionary success in the changes it wrought in the social composition of the working class. The mobilisation of skilled men, together with the increase in the numbers of women, older peasants and *meshchane* (petty-bourgeois) elements employed, further reduced the cadre of hereditary proletarians and increased the weight of the less urbanised unskilled and semi-skilled. The Bolsheviks' cells continued to be recruited overwhelmingly from the ranks of skilled male engineering workers. A mere 18 of 112 members of the PK during the war were not proletarian by origin. All of the 29 operatives whose trade could be discovered were skilled metalworkers.[142]

In the light of the foregoing analysis it must be concluded that the radicalisation of the Petrograd working class in the war owed very little to the endeavours of the revolutionary parties. The workers' final alienation from the regime, so visibly evident by the autumn of 1916, was rather the product of the economic and social dislocations of urban life caused by the war and the crisis of high politics which destroyed the monarchy's last shreds of popularity.

Chapter 14

THE WARTIME STRIKE MOVEMENT,
JULY 1914 – 22 FEBRUARY 1917

I

One of the most remarkable features of the labour movement after Russia's declaration of war against Germany on 19 July 1914 was a sharp decline in the frequency of strikes both in Petrograd province and the Empire as a whole. During the first six months of 1914 the number of industrial stoppages in the Empire had reached the unprecedented total of 4,098 and the number of strikers almost one and a half million. By contrast, in the last six months of the year the respective numbers fell to just 68 and 35,000. The period of industrial peace lasted until May and June 1915 when strikes in the textile towns of Shuia and Ivanovo-Voznesensk in Vladimir province ushered in a new era of industrial unrest.[1] During the year 1915 the number of strikes recorded in the Empire totalled 1,034 and the number of strikers 539,528: in 1916 1,576 and 957,075.[2] In Petrograd province the trend was similar though even more pronounced, the number of strikes and strikers rising from 25 and 19,741 between August and December 1914 to 170 and 173,833 in 1915, and 401 and 513,737 in 1916.[3] In the period August–December 1914 Petrograd province accounted for 36.8 per cent of all the country's strikes and 16 per cent of all its strikers. By 1916 the ratios had increased to 82 per cent and 56 per cent. Despite this, it must be stressed that levels of industrial unrest in Petrograd province during the war years remained far below those of 1905 and 1912–July 1914.

Contrary to the view of the Soviet historians I. I. Krylova and I. P. Leiberov, Petrograd province did not dominate the wartime strike movement.[4] Whilst in the first months of the war the great majority of strikers came from Kostroma province, in 1915, according to the factory inspectorate, the provinces of Moscow and Vladimir were both more racked by labour disturbances than Petrograd. In 1916 alone did the capital and its province revert to their place of pre-eminence.

As Table 14.i shows, the incidence of wartime strikes in the province varied greatly from industry to industry.

The gradual breakdown of industrial discipline, which set in in Petrograd with the first serious economic conflicts in metalworking plants in July 1915, once more as before the war brought to a position of pre-eminence within the revived strike movement workers in the capital's metalworking and machine construction plants. Metalworkers were responsible for 72 per cent of all strikes and 84 per cent of all strikers in the wartime period, in contrast to the pre-war ratios (1912–July 1914) of 39 per cent and 62 per cent respectively. Textiles, on the other hand, came a very poor second, furnishing only 10–13 per cent of all strikes and strikers. All other sectors of manufacturing had a scarcely visible presence.[5] They contributed a mere 6 per cent of all the city's strikers, in contrast to the 30 months before the outbreak of hostilities when 22 per cent of strikers came from the 'other industries' category. Outside of manufacturing, servants, commercial–industrial employees, post and telegraph workers held aloof from the renewed unrest.

Confirmation of the relative extent of strike action in the metal/machine and textile industries is given in Table 14.ii. No other branch of industry suffered from quite such an intensity of strikes as metalworking, particularly in 1916. After lagging behind this sector in 1915, textiles did approach it in the level of disputes the following year. However, although the strike propensity of Petrograd factory

Table 14.i: *Petrograd Province: Strikes and Strikers, by Industry, 19 July 1914–22 February 1917 (number (000s) and % of total)*

Industry	Strikes		Strikers	
	no.	%	no.	%
Animal products	36	4.6	28,880	3.0
Chemicals	5	0.6	1,969	0.2
Communications	5	0.6	4,862	0.5
Food/drink/tobacco	27	3.4	7,186	0.7
Metals and machines	568	71.8	807,061	83.6
Mineral products	6	0.8	1,123	0.1
Paper and printing	23	2.9	10,810	1.1
Textiles	105	13.3	100,482	10.4
Woodworking	16	2.0	3,107	0.3
TOTAL	791	100.0	965,480	99.9

Table 14.ii: Petrograd Province: Total Number of Strikers Each Year as % of Total Factory Labour Force, by Industry, 19 July 1914–22 February 1917

Industry	19 July – 31 Dec. 1914	1915	1916	1 Jan. – 22 Feb. 1917
Animal products	17.5	57.8	133.4	26.8
Chemicals	–	–	3.2	1.2
Food/drink/tobacco	1.3	13.7	26.3	3.6
Metals and machines	10.1	63.7	176.1	58.0
Mineral products	–	0.4	24.8	–
Paper and printing	–	0.2	30.3	8.6
Textiles	19.7	28.5	130.8	50.7
Woodworking	0.002	–	29.1	17.1
All factory labour	8.1	44.3	130.8	65.7

Note: The percentages for 19 July–31 December 1914 have been calculated as a proportion of the factory labour force as of 1 January 1914. In the absence of data for the number of employees in particular industries in 1915 and 1916, the estimates for these two years have been based on the figures available for 1 January 1917. As there is no information on the aggregate of workers in communications and on the total hired labour force in the war years, these have had to be omitted from the calculations.

workers rose during the war, it was distinctly lower, even for metalworkers, than between 1912 and July 1914, when between 240 per cent and 326 per cent of the city's labour force downed tools.

II

As between 1913 and 1914, a particularly significant feature of war-time strikes in Petrograd province was the growing frequency with which they were associated with political objectives.[6]

Although Petrograd province did not assume the foremost place in wartime industrial unrest on an all-Russian scale to 1916, it did play such a role in political action from the onset of belligerency. In 1915 the capital and its province already accounted for 69 per cent of nationwide stoppages of a political nature. A year later the ratio rose to an extraordinary 96 per cent. These figures were almost identical to its share of national political protest in 1912 and 1913. As Table 14.iii reveals, in the last thirty months of the old regime's existence three fifths of all strikes and two-thirds of all strikers were associated with mass walk-outs of a political nature. In this respect there was a

Table 14.iii: Petrograd Province: Number of Political Strikes and Strikers as % of All Strikes and Strikers, by Industry, 19 July 1914–22 February 1917

Industry	Strikes %	Strikers %
Animal products	50.0	46.7
Chemicals	40.0	5.1
Communications	–	–
Food/drink/tobacco	29.6	37.0
Metals and machines	66.2	71.6
Mineral products	33.4	14.0
Paper and printing	52.2	34.2
Textiles	41.9	44.3
Woodworking	68.7	78.7
ALL INDUSTRIES	59.4	67.8

pronounced difference between the metal and machinery industries and light industry, i.e. textiles and food processing (see Table 14.iii). Moreover, in contrast to the years before the war, these shutdowns were for the most part more drawn-out affairs. Of the fifteen stoppages classed as political, only eight could be described loosely as being of a mass demonstrative nature. Five of the eight lasted three to four days, whilst three alone followed the pre-war pattern of one day's duration.[7] Even more so than in the earlier, pre-war era of mass political action these political strikes formed workers' sole powerful weapon against the regime. In the complete absence of legal labour organisations it would scarcely be an exaggeration to state that these political stoppages comprised the essentials of the labour movement during the war. The prevalence of political protest in the Petrograd strike wave during the war ran sharply against the national trend. Both in 1915 and 1916 participants in political strikes constituted only a third of all Russian strikers.[8]

Whilst the extent of political striking varied little over the period 19 July 1914–December 1916, there occurred a pronounced increase in the frequency of political strikes in the first seven weeks of 1917. Approximately 85 per cent of all strikes and strikers were accounted for by the anniversary of Bloody Sunday on 9 January and the protests orchestrated by the Labour Group of the Central War-Industries Committee to mark the reopening of the State Duma (see Chapter 13).

Politically motivated industrial unrest in the capital during war-

Table 14.iv: Petrograd Province: Political Strikes and Strikers, by Industry, 19 July–22 February 1917 (number (000s) and % of total)

Industry	Strikes		Strikers	
	no.	%	no.	%
Animal products	18	3.8	13,475	2.1
Chemicals	2	0.4	100	0.003
Communications	–	–	–	–
Food/drink/tobacco	8	1.7	2,661	0.4
Metals and machines	376	80.0	577,847	89.6
Mineral products	2	0.4	157	0.005
Paper and printing	12	2.6	3,694	0.6
Textiles	41	8.7	44,560	6.9
Woodworking	11	2.3	2,446	0.3
TOTAL	470	99.9	644,940	99.908

time was dominated by workers in the metal and machinery industries, which were responsible for eight out of every ten political strikes and nine out of every ten political strikers (see Table 14.iv). In this respect, the dominance of these industries was even greater than it had been before the outbreak of the war. By contrast the textile industries, the next most important source of political strikes, accounted for fewer than one in ten of all political strikes and strikers. The contribution of other industries to politically motivated unrest was negligible.

The metalworking and machine construction industries, too, were noteworthy for the intensity of political disputes, involving 43 per cent of their employees in 1915 and 85 per cent in the first seven weeks of 1917 (see Table 14.v). An astonishing 90 per cent of participants in the eight mass wartime political stoppages were metalwokers.[9] Thus the political colouring of the wartime strike movement in the capital derived almost exclusively from the overwhelming political nature of metalworkers' protests. However, the incidence of political striking among metalworkers during the war was far below the levels reached in the period 1912 to 1914, when between 300 and 450 per cent of the labour force in this sector were involved in walk-outs of a political coloration. Furthermore, even within this branch of manufacturing participation was far from uniform throughout the various sub-sectors or engineering districts. The almost complete abstinence from political striking by the employees of the large state-owned munitions plants is particularly

Table 14.v: Petrograd Province: Total Number of Political Strikers Each Year as % of Total Factory Labour Force, by Industry, 19 July 1914–22 February 1917

Industry	19 July–31Dec. 1914	1915	1916	1 Jan.–22 Feb. 1917
Animal products	12.5	15.2	60.9	27.8
Chemicals	–	–	0.001	0.001
Food/drink/tobacco	–	6.4	6.8	3.6
Metals and machines	8.3	42.8	67.8	84.9
Mineral products	–	4.0	–	–
Paper and printing	–	0.5	5.0	8.4
Textiles	7.5	5.4	47.6	41.3
Woodworking	–	–	19.4	17.1
All factory labour	5.1	27.3	76.0	57.8

worthy of note. The Arsenal (4,000 workers in January 1917), Baltic Shipyards (7,500), Izhora arms-works (9,000), Petrograd Cartridges (8,000), Petrograd Pipes (19,000), Obukhov (10,600) and Ordnance (3,000) either participated in none of the political strikes during the war or only once. The brunt of political unrest in the heavy-goods sector – indeed in all manufacturing industry – rested upon a group of particular privately owned plants in the medium-sized range of 500–2,000 employees. Thus twenty factories were each hit by more than two of the eight mass political stoppages.[10] Ten establishments employing between 2,000 and 6,000 workers also fell into this category.[11] Nor did relatively small metalworking establishments remain immune. Fifteen factories with payrolls numbering 100–500 each endured two or more politically inspired walk-outs.[12] Political strikes in heavy industry were not spread uniformly among the various district centres of the sector. Vyborg occupied a dominant position (52 per cent of all political strikers during the war came from this district) precisely because its medium-sized metalworking and machine construction plants were to the fore in political unrest. In contrast, the Neva district, despite its large number of engineering works, contributed a mere 8 per cent of all political strikes, whilst Vasil'evskii Island's share was a minute 6 per cent.

The intensity of strikes in textiles always remained at a level significantly below that in metals and machines. Yet even in textiles the year 1916 witnessed a dramatic surge in the percentage of political strikers, a momentum continued into the first month and a half of the following year (see Table 14.v).

III

As was the case before the First World War, the capital did not occupy such a pre-eminent place within wartime economic conflicts in the Russian Empire as it did in political protest. In 1915 it accounted for 15 per cent of Empire-wide participants in economic strikes, a record overtaken by the provinces of Vladimir (26 per cent) and Moscow (31 per cent). Although the capital's share of economic strikes doubled the following year, the three Central Russian textile provinces of Kostroma, Moscow and Vladimir were responsible together for 48 per cent of participants in disputes of an economic nature.[13]

Between July 1914 and February 1917 only four out of every ten strikes and less than one third of all strikers in Petrograd were economically motivated (see Table 14.vi) – figures well below those for the Empire as a whole, where around two-thirds of all strikers walked out for economic reasons and well below those for politically motivated strikes and strikers in the province. As in the pre-war period, during the war years political rather than economic motives dominated the Petrograd strike movement. Furthermore, a higher percentage of economic strikes during the war years (76 per cent in 1915 and 54 per cent in 1916) were partial rather than total walk-outs than had been the case between 1912 and 1914 when the figures ranged from only 27 to 40 per cent. Within the war period itself, however, there were significant variations in the importance of economic strikes in Petrograd. Throughout the first two and a half years of the war the proportion of Petrograd strikes and strikers

Table 14.vi: *Petrograd Province: Number of Economic Strikes and Strikers as % of All Strikes and Strikers, by Industry, 19 July 1914–22 February 1917*

Industry	Strikes %	Strikers %
Animal products	50.0	53.3
Chemicals	60.0	94.9
Communications	100.0	100.0
Food/drink/tobacco	70.4	63.0
Metals and machines	33.8	28.4
Mineral products	66.6	86.0
Paper and printing	47.8	65.8
Textiles	58.1	55.7
Woodworking	31.3	21.3
ALL INDUSTRIES	40.6	32.2

classified as economic remained constant, at around 50 per cent in the case of the former and 40 per cent in the case of the latter. By contrast in January and February 1917, the percentage of strikes and strikers acting for economic reasons fell to just 18 per cent and 12 per cent respectively.

The inter-industry pattern of economic strikes/strikers differed considerably from that of political strikes and strikers.

The contribution of metalworkers to wartime economic discontent was less than it was to political stoppages. Although the metalworking and machine construction industries continued to occupy first place, they were responsible for three-fifths of all economic strikes and seven-tenths of economic strikers in the capital (see Table 14.vii). This also stood in contrast to pre-war economic unrest when they accounted for a quarter of economic strikes and two-fifths of economic strikers. As with political stoppages, the weight of economic protest in this sector was carried by plants employing labour forces in the range 500–6,000 workers. Such establishments contributed two-thirds of all economic strikes in this industry. Textile workers, on the other hand, more than doubled their share to approximately a fifth of all economically motivated strikes and strikers. Despite the dominance of political over economic strikes in the metal/machines industries and their increasing importance in the textile industry (above all early in 1917), these sectors nevertheless together accounted for almost four-fifths of all economic strikes and nine out of every ten economic strikers in the province during the war. Thus the contribution made by all other industries to economic

Table 14.vii: *Petrograd Province: Economic Strikes and Strikers, by Industry, 19 July – 22 February 1917 (number (000s) and % of total)*

Industry	Strikes		Strikers	
	no.	*%*	*no.*	*%*
Animal products	18	5.6	15,405	4.8
Chemicals	3	0.9	1,869	0.6
Communications	5	1.6	4,862	1.5
Food/drink/tobacco	19	5.9	4,525	1.4
Metals and machines	192	59.8	229,214	71.5
Mineral products	4	1.2	966	0.3
Paper and printing	11	3.4	7,116	2.2
Textiles	64	19.9	55,922	17.4
Woodworking	5	1.6	661	0.2
TOTAL	321	99.9	320,540	99.9

Table 14.viii: Petrograd Province: Total Number of Economic Strikers Each Year as % of Total Factory Labour Force, by Industry, 19 July 1914– 22 February 1917

Industry	19 July–31 Dec. 1914	1915	1916	1 Jan.–22 Feb. 1917
Animal products	5.0	45.5	79.2	0.4
Chemicals	–	–	3.1	1.5
Food/drink/tobacco	1.3	7.3	19.5	–
Metals and machines	1.7	20.9	63.9	11.0
Mineral products	–	–	24.8	–
Paper and printing	–	1.4	25.3	0.02
Textiles	1.2	23.1	83.2	9.4
Woodworking	0.002	–	1.0	–
All factory labour	3.0	17.0	54.8	7.9

discontent remained small. Servants and commercial industrial employees, too, failed to resort to a withdrawal of labour as a means to improve their deteriorating economic position.

As Table 14.viii demonstrates, in metals and machines the intensity of economic strikes was less than for political stoppages, particularly in 1915. This divergence was at its worst in the first month and a half of 1917 when the surge of politically inspired stoppages in metalworking led to a dramatic decline in the intensity of the industry's economic disputes. In textiles, however, the predominance of economically motivated strikes in 1915 and 1916 ensured that the reverse was the case with regard to the intensity of economic striking, in particular in 1916 (see Table 14.viii). The first seven weeks of 1917 alone witnessed the greater attractiveness of political protest to mill hands.

In striking contrast to the pre-war period, wartime economic strikes in Petrograd were of considerably shorter duration. Whereas a third of disputes had lasted over a month in 1913, throughout the two and a half years of the war not a single stoppage exceeded 30 days in length. Even conflicts of intermediate length (8–30 days) were less common. In the years 1912 to 1914 a third to two-fifths of strikes had fallen into this category. As Table 14.ix reveals, the ratio of walk-outs lasting between 8 and 30 days oscillated between 22 per cent and 36 per cent in 1915 and 1916. Consequently strikes lasting less than eight days contributed a far higher proportion of shutdowns, touching 78 per cent of the aggregate of all economic clashes in 1915, with a modest decline to 64 per cent the following year. One reason for this notable turnaround in the length of stoppages of an

Table 14.ix: *Petrograd Province: Length of Economic Strikes, by Industry, 19 July 1914–22 February 1917**

19 July – 31 December 1914 Industry	1 day	2–7	8–30	Total	No.
Animal products	100.0	–	–	100.0	184
Chemicals	–	–	–	–	–
Communications	–	–	–	–	–
Food/drink/tobacco	–	–	–	–	–
Metals and machines	60.4	39.1	–	100.0	1,375
Mineral products	–	–	–	–	–
Paper and printing	–	–	–	–	–
Textiles	100.0	–	–	100.0	800
Woodworking	–	–	–	–	
ALL INDUSTRIES	76.9	23.1	–	100.0	2,359

1915	1 day	2–7	8–30	Total	No.
Animal products	4.3	–	95.7	100.0	5,225
Chemicals	–	–	–	–	–
Communications	–	–	–	–	–
Food/drink/tobacco	47.8	52.2	–	100.0	1,150
Metals and machines	42.8	43.1	14.1	100.0	46,264
Mineral products	–	–	–	–	–
Paper and printing	5.4	–	94.6	100.0	370
Textiles	40.2	38.2	21.6	100.0	11,979
Woodworking	–	–	–	–	
ALL INDUSTRIES	39.1	38.6	22.3	100.0	64,988

1916	1 day	2–7	8–30	Total	No.
Animal products	28.3	71.7	–	100.0	9,504
Chemicals	–	10.4	89.6	100.0	1,249
Communications	29.3	44.0	26.7	100.0	4,862
Food/drink/tobacco	50.6	49.4	–	100.0	3,080
Metals and machines	28.4	36.1	35.5	100.0	153,160
Mineral products	15.5	84.5	–	100.0	966
Paper and printing	45.5	0.1	54.4	100.0	6,706
Textiles	2.1	46.9	51.0	100.0	31,557
Woodworking	68.0	–	32.0	100.0	650
ALL INDUSTRIES	25.3	38.5	36.3	100.0	211,734

1 January–22 February 1917

Industry	1 day	2–7	8–30	Total	No.
Animal products	–	100.0	–	100.0	48
Chemicals	–	100.0	–	100.0	620
Communications	–	–	–	–	–
Food/drink/tobacco	–	–	–	–	–
Metals and machines	48.9	32.5	18.5	99.9	24,281
Mineral products	–	–	–	–	–
Paper and printing	–	–	100.0	100.0	40
Textiles	19.1	48.5	32.4	100.0	4,848
Woodworking	–	–	–	–	–
ALL INDUSTRIES	42.9	36.6	20.5	100.0	29,837

*Percentages are based on the total number of strikers, where known.

economic nature lay in the higher proportion of strikes won outright
by workers during the war (see p. 416). It is probable, too, that in the
circumstances of the war working people had even fewer financial
reserves to withstand prolonged periods of unemployment. Within
metalworking and textiles, as overall, there was a pronounced
tendency for economic clashes to become more stubborn as the war
advanced. Thus, whilst, only 14 per cent of such disputes in heavy
industry were of 8 to 30 days' duration in 1915, the ratio had risen to
36 per cent the following year. In textiles, too, their share doubled.
This phenomenon, however, did not reflect an increase in the
number of conflicts lost by workers.

An analysis of the outcome of economic protest during the war
in the capital reveals another equally striking difference from the
pattern of unrest immediately prior to the First World War. Thus,
whereas Petrograd workers won only a minute proportion of economic disputes in the years 1912 to 1914, ranging from 13 per cent of
the total in 1912 to 4 per cent in 1914, their success rate wavered
between a quarter to a third of the aggregate of economic strikes
during the war (see Table 14.x). Indeed, in 1915 Petrograd workers
fared far better in this respect than strikers elsewhere in Russia.
According to the factory inspectorate only 19 per cent of stoppages
on the national scale represented workers' victories.[14] Conversely
strikers in the capital lost far fewer disputes in 1915 and 1916 than
previously. As Table 14.x shows, in both years employers defeated
outright a third of economically inspired walk-outs. The first seven
weeks of 1917 marked a distinct departure from this pattern in that
workers failed to secure gains in 70 per cent of all clashes. Compromise settlements were also more acceptable to Petrograd employers

Table 14.x: Petrograd Province: Outcome of Economic Strikes, by Industry, 19 July 1914–22 February 1917*

19 July – 31December 1914 Industry	W	L	C	Total	No.
Animal products	34.8	65.2	–	100.0	184
Chemicals	–	–	–	–	–
Communications	–	–	–	–	–
Food/drink/tobacco	–	–	–	–	–
Metals and machines	–	100.0	–	100.0	1,375
Mineral products	–	–	–	–	–
Paper and printing	–	–	–	–	–
Textiles	–	100.0	–	100.0	800
Woodworking	100.0	–	–	100.0	11
ALL INDUSTRIES	3.2	96.8	–	100.0	2,370

1915	W	L	C	Total	No.
Animal products	4.3	–	95.7	100.0	5,225
Chemicals	–	–	–	–	–
Communications	–	–	–	–	–
Food/drink/tobacco	–	100.0	–	100.0	1,150
Metals and machines	42.3	30.8	26.9	100.0	46,172
Mineral products	–	–	–	–	–
Paper and printing	94.6	5.4	–	100.0	370
Textiles	20.0	50.1	29.9	100.0	10,922
Woodworking	–	–	–	–	–
ALL INDUSTRIES	34.9	32.6	32.4	99.9	63,839

1916	W	L	C	Total	No.
Animal products	42.6	54.0	3.4	100.0	9,384
Chemicals	89.6	10.4	–	100.0	1,249
Communications	–	52.7	47.3	100.0	2,962
Food/drink/tobacco	25.3	44.9	29.7	99.9	1,580
Metals and machines	21.8	31.9	46.3	100.0	153,594
Mineral products	15.5	84.5	–	100.0	966
Paper and printing	37.0	57.9	5.1	100.0	5,917
Textiles	37.5	43.4	19.1	100.0	30,794
Woodworking	96.6	3.4	–	100.0	650
ALL INDUSTRIES	25.8	35.8	38.4	100.0	207,096

1 January – 22 February 1917

Industry	W	L	C	Total	No.
Animal products	–	100.0	–	100.0	48
Chemicals	100.0	–	–	100.0	620
Communications	–	–	–	–	–
Food/drink/tobacco	–	–	–	–	–
Metals and machines	21.2	77.1	1.7	100.0	17,004
Mineral products	–	–	–	–	–
Paper and printing	–	100.0	–	100.0	40
Textiles	24.8	49.9	25.3	100.0	3,748
Woodworking	–	–	–	–	–
ALL INDUSTRIES	24.0	70.2	5.8	100.0	21,460

* Percentages are based on total number of strikers, where known.

Symobls: W – all major demands secured by striking workers.

L – all major demands rejected by employers: workers lost the strike.

C – compromise: both strikers and factory owners made mutual concessions.

during the war than before.[15] In 1915 and 1916 alike around a third of all disputes ended in such agreements. The metalworking industry followed closely the trend just delineated. In 1915 42 per cent of strikes in this sector ended in victories for their participants and 27 per cent in compromises. Whilst there was a decline in the following year in the ratio of conflicts registering workers' success to 22 per cent, conversely 46 per cent ended in mutual concessions. Textiles, however, displayed a dissimilar trend. Whereas the proportion of economic conflicts won outright by workers in this sector doubled between 1915 and 1916, the share of compromise settlements fell by a third. On the other hand, the longer the dispute in both these branches of manufacturing the greater the likelihood of failure, a tendency replicating the pre-war pattern. Thus, in metalworking eleven of twenty-one wartime stoppages lasting between eight and thirty days were lost by the strikers. In textiles almost half similarly resulted in defeat.

There were several reasons why the noticeably hard-faced Petrograd industrial community showed a greater spirit of conciliation towards strikers than its previous intransigent record would have predicted. Wartime profits were high and order books full. Employers could afford to be generous, at least until they started to run into liquidity problems and raw materials shortages late in 1916 and early 1917. After all the increased costs could be passed on to the government in the form of higher prices. Strict deadlines for deliveries also put pressure on industrialists to avoid lengthy shutdowns of production. There was intermittent pressure from the military, the Okhrana and bureaucrats to avoid unnecessary interruptions to the smooth functioning of assembly lines. The acute dearth, too, of skilled specialists and the latter's consequent ability to move at will between plants made factory owners extremely anxious to placate and retain such people. The hardening of employers' attitudes came early in 1917 precisely because the circumstances propelling them towards concessions began to alter for the worse. On the eve of the February revolution they started to face the bleak prospect of being squeezed between financial deficits and spiralling wage demands.

As Table 14.xi reveals, the two main causes of economic stoppages continued to be issues of authority at work and wages.[16] In 1915 and

Table 14.xi: *Petrograd Province: Causes of Economic Strikes, by Industry, 19 July 1914–22 February 1917**

19 July–31 December 1914

Industry	A	H	Wk	Wg	Total	No.
Animal products	–	65.2	–	34.8	100.0	184
Chemicals	–	–	–	–	–	–
Communications	–	–	–	–	–	–
Food/drink/tobacco	–	–	–	–	–	–
Metals and machines	39.1	–	–	60.9	100.0	1,375
Mineral products	–	–	–	–	–	–
Paper and printing	–	–	–	–	–	
Textiles	–	–	–	100.0	100.0	800
Woodworking	–	–	–	–	–	
ALL INDUSTRIES	23.1	5.1	–	71.8	100.0	2,359

1915

Industry	A	H	Wk	Wg	Total	No.
Animal products	–	–	–	100.0	100.0	5,225
Chemicals	–	–	–	–	–	–
Communications	–	–	–	–	–	–
Food/drink/tobacco	60.0	–	6.7	33.3	100.0	1,500
Metals and machines	26.5	1.9	0.7	70.9	100.0	46,426
Mineral products	–	–	–	–	–	–
Paper and printing	–	–	–	100.0	100.0	370
Textiles	21.2	10.6	5.8	62.5	100.1	15,598
Woodworking	–	–	–	–	–	–
ALL INDUSTRIES	23.9	3.7	1.9	70.5	100.0	69,119

1916

	A	H	Wk	Wg		
Animal products	4.1	–	4.4	91.5	100.0	9,804
Chemicals	–	–	–	100.0	100.0	1,249
Communications	–	–	–	100.0	100.0	4,862
Food/drink/tobacco	–	32.8	10.1	57.2	100.1	4,580
Metals and machines	30.0	1.4	1.6	67.1	100.1	183,795
Mineral products	–	–	–	100.0	100.0	966
Paper and printing	8.7	8.7	8.7	73.8	99.9	8,530
Textiles	4.5	–	5.7	89.8	100.0	26,819
Woodworking	–	–	–	100.0	100.0	1,070
ALL INDUSTRIES	24.0	1.9	2.3	71.8	100.0	241,675

1 January–23 February
1917

	A	H	Wk	Wg		
Animal products	–	–	–	100.0	100.0	48
Chemicals	–	–	–	–	–	–
Communications	–	–	–	–	–	–
Food/drink/tobacco	–	–	–	–	–	–
Metals and machines	33.5	1.3	12.9	52.3	100.0	31,753
Mineral products	–	–	–	–	–	
Paper and printing	–	–	–	–	–	
Textiles	12.3		–	87.7	100.0	5,678
Woodworking	–	–	–	–	–	
ALL INDUSTRIES	30.2	1.2	10.9	57.8	100.1	37,479

*Percentages are based on the total number of strikers, where known.
Symbols: A – Authority strikes
          H – Hours
          Wk – Working conditions
          Wg – Wages

1916, 70 per cent of all economic disputes concerned matters of pay, whilst a further 25 per cent arose from challenges to the prerogatives of management. On the other hand, strikes involving conflicts over hours of work, sanitary and hygiene conditions were relegated by workers to the back burner.

The overwhelming predominance of wages as the occasion for walk-outs in Petrograd stood out in sharp relief to the pre-war years when such disputes constituted only a third of the total of economic strikes. On the other hand, the capital followed a national trend, as in

1915 60 per cent of all economic stoppages nationwide were occasioned by issues of pay, a share rising to 79 per cent the next year.[17] The city's heavy industrial sector mirrored almost exactly the general pattern (see Table 14.xi). In textiles, the share of the aggregate of strikes deriving from disputes over wages grew over time, from 63 per cent in 1915 to 90 per cent a year later precisely as the already low real earnings of mill hands fell even further. The reasons for the pre-eminent position occupied by wage demands have to be sought in the deteriorating working-class standard of living described in Chapter 11. As the factory inspectorate reported in the spring of 1916, 'the cause of the upsurge of economic unrest lies in the significant and universal rise in the cost of living'.[18]

Another striking dissimilarity from the pattern of pre-war labour unrest concerned disputes arising over hours of work and conditions at the workplace. Whereas between 16 per cent and 23 per cent of economic stoppages in the years immediately before the war had arisen over the length of the working day, in particular overtime, a mere 2–3 per cent of the total of economic disputes during the war were occasioned by this cause. The explanation for this difference cannot be the absence of overtime in the capital's wartime industries. Indeed, the reverse was the case. It may be that workers, increasingly desperate to make ends meet, could not object to a practice which helped raise incomes. A mere five disputes arose during the war in relation to overtime.

The proportion of wartime economic strikes attributable to issues of authority remained approximately comparable with pre-war levels, i.e. in the range of a quarter to a third of all disputes. This was especially so in the metalworking industry. In textiles, on the other hand, the share of such conflicts declined from 21 per cent in 1915 to 5 per cent in 1916. For certain groups of workers, mainly in metalworking and machine construction the untrammelled use of their powers by private owners, managers and factory personnel remained unacceptable practice. Among the possible motives for disruption to production under this heading, some gave rise to few protests.[19] Arrests of colleagues by the police, factory regulations, fines and searches were not major stimuli to unrest. A mere 6 per cent of wartime disputes in this category (as measured by the number of strikers) were occasioned by detentions, whilst the corresponding figure for fines was 2 per cent. In contrast to the years before hostilities, during the war the POZF abandoned its previous practice of exacting monetary penalties from the labour force for participation in political stoppages.

Far more than in the pre-war period, the hiring and firing of labour became the major reason for authority disputes. Between 19

July 1914 and 22 February 1917 45 per cent of all stoppages character-ised as 'authority at work' arose over the sacking of workers. This was a phenomenon almost exclusively of the capital goods sector, which furnished 38 of the 44 disputes. At the Mines factory of the Russian Society, for example, 1,000 employed in the new shrapnel department downed tools on 23 October 1915 to demand the rehir-ing of two sacked colleagues. And at Aivaz 3,000 walked out at the end of March 1916 to press for the taking back of ten reservists called up to the army after being given their books.[20] Employers remained as jealous of their prerogatives in this sphere of management as before. Thus 28 of the 44 such disputes ended in total defeat for the strikers. Five alone witnessed victory by the workers. It may be that during the war solidarity walk-outs in support of fellows held to have been unjustly dismissed acted as a surrogate for other forms of authority protest, such as fines or courteous treatment. Demands for the latter occurred in a mere 5 per cent of authority conflicts. The termination of a worker's livelihood was the most awesome power of management and the most likely to be abused, as well as having the greatest potential for misunderstanding and resentment. Dr Steffens has made the interesting suggestion that frequent job changes strengthened ties between plants and encouraged solidarity.[21]

In the same way supervisory staff became a greater target for workers' distrust in the war years. Almost a quarter of all authority disputes comprised demands for the sacking of workshop foremen or other management personnel. Clearly the data underestimate the disruptive consequences of the actions of foremen as many clashes arising over dismissals, fines and courteous treatment owed their origins to their decisions. Early in October 1915 at Aivaz the entire labour force refused to work, complaining that the Latvian foreman wrongly sacked workers and restricted hiring to his countrymen. When a youth was killed in an accident at the steel department of the Russian Society in November 1916, the entire plant of 5,000 ground to a halt to request the removal of the section head, whose negligence was held to be responsible for the fatality.[22] Plant staff found stout protectors in higher management. In engineering thirteen of nineteen such conflicts witnessed employers' triumphs.

Demands for worker representation were a relatively rare phenomenon in wartime. A mere five shutdowns, all in heavy industry, arose over this issue. In three, strikers requested the institution of factory elders and in two a rates commission of elected workers' representatives. In view of the involuntary demise of the trade unions after the outbreak of the First World War, it is scarcely surprising that no role was accorded them by strikers. What is noteworthy is the apparent lack of importance strikers attached to

Table 14.xii: Petrograd City: All Strikes, by Districts, 19 July 1914–22 February 1917 (% of total)

District	19 July–31 Dec. 1914 No.	%	1915 No.	%	1916 No.	%	1 Jan–22 Feb. 1917 No.	%	Total 19 July 1914–22 Feb. 1917 No.	%
Admiralty	–	–	–	–	–	–	–	–	–	–
Kazan	–	–	1	0.6	1	0.3	–	–	2	0.3
Kolomna	–	–	–	–	5	1.3	1	0.5	6	0.8
Lesnoi	–	–	–	–	–	–	–	–	–	–
Liteinii	–	–	–	–	3	0.8	3	1.6	6	0.8
Moscow	1	4.3	17	10.9	46	12.0	17	8.9	81	10.8
Narva	2	8.7	11	7.1	33	8.6	11	5.8	57	7.6
Neva	3	13.0	19	12.7	30	7.8	29	15.2	81	10.8
Okhta	–	–	5	3.2	2	0.5	3	1.6	10	1.3
Peterhof	–	–	8	5.1	8	2.1	7	3.7	23	3.1
Petrograd Side	–	–	17	10.9	79	20.6	44	23.0	140	18.6
Poliustrovo	–	–	–	–	1	0.3	–	–	1	0.1
Rozhdestvo	1	4.3	2	1.3	3	0.8	1	0.5	7	0.9
Spasskaia	–	–	–	–	–	–	–	–	–	–
Vasil'evskii Island	1	4.3	7	4.5	36	9.4	12	6.3	56	7.4
Vyborg	15	65.2	59	37.8	130	33.9	58	30.4	262	34.7
Staraia and Novaia Derevnia	–	–	4	2.6	5	1.3	2	1.0	11	1.5
Environs	–	–	6	3.8	1	0.3	3	1.6	10	1.3
TOTAL	23	99.8	156	100.5	383	100.0	191	100.1	753	100.0

matters of representation in 1915 and 1916 in view of the much greater weight given to elected forms of consultation in the 1905–7 revolution, between 1912 and 1914 and, of course, after the February revolution. Again, job security and incomes were given far higher priority. As was the case with courteous treatment, it may be surmised that workers felt such demands stood no chance of realisation in the exigencies of wartime with martial law in the capital.

The geographical incidence of labour unrest in Petrograd during the war was even more distorted than previously. Thus, whilst the districts of Vyborg and Petrograd Side together accounted for 36 per cent of the aggregate of all stoppages (political and economic) in the thirty months before the First World War, these two quarters were responsible for 53 per cent of the total in the two and a half years before the fall of the monarchy (see Table 14. xii). Indeed Vyborg alone carried almost the entire weight of the increase, Petrograd Side contributing a mere 1 per cent of the growth. In contrast, the role of the central city wards (Admiralty, Kazan, Kolomna, Liteinii, Rozhdestvo and Spasskaia) underwent a marked diminution from 13 per cent of the sum total of all disputes between January 1912 and 3 July 1914 to 3 per cent in the thirty months after the declaration of war. Three wards (Admiralty, Lesnoi and Spasskaia) recorded no walkouts whatsoever. The part played by the outer quarters (Lesnoi, Okhta, Poliustrovo, Staraia and Novaia Derevnia and the Environs) remained very limited, their share totalling just 4 per cent of all conflicts. After Vyborg and Petrograd Side, three districts each contributed approximately 11 per cent of the aggregate of wartime stoppages. As before, these were Moscow, Neva and Narva plus Peterhof (which constituted a single industrial unit). In contrast to the pre-war confrontations, however, Vasil'evskii Island's significance as a focus of unrest diminished considerably. This general geographical pattern was broadly similar for disputes of both a political and an economic provenance, although Vyborg and Petrograd Side were even more prominent in the former case. If these two quarters combined recorded 41 per cent of the aggregate of economic strikes, their share of the total of political protests was 20 per cent higher. As the analysis of the sectoral distribution of disturbances has shown, the key to the wartime geographically distorted pattern of stoppages lies in the predominant part played by the mainly privately owned, medium-sized machine construction and electrical equipment firms of Vyborg and Petrograd Side in all forms of action. Even in the second-rank districts (Moscow, Narva, Neva and Peterhof) those plants afflicted by shutdowns were almost exclusively in heavy industry. In all districts textiles and 'other industries' were far less prone to labour protests.

IV

During the war the strike movement in Petrograd remained the monarchy's most visible source of opposition. The peasantry superficially at least continued to stifle their aspirations for the gentry's estates. Peasants refrained from open expressions of discontent. Isolated incidents apart in the Baltic Fleet in the middle of 1915 and among the troops quartered in Vyborg district, the garrison of the capital seemed to be loyal. After the president of the Council of Ministers, I. L. Goremykin, and the Tsar had outmanoeuvred the newly formed Progressive Bloc in August–September 1915, the liberals' growing disenchantment with the prosecution of the war could not be translated into effective political opposition. Weakened as before by internal divisions and their refusal to contemplate a non-parliamentary course of action, the liberal parties remained effectively powerless to effect change peacefully. In this situation certain sections of the work-force of the capital remained the most immediate source of challenge to the regime's power. In the absence of legal labour organisations and the failure of all revolutionary parties to establish during the war the mechanisms to translate growing working-class disenchantment with the monarchy into organised channels via the revolutionary underground, strikes continued to be the most significant form of the labour movement.

But there were significant differences, as well as similarities, between industrial unrest in the capital in wartime and in the years immediately preceding the declaration of war. In the first place the incidence of disputes was far less. The number of strikes was only a fifth of the pre-war level and the number of strikers declined by half.[23] Nor did the capital and its province dominate the national strike movement to the same extent as before. Stoppages fell precipitately during the first year of hostilities due to the suppression of the trade unions, the labour and socialist press and the revolutionary underground, the potential mechanisms of mobilisation. The initial call-up by the military also took away many of the surviving activists, whilst the fear of being drafted into the army as a punishment for striking constituted a powerful deterrent. The initial rise in real wages for those employed in the defence industries and, for an undisclosed number, a sense of patriotic duty also acted as disincentives to striking for either political or economic motives. On the other hand, the number of strikes increased greatly from July 1915 onwards, particularly early in 1917. Politically inspired stoppages continued to occupy an unusually important position in wartime industrial disturbances in Petrograd, especially at the end of the monarchy's existence. In this respect the capital led all Russia. Whilst economic disputes accounted for far fewer strikes and strikers than political walk-outs, were more partial in nature and shorter in duration than before the war, participants therein were more likely either to have their demands met outright or to reach compromise settlements than previously. Walk-outs of an economic nature, furthermore, were occasioned much more by dissatisfaction with wages than hours or conditions of work. In heavy industry at least, however, managerial omnipotence was still questioned by skilled and experienced metalworkers who continued to seek some representative voice in issues affecting hiring and firing and rates of pay. All forms of protest, economic as well as political, were dominated to an even greater extent than before the war by workers in the metals and machinery industries, although the intensity of disputes in this sector was lower than earlier. This fact bears witness to the deep political alienation of key groups of skilled metalworkers in medium-sized, metalworking, machine construction and electrical equipment companies, primarily in the Vyborg and Petrograd Side districts. The most urbanised, politically aware and proletarianised workers still rejected the monarchical system and remained committed to revolution. A lowly second place in wartime discontent was occupied by textile workers, above all in politically inspired stoppages, although 1916 and the start of 1917 saw mill hands increasingly drawn into protest. To an even greater extent than pre-war all other branches of manufacturing and all other sectors of the capital's economy (commerce, service, transport) played an insignificant part in unrest. The unskilled and women, too, were far less involved than their numbers warranted.

As with the pre-war strike movement in St Petersburg, the incidence and intensity of political and economic stoppages within particular branches of production and districts of the city during the war were influenced by a range of variables, which themselves had been modified by the changes in the social complexion of the labour force brought about by the rapid expansion of the defence industries.

The earlier discussion of the respective roles of the metalworking and textile industries once more illustrates clearly that high concentration of workers in large units of production did not of itself guarantee the capacity to mobilise them in protest. Medium-sized engineering factories rather than gigantic enterprises were to the fore in all forms of protest in part precisely due to the fact that their intermediate size facilitated prompt mobilisation of employees.

Whilst female unskilled or semi-skilled wage earners in animal products, food processing and textiles had been increasingly drawn into the strike movement before the war, a reverse process occurred after July 1914, a major factor behind the lesser role played by these industries in wartime unrest. In the war years women workers were responsive for the most part merely to short-term economic goals, shunning political protest. The reasons for this development are diverse. On the one hand, in the aforementioned industries, as well as in woodworking there was a pronounced increase after 1914 in the employment of new female operatives. In food and tobacco, leather and shoes, chemicals and textiles many of these were in fact young girls aged 12 to 15. These women and girls were either rural migrants or the wives and daughters of factory workers called to the colours. There were, therefore, higher ratios than before of non-urbanised, unskilled or semi-skilled women, with little commitment either to the mill or plant or to their work. In textiles, too, periodic shortages of raw materials led to cuts in the working week and reductions in pay, a disincentive to striking. Furthermore, the decline in real incomes in all sectors of manufacturing other than in heavy industry and chemicals and the widening gap in differentials in wages between men and women were major hurdles to persuading female workers to participate in stoppages, particularly of a political nature.

Levels of skill and urban roots still remained basic determinants of strike militancy, with special reference to political stoppages. The medium-sized metalworking firms continued to hold the highest ratios of skilled, urbanised, more politically conscious proletarians because their specialists received more deferments from military service than other categories of workers. They also manufactured a range of munitions which included sophisticated machine tools and electrical equipment as well as shells and shrapnel. The new aircraft industry was particularly to the fore in political actions. Moreover, the extreme shortage of skilled metals operatives and their rising rates of real income until the autumn of 1916 placed them in a powerful bargaining position vis-à-vis their employers. The threat of the sack as a punishment for participation in political or economic protest carried little meaning for them. Women, who were employed in increasing numbers in these plants, were carried along by their male colleagues in all forms of strikes. In the gigantic state-owned plants the proportions of skilled, semi-skilled and unskilled were more unevenly distributed. The last two categories were more numerous. As was argued in Chapter 11, wartime mechanisation of production had not undercut the power of skilled workers in engineering. In the case of printing, as well as the restraining influence exercised by the compositors, two new factors acted to constrain its labour force from joining in strikes. The contraction of the trade after 1914 and the savage decline in real earnings of a third in the course of the war were major obstacles to action. Printers understandably were apprehensive of losing their jobs.

On the other hand, both wartime economic and political protest was as little consciously planned or co-ordinated by revolutionary groups as in the pre-war wave of disturbances. None of the socialist parties, including the Bolsheviks, succeeded in establishing permanent organisations of mass support during the war, or in providing effective leadership to the diffuse working-class discontent with the regime or much in the way of widespread agitation before the political walk-outs. The reports of the Okhrana likewise scarcely ever mention an organisational and initiative role on the part of the revolutionary parties, including the Bolsheviks, during economic disputes, with the exception of a few noteworthy conflicts such as the first Putilov walk-out in February 1916 or the New Lessner stoppage a month later. The numerical size of factory cells was exiguous for the most part, membership was in constant flux, and the network was distorted geographically. Indeed the extremely short duration of many wartime stoppages precluded the need for much in the way of organisational structures. On these occasions *ad hoc* workers' delegations fulfilled a representational function. On the other hand, in the autumn of 1915, and February 1916, the short-lived 'food commissions' or strike committees, in which revolutionary activists of all factions co-operated, may have played a role in individual stoppages. It is probably not completely accidental that heavy industry, above all in Vyborg, came to have in the spring of 1916 and again early in 1917, the highest concentration of revolutionary factory cells, if numerically thin, on the part of Bolsheviks, Menshevik internationalists, the Mezhraionka and SR-internationalists. Individual members may well have been to the fore as strike activists. In contrast, in the late spring and summer months of 1916 the factory underground of all socialist parties had been persecuted to vanishing point. On the other hand, general meetings remained an important means of communication and leadership for particular disputes.

In conclusion, it could be argued that the immediate threat posed to the dynasty by labour unrest in the capital in 1915 and 1916 was less than it seems at first sight. Wartime social changes within the labour force acted as a constraining factor upon protest. The sectoral, geographical and social basis of the strike movement was comparatively narrow, being confined by and large to skilled male workers in medium-sized metals and machine construction plants in Vyborg and Petrograd Side. This was particularly the case with reference to stoppages of a political nature. Only to the most limited extent was the movement broadening out its parameters by early 1917. The intensity of unrest, especially of politically motivated walk-outs, was far below pre-war levels, even in metalworking. Economic strikes were of shorter duration. The employers, too, displayed more sense in some ways in that they sought in effect to buy off discontent by rapidly conceding all or many of workers' demands. The strike and labour movements remained divorced from the liberal opposition.

Yet, paradoxically, the impact of the war on Petrograd undercut the regime's last foundations. As became increasingly clear from the autumn of 1916, the progressive deterioration of living standards and the incipient disintegration of normal industrial processes made it impossible for ministers, generals and industrialists alike to hope to continue containing rising political and economic disaffection merely by further pay rises. The months after the February revolution were to show that employers were increasingly unable to meet workers' inflated expectations concerning wages. And the break-up of the national economy, itself a consequence of the very success of industrial mobilisation by 1916, rendered more and more bleak the prospects of feeding, heating and employing the swollen Petrograd labour force. In these circumstances any new, sudden and severe interruption to food supplies could act as the trigger for an explosion of mass discontent. Although the forces of law and order had in fact coped relatively satisfactorily from their point of view in 1915 and 1916 with strikers, labour activists and socialists agitators alike, the most invidious and covert consequence of the war was the subterranean social changes in the Petrograd garrison, undermining its trustworthiness as an agent of repression. Late in February 1917 these three factors interacted to bring down the 300-year-old dynasty in under a week.

Chapter 15

GOVERNMENT, EMPLOYERS AND LABOUR DURING THE WAR

The endeavours of both Petrograd employers and bureaucrats to fashion a commonly acceptable approach to the myriad difficulties of factory life were gravely complicated during the war by the emergence of new rival sources of authority in the sphere of labour policy-making in the form of the Central War-Industries Committee (TsVPK) and the military authorities, in the person of the Minister of War as chairman of the Special Council for Defence (OSO) and the commander of the Petrograd Military District (PVO). A multiplicity of interests, therefore, became concerned with the formulation of governmental and industrialist response to wartime labour unrest, itself an important factor hindering the evolution of co-ordinated, efficacious, mutually agreed solutions. In many respects Petrograd employers successfully defended their economic interests during the war against the challenge of their economic competitors grouped around the TsVPK and the interventionist activities of the OSO, from which they were excluded. The TsVPK was to become an irrelevance so far as the Petrograd industrial and financial community was concerned in the distribution of contracts. The new state economic regulatory apparatus established in August 1915 brought the capital's manufacturers positive advantages in that it accorded them the highest priority after the army in the delivery of scarce resources of fuel and raw materials. The POZF, however, faced a potentially more dangerous threat to its exclusive control over factory affairs from the leadership of the TsVPK with its unacceptable schemes of labour reform. They also had to cope, as before the outbreak of hostilities, with continuing inter-ministerial differences concerning industrial relations, gravely exacerbated by the new responsibilities assumed by the military in this sphere. In the short run the POZF proved remarkably successful both in defending the *ancien régime* within the factories and in wrecking the liberal labour

programme of the TsVPK. In the long run this success was purchased at a very high price, namely the emergence of the factory
committee movement in 1917 and workers' growing responsiveness
in that year to the solutions propounded by the Bolsheviks. Even
more central to the regime's failure to direct the labour movement
along legal channels were the inconsistencies and uncertainties of the
approach to labour troubles on the part of officialdom and the military. Equivocation and confusion characterised official policy-making.
Bureaucrats and generals pursued in a half-hearted, inconsistent
manner three different, mutually exclusive courses at different times
in 1915 and 1916 – punitive repression, state-directed paternalism,
political and social reforms. The inevitable consequence was a series
of contradictory, *ad hoc* measures which never amounted to a properly conceived and sensibly executed labour programme.

I

THE WARTIME ECONOMIC REGULATORY APPARATUS

From at least the 1880s there had existed intense rivalry and distrust
between industrial circles in St Peterburg and Moscow. This reflected
their different and conflicting economic interests. In contrast to the
significant role played within the manufacturing sector of the capital
by heavy industry, with its growing dependence on the state for its
economic well-being and foreign infusions of capital, Moscow and
its hinterland constituted the textile centre *par excellence*. Its native-
born mill owners (many of them of serf origins and professing the
Old Believer faith) relied far more upon the domestic (i.e. peasant)
market and financed their operations from profits and indigenous
sources of capital. Moscow, too, was the Empire's commercial heart.
After 1905 a political dimension was added to the ingrained Muscovite
suspicion of bureaucratic St Petersburg and its foreign-connected
industrialists. Whilst the POZF had eschewed participation in State
Duma politics, a younger generation of Moscow textile manufacturers and merchants, imbued with the desire for political power
for the bourgeoisie, antagonistic to the continuation of gentry predominance over the political structure, enthusiastically plunged into
the new world of parliamentary politics. In 1912 they formed the
moderately liberal Progressist party, which secured 47 seats in the
elections to the Fourth State Duma. The leaders of the new party
were Peter P. Riabushinskii, from a well-established Moscow Old
Believer cotton manufacturing family, chairman of the Society of
Cotton Manufacturers of the Moscow Region and of the board of the
Moscow Bank, and his political ally, Alexander Konovalov, a cotton
manufacturer from Kostroma province and leader of the Progressist
faction in the Fourth Duma. Even before 1914 the Progressists were

strong supporters of a revived Great Russian nationalism, implacably anti-German and proponents of Russian expansion in the Near East. A further source of discord between the industrialist élites of the two capitals after the 1905 revolution lay in the foundation of the Association of Industry and Trade (AIT) in 1906 as the all-Russian representative organ of industry and commerce. The AIT was controlled from its inception by St Petersburg heavy industry and finance and the southern coal and steel entrepreneurs. Moscow's employers and merchants played a secondary role within it. The Muscovites disliked its location in the capital, its 'domination' by the syndicates, its apolitical 'petitioning' approach to the bureaucracy and its lack of institutional power. Labour policy, too, had become a divisive issue between the St Petersburg and Moscow industrial communities in the years prior to the war. In 1914, for example, the Moscow Society of Mill and Factory Owners recognised the existence of trade unions and proposed that May Day should be declared a holiday.[1]

The political and economic complexion of Moscow's industrialist community helps explain the fierce reaction of its textile magnates and merchants to the incompetent conduct of the war made manifest in the retreat of the Imperial army from the recent conquest of Galicia in May 1915. The poor performance of the troops and the alarmist reports of military inadequacies, in particular the shortage of shells, led the Muscovites to throw the blame upon the groups and institutions they had long disliked: an inept, corrupt bureaucracy, in particular the GAU for its failure to make effective use of native industry in its procurement policies; their Petrograd rivals who had monopolised hitherto the domestic contracts awarded by the GAU; the AIT for failing to press effectively for a far greater share for non-Petrograd private enterprise in munitions production. It is also probable that the Muscovites were spurred to action by the formation on 14 May 1915 of the clumsily titled Special Council for the Co-ordination of Measures to Guarantee the Supply of Munitions and other Material to the Army with the aid of private industry, as the minority representation of the manufacturing interest was restricted to the Petrograd financial–industrial oligarchy.[2] A mixture of motives, therefore – genuine anxiety for the safety of the country and a more forceful prosecution of the war, as well as a desire to share in profitable war orders – impelled Moscow industrialists to make a bid to wrest the leadership of the organisation of war production from both the central bureaucracy and Petrograd heavy industry.

The behind-the-scenes struggle for a fairer and wider distribution of contracts burst forth into the public domain at the ninth congress of the AIT held in Petrograd between 26 and 28 May 1915. The leaders of the AIT, the chairman, N. S. Avdakov (ex-head of the

Association of Southern Coal and Steel Producers and chairman of the coal syndicate Produgol) and vice-chairman V. V. Zhukovskii (head of the Polish Coal and Steel Association) were satisfied with the existing narrow representation for employers on the new Special Council. Accordingly they had omitted from the congress agenda the issue of wartime industrial mobilisation. Although E. L. Nobel', president of the POZF, was elected to the congress praesidium, not a single Petrograd factory owner spoke even once during the three days' debates. It may be summarised that the POZF relied either upon the AIT to defend its interests, or upon the bureaucracy to continue Moscow's exclusion from the Special Council. In the event their trust proved misplaced. Contemporary press reports agree that it was the non-scheduled, highly emotional speech of Peter P. Riabushinskii on the second day of proceedings which upset the plans of the AIT leadership. He made an impassioned plea for the organisation of the rear without suggesting any specific scheme. In fact his call for the 'self-mobilisation of industry' had been given concrete content in the Progressist mouthpiece, *Utro Rossii*, the day before; the paper recommended the creation of a central organ of Russian industry to assign state orders to factories, exercise control over their fulfilment, supply raw materials and fuel. After he had spoken, two other members of the Progressist party, M. M. Fedorov (chairman of the board of the Azov-Don bank) and Iu I. Poplavskii (vice-chairman of the Moscow Society of Mill and Factory Owners) proposed in concrete form the formation of the TsVPK with a network of regional and local war-industries committees. Yet if the Muscovites had won this skirmish, they had lost the particular battle. In order to secure the assent of the AIT to the proposal, its opponents had made two significant concessions. The TsVPK was to be located in Petrograd rather than Moscow and its arrangement was entrusted to the AIT.[3] The latter hastened to consolidate its victory. At the very first session of the TsVPK on 4 June 1915, Avdakov and Zhukovskii were elected chairman and vice-chairman. This decision effectively excluded proper representation for both Petrograd and Moscow, who were reduced to two and one member respectively.[4]

Moscow industrialists and provincial and small medium industry, which was well represented in the newly formed local war-industries committees, quickly condemned the new body as the instrument of the AIT and big industry for the monopolisation of military contracts.[5] The two groups formed a tacit alliance which swept to power at the First All-Russian Congress of War-Industries Committees held in Petrograd, 25–27 July 1915. As with the ninth congress of the AIT, there was a deafening silence from the capital's industrialists, who were represented by a mere three members of the POZF amongst the 1,000 delegates from 85 war-industries committees.[6]

Alexander Guchkov, who had been invited to join the praesidium (or Bureau) of the TsVPK on 16 June, was elected congress chairman.[7] His advent marked a significant shift within the TsVPK from the traditional 'apoliticism' of the AIT leadership to a more overtly political stance. As erstwhile leader of the splintered Octobrist party, former president of the Third State Duma, and scion of a Moscow wool-manufacturing dynasty with independent business interests (a board member and shareholder of the Rossiia Insurance Company, Skorokhod Shoes, the 'Novoe Vremia' publishing company), Guchkov was a professional politician. In a sense he had been searching for a new political role after the loss of his Moscow seat in the elections to the Fourth State Duma in the autumn of 1912 and the effective disintegration of the Octobrist party early in 1914.[8] Later events make clear that Guchkov felt he had found his new political platform in the TsVPK. Neither the praesidium of the congress nor the chairmanships of its sections included Petrograd representatives.[9] The protocols of the proceedings reveal that not a single Petrograd factory owner contributed to the discussions. The delegates plunged into the high politics of defence with calls for a responsible ministry from the Progressist leaders Peter P. Riabushinskii and E. I. Efremov. The proposal of the AIT leadership that the new TsVPK should include its existing praesidium (i.e. that the TsVPK should continue to be controlled by the AIT) met with fierce resistance. Riabushinskii openly insisted on their separation. The opposition carried the day. The final version of the statutes of the TsVPK reduced AIT representation to ten, whilst assigning four representatives each to the Moscow and Petrograd committees and two apiece to the regional committees.[10] The Moscow takeover was brought to a triumphant conclusion on the last day with the election of Guchkov as chairman and Konovalov as vice-chariman of the new TsVPK.[11]

The true focus of power in the TsVPK was to reside in its Bureau rather than its plenary sessions, which convened on only 25 occasions between August 1915 and September 1916 and ceased to be summoned thereafter. An analysis of the composition of the Bureau, which met 398 times from August 1915 to the close of the following year, and of the frequency with which members attended and contributed to debates, indicates that a mere nine individuals out of the twenty-four represented exercised predominant influence in the TsVPK. None acted as spokesmen for the interests of Petrograd industry. Moscow and the Progressists were indeed the dominating influence, with Guchkov, Fedorov, Konovalov and A. A. Bublikov, a Moscow industrialist and Progressist deputy in the Fourth Duma. A minority of the leadership of the Bureau derived from the AIT, namely N. N. Iznar (the representative of the Association of Baku oil producers in the capital), P. P. Kozakevich and Zhukovskii (who died in August 1916). Although Nobel' and Bachmanov of the POZF were members of the Bureau, they rarely attended its meetings.[12] In view of Guchkov's long absence from the TsVPK in the first half of 1916 due to a heart attack, leadership devolved upon Konovalov, assisted by N. N. Iznar and D. S. Zernov (a former director of the Petrograd Technical Institute). The supremacy of the Muscovites in the TsVPK ensured that the latter was to be as much concerned with high politics as with the economics of defence: the TsVPK, it was hoped, would serve as the agent of the Progressist bourgeoisie's bid for political power.[13]

The effective exclusion of the Petrograd employers from the TsVPK, the demise of the AIT as a potential instrument of protection for the capital's concerns as well as the avowedly political stance of the new TsVPK leadership, all combined to compel the city's industrialists and their financial backers to seek new methods of advancing their cause. Accordingly, in what can only be regarded as a pre-emptive move, the Council of the POZF resolved on 20 June 1915 to establish a Petrograd Regional War-Industries Committee. It minuted that the members of the Council should become the office-bearers of the new institution, which covered the provinces of Novgorod, Olonets, Petrograd, Pskov and Vitebsk.[14] Thus the president of the POZF, Nobel', became chairman of the new body and I. K. Komissarov acted as secretary to both. The council of the Petrograd Regional War-Industries Committee, elected at a plenum on 28 October 1915, was replete with stalwarts of the Council of the POZF.[15] Whatever the impact of the new organisation on the industrial life of the other northern provinces, it exerted little influence on the capital.

Eight months after the creation of the Petrograd Regional War-Industries Committee, the city's capital goods manufacturers made another effort to bypass the TsVPK. In alarm at the labour policies of the TsVPK and the OSO and the plan of GAU to construct new state arms-works, Petrograd industrialists joined forces with their central Russian and southern competitors to establish a distinctive organisation of heavy industry. At a congress convoked in Petrograd from 29 February to 1 March 1916 an Association of the Metalworking Industry was created. Moscow was conspicuous by its absence. The capital's armament firms were to the fore both in the number of delegates they sent (31 of the total of 95 present) and in the proportion of seats accorded them on the council of the new institution (nine of twenty-seven places). However, the congress rather oddly chose as chairman of the Association A. D. Protopopov, the Octobrist vice-president of the State Duma, a Simbirsk landowner and a clothing factory owner, who was also a director of Hartmann Engineering in Lugansk. Speakers at the gathering complained bitterly at the exclusion of the metalworking sector from the OSO, and subjected the TsVPK to trenchant criticism for its absorption of the AIT and its ill-judged attitude to labour. The Congress's resolution requesting the new organ's admission to the Special Councils was ignored by the government.[16]

Thus the relationship between the TsVPK and the capital's industrialists and their financial backers was to be one of mutual suspicion and distrust. If Petrograd employers' apparently studied indifference to the formation of the TsVPK concealed apprehensions that the new grouping might successfully challenge their hitherto dominant position in armaments manufacture, their misgivings soon proved to be unwarranted. After the TsVPK failed in August 1915 in its bid to become the directing force in the distribution of contracts – that role was preserved by the government for the state in the form of the Special Council for Defence – its overall contribution to the war effort was far from impressive. Dr Siegelbaum has calculated that between June 1915 and May 1916 the TsVPK received a mere 8 per cent of all wartime orders, whilst the Soviet historian A. G. Pogrebinskii offers the even lower estimate of 2–3 per cent.[17] The Petrograd Regional War-Industries Committee had disbursed contracts worth a mere 17 million roubles by 1916. Its textile and transport sections received none at all.[18] The capital's firms and banks bypassed both the TsVPK and its Petrograd subsidiary, receiving the vast bulk of their business from GAU through the intermediary of the OSO. To the horror of the POZF, however, the leaders of the TsVPK allowed political considerations to dictate their attitude to the working class. The TsVPK's adoption of a liberal labour policy posed a new and direct challenge to the interests and prerogatives of the city's factory owners and managers.

A further setback to the powerful position of the POZF came with the formation of the Special Council for Defence on 17 August 1915.[19] The single representative organ of Russian industry or commerce to be accorded membership of the OSO was the TsVPK (four places, occupied by Guchkov, Konovalov, Kozakevich and Zernov), whose delegates were far outnumbered by those of the legislature (the presidents of and nine elected members each from the State Council and State Duma) and the bureaucracy (ten representatives). Thus the OSO contained not even one representative of the Petrograd industrial and financial community.[20] The decisive role in the OSO, whose Council possessed only advisory functions, fell to its chairman, the Minister of War and the bureaucrats. The sweeping powers vested in the chairman by the statutes represented a potentially severe restriction on the freedoms of the capital's employers. The Minister of War as head of the new institution possessed the authority to order the sequestration of plants; requisitions; reviews of individual establishments with access to the accounts; the deter-mination of wage rates; and the removal of the directors and board members of private companies.[21] These articles foresaw a new and far-reaching intervention by the state (in effect the military author-ities) into the concerns of private enterprise. Under supplementary regulations of 10 September 1915, a Petrograd regional commission-er of the OSO was appointed in the person of General A. Myshlaevs-kii, a former chief of the General Staff, and a consultative organ, the Petrograd Factory Conference, was established covering six pro-vinces. The powers and duties of the regional commissioner were analagous to those of the chairman of the OSO.[22] At one level the exclusion of Petrograd industrialists from the OSO scarcely mat-tered. The latter continued to assign innumerable war contracts to the city's firms; Petrograd arms manufacturers' long-established and secret contacts with leading officials, as well as the proven expertise of their plants, stood them in good stead. As Chapter 11 has shown, the work of all four Special Councils established in the summer of 1915 proved of enormous benefit to the capital's industries in fur-nishing them as a top priority with dwindling resources of fuel and raw materials. But as with the TsVPK, the real danger to factory administrations' control of industrial affairs lay in the intervention of the OSO and the generals in labour relations.

II

EMPLOYERS AND THE 'LABOUR QUESTION': (I) THE CENTRAL
WAR-INDUSTRIES COMMITTEE

The latent economic and political antagonisms between the leader-ships of the POZF and the TsVPK imparted a special bitterness to the contradictory solutions propounded by the respective groups to the 'labour question' in 1915 and 1916. The conflict between them focused on the adoption by the TsVPK of a policy of 'class collabora-tion' between bourgeoisie and proletariat symbolised by the inclu-sion of factory workers' elected representatives in the war-industries committees, and the consequent attempted implementation of a pro-gramme of social reforms as apparent proof of the tangible benefits of the cessation of class warfare between capital and labour.

In view of the fragmentary evidence available to the historian, it is impossible to clarify satisfactorily the timing of the proposal, the reasons for, and identity of the proponents of, the admission by the TsVPK of workers' delegates to its central and provincial organs. At the Ninth Congress of the AIT in May 1915 neither a single contributor nor the final resolution proposing the establishment of the war-industries committees made any reference to the inclusion of representatives from the factories. The second meeting of the

TsVPK, which approved its statutes on 4 June 1915, passed over the issue in silence. At the First All-Russian Congress of War-Industries Committees at the end of July, the compromise leadership of the TsVPK put forward for consideration at the third session on 26 July a scheme of membership of the TsVPK excluding workers. This particular omission was criticised only by a solitary delegate from Novocherkassk. The Section on the Labour Question never discussed the matter. Yet, for reasons that remain obscure, at the seventh plenary gathering the next day the Bureau presented a revised version which accorded five places to workers' delegates. The change of mind could scarcely have been in response to public pressure from the floor of the congress. Indeed V. V. Zhukovskii openly opposed the proposal. The sole alteration made during the debate was to increase the number of labour representatives to ten.[23]

According to the normally well-informed Colonel A. P. Martynov, chief of the Moscow Okhrana, in a review of the Labour Groups written on 12 May 1916, 'the real initiative behind the formation of the Labour Groups lay with A. I. Konovalov'. The latter's consistent support from August 1915 for workers' representation in the war-industries committees lends substance to this supposition, but Konovalov never spoke at the First Congress – indeed it is not evident whether he even attended it.[24] On the other hand, in the spring of 1914, the Progressist leader had taken the first steps towards re-establishing the links between the radical intelligentsia and the working class, sundered after 1905, by bringing together Progressists, Left Kadets, Mensheviks, Popular Socialists and Bolsheviks in a short-lived Moscow Information Committee.[25] Although A. Guchkov had confined his political opposition before the war to the legal channel of parliamentary pressure on the regime, by the summer of 1915 the former Octobrist chairman, excluded as he was from the Fourth State Duma, seems to have concluded that the force of public opinion as manifested in the public organisations would provide the requisite extra-parliamentary weight to the Progressive Bloc's bid for power. In view of the apparent opposition of the AIT members of the TsVPK to the admission of workers to their institution, it may be surmised that Guchkov and Konovalov were instrumental in forcing the desired alteration to the composition of the TsVPK.

Moreover, the method of securing working-class attendance at the TsVPK was far from being self-evident as, in the words of Konovalov at the plenary session of the Committee on 24 August 1915, 'the labour force possessed at present no organisation with whose aid such representation might be realised'. In the absence of the suppressed trade unions, Guchkov and Konovalov hoped that the sickness insurance funds would act as the agency for the workers' choice of candidates. The refusal of the *kassy* constrained the leaders of the TsVPK to adopt the more risky course politically of attempting themselves to persuade Petrograd industrialists, the government and the generals to allow direct elections from the factories.[26]

Although the leaders of the TsVPK permitted the ten workers' delegates to constitute an independent Labour Group in December 1915 with its own premises, an initial budget of 1,725 roubles and the right to form commissions including outside experts, they also exerted pressure to circumscribe the Labour Group's more overtly political actions in order to deprive the authorities of a pretext for eliminating working-class representation. When at the first plenum of the TsVPK attended by the Labour Group on 3 December 1915, K. A. Gvozdev, the Group's leader, read out the political resolutions passed at the election meeting of 29 November, Guchkov reminded the newcomers that, as the war-industries committees were not political organisations, the political issues raised in the declaration were beyond their competence. In the preparations for the Second Congress of War-Industries Committees, the Bureau received and made several amendments to the reports prepared by the Labour Group. It also prohibited the latter from distributing to delegates the political resolutions of 29 November 1915 and excised all reference to them from the published proceedings of the Congress.[27] After a session of the Bureau on 18 March 1916, henceforth all correspondence between the Labour Group and state and public institutions had to be forwarded to the secretariat of the TsVPK which opened and registered its contents. On occasions the Bureau held back communications, the tenor of which it disapproved. The Bureau attempted to censor the third bulletin issued by the Labour Group; the ensuing bitter recriminations long delayed the publication of issue number four.[28]

It is instructive to note that the initiative of Konovalov did not meet with the sympathy of his political colleagues in the Moscow War-Industries Committee. Peter P. Riabushinskii, who had failed to endorse the plan for labour representation at the First Congress, S. N. Tretiakov, I. I. Poplavskii and Iu P. Guzhon (of the Moscow Society of Mill and Factory Owners) rejected the entire programme of the Labour Groups. The direct intervention of Konovalov alone ensured a compromise whereby an independent labour sub-department was formed within the department of industrial labour of the Moscow War-Industries Committee.[29]

Several assumptions underlay the labour policies of Guchkov and Konovalov, and the distinct minority in the industrial community supporting them. In the first instance social peace – the absence of domestic class conflict – was the prerequisite for the successful mobilisation of all strata for victory over Germany. 'Only by the friendly unity of social forces . . . ,' Guchkov wrote in an open letter to K. A. Gvozdev on 11 March 1916, 'can we save our motherland from danger'. 'The war-industries committees,' emphasised the journal of the Moscow War-Industries Committee, 'are based upon the broad social principle of the co-operation of all elements of the organised rear, including the workers'. The proletariat, therefore, could not be excluded, the organ believed, because 'of the connection between the victory of Russia and the interests of the,labouring masses'. It was axiomatic, as far as the leaders of the TsVPK were concerned, that, in Guchkov's words, 'I believe in the patriotism of the working class – defeatism is alien to it'.[30] In the second instance, the two Muscovites were profoundly alarmed by the revival of the strike movement, not because they interpreted it as the harbinger of a Bolshevik-led revolution or as sounding the death-knell of Russian capitalism (as Soviet historians claim), but because of the consequent disorganisation of war production and lost working days.[31] In a careful evaluation of the causes of labour unrest, a memorandum written by Konovalov at the request of the regional conference of war-industries committees on 23–25 May 1916 ascribed the upsurge in stoppages not only to inflation and deteriorating economic conditions but also to the working class's lack of political rights. In the absence of their own free institutions and of authoritative leaders, workers sought a remedy for their grievances in disorganised, elemental strikes. The solution to this problem was not to be found in repression. The path to peaceful industrial relations, he emphasised, lay in the concession of genuine trade unions, a system of arbitration and a programme of social reform. 'The presence of labour organisations would ensure conflicts took place within well-defined limits.' His conclusion must have made unpleasant reading for bureaucrats and Petrograd industrialists alike. 'The thought that the future of Russia is closely linked to the future of the working class must become the guiding principle of the activity of the Russian state.'[32]

In addition to the publicly expressed and genuine desire for the restoration of industrial harmony in the factories, Konovalov, and perhaps Guchkov, was playing a concealed and more dangerous political game, integral to which were the Labour Groups. In a series of devastating exposés of the left-liberal machinations, Colonel Martynov, in his reports of the spring of 1916 to his superiors, revealed that the Progressists and Left Kadets, disillusioned with the Progressive Bloc and the legal, parliamentary form of opposition, had resolved to revive the Union of Unions of 1905 through the formation of all-Russian peasant, labour, co-operative and commercial–industrial unions as well as a central food supply organ, which, joining forces with the public organisations, would be able to put overwhelming extra-parliamentary pressure upon the government and Tsar in order to compel them to make concessions, as had happened in October 1905. At a secret conference of the left-wing liberals during the congress of the All-Russian Union of Towns in March 1916, Konovalov explicitly stated that in his view the purpose of the Labour Groups was to revive working-class institutions and to convoke an All-Russian Labour Congress which would establish 'an all-Russian union of workers . . . as it were, a soviet of workers' deputies'. In this way the pressure of the working-class movement would be brought to bear on Tsardom. It seems inconceivable that the proponents of this course of action would have suggested it if they dreaded a revolutionary explosion.[33]

As early as the first sessions of the newly formed department of labour supply of the TsVPK in June 1915, at the suggestion of the Kadet A. I. Shingarev, a sub-committee was created to draft bills guaranteeing the freedom of trade unions and *kassy*.[34] However, the formulation of concrete measures of labour reform did not occur until after the establishment of the Labour Group of the TsVPK in December 1915. With the support of Konovalov and Guchkov, the latter drew up a programme comprising *inter alia* the convocation of an All-Russian Labour Congress, the creation of an All-Russian Labour Exchange, arbitration chambers and factory elders. These proposals received the imprimatur of the Second All-Russian Congress of War-Industries Committees thereby becoming, theoretically, the official policies of the organisation.

Whatever the motives of Konovalov and the Labour Group for the summoning of an All-Russian Labour Congress, the TsVPK plenum on 21 December 1915 lent whole-hearted, if somewhat sceptical, support to the concept. It also accepted the arguments advanced by the Labour Group in favour of periodic meetings with its constituents. At the start of January 1916 Konovalov wrote to the Minister of the Interior, A. N. Khvostov, and the commander of the PVO, General Prince N. V. Tumanov, seeking permission for such gatherings on the twenty-fourth of that month. The authorities successfully sabotaged the plan by imposing the unacceptable conditions of the attendance of the police and the imposition of censorship on the reports of prospective speakers.[35] When Konovalov and Gvozdev visited B. V. Stürmer, in his capacity as Minister of the Interior on 8 April, they encountered the same ultimatum from him as from his predecessor. A similarly effective obstacle was deployed a third time when Konovalov proposed to arrange a private gathering of the Labour Group with its electors on 5 June. Although the Second

Congress of War-Industries Committees passed without debate a motion approving the convocation of an All-Russian Labour Congress, ministers and police, fully appraised of the ulterior designs of its advocates, prohibited it.[36]

As employers and workers alike suffered from the malfunctioning of the labour market, both expressed interest in the creation of a central network of urban and rural labour exchanges. In addition the Labour Group was insistent upon the participation of equal numbers of elected representatives from industrialists and workers on existing and future municipal labour exchanges. At the Second Congress, P. P. Kozakevich, chairman of the department of labour supply, presented a report embodying these proposals, as well as a call for the free development of trade unions and industrial organisations. All these desiderata were included in an appropriate resolution. Delegates, however, in effect condemned the scheme to death at the outset by accepting that it should be implemented by means of a parliamentary bill: neither the Ministry of Trade and Industry nor the State Duma showed the slightest inclination to accommodate the wishes of the Congress.[37]

The gauge of class collaboration was intended to be the establishment of arbitration chambers. The purpose of these new organs, according to the Moscow War-Industries Committee, was 'to guarantee lasting social peace'. As Konovalov emphasised in a letter to the Minister of War, A. A. Polivanov, on 10 March 1916, 'repressive measures taken against workers who stop work ... do not achieve their aims', whereas the proposed mediatory institutions 'would obviate conflicts'.[38] Although Guchkov had made such a proposal in the OSO on 12 December 1915, the Bureau of the TsVPK considered it more appropriate that a concrete plan should be drafted in the first instance by the new Labour Group, as the scheme would be unworkable without workers' acquiescence. The blueprint presented to the Second Congress and passed by it embodied the initial creation in Petrograd of an arbitration chamber comprising eight elected industrialist and eight labour members (the latter chosen by the Labour Groups of the TsVPK and Petrograd Regional War-Industries Committee in the absence of trade unions). This body, at the invitation of both sides in a dispute, could set up an arbitral court, whose decisions would be non-binding. As the legislative process involved a lengthy procedure, the Labour Group envisaged the establishment of a temporary arbitration chamber attached to the TsVPK. However, at the Second Congress the Bureau carried an amendment, against the protests of the Labour Group, that in the first instance the OSO should use its powers to set up the new institution.[39]

Despite the insistent pleading of the Labour Group, the Bureau of the TsVPK followed the instructions of the Second Congress by dispatching its resolution to the OSO, although the latter had evaded the issue in December 1915 by its declaration that the matter fell within the competence of the Ministry of Trade and Industry (MTP). In the absence of action by the MTP and under pressure by the delegates to the third regional conference of war-industries committees, 4 July 1916, the Bureau proceeded to take the initial steps towards the formation of an optional ('facultative') arbitration chamber attached to the TsVPK.[40] The overwhelming repudiation of this cardinal element in the reform programme of the TsVPK by Petrograd and other industrialists (discussed in the next section) ensured not only that no more was heard of the scheme but also highlights how divorced the leaders of the TsVPK were from the vast majority of their own constituency.

Perhaps aware at the outset of the difficulties of securing the employers' consent to the creation of arbitration chambers, the Labour Group and the luminaries of the TsVPK endeavoured with more success to secure wider recognition by factory owners of the 1903 law on factory elders, maybe seeing in this proposal the lowest common denominator on which agreement might be possible. Thus at the Second Congress of War-Industries Committees the Labour Group introduced a motion, passed in an amended form, demanding that 'the TsVPK take measures to ensure a constitutional regime in the factories', including 'the institute of factory elders'. After deleting from the proposal any reference to a 'constitutional regime' in plants, delegates passed an appropriate resolution. At the above-mentioned third conference of regional war-industries committees, those attending approved non-obligatory 'model statutes of factory elders', which, drafted by the TsVPK, set the minimal period of electoral qualification for an elder at one month's employment in the factory.[41]

In the light of the TsVPK leadership's commitment to social reform and the search for a political alliance with the working class, it is scarcely surprising that the plenum of the TsVPK rejected the government's draft bill of 10 August 1915 on the militarisation of labour or that the Second Congress of War-Industries Committees condemned a revised version of the measure. Memoranda were dispatched to the Council of Ministers expressing the opposition of manufacturers, who were apprehensive lest 'enserfment' of workers would aggravate industrial relations by preventing the free transfer of labour between factories. 'It is quite erroneous to believe,' the document warned bureaucrats, 'that the militarisation of plants will end labour disputes'. Objections were also raised to the proposed intervention by the state under the measure in the sphere of hiring and firing and the determination of wage rates.[42]

III

EMPLOYERS AND THE 'LABOUR QUESTION': (II) THE POZF

Although the TsVPK encountered great obstruction on the part of the authorities to its liberal labour policies, the *coup de grâce* which ensured their abject failure was administered by fellow industrialists. The POZF put up the fiercest and ultimately successful resistance to the endeavours of the TsVPK to introduce a pacific regulation of factory relations. Petrograd's employers bitterly resented the incursion by their detested economic Muscovite rivals into what they regarded as their exclusive sphere of competence. The relationship, on the other hand, between the POZF and the civilian and military authorities during the war with respect to the handling of industrial disputes was more complex. The factory owners were prepared to use the PVO's support for their authoritarian attitude towards strikes and to let the military authorities shoulder the responsibility for unpopular, if effective, means of repression. They were not prepared to go further and permit the generals to intervene in the day-to-day handling of labour affairs.

In the light of the POZF's long-established hostility to any form of independent working-class organisations and of its distrust from the outset of the TsVPK, it is difficult to explain the apparent paradox of its voluntary acceptance of the scheme of labour representation in the war-industries committees. The minutes of the two meetings of the Council which discussed the issue (11 August and 22 September 1915) cast no light at all upon the reasoning of the employers. The first session merely resolved that the elections should be arranged through the medium of the *kassy*. When this project collapsed, it would seem that no gathering of the Council was convoked to fashion the Society's response to the new plan for direct factory elections. The solitary member of the POZF to declare outright hostility to the general elections of workers' representatives, in public at any rate, was its secretary, I. K. Komissarov. It is possible that the POZF was simply indifferent to the whole endeavour, although this seems rather unlikely. It may be that Petrograd factory owners believed that resistance to an arrangement which had secured the approval of the Council of Ministers and the Ministry of War would be pointless. If industrialists had been strangely mute on this occasion, their opposition to the TsVPK programme of labour reforms was soon swift to emerge, highly vocal, and deadly.[43]

The centrepiece of the TsVPK labour platform was the attempt to establish arbitration chambers. The endemic suspicion entertained by the POZF towards its rivals erupted in force around this issue. On the eve of the Second Congress of War-Industries Committees, two joint sessions of the Councils of the POZF, which prior to the war had opposed a similar project emanating from the Council of Ministers, again rejected the concept as 'untimely' on the ironic grounds that workers would not accept the tribunals' decisions as no trade unions existed to secure their members' compliance. At the Congress V. V. Diufur and B. A. Efron argued that the TsVPK rather than the POZF should assume responsibility for the election of industrial delegates to the chamber, and raised objections to the workers' representatives being chosen by the Labour Groups. 'You cannot,' Efron bluntly warned the assembly 'force the industrialists to attend'. In a further discussion of the scheme in the Councils of the POZF in March 1916, it was turned down by a conclusive vote of thirty-two to seven. A separate meeting of large private engineering firms castigated chambers as 'completely inappropriate and harmful'.[44] The POZF proceeded to inflict the death-blow by rejecting Guchkov's request to start on the election of its representatives to an optional arbitration chamber attached to the TsVPK. The opposition of the capital's employers secured powerful backing from the Association of the Metalworking Industry in August 1916 and the Moscow Society of Manufacturers and the Moscow Stock Exchange Committee. As in the past, Moscow's Progressist business leaders' bold claims to represent a broad section of industrialist opinion had been shown once more to be false.[45]

The POZF, moreover, revealed scant sympathy for another of the TsVPK's liberal notions, viz., the broader application of the hitherto neglected 1903 law on factory elders. The Council of the Society, meeting on 29 March 1916, reiterated its traditional hostility to the institution. The POZF and its sister grouping in Moscow both objected to the 'model statutes of factory elders' approved at the third conference of regional war-industries committees in the summer of 1916. On this issue at least, however, the official leadership of the capital's organised industrialists did not reflect unanimity of opinion. It is evident that some Petrograd firms could see no harm in granting such a minor concession. Indeed in the autumn of 1915 a meeting of 35 Petrograd companies' representatives had agreed to concede any requests by workers for the election of elders. A year later four firms in heavy industry (Aivaz, Erickson, Petrograd Pipes and Siemens and Halske) and one cotton mill had consented to the introduction of elders.[46]

A fundamental, if covert, objection on the part of Petrograd employers towards the proposed arbitration chambers was the potential challenge they posed to factory managements' unimpeded control of all matters within their plants. They realised that an unspoken assumption behind the plan was the removal of all restrictions on the existence of genuinely independent trade unions, towards which the POZF displayed an unremitting hostility during the war. It continued to reject interference by elected labour delegates in any sphere of management prerogatives. Factory directors undoubtedly welcomed the complete absence of intervention in disputes by the few, powerless, surviving trade unions in 1915 and 1916. This stance of principled opposition was upheld in a dispute at New Lessner's shell department in July 1915. When the company board seemed prepared to concede the demand of 700 operatives for the election of workshop representatives to participate with management in the review of rates of pay, an extraordinary general meeting of the POZF's Engineering Section, convoked in great haste, rejected such a radical step. 'We must fight,' warned the managing director of Neva Shipyards, 'against the pretensions of workers by all means'.[47]

In the same way, Petrograd manufacturers sought to maintain their grip on the sickness insurance funds and to defend the rights imposed by the statute of 1912. Thus, when in May 1915 the directors of the Swedish-controlled Erikson electrical equipment company proposed to renounce the firm's chairmanship of the executive board of the factory's *kassa* and its power to appoint management delegates, the POZF's insurance commission voted by fifteen votes to three to reaffirm the Society's policy that factory owners 'retained the leadership of the sickness funds'. A year later, on 12 July 1916, the Council reconfirmed this decision. The employers' organisation likewise distrusted the efforts of some funds' executive boards to secure premises outside factory grounds. As A. A. Bachmanov, the Lessner director, warned his colleagues, managers would be unable to supervise meetings in external surroundings and the fund boards could become 'secret committees' discussing political and social issues (the very purpose of revolutionary activists in proposing this course of action).[48] The unanimity of employers, however, broke down over the new issue of the endeavours of individual sickness funds in 1915 and 1916 to pool their resources to found district hospitals. A session of the insurance commission on 10 February 1915 failed to come to any firm conclusion. Eighteen months later a circular was forced to concede that the construction of hospitals by funds was legal. Yet in February 1916 the insurance commission condemned unreservedly the plans of some *kassy* boards to transfer medical treatment from the responsibility of the management to the workers themselves.[49]

In the matter of the TsVPK's schemes for arbitration chambers and other labour reforms, in their handling of trade unions and *kassy*, the POZF had found itself at one with the majority of officialdom (excluding the bureaucrats of the MTP). These issues had given rise to no complications in the relations between Petrograd industrialists and the authorities. The re-emergence of the strike movement in the summer of 1915, however, brought to the fore once more the same divisiveness between the two sides as in the years immediately prior to the war. Although the POZF discovered a new source of support for its firm stance in labour disputes in the form of the military authorities, it also quickly found to its dismay that its new allies in fact entertained an ambivalent attitude towards labour. Whilst the POZF was prepared to entertain the greater intervention of outside agencies than before the war in its hitherto exclusive control over affairs behind factory gates, it sought to restrict such interference to the sphere of industrial disputes. Beyond that limit, it struggled hard and with success to prevent the military from meddling in day-to-day labour matters.

As the strike movement revived in July 1915 after a year of industrial peace, Petrograd factory administrations had recourse to their standard measures of repression against stoppages of an economic character – closure of plants and sacking of workers, arrests of strikers, blacklists and filtration of the labour force on the return to work. In the course of 53 of the 321 economic disputes in the city between the declaration of war and the February revolution, employers in heavy industry, textiles, the leather, food and printing sectors shut down their establishments and paid off the labour force as soon as it downed tools. Moreover, there were twenty-three instances during stoppages in engineering and six in other branches of production when managers prevailed on the police to arrest 'ringleaders' or refused to rehire strikers at the end of a conflict. After a strike at the Mines Factory of the Russian Society in October 1915, for example, 160 were not rehired; the March 1916 dispute at New Lessner ended with 800 losing their jobs; at Russian-American Rubber 350 women were refused readmittance at the close of a pay dispute in February 1916. In the course of the second stoppage at Putilov in February 1916 150 were arrested.[50] On the other hand firms refrained from imposing the type of punitive lock-out to which a minority had resorted in the 1912–1914 period, presumably because the exigencies of wartime production rendered a lengthy cessation of output too unprofitable and ran the risk of provoking the wrath of the military authorities.

The first serious interruptions to munitions production in the city's manufactories in the summer of 1915 brought the POZF new and unexpected support for its hardline stance from the Petrograd Military District. The earliest instances of military intervention in industrial relations occurred early in July 1915. In the course of wage disputes at Erikson and Neva Shipyards, in which the POZF's Engineering Section had refrained from interference, General A. P. Frolov, commander of the PVO, broke the two strikes on his own initiative by posting up in the plants warnings that all refusing to return to work would be sacked and all reservists with military deferments would be recalled to the colours.[51] This unexpected act did not lead at once to a co-ordinated response on the part of industrialists and the PVO, as was revealed by their disjointed reaction to the stoppages occurring in the capital between 17 and 20 August (16,000 ceased working in 18 plants) in protest against the shootings of workers in the textile towns of Ivanovo-Voznesensk and Kostroma in the Central Industrial Region. At two sessions of the Engineering Section of the POZF on 19 and 21 August members could not agree on either a request to the TsVPK to publish an appeal to the strikers or a lock-out. A solitary individual (A. D. Lebedev, the owner of a sawmill) urged the latter course on his colleagues: his proposal evoked no sympathy. A mission was dispatched to General Frolov to ascertain his views. Having been warned by the Special Council for Defence to exercise the greatest restraint in the choice of measures against industrial stoppages, the head of the PVO refused to express an opinion to the delegation. As a consequence no punitive action was taken.[52] These hesitations and doubts quickly disappeared when the first large-scale walk-outs of a political nature took place in Petrograd between 2 and 6 September 1915 in opposition to the arrests of 30 labour activists at Putilov and the proroga-tion of the State Duma: 79,000 left their benches.[53] The POZF again sent a deputation to General Forlov, this time bearing a memoran-dum impressing upon him the necessity of repeating the stern measures deployed in July. The industrialists pushed at an open door. On 4 September the PVO issued a public warning that plants would be closed and reservists would lost their exemptions in the event of the non-resumption of work within 24 hours. The threats alone were a sufficient inducement to persuade strikers to return, and did not have to be implemented.[54]

After the events of the summer of 1915, Petrograd factory owners were apparently content to let the military authorities shoulder the responsibility for unpopular, if effective, measures of repression against strikes and welcomed their backing for the POZF's hardline stance towards labour troubles. They made no protest at the PVO's resort to the threat of or the actual call-up of worker reservists in order to smash stoppages of a political or non-economic character.

Relying upon the military to wield the threat of losing military exemption as the most powerful, if ultimate, weapon to break strikes, the POZF leadership, in stark contrast to the pre-war years, devoted remarkably little consideration to discussion of the appropriate, co-ordinated reaction to labour disputes. Nor did indi-vidual firms resort to the imposition of fines or the adoption of lock-outs. The Council of the POZF found it unnecessary (in 1916) to react in any way to the likelihood of unrest on the anniversaries of

Bloody Sunday, the Lena massacre and May Day. When some 89,000 downed tools between 17 and 21 October 1916 in anger over food shortages, the Council felt compelled to admit the justness of workers' bitterness and decided to show discretion by refraining from any response.[55]

The POZF's espousal of what may be termed the 'military solution' to the labour question found clearest expression in its considerable attention to and sympathy for schemes concerning the militarisation of labour, either as a device to remedy the lack of specialists or as an instrument to forestall stoppages of work. As early as January 1915 the Engineering Section proposed the application of military discipline and courts martial to factory workers. The New Lessner and Erikson strikes at the start of July constrained the Section to vote in favour of the suggestion of L. B. Krasin (the defensist Bolshevik managing director of Siemens-Schukkert) of setting up a commission to draft a parliamentary bill for the militarisation of all factories working for state defence. It fashioned its own plan in contradiction to that of the MTP. The POZF-outlined legislative proposal differed significantly from the governmental project in that the former deprived the factory inspectorate of the strengthened powers, envisaged for it by the latter, to intervene in labour disputes.[56] The Petrograd industrialists' enthusiasm for the militarisation of labour constituted another source of friction between them and the TsVPK with its dislike of such a measure.

The POZVF's benevolent attitude towards intervention by the PVO in industrial relations did not encompass spheres of action beyond threats to the continuity of production. The two sides fell out over the military's unexpected meddling in the determination of rates of pay. The issue first arose during a strike for a rise in wages at the New Lessner plant at the start of July 1915. To the horror of the management, a commission from the staff of the Sixth Army, fortuitously visiting the plant, took the strikers' side and browbeat the director into conceding a 'wartime allowance'. In the OSO, industrial representatives at once indignantly rejected as 'irrational any influence by the government upon the establishment of rates of pay'. The action of the Sixth Army proved to be the harbinger of stronger pressure upon employers, as on 11 July General Frolov insisted that they improve pay 'as their profits were high'. To the relief of the POZF, thereafter the military authorities lapsed into silence on this issue for several months. The matter arose again as a consequence of the two Putilov strikes in February 1916. In its response to these events the State Duma called upon the OSO to utilise its powers to regulate the size of wages. The parliamentary representatives in this body, led by the Kadet leaders P. N. Miliukov and A. I. Shingarev, persuaded a majority to vote in favour of the principle on the grounds that, in Shingarev's words, 'such a measure will prevent working-class disturbances arising out of economic necessity'. When the Supervisory Commission of the OSO renewed the proposal two months later, the industrialists repudiated the suggestion. There is no evidence that the OSO ever intervened to regulate wage rates in the capital.[57]

IV

BUREAUCRATS, GENERALS, AND THE 'LABOUR QUESTION'

In the attempted formulation of a co-ordinated response to the labour movement and industrial unrest during the war on the part of Petrograd industrialists, the new TsVPK, the military authorities, and central officialdom, fundamental responsibility lay with the latter. In the last resort ministers and the Tsar alone could take the political decisions required to alter endemic state distrust of and hostility towards legal working-class organisations and make the requisite concessions. But the outbreak of war left high bureaucrats no longer master in their own house. On the one hand, the bifurcation of authority in general between the government and *Stavka* meant that the capital, including the Imperial administration, being in the theatre of military action, became subordinate in all affairs to the commander of the Sixth Army (Northern Front) and to his representative, the commander of the Petrograd Military District. Moreover, the Minister of War, as chairman of the OSO, was endowed with formidable, theoretical powers of intervention in all aspects of factory life. Ministers and officials, therefore, had to take into account in policy-making the views of the generals and endure independent actions by military men taken without consulting the Council of Ministers. On the other hand, the leaders of the TsVPK also entertained pretensions in the sphere of industrial relations with a liberal programme of social reforms abhorrent to the majority of officials. The divergence of views among and within ministries, the existence of several competing agencies with contradictory goals and the intermittent nature of the interference by the generals in the arena of labour relations rendered the fashioning of a consistent, coherent and carefully considered labour strategy almost impossible. The official approach to industrial problems was marked by equivocation, confusion, inconsistency and uncertainty. In the absence of mutually agreed solutions bureaucrats and generals pursued contradictory, essentially *ad hoc* measures. The official labour policies of the regime, or perhaps more accurately their absence, remained the fundamental blockage to the evolution of a legal labour movement and the incorporation of labour into Tsarist society.

The prevarication at the centre of wartime official policy-making in the field of industrial relations and the variety of action taken do not render easy the historians' task of exposition. At the risk of imposing even a minimal pattern on the bewildering kaleidoscope of initiatives taken and plans considered and rejected, three trends at least may be discerned – political and social reforms, punitive repression and state-directed paternalism. Officials and the military pursued all three, mutually exclusive courses in a thoroughly inconsistent and half-hearted manner.

In the first place, the possibility of a radical change of direction in the state's labour policies depended on the course of 'high politics' during the war. For a brief time, during the political crisis of the summer of 1915, the likelihood of such a volte-face did not seem impossible. After the Tsar had replaced the most reactionary ministers by more reasonable men in June 1915, a majority within the Council of Ministers emerged in favour of close collaboration with moderate elements within society and concessions to the liberal opposition, in particular to the demand for a 'ministry of confidence'. This group centred on the new Minister of War, A. A. Polivanov, who had worked closely before the war with the erstwhile Octobrist leader Guchkov and the Third State Duma's Commission on State Defence; the new Minister of Internal Affairs, Prince N. B. Shcherbatov; and A. V. Krivoshein, the Minister of Agriculture, the *éminence grise* of the Council.[58] A potentially less authoritarian attitude towards labour began to manifest itself in the highest spheres.

Political, as much as economic, considerations, for example, induced the emergent 'liberal' majority within the Council of Ministers to incline towards sanctioning both the statutes of the TsVPK and the proposed election of workers' representatives to it. Such an unprecedented concession, it was hoped, would be interpreted by the liberal opposition as an earnest of ministers' desire for fruitful joint work with moderate society in the course of better prosecution of the war. Thus Polivanov defended the scheme to his colleagues in the session of the Council held on 24 August 1915 on the grounds that 'the mobilisation of industry is impossible without the co-operation of the workers'; 'it would be most careless,' he chided, 'to stir up the workers by denying them participation in a guiding organisation'. Despite the opposition of the outright reactionary minority of ministers and the prescient warning of the Minister of Justice, A. A. Khvostov, that the workers' elections would be exploited by revolutionary activists 'to fill the gap in their organisations', the Council gave its consent both to the statutes of the TsVPK and to the workers' elections.[59] In the absence of reliable archival evidence, it may be argued that political factors were uppermost in ministers' minds. The granting of legal recognition to the TsVPK, which provided an extra-parliamentary dimension to the Duma opposition, would mollify the emergent Progressive Bloc, a coalition of liberal and moderate political parties within the State Duma and State Council. It was also a relatively harmless step from the economic point of view as control of the war economy had been invested in the four Special Councils established a week earlier, thereby defeating the TsVPK's attempt to take it over from the state apparatus. And the possibility of preserving industrial calm in the factories may have outweighed the dangers of allowing liberal industrialists and workers to come together in the committees. In addition, if the simultaneous ministerial design for the militarisation of labour was implemented (see pp. 455–56], the competence and influence of the war-industries committees and their working-class members would suffer further drastic diminution.

Political tactics, furthermore, lay behind the startling reversal displayed by the Council of Ministers towards trade unions two days after the ratification of the TsVPK regulations. The journal of the Council noted that it was resolved 'to permit labour unions'. In view of the fact that paragraph eight of the programme of the Progressive Bloc demanded the restoration of labour organisations and press, P. A. Kharitonov, the State Comptroller, argued that this verbal concession 'would serve as a vivid example of the softening of government policy'.[60]

The chance of a genuine accommodation between the regime and its liberal opponents, and hence of the implementation of reforms in the sphere of labour relations, was dealt a death-blow with the prorogation of the State Duma on 3 September 1915 and Nicholas II's rejection of a compromise with the Progressive Bloc. The replacement of Shcherbatov as Minister of Internal Affairs in September 1915 by the more robustly conservative A. N. Khvostov, a former provincial governor and leader of the fraction of the Right in the Fourth State Duma since 1912, as well as the government's turn to a course of action hostile to the public organisations, marked the reassertion of the regime's tutelary habits towards labour.

In the absence of an official programme of political and social reforms traditional authoritarian habits in the handling of the labour question remained unchecked and continued to mould bureaucrats' suspicious attitudes towards independent working-class institutions. Indeed at one level the war offered officials with this cast of mind an unparalleled opportunity to devise a carefully modulated strategy of punitive repression in place of the hitherto largely unthinking reaction to working-class initiatives. The new role accorded the military within labour policy-making raised the possibility of the application of military discipline to the factories. For a variety of reasons to be explored later the militarisation of labour did not occur. As in the years prior to hostilities an uncoordinated, disjointed, and at best partially effective, set of repressive measures was adopted.

As far as the government's policies on legal labour institutions were concerned, the Ministry of Internal Affairs remained the dominant and illiberal influence. As the police had used the occasion of the St Petersburg general strike in July 1914 to suppress almost all trade unions and their journals as well as educational societies, the solitary legal trade union continuing to function in the city during the war was the uninfluential union of pharmaceutical employees. All efforts by workers to revive their professional organisations were blocked by the authorities. The Petrograd Municipal Bureau for Union Affairs declined to register the charters of a union of metalworkers and a 'union of workers in fibrous products' in the spring of 1916, having previously turned down a plan for a union of commercial–industrial employees the previous December. When the union of metalworkers, whose revised charter had secured approval in June 1916, quickly enrolled some 3,160 members, it was closed down before its first general meeting. The new union of printers met an identical fate. Permission was granted for only two new professional publications, the textile workers' *Tekstil'shchik* and the commercial–industrial employees' *Sluzashchii*.[61]

The officials of the Ministry of Internal Affairs (MVD) and the Department of the Police also feared, with good reason, that the sickness insurance funds, being the sole legal workers' institutions after July 1914, would afford a legal covering for socialist party activists. When instances came to the Okhrana's attention it did not hesitate to act. Thus elected representatives of the Putilov *kassa* were arrested at the close of August 1914 and exactly one year later. The large-scale protest strikes to which the latter gave rise in the first week of September 1915 seem to have served as a warning to bureaucrats to act more cautiously in their treatment of the *kassy*. Thus a conference of the governors of the Central Region in April 1916 admonished local administrations against resort to the mass arrests of *kassy* members.[62]

The defeat of the Progressive Bloc's bid for political power in the late summer of 1915 and the swift return to a reactionary internal course inevitably altered officialdom's early tolerance of the TsVPK. The Second Congress of the latter, which publicly symbolised the incipient alliance between liberal employers and the defensist socialist leaders of the working class with the adoption of a programme of labour reforms, turned mounting distrust on the part of ministers into outright hostility. The dismissal of Polivanov, the strongest defender of the committees in the highest spheres, on 13 March 1916 presaged intensifying right-wing pressure to restrict both the political and economic activities of the committees.[63] As for the labour policies of the TsVPK, ministers, fully apprised of the covert political motives of Guchkov and Konovalov thanks to the secret police, were as determined as Petrograd industrialists to thwart their implementation. B. V. Stürmer, who was both president of the Council of Ministers from January 1916 and head of the MVD from March of the same year, and General E. K. Klimovich, the director of the Department of Police, sought the suppression of the Labour Groups. Colonel A. P. Martynov, the chief of the Moscow Okhrana, assured ministers that such a drastic course of action would meet with the secret approval of most employers. The authorities took great care to prevent the convocation of the All-Russian Congress of Labour or gatherings of Labour Groups with their constituents. The Minister of Trade and Industry rejected the immediate introduction of arbitration chambers. In March 1916 a commission in the MTP considered the TsVPK proposal for such a body. On account of the opposition of the representatives from the POZF and its counterpart in Moscow, the commission rejected the immediate introduction of arbitration chambers owing to the lack of working-class professional organisations. In the light of the pre-war divisions among officials over this issue, it is scarcely surprising that Prince V. N. Shakhovskoi, the Minister of Trade and Industry, upheld the committee's findings.[64] The Okhrana also maintained a vigorous supervision of the activities of the Labour Groups, culminating in the arrest of the Labour Group of the TsVPK in January 1917.

The wartime period, moreover, brought no alteration for the better in the regime's harsh treatment of strikes and their participants. Circulars from the MVD to provincial gendarme administrations in May and July 1915 reminded them of the standard practice of 'removing from circulation' strike leaders.[65] In fact the arrests and exiling of strikers from Petrograd, by either the police or the military, seems to have been a comparatively rare phenomenon during the war. Out of 167 wartime stoppages (to the February revolution) on which detailed information is available, such methods were used only on nine occasions, six of them between July and October 1915. The numbers involved reached over the hundred limit three times – the Erikson stoppage in July 1915 and the two Putilov strikes in February 1916.

Furthermore, the PVO's use of the revocation of workers' exemptions from serving with the colours as a method of strikebreaking never amounted to a definite strategy, consistently applied. Resort was had to it in a mere twenty-three instances, all except one concerning plants in heavy industry. On occasions, however, the number of strikers suffering this penalty were considerable. In a dispute at Phoenix Engineering in October 1915 430 received summonses to the army. During the strike at the Admiralty Shipyards in

January 1916 the Ministry of the Navy revoked the exemptions of 350 reservists. When around 87,000 stopped work in protest against the trial of Baltic sailors on a charge of mutiny at the end of October 1916, General S. S. Khabalov, the commander of the PVO, ordered the closure of ten large plants in the capital goods sector and mobilised the 1,750 reservists working therein.[66] The call-up of worker reservists serving in factories was at most an intermittent, *ad hoc*, response by the commanders of the PVO to a few large-scale mass labour disturbances, such as those which occurred early in September 1915, February 1916 and the close of October 1916. Indeed of the twenty-three cases, seven involved merely a warning that was never implemented.

Various attempts to secure better co-ordination of the actions of the military and civilian authorities and to mould them into a proper systematic response to industrial unrest came to naught. A special committee to co-ordinate measures against strikes in the capital was set up in the summer of 1915. In May 1916 a special conference met in the MVD 'to unify the actions of the governmental authorities for the prevention and resolution of strikes'.[67] An analysis of individual stoppages in Petrograd suggests that these bureaucratic devices brought no greater degree of uniformity of approach by the various official bodies involved: the police, the PVO and the factory inspectorate continued to intervene in a haphazard, occasional manner. Nor was the Special Council for Defence able to sort out the muddle. A special session of the OSO devoted to the issue in May 1916 revealed such deep divisions of opinion that it failed to come to any official conclusion at all. Whilst the more conservative members favoured the application of harsh penalties against walk-outs in defence plants, in the words of S. I. Timashev, 'as the single method capable of stopping the menacing spread of strikes', the representatives of industry, the TsVPK and the liberal parties rejected repressive measures on the grounds that these 'would conjure up the spectre of a general strike'.[68]

From the state's point of view these defects in its treatment of industrial disturbances could have been remedied if it had pushed through the militarisation of labour. Several variant drafts of such schemes emanated from the Ministry of War in July and December 1915, as well as the MTP in August of the same year. Although the second of the two Ministry of War bills was submitted to the State Duma in February 1916, no more was heard of it thereafter. The Council of Ministers had refused to implement it by decree under Article 87 of the Fundamental Laws; the proper legislative procedure had to be pursued so that an inherently unpopular measure might stand a better chance of securing the assent of an industrial community (whose views on its efficacy were divided) and the work-force.[69]

In view of the powerful support for the bill by the right in general and the majority of the OSO, the reluctance of the authorities to press the bill as a matter of urgency in the legislature or in the last resort to enact it by emergency powers remains enigmatic. It is evident that the liberal parties in parliament and the TsVPK entertained a common distaste for a measure which probably would embitter deteriorating industrial relations. A conference of both groups rejected the proposals in July 1916.[70] It is possible that many high bureaucrats and generals privately shared these apprehensions.

In clear contradiction to the variety of punitive responses to industrial unrest, what may be termed the 'state-paternalist' approach survived within the bureaucratic apparatus. Even within the MVD, for example, this tradition lingered on. General K. I. Globachev, the chief of the Petrograd Okhrana, for example, sought to persuade the MVD in a letter of 11 July 1915 that the most suitable antidote to the poison of the strike movement would be to meet, in part or in full, workers' economic demands.[71] There exists no evidence, however, in the archives of the POZF or the Okhrana that the police in the capital put official pressure on employers to concede workers' claims for higher wages.

Within the bureaucracy, the MTP continued to remain the chief bastion of more open-minded labour policies. Shakhovskoi, who replaced Timashev as head of the ministry in February 1915, paid at least lip-service to the value of trade unions and sickness benefit funds as vehicles for mitigating labour friction. In the Council of Ministers on 26 August 1915, he argued that their destruction by the military and provincial administrations 'is one of the chief causes of discontent and unrest among the workers'.[72]

In the atmosphere of reaction prevailing in the highest circles from the autumn of 1915 onwards, it proved impossible for Shakhovskoi to translate his fine sentiments, if he genuinely believed in them, into a conscious, carefully elaborated, scheme of social improvements. At most certain limited legislative proposals emerged from the MTP to widen the scope of legal workers' organisations in a modest manner. In Shakhovskoi's own view, moreover, the government should react to the challenge of the TsVPK labour programme not only by administrative means but also by the consideration of cautious concessions.

The narrow cope of the MTP's reforms is revealed by a brief summary of its legislative programme and its fate in the course of the war. A bill authorising municipalities and *zemstvos* (the provincial and district organs of local self-government) to establish free 'offices of hire' with subsidies from the state remained hidden in the recesses of the ministerial chancellery.[73] An inter-ministerial commission within the MTP drafted new, less restrictive, model regulations for consumer co-operatives. The State Council threw out the measure in the autumn of 1916.[74] Shakhovskoi's proposed minor changes to the 1903 law on factory elders encountered such fierce opposition within bureaucratic circles, in particular the MVD and the Ministry of Justice, that nothing of substance came of this scheme.[75] The minister himself blocked the plan to establish arbitration chambers.

Another and potentially significant opportunity for the state to reveal solicitude for workers' interests presented itself in the broad powers of intervention in industrial affairs accorded the Minister of War under the statute establishing the Special Council for Defence in August 1915. Thus Polivanov personally endorsed a suggestion by the Octobrist and Kadet members of the OSO in the summer of 1915 that special commissions (embracing representatives of the government, employers and workers) should be formed to regulate the size of wages, the length of the working day and conditions of labour. Nothing more was heard of the project. Nor did the Minister of War's endorsement of the TsVPK scheme for arbitration chambers save it from the bureaucratic axe.[76] The chairman of the OSO, as far as is known, never used his statutory right to regulate wages in Petrograd industry. It may be that in the light of the bitter hostility of the capital's industrialists to all these notions the Ministry of War felt that it was more discreet to mollify the captains of a sector so crucial to the war effort.

V

In the short term at least as far as the Petrograd employers and their organisation, the POZF, were concerned, the challenges posed to their control over their plants and work-forces by the appearance of new governmental (the OSO) and private (the TsVPK) regulatory agencies with the authority as well as aspirations to meddle in industrial affairs were successfully defeated. Despite their exclusion from the TsVPK and the OSO, the capital's manufacturers were able to avail themselves of their well-established connections with high bureaucrats and generals in order to sustain their important share of war contracts. They discovered that the new state economic regulatory apparatus could work in their favour, at least with regard to scarce supplies of fuel and raw materials. They benefited without any direct effort on their part from the government's defeat of the TsVPK's quest for a dominating role in the war economy. Factory administrations, moreover, proved more than capable of warding off the threats to managerial prerogatives posed by the TsVPK labour reform programme and the interventionist powers of the OSO. With the covert help of the authorities all Konovalov's schemes for an All-Russian Labour Congress, an All-Russian Labour Exchange, arbitration chambers and revision of the 1903 law on factory elders came to naught. The OSO failed to regulate wages. Indeed the actions of the military authorities in intervening in strikes brought the POZF a new and welcome source of support in its struggle against labour troubles. By a mixture of this succour and timely concessions concerning wages, employers were able to contain war-time industrial unrest and prevent it inflicting unacceptable damage upon the continuity of production.

From the longer perspective of 1917 the success of the POZF in upholding the *ancien régime* in the factories was purchased at a short-sighted price. The refusal of the POZF to contemplate the labour and social reforms proposed by the TsVPK leadership consti-tuted a profound error of judgement. As the factory committee movement of 1917 revealed, Petrograd operatives were not desirous of taking over direct control of their workplace or expropriating their employers but did seek a 'constitutional factory régime', i.e. the right of workers to be consulted on issues of immediate concern to them, namely pay, hiring and firing and the behaviour of foremen. It is at least arguable that full and genuine implementation of the TsVPK programme, together with rapid improvements in working conditions, would have helped bridge the gulf between labour and capital.

The real impediment, however, to the realisation of the TsVPK's plans, even if the Petrograd industrialists had not been so myopic, lay with the central authorities. The Imperial government, and above them Nicholas II, alone could have made the crucial concessions which might have directed labour along legal channels – the right to form genuinely independent trade unions, a working-class press and political parties. The failures of official labour policies, the absence of a coherent, properly conceived, sensibly executed programme, con-stituted more of a blockage to the evolution of a non-revolutionary labour movement than the actions of factory owners. Bureaucrats and generals failed to choose between the three options available to them; instead they pursued all of them simultaneously or in different combinations. The 'high politics' of the war years militated against an alliance between ministers and the moderate liberal opposition to implement a series of political and social reforms except for a brief period in the summer of 1915. The lip-service paid to state-directed paternal guardianship of the interests of workers was never translated into any consistent set of measures, by either the MVD, OSO or even the MTP. Nor was a carefully modulated strategy of punitive repression adopted in a systematic manner. Contrary to the opinion of M. Balabanov that 'all wartime measures amounted to a *de facto* militarisation of labour', almost the reverse was the case.[77] The MVD and PVO intervened comparatively rarely in stoppages in the capital. The various attempts to introduce militarisation of labour were frustrated by a combination of the opposition of many industrialists outside Petrograd, the lukewarm attitude of the State Duma and ministers' fears of aggravating industrial relations. Yet the punitive measures, which were implemented, and the militarisation of labour, which was not, both deepened working-class suspicion of and hostility to the authorities. The erratic and unpredictable nature of such repression probably increased workers' discontent.

Epilogue

THE FEBRUARY REVOLUTION

This monograph has been an examination of the labour movement in its diverse aspects in St Petersburg/Petrograd during the last ten years of the *ancien régime*. The investigation, however, would be incomplete without some consideration of the role played by workers and revolutionary parties in the dramatic events between 23 and 26 February 1917 which presaged the downfall of the monarchy in its capital. On the other hand, as the February revolution in Petrograd has been the subject of at least five detailed tomes, it would be otiose to repeat at length that particular exercise.[1] Instead, the focus of attention will be on the ways in which the developments of late February help to illuminate and corroborate many of the themes of this particular work.

The stoppages which began at textile mills in the Vyborg district in the morning of 23 February quickly acquired unprecedented dimensions.[2] As Table E.i shows, within two days over 270,000 workers had downed tools in around 200 enterprises.

An analysis of the sectoral, geographical and social base of the February strikes reveals significant contrasts as well as similarities with the patterns of labour unrest in the capital in the five years after the Lena goldfields massacre of April 1912. These differences explain the unparalleled scope of the protests and the unexpected dangers faced by the Tsarist authorities.

In the first place, the February walk-outs in Petrograd very quickly assumed the dimensions of a genuine general strike. Whereas in the previous worst bout of unrest in July 1914, factory disturbances had embraced at their greatest scarcely over a quarter of the manufacturing labour force, even on the second day (24 February) half of all factory employees had already left their benches. Twenty-four hours later the proportion had reached 69 per cent. By the last

Table E.i: *Petrograd City: Growth of the Strike Movement, 23–7 February 1917**

	Strikes	Strikers
23 February	48	99,700
24 February	147	196,631
25 February	206	271,211
27 February	216	314,439

* 26 February was a Sunday. Consequently all factories were closed on that day.

Table E.ii: *Petrograd City: Strikes and Strikers, by Industry, 23–7 February 1917 (number and % of total)*

Industry	Strikes		Strikers	
	No.	%	No.	%
Animal products	14	5.2	27,192	8.6
Chemicals	6	2.2	18,891	6.0
Communications	2	0.7	2,000	0.6
Food/drink/tobacco	11	4.1	6,537	2.1
Gold/silver/bronze	1		100	0.6
Metals and machines	154	57.7	201,680	64.1
Mineral products	4	1.5	3,849	1.2
Miscellaneous*	1	0.3	340	0.01
Paper and printing	25	9.4	11,543	3.7
Textiles	34	12.7	38,968	12.4
Woodworking	15	5.6	3,339	1.1
TOTAL	267	99.4	314,439	100.41

* The 'miscellaneous' category refers to public utilities owned by the Petrograd Municipality.

day of the monarchy's existence in its capital (27 February) a staggering 80 per cent had ceased working.

Secondly, although metalworkers continued as before to furnish the highest ratio of strikers (64 per cent of all participants in stoppages between 23 and 27 February), the movement's strength derived from the fact that it began to draw in larger groups of hands in all other industrial sectors than had been the case hitherto (see Table E.ii). Whereas the non-metalworking branches of production had accounted for a mere 16 per cent of all strikers between 19 July 1914 and 22 February 1917, their contribution to the aggregate of strikers during the February revolution rose to 36 per cent. Within several industries, too, the stoppages became almost total, as in animal products, metals and machines, mineral products and textiles (See Table E.iii). This was in part due to the fact that for the first time the gigantic state-owned plants in chemicals and engineering were sucked into civil disobedience.[3] It was also the consequence of a greater propensity to strike by workers in small enterprises, in particular in engineering, printing and textiles. These changes brought into the movement far greater numbers of women and unskilled than had been the case before.

The geographical scope of the disturbances was distinctly less narrow than in the earlier pattern of unrest. Whereas Vyborg and Petrograd Side had borne the brunt of industrial conflicts in 1915 and 1916, accounting for 53 per cent of all disputes, their joint share of the aggregate of strikers fell during the February days to 32 per cent (see Table E.iv). The incidence of walk-outs was more uniformly spread throughout the manufacturing districts, reflecting the enlargement of disaffection to embrace industrial sectors and categories of the labour force other than, as before, skilled male workers employed in privately owned, medium-sized machine construction and electrical equipment firms, primarily in Vyborg and Petrograd

Table E.iii: Petrograd City: Strikers as % of Total Factory Labour Force in Each Industry, 23–7 February 1917

Industry	%
Animal products	215.8
Chemicals	47.1
Food/drink/tobacco	41.4
Metals and machines	85.0
Mineral products	98.7
Paper and printing	43.6
Textiles	88.4
Woodworking	49.8
TOTAL	80.1

*Percentages have been worked out on the basis of the labour force in each industry on 1 January 1917 (see Table 11.i, p. 328). Owing to lack of exact data on the labour force employed in communications, gold and silver, miscellaneous, no calculations could be made.

Table E.iv: Petrograd City: Number of Strikers, and Number of Strikers as % of Total, by District, 23–7 February 1917

District	No.	%
Kazan	436	0.1
Kolomna	7,750	2.5
Lesnoi	610	0.2
Liteinii	6,200	2.0
Moscow	15,419	4.9
Narva	39,340	12.5
Neva	43,574	13.9
Okhta	4,316	1.4
Peterhof	25,000	8.0
Petrograd Side	24,981	7.9
Poliustrovo	11,883	3.8
Rozhdestvo	8,267	2.6
Vasil'evskii Island	48,052	15.3
Vyborg	76,221	24.2
Staraia and Novaia Derevnia	2,390	0.8
	314,439	100.1

Side. Thus Neva and Vasil'evskii Island each contributed about 15 per cent of the total of February strikers, whilst Narva/Peterhof accounted for a fifth of all participants. The extraordinary scope of discontent is reflected, furthermore, in the fact that many working-class districts experienced a complete shutdown of all their enterprises, such as Narva, Neva, Okhta, Vasil'evskii Island and Vyborg (see Table E.v). Indeed, with the exception of the remote Lesnoi quarter, there was not a single manufacturing district in which less than two-thirds of the work-force downed tools.

Thus, the broad sectoral nature of the work stoppages after 23 February, their enhanced geographical range and greater social diversity marked them out from all preceding periods of labour unrest in the capital. The months of January and October 1905 alone bore comparison in this respect. Indeed the analogy with October 1905 became all the more apt from 25 February when the social basis of the opposition in Petrograd moved beyond the working class for the first time in twelve years. In the afternoon of that day students at all the higher educational institutes held meetings, after which they walked out in sympathy. On 24 and 25 February tramway staff and cabdrivers, partly as a result of many attacks on them by demonstra-

Table E.v: *Petrograd City: Strikers as % of Total Work-force, by District, 23–7 February 1917**

District	%
Kolomna	73.4
Lesnoi	8.9
Moscow	73.1
Narva	101.4
Neva	114.0
Okhta	101.0
Peterhof	69.2
Petrograd Side	69.1
Poliustrovo	62.8
Rozhdestvo	80.8
Vasil'evskii Island	92.6
Vyborg	110.5
Staroe and Novoe Derevnia	77.5
TOTAL	69.0

* The calculations are based on the figures for district work-forces provided by Z. V. Stepanov in *Rabochie Petrograda v period podgotovki i provedenie oktiabr'skogo vooruzhennogo vosstaniia* (Moscow, 1965), Table 3, p. 30. Owing to lack of data, the districts of Kazan and Lesnoi have been omitted from the table.

tors, brought city transport to a halt. By 26 February, as eyewitnesses testify, members of the professions and civil service, artisans and domestic servants began to join the street demonstrations. A popular rather than a purely working-class general strike began to take shape.[4]

The dimensions of the strike wave were not the only feature of the February days distinguishing them from earlier disturbances. The mass stoppages of work were accompanied by, interwoven with and powerfully reinforced by street demonstrations on a scale unprecedented since 1905. Whilst street manifestations in working-class quarters were confined almost solely to Vyborg on the first day of the general strike, the following day they erupted in Moscow, Petrograd Side and Vasil'evskii Island districts and on 25 February spread to Neva. This repeated the pattern of the July 'general' strike in 1914. However, the crucial and novel element of the February marches was the persistent and increasingly successful attempt of protestors to penetrate to Nevskii Prospekt in the city centre, the symbolic heart of the government. Due to the heavy cordon of police and troops at the Aleksander II bridge linking Vyborg to the

Liteinii district, on 23 February only small groups, numbering 100 to 200, of mostly working-class women and youths managed to cross the ice of the Neva to reach the city's heart by late afternoon.[5] The following day, between eight and ten o'clock in the morning, up to 10,000 Vyborg workers attempted thrice to break through the forces guarding the bridge. Many succeeded. At least six mass demonstrations, involving around 3,000 workers, occurred on the central thoroughfare between eleven in the morning and eight in the evening.[6] A similar pattern was noticeable on 25 and 26 February (a Sunday), when seven and six large demonstrations, respectively, embracing from 1,000 to 5,000 people took place on Nevskii Prospekt.[7]

The rapid spread of walk-outs and the persistence of street demonstrations in turn revealed an ominous change in the mood of Petrograd workers in comparison with all other protests since the spring of 1912 (with the exception of the July days of 1914). As early as 23 February an internal Okhrana memorandum remarked in alarm that strikers and demonstrators 'displayed great stubbornness'. Crowds, dispersed by mounted police and gendarmes, quickly regrouped.[8] The new and desperate determination of workers was revealed by the fact that on this first day of the incipient revolution at least thirteen clashes with police took place as they attempted to disperse columns of strikers or throngs of demonstrators. Hatred for the symbols of authority and discontent occasioned by food shortages burst forth in four instances of attacks on policemen, nine attempts to stop or overturn tramcars and five cases of plundering of food stores.[9] The next day the crowds' temper had become more excited, as people were more ready to offer violent resistance to orders to disperse. During three of a minimum of fifteen skirmishes with the forces of law and order, stones and lumps of ice were flung at the police and on Kamennoostrovskii Prospekt (Petrograd Side) shots were fired at them.[10] On nine occasions (widely scattered throughout all districts) tram movement was halted and keys removed. Attacks on retail outlets reached their apogee with sixteen such occurrences, mostly in the Moscow and Petrograd Side quarters.[11] On 25 February the disposition of demonstrators became much uglier. A report by one of the secret police's most trusted and percipient agents, 'Limonin', (the Bolshevik V. E. Shurkanov) noted that due both to growing instances of Cossacks' refusing to obey orders to break up columns of demonstrators and to the authorities' patent inability to prevent workers' penetrating the city centre 'the masses have become convinced of their impunity'. The belief had become widespread, he remarked, that revolution had begun and that very soon the soldiers would come over to the workers' cause. N. Sukhanov, too, observed 'the extreme excitement' of the multitude, whilst the French journalist Claude Anet discovered that 'the crowd was in a dangerous mood'.[12] Workers and students, emboldened by their sense of the soldiers' wavering, stepped up assaults on individual, isolated policemen (there were ten instances of disarming or beating up constables) and, on at least six occasions, shots were fired from crowds at the police. In all there were fourteen skirmishes with the upholders of law and order. There were also two examples in the city centre of crowds freeing arrested demonstrators. On the other hand, food riots had died out.[13] Even the shootings and consequent fatalities on 26 February on Nevskii Prospekt failed to dampen protestors' enthusiasm or hostility. One of the very last documents written by the Tsarist police remarked that crowds merely laughed at the troops' orders to disperse and that, even after live shot was used, demonstrators soon reformed, throwing stones and blocks of ice.[14]

The fundamental difference between the course of events unfolding from 23 February and previous disorders, in particular the July 'general' strike of 1914, lay in the response of the soldiers. According to the Military Commmission of the Provisional Government there were 170,000 troops in the capital and 151,000 in surrounding towns.[15] But the majority comprised uninstructed new recruits and recuperating veterans in the reserve battalions of the fourteen guards regiments, which were poorly provided with officers.[16] As events soon revealed, these men shared workers' loathing of the police and the government. As early as the first day, vacillation and indecisiveness characterised the attitude of troops on the streets. Cossacks proved reluctant to fulfil commands or did so with a distinct lack of enthusiasm. These signs became more and more marked on 24 and 25 February as the authorities were compelled to make greater use of cavalry, Cossacks and soldiers. Eyewitnesses such as Sukhanov commented on the fact that Cossacks performed their duties 'without any energy or zeal and after lengthy delays'.[17] There were some isolated instances of Cossacks refusing to disperse demonstrators. On the afternoon of 24 February, for example, they allowed a meeting to take place on Znamia Square. In the same place the following day a famous incident occurred when a Cossack either sabred or shot a police officer as he tried to restore order.[18] By 25 February lower military ranks and ensigns began to join the crowds on Nevskii Prospekt.[19] There is some evidence that officers, particularly NCOs, shared their men's sympathies for the crowds' aims. On Znamia Square, for example, on 25 February the commanding officer of the First Don Cossack Regiment refused a police request to disperse the crowd, whilst on Kazanskaia Street the officer in charge of the Fourth Don Cossack Regiment liberated workers arrested by the police.[20] In addition to the longer-term subterranean influences of discontent with the government and the war, the soldiers on duty were also affected by the crowds' efforts at fraternisation. When Cossacks refused to disperse demonstrators they were greeted with shouts of hurrah. Instances grew of members of the public talking to soldiers' pickets, explaining their grievances and demands. Soldiers drawn from the lower classes found themselves being put in the impossible situation of firing on workers, including women, demanding bread.[21]

The rapid enlargement of the strike movement and the eruption of popular fury into violent street demonstrations, attacks on police, tramcars and shops must be explained in the first instance by the extremely embittered and nervous mood of all sections of Petrograd's population in the last weeks of 1916 and the first of 1917. In an acute internal memorandum written some time late in January 1917 the Okhrana analysed the causes of what it described as a popular temperament 'of an exceptionally alarming character'. The particularly steep rise in prices which set in from October 1916, the increasing shortage of all necessities, the growing occurrence of partial shutdowns of plants due to a dearth of raw materials, together with the perceived failure of all governmental measures to improve food supplies, immeasurably strengthened the antagonism of all social strata towards both the ministry and even the dynasty itself.[22] In this atmosphere the famous session of the State Duma on 1 November 1916, together with the wide distribution of the banned speeches of Miliukov and other politicians, evoked great sympathy and support for that body as 'the representative of all Russia'. The city's inhabitants lived on rumours – of an approaching palace *coup d'état*, of the imminent implementation of reactionary measures by the government, of the existence of a German party which was on the point of seizing power, of terrorism. Above all, the diverse political and social groups were in agreement that 'the present political moment is very similar to events preceding the revolutionary excesses of 1905'. Given the widespread assumption of the imminence of revolution, the secret police expressed particular alarm at the fact that 'the idea of a general strike . . . has become as popular as in 1905'. Thus the initial stoppages of 23 February in Vyborg district occurred in an atmosphere peculiarly conducive to evoking the broadest possible support amongst not only workers of manufacturing quarters but also, for the first time since 1905, among bourgeois strata.[23]

As is well known, the general strike began among women textile hands in Vyborg on the morning of 23 February as a protest against the shortage of bread. The evidence concerning the extent of the bread crisis and its causes is not clear-cut. On the eve of the February revolution, the city's granaries were not in fact empty. The chairman of the Municipal Food Supply Commission confirmed at a public meeting on 25 February that the municipal and public authorities jointly had reserves of flour for another two weeks. General Knox, the British military attaché, reported that there were nearly half a million *puds* of rye flour in store, but none of wheat flour or oats or hay.[24] On the other hand, from the middle of February, in the working-class districts, particularly Vyborg, shortages of white bread for sale did take place, in part because bakers were unable to obtain wheat flour and in part because they found it more profitable to sell off their stocks of rye bread to horse-owners who bought it in place of missing oats.[25] The situation was compounded by the fact that many petty retail outlets had ceased to function due to the problems of supply and those still open curtailed their hours of business. As a consequence long queues of women and children stood for up to four hours in temperatures as low as −15° centigrade.[26] Rumour, too, played a damaging role. Press discussion of the possible introduction of rationing produced a rush on the shops in panic stockpiling.[27] On the other hand, it would be erroneous to conclude that the revolution started as an old-fashioned bread riot. The first attacks on foodshops began only at three o'clock in the afternoon of 23 February in the Petrograd Side and were relatively few.[28] It was only when the strike spread to other districts the following day that such pillaging became common. Furthermore, whilst police reports reveal that the slogan 'Give Us Bread' was the most commonly heard on the streets on 23 February, in the subsequent two days more overtly political slogans such as 'Down with the Tsar', 'Down with the Government' and 'Down with the War' came to the fore.[29] In the highly charged atmosphere of the capital, therefore, the sudden bread crisis acted as the trigger for the outpouring of workers' and bourgeois inhabitants' political alienation from the regime.

The participation, moreover, of particular factories in the strike movement was not always a matter of free choice. As on previous occasions in the past, pressure was applied from outside by workers in plants which were the first to come to a halt. This phenomenon happened on at least thirty-two occasions in the first three days of the revolution.[30] At noon on 23 February, for example, strikers from Erikson, New Lessner, Neva Thread and the Russian Society surrounded the Arsenal, throwing stones and lumps of ice at its windows. The adherence of most of the large state-owned concerns to the stoppages was the product of such external influences. It took several attempts over three successive days to force out the gigantic Petrograd Pipes works.[31] On the other hand, contrary to some accounts, the partial strikes which began at Putilov on 17 February did not act as a catalyst to the later wave of confrontations as the administration locked out the entire labour force of 26,000 five days later, depriving the workers of a base for meetings and agitation.[32]

The part played by the revolutionary organisations in the gestation of the February revolution has been a subject of intense controversy ever since it happened. Soviet historiography of 1917, including the February revolution, has always been influenced by current political considerations. In the 1920s Soviet scholars emphasised the spontaneity and leaderless character of the February events, and the absence of definite Bolshevik leaders and organisers. In Leon Trotskii's celebrated dictum 'conscious and tempered workers educated for the most part by the party of Lenin' led the February revolution.[33] From the 1930s Stalinist orthodoxy imposed a complete turnaround in interpretation, elevating the Bolshevik party to the exalted and exclusive role of leader of the masses in the final assault upon Tsardom. Western historians, reliant upon the archival sources and memoirs published by the Soviet authorities, which in fact have been carefully selected to bolster current interpretation of events, have tended to follow changes in Soviet presentation. Thus, in his influential study, first published in 1935, William H. Chamberlin could write that 'the collapse of the Romanov autocracy in March 1917 was one of the most leaderless, spontaneous, anonymous revolutions of all time'. Tsuyoshi Hasegawa has recently attacked both the concept of the spontaneous nature of the February revolution and the theory of Bolshevik leadership, whilst nevertheless attributing a special role to the Bolsheviks' Vyborg organisation.[34] The researcher is also confronted with the fact that participants' later accounts were undoubtedly coloured by their retrospective knowledge of the February revolution's ultimate success and by their own subsequent personal political history. The rapid disintegration of the Okhrana's information network from 25 February and the destruction of part of its archives has further deprived historians of much valuable material.[35]

The February revolution was 'spontaneous' only in the sense that none of the revolutionary organisations actually planned the strikes and demonstrations which erupted on 23 February and took their leaders by surprise. The well-informed Shurkanov assured his paymasters that 'the movement which has arisen exploded without any party preparation and without a preliminary discussion of a plan of action'.[36] Although 23 February was International Women's Day, only the Vyborg district committee among authoritative Bolshevik organs attempted to arrange meetings of women workers that morning with speeches devoted to the war, inflation and the condition of women. No leaflets were published. Indeed local Bolshevik leaders were actively seeking to restrain workers from dissipating their energies in partial stoppages.[37] The Mezhraionka alone was more successful in that it succeeded in publishing and distributing a leaflet. The exact contents of this document, however, are a subject of controversy. A police report stated that it specifically called for a stoppage on 23 February. Yet the version published in Soviet sources contains no such injunction.[38] In view of the uncertainty of the evidence it would be unwise to conclude conclusively that the Mezhraionka sought to utilise International Women's Day to spark a revolutionary outbreak.[39]

As in the July 'general' strike of 1914, the swift onrush of events meant that the socialist leaders in exile, including Lenin, could exert absolutely no influence upon developments. But it would be erroneous to deduce from this fact, as Sukhanov did, that 'the organised Socialist centres were not controlling the popular movement'.[40] In the absence of immediate directives either from the *émigrés* or from local leadership organs, second-rank party activists in the factories responded on their own to the initial walk-outs by female textile hands and the rapid spread of stoppages on 23 and 24 February. Moreover, contrary to the distorted accounts of Bolshevik participants, who suffered collective amnesia about the existence and contributions of rival socialist groupings, the very thin distribution of revolutionary factory cells, as in the past, compelled the different revolutionary collectives to co-operate in fashioning a response. The reaction of party activists of internationalist beliefs was strongly influenced by the highly charged atmosphere in the capital, their own and workers' expectations of imminent revolution which they had long anticipated and the previous history of attempting to launch both a general political strike and an armed uprising. Thus when striking mill hands came to the Erikson plant, the Bolsheviks, Menshevik internationalists and Left SRs jointly resolved to support them, to bring out other plants and to lead demonstrations.[41] At other factory meetings in the next two days, these three groups along with members of the Mezhraionka worked together to persuade workers to leave their benches and process to the city centre. The political slogans directed against the war and the autocracy, heard increasingly from 24 February, emanated in part from revolutionary orators.[42] Furthermore, it would not be unreasonable to conclude, by analogy with previous stoppages, that the February strike wave itself, given the extraordinary depth of popular disaffection, brought forth new non-party working-class leaders. In this connection, the role of factory meetings was of cardinal importance. In the almost complete absence of revolutionary proclamations and socialist newspapers, factory mass meetings, held in the mornings of 24 and 25 February, acted, in the words of police agent 'Limonin' 'as information centres for the masses'. At these gatherings revolutionary activists of all hues were able to agitate for a general strike, exhort listeners to march to the city centre and propagate their slogans.[43]

At the level above the factories, certain revolutionary city and district organisations also endeavoured to provide co-ordination and leadership. Among Petrograd Bolsheviks the differences and tensions which existed before the outbreak of the revolution between the Russian Bureau and the PK and district committees were exacerbated by their different responses to unfolding events. A close reading of Shliapnikov's memoirs reveals that the three members of the Bureau did not speak at factory meetings or lead demonstrations or attempt to fraternise with soldiers in the course of the four days before 27 February. Although Shliapnikov claimed in his reminiscences that by the second day 'for all it was clear the revolution had begun', his actions and that of the Russian Bureau belie his statement.[44] The Russian Bureau only met for the first time on the evening of 24 February. Under intense pressure from Vyborg and PK comrades disappointed 'at the lack of general leadership' the Bureau drafted a proclamation, which the PK approved the following day. However, this document offered no concrete suggestions for action to workers apart from establishing Social Democratic committees in factories and districts and the slogan 'To the Streets'.[45] Indeed, it is almost certain that the 'PK' leaflet, which appears in Soviet collections, was not in fact published.[46] The hesitancy of the Russian Bureau derived from its assessment that the decisive battle against Tsardom had not in fact begun. It felt that the party did not have the resources for an ill-prepared strike. Both the Vyborg Bolsheviks and the PK, in closer touch with ordinary workers, were more attuned to the popular mood. Thus at meetings on the nights of 23 and 24 February the Vyborg district committee resolved to launch a general political strike, to hold demonstrations on Nevskii Prospekt, to agitate among the soldiers, disarm the police and acquire weapons.[47] The PK, assembling on the evening of 25 February, decided that within two days, in the absence of countermeasures by the authorities, it would launch in effect an armed uprising by constructing barricades and cutting off public utilities.[48] This desire of many Bolsheviks to initiate an armed uprising was the cause of a further rift with the Russian Bureau. It refused to sanction their insistent demands to seize arms on the grounds that the sole way to secure the overthrow of the autocracy was to attract the garrison into the uprising through fraternisation and the worsening of the struggle on the streets.[49] It is impossible to discover the opinions and actions of the other Bolshevik district committees, as neither police archives nor published memoirs throw any light upon them. Sources disagree, too, concerning the impact of the shootings on 26 February on the Bolshevik leadership. Kaiurov asserts that at the meeting of the Vyborg committee that evening many were discouraged and inclined to call a halt to the movement, whereas Sveshnikov relates that the decision was taken to transform the struggle into an armed uprising. A police agent reported that an assembly of Vasil'evskii Island Bolsheviks and members of the Mezhraionka resolved both to continue the strike and to form fighting detachments.[50]

The Mezhraionka committee displayed as much activity as Bolshevik organs. In the field of publicity, indeed, it had no rivals as it alone had access to a secret printing press. Apart from the leaflet for International Women's Day, it published a proclamation on 24 February calling for a three-day general strike. And on 26 February, jointly with the Left SRs, it printed and distributed (in the early hours of the next day) two leaflets, one to the workers, urging a continuation of the stoppages, and one to the soldiers, exhorting them to refrain from attacking the demonstrators.[51] Whilst the content of the proclamation of 24 February reveals that the Mezhraionka sought to capitalise on the unfolding situation, the fact that the object of the strike was declared to be a protest against the Putilov lock-out would suggest that the Mezhraionka leaders shared the Russian Bureau's scepticism concerning the suitability of the hour for launching the final assault on the Tsarist citadel.[52] At no time did the Mezhraionka openly call for an armed uprising. Iurenev states that his group was apprehensive lest the movement turn into an elemental explosion of the unorganised masses. He apparently told a gathering of socialist leaders in A. F. Kerenskii's flat on the evening of 26 February that 'there is no revolution, nor will there be any'.[53]

The other two internationalist leaderships displayed much less dynamism. The Central Initiative Group never met nor published any leaflets. Lacking an all-city organisation the Left SRs' leaders could offer their followers no centralised direction. In both cases, however, rank and file members participated without offical orders in the movement.[54]

The standard argument among Soviet scholars, supported by some Western historians, that the Menshevik and SR defensist activists reacted with hostility and equivocation to the stoppages and demonstrations requires modification.[55] In the first instance the Labour Group's dramatic turn to the left from November 1916 and its organisation of the mass stoppages of 14 February 1917 would logically suggest that they, too, would seek to support the February strikes once they had begun. Secondly, on the evening of 23 February, the moderate Menshevik and SR leaders of the Petrograd Union of Consumer Organisations convoked an assembly of representatives of *kassy*, co-operatives and 'assistance groups' of the Labour Group which resolved to endorse both the work and street protests. In view of the size of *kassy* and co-operative membership in comparison with that of revolutionary cells this decision was as important as any taken by the revolutionary left activists. On the other hand, whereas the internationalists sought to direct demonstrators towards the Nevskii Prospekt, the socialist moderates, faithful to the Menshevik and Trudovik policy of seeking to revolutionise the liberal opposition through working-class pressure, urged workers to go to the Tauride Palace with the slogan 'Bread and Peace'. Attempts were made to put this resolution into effect. At a meeting at Aivaz on the morning of 24 February orators exhorted their listeners to demonstrate outside the State Duma with the demand for the removal of the government. And a delegation of workers did meet the Menshevik deputy Skobelev.[56] On 25 February speakers at a mass meeting on Znamia Square called for support for the State Duma.[57] As Hasegawa has pointed out, the fact that mass demonstrations did not occur at the Tauride Palace before the soldiers' uprising of 27 February does not in itself mean that the moderates' recommendation was unpopular with workers. It would be more accurate to state that the huge concentration of barracks and police around the State Duma acted as a powerful deterrent, as it had done a week previously.[58]

Both wings of the socialist camp also attempted to provide some form of overarching institutional framework which could furnish central guidance to strikers and demonstrators. Some time between 23 and 25 February, on the initiative of the Mezhraionka, a leftist inter-party informational and contact bureau was established linking the Bolsheviks, Left SRs, Central Initiative Group and Mezhraionka. It met three or four times. However, the Bolsheviks attended only the first meeting.[59]

The moderate, defensist Menshevik and SR leaders (the Labour Group, the parliamentary deputies, the co-operative activists) were also far from being swept aside by the labour movement as Soviet critics maintain. Following their long-established policy of co-operating with the progressive bourgeois opposition against the autocracy, they endeavoured to utilise the stoppages and demonstrations to frighten the Progressive Bloc to adopt a more radical stance. In speeches in the State Duma Kerenskii and Chkheidze both exhorted the liberals to press for the government's resignation. It was to the same end that the Mensheviks and SRs had endeavoured to organise mass processions to the Tauride Palace. Attempting to establish a bridge between the working class and the liberal parliamentarians, they also tried to co-ordinate the actions of all socialist groups. At least three conferences of representatives of the socialist parties were held in Gorkii's flat.[60] Most significantly of all, the Mensheviks took the lead in attempting to create a popular centre for the strike movement in the form of a Soviet of Workers' Deputies.

On the afternoon of 25 February the Menshevik parliamentary fraction and the Petrograd Union of Consumer Societies convoked a meeting of district labour representatives. This adopted the resolution of F. A. Cherevanin to establish a soviet.[61] In all these respects the socialist moderate leaders revealed as much initiative and daring as internationalists. Indeed, in their realisation that the autocracy would finally fall only if the liberal parliamentary opposition could be persuaded to side with the revolutionary cause, they displayed more acumen than the left socialists with their sterile hostility to the State Duma.

If the revolutionary parties of all hues did not trail behind the strike movement, neither can it be said that they were able to offer clear-cut, consistent, regular and effective leadership. In the first place, the efforts to set up central all-party mechanisms foundered. Contrary to the assertion that the leftist information bureau acted as a co-ordinating centre, it functioned rather as a vehicle for the exchange of information.[62] Apart from the fact that the Bolsheviks attended only a single meeting and that its other component groups had miniscule ties to factories, its members failed to agree on a slogan for the movement. Whilst the Central Initiative Group favoured a Constituent Assembly, the Mezhraionka and the Left SRs rejected a call for elections to a soviet as premature.[63] The Bolsheviks were ambivalent in their attitude towards the formation of a soviet. Whilst Pozhello supported it at the first gathering of the left's informational bureau, the Russian Bureau's draft proclamation of 25 February conspicuously kept silent on the matter. Meeting the same day, the PK had proposed the immediate establishment of factory committees which would send representatives to an Information Bureau. This body would transmit the directives of the PK.[64] Contrary to the assertions of Soviet researchers that this decision proves that the Bolsheviks had resolved to head the organisation of the soviet, the police memorandum actually shows that the PK did not regard the creation of the soviet as a matter of urgent necessity. The PK resolved that the projected Information Bureau would endeavour to create the soviet 'in the near future'.[65] On the other hand, in the light of Bolshevik activists' previous efforts during the war to establish a soviet, it is not inconceivable that they took independent steps in this direction.[66] The arrests by the Okhrana of 100 revolutionary activists on the night of 25–26 February, including many of the participants at the Mensheviks' assembly, interrupted all efforts to arrange elections to the soviet. As Iu. S. Tokarev has pointed out there exists no contemporary documentary proof that elections were held.[67]

The efforts of moderate socialists to unite all revolutionary groups irrespective of attitudes to the war were likewise fruitless. The ideological divisions over the war, the purposes of a 'bourgeois' revolution and the role therein of the liberal opposition were too deep to be overcome. At the first such conference on 24 February, Iurenev, Pozhello and Grinevich (Central Initiative Group) rejected Gorkii's proposal to issue jointly an illegal informational leaflet, instead demanding money to publish their own party literature. At the meeting in Kerenskii's flat on the evening of 26 February the various factional representatives fell out over their evaluation of the future course of events. Zenzinov's assertion, therefore, that these assemblies 'laid claim to something like the role of general headquarters of the revolution' is a gross exaggeration.[68] Although a maverick internationalist like Sukhanov was prepared to play down the anti-war aspect of the revolutionary movement in order not to alienate the liberal parties, whose opposition to Tsardom rested upon its inefficient conduct of the war, the Bolshevik, Mezhraionka and Central Initiative Group leaders refused to accept his arguments.[69]

In the absence of regular or specific directives from central party bodies, the strikes and street movements lacked central direction. Although lower-level district committees and factory collectives of all revolutionary groups sought to fill this void, their cells were too thinly spread and their membership too insignificant to be able to offer coherent guidance.[70] The Mezhraionka leaflets aside, party literature was significant by its absence. There were no socialist newspapers. From the evening of 24 February when the tram service ceased to function, direct communication between party leaders and district activists became even more difficult to achieve, as they were compelled to walk long distances. The revolutionary rank and file, where they existed, might help at most to initiate a series of uncoordinated mass actions. Above all, the movement expanded so rapidly as to involve not only huge numbers of workers but also other social strata with whom the revolutionary parties had no ties whatsoever that it was physically impossible for isolated nuclei of activists and socialist leaders to direct it in a meaningfully organised manner. The depth of popular disaffection was so deep, the expectation of revolution and a general strike so widespread, that workers reacted instinctively to the first strikes on 23 February.

The final difference between the events of 23–26 February and previous bouts of labour unrest in Petrograd since 1907 lay in the reactions of the authorities and the employers. With respect to the latter, there is unfortunately a complete dearth of evidence. The POZF apparently did not meet. One may speculate that the rapidity of events as well as the awesome scale of the stoppages made any considered reaction impossible. At any event no thought was apparently given to lock-outs. Both the employers and the government committed a serious blunder in allowing workers to use factory yards as meeting places. As agent 'Limonin' shrewdly pointed out, the temporary closure of factory premises would have deprived revolutionary and non-party activists of platforms and the mass of workers of information centres.[71] It is possible that, as in the October days of 1905, by this stage many industrialists in secret sympathised with their workers' political protests against the regime. As to the officials of the *ancien régime*, they had lost that inner conviction in the justness of their cause which had enabled them to react with such determination to the 'general' strike in July 1914. Hasegawa and Burdzhalov have both shown that the response of the military and police chiefs was marked by confusion, lack of vigour and ineptness, based in part on their distrust of the loyalty of the bulk of the garrison.[72]

By the late evening of 26 February the struggle between the workers, bourgeois sympathisers and revolutionaries, on the one hand, and the authorities on the other had reached an impasse. As the reaction of the crowds on that day and the refusal of the strikers to return to work at the normal time on the morning of 27 February revealed, there was no slackening in the determination of workers to press on with the strike and street battles. The movement had not run into the sands, nor had it passed its peak. The Tsar's ministers had refused to consider political concessions, unlike October 1905, spurning even the Progressive Bloc's moderate call for a ministry of confidence. Rejecting a political solution, the authorities had been compelled to resort to physical force. The shootings of 26 February, however, broke the last threads of loyalty on the part of much of the garrison, driving the soldiers to choose between obedience to orders or slaughtering unarmed civilians whose grievances and aspirations they shared. The revolt of the garrison the following day sealed the monarchy's fate in its capital.

Conclusion

From the 1860s onwards labour protest in Europe was modernised. Instead of pre-industrial forms of dissent, localised riots, or the methods of the early modern era, such as machine smashing, new forms of articulation of working-class discontent emerged – the strike, the political party and the trade union. These organisations for the first time endeavoured to involve masses of workers on a national scale and give expression to an emergent working-class consciousness. In the decade between the revolutions of 1905–7 and February 1917, the St Petersburg labour movement (the legal working-class institutions, the revolutionary socialist parties, the mass industrial stoppages) was part of that wider modernisation of labour protest. Its strengths and weaknesses, however, were as much the product of the city's distinctive economic and social features.

The most fundamental determinant of the St Petersburg labour movement was the character of the capital's economy. In Soviet and some Western historical accounts the impression is given that the economy was distinguished by the dominance of modern industry (in particular the capital goods sector), monopoly capital and large-scale enterprises. All three suppositions require modification.

The city's economy (and its labour force) was marked by sectoral (and occupational) diversity. Until the First World War at least, by value of output, commerce rather than manufacturing occupied first place and the service sector accounted for over a third of all jobs. This fact created one of the greatest, if unacknowledged, obstacles to the growth of the socialist parties and powerful legal labour organisations, as commercial–industrial employees and domestic servants proved impossible to organise or attract into the strike struggle. Furthermore, within manufacturing, there existed a flourishing artisanal sector (until 1914 at any rate), whose members contributed much to legal labour institutions and revolutionary parties. Even within factory-based industry the capital goods sector was responsible only for 40 per cent of its labour force in 1913, whilst all other branches accounted for 60 per cent. On the other hand, St Petersburg's economy was distinguished from other Russian cities precisely because its metalworking sector was greater than elsewhere, a weight greatly increased by the First World War. Thus skilled metalworkers were to play a dominant, although not exclusive, part in all manifestations of the labour movement in this period. Moreover, neither in 1914 nor 1917 did bank capital, either native based or foreign, dominate the urban economy as a whole. Its influence was marked only in heavy industry. On the other hand this fact itself probably contributed to the hardline stance of the Petrograd employers' organisation, the POZF, against any infringement of the autocratic regime in the factories, as the leaders of this body were all non-Russians, as were many plant managers.

As for the contribution made by large enterprises towards collective action and labour mobilisation, this, too, was less than has been claimed. In the first place, if the entire city economy is considered, small-scale rather than large units of production predominated before the outbreak of war in 1914. The history of the trade unions after 1906 reveals that the most successful were either in artisanal trades such as baking, printing and tailoring, where workshops were overwhelmingly small or, in the case of the union of metalworkers, in medium-sized firms (of around 1,000 workers) in machine construction and electrical equipment sectors (with many small workshops) rather than in the gigantic mixed-production plants. This finding is confirmed by an analysis of the pattern of strikes both in the pre-war years of 1912–14 and in 1915–16. In metalworking, particularly with respect to walk-outs of a political nature, those establishments most liable to suffer disruption were privately owned machine construction and electrical goods manufacturers, employing 500 to 2,000 hands rather than the enormous state-owned mixed production, ordnance plants and shipyards, whose labour forces were in excess of 5,000.

The history of the capital's economy between 1907 and 1917 also exerted a decisive influence on the development of labour protest. The industrial depression of 1906–1910/11 compelled industrialists, particularly in metalworking, to adopt cost-cutting policies in order to raise competitiveness. To this end they launched a counter-attack on the gains secured by workers in the 1905 revolution, namely the eight-hour day, wage rises and restrictions on the unlimited powers of managers and foremen. There occurred mass lay-offs, cuts in pay, the covert lengthening of the working day through the wider adoption of overtime, the replacement of men by women and adolescents (although the position of the skilled was not threatened in a significant way), wage reforms which lowered rates of pay and intensified the pace of work and the better utilisation of working time. In the short run these policies, which restored the *ancien régime* in the factories, created formidable obstacles to unionisation, revolutionary organisation and industrial militancy. In the longer run they signally failed to pacify the Petersburg labour force, helping to nourish that very outpouring of unrest in the factories in 1912–14 which they had been designed to prevent.

Like all periods of economic recovery the pre-war boom, which in the case of heavy industry rested on rearmament, created apparently favourable conditions (such as low unemployment and high profits) for workers to press for improvements to their conditions and to fight back belatedly against the employers' counter-offensive. The shortage of skilled labour and the dependence of employers in the capital goods' sector upon state contracts, with stiff penalties for delays in delivery, undercut the POZF's efforts to fashion a hardline response to the new wave of disruptions to production, as industrialists were apprehensive of applying punitive measures out of fear of conferring advantages upon their competitors. The new industrial unrest before the First World War was also a matter of dashed expectations, in that as a result of modest inflation real wages stagnated.

At one level the war brought enormous benefits to the Petrograd economy, industrialists and certain groups of workers. The rapid expansion of some industrial sectors rested upon state orders, making the welfare of employers and employees alike dependent on the government and the war effort. Heavy industry in particular experienced rapid and enormous growth, whilst the artisanal, brewing and printing sectors endured contraction. Real wages for skilled workers in metalworking and chemicals rose without interruption until the autumn of 1916. High profitability, strict deadlines for prompt delivery and a dearth of skilled hands all drove employers to be more accommodating in meeting workers' wage demands. On the other hand, the wartime expansion proved fatal for the regime in its economic and social consequences. By late 1916 the city's economy began to break down; inflation took off; shortages of fuel and food supplies became acute, affecting all social strata; rents tripled; housing became even more overcrowded; real wages for the unskilled, women and apprentices fell continuously from early 1915; working conditions worsened; temporary unemployment became more common. All these factors immeasurably strengthened working-class alienation from the monarchy and proved a powerful stimulus to the revival of labour unrest from the summer of 1915, in particular to the political character of protest in the first seven weeks of 1917.

The social composition of the Petersburg working class, itself the product of the capital's economy, acted both to facilitate the growth of labour and revolutionary organisations and to create formidable barriers to their success.

Contrary to the Soviet view that the existence of a mature, hereditary, urbanised proletariat explains the emergence of a militant, class-conscious labour movement which was captured by the Bolsheviks on the eve of the war, even before 1914 the capital's working class was not overwhelmingly proletarian in the Marxist sense. Because the labour force grew by the continuous migration of peasants to the city, mainly young unmarried males from the North-Western and Central Industrial regions, the dominant weight of the peasant element in the labouring population exerted a decisive impact on the structure of the working class. Men outnumbered women; the bulk of the labour force was aged 16–40; single workers were more numerous than married; most were literate, although only a small number were in any sense properly educated. Before 1914 cadre workers were a minority. Yet these hereditary, class-conscious workers, integrated into urban culture with their families resident in the city and cut off from their rural roots, for the most part skilled factory and artisanal operatives, furnished to a great degree the ranks of labour and revolutionary activists. They constituted the solid proletarian core of all the socialist parties, particularly the Bolsheviks. They also formed the workers' intelligentsia, whose numbers grew after 1905. But a majority of the labour force were still peasant workers, for the most part unskilled or semi-skilled, who retained ties to the land as a form of social security. On the other hand, both the traditions of rural migration and urban work in the provinces from which so many Petersburg migrants came and the institution of the *zemliachestvo* may have helped ease newcomers' adoption to city and industrial life, lessening their psychological disorientation and social anomie. If the capital's working class was still at the transition stage towards a hereditary proletariat, the First World War altered the balance between cadre and peasant workers to the detriment of the former. The weight of cadre workers was reduced by conscription, the immigration of new peasant workers and refugees, as well as the increased hiring of women and operatives from other social strata. On the eve of the February revolution the Petrograd labour force was distinctly less proletarian in nature than three years earlier.

The emerging labour force, moreover, was marked by social stratification. A fundamental division lay between skilled and semi- and unskilled operatives. An examination of the membership of legal labour organisations, revolutionary parties and participants in strikes reveals the pivotal role played within them by young, skilled, single male workers, both factory and artisanal. The 'successful' trade unions and educational societies were precisely those in which this group predominated. The 'proletarianisation' of the Petersburg Bolshevik party after 1907 owed everything to their influx into its ranks. The predominance of machine construction and electrical equipment plants in work protests in 1912–17 is to be explained by the high ratios therein of skilled, well-paid, literate younger men. The greater remuneration of skilled operatives and slightly shorter hours of work gave them the resources and time to organise and act. They were more assimilated to urban life and culture, possessing a stronger sense of trade identity, self-respect and personal independence. Semi-skilled machine operators and unskilled day labourers, on the other hand, lagged far behind the skilled in commitment to labour or revolutionary institutions and industrial militancy. Their lowly rates of pay, lengthy hours of toil, low expectations, minimal literacy and exhaustive work all acted against long-term commitments to organisation while their lack of skills deprived them of bargaining power. For these reasons industries containing large numbers of the semi-skilled or unskilled (animal products, factory-based food processing, mineral products, textiles), as well as the service sector, were almost impossible to unionise or to attract in a meaningful way into the strike struggle. Similar factors explain the low participation rates of women, who, for the most part, were employed as domestic servants, sweated outworkers in the service sector and, increasingly in the war years, as unskilled or semi-skilled machine operators in chemicals, food processing and textiles. In addition most women workers were younger than men, often in fact young girls aged 15–20. Treated as social inferiors by both bosses and fellow male workers, they had a far weaker sense of themselves as factory workers than did skilled males. Like the male unskilled, women could be drawn into short-term economic protest, but not into longer-term organisation.

Residential distribution and the urban environment contributed in different ways to social unrest and class antagonisms. In the central city districts, workers, mostly artisanal and service, lived in propinquity to the rich and powerful. On the other hand, there were evolving more distinctly proletarian quarters such as Narva, Neva, Vasil'evskii Island and Vyborg. There were also distinct disparities in amenities between working-class housing and the homes of the bourgeoisie and gentry. The Vyborg district particularly stood out on account of its high concentration of skilled, better-educated metalworkers.

Experience at the place of employment and conditions therein had a significant effect on the outlook of Petersburg workers. The attitudes of employers and state towards employees helped mould working-class consciousness and contributed to operatives' alienation from the regime.

The autocratic power of managers and foremen in factories, as well as of petty artisanal employers, together with the restoration of the old order in plants after 1907 with its fines, searches, factory regulations and assault upon human dignity, gave rise both in the first revolution and, most spectacularly in 1917, to the demand for a 'constitutional factory order'. In this respect the pre-war and wartime labour unrest revealed certain elements of continuity. Thus in 1912–14, 31 to 41 per cent of economic disputes concerned 'authority at work', whilst the ratio during the war years remained as high as a quarter. Such strikes were especially common in metalworking, printing and textiles before the war, and in heavy industry during the war. The actions of foremen in imposing fines, in matters of hiring and firing, and derogatory attitudes towards operatives, were a prime cause of such walk-outs. On the other hand, calls for the institution of a constitutional factory order rarely included demands for some form of worker representation. In the main they amounted rather to a desire to reform management style than to challenge the existence of private ownership and control of management's generally accepted functions.

The hostility of the employers, represented by the POZF, towards all labour organisations and their claims, as well as the methods adopted to cope with labour unrest, contributed towards the estrangement of workers. The POZF, almost the exclusive tool of the captains of heavy industry, always refused to grant recognition to trade unions or collective bargaining or arbitration chambers. The concept of a pacific regulation of labour relations was alien to it. Thus the POZF reacted bitterly to the tactics of class collaboration and liberal labour reforms propounded by the TsVPK during the war and fought successfully to squash all the sensible and moderate proposals emanating from Konovalov and the Labour Group of the TsVPK. During strikes the POZF's members resorted to a battery of repressive measures, embracing fines and lock-outs before the First World War, whilst they welcomed the intermittent intervention of the military in the war years to crush certain stoppages through the call-up of strikers enjoying deferment from military service. Yet these were essentially *ad hoc* devices, as the POZF failed to elaborate any mutually acceptable set of punitive measures or apply them in a consistent manner. At one level this scarcely mattered since before the war the industrialists more and more defeated outright the vast majority of economically inspired stoppages, whilst during the war a combination of greater conciliatoriness (at least concerning demands for pay rises) and repression likewise contained labour unrest. But from the perspective of 1917 the short-sighted policies of the capital's employers and their rejection of all concessions to workers contributed immeasurably to the peculiar explosiveness of labour unrest in that year and to the popularity of the factory committee movement.

The ambivalent attitude of the state towards labour was a further powerful factor precluding the emergence of a legal labour movement on West European lines. Ministers, bureaucrats, the police and, during the war, the military, whose powers were enshrined in the Special Council for Defence, failed to pursue any consistent, coherent set of policies, oscillating between political and social reforms, paternalism and repression. The formulation of state labour policies was hindered by systemic constraints, the institutional weakness of the Council of Ministers, the social composition of the upper bureaucracy (its landed roots), the impact of high politics and the endemic bureaucratic rivalry between the Ministries of Internal Affairs (MVD) and Trade and Industry (MTP). Despite the grant of the vote to many workers in December 1905, the legalisation of trade unions in March 1906 and the passing of the Social Insurance Laws in 1912, political circumstances were firmly against the reformist option. The MTP defended state-directed paternalism, on the grounds that labour conflicts were an inevitable by-product of an economic upsurge and that repression was futile. Its course found little support in the upper echelons of government, where the politically more powerful MVD contributed most to the evolution of official labour policy-making. Distrusting working-class spontaneity and self-activity and fearful of the use revolutionaries might make of legal organs, the MVD and the Department of Police constantly sought to keep trade unions, educational societies and sickness funds within the narrowest confines of strictly interpreted laws. Yet even in the war an outright repressive course could not be fashioned; the militarisation of labour was much discussed but never enacted. The ambivalent labour policies of the state after 1907 reinforced its already existing identification in the eyes of workers as the firm ally of the employers. The actions of industrialists, bureaucrats and police all helped undermine skilled workers' confidence in the value of the legal path to change and the pursuit of reformist labour policies. The decline in the attraction of Menshevism and the rise in that of Bolshevism for skilled worker activists in 1913 and 1914 owed much to the state's and employers' discrediting of the purposes of trade unionism and parliamentary representation.

The role played by the revolutionary parties, in particular the Bolsheviks, in promoting political radicalism among Russian workers has long been a matter of partisan controversy. Most Western historians, concentrating on the exiled sections of the socialist parties, have tended to portray the revolutionary movement as undergoing irretrievable decline after 1907, hastened by ideological divisions. Soviet scholars have oscillated, according to changes in ideological dictates, between depicting a Bolshevik party in disarray and decay and the picture of a resurgent party, led by Lenin from Western Europe. Both approaches have lost sight of the other socialist factions.

In St Petersburg (Petrograd) there always existed between 1907 and 1917 a bewildering variety of socialist groups, of whom the Bolsheviks were only one and by no means always the dominant. Contrary to Lenin's and Soviet researchers' aspersions all the socialist factions were unambiguously revolutionary in that they sought the immediate goal of the overthrow of Tsardom and the longer-term vision of a socialist society. Indeed concentration of attention upon the divisions between Bolsheviks, Mensheviks and Socialist Revolutionaries has obscured the fragmention that occurred within these parties after 1907. The new internal divisions arose out of their intellectual leaders' response to the defeat of the 1905 revolution and the new perspectives opened up for legal labour institutions under the 1906 constitution. Thus, within Bolshevism, Lenin and his adherents were only one of several factions, whose gamut included Otzovists, Ultimatists, Vperedists and Bolshevik Conciliators. The issue of 'Liquidationism' put severe strain, too, upon Menshevism, opening up differences between the exiles grouped around *Golos sotsial-demokrata*, the intellectual progenitors of *Nasha zaria* and the *'praktiki'*, the labour leaders of the trade unions and educational societies. The issue of future tactics likewise polarised SRs into a left, an evolving reformist right and a central leadership clinging to former tactical precepts.

The revolutionaries' ideological reaction to the outbreak of war in July 1914 deepened factional infighting. Whatever the positions of the socialist leaders in exile, there were few outright defensists or defeatists in the ranks of the socialist intellectuals and labour activists in the capital. Almost all revolutionary groups rejected the concepts of social peace and class collaboration. Most, including Mensheviks, argued for the continuation of the revolutionary struggle. Petrograd Bolsheviks were not the sole or most consistent socialist opponents of the war. Indeed they can scarcely be classed as Leninist at all in their position on the war, rejecting or ignoring their leader's concepts of defeatism, civil war and the Third International. It would be more accurate to state that they, along with the Menshevik Central Initiative Group and the Left SRs, evolved an internationalist stance. On the other hand most Mensheviks and some SRs adopted the distinctive position of self-defence as conceived by A. N. Potresov. Two new realignments began to take shape amongst Petrograd socialists. Whilst they differed drastically in their assessment of the purposes of the forthcoming revolution, they were united in practical action for the promptest overthrow of the dynasty.

Even in the more favourable circumstances of the period from 1907 to 1914, when communications and correspondence with Russia were relatively uncomplicated and regular, none of the exiled socialist leaders could or did exercise effective, daily control over their parties or groups in the capital. They remained divorced from developments in the city. None succeeded in establishing permanent, organisational links to St Petersburg. Lenin proved no exception in this respect. He was unable to exert more than minimal leverage on either the Bolshevik party as a whole or his own grouping within it. The Russian Bureau, set up in August 1908, met rarely, collapsing within a year. It was not reformed effectively until January 1916, lasting then a mere month. The Central Committee, elected at the schismatic Prague Conference, was soon scattered by arrests and never offered effective leadership. Shortage of funds precluded Lenin's regular dispatch of agents and adequate copies of the infrequently published *Sotsial-demokrat*. His few emissaries were soon arrested, such as Inessa Armand or Iu. Sverdlov, or acted in an independent manner, as did Stalin and Shliapnikov. Lenin played scarcely any role in the launching of *Zvezda* and *Pravda*, nor did he secure control of the editorial board of the new daily or the Bolshevik parliamentary fraction until late 1913. He exercised no personal influence at all over the affairs of trade unions or sickness insurance funds. The circumstances of the war left him even more isolated in Switzerland, with exiguous contact with or influence over Petrograd Bolsheviks and their policies. In similar fashion and for the same reasons the Menshevik luminaries in Western Europe, and the Organisational Committee elected at the August conference 1912, were reduced to ineffectual spectators, their relations with the 'Liquidationist' and 'self-defensists' literati inside the capital constantly strained and tense.

The true leaders of the Petersburg labour movement in its legal and covert forms were the local activists, who constituted a revolutionary sub-élite. These secondary-rank bosses, for the most part workers or worker–intellectuals, were not the mere executants of decisions taken outside Russia. Both Bolshevik and Menshevik, as well as SR cadres, resented and rejected both the claim of the intellectual exiles to leadership, and in particular, their unquenchable thirst for sterile factional infighting. Working-class militants, desirous of self-organisation, opposed the intellectuals' striving to control workers. Throughout the entire decade, these secondary local leaders pursued their own policies. The Bolsheviks' commitment to a national general political strike from the summer of 1913, the electoral strategy in the Fourth Duma elections, the decision to launch an attack on Menshevik union positions in the spring of 1913 and the resurrection of the slogan of a soviet in October 1915 were all cases where the activists took the lead. Lenin later either gave them retrospective sanction or opposed them in vain.

Within the ranks of Social Democracy, the local sub-élite gave repeated proof of its commitment to the restoration of party unity, from the time of the meeting of the expanded editorial·board of *Proletarii* in June 1909 when the Petersburg representatives opposed Lenin's motion to expel the Otzovists and Ultimatists, to the Prague Conference in January 1912 which local Vperedists and Bolshevik Conciliators condemned. The initiators and editors of *Pravda*, too, sought a non-factional newspaper and autonomy from Lenin; they pursued a conciliatory line on party unity and in the Fourth Duma elections. Trotskii's newspaper *Pravda* (Vienna), which preached party unity, was popular among activists. In the elections to the new central insurance organs in the spring of 1914 there were united Social Democratic slates and a single *nakaz* (mandate). The Social Democratic fractions of the Third and Fourth State Dumas struggled to 1913 to remain united and independent of foreign control. The longer European hostilities dragged on, this desire for party unity, initially weakened by the ideological divisions over the war, resurfaced. Local Bolshevik illegal literature kept an eloquent silence about the 'sins' of Menshevik and SR 'social patriots'. Such longings found expression in repeated efforts to set up united Social Democratic groups, from the Central Group of Social Democratic Workers in 1911–12 to the Mezhraionka. It is no accident that both were the only relatively 'successful' socialist groups between 1908 and 1914.

Furthermore, contrary to the increasingly bitter relations between the various socialist leaders living abroad, the realities of the underground compelled all local revolutionary groups to co-operate, particularly in preparations for political strikes. Until 1913 elections to union executives took place on a non-partisan basis, whilst Bolsheviks and Mensheviks initially worked together in the insurance campaign in 1913. The two Social Democratic fractions drew up a joint parliamentary declaration on the war in July 1914. In late 1916 all the internationalist groupings endeavoured to set up an Information Bureau.

In attempting to assess the influence of the many socialist groupings in St Petersburg, the historian has to examine the potential mechanisms available for reaching out to the masses. Throughout this period neither illegal structures nor the new legal institutions provided effective means of revolutionary mass mobilisation. Neither enabled revolutionary cadres to exercise continuing or central control over the labour movement. Whether in the years of depression after 1907 or in the pre-war or wartime boom, the Bolsheviks signally failed to establish viable underground networks, either permanently functioning all-city or district committees. The absence of a PK or district committees for lengthy periods deprived activists of instruments capable of furnishing leadership and direction. The party at best was reduced to a cellular existence. Yet even in this form Social Democratic factory collectives were present for the most part only in machine construction and electrical goods industries, primarily in Vyborg, Narva and Neva districts in the 1911–14 period. All revolutionary groupings, including the Bolsheviks, suffered severely from the depredations of the Okhrana, thanks to its secret agents, working–class disillusionment and fear of provocation, leading to a distaste for underground work, an acute shortage of finance, secret printing presses and illegal literature, as well as the flight of much of the intelligentsia from revolutionary work with a consequent chronic dearth of agitators, propagandists and organisers. Within Petersburg Bolshevism, the Leninists were a minority to 1912, outnumbered by Left Bolsheviks and Bolshevik Conciliators. In 1913–14 Leninists probably came to predominate as Vperedism disintegrated and Bolshevik Conciliators possessed no organisations of their own. Both in 1913 and 1914, as well as in 1915–16, the local Bolsheviks failed to spark a national general political strike or mass street demonstrations or create a Soviet of Workers' Deputies. Within Menshevism, Party Mensheviks were few. The Menshevik underground had self-destructed in 1908 as most of its members abandoned it for legal work. Revived as the Central Initiative Group in 1911, its activity was minimal before the war. The new body was weakened by tensions between 'Liquidationist' intellectuals and *praktiki*. Dissolved at the start of the war, the Central Initiative Group was revived only in mid-1916. The SRs' decentralised organisation had almost completely expired by 1910. Between then and the outbreak of hostilities, illegal SR district networks functioned only in the first months of 1913. During the war their district groupings, which were SR-internationalist, existed for a few brief months in late 1915 and early 1916. The Mezhraionka, after its foundation in October 1913, quickly made an appeal to cadres through its resolute hostility to factionalism. In the spring and autumn of 1914, and again in 1916 it succeeded in establishing, however briefly, a more durable committee structure than any other underground faction. Membership of all socialist groups was in a state of constant flux and remained minute. With the exception of the Baltic Fleet in 1912 and late 1915, none of the parties succeeded in establishing links with the garrison or navy.

In one respect alone did the Bolsheviks enjoy some measure of success over their Menshevik rivals, namely their gains in the legal labour sphere in 1912 to 1914. The Bolshevik Badaev was elected as the representative of St Petersburg workers to parliament in the autumn of 1912; *Pravda* was launched six months before its Menshevik rival *Luch* and always enjoyed a higher circulation; perhaps eleven and a half out of fifteen trade-union boards whose allegiance is known fell to the Bolsheviks, as did three educational societies' executives; the Bolsheviks split the united insurance campaign in late 1913 and a Pravdist list swept to victory in the elections to two of the three central insurance organs in March 1914. The Bolsheviks' ability to wrest from the Mensheviks their hold on the legal activist minority was the product not only of tactical factors such as voting by factional lists and the use of the mandate (*nakaz*) but also of the conditions in which skilled young male workers, factory and artisanal, found themselves between 1912 and 1914. The Mensheviks basically lost the confidence of their erstwhile constituency because their policies of moderation, of gradualism, of working within the new legal system and of caution in industrial disputes seemed to make less and less sense. The ambivalent attitude of the state towards labour organisations and the resistance of employers to skilled workers' demands in the disputes of 1912 and 1914 drove this group to lose faith in 'legal opportunities' and the legitimacy of trade unionism. The Bolsheviks' militancy and forceful articulation of workers' interests, as well as their vision of imminent revolution, more and more appealed to skilled, hereditary workers.

Yet one must not exaggerate the scale and importance of the Bolsheviks' conquests from 1912 to 1914, or interpret them as specific victories by Lenin and his local supporters. Many of the gains were rather illusory and tell one little about the political views, if any, of the majority of workers. In the Fourth Duma and central insurance elections, for example, entire categories of the labour force were disenfranchised by law; the campaigns and voting were marked by ambiguity, the desire on the part of Social Democratic activists for party unity and their hostility to Leninist factionalism; the SRs quixotically boycotted the polls; electors represented the activist minority, drawn in the main from skilled workers in privately owned heavy industry. Only a minority of operatives, worker–intellectuals, skilled male workers in engineering and printing and artisans, read the socialist press. Most workers preferred commercial fiction and *Gazeta kopeika*. Furthermore the real victors were not so much Leninists as Bolshevik Conciliators and members of the Mezhraionka. These Bolshevik legal cadres proved unamenable to domination by Lenin abroad and articulated their own policies. Indeed once in control of trade unions and *kassy* they tended to pursue in practice the policies of their Menshevik predecessors.

At a more fundamental level the Bolsheviks' gains were of limited value to their cause because, contrary to the Mensheviks' vision of a

'Europeanisation' of the labour movement, the legal labour institutions proved to be a feeble vehicle of revolutionary outreach to the masses. In sharp contrast to Imperial Germany, where after 1890 the free trade unions became the bedrock of the Social Democratic Party, professional organisations in the capital signally failed to establish their legitimacy among the rank and file. The scope of union allegiance was severely limited. Even after some measure of recovery from their nadir of membership in 1910 (12,000), their appeal encompassed a mere 28,000 in 1914. Unions remained organisationally and financially feeble. The attitudes of the state and St Petersburg employers towards professional organisations also contributed greatly to their emasculation. Trade unions, therefore, failed to form a broad popular basis for an open mass party. Neither could they act as surrogates for the Bolshevik underground. The State Duma Social Democratic fraction likewise was a weak instrument of revolutionary propaganda and political education of the masses. Its deputies stood no chance of securing positive legislative achievements. The Menshevik parliamentary representatives, who lacked internal cohesion, held aloof from the underground, whilst the Bolshevik deputies played a minor role in illegal activities until late 1913 and were soon weakened by the Malinovskii affair. The functions of the *kassy* were severely limited by the authorities and the employers. Workers were in general apathetic towards parliamentary affairs and the legal congresses of 1908 to 1912. The labour groups at these gatherings left no organisations behind them. Unlike the German Social Democrats, their Russian counterparts proved unable to erect a series of ancillary organisations which could create an entire working-class sub-culture, an alternative society.

During the war, the depredations of the authorities reduced the chances of legal activity almost to nil. The Bolshevik deputies were arrested in November 1914; no legal daily socialist press existed; trade unions all but expired; the *kassy* could not replace them. The decision of the TsVPK leadership to establish a Labour Group provided Mensheviks with an unlooked for opportunity to recoup their fortunes. But the elections of the Group in the autumn of 1915 and its actions thereafter deepened factional infighting, even within Menshevism itself. Lacking legitimacy in the eyes of its constituents owing to the contested method of its selection and the distortion of its views by its opponents, the Labour Group set out to secure support by a programme of labour reforms. This initial legalist strategy had the opposite effect by the summer of 1916. However, when the Group altered its stance late in 1916 in favour of an illegal, revolutionary course it soon evoked a warm response, as the strikes of 14 February 1917 testified.

Due to the manifold weaknesses of the revolutionary underground and of the legal labour institutions between 1907 and 1917, work stoppages became the main form of opposition on the part of the capital's working-class to the regime. Both in the period April 1912 to July 1914 and, at a much lower level, in the months between August 1915 and February 1917, the monarchy faced its gravest threat in its capital from a steadily rising wave of walk-outs, the majority of which were of a political nature. In 1912–14, 61 per cent of all strikes and 83 per cent of all strikers were politically inspired, whilst the corresponding ratios for the period August 1914 to 22 February 1917 were 59 per cent and 68 per cent respectively. Moreover, the metalworking industries, so crucial to national defence, were by far the worst affected throughout the two periods of labour turbulence. In 1912 to 1914, 88 per cent of all strikers in heavy industry participated in politically motivated walk-outs; in 1914–17, 71 per cent. Indeed the prevalence of disputes of a political nature in its capital goods sector made St Petersburg the epicentre of all Russian labour protest in the pre-war years and again in 1916. These political stoppages provided the main outlet for a diffuse and growing opposition by more and more workers to the existing political system. They reveal that the political and economic concessions of 1905 to 1906 had not allayed the hostility of the capital's operatives to the monarchy.

Economic disputes, too, provided cause for anxiety on the part of the authorities and industrialists. They were responsible for the bulk of lost working days. In the years from 1912 to 1914 they became more persistent and stubborn, although during the war they were of shorter duration. Whilst wage rates remained the single most important cause of economically motivated walk-outs throughout the time span 1907–1917, many industrial actions represented a genuine challenge to managerial authority and an attempt to regain the concessions lost in the employers' counter-offensive of 1907 to 1911.

Furthermore, whilst the authorities' fears about the degree of revolutionary involvement in strikes, especially of a political nature, proved to be greatly overdrawn, it would be equally erroneous to conclude that the labour unrest was completely 'spontaneous'. In place of socialist collectives and trade unions, surrogate forms of organisation were created during disputes in the form of temporary strike committees and general meetings. Both strengthened workers' allegiance to their factories. In the years from 1912 to 1914 the socialist daily press played an especially vital function as a source of news, moral and material support. Strikes created their own leadership, often very young workers without a revolutionary past or worker–intellectuals who had joined the revolutionary movement in 1905–7 and subsequently abandoned it.

Yet the strike movement also suffered from defects which made it a less effective vehicle for political change. As the earlier discussion has revealed, the geographic and sectoral basis of stoppages within St Petersburg was very one-sided. The entire service sector, communications and construction were noteworthy by their absence. Within manufacturing, light industry, printing, chemicals, animal and mineral products, and artisanal trades lagged far behind the metalworking sector, both in political and in economic strikes. During the pre-war unrest Vyborg and Petrograd Side districts accounted for 36 per cent of all strikes, a ratio rising to 53 per cent during the war. In 1912 to 1914 and in 1916 the rest of the country was far less affected by industrial conflicts than the capital. Thus the city's vanguard role was a distinct weakness. The July 1914 'general' strike in St Petersburg remained an isolated phenomenon. Atrophied revolutionary factory collectives, enfeebled trade unions and transient strike organs could neither guide working-class opposition as expressed in politically inspired strikes into mass support for specific political goals nor utilise the stoppages to create permanent structures. The political walk-outs of 1912 to 1917 were marked by a general absence of concrete political demands. The strikes, like the legal labour institutions, do not reveal a commitment on the part of a majority of the capital's workers to one particular revolutionary party or group. Thus workers' revolutionary consciousness, which was developed above all by their own experience, was limited. On the eve of 1917, although workers profoundly desired political change, and the end of the *ancien régime*, their consciousness did not embrace the acceptance of any alternative socialist political philosophy. In that fact lay the Bolsheviks' greatest opportunity in 1917. Whatever the longer-term consequences for themselves, in the short term the authorities and the employers were able to cope with labour unrest. From 1912 to 1914 the members of the POZF defeated outright most strikes. During the war high profits let them appear more conciliatory towards wage demands.

Finally, a comparison between the events of the first half of July 1914 in the capital and those of the last six days of February 1917 highlights the general strengths and weaknesses of the St Petersburg labour movement. It also illuminates the reasons for the monarchy's survival in the earlier but not the later outburst of working-class protest.

The stoppages of 3–15 July 1914 never assumed a truly 'mass' character. At their peak a mere 28 per cent of the manufacturing labour force was involved. The sectoral scope remained limited. The service sector, shop personnel, railwaymen, port and construction workers did not participate, whilst textiles, baking, wood and printing were under-represented. Workers in both petty and gigantic establishments were far less involved. In sharp contrast, at their height the February 1917 walk-outs embraced 80 per cent of all manufacturing workers, enveloping for the first time on a broad scale operatives in all the non-metalworking sectors. Far more women and unskilled, as well as employees in small and very large enterprises, were swept into the protests. Geographically, too, the February strike movement was more evenly spread across all the city districts. Furthermore, whereas the police successfully prevented mass demonstrations in the city centre in July 1914, they signally failed to do so from the very outset of the February events.

The July 1914 'general' strike noticeably failed to evoke the sympathy of other social strata. The parliamentary liberal opposition remained indifferent. On the other hand, February 1917 became a truly popular movement, swiftly embracing in its revolutionary *élan* students, members of the professions, artisans and service employees. Most crucially of all, in the afternoon and evening of 27 February the liberals in the State Duma deserted the government.

If none of the revolutionary parties was responsible for the initial events which sparked the respective general strikes, (the Putilov incident on 3 July 1914 and the walk-outs of textile women workers on 23 February 1917) the two mass stoppages cannot be dismissed either as merely 'elemental' outbursts. On the other hand, revolutionary leadership was not the exclusive prerogative of the Bolsheviks, nor was it clear-cut, consistent or very effective. On both occasions local cadres of all different socialist groups co-operated, forming joint factory committees and attempting to provide a focus to demonstrations. Whereas only a minority of activists interpreted the Putilov shootings of 3 July 1914 as the opportunity to launch an armed uprising, expectations were much higher among far more cadres in February 1917 due to the more embittered, extreme mood of workers and middle classes alike. Many revolutionary activists regarded the developments of 23–4 February as marking the prelude to the final assault against Tsardom by a general political strike and armed insurrection. Both events brought to the surface differences between the local Bolshevik leadership and their rank and file, rendering impossible the fashioning of a coherent party response. Due to the thin spread of revolutionary collectives in factories and the inability to create a Soviet of Workers' Deputies, at least before the evening of 27 February, or other forms of inter-party co-operation, the socialist factions were unable to furnish overall or coherent direction to both movements.

The reactions of the authorities and employers also proved to be extremely different. Whereas in July 1914 none felt the regime to be in danger and all acted without vacillation, three years later the response of both fatally proved to be confused and inept.

The attitude of the garrison was decisive on both occasions. Whilst the regime had been able with equanimity to use force to break the July 1914 'general' strike, from the very outset of the February days the loyalty of the troops was in doubt. The changes in the composition of the garrison during the war, the ambivalent attitudes of many soldiers and even junior officers towards the demonstrators, the impact of fraternisation all acted to dissolve the oath of allegiance. The order to shoot on 26 February was the turning point in the sympathies of a crucial minority of soldiers.

The history of the labour movement in St Petersburg in the last decade of Tsarist rule left a legacy which deeply affected the relations between labour and capital in 1917 and the fortunes of the revolutionary parties. The efforts of the moderate Menshevik and SR leaders of the Petrograd Soviet of Workers' and Soldiers' Deputies and of A. I. Konovalov, the Minister of Trade and Industry in the First Provisional Government, to construct a West European style of labour relations based on mechanisms of conciliation and arbitration, the legalisation of workers' organisations and economic concessions to workers foundered not only on the deepening economic crisis but also on the Tsarist inheritance.[1] The Mensheviks' labour programme, which was predicated on collaboration with the progressive bourgeoisie, was moulded both by their experience of the 1905 revolution and by the Labour Group's participation in the TsVPK. It was in part wrecked by the policies of the Petrograd employers. In view of the POZF's record of total hostility to and non-cooperation with labour organisations, as well as its very recent subversion of the TsVPK reform proposals, the sincerity of its signature on its accord of 10 March with the Petrograd Soviet and its new-found enthusiasm for the reconstruction of labour relations on a new legal basis must be questioned. It is more likely that the sudden removal of the apparatus of repression and the necessity of recognising *faits accomplis* lay behind the volte-face of accepting factory committees and conciliation chambers and granting the eight-hour day. The later actions of the POZF bear out this interpretation.[2] Furthermore, the alienation of workers from their employers' methods of management had become so deep as a consequence of their pre-1917 experience of authority in the workplace and the support of state power for the owners' strikebreaking proclivities that the factory committee movement at once took deep root among operatives, the expression of a longing for a say in decisions affecting their lives. Petrograd workers' demands and actions in March–April 1917, then, were not merely a by-product of the fall of the *ancien régime* in state and factory. Wage rises, the introduction of the eight-hour day and polite treatment, removal of hated foremen and managers, some measure of control by factory

committees over overtime and hiring and firing, widespread phenomena in the early spring of 1917, all reflected pent-up desires with
lengthy antecedents.[3] Yet as the history of authority disputes in the
pre-war years and 1915–16 reveals, workers had not wanted before
the February revolution to run the factories themselves or expropriate
the owners. Although the character of the movement for 'workers'
control' changed radically and swiftly in the summer and autumn of
1917, it, too, was in no sense a syndicalist movement. Just as the
origins of authority conflicts before 1917 lay in workers' direct
experiences at the workplace, so in the course of 1917 the widening
scope of demands for 'workers' control' reflected workers' response
to economic collapse and the spectre of unemployment.[4]

As far as the revolutionary parties were concerned, they emerged
from the last ten years of Tsardom with little concrete to show for
their efforts. None of the socialist groups, including the Bolsheviks,
entered the new free Russia with solid legal or illegal structures or
anything other than a minute following among a minority of skilled
male workers. In that sense the revolutionary politics of 1917 began
in a vacuum with each of the three contenders, Bolsheviks, Mensheviks and Socialist Revolutionaries, starting on an equal footing in the
emerging struggle for power. The development of mass revolutionary consciousness in the form of a commitment to a specific socialist
party or political philosophies was fundamentally a phenomenon of
the months after the fall of Nicholas II, when the politicisation of the
masses began in earnest.

Appendix I

POLITICAL MASS STRIKES IN ST PETERSBURG, APRIL 1912–3 JULY 1914

Date	Purpose of Stoppage	Estimates of Numbers of Strikers		
		Author's	*Police*	*Socialist press*
1912				
14–22 Apr.	Protest against the Lena massacre	72,395	140,000	200,000
1 May	May Day	63,546	150,000	200,000
5–16 Oct.	Cassation of elections from workers' curiae to the Fourth State Duma	51,707	50,000	100,000
29–31 Oct.	Court martial of Sevastopol naval mutineers	72,761	60,000	100,000
15 Nov.	Opening of the Fourth State Duma	36,110	23,000	40,000
14 Dec.	Social Democratic interpellation in the State Duma concerning repressions of trade unions	13,610	55,000	61,000
TOTAL		310,129	478,000	701,000
1913				
9 Jan.	Anniversary of Bloody Sunday, 1905	70,950	60,000	72,000
4 Apr.	Anniversary of the Lena massacre	77,778	60,000	85,000
1 May	May Day	135,412	110,000	250,000
17–19 June	The court martial of Baltic Fleet sailors	35,711	34,000	70,250
1–3 July	Repression of the labour press	29,945	26,613	62,000
25–27 Sept.	Repression of the labour press in Moscow	51,998	62,000	100,000

APPENDIX I

Date	Purpose of Stoppage	Estimates of Numbers of Strikers		
		Author's	Police	Socialist press
17–18 Oct.	Anniversary of the October Manifesto, 1905	7,367	–	9,150
6–7 Nov.	Trial of strikers at the Obukhov arms plant	68,039	83,500	110,569
3–5 Dec.	Fine levied upon the State Duma deputy from St Petersburg, A. E. Badaev	1,577	2,800	5,635
TOTAL		478,777	438,913	764,604
1914				
9 Jan.	Anniversary of Bloody Sunday, 1905	113,590	110,000	141,238
19 Feb.	Anniversary of the Emancipation of the Serfs, 1861	19,420	–	15,300
4 Mar.	Secret conference on rearmament between the government and State Duma on 1 March	3,000	4,300	5,340
6–12 Mar.	Repression of the labour press and trade unions	20,336	26,611	35,132
13–14 Mar.	Social Democratic interpellation in the State Duma concerning the Lena massacre	55,249	55,300	66,372
17–20 Mar.	Protest against the mass faintings of women workers in the Treugol'nik rubber plant	83,889	130,000	156,030
23–26 Apr.	Exclusion of left-wing deputies from the State Duma	64,762	55,800	75,431
1 May	May Day	170,030	125,000	215,000
19–20 May	Second trial of Obukhov strikers	88,673	72,000	112,825
9–11 June	Trial of St Petersburg lawyers defending Mendel Beilis, and trial of a worker at St Petersburg Pipes	26,775	22,574	35,660
1–2 July	Solidarity with Baku oil workers' stoppages	9,038	3,100	11,901
TOTAL		654,762	604,685	870,229

Appendix II

POLITICAL MASS STRIKES IN PETROGRAD, 19 JULY 1914–22 FEBRUARY 1917

| | | *Estimates of Numbers of Strikers* | | |
Date	Purpose of Stoppage	Author's	Police	Factory Inspectorate
July–Dec. 1914				
19–20 July	Protest against the war	11,320	27,360	
12 Nov.	Arrest of Bolshevik deputies to the State Duma	1,050	1,050	
1915				
9 Jan.	Anniversary of Bloody Sunday, 1905	2,346	2,528	1,791
10–13 Feb.	Trial of the Bolshevik Duma Deputies	167		
1 May	May Day	845	380	605
17–20 Aug.	Protest against the shooting of workers at Ivanovo and Kostroma	16,404	9,144	12,574
2–6 Sept.	Protest against arrests of workers and prorogation of the State Duma	79,209	60,696	62,221
1916				
9 Jan.	Anniversary of Bloody Sunday, 1905	60,507	66,767	45,155
29 Feb.– 4 Mar.	Support for Putilov strikers	49,921	60,320	57,536
4 Apr.	Anniversary of the Lena massacre	8,490	8,090	8,000

Date	Purpose of Stoppage	Estimates of Numbers of Strikers		
		Author's	*Police*	*Factory Inspectorate*
17–21 Oct.	Food shortages	89,542		
26 Oct.– 1 Nov.	Protest against the trials of soliders of 181st Infantry Regiment and of Baltic sailors	87,695		
Both October strikes together		177,237	246,937	137,867
1917				
9 Jan.	Anniversary of Bloody Sunday, 1905	142,415	137,536	94,887
14–15 Feb.	Reopening of the State Duma	84,695	95,319	64,330

NOTES

Chapter 1

1. St Petersburg comprised the city proper and the suburbs of Peterhof and Shlissel'burg to the south-west and south-east respectively, and across the Neva, Okhta and Poliustrovo to the east, Lesnoi to the north, and Staraia and Novaia Derevnia to the north-west (see Map). The suburbs did not come under the jurisdiction of the Governor General of St Petersburg and the St Petersburg Municipal Duma, but the Governor of St Petersburg province (*guberniia*) and the district *zemstvo*. As these environs formed in fact an integral part of the capital's economy and social structure, throughout this book, unless otherwise stated, the term 'St Petersburg' will refer to the city and the suburbs inclusive. The capital was split into the administrative divisions of districts (*chasti*), which in turn were subdivided into wards (*uchastki*).

2. Henry Norman, *All the Russias* (London, 1902), p. 8.

3. Charles Dobson, *St Petersburg* (London, 1910), pp. 112, 115, 122–3; Karl Baedeker, *Russia, with Teheran, Port Arthur and Peking* (London, 1914), pp. 88–90, 95–7; *Ocherki istorii Leningrada. Tom tretii. Period imperializma i burzhuazno-demokraticheskikh revoliutsii 1895–1917gg.* (Moscow-Leningrad, 1956), pp. 838, 904, 910, 912.

4. Baedeker, *Russia*, op. cit., p. 102.

5. Ibid., p. 99. There is an excellent description of Moscow in Joseph Bradley, *Muzhik and Muscovite. Urbaniza-* tion in Late Imperial Russia (Berkeley, 1985). The theme of the 'dual city' is also explored by the contributors to Michael F. Hamm (ed.), *The City in Late Imperial Russia* (Bloomington, 1986).

6. Thomas S. Fedor, *Patterns of Urban Growth in the Russian Empire in the Nineteenth Century* (Chicago, 1975), pp. 145, 173–8.

7. The table is based on A. G. Rashin, *Naselenie Rossii za sto let* (Moscow, 1956), Table 74, p. 114.

8. *Svod otchetov fabrichnykh inspektorov za 1912 god* (St Petersburg, 1913), p. 26; TsGIA, f.1284, op.194, 1913g., d.128, l.13. In Moscow province, by contrast, in 1902 37 per cent of the industrial labour force had found work in the city itself but 63 per cent in manufacturing establishments in the province outside the metropolis (Robert E. Johnson, *Peasant and Proletarian: The Working Class of Moscow in the Late Nineteenth Century*, Leicester, 1979, p. 25).

9. *Petrograd po perepisi 15 dekabria 1910 goda* (Petrograd, 1914), tom 2, pp. 1–23. Due to the deficiencies of all other statistical surveys of the city's labour force, in particular those of the factory inspectorate (see note 12), the four decennial censuses of the capital carried out by the St Peterburg Municipal Board between 1881 and 1910 furnish the most reasonably accurate and comprehensive picture of wage earners at the moment each was taken. Unfortunately the data of the 1910 census took a long time to work out

and were never published in full (S. N. Semanov, 'Sostav i polozhenie rabochikh Peterburga po dannym gorodskikh perepisei', in L. M. Ivanov (ed.), *Rabochii klass i rabochee dvizhenie v Rossii, 1861–1917*, Moscow, 1966, pp. 394–403).

10. James H. Bater, *St Petersburg. Industrialization and Change* (London, 1976), p. 223; *Ocherki*, op.cit., p. 73.

11. Bater, *St Petersburg*, op.cit., p. 223. According to the factory inspectorate, in St Petersburg province in 1913 the comparative share of heavy and light industry was 30.8 and 31.1 per cent of the factory labour force ('Polozhenie promyshlennosti v Petrogradskoi gubernii 1913g.', *Vestnik finansov, promyshlennosti i torgovli*, no. 38 (1914), p. 38). As the factory inspectorate excluded state-owned enterprises from its scope, these figures underestimated the overall share of heavy industry.

12. The major source of official statistical materials are the annual reports of the factory inspectorate, published from 1901 as *Svod otchetov fabrichnykh inspektorov*. Their fundamental defect lay in the lack of a clear and consistent definition of a factory or a mill, with a consequent tendency to omit smaller units of production. With particular reference to St Petersburg, the *Svody* covered the entire province and did not distinguish the city. They also omitted state-owned plants from their purview (S. I. Antonova, 'Statistika fabrichnoi inspektsii kak istochnik po istorii proletariata', in L. M. Ivanov, *Rabochii klass*, op.cit., pp. 314–44; Olga Crisp, 'Labour and industry in Russia', Chapter 7 of the *Cambridge Economic History of Europe*, Vol. 7, Part 2, Cambridge, 1978, pp. 341–4; Victoria E. Bonnell, *Roots of Rebellion. Workers' Politics and Organization in St Petersburg and Moscow, 1900–1914*, Berkeley, 1983, pp. 21–3).

13. Bonnell, *Roots of Rebellion*, op.cit., p. 23. The category *'odinochki'* used in the city censuses referred to individual garret masters: by excluding a separate category of urban non-factory artisans, the censuses seriously underestimated the numbers so employed. And the 11,033 artisanal workshops registered with the Artisanal Board in 1910 referred only to master artisans (Bradley, *Muzhik and Muscovite*, op.cit., p. 96; U. A. Shuster, *Peter-*

burgskie rabochie v 1905–1907gg., Leningrad, 1976, p. 8. Shuster is one of the few Soviet investigators to make serious reference to artisans).

14. There exist, unfortunately, no statistical data on the exact division of the city's manufacturing labour force between artisanal and factory workers in the period 1908 to 1914. An analysis of the size of enterprises (see Chapter 2) affords some approximation of the weight of each group in particular branches of production.

15. *Ocherki*, op.cit., pp. 73–83; Bater, *St Petersburg*, op.cit., pp. 264–5.

16. In addition the following came under the care of the state: the Expedition of State Papers, the Imperial Porcelain and Glass, and Imperial Paper factories, Imperial Court Carriages and the railway workshops of the Warsaw and Nikolaev railroads.

17. *Ocherki*, op.cit., p. 36; Bater, *St Petersburg*, op.cit., p. 223; E. E. Kruze, *Peterburgskie rabochie v 1912–1914 godakh* (Leningrad, 1961), p. 34.

18. A. L. Sidorov, *Istoricheskie predposylki velikoi oktiabr'skoi sotsialisticheskoi revoliutsii* (Moscow, 1970), pp. 64, 67–8, 87; Kruze, *Peterburgskie rabochie*, op.cit., p. 33. Sidorov's essay, bearing the same title as his *Istoricheskie predposylki*, and the comments upon it by P. V. Volobuev and I. F. Gindin furnish an excellent example of this approach, as does I. F. Gindin's essay 'Sotsialno-ekonomicheskie itogi razvitie rossiiskogo kapitalizma i predposylki revoliutsii v nashei strane', in *Sverzhenie samoderzhaviia. Sbornik statei* (Moscow, 1970), pp. 39–88.

19. Olga Crisp, 'Banking in the industrialisation of Tsarist Russia, 1860–1914', in Olga Crisp, *Studies in the Russian Economy before 1914* (London, 1978), pp. 111–58. By 1916 foreign participation in the capital of the ten largest joint-stock commercial banks, nearly all located in the capital, reached 45 per cent of the total (ibid., p. 147). In the case of those banks most heavily involved in St Petersburg industry it was: Russo-Asiatic, 79 per cent (65 per cent French); St Petersburg Private Commercial, 58 per cent (exclusively French); St Petersburg Loan and Discount, 13 per cent (purely German); St Petersburg International, 40 per cent (33 per cent German) (ibid., Table 5.17, p. 148).

20. V. I. Bovykin, 'Banki i voennaia pro-myshlennost' Rossii nakanune pervoi mirovoi voiny', *Istoricheskie zapiski*, vol. 64 (1959), pp. 82–135.

21. Ibid., pp. 96–8, 124. Baranovskii manufactured time fuses, explosives and cartridge cases. A third case of takeover by the Russo-Asiatic and the Banque de l'Union Parisienne occurred in 1912 with the newly established Russian Society for the Preparation of Shells, and Munitions, when it required capital to construct a ship-yard (ibid., p. 93).

22. V. S. Diakin, *Germanskie kapitaly v Rossii: elektroindustriia i elektricheskii transport* (Leningrad, 1971), pp. 32, 35, 131, 140, 220. In a similar way, 'The Russian Company Westinghouse' had been founded in 1906 as a branch of the well-known American electrical company (but financed by the Société Générale of Paris), and Geisler was an offshoot of Western Electric of Chicago (Diakin, *Germanskie kapitaly*, op.cit., pp. 100, 144).

23. Kruze, *Peterburgskie rabochie*, op.cit., Table I, p. 34. Among the engin-eering enterprises financed by the Russo-Asiatic bank were Baranovskii, Donets-Iur'ev Metals, Reks, the Rus-sian Society for the Preparation of Shells and Munitions and St Peters-burg Wagons; those under the aegis of the St Petersburg Loan and Dis-count included Baranovskii (to 1914), Donets-Iur'ev Metals, Lessner, Phoenix and the Russian Society of Wireless Telegraphy and Telephone.

24. Kruze, *Peterburgskie rabochie*, op.cit., Table I, p. 35; Victoria A. P. King, 'The emergence of the St Petersburg industrialist community, 1870 to 1905: the origins and early years of the St Petersburg Society of Manufacturers' (Berkeley, Ph.D., 1982), pp. 12, 13, 18. In Moscow, however, the textile industry was financed by native capital and its textile barons constituted the core of Russia's native bourgeoisie (Diane Koenker, *Moscow Workers and the 1917 Revolution*, Princeton, 1981, p. 21).

25. Kruze, *Peterburgskie rabochie*, op.cit., Table I, pp. 34, 35.

26. At Neva Shipyards and Engineering, for example, daily pay for a skilled metalworker rose from 2 roubles in 1904 to 2 roubles 48 kopecks in 1905, to 2 roubles 86 kopecks in 1906, and at Franco-Russian from 1 rouble 36 kopecks to 1 rouble 68 kopecks to 2 roubles 20 kopecks. The nine-hour day was introduced into state-owned plants (*Materialy ob ekonomicheskom polozhenii i professional'noi organizatsii Peterburgskikh rabochikh po metallu*, St Petersburg, 1909, pp. 106–7, 121).

27. *Nadezhda*, no. 1 (31 July 1908), p. 6; *Edinstvo*, no. 4 (23 April 1909), p. 19; no. 9 (18 September 1909), pp. 7–8; *Professional'nyi vestnik*, no. 21 (24 January 1909), p. 24; *Biulleten'* no. 7 of the Moscow Society of Factory Own-ers (April 1908), (TsGIA, f.150, op.1, d.665, l.21). An examination of the journals of the St Petersburg union of metalworkers between 1907 and 1910 yields a list of 37 plants in the heavy industrial sector in which dismissals took place. At the eight largest private engineering plants the total work-force fell from 22,310 to 14,280 in the course of 1907 alone (*Kuznets*, no. 8 (3 March 1908), p. 4).

28. *Kuznets*, no. 8 (3 March 1908), p. 10; *Edinstvo*, no. 2 (5 March 1909), p. 10; no. 9 (18 September 1909), p. 8; *Profes-sional'nyi vestnik*, no. 21 (24 January 1909), pp. 22, 24. In engineering, some 30 establishments reduced wages between 1907 and 1911, including both state-owned plants (such as the Admiralty, Baltic Shipyards, Obu-khov, Pipes) and private firms both large (Putilov, St Petersburg Metals) and small (Glebov, Niedermeier, Vegman).

29. *Kuznets*, no. 3–4 (20 December 1907), pp. 13, 14; no. 5–6 (1 January 1908), p. 27.

30. *Rabochii po metallu*, no. 17 (12 July 1907), p. 14; *Kuznets*, no. 5–6 (1 Janu-ary 1908), p. 27; no. 8 (3 March 1908), p. 10; *Edinstvo*, no. 9 (18 September 1909), p. 8; *Biulleten'* no. 6 of the Moscow Society of Factory Owners (January 1908) (f.150, op.1, d.665, l.15).

31. *Edinstvo*, no. 9 (18 September 1909), p. 8; no. 10 (22 October 1909), p. 10; *Biulleten'* no. 11 of the Moscow Soci-ety of Factory Owners (April 1909) (f.150, op.1, d.665, l.46); *Materialy ob ekonomicheskom polozhenii*, op.cit., pp. 121, 123. Firms reintroducing overtime paid at ordinary rates in 1909 included Armature-Electrical, Langenzippen, Pipes and Rozenk-rants.

32. This has been thoroughly studied by Heather Hogan in her excellent dissertation 'Labour and management in conflict: the St Petersburg metal-working industry, 1900–1914' (Michigan, Ph.D., 1981).

33. *Edinstvo*, no. 9 (18 September 1909), p. 8; *Nash put'*, no. 3 (25 June 1910), p. 12; Hogan, 'Labour and Management', op.cit., pp. 112, 138.

34. *Professional'nyi vestnik*, no. 21 (24 January 1909), p. 23; *Biulleten'* no. 10 of the Moscow Society of Factory Owners (December 1908) (f.150, op.1, d.665, l.7); Bonnell, *Roots of Rebellion*, op.cit., p. 66.

35. It is likely that the workshop reforms and technical innovations did lead to an expansion of technical and administrative personnel, but there is little substantive data for this phenomenon in St Petersburg before the First World War.

36. TsGIA, f.23, op.19, d.321, l.4; *Biulleten'* no. 10 of the Moscow Society of Factory Owners (December 1908) (f.150, op.1, d.665, l.7); Rose L. Glickman, *Russian Factory Women. Workplace and Society, 1880–1914* (Berkeley, 1984), Table 7, p. 82.

37. *Edinstvo*, no. 15 (12 March 1910), p. 3; *Nash put'*, no.3 (25 June 1910), p. 12; *Metallist*, no. 4 (10 November 1911), p. 11; no. 2/26 (22 May 1913), p. 4; no. 13/37 (14 December 1913), p. 2; *Rabotnitsa*, no. 2 (1914), p. 8.

38. *Petrograd po perepisi*, op.cit., tom 2, p. 4; Z. V. Stepanov, *Rabochie Petrograda v period podgotovki i provedeniia oktiabr'skogo vooruzhennogo vosstaniia* (Moscow, 1965), Table 5, p. 34.

39. *Metallist*, no. 13/37 (14 December 1913), p. 2.

40. *Rabochii po metallu*, no. 15 (13 June 1907), p. 14; *Edinstvo*, no. 7 (10 July 1909), p. 14; *Nash put'*, no. 14 (4 March 1910), p. 13; Hogan, 'Labour and Management', op.cit., pp. 154, 155, 168, 172.

41. *Nadezhda*, no. 1 (31 July 1908), p. 13; *Edinstvo*, no. 16 (1 April 1910), p. 22; *Materialy ob ekonomicheskom polozhenii*, op.cit., p. 108; Hogan, 'Labour and Management', op.cit., pp. 172–3.

42. *Edinstvo*, no. 2 (5 March 1909), p. 14; no. 7 (10 July 1909), p. 14; *Metallist*, no. 7 (30 December 1911), p. 13; no. 9 (26 January 1912), p. 14; *Materialy ob ekonomicheskom polozhenii*, op.cit., pp. 121–2.

43. *Metallist*, no. 6 (17 December 1911), p. 6; no. 7 (30 December 1911), p. 13. Semenov's was a machine construction firm. His lecture on the Taylor system to St Petersburg engineers in March 1913 caused a flurry of interest in the left-wing press.

44. TsGIA, f.32, op.1, d.60, l.44. The annual report of the St Petersburg factory inspectorate for 1912 remarked that 'first place in the revival of the city's industry must be accorded to state contracts...' (f.23, op.19, d.321, l.1).

45. Peter Gatrell, 'Russian heavy industry and state defence, 1908–1918: pre-war expansion and wartime mobilisation' (Cambridge, Ph.D., 1979), p. 25; K. F. Shatsillo, *Russkii imperializm i razvitie flota nakanune pervoi mirovoi voiny (1906–1911gg.)* (Moscow, 1968), pp. 66–78 and 121–34.

46. Bovykin, 'Banki', op.cit., pp. 87–90, 92, 94, 103, 125; f.23, op.12, d.1134, l.74; ibid., op.19, d.321, l.2. Other private firms which were the recipients of state orders between 1910 and 1914 included Baranovskii, Langenzippen, Lessner, Nobel, Phoenix, Russian Society, St Petersburg Engineering and St Petersburg Metals.

47. Bovykin, 'Banki', op.cit., pp. 94, 96, 98; Hogan, 'Labour and Management', op.cit., p. 114.

48. Bovykin, 'Banki', op.cit., p. 96; *Gorno-zavodskoe delo*, no. 27 (8 July 1915), pp. 11392–3; *Novyi ekonomist*, no. 24 (11 June 1916), p. 12; *Letopis'*, no. 1 (January 1917), pp. 278, 279.

49. *Ocherki*, op.cit., pp. 36, 43, 47, 49, 53.

50. f.23, op. 19, d.321.

51. *Svod otchetov fabrichnyh inspektorov za 1909 god*, pp. 38, 42–3; *za 1910 god*, pp. 88–9; *za 1911 god*, pp. 80–1; *za 1912 god*, p. 26 (St Petersburg, 1910 to 1914 respectively): *Otchet otdela promyshlennosti za 1913 god* (St Petersburg, 1914), p. 179.

52. Kruze, *Peterburgskie rabochie*, op.cit., Table 4, p. 69.

53. *Svod otchetov fabrichnykh inspektorov za 1910 god* (St Petersburg, 1911), p. 41; 'Polozhenie promyshlennosti v Petrogradskoi gubernii 1913g.', *Vestnik promyshlennosti i torgovli*, no. 38 (1914), p. 381.

54. *Otchet otdela promyshlennosti za 1913 god* (St Petersburg, 1914), p. 183; Koenker, *Moscow Workers*, op.cit., p. 23.

55. *Petrograd po perepisi*, op.cit., tom 2, pp. 1–23.

56. Table 1.vi is from Rashin, *Naselenie*, op.cit., Table 108, p. 144; Table 1.vii, from *Ocherki*, op.cit., p. 105. In Moscow, the city census of 1902 revealed that 73 per cent of the population were migrants (Johnson, *Peasant and Proletarian*, op.cit., p. 31).

57. Rashin, *Naselenie*, op.cit., pp. 234–6; Z. Frenkel, 'Neskol'ko dannykh o sanitarnom sostaianii Moskvy i Peterburga za 1909g.', *Gorodskoe delo*, no. 20 (15 October 1910), p. 405. These figures compared with a birth rate of 41 per 1,000 and a death rate of 25.3 for the Empire in 1914 (W. E. Eason, 'Population changes', in Cyril E. Black (ed.), *The Transformation of Russian Society: Aspects of Social Change since 1861*, Cambridge, Mass., 1960, p. 74).

58. It is one of the misfortunes of Imperial Russian censuses that they still used the old estate or *soslovie* designations (gentry, honorary citizens, merchants, *meshchanstvo*, and peasant) which no longer corresponded to the emergent social classes. The category of *meshchanstvo* was particularly amorphous and the term 'petty bourgeoisie' is only a rough approximation. The few contemporary investigations that were made suggest that the majority of the working class was derived from the peasant estate. Thus at the Baltic Shipyards in 1901, 80 per cent of the workers were from the peasant estate and 17 per cent the *meshchanstvo*, whereas 92 per cent of textile operatives surveyed in 1900–2 classed themselves as peasants (S. N. Semanov, *Peterburgskie rabochie nakanune pervoi russkoi revoliutsii*, Moscow, 1966, pp. 40–1).

59. *Petrograd po perepisi*, op.cit., tom 2, Table 1, p. 3; Table 10, pp. 150–5 and Table 14, p. 290; Rashin, *Naselenie*, op.cit., Table 109, p. 144; Leopold Haimson and Eric Brian, 'Changements démographiques et grèves ouvrières à Saint-Pétersbourg, 1905–1914', *Annales ESC*, no. 4 (July–August 1985), p. 791; David F. Crew, *Town in the Ruhr. A Social History of Bochum, 1860–1914* (New York, 1979), pp. 62–3. In the age cohort 6–20, 30 per cent of peasant men had been born in the city, but 43 per cent of peasant women; in the band aged 21–30 the respective figures were 6

per cent and 11 per cent; and between the ages of 31 and 40, 4 per cent and 9 per cent respectively (*Petrograd po peripisi*, op.cit., tom 2, Table 10, pp. 150–85).

60. In Table 1.viii, the column for 1869 is taken from Reginald E. Zelnik, *Labor and Society in Tsarist Russia. The Factory Workers of St Petersburg, 1855–1870* (Stanford, 1971), pp. 224, 237; the 1900 column from Semanov, *Peterburgskie rabochie*, op.cit., p. 41; the 1910 figures from *Petrograd po perepisi*, op.cit., tom 1, Part 2, Table 14, p. 290.

61. Barbara A. Anderson, *Internal Migration during Modernization in Late Nineteenth-Century Russia* (Princeton, 1980), pp. 98, 99, 104, 105, 108, 115, 119.

62. P. Timofeev, 'What the factory worker lives by', in Victoria E. Bonnell (ed.), *The Russian Worker. Life and Labor under the Tsarist Regime* (Berkeley, 1983), pp. 76, 84; *Novaia rabochaia gazeta*, no. 19 (30 August 1913), p. 1. When the Moscow patternmaker Semën Kanatchikov came to St Petersburg to find work in the autumn of 1898, he sought out a distant relative who lived in the Nevskii district (Reginald E. Zelnik (ed.), *A Radical Worker in Tsarist Russia. The Autobiography of Semën Kanatchikov*, Stanford, 1986, pp. 79, 83–4).

63. James H. Bater, 'Transience, Residential Persistence, and Mobility in Moscow and St Petersburg, 1900–1914', *Slavic Review*, vol. 39, no. 2 (June 1980), pp. 242–3; Crew, *Town in the Ruhr*, op.cit., pp. 60–2. In his study of Moscow, Robert Johnson discovered a similar 'constant two-way movement between the countryside and urban centres' (*Peasant and Proletarian*, op.cit., p. 50).

64. *Petrograd po perepisi*, op.cit., tom 1, Table 3, pp. 4–5; ibid., Part 2, Table 7, pp. 26–35; ibid., tom 2, pp. 1–12; *Svod otchetov fabrichnykh inspektorov za 1912 god* (St Petersburg, 1913), p. 26. In Moscow in 1912 the proportion of female workers followed a similar pattern to the capital: women constituted 21 per cent of all wage earners and 30 per cent of factory operatives (Bradley, *Muzhik and Muscovite* op.cit., Table 5, pp. 146–7).

65. *Svod otchetov fabrichnykh inspektorov za 1913 god* (St Petersburg, 1914),

pp. 24–81; Semanov, *Peterburgskie rabochie*, op.cit., p. 25. In 1897 domestic service employed 87,777 women; there exist no exact statistics for the pre-war period, but the numbers can scarcely have been less (Glickman, *Russian Factory Women*, op.cit., p. 60).

66. Semanov, *Peterburgskie rabochie*, op.cit., p. 45. The distribution of the general city population by age in December 1910 was: under 16 years, 26 per cent; 16–30, 38 per cent; 30–40, 17 per cent; 41–60, 15 per cent ; over 61, 3 per cent (*Petrograd po perepisi*, op.cit., tom 1, Tables 3 and 4, pp. 4–9).

67. M. F. Desjeans, 'The common experience of the Russian working class: the case of St Petersburg, 1892–1904' (Duke, Ph.D., 1978), Tables 3–10, p. 95; *Trudy pervogo vserossiiskogo zhenskago s"ezda, 10–16 dekabria 1908* (St Petersburg, 1909), p. 341. In the union of metalworkers 78 per cent of members were aged 16 to 34 in January 1908 (*Materialy ob ekonomicheskom polozhenii*, op.cit., p. 79).

68. *Svod otchetov fabrichnykh inspektorov za 1912 god* (St Petersburg, 1913), pp. 26, 30–4, 36; *Otchet otdela promyshlennosti za 1912 god* (St Petersburg, 1913), p. 157; Desjeans, 'Common Experience' op.cit., p. 95; *Trudy pervogo*, op.cit., p. 310; G. Zinoviev, 'Remesslennyi s"ezd', *Mysl'*, no. 3 (February 1911), p. 38.

69. *Petrograd po perepisi*, op.cit., tom 1, Part 2, Table 1, p. 3; Table 7, pp. 26–35; Table 10, pp. 150–85.

70. *Materialy ob ekonomicheksom polozhenii*, op.cit., pp. 84–7; S. N. Prokopovich, *Kooperativnoe dvizhenie v Rossii. Ego teoriia i praktika* (Moscow, 1913), p. 309.

71. L. Kuprianova, 'Rabochii Peterburg', in *S. Peterburg i ego zhizn'* (St Petersburg, 1914), pp. 185–6; Semanov, *Peterburgskie rabochie*, op.cit., pp. 49–50; *Zvezda*, no. 27 (29 October 1911), p. 4.

72. Haimson and Brian, 'Changements', op.cit., pp. 796–8; Rashin, *Naselenie*, op.cit., Table 181, p. 235.

73. *Svod otchetov fabrichnykh inspektorov za 1910 god* (St Petersburg, 1911), p. 82; Prokopovich, *Kooperativnoe Dvizhenie*, op.cit., p. 309; Kuprianova, 'Rabochii Peterburg', op.cit., p. 190.

74. *Petrograd po perepisi*, tom 1, Table 8, pp. 40–1; Haimson and Brian, 'Changements', op.cit., p. 794. In Moscow in 1912 67 per cent of all male wage earners were literate and 27 per cent of women (Bradley, *Muzhik and Muscovite* op.cit., p. 150).

75. Tables 1.ix and 1.x are calculated from *Petrograd po perepisi*, tom 2, Table 10, pp. 150–85.

76. A. G. Rashin, *Formirovanie rabochego klassa Rossii. Istoriko-ekonomicheskie ocherki* (Moscow, 1958), p. 591; Semanov, *Peterburgskie rabochie*, op.cit., p. 55; Bonnell, *Roots of Rebellion*, op.cit., p. 58; *Put' pravdy*, no. 20 (23 February 1914), p. 3.

77. Stepanov, *Babochie Petrograda*, op.cit., p. 45. Gerald Surh, too, stresses the importance of the literacy of younger workers: *1905 in St Petersburg. Labor, Society, and Revolution* (Stanford, California, 1989) p. 33.

78. Jeffrey Brooks, *When Russia Learned to Read. Literacy and Popular Culture, 1861–1917* (Princeton, 1985), pp. 35, 36, 46, 49; Crisp, 'Labour and industry in Russia'. op.cit., pp. 392–3; Semanov, *Peterburgskie rabochie*, op.cit., p. 56; S. A. Smith, *Red Petrograd. Revolution in the Factories, 1917–1918* (Cambridge, 1983), pp. 34–5.

79. L. Kleinbort, 'Ocherki rabochei demokratii: umstvennyi pod"em', *Sovremennyi mir*, no. 2, 2nd edn (May 1913), pp. 113–15, 121, 134. Kleinbort, as a Marxist, dismisses the importance of artisanal enterprises as a source of 'labour-intellectuals' (ibid., p. 118), but a study of the membership of the pre-war educational societies reveals that printers, tailors, joiners and gold- and silversmiths were well to the fore in such bodies (see Chapter 7).

80. In English, the problem of internal differentiation within the Russian working class has received illuminating treatment in Victoria E. Bonnell, 'Urban working-class life in early twentieth-century Russia: some problems and patterns', *Russian History/Histoire Russe*, vol. 8, part 3 (1981), pp. 360–78; and in S. A. Smith, 'Craft consciousness, class consciousness: Petrograd 1917', *History Workshop*, vol. 11 (1981), pp. 86–123.

81. A. Blek, 'Usloviia truda rabochikh na peterburgskikh zavodakh po dannym 1901 goda (Baltiiskii i drugie desiat' zavodov)', *Arkhiv istorii truda v Rossii*, Book 2 (1921), pp. 78–9; E. E. Kruze, *Polozhenie rabochego klassa Rossii v*

1900–1914gg. (Leningrad, 1976), p. 173.

82. Blek, 'Uslovia truda' op.cit., pp. 81, 82; A. I. Davidenko, 'K voprosu o chislennosti i sostave proletariata Peterburga v nachale XX veka', in *Istoriia rabochego klassa Leningrada. vypusk II* (Leningrad, 1963), p. 106. At Obukhov 13 per cent of the work-force over the period 1901–15 came from the *meshchanstvo* (ibid., p. 109).

83. Lenard R. Berlanstein, *The Working People of Paris, 1871–1914* (Baltimore, 1984), pp. 15–21; E.A. Oliunina, *The Tailoring Trade in Moscow and the Villages of Moscow and Riazan Provinces* in Bonnell (ed.), *The Russian Worker*, op.cit., pp. 154–9; Bonnell, 'Urban working-class life', op.cit., p. 372.

84. The best contemporary description of the world of the skilled factory worker – and the major source of observations made in this paragraph – is the auto-biography of Semën Kanatchikov (see note 62).

85. Kruze, *Polozhenie*, op.cit., p. 144; Semanov, *Peterburgskie rabochie*, op.cit., p. 43. With regard to the em-ergence of an all-Russian modern in-dustrial class, the Soviet point of view is set out with admirable clarity in L. M. Ivanov's article 'Preemstvenost' fabrichno-zavodskogo truda i formir-ovanie proletariata v Rossii', in L. M. Ivanov, *Rabochii klass*, op.cit., pp. 58–140.

86. Smith, *Red Petrograd*, op.cit., p. 20; Surh, *1905 in St Petersburg*, op.cit., p. 120; Johnson, *Peasant and Proletarian*, op.cit., Chapter 2.

87. *Petrograd po perepisi*, op.cit., tom 2, pp. 85–149; Haimson and Brian, 'Changements', op.cit., p. 791; Shus-ter, *Peterburgskie rabochie*, op.cit., p. 23; V. Z. Drobizhev, A. K. Sokolov and V. A. Ustinov, *Rabochii klass sovetskoi Rossii v pervyi god proletarskoi diktatury* (Moscow, 1975), p. 93. The 1918 census suffers from several grave defects, which render it a less than trustworthy source on the capital's working class before 1914 and 1917. It covered only 107,262 Petrograd wage earners; for the years prior to 1914, its data are distorted by the massive influx into the capital during the war; it was held in autumn 1918 during a period of intense de-urbanisation and de-industrialisation, with a conse-quent large-scale exodus of workers from the city.

88. Davidenko, 'K Voprosu', op.cit., p. 106; Rashin, *Formirovanie*, op.cit., p. 503; *Materialy ob ekonomicheskom polozhenii*, op.cit., pp. 81, 82.

89. For example, 11 per cent of Tver' province migrants returned from the capital for field work in 1910 (Davidenko, 'K Voprosu', op.cit., p. 104). The 1918 census finding that a mere 4 per cent left for field work, in the light of the circumstances under which it was taken, is a serious under-estimate.

90. *Trudy pervogo*, op.cit., p. 311; *Metal-list*, no. 10/34 (25 October 1913), p. 8.

91. Blek, 'Usloviia truda', op.cit., p. 80; Drobizhev et al., *Rabochii klass*, op.cit., p. 97; Semanov, *Peterburgskie rabochie*, op.cit., p. 42. In his memoirs P. Timofeev remarks that 'as for skilled workers, the majority probably feel that the village is nothing but a burden' (Timofeev, 'What the factory worker lives by', op.cit., p. 82).

92. Bater, 'Transience, residential persist-ence and mobility', op.cit., p. 242; Kuprianova, 'Rabochii Peterburg', op.cit., p. 185. P. Timofeev observes that the low pay of the unskilled worker and the constant threat of un-employment 'makes him unwilling to give up his ties to the village' ('What the factory worker lives by', op.cit., p. 78).

93. Blek, 'Usloviia truda', op.cit., p. 80; Semanov, *Peterburgskie rabochie*, op.cit., p. 51.

94. Prokopovich, *Kooperativnoe Dvizhe-nie*, op.cit., p. 311; M. Davidovich, *Peterburgskii tekstil'nyi rabochii v ego biudzhetakh* (St Petersburg, 1912), p. 8; Timofeev, 'What the factory worker lives by', op.cit., pp. 78, 84.

95. Smith, *Red Petrograd*, op.cit., p. 21.

Chapter 2

1. Table 2.i is calculated from *Svod otche-tov fabrichnykh inspektorov za 1912 god* (St Petersburg, 1913), pp. 88–99, 112, 113, 124, 125, 158, 159, 172, 173. These figures distort the degree of concentration within manufacturing, because they omit both the large-scale state armaments plants (which would raise the percentage of opera-tives in metalworking establishments with over 500 employees) and many medium and small units of production

(whose inclusion would lower the overall level of concentration).

2. *Trudy pervogo vserossiiskogo zhenskogo s'ezda* (St Petersburg, 1909), p. 310; *Proletarskaia pravda*, no. 12/30 (16 January 1914), p. 3.

3. Laura Engelstein, *Moscow, 1905. Working-class Organization and Political Conflict* (Stanford, California, 1982), p. 34.

4. P. Timofeev, 'What the factory worker lives by', in Victoria E. Bonnell (ed.), *The Russian Worker. Life and Labour under the Tsarist Regime* (Berkeley, 1983), pp. 73–4.

5. Timofeev, 'What the factory worker lives by', op.cit., pp. 75, 195; S. N. Semanov, *Peterburgskie rabochie nakanune pervoi russkoi revoliutsii* (Moscow 1966), pp. 116, 119–20.

6. *Otchet otdela promyshlennosti za 1910 god* (St Petersburg, 1911), p. 202; U. A. Shuster, *Peterburgskie rabochie v 1905–1907gg.* (Leningrad, 1976), p. 47.

7. A. M. Gudvan, 'Essays on the history of the movement of sales-clerical workers in Russia' in Bonnell (ed.), *The Russian Worker*, op.cit., pp. 194–6.

8. Timofeev, 'What the factory worker lives by', op.cit., p. 107; L. Kleinbort, 'Ocherki rabochei demokratii; stat'ia pervaia', *Sovremennyi mir*, no. 4 (April 1913), pp. 27–31.

9. *Put' pravdy*, no. 20 (23 February 1914), p. 3; no. 46 (26 March 1914), p. 1; *Mysl'*, no. 3 (February 1911), p. 39; Z. Frenkel, 'Narodnoe zdorov'e v gorodakh Rossii po offitsial'nym dannym', *Gorodskoe delo*, no. 5 (1 March 1910), p. 279; *Vestnik prikazchika*, nos. 14–15 (1914), p. 22.

10. *Svod otchetov fabrichnykh inspektorov za 1909 god* (St Petersburg, 1910), p. 78; TsGIA, f.23, op.19, d.321, l.9; E. E. Kruze, *Peterburgskie rabochie v 1912–1914 godakh* (Leningrad, 1961), pp. 124, 126.

11. Iu. I. Kirianov, *Zhizennyi uroven' rabochikh Rossii* (Moscow, 1979), pp. 55, 68.

12. *Novoe pechatnoe delo*, no. 7 (18 July 1913), p. 7; *Put' pravdy*, no. 20 (23 February 1914), p. 3.

13. *Pravda*, no. 159 (3 November 1912), p. 4; no. 55/259 (7 March 1913), p. 4; *Severnaia pravda*, no. 18 (23 August 1913), p. 4; *Golos bulochnika i konditera*, no. 1/12 (1912), p. 15.

14. Kirianov, *Zhizennyi uroven'*, op.cit., pp. 76, 77; M. Gordon, 'Iz zhizni rabochikh i sluzhashchikh na gorodskikh zheleznykh dorogakh Petrograda', *Arkhiv istorii truda v Rossii*, vol. 8 (1923), p. 90.

15. E. E. Kruze, *Polozhenie rabochego klassa Rossii v 1900–1914gg.* (Leningrad, 1976), p. 168. The table is based on the annual reports of the factory inspectorate; it embraced only those firms under its purview which levied fines.

16. Kirianov, *Zhizennyi uroven'*, op.cit., p. 118; *Otchet otdela promyshlennosti za 1912 god* (St Petersburg, 1913), p. 158; E. H. Hunt, *British Labour History, 1815–1914* (London, 1981), pp. 74–6; Roger Price, *A Social History of Nineteenth Century France* (London, 1987), p. 216.

17. Kirianov, *Zhizennyi uroven'*, op.cit., pp. 97, 98, 99, 143; Shuster, *Peterburgskie rabochie*, op.cit., p. 45; *Svod otchetov fabrichnykh inspektorov za 1912 god* (St Petersburg, 1913), pp. 30, 36, 42, 48, 65, 72.

18. *Severnaia pravda*, no. 17 (22 August 1913), p. 3; no. 43 (24 November 1913), p. 3; TsGAOR, f.D.P., 4d-vo., 1913g., d.61, ch.2, t.1., l.107.

19. M. Davidovich, *Peterburgskii tekstil'nyi rabochii v ego biudzhetakh* (St Petersburg, 1912), p. 5; *Materialy ob ekonomicheskom polozhenii i professional'noi organisatsii Peterburgskikh rabochikh po metallu* (St Petersburg, 1909), p. 103; Hartmut Kaelble, *Industrialisation and Social Inequality in Nineteenth Century Europe* (Leamington Spa, 1986), pp. 42–3.

20. Davidovich, *Peterburgskii tekstil'nyi rabochii*, op.cit., pp. 5–6; S. N. Prokopovich, *Kooperativnoe dvizhenie v Rossii. Ego teoriia i praktika* (Moscow, 1913), p. 309; L. Kuprianova, 'Rabochii Peterburg', in *S. Peterburg i ego zhizn'* (St Petersburg, 1914), p. 190.

21. *Petrograd po perepisi 15 dekabria 1910 goda* (Petrograd, 1914), tom 2, Table 4, pp. 12–13. The term 'bourgeoisie' embraces the legal estates of 'honorary citizens', 'merchants' and 'meshchane'. The percentages under the columns gentry, 'bourgeoisie' and peasants do not add up to 100 in each district as the table omits the categories of clergy and foreign residents.

22. Leopold Haimson and Eric Brian, 'Changements démographiques et

grèves ouvrières à Saint-Pétersbourg, 1905–1914', *Annales ESC.*, no. 4 (July-August 1985), pp. 799–801; James H. Bater, *St Petersburg, Industrialization and Change* (London, 1976), pp. 276, 280, 373–5, 379; Michael F. Hamm (ed.), *The City in Late Imperial Russia* (Bloomington, 1986), pp. 66–73.

23. M. Fedorov, 'Finansovoe polozhenie Peterburga', *Gorodskoe delo*, no. 1 (1 January 1909), p. 12; Charles Dobson, *St Petersburg* (London, 1910), p. 119; Semanov, *Peterburgskie rabochie*, p. 107.

24. TsGIA, f.1284, op.194, 1913g., d.95, l.2; Fedorov, 'Finansovoe polozhenie', op.cit., p. 12; Dobson, *St Petersburg*, op.cit., pp. 85, 86, 109; *Nadezhda*, no. 2 (28 September 1908), p. 2.

25. Bater, *St Petersburg*, op.cit., pp. 352, 353, 357, 359, 360, 363.

26. Frenkel, 'Narodnoe zdorov'e', op.cit., p. 279; Z. Frenkel, 'Neskol'ko dannykh o sanitarnom sostaianii Moskvy i Peterburga za 1909g.', *Gorodskoe delo*, no. 20 (15 October 1910), p. 1406; A. I. Rammul, 'O vodosnabzhenii S. Peterburga', *Gorodskoe delo*, no. 22 (15 November 1910), p. 1588; A. G. Rashin, *Naselenie Rossii za sto let* (Moscow, 1956), Table 183, p. 237.

27. Kirianov, *Zhizennyi uroven'*, op.cit., p. 227; Semanov, *Peterburgskie rabochie*, op.cit., p. 164; Gordon, 'Iz zhizni', op.cit., pp. 100–1; E. E. Kruze, *Usloviia truda i byta rabochego klassa Rossii v 1900–1914 godakh* (Leningrad, 1981), p. 91; TsGIA, f.1450, op.530, d.824, l.73.

28. *Luch*, no. 35 (26 October 1912), p. 4; no. 64 (1 December 1912), p. 3; no. 9/95 (12 January 1913), p. 3; *Pravda*, no. 36 (10 June 1912), p. 2.

29. Franz J. Brüggemeier and Lutz Niethammer, 'Lodgers, schnapps-casinos and working-class colonies in a heavy-industrial region', in Georg Iggers (ed.), *The Social History of Politics. Critical Perspectives in West German Historical Writing since 1945* (Leamington Spa, 1985), pp. 226–7.

30. Bater, *St Petersburg*, op.cit., p. 319; Semanov, *Peterburgskie rabochie*, op.cit., p. 161; K. Pazhitnov, 'Kvartirnyi vopros v Peterburge', *Gorodskoe delo*, no. 20 (15 October 1910), pp. 1375–6.

31. K. Pazhitnov, 'Zhilishchnaia politika gorodskoi dumy goroda Peterburga',

Izvestiia Moskovskoi gorodskoi dumy, no. 37 (10 October 1914), p. 40; *Ocherki istorii Leningrada. Tom tretii. Period imperializma i burzhuazno-demokraticheskikh revoliutsii 1895–1917gg.* (Moscow–Leningrad, 1956), p. 897; *Izvestiia S. Peterburgskoi dumy*, no. 13 (March 1911), p. 2433.

32. Kuprianova, 'Rabochii Peterburg', op.cit., p. 192; Kirianov, *Zhizennyi uroven'*, op.cit., pp. 237–9. In Germany, too, from 1890 to 1914, the line between skilled and unskilled workers in housing was strong (Kaelble, *Industrialisation*, op.cit., p. 124).

33. *Petrograd po perepisi*, op.cit., tom 1, pp. 12–13; f.1284, op.194, 1913 god, d.95, l.7; *Nash put'*, no. 19 (July 1911), pp. 6–7.

34. D. Polupanov, 'K kvartirnomu krizisu Peterburga', *Gorodskoe delo*, no. 20 (15 October 1913), pp. 1356–7; *Izvestiia S. Peterburgskoi dumy*, no. 32 (1910), p. 1855; Kruze, *Usloviia*, op.cit., p. 93.

35. *Izvestiia S. Peterburgskoi dumy*, no. 13, (March 1911), p. 2435; Kirianov, *Zhizennyi uroven'*, op.cit., p. 260; Davidovich, op.cit., p. 10; Kaelble, *Industrialisation*, op.cit., p. 107. In the Ruhr in the two decades before the First World War, rent consumed over 15 per cent of workers' incomes (S. H. F. Hickey, *Workers in Imperial Germany. The Miners of the Ruhr*, Oxford 1985, p. 39.)

36. Prokopovich, *Kooperativnoe divzhenie*, op.cit., p. 311; *Materialy ob ekonomicheskom polozhenii*, op.cit., pp. 115–17; Davidovich, *Peterburgskii tekstil'nyi rabochii*, op.cit., pp. 14–16, 19; Kirianov, *Zhizennyi uroven'*, op.cit., pp. 189, 192, 194, 210, 211.

37. V. Miliutin, 'Rabochaia gruppa na s'ezde po bor'be s alkogolizmom', *Vozrozhdenie*, no. 2 (February 1910), pp. 51–2; B. Magidov, 'Alkogolizm sredi S. Peterburgskikh rabochikh (po dannym ankety)', *Edinstvo*, no. 16 (1 April 1910), p. 9; *Luch*, no. 128/214 (6 June 1913), p. 1.

38. Kh, 'Prostitutsiia, eia prichiny i mery bor'by s nei', *Edinstvo*, no. 15 (12 March 1909), pp. 5, 6; Gudvan, 'Essays on the history', op.cit., pp. 195, 197; *Vestnik prikazchika*, no. 13 (1914), p. 3; Richard Stites, 'Prostitute and society in pre-revolutionary Russia', *Jahrbücher für Geschichte Osteuropas*, Vol. 31, Part 3 (1983), pp. 348–64.

39. Jean Neuberger, 'Crime and culture: hooliganism in St. Petersburg, 1900–1914' (Stanford, Ph.D., 1985), pp. 98–117, 150–1.

Chapter 3

1. The new electoral law of 3 June 1907 and the political system built upon it by P. A. Stolypin have received illuminating treatment by Western and Soviet historians. Among the many works available, the following may be recommended in particular: Alfred Levin, *The Third Duma, Election and profile* (Hamden, Conn., 1973); Geoffrey Hosking, *The Russian Constitutional Experiment* (Cambridge, 1973); M. Conroy, *P. A. Stolypin, Practical Politics in Late Tsarist Russia* (Boulder, Col., 1976); A. Ia. Avrekh, *Stolypin i tret'ia duma* (Moscow, 1968); V. S. Diakin, *Samoderzhavie, burzhuaziia i dvorianstvo v 1907–1911gg.* (Leningrad, 1978).

2. V. I. Lenin, *Collected Works* (Moscow, 1963–9), Vol. 13, pp. 114–22 ('Revolution and counter-revolution', *Proletarii*, no. 17 (20 October 1907)); Vol. 15, pp. 50–62 ('The assessment of the Russian revolution', *Proletarii*, no. 30 (23/10 May 1908)). Hereafter *CW*.

3. Lenin, *CW*, Vol. 15, pp. 321–24 ('Draft resolution on the present movement and the tasks of the party', for the Fifth All-Russian Conference, December 1908; Vol. 15, pp. 40–7 ('On the beaten track', *Proletarii*, no. 29 (29/16 April 1908)).

4. Lenin, *CW*, Vol. 15, pp. 17–21 ('On to the straight road', *Proletarii*, no. 26 (1 April/19 March 1908)); Vol. 16, pp. 147–55 ('Towards unity', *Sotsial-demokrat*, no. 11 (26/13 February 1910)).

5. Lenin, *CW*, Vol. 15, pp. 345–55 ('On the road', *Sotsial-demokrat*, no. 2 (10 February/28 January 1909)); Vol. 15, pp. 452–60 ('The liquidation of Liquidationism', *Proletarii*, no. 46 (24/11 July 1909)).

6. Lenin, *CW*, Vol. 15, pp. 356–9 ('On the article "Questions of the Day"', *Proletarii*, no. 42 (25/12 February 1909)); Vol. 15, pp. 383–94 ('A caricature of Bolshevism', *Proletarii*, no. 44 (17/4 April 1909)); Vol. 16, pp. 95–102 ('Methods of the Liquidators and party tasks of the Bolsheviks', *Proletarii*, no. 50 (11 December/28 November 1909)).

7. Dietrich Geyer, *Kautsky's Russisches Dossier (1910–1915)* (Frankfurt am Main, 1981), pp. 10–11.

8. Robert C. Williams, *The Other Bolsheviks. Lenin and His Critics, 1904–1914* (Bloomington, Ind., 1986).

9. A. A. Bogdanov and L. B. Krasin, *Otchet tovarishcham bol'shevikami ustranennykh chlenov rasshirennoi redaktsii 'Proletariata'* (Paris, 1909) in Geoff Swain (ed.), *Protokoly soveshchaniia rasshirenoi redaktsii 'Proletariia' Iiun' 1909* (Moscow, 1934; repr. Millwood, NY, 1982), pp. 241–50; 'Rezoliutsiia Peterburgskikh Otzovistov', *Proletarii*, no. 44 (17/4 April 1909), supplement, p. 1.

10. Robert Service, *Lenin: A Political Life. Volume I. The Strengths of Contradiction* (London, 1985), pp. 148, 154–5; Alfred Levin, *The Second Duma. A Study of the Social Democratic Party and the Russian Constitutional Experiment* (Hamden, Conn., 1966), pp. 42–4; K. Ostroukhova, 'Sotsial-demokratiia i Vybory v 3-iu gosudarstvennuiu dumu', *Proletarskaia revoliutsiia*, vol. 25 (1924), p. 90. At both the Fourth Congress and the Second All-Russian Conference, the Bolshevik boycottists (a majority in the faction's delegations) were defeated by the combined votes of the Mensheviks and national Social Democratic parties (Bund, Poles, Latvians), whose resolutions in favour of participation in the State Duma were supported by Lenin.

11. I. Voitinskii, 'Boikotizm, otzovizm, ul'timatizm', *Proletarskaia revoliutsiia*, vols. 91–2 (1929), p. 36; *Proletarii*, no. 44 (17/4 April 1909), supplement, p. 1; Ostroukhova, 'Sotsial-demokratiia', op.cit., p. 87; Service, *Lenin*, op.cit., pp. 160–1, 169.

12. *Proletarii*, no. 31 (17/4 June 1908), p. 6.

13. G. Aleksinskii, 'Chto zhe dal'she?', *Proletarii*, no. 34 (7 September/25 August 1908), pp. 2–3.

14. Robert Williams provides the best account of the philosophical debates within the Bolshevik faction at this time. His interpretation, however, has not met with universal assent among specialists, in particular his imputation of syndicalist views to

Bogdanov. As always with Lenin, his onslaught on Bogdanov as a philosopher (his *Materialism and Empirio-criticism*, published in April 1909) served the political purpose of discrediting his arch-rival within Bolshevism by attacking his status as a Marxist thinker.

15. The most thorough investigation of the Schmidt affair may be found in Geyer, *Kautsky*, op.cit., pp. 21–5; Williams, *The Other Bolsheviks*, op.cit., pp. 114–19.

16. On the expanded meeting of the editorial board of *Proletarii*, June 1909, consult Swain, *Protokoly*, op.cit., pp. xxvi–xxxix.

17. John Biggart, '"Anti-Leninist Bolshevism": the forward group of the RSDRP', *Canadian Slavonic Papers*, vol. 23, no. 2 (1981), pp. 134–53, V. Voitinskii, 'O gruppe "Vpered" (1909–1917)', *Proletarskaia revoliutsiia*, vol. 95 (1929), pp. 59–119; Williams, *The Other Bolsheviks*, op.cit., pp. 155–7.

18. S. A. Oppenheim, 'The making of a Right Communist – A. I. Rykov to 1917', *Slavic Review*, vol. 26, no. 3 (1977), pp. 434–5; Geoffrey Swain, *Russian Social Democracy and the Legal Labour Movement, 1906–14* (London, 1983), p. 92.

19. F. Dan, 'Proletariat i russkaia revoliutsiia', *Golos sotsial-demokrata*, no. 3 (March 1908), pp. 4–5.

20. L. Martov, 'Zametki publitsista: "Likvidatorstvo" i "Perspektivy"', *Zhizn'*, no. 8 (1912), pp. 242–5; F. Dan, 'Burzhuaziia i konstitutsionnyi rezhim', *Golos sotsial-demokrata*, no. 13 (April 1909), p. 5.

21. L. Martov, 'Burzhuaziia i kontr-revoliutsiia', *Vozrozhdenie*, nos. 5–6 (April 1909), pp. 25–32; Martov, 'Ob istoricheskoi neobkhodimosti', *Vozrozhdenie*, no. 6 (April 1910), pp. 3–18; Dan, 'Burzhuaziia i konstitutsionnyi rezhim', op.cit., pp. 5–8; B. Sapir (ed.), *Theodore Dan. Letters (1899–1946)* (Amsterdam, 1985), letter of A. N. Potresov to Iu. Martov, 15 April 1909, note 6, p. 217.

22. F. Dan, 'Krizis', *Sovremennyi mir*, no. 9 (May 1914), pp. 59–64; *Nasha zaria*, nos. 7–8 (1911), pp. 47–50.

23. A. N. Potresov, 'Kriticheskie nabroski', *Nasha zaria*, no. 2 (1910), pp. 50–62 and no. 4 (1910), pp. 92–8; V. Levitskii, 'Na temu dnia: likvidatsiia

ili vozrozhdenie?', *Nasha zaria*, no. 7 (1910), pp. 91–103; V. Ezhov, 'Ocherednye voprosy rabochego dvizheniia', *Vozrozhdenie*, nos. 9–10 (June 1910), pp. 11–32; E. Maevskii, 'Chto takoe likvidatorstvo?', *Nasha zaria*, nos. 11–12 (1910), pp. 46–59.

24. S. H. Baron, *Plekhanov, the Father of Russian Marxism* (London, 1963), pp. 282–5; *Za partiiu*, no. 1 (16 April 1912), p. 1; *Sotsial-demokrat*, no. 12 (5 April/23 March 1910), pp. 1–2.

25. Geyer, *Kautsky*, op.cit., pp. 11–12.

26. L. Martov, 'Posle buri', *Golos sotsial-demokrata*, nos. 1–2 (February 1908), pp. 1–3; Martov, 'Kuda idti?', *Golos sotsial-demokrata*, no. 13 (April 1909), pp. 4–5; Martov, 'O likvidatorstve', *Golos sotsial-demokrata*, nos. 16–17 (August 1909), pp. 2–4.

27. *Pravda* (Vienna), no. 1 (16/3 October 1908), pp. 1–2; ibid., no. 4 (14/1 June 1909), pp. 1–2; Geyer, *Kautsky*, op.cit., pp. 16–17. The best treatment of Trotsky's pre-1917 intellectual odyssey is to be found in Baruch Knei-Paz, *The Social and Political Thought of Leon Trotsky* (Oxford, 1979).

28. Manfred Hildermeier, *Die Sozialrevolutionäre Partei Russlands: Agrarsozialismus und Modernisierung im Zarenreich (1900–1914)*, (Cologne, 1978), p. 317. Hildermeier is the indispensable guide to the history of the Socialist Revolutionary party before 1914.

29. Ibid., pp. 324–5.

30. Ava (pseudonym of L. M. Amand), 'Chto teper' nuzhno?', *Izvestiia oblastnogo zagranichnago komiteta*, no. 10 (March 1909), pp. 11–24; Al. Kliuev (V. M. Zenzinov), 'O partiinykh zadachakh', *Znamia truda*, no. 27 (April 1910), pp. 9–14; Ant. Savin (A. V. Shimanovskii) 'Bol'nichnye voprosy', *Izvestiia oblastnogo zagranichnago komiteta*, no. 12 (November 1910), pp. 1–4.

31. Ant. Savin, 'Bol'nye voprosy', *Izvestiia oblastnogo zagranichnago komiteta*, no. 15 (April 1911), pp. 1–9; Nurit Schleifman, *Undercover Agents in the Russian Revolutionary Movement. The SR. Party, 1902–14* (London, 1988), pp. 102–3. A detailed account of the Azef affair may be found in Boris Nikolaevsky, *Azeff the Spy: Russian Terrorist and Police Stool* (New York, 1934).

32. A. Voronov (B. N. Lebedev), 'Rabochaia organizatsiia (zametki propagandista)', *Znamia truda*, no. 16 (4 March 1909), pp. 5–8; Voronov, 'Ekonomicheskaia bor'ba v podpol'e', *Znamia truda*, no. 18 (18 May 1909), pp. 3–7; Voronov, 'Kak vosstanovit' partiinuiu rabotu', *Izvestiia oblastnogo zagranichnago komiteta*, no. 12 (November 1910), pp. 4–12.

33. N. M. (pseudonym of A. I. Rakitnikov), 'Ocherki po organizatsionnym voprosam', *Znamia truda*, no. 16 (14 March 1909), pp. 3–5 and ibid., no. 17 (27 April 1909), pp. 6–10; Hildermeier, *Die Sozialrevolutionäre Partei*, op.cit., p. 331.

34. P. Gooderham, 'The anarchist movement in Russia, 1905–1917' (Bristol, Ph.D., 1981), pp. 172, 179–97, 206–7.

35. Sections II to V of Chapter 3 are the sole parts of this work for which the author was unable to obtain access to the Soviet archives. These sections have had to be based upon published memoirs and documentary collections as well as the contemporary socialist and labour press. *Émigré* newspaper accounts of the underground should be treated with caution as they attempted on occasions to put as best gloss as possible upon their factions' positions (see note 47, for example). The Okhrana's reports covering the period 1911–17 provide confirmation of the existence of this practice.

36. R. Arskii, 'Epokha reaktsii v Petrograde (1907–1910gg.)', *Krasnaia letopis'*, no. 9 (1924), p. 72; *Proletarii*, no. 22 (3 March/19 February 1908), p. 6; G. Shidlovskii, 'V Peterburgskikh partiinykh riadakh vesnoi i letom 1910 goda (ocherk)', *Krasnaia letopis'*, nos 5–6 (1931), p. 180. These figures must be regarded as crude approximations since no accurate membership lists could be kept, for conspiratorial reasons. The number of 1,000 members in January 1909 is quoted in *Istoriia rabochego klassa SSSR. Rabochii klass Rossii. 1907–fevral' 1917g.* (Moscow, 1982), p. 135. But a report in *Proletarii*, no. 42 (25/12 February 1909), p. 7 furnishes an estimate of 520 members.

37. Arskii 'Epokha reaktsii v Petrograde', op.cit., pp. 72–3, 75; *Ocherki istorii Leningradskoi organizatsii KPSS* (Leningrad, 1980), p. 175; *Proletarii*, no. 33 (5 August/23 July 1908), p. 5; *Sotsial-demokrat*, no. 2 (10 February/28 January 1909), p. 9.

38. P. Kudelli, 'Iz zhizni Peterburgskoi organizatsii RSDRP (B) v period reaktsii', *Krasnaia letopis'*, no. 14 (1925), p. 221.

39. *Proletarii*, no. 33 (5 August/23 July 1908), p. 5; *Sotsial-demokrat*, no. 2 (10 February/28 January 1909), pp. 9, 10; no. 5 (6 May/23 April 1909), p. 9; *Peterburgskii komitet RSDRP. Protokoly i zasedanii. Iiul 1902–Ferral 1917* (Leningrad 1986), pp. 347–48.

40. In addition to the sources listed in note 39, *Proletarii*, no. 38 (14/1 November 1908), p. 9.

41. M. Akhun and V. Petrov, 'Voennaia organizatsiia pri Peterburgskom komitete RSDRP v 1907–1908gg.', *Krasnaia letopis'*, no. 19 (1926), pp. 124–37; Kudelli, 'Iz zhizni', op.cit., p. 222.

42. Arskii 'Epokha reaktsii v Petrograde', op.cit., pp. 78, 81; *Proletarii*, no. 21 (26/13 February 1908), p.4; *Peterburgskii komitet*, op. cit., p. 329.

43. A. Golubkov, 'Iz epokhi reaktsii (otryvki iz vospominanii)', *Proletarskaia revoliutsiia*, vol. 80 (1928), pp. 121–4; *Ocherki*, op.cit., p. 190.

44. *Proletarii*, no. 21 (26/13 February 1908), p. 4; no. 22 (3 March/19 February 1908), p. 6; no. 33 (5 August/23 July 1908), p. 4; *Ocherki*, op.cit., p. 170; *Peterburgskii komitet*, op. cit., p. 332.

45. R. C. Elwood, 'Trotsky's questionnaire', *Slavic Review*, vol. 29, no. 3 (1970), pp. 296–301. Trotsky received 92 responses from 27 cities; none were returned from St Petersburg. (*Pravda* (Vienna), no. 16 (6 October/24 September 1910), p. 2).

46. *Sotsial-demokrat*, no. 6 (17/4 June 1909), p. 7.

47. K. Ostroukhova, 'Iz perepiski mestnykh organizatsii s zagranichnym bol'shevistskim tsentram v 1909g.', *Proletarskaia revoliutsiia*, no. 80 (1928), p. 182. Fedorov's letter provides an excellent example of the ways in which editors of Bolshevik *émigré* publications at times manipulated the information sent them by correspondents from Russia. The Bolshevik majority on the editorial board of *Sotsial-demokrat* in 1909 (Lenin, Kamenev and Zinoviev) de-

liberately omitted from the issue, (no. 10) in which there appeared a report (based on Fedorov's letter) on the Petersburg organisations, all his references to the non-existence of party groups in the Moscow, Neva and Vyborg districts.

48. *Sotsial-demokrat*, no. 10 (6 January 1910/24 December 1909), p. 6.

49. Ostroukhova, 'Iz perepiski mestnykh organizatsii', op.cit., pp. 162, 172, 181; *Proletarii*, no. 50 (24/11 December 1909), p. 7; *Sotsial-demokrat*, no. 6 (17/4 June 1909), p. 7.

50. *Bor'ba*, no. 1 (27 July 1908); N. I. Kats, 'Professional'nye soiuzy Peterburga v gody reaktsii (1907–1910gg.)', *Istoriia rabochego klassa Leningrada. Vypusk II* (Leningrad, 1963), p. 139; Swain, *Russian Social Democracy*, op.cit., pp. 45–6.

51. *Proletarii*, no. 36 (16/3 October 1908), p. 8; W., 'Vserossiiskii zhenskii s''ezd i rabochaia gruppa (pism'o iz Peterburga)', *Golos sotsial-demokrata*, no. 12 (March 1909), p. 8; *Peterburgskii komitet*, op. cit., pp. 359, 363.

52. Ostroukhova, 'Iz perepiski mestnykh organizatsii', op.cit., p. 179 (letter of S. Ia Bagdat'ev to the Bolshevik Centre, 11 November 1909); *Pravda* (Vienna), no. 11 (31/18 March 1910), p. 3.

53. *Ocherki*, op.cit., pp. 193, 197; *Proletarii*, no. 50 (24/11 December 1909), p. 7; Ostroukhova, 'Iz perepiski mestnykh organizatsii', op.cit., p. 175. Contemporary observers obfuscated matters further by using the terms Otzovism and Ultimatism interchangeably.

54. *Sotsial-demokrat*, no. 6 (17/4 June 1909), p. 7.

55. Swain, *Protokoly*, op.cit., pp. 28–38. It is interesting to note that A. I. Rykov, a future leader of the Bolshevik Conciliators, supported the resolution on Otzovism at the Paris meeting.

56. Ostroukhova, 'Iz perepiski mestnykh organizatsii', op.cit., p. 166 (letter of Goloshchekin to Zinoviev, 25 July 1909); p. 170 (letter of Rykov to the Bolshevik Centre, 10 August 1909); p. 173 (letter of V. O. Volosevich to the Bolshevik Centre, September 1909); *Ocherki*, op.cit., p. 196.

57. *Sotsial-demokrat*, no. 11 (13 February/31 January 1910), pp. 10–11. The best survey of the January 1910 Plenum of the TsK may be found in Geyer, *Kautsky*, op.cit., pp. 25–45.

58. This point has to remain a conjecture as the minutes of the Plenum have never been published. But in the light of the known views of Gol'denberg-Meshkovskii and his role in local party politics during the by-election to the State Duma in the capital in the autumn of 1909 (see Section III of this chapter), the hypothesis does not appear without foundation.

59. *Pravda* (Vienna), no. 17 (3 December/20 November 1910), p. 3; nos. 18–19 (11 February/29 January 1911), p. 6; Arskii, 'Epokha reaktsii v Petrograde' op.cit., pp. 93, 94, 102; *Sotsial-Democrat*, nos. 15–16 (25/12 September 1910), p. 13.

60. *Sotsial-demokrat*, no. 14 (5 July/22 June 1910), p. 9; nos. 15–16 (25/12 September 1910), p. 13; *Pravda* (Vienna), nos. 18–19 (11 February/29 January 1911), p. 6; Shidlovskii, 'V. Peterburgskii partiinykh riadakh', op.cit., pp. 177, 180, 181, 184; Arskii, 'Epokha reaktsii v Petrograde', op.cit., pp. 93, 94, 102.

61. *Sotsial-demokrat*, nos. 15–16 (25/12 September 1910), p. 13; *Pravda* (Vienna), no. 17 (3 December/20 November 1910), p. 3; nos. 18–19 (11 February/29 January 1911), p. 6; R. Arskii, 'O partiinoi rabote v 1910 godu v Peterburge (iz vospominanii)', *Krasnaia letopis'*, no. 4 (1932), pp. 101, 102.

62. M. A. Tsiavlovskii (ed.), *Bol'sheviki: dokumenty po istorii bol'shevizma s 1903 po 1916 god byvsh. Moskovskogo okhrannago otdeleniia* (Moscow, 1918), pp. 44–5; Arskii, 'O partiinoi rabote', op.cit., p. 110. On the Capri and Bologna schools, at which the 'Left Bolsheviks' hoped to train organisers and propagandists for Russia, consult: R. C. Elwood, 'Lenin and the Social Democratic schools for underground party workers, 1909–1911', *Political Science Quarterly*, vol. 81 (September 1966), pp. 371–9; Williams, *The Other Bolsheviks*, op.cit., pp. 149–53, 155–6, 158–9.

63. *Pravda* (Vienna), no. 5 (3 October/20 September 1909), supplement, p. 4; no. 7 (7 December/24 November 1909), p. 3; Ostroukhova, 'Iz perepiski mestnykh organizatsii', op.cit.,

p. 180 (letter of S. Ia. Bagdat'ev to the Bolshevik Centre, 11 November 1909); Swain, *Protokoly*, op.cit., pp. 109–11.

64. F. Dan (ed.), *Materialy po istorii russkogo revoliutsionnogo dvizheniia. vol. II. Iz arkhiva P. B. Aksel'roda: pis'ma P. B. Aksel'roda i Iu O. Martova, 1901–1916* (Berlin, 1924), letter of Iu. O. Martov to P. B. Aksel'rod, 26 June 1907, p. 164 and note 1, p. 183; Sapir, *Theodore Dan*, op.cit., letter of F. I. Dan to P. B. Aksel'rod, 6 December 1907, p. 183, and note 7, p. 184; *Sotsial-demokrat*, no. 2 (28 January/10 February 1909), p. 9; *Golos sotsial-demokrata*, nos. 8–9 (July–September 1908), p. 31; *Peterburgskii komitet*, op. cit., p. 348.

65. *Sotsial-demokrat*, no. 5 (6 May/23 April 1909), p. 9; no. 10 (6 January 1910/24 December 1909), p. 6; no. 14 (5 July/22 June 1910), p. 9; no. 15–16 (25/12 September 1910), p. 13.

66. Sapir, *Theodore Dan*, op.cit., letter of F. I. Dan to P. B. Aksel'rod, 28 February 1908, p. 194; letter of F. I. Dan to P. B. Aksel'rod, 3 May 1909, p. 121.

67. Dan, *Materialy*, op.cit., letter of Iu. O. Martov to P. B. Aksel'rod, 21 March 1908, p. 184; letter of Iu. O. Martov to P. B. Aksel'rod, 18 August 1909, p. 194.

68. Tsiavlovskii, *Bol'sheviki*, op.cit., pp. 37, 40; 'Razrushennaia legenda', *Golos sotsial-demokrata*, no. 24 (February 1911), supplement, p. 3; *Sotsial-demokrat*, no. 13 (9 May/26 April 1910), p. 11.

69. *Trud*, no. 17 (October 1907), p. 15; no. 19 (February 1908), p. 8.

70. 'Polozhenie del v Peterburgskoi organizatsii, sentiabr' 1908g.', Archives of the Socialist Revolutionary Party (Amsterdam), folder 430; 'Stenograficheskii otchet piatogo soveta partii S. R.', Archives of the Socialist Revolutionary Party, folder 792, pp. 7, 8; *Trud*, no. 20 (March 1908), p. 13.

71. Hildermeier, *Die Sozialrevolutionäre Partei*, op.cit., p. 314. The author's conclusion that the 'foundation of the metropolitan organisation was still lively' is curiously at odds with his own data.

72. 'Peterburg, 25 – oe avgusta 1909g.', Archives of the Socialist Revolutionary Party, folder 757; *Znamia truda*,

nos. 21–2 (September 1909), pp. 22–3; nos. 23–4 (December 1909), pp. 29–30.

73. Archives of the Socialist Revolutionary Party, folder 430; 'Stenograficheskii otchet piatogo soveta partii S. R.', ibid., folder 792, pp. 10–11; *Znamia truda*, nos. 21–2 (September 1909), p. 23; nos. 23–4 (December 1909), p. 29.

74. *Znamia truda*, no. 26 (February 1910), p. 22; C. Rice, 'The Socialist Revolutionary Party and the urban working class in Russia, 1902–1914' (Birmingham, Ph.D., 1984), p. 279.

75. Two works devote exclusive attention to the legal activists in this period. They are Swain, *Russian Social Democracy*, op.cit., and P. B. Barchugov, *Revoliutsionnaia rabota bol'shevikov v legal'nykh rabochikh organizatsiiakh* (Rostov-na-donu, 1963).

76. 'Arkhivnye dokumenty i biografii V. I. Lenina (1887–1914gg.) Revoliutsiia 1905–1907gg.', *Krasnyi arkhiv*, vol. 2, no. 62 (1934), pp. 209–10; Lenin, *CW*, op.cit., Vol. 13, pp. 15–49 ('Against boycott', 26 June 1907); pp. 60–1 (Draft Resolution on Participation in the Elections to the Third Duma, presented to the Second All-Russian Conference); K. Ostroukhova, 'Sotsial-demokratiia v vybory', op. cit., pp. 87, 90; *Trud*, no. 16 (August 1907), pp. 1–3.

77. Rice, 'Socialist Revolutionary Party', op.cit., pp. 225–33.

78. The elections in the labour curia of St Petersburg were indirect. Eligible working-class voters first chose delegates who in turn selected six electors. The latter attended the provincial electoral assembly at which the predominant landed and middle-class elements made the final choice of the working-class deputy (cf. Levin, *The Third Duma*, op.cit.).

79. 'Vybory po rabochei curii v Peterburge', *Trud* (October 1907), pp. 1–3; *Proletarii*, no. 17 (20 October 1907), p. 6; Levin, *The Third Duma*, op.cit., pp. 70–1; *Peterburgskii komitet* op. cit., pp. 317–18, 320–21.

80. G. I. Zaichikov, *Dumskaia taktika bol'shevikov (1905–1917gg.)* (Moscow, 1975), p. 126; M. K. Korbut, 'Rabota N. G. Poletaeva v 3-i Gos. Dume', *Krasnaia letopis'*, no. 2 (1931), p. 170, note 1.

81. Lenin, *CW*, op.cit., Vol. 13, pp.

135–7 ('Report on the Third State Duma to a Conference of the St Petersburg Organisation of the RSDLP', *Proletarii*, no. 20 (19 November 1907)); pp. 138–9 ('Resolution on the Third State Duma', *Proletarii*, no. 19 (5 November 1907)).

82. Ralph Carter Elwood, *Resolutions and Decisions of the Communist Party of the Soviet Union. Volume 1. The Russian Social Democratic Labour Party. 1898–October 1917* (Toronto, 1974), pp. 113–14 and 131–4.

83. L. M. (Martov), 'Pered dumskoi sessii', *Golos sotsial-demokrata*, nos. 8–9 (July–September 1908), pp. 8–9.

84. Lenin, *CW, op.cit.*, Vol. 15, pp. 286–302 ('Two letters', *Proletarii*, no. 39 (26/13 November 1908)). Soviet historians adopt the same interpretation: cf. Zaichikov, *Dumskaia taktika* op.cit., p. 127.

85. *Proletarii*, no. 28 (15/2 April 1908), p. 2; *Proletarii*, no. 31 (17/4 June 1909), p. 2. In late December 1907 the PK had already attacked the faction's Duma activities as indecisive.

86. Swain, *Russian Social Democracy*, op.cit., p. 42.

87. Dan, *Materialy*, op.cit., letter of Iu. O. Martov to P. B. Aksel'rod, 3 September 1908, p. 189, note 1.

88. Swain, *Protokoly*, op.cit., pp. 82–3; Zaichikov, *Dumskaia taktika* op.cit., p. 138; *Peterburgskii komitet*, op. cit., p. 357.

89. Zaichikov, *Dumskaia taktika*, op.cit., p. 137.

90. *Sotsial-demokrat*, nos. 7–8 (21/8 August 1909), pp. 2, 6.

91. Zaichikov, *Dumskaia taktika*, op.cit., p. 118.

92. *Pravda* (Vienna), no. 17 (3 December/20 November 1910), p. 1; *Sotsial-demokrat*, no. 13 (9 May/26 April 1910), p. 10.

93. *Biulleten'* no. 8 of the Moscow Society of Factory Owners (July 1908), (TsGIA, f.150, op.1, d.665, l.28): ibid., no. 12 (September 1909) (ibid., l.55).

94. *Biulleten'* no. 1 of the Moscow Society of Factory Owners (31 July 1907), (f.150, op.1, d.665, l.2); V. Miliutin, 'Rabochaia zhizn'', *Vozrozhdenie*, no. 1 (January 1910), p. 100.

95. *Nadezhda*, no. 1 (31 July 1908), p. 5; *Metallist*, no. 10 (11 February 1912), p. 2; *Professional'nyi vestnik*, no. 22 (4 March 1909), p. 15; *Zvezda*, no. 12 (5 March 1911), p. 4.

96. *Professional'nyi vestnik*, no. 25 (18 August 1909), p. 22.

97. *Biulleten'* no. 4 of the Moscow Society of Factory Owners (31 October 1907), (f.150, op.1, d.665, l.2); *Professional'nyi vestnik*, no. 22 (4 March 1909), p. 29.

98. 'Professional'nye soiuzy v Rossii', *Vozrozhdenie*, no. 1 (December 1908), pp. 61–5; G. Smolin, 'Iz zhizni professional'nykh soiuzov', ibid., no. 6 (14 April 1910), pp. 63–71.

99. *Edinstvo*, no. 10 (22 October 1909), p. 9; *Zvezda*, no. 20 (30 April 1911), p. 4; *Metallist*, no. 10 (11 February 1912), p. 2.

100. K. Dmitriev (pseudonym of P. N. Kolokol'nikov), 'Peterburgskie profsoiuzy v pervuiu polovinu 1910', *Nasha zaria*, nos. 11–12 (1910), p. 115.

101. Ibid., p. 118.

102. *Vozrozhdenie*, no. 6 (14 April 1910), p. 63; *Professional'nyi vestnik*, no. 22 (4 March 1909), p. 15.

103. *Nash put'*, no. 13 (January 1911), p. 12; *Vozrozhdenie*, nos. 5–6 (April 1909), p. 50.

104. *Materialy ob ekonomicheskom polozhenii i professional'noi organizatsii Peterburgskikh rabochikh po metallu* (St Petersburg, 1909), pp. 75, 77. Thus 24 per cent of workers in electro-mechanical factories and 26 per cent in machine construction had enrolled in the union, but only 11 per cent in shipbuilding, 7 per cent in metal rolling and 3 per cent in nails.

105. Ibid., pp. 79, 84, 89.

106. Ibid., pp. 78, 95.

107. *Zvezda*, no. 12 (5 March 1911), p. 4; *Golos portnogo*, no. 6 (1 March 1911), p. 10; *Vestnik portnykh*, no. 1 (6 June 1911), p. 9. Possible explanations for the lowly unionisation of women are explored in Chapter 7 in relation to the trade-union movement in the years 1912–1914.

108. *Edinstvo*, no. 9 (18 September 1909), p. 3; *Nash put'*, no. 3 (25 June 1910), p. 11; *Professional'nyi vestnik*, no. 21 (24 January 1909), p. 24.

109. M. Kheisin, 'V mire rabochikh', *Nasha zaria*, no. 1 (1910), pp. 62–8; Dmitriev, 'Peterburgskie profsoiuzy', op. cit., pp. 115–25; Resolution on Trade Unions, Fourth Con-

110. gress of the RSDLP, April 1906 (Elwood, *Resolutions and Decisions*, op.cit., Vol. 1, p. 102).

110. Lenin, *CW*, op.cit., Vol. 13, p. 61. (Outline of a Draft Resolution on the All-Russian Congress of Trade Unions, July 1907); Elwood, *Resolutions and Decisions*, op.cit., Vol. 1, pp. 115, 121–2; Barchugov, *Revoliutsionnaia rabota*, op.cit., pp. 177–81; *Peterburgskii komitet*, op. cit., p. 314.

111. Rice, 'Socialist Revolutionary Party', op.cit., pp. 255–6, 419–44; 'Professional'nye soiuzy i partiia sotsialistov-revoliutsionerov', *Trud*, no. 17 (October 1907), pp. 3–6.

112. 'Polozhenie del v Peterburgskoi organizatsii, sentiabr' 1908g.', Archives of the Socialist Revolutionary Party, folder 430.

113. Kats, 'Professional'nye soiuzy', op.cit., p. 140. Kats reaches his conclusion by erroneously equating contemporary estimates of unionists' Social Democratic sympathies as support for the Bolsheviks (ibid., p. 141).

114. F. Bulkin, 'Departament politsii i soiuz metallistov (okonchanie)', *Krasnaia letopis'*, no. 8 (1923), pp. 220–33.

115. This episode is discussed in Chapter 4.

116. Kats, 'Professional'nye soiuzy', op.cit., p. 141.

117. S. Kanatchikov, 'Kul'turno-prosvititel'naia deiatel'nost' v Peterburgskikh professional'nykh soiuzakh', *Vozrozhdenie*, nos. 5–6 (April 1909), p. 54; *Zvezda*, no. 9 (12 February 1911), p. 4; V. M., 'Rabochee dvizhenie', *Vozrozhdenie*, nos. 9–12 (September 1909), p. 145.

118. L. K-ova, 'Rabochie obshchestva samoobrazovaniia', *Professional'nyi vestnik*, no. 22 (4 March 1909), pp. 23–5.

119. *Zvezda*, no. 33 (10 December 1911), p. 4; 'Rabochee dvizhenie', *Zaprosy zhizni*, no. 5 (15 November 1909), p. 17.

120. *Professional'nyi vestnik*, no. 26 (31 October 1909), p. 36; V. M., 'Rabochee dvizhenie', op.cit., p. 145; *Nash put'*, no. 4 (15 July 1910), p. 8.

121. *Nash put'*, no. 7 (1910), p. 9.

122. E. Adamovich, 'Legal'nye vozmozhnosti i partiinaia rabota v Peterburge v 1908–1909gg.', *Krasnaia letopis'*, no. 4 (1930), pp. 28, 32, 34,

35; A. Tsvetkov-Prosveshchenskii, *Mezhdu dvumia revoliutsiamii (1907–1916gg.)* (Moscow 1957), pp. 10, 13.

123. Barchugov, *Revoliutsionnaia rabota*, op.cit., p. 249; Michael S. Melancon, 'The Socialist Revolutionaries from 1902 to February 1917: a party of the workers, peasants and soldiers' (Indiana, Ph.D., 1984), p. 79.

124. Kanatchikov, 'Kul'turno-prosvititel'naia deiatel'nost'', op.cit., p. 53.

125. B. I. Nikolaevskii, *Materialy* (Papers) (Oxford), Vol. 3, item 47, letter of A. N. Potresov to Iu. O. Martov, 23 October 1910; item 53, letter of A. N. Potresov to Iu. O. Martov, 15 December 1910; Vol. 5, note 114, p. 58; Dan, *Materialy*, op.cit., letter of P. B. Aksel'rod to Iu. O. Martov, 3 October 1910, p. 206.

126. Swain, *Protokoly*, op.cit., pp. 85, 87; Nikolaevskii, *Materialy*, op.cit., Vol. 3, note 26, p. 17.

127. Nikolaevskii, *Materialy*, op.cit., Vol. 3, item 50, letter of A. N. Potresov to Iu. O. Martov, 13 November 1910; item 52, letter of Iu. O. Martov to A. N. Potresov, 30 November 1910; note 43, p. 23.

128. Ibid., Vol. 3, item 80, letter of A. N. Potresov to Iu. O. Martov, 24 May 1911; note 222, p. 102; Vol. 4, item 96, letter of A. N. Potresov to Iu. O. Martov, 1 July 1911; note 98, p. 31; Vol. 5, note 45, p. 33.

129. *Trudy pervogo vserossiiskago zhenskago s"ezda, 10–16 dekabria 1908 goda* (St Petersburg, 1909), pp. 310–42, 571–9. The women's movement and the congress's broader work are examined in Linda Edmondson's article 'Russian feminists and the First All-Russian Congress of Women', *Russian History/Histoire Russe*, vol. 3 no. 2 (1976), pp. 123–49.

130. V. Miliutin, 'Rabochaia gruppa na s"ezde po bor'be s alkogolizmom', *Vozrozhdenie*, no. 2 (February 1910), p. 51; 'S"ezd po bor'be s pianstvom', *Edinstvo*, no. 14 (16 February 1910), p. 8.

131. *Golos sotsial-demokrata*, nos. 10–11 (November–December 1908), p. 25; *Pravda* (Vienna), no. 2 (30/17 December 1908), p. 11; no. 8 (21/8 December 1909), p. 3.

132. N. I. Letunovskii, *Leninskaia taktika ispol'zovaniia legal'nykh vserossiiskikh s"ezdov v bor'be za massu v 1908–1911 godakh* (Moscow, 1970), p. 6.

133. *Proletarii*, no. 33 (5 August/23 July 1908), p. 2; *Pravda* (Vienna) no. 8 (21/8 December 1909), p. 3.

134. *Pravda* (Vienna), no. 12 (16/3 April 1910), p. 1.

135. Iu. Chatskii (pseudonym of P. A. Garvi), 'Zhizn' pobezhdaet', *Nasha zaria*, no. 5 (1911), pp. 86–7; F. Dan, 'Promyshlennyi pod"em', *Golos sotsial-demokrata*, no. 23 (November 1909), pp. 2–3; L. Martov, 'Bor'ba za svobodu koalitsii'; ibid., no. 25 (May 1911), pp. 6–8; G. Baturskii, 'Mertvyi khvataet zhivoe', *Delo zhizni*, no. 4 (1911), pp. 21–32.

136. S. V. (Volskii), 'Petitsionnaia kampaniia', *Vpered*, no. 3 (May 1911), pp. 40–5; *Pravda* (Vienna), no. 26 (25 June–8 July 1911), p. 5; no. 23 (23/10 December 1911), p. 5; G. E. Zinoviev, *Sochineniia*, vol. 2 (Moscow 1923), pp. 208–47 (*Voprosy taktiki po povodu "petitsionnoi kampanii"*); *Rabochaia gazeta*, nos. 4–5 (28/15 April 1911) p. 4.

137. Nikolaevskii, *Materialy*, op.cit., Vol. 3, no. 73, letter of A. N. Potresov to Iu. O. Martov, 22 April 1911; *Zvezda*, no., 24 (27 May 1911). The authors of the two articles were P. N. Dnevnitskii (pseudonym of Martov's cousin F. I. Tsederbaum), Plekhanov's secretary and N. Iordanskii.

138. Iu. Chatskii, 'Zhizn' pobezhdaet', *Nasha zaria*, no. 5 (1911), pp.86, 88; G. Kuznetsov, 'Rabochie i politicheskaia zhizn', *Zhivoe delo*, no. 6 (24 February 1912), p. 2; *Nash put'*, no. 17 (23 May 1911), pp. 10, 11; *Zvezda*, no. 28 (5 November 1911), p. 4.

139. *Svod otchetov fabrichnykh inspektorov za 1909 god* (St Petersburg, 1910), pp. 162, 174; ibid., *za 1910 god* (St Petersburg 1911) pp. lxx–lxxi, 294; V. Nardova, 'Proletariat stolitsy v gody reaktsii', in *Istoriia rabochikh Leningrada. Tom Pervyi. 1703–fevral' 1917* (Leningrad, 1972), p. 354.

140. In 1905, according to the factory inspectorate, 22 per cent of all strikes in the Empire came from St Petersburg province, and 38 per cent in 1907. In 1906, however, the Polish province of Petrokovskaia (Piotrkow) occupied first place, with 38 per cent; St Petersburg province furnished 16 per cent of the total of strikers. (U. A. Shuster, *Peterburgskie rabochie v 1905–1907gg.*, Leningrad, 1976, pp. 275–6).

141. M. S. Balabanov, *Ot 1905 k 1917 godu; massovoe rabochee dvizhenie* (Moscow, 1927), p. 112.

142. *Biulleten'*, no. 5 of the Moscow Society of Factory Owners (24 December 1907), (f.150, op.1, d.665, l.11); *Ocherki*, op.cit., p. 364; *Proletarii*, no. 42 (25/12 February 1909), p. 7; *Sotsial-demokrat*, no. 6 (17/4 June 1909), p. 7; no. 13 (9 May/26 April 1910), p. 1; nos. 15–16 (25/12 September 1910), p. 13.

143. As note 135.

144. *Professional'nyi vestnik*, no. 24 (24 June 1909), p. 23.

145. Nardova, 'Proletariat stolitsy', op.cit., pp. 360–1; *Vozrozhdenie*, no. 7 (May 1909), pp. 71–2.

146. Theodore Steffens, *Die Arbeiter von Petersburg 1907 bis 1917. Sociale Lage, Organisation und Spontaner Protest zwischen zwei Revolutionen* (Freiburg, 1985), p. 532.

Chapter 4

1. Such falsely optimistic reports appeared in *Sotsii-demokrat*, no. 23 (14/1 September 1911); *Pravda* (Vienna), no. 20 (29/16 April 1911), p. 5.

2. *Sotsial-demokrat*, no. 24 (31/18 October 1911); B. I. Nikolaevskii, *Materialy*, (Papers) (Oxford), Vol. 4, item 101, letter from F. I. Kalinin to G. A. Aleksinskii, 4 July 1911.

3. Trotskii's newspaper reported that an unsuccessful attempt occurred late in October 1911 to re-establish a PK, whilst *Sotsial-demokrat* mentioned the existence of a Technical Commission, 'which to some degree replaced the PK'. *Pravda* (Vienna), no. 24 (27/14 March 1912), p. 5; *Sotsial-demokrat*, no. 25 (21/8 December 1911).)

4. These included: N. P. Bogdanov, police agent, a pupil at the second Vperedist school in Bologna, and secretary of the union of woodworkers; N. M. Shvernik, Bolshevik, a dominant personality in the Sampsonievskii Educational Society; I. A. Akulov, Bolshevik, a member of the board of the union of accounting clerks, (Nikolaevskii, *Materialy*, op.cit., Vol. 6, note 130, p. 70).

5. M. A. Tsiavlovskii (ed.), *Bol'sheviki: dokumenty po istorii bol'shevizma s 1903 po 1916 god byvsh. Moskovskago okhrannago otdeleniia* (Moscow, 1918), p. 57; *Pravda* (Vienna), no. 24 (27/14 March

1912), pp. 5, 6.

6. *Listok golosa sotsial-demokrata*, no. 1 (25 June 1911), p. 3. The constantly changing membership of the Initiative Group in 1911 included at one time or another such intellectual literary luminaries as I. A. Isuv, V. Ezhov, (Martov's younger brother and editor of *Delo zhizni*), I. S. Astrov, P. A. Garvi and working-class trade unionists such as K. A. Gvozdev, president of the union of metalworkers, 1910–11, A. N. Smirnov, vice-president of the same union and V. M. Abrosimov, police agent. (Nikolaevskii, *Materialy*, op.cit., Vol. 3, no. 68, note 117, p. 59 and Vol. 6, no. 169, note 66, p. 25).

7. Ibid., Vol. 5, item 142, letter from S. Vol'skii to F. I. Kalinin, pre-14 September 1911; *Pravda* (Vienna), no. 23 (23/10 December 1911), p. 2; no. 24 (27/14 March 1912), p. 5. The point of view of the legal activists found clear expression in an uncensored article written by Iu. Larin in the St Petersburg journal *Delo zhizni*, which called for 'both open political activity and closed circles of leading workers' (Larin, 'Puti sozdaniia', *Delo zhizni*, no. 7 (1911), pp. 13–20). The practice of the Initiative Groups also approximated closely to Iu. Martov's vision of the party pursuing the path the German Social Democrats had trod in the decade of the Exceptional Laws in the 1880s.

8. *Rabochaia gazeta*, nos. 4–5 (28/15 April 1911), p. 4; I. Iurenev, 'Mezhraionka (1911–1917gg) (Vospominaniia)', *Proletarskaia revoliutsiia*, vol. 24 (1924), p. 114.

9. I. Iakovlev, 'Aprel'sko-maiskie dni 1912 goda v Peterburge', *Krasnaia letopis'*, no. 3 (1925), p. 228; *Pravda* (Vienna), no. 24 (27/14 March 1912), p. 5; Nikolaevskii, *Materialy*, op.cit., Vol. 6, note 134, p. 79; TsGIA, f.1405, op.530, d.824, l.56.

10. f.1405, op.530, d.824, ll.56 and 57; TsGAOR, f.102, DPOO., 1913g., d.5, ch.57, l.69; *Znamia truda*, no. 42 (April 1912), pp. 10–12; no. 43 (May 1912), pp. 13–14.

11. P. Gooderham, 'The anarchist movement in Russia, 1905–1917' (Bristol, Ph.D., 1981), p. 222; *Pravda* (Vienna), no. 25 (6 May/23 April 1912), p. 4.

12. *Rabochaia gazeta*, no. 6 (6 October/22 September 1911), p. 4; *Pravda* (Vienna), no. 24 (27/14 March 1912), p. 5;

'Protokoly vi (Prazhskoi) vserossiiskoı kon ferentsii RSDRP', *Voprosy istorii KPSS*, no. 5 (1988), p. 52.

13. f.1405, op.530, d.824, ll.84–6; *Istoriia rabochikh Leningrada. Tom pervyi 1703–fevral' 1917* (Leningrad, 1972), p. 422.

14. O. Piatnitskii, *Memoirs of a Bolshevik* (London, 1933), pp. 133–43; G. A. Arutiunov, 'Rasprostranenie "Sotsial-demokrata" i "Rabochei Gazety" v Rossii (1910–1912)', *Voprosy istorii KPSS*, no. 12 (1984), pp. 57–63; *Pravda* (Vienna), no. 21 (8 July/25 June 1911), p. 5; no. 22 (29/16 November 1911), p. 3; *Rabochaia gazeta*, nos. 4–5 (28/15 April 1911) p. 4; no. 6 (6 October/22 September 1911), p. 4; *Znamia truda*, no. 42 (April 1912), p. 11.

15. Tsiavlovskii, *Bol'sheviki*, op.cit., pp. 59–70; Nikolaevskii, *Materialy*, op.cit., Vol. 4, no. 84, letter from D. Z. Manuilskii to G. A. Aleksinskii, 11 June 1911 and no. 113, letter from F. I. Kalinin to G. A. Aleksinskii, 31 July 1911; Vol. 5, no. 141, report on the school in Longjumeau (by Grott), September 1911; R. C. Elwood, 'Lenin and the Social Democratic schools for underground party workers, 1909–1911', *Political Science Quarterly*, vol. 81 (September 1966), pp. 380–8.

16. *Listok zagranichnago biuro tsentral'nago komiteta*, no. 1 (8 September 1911); *Sotsial-demokrat*, no. 23 (14/1 September 1911); no. 24 (31/18 October 1911).

17. L. I. Zharov and N. I. Kuznetsov, 'O podgotovke Prazhskoi konferentsii RSDRP', *Istoricheskii arkhiv*, vol. 6, no. 5 (1958), p. 12; K. Popov, 'K istorii Prazhskoi konferentsii', *Krasnyi arkhiv*, vol. 6/97, (1939), pp. 101–2; *Pravda* (Vienna), no. 25 (6 May/23 April 1912), p. 3.

18. E. Onufriev, *Vstrechi s Leninym* (Moscow, 1959), pp. 9–11; M. D. Rozanov, *Obukhovtsy* (Leningrad, 1965), pp. 231–3, 241 (which disingenuously described Onufriev as 'a sufficiently visible figure' and absurdly claims that 'in his words Lenin heard entire proletarian Piter [i.e. Petersburg]'); *Vserossiiskaia konferentsiia Ros.Sots-dem. Rab. Partii 1912 goda* (Paris, 1912; repr., New York, 1982), p. 7. Although the Social Democratic fraction in the State Duma refused to send a delegation to Lenin's conference, two of its number, N. G. Poletaev and

V. E. Shurkanov, left for Prague without their colleagues' authorisation. They arrived after the finish of proceedings (Nikolaevskii, *Materialy*, op.cit., Vol. 6, note 64, p. 25).

19. V. I. Lenin, *Polnoe sobranie sochinenii* (Moscow, 1958–65), Vol. 48, item 40, p. 49 and item 65, pp. 83–5; Nikolaevskii, *Materialy*, op.cit., Vol. 6, no. 185; *Za partiiu* no. 1 (29 April 1912); Tsiavlovskii, *Bol'sheviki*, op.cit., pp. 94, 96; *Vserossiiskaia konferentsii*, op.cit., pp. 28–9; 'Protokoly', op.cit., *Voprosy istorii KPSS*, no. 6 (1988), pp. 52–5; no. 7 (1988), pp. 32–5.

20. *Vserossiiskaia konferentsii*, op.cit., pp. 16. 18, 22; V. I. Lenin, *Collected Works* (Moscow 1963–9), Vol. 41, p. 251.

21. *Iz epokhi 'Zvezdy' i 'Pravdy' (1911–1914)* (Moscow, 1921), Vol. 3, pp. 184, 230, 234–5; I. Iurenev, 'Mezhraionka', op.cit., p. 111; *Pravda* (Vienna), no. 25 (6 May/23 April), 1912, pp. 3–4; *Rabochaia gazeta*, no. 8 (17 March 1912); 'V. I. Lenin v 1912–1914gg', *Krasnyi arkhiv*, vol. 2/62 (1934), p. 229.

22. f.1405, op.530, d.824, 1.56. A survey of the resolutions and the lists of contributors to the 'Lena fund' published in *Zvezda* and *Pravda* reveals that all sectors of manufacturing, artisanal as much as factory, small as well as large establishments, state-owned in addition to private plants, felt instinctive solidarity with the oppressed gold workers. Protests and monetary donations came from workers in shipbuilding, engineering, leather, paper, printing, baking, confectionery, tailoring, woodworking, transport, and jewellery. The one noticeable exception is textiles. [*Zvezda*, no. 29/65 (12 April 1912); no. 30/66 (15 April 1912); no. 31/67 (17 April 1912); no. 32/68 (19 April 1912); *Pravda*, no. 5 (27 April 1912); no. 12 (6 May 1912); no. 18 (20 May 1912).]

23. 'Arkhivnye materialy o revoliutsionnoi deiatel'nosti I. V. Stalina, 1908–1913gg.', *Krasnyi arkhiv*, vol. 2/105 (1941), pp. 25–6. Kruze asserts that the PK suffered arrest after 15 April 1912: *Istoriia rabochikh Leningrada*, op.cit., p. 425. Yet G. A. Pochebut states that the PK was broken up by the police in March: *Ocherki istorii Leningradskoi organizatsii KPSS. Chast' I. 1883-oktiabr' 1917g.* (Leningrad,

1962), p. 321. The police archives contain no reference to the existence of a PK in April, or to the leaflet Kruze claims it published, calling on workers to demonstrate on 15 April.

24. f.1405, op.530, d.824, ll.53, 56–7, 61, 64–5; f.102, DPOO., 1912g., d.61, ch.2, t.2, l.55; *Zvezda*, no. 30/66 (15 April 1912). The Okhrana claimed that the appeal for preparations for a general armed uprising emanated in the university from a 'non-party' group entitled 'the Foundation Group of the Revolutionary Union'. The nature of the appeal, however, suggests the existence of some sympathy for the extreme left wing of the Socialist Revolutionary party.

25. f.1405, op.530, d.824, ll.61–3; *Zvezda*, no. 31/67 (17 April 1912); *Pravda* (Vienna), no. 25 (6 May/23 April 1912), p. 3.

26. f.1405, op.530, d.824, ll.82, 88; f.102, DPOO., 1912g., d.341, l.108; Iakovlev, 'Aprelsko-maiskie dni', op.cit., pp. 230–7. The contention of Soviet historians that the creation of the '1 May committees' and the 'Central Bureau' was the work solely of Bolshevik cells is refuted by Iakovlev's testimony (cf. *Istoriia rabochikh Leningrada*, op.cit., p. 322).

27. f.1405, op.530, d.824, ll.84–6, 90–2; f.102, DPOO., 1912g., d.101, ll.25, 74, 78, 147–9; *Pravda*, no. 8 (1 May 1912); no. 9 (3 May 1912); *Listovki Peterburgskikh bol'shevikov 1902–1917. Tom vtoroi. 1907–1917* (Leningrad, 1939), pp. 64–5; Iakovlev, 'Aprel'sko-maiskie dni', op.cit., pp. 232, 234–5.

28. f.102, DPOO., 1912g., d.341, ll.136–7, 161, 181; d.101, ll.81, 225–6.

29. f.1405, op.530, d.824, l.102; Iurenev, 'Mezhraionka', op.cit., pp. 133–4; *Listovki*, op.cit., pp. 65–6; *Iz epokhi*, op.cit., Vol. 3, p. 127. Since the 1920s Soviet scholars have kept silent concerning the Vperedist character of the Narva committee.

30. Piatnitskii, *Memoirs*, op.cit., p. 144; 'Pis'ma N. Krupskoi K. G. L. Shklovskomu, 1910–1916gg.', *Proletarskaia revoliutsiia*, vol. 43 (1925), p. 123.

31. f.1405, op.530, d.824, ll.103–4; *Iz epokhi*, op.cit., Vol. 3, pp. 126–7; *Sotsial-demokrat*, nos. 28–9 (18 November 1912 n.s.). The claim presented in the official history of the Leningrad party that Lenin provided direct

leadship of the underground at this period is absurd (cf. *Ocherki*, op.cit., pp. 326–7).

32. In his memoirs, published in 1921, Safarov asserted that he had reformed a PK. But the contemporary Okhrana and *Sotsial-demokrat* reports make no mention of one. Soviet historians give various and conflicting dates for the re-emergence of a PK – in September or October or November 1912.

33. *Sotsial-demokrat*, nos. 28–9 (18 November 1912n.s.); Iurenev, 'Mezhraiorka', op.cit., p. 111; A. Tsvetkov-Prosveshchenskii, *Mezhdu dvumia revoliutsiiami (1907–1916gg)* (Moscow, 1957), pp. 47–9. (The latter omits to mention the 'conciliatory' nature of the 'Central Petersburg Group'.)

34. *Ocherki*, op.cit., p. 324; *Sotsial-demokrat*, no. 30 (25/12 January 1913). This version has been repeated over several decades by Soviet historians: cf. M. Mitel'man, B. Glebov, A. Ul'ianskii, *Istoriia Putilovskogo zavoda* (Moscow, 1941), p. 331; G. A. Arutiunov, *Rabochee dvizhenie v Rossii v period novogo revoliutsionnogo pod"ema 1910–1914gg.* (Moscow, 1975), p. 175.

35. N. A. Ivanova, 'Oktiabr'sko-noiabr'skie stachki 1912g. v. Rossii', *Istoriia SSSR*, no. 2 (1965), pp. 138–40; f.102, D.P., 4 d-vo., 1912g., d.62, ch.2, t.2., l.180.

36. f.102, DP., 4 d-vo., 1912g., d.61, ch.3, ll.5, 9; d.62, ch.2, t.2, l.208; *Listovki*, op.cit., pp. 68–71; *Luch*, no. 49 (13 November 1912), p. 3; *Pravda*, no. 109 (15 November 1912), p. 1. Tsvetkov asserts in his memoirs that his 'Bolshevik' 'Central *Petersburg* Group' conceived the scheme of a demonstration on 15 November (Tsvetkov, *Mezhdu*, op.cit., p. 52). It is not inconceivable that this, in reality a factionally mixed group, played some role, but its name does not appear among the signatories of the appeal. Whereas Kruze falsely and illogically assigns the leading role to the Bolsheviks, Arutiunov alone of recent Societ commentators affords an accurate picture of events.

37. A. Badaev, *The Bolsheviks in the Tsarist Duma* (London, n.d.), pp. 51–4; f.102, D.P., 4 d-vo., 1912g., d.62, ch.2, t.2, l.237; f.102, DPOO., 1913g., d.5. ch.57, ll.20, 77.

38. *Izveshchenie o konferentsii organizatsii*

RSDRP (Paris, 1912; repr., New York, 1982), p. 10; TsGAOR, f.DPOO., 1913g., d.5, ch.57, l.74; B. Sapir (ed.), *Theodore Dan. Letters (1899–1946)* (Amsterdam, 1985), letter of F. I. Dan to P. B. Aksel'rod, 11 May 1912, p. 261.

39. Sapir, *Theodore Dan*, op.cit., letter of F. I. Dan to P. B. Aksel'rod, 24 January 1912, pp. 245–6; ibid., 14 September 1912, p. 274; F. Dan (ed.), *Materialy po istorii russkogo revoliutsionnogo dvizheniia. vol. II. Iz arkhiva P. B. Aksel'roda: pis'ma P. B. Aksel'roda i Iu. O. Martova, 1901–1916* (Berlin, 1924), letter of Iu. Martov to P. Garvi, April 1912, p. 223 and 13 August 1912, pp. 252–3. From 1911 to 1913 prominent St Petersburg 'Liquidators' (F. A. Cherevanin, I. A. Isuv, M. A. Kheisin, V. D. Levitskii) lived in exile in Pskov: these men were all associated with the 'thick' monthly St Petersburg periodical *Nasha zaria*.

40. Sapir, *Theodore Dan*, op.cit., letter of F. I. Dan to P. B. Aksel'rod, 3 February 1912, pp. 247–8 and 2 March 1912, p. 254.

41. *Izveshchenie*, op.cit., pp. 5, 10–11; *Listok organizatsionnogo komiteta po sozyvu obshchepartiinoi konferentsii*, no. 1 (2 June/20 May 1912), pp. 1, 3; no. 4 (29/16 August 1912), p. 3; P. Garvi, *Vospominaniia 1912g. Petersburg – Odessa – Vena* (Newtonville, Mass., 1982), p. 166.

42. Issue may be taken with Dr G. Swain's view that 'only the Initiative Group could fairly claim to represent Russian opinion' (Swain, *Russian Social Democracy and the Legal Labour Movement, 1906–1914*, London, 1983, p. 146.) Although Abrosimov and Smirnov could plausibly pretend to represent Menshevik legal activists, the Initiative Group was only one of several non-Leninist factions in the city and there were Bolshevik and Vperedist trade-union leaders. Apart from this the proportion of trade unionists who were Social Democrats, let alone Mensheviks, is unknown. As Chapter 7 will show, membership of trade unions involved only a fraction of the working class.

43. *Listok OK*, op.cit., no. 3 (19/6 July 1912), p. 1; *Izveshchenie*, op.cit., pp. 28–9, 41–2; Tsiavlovskii, *Bol'sheviki*, op.cit., p. 114. The OK was the institutional expression of the 'August

Bloc' formed at the conference between Trotskii, the Bund, the Mensheviks, the Caucasian and Latvian Social Democrats.

44. *Izveshchenie*, op.cit., pp. 33–4; G. Baturskii, 'Stachechnaia bor'ba i professional'nye obshchestva', *Nevskii golos*, no. 2 (23 May 1912), p. 3; *Luch*, no. 53 (17 November 1912), p. 1.

45. f.102, DPOO., 1913g., d.5, ch.57, l.69; *Znamia truda*, no. 43 (May 1912), pp. 14–15; no. 48 (January 1913), p. 13; Archives of the Socialist Revolutionary Party (Amsterdam), folder 757.

46. f.102, DPOO., 1913g., d.5, ch.57, l.67; Gooderham, 'The anarchist movement', op.cit., p. 223.

Chapter 5

1. The *émigrés* were Lenin, Krupskaia, Zinoviev, V. N. Lobova, A. A. Troianovskii and his wife E. F. Rozmirovich; the deputies were A. E. Badaev, R. V. Malinovskii, G. I. Petrovskii, N. R. Shagov; somehow or other a worker delegate, a certain turner named Medvedev, arrived from St Petersburg. Lenin could not convoke a formal Plenum of his TsK as five of its members had been arrested in 1912.

2. V. I. Lenin, *Collected Works* (Moscow, 1963–69) Vol. 18, pp. 102–6 ('The revolutionary upswing', *Sotsial-demokrat*, no. 27, 17 June 1912); Vol. 16, pp. 395–406 ('Strike statistics in Russia', *Mysl'*, nos. 1 and 2, December 1910 and January 1911); Vol. 18, pp. 450–3 and 456–8 (Cracow resolutions). The strikes on 9 January and 1 May 1913 for Lenin merely confirmed the correctness of his analysis. Commenting on them in an article in *Sotsial-demokrat* in June he observed that 'a nationwide political crisis is in evidence in Russia ...' (*CW*, Vol. 19, pp. 219–22). Hereafter C. W.

3. Lenin, *CW*, op.cit., Vol. 18, pp. 458–60, 463–5 (Cracow resolutions); A. Badaev, *The Bolsheviks in the Tsarist Duma* (London, n.d.), p. 63; S. M. Goncharova, 'Neopublikovannye resheniia Krakovskogo soveshchaniia TsK. RSDRP s partiinymi rabotnikami', *Voprosy istorii KPSS*, no. 7 (1967), pp. 81–3. The resolutions of the conference concerning the party's legal activities are discussed in Chapter 6.

4. It is possible that there may be some substance to the gossip current among Mensheviks living abroad that Badaev was 'a very uncultured person and a bitter drunkard' (B. Sapir (ed.), *Theodore Dan. Letters (1899–1946)*, Amsterdam, 1985, letter of F. I. Dan to P. B. Aksel'rod, 16 November 1912, p. 282).

5. TsGAOR, f.102, DPOO., 1913g., d.5, ch.57, 1.20; *Listovki Peterburgskikh bol'shevikov. 1902–1907. Tom Vtoroi 1907–1917* (Leningrad, 1939), pp. 74–5; 'Lenin i "Pravda", 1912–1913gg.: Perepiska', *Krasnaia letopis'*, no. 10 (1924), p. 71; *Pravda*, no. 8/212 (11 January 1913), p. 2. Soviet historians find this episode embarrassing. G. A. Pochebut makes the false assertion that the Bolsheviks prepared mass strikes and demonstrations on 9 January (*Ocherki istorii Leningradskoi organizatsii KPSS. Chast'I. 1883-oktiabr' 1917g.*, Leningrad, 1962, p. 333), whilst E. E. Kruze omits to mention in her analysis of the PK leaflet that the document failed to mention a strike (*Istoriia rabochikh Leningrada. Tom pervyi. 1703–fevral' 1917*, Leningrad, 1972, p. 431).

6. V. I. Lenin, *Polnoe sobranie sochinenii* (Moscow, 1958–65), Vol. 48, item 128, p. 156.

7. TsGIA, f.150, op.1, d.58, ll.20–2, 24–5; TsGAOR, f.102, DPOO., 1913g., d.5, ch.57, ll.52, 90, 100; d.307, 1.51; *Listovki*, op.cit., pp. 78–9.

8. TsGIA, f.1405, op.530, d.859, ll.7–9, 18–20; *Listovki*, op.cit., pp. 77–8; *Sotsial-demokrat*, no. 31 (28 June 1913 n.s.).

9. f.1405, op.530, d.859, 1.77; f.102, DPOO., 1913g., d.5, ch.57, l.189.

10. Of the fourteen members of the PK in the spring of 1913, whose biographies are available, only two were students. Of the remaining twelve, eleven were factory workers and one a commercial employee: ten were skilled metalworkers and one an engraver. The new PK derived its strength from the revival of the union of metalworkers in April 1913; from the latter the president (A. A. Kiselev), assistant secretary (A. A. Mitrevich), and two board members (P. A. Mel'nikov and P. I. Ignat'ev, a police spy) also sat on the PK. Of 105 members and organisers of district committees in the first half of 1913, on whom there exists in-

formation, a mere three were students.

11. f.102, DPOO., 1913g., d.307, ll.43, 117; d.5, ch.57, l.188; M. A. Tsiavlovskii, *Bol'sheviki: dokumenty po istorii bol'shevizma s 1903 po 1916 god byvsh. Moskovskogo okhrannogo otdeleniia* (Moscow, 1918), p. 129. It was perhaps no accident that, in the light of the continuing conciliatory actions of the other five Bolshevik deputies (see Chapters 6 and 7), Malinovskii alone – the deputy whom Lenin trusted above all others – attended the gathering in Poronin on 27 July 1913.

12. f.102, DPOO., 1913g., d.307, ll.301–9; Tsiavlovskii, *Bol'sheviki*, op.cit., p. 135; *Iz epokhi 'Zvezdy' i 'Pravdy' (1911–1914)* (Moscow, 1921), Vol. 3, p. 222.

13. f.1405, op.530, d.859, l.3; *Luch*, no. 41/127 (19 February 1913), p. 2; Rose L. Glickman, *Russian Factory Women. Workplace and Society, 1880–1914* (Berkeley, 1984), pp. 274–5.

14. f.1405, op.530, d.859, ll.56–7, 64, 72–5; f.102, DPOO., 1913g., d.5, ch.57, ll.66, 154, 190; d.307, ll.472–7; *Listovki*, op.cit., pp. 80–2; *Luch*, no. 80/166 (6 April 1913), p. 1.

15. f.1405, op. 530, d.859, ll.77–8, 82, 84–7; f.102, 1913g., d.101, l.97; f.102, DPOO., 1913g., d.5, ch.57, l.177; *Listovki*, op.cit., pp. 82–4; *Pravda*, no. 100/304 (3 May 1913), p. 3; *Luch*, no. 100/86 (3 May 1913), p. 2. The author calculates that 135,000 workers struck on May Day 1913 in the capital.

16. f.1405, op.530, d.859, ll.89–90; f.102, DP., 4d-vo., 1913g., d.61, ch.2, t.2, ll.61, 67.

17. f.102, DP., 4d-vo., 1913g., d.61, ch.2, t.2, ll.92, 101, 106; *Listovki*, op.cit., pp. 84–5; E. E. Kruze, *Petersburgskie rabochie v 1912–1914 godakh* (Leningrad, 1961), pp. 276–7.

18. f.102, DP., 4d-vo., 1913g., d.61, ch.2, t.2, ll.178–9; *Listovki*, op.cit., pp. 86–8. Among those involved in planning the general strike were two Bolshevik members of the board of the union of metalworkers, A. S. Kiselev, its president, and M. S. Lebedev, as well as K. S. Eremeev, who was in charge of the workers' chronicle section in *Pravda*, and A. V. Shotman; Kiselev and Eremeev were Bolshevik Conciliators (*Ockherki*, op.cit., p. 366).

19. Lenin, *CW*, op.cit., Vol. 19, pp. 422–3; A. M. Volodarskaia, 'Poroninskoe soveshchanie TsK RSDRP s partiinymi rabotnikami v 1913g.', *Istoricheskie zapiski*, vol. 59 (1957), pp. 138, 143, 146. Given the presence of the police agents Malinovskii and A. I. Lobov at the meeting, there may have been an element of police provocation in the decision for a general strike.

20. f.102, DPOO., 1913g., d.5, ch.57, ll.308–9; d.341, prod.II, ll.218–20; prod.III, l.266. It is instructive to note that the standard Soviet studies of the Leningrad party pass over in silence the organisational history of the last five months of 1913.

21. f.1405, op.530, d.859, l.101.

22. Tsiavlovskii, *Bol'sheviki*, op.cit., p. 129; Lenin, *CW*, op.cit., Vol. 41, p. 298 and Vol. 43, p. 373; Volodarskaia, 'Poroninskoe soveshchanie', op.cit., p. 146; f.102, DPOO., 1913g., d.307, prod.IV, l.114; S. T. Beliakov et al., 'Iz perepiski TsK RSDRP s mestynmi partiinymi organizatsiiami (1912–1914gg.)', *Istoricheskii arkhiv*, vol. 6 no. 2 (1960), p. 30.

23. f.102, DPOO., 1913g., d.341, prod. II, ll.218–20, 226; *Pravda truda*, no. 14 (26 September 1913), p. 3.

24. f.102, DPOO., 1913g., d.341, prod. III, l.1.

25. Ibid., ll.6, 37–8, 133; d.5, ch.57, l.265; *Severnaia rabochaia gazeta*, no. 77 (8 November 1913), pp. 1, 2; A. M. Volodarskaia and N. V. Orlova, 'Rabochee dvizhenie v 1913–1914gg.', *Istoricheskii arkhiv*, vol. 1, no. 5 (1955), pp. 72–8.

26. f.102, DPOO., 1913g., d.341, prod. III, l.65.

27. Tsiavlovskii, *Bol'sheviki*, op.cit., pp. 124, 128; letter of Iu. Martov to P. Aksel'rod, 3 February 1913 (Institute of International Social History, Amsterdam).

28. f.102, DPOO., 1913g., d.5, ch.57, ll.2, 166, 190, 274–5, 310–31.

29. Ibid., ll.190, 201, 311–12.

30. Tsiavlovskii, *Bol'sheviki*, op.cit., p. 124; I. Iurenev, '"Mezhraionka" (1911–1917gg.) (Vospominaniia)', *Proletarskaia revoliutsiia*, vol. 24 (1924), pp. 115–20.

31. f.102, DPOO., 1913g., d.307, prod. III, l.116.

32. Ibid., d.5, ch.57, ll.274–5; Sapir, *Theodore Dan*, op.cit., letter of F. I. Dan to Iu. Martov, 22 January 1913, p. 290; N. Garvi, 'Nachalo lokautnoi

epidemii', *Nasha zaria*, no. 2 (1913), pp. 19–23; *Luch*, no. 149/235 (2 July 1913), p. 4.

33. f.1405, op.530, d.859, ll.13–16, 22, 56–7, 59–64; *Znamia truda*, no. 53 (April 1914), p. 10.

34. *Znamia truda*, no. 52 (November 1913), p. 10; no. 53 (April 1914), pp. 8–10.

35. f.102, DPOO., 4 d-vo., 1913g., d.61, ch.9.

36. Ibid., 1913g., d.5, ch.57, ll.23–4; *Rabochii mir*, no. 5 (15 February 1913), p. 1; *Pravda*, no. 23/227 (29 January 1913), p. 3; P. Gooderham, 'The anarchist movement in Russia, 1905–1907' (Bristol, Ph.D., 1981), pp. 210–19.

37. V. T. Loginov et al., 'Perepiska TsK RSDRP s mestnymi partiinymi organizatsiiami v gody novogo revoliutsionnogo pod"ema', *Istoricheskii arkhiv*, vol. 3, no. 1 (1957), pp. 17–18, 22–3, 24–5; f.102, DPOO., 1914g., d.5, ch.57, t.1, ll.57, 84–5; d.5, ch.57, t.2, l.24.

38. Among the eight members of the PK arrested on 20 February 1914 were E. I. Nekliudov (employed at the Pipes works; treasurer of the Vasil'evskii Island branch of the union of metal-workers); P. I. Ignat'ev (police agent, worker at Okhta Gunpower, 32 years of age, member of the PK in 1912 and president of the union of metal-workers from January 1914); V. I. Shurkanov (police agent, aged 37, vice-president of this union and a Menshevik deputy in the Third State Duma); V. V. Schmidt (employed at New Lessner, aged 27, assistant secretary of this union); Iu. Ia. Prafrod (worker at New Lessner, member of the PK and Vyborg committee in 1912 and 1913).

39. f.1405, op.530, d.883, ll.2–5, 6; *Listovki*, op.cit., pp. 88–90; *Proletarskaia pravda*, no. 8/26 (11 January 1914), p. 3; *Novaia rabochaia gazeta*, no. 8/26 (11 January 1914), p. 3.

40. *Bor'ba*, no. 2 (18 March 1914), p. 34; *Rabotnitsa*, no. 2 (1914), p. 3; *Severnaia rabochaia gazeta*, no. 14 (25 February 1914), p. 2; f.102, DPOO., 1914g., d.5, ch.57, t.1, l.39. *Rabotnitsa*, the Bolshevik journal for women workers launched in February 1914, is discussed in Chapter 6.

41. A. F. Bessonova, 'K istorii izdanii zhurnala "Rabotnitsy", 1914', *Istoricheskii arkhiv*, vol. 1, no. 4 (1955), pp.

25–53; *Rabotnitsa*, no. 1 (23 February 1914), p. 1; Glickman *Russian Factory Women*, op.cit., pp. 276–7.

42. f.102, DPOO., 1914g., d.5, ch.57, t.1, l.106; G. Shidlovskii, 'Peterburgskii komitet bol'shevikov v kontse 1913g. i v nachale 1914g.', *Krasnaia letopis'*, no. 17 (1926), p. 129. The assertion of E. E. Kruze that the strikes broke out 'at the summons of the Bolshevik party' is erroneous (*Peterburgskie rabochie*, op.cit., p. 294).

43. f.102, DPOO., 1914g., d.5, ch.57, t.1, ll.118–19; d.307, prod.I, ll.88, 98; *Listovki*, op.cit., pp. 95–6; *Severnaia rabochaia gazeta*, no. 29 (14 March 1914), p. 1; *Put' pravdy*, no. 36 (14 March 1914), p. 3. Another possible reason for the switch of date from 4 April to 13 March was that the militants suddenly remembered that 4 April coincided with a public holiday, as it was Good Friday.

44. f.1405, op.530, d.883, ll.14, 16–18; *Severnaia rabochaia gazeta*, no. 30 (15 March 1914), p. 2; *Put' pravdy*, no. 39 (18 March 1914), p. 3; no. 40 (19 March 1914), p. 3; no. 42 (21 March 1914), p. 3; Badaev, *Bolsheviks*, op.cit., pp. 137–41; *Istoriia*, op.cit., p. 454.

45. TsGAOR, f.DPOO, 1914g., d.5, ch.57, t.1, l.162; *Put' pravdy*, no. 42 (21 March 1914), p. 1.

46. f.102, DPOO., 1914g., d.5, ch.57, t.1, ll.163, 175, 221, 283; *Listovki*, op.cit., pp. 102–3; Shidlovskii, '*Peterburgskii komitet*' op.cit., pp. 137–8.

47. All the standard Soviet histories of the party in the capital make no reference to any district committees after March 1914.

48. f.102, DPOO., 1914g., d.5, ch.57, t.2, ll.22–5; t.1, ll.263, 267–8, 281, 287; d.307, prod.I, ll.296–300.

49. A. M. Volodarskaia and T. V. Shapeleva, 'Zasedaniia TsK RSDRP, 15–17 aprelia 1914 goda', *Voprosy istorii KPSS*, no. 4 (1957), pp. 115–200; f.102, DPOO., 1914g., d.5, ll.238–41; A. M. Volodarskaia, 'Podgotovka s"ezda bol'shevistskoi partii v 1914g.', *Istoricheskii arkhiv*, vol. 4, no. 6 (1958), p. 26; A. M. Volodarskaia, 'Podgotovka bol'shevikami s"ezda RSDRP v 1914g.', in *Bol'shevistskaia pechat' i rabochii klass Rossii v gody revoliutsionnogo pod"ema*, 1910–1914 (Moscow, 1965), p. 191.

50. *Ocherki*, op.cit., p. 372.

51. This episode is treated in detail in R. B. McKean, 'Russia on the eve of the Great War. Revolution or evolution?', (East Anglia, Ph.D., 1971), pp. 144–54.

52. f.102, DPOO., 1914g., d.307, prod.I, ll.272, 275–7; d.5, ch.57, t.1, l.285; *Severnaia rabochaia gazeta*, no. 58 (19 April 1914), p. 1; *Put' pravdy*, no. 71 (26 April 1914), p. 3.

53. *Put' pravdy*, no. 72 (27 April 1914), p. 1.

54. f.1405, op.530, d.883, ll.22–4; f.102, DPOO., 1914g., d.5, ch.57, t.1, ll.200–1, 212, 285; lit.G, l.8; d.307, prod.I, l.300; *Nasha rabochaia gazeta*, no. 1 (3 May 1914), p. 2; *Put' pravdy*, no. 76 (3 May 1914), p. 2; *Listovki*, op.cit., pp. 104–5.

55. f.102, DPOO., 1914g., d.5, ch.57, t.1, ll.229, 245–55, 286; *Listovki*, op.cit., pp. 105–6; *Put' pravdy*, no. 92 (21 May 1914), p. 2.

56. *Trudovaia pravda*, no. 11 (10 June 1914), p. 1; no. 13 (12 June 1914), p. 3; f.102, DP., 4 d-vo., 1914g., d.61, ch.2, t.2, lit.A, ll.55, 58, 76.

57. Loginov, 'Perepiska', op.cit., p. 26; Lenin, *CW*, op.cit., Vol. 43, pp. 377, 382, 389.

58. Presumably due to Malinovskii, Lenin's analysis appeared in a memorandum of Colonel Martynov of the Moscow Okhrana dated 27 April 1914 (f.102, DPOO., 1914g., d.307, prod. I, ll.296–300; this is reprinted in Volodarskaia, 'Podgotovka s''ezda', op.cit., 4, no. 6, pp. 9–11).

59. f.102, DPOO., 1914g., d.307, prod. II, ll.80–1; d.5, ch.46, lit.B, prod. I, l.188 i ob; A. M. Volodarskaia, 'Otvet V. I. Lenina na pis'mo I. I. Skvortsova-Stepanova', *Istoricheskii arkhiv*, vol. 5, no. 2 (1959), p. 11–18.

60. R. C. Elwood, 'The congress that never was. Lenin's attempt to call a "Sixth" Party Congress in 1914', *Soviet Studies*, vol. 31, no. 3 (July 1979), pp. 355–7; Elwood, *Roman Malinovsky. A Life Without a Cause* (Newtonville, 1977), p. 56.

61. f.102, DPOO., 1914g., d.5, ch.57, t.2, ll.26–7; t.1, ll.53, 216.

62. f.102, DPOO., 1914g., d.307, ll.207, 385–6; prod.I, l.260; *Severnaia rabochaia gazeta*, no. 48 (5 April 1914), p. 1.

63. *Severnaia rabochaia gazeta*, no. 13 (23 February 1914); f.102, DPOO., 1914g., d.5, ch.57, lit.B, ll.141–2.

The single reference after 23 February in the Menshevik press to women's issues concerned Kollontai's draft resolution for the protection of maternity, which was to be presented to the Third Conference of Socialist Women in Vienna in August 1914 (*Nasha rabochaia gazeta*, no. 26 (4 June 1914), p. 2).

64. Iurenev, '"Mezhraionka"', op.cit., pp. 119, 120, 124; f.102, DPOO., 1914g., d.307, l.68.

65. Iurenev, '"Mezhraionka"', op.cit., pp. 120, 125; f.102, DPOO., 1914g., d.5, ch.57, lit.B, ll.172–3, 185–6, 187–8, 242–4.

66. f.102, DPOO., 1914g., d.5, ch.57, lit.B., ll.9, 12, 26; Iurenev, '"Mezhraionka"', op.cit., p. 125; *Bor'ba*, no. 3 (1914), pp. 34–9.

67. *Nasha zaria*, no. 4 (1914), pp. 60–3; f.102, DPOO., 1914g., d.5, ch.57, t.1, ll.9 51; Tsiavlovskii, *Bol'sheviki*, op.cit., p. 145; *Informatsionnyi listok zagranichnoi organizatsii bunda*, no. 7 (January 1915), p. 14. The best treatment of the Brussels 'Unity' Conference is provided by R.C. Elwood, 'Lenin and the Brussels "Unity" Conference of July 1914', *Russian Review*, vol. 39 (January 1980), pp. 32–49.

68. *Luch*, no. 1/87 (1 January 1913), p. 1; *Novaia rabochaia gazeta*, no. 119 (1 January 1914), p. 1; L. Martov, 'Vmeshatel'stvo Internatsionala i s-d edinstvo v Rossii', *Nasha zaria*, no. 1 (1914), p. 110; Martov 'Na pereput'i', *Sovremennik*, vol. 5 (March 1914), pp. 63–71; *Severnaia rabochaia gazeta*, no. 21 (5 March 1914), p. 2.

69. f.102, DPOO., 1914g., d.5, ch.57, t.1, ll.108–12; d.307, prod.I, ll.259–60; F.D., 'Burnye dni', *Nasha zaria*, no. 4 (1914), pp. 93–100; *Severnaia rabochaia gazeta*, no. 41 (28 March 1914), p. 1; N. M. Egorov, 'Uroki rabochago dvizheniia v Peterburge za mart 1914 god', *Bor'ba*, no. 6 (1914), pp. 35–40.

70. f.102, DPOO., 1914g., d.5, ch.57, t.1, ll.191, 202; *Znamia truda*, no. 53 (April 1914), pp. 1–2.

71. Gooderham, 'The Anarchist Movement', op.cit., p. 218; *Rabochii mir*, no. 8 (20 September 1913), p. 4; ibid., series II, no. 3 (April 1914), pp. 10–11.

72. This section is based on a variety of sources – archives, memoirs, secondary studies, the contemporary legal

socialist press. With regard to the latter, the publication of resolutions concerning clear factional issues (e.g. the split in the Social Democratic fraction in the autumn of 1913) may be taken as proof of the existence of appropriate Bolshevik or Menshevik groups in the factory in whose name the document was submitted to the relevant newspaper. It would be erroneous, however, to treat workers' contributions to the socialist press as *prima facie* evidence of factional allegiance.

73. Due to the non-availability of the legal Socialist Revolutionary press, the figure of five is an underestimate. The factories were: New Aivaz (machines, payroll of 1,500); Koppel' (machines, 700); Neva Shipyards (mixed production 6,500); Semenov (machines, 400); Siemens and Halske (electrical, Narva branch: 1,000).

74. In chemicals, both Social Democratic factions set up cells in Neva Stearine (1,200 workers) and the Bolsheviks alone at Tentelevskii (800); in textiles, the Bolsheviks maintained groups at K. Ia. Pal' (2,000) and at Thornton (1,700), and the Mensheviks at Petrovskaia (2,000) and one of the six mills (unidentified) of Voronin, Liuts and Chesher.

75. Among machine construction plants, both Bolsheviks and Mensheviks established cells *inter alia* in New Aivaz (1,500 operatives), New Lessner (1,000), Nobel' (980), St Petersburg Engineering (1,000) and St Petersburg Metals (4,000). The Bolsheviks alone set up groups in: Atlas-Herman (300), Baranovskii (800), Eklund (160), Ekval (300) and Semenov (400). The following electrical goods firms witnessed groups from both Social Democratic factions: Erikson (1,200), Geisler (700), Siemens and Halske (Narva plant, 1000: Vasil'evskii Island plant, 650) and the 1886 Electricity Station (around 500).

76. The four were: Franco-Russian (2,500 wage earners), Obukhov (6,000), Neva Shipyards (6,500) and Putilov (over 11,000).

77. Social Democratic groups at some time existed, among others, in: Baltic Shipyards (a Menshevik cell: 7,500 workers in the factory); Okhta Gunpowder (a Bolshevik cell: 4,000 workers); the Russian Society (1,200) and St Petersburg Nails (over 2,000).

Chapter 6

1. V. I. Lenin, *Collected Works* (Moscow, 1963–9), Vol. 20, p. 502. Hereafter *CW*.

2. Under the electoral law of 3 June 1907, in St Petersburg all males who met the appropriate electoral qualifications (women did not possess the vote, nor men under 25 years of age or employed in plants with under 50 hands) were split into three electoral colleges or curiae: the first urban curia, numbering 3,969 in 1912, was restricted to the wealthiest electors; the second urban curia, with 70,824 voters, embraced the less well-to-do members of the middle classes, including many commercial–industrial employees; the labour curia covered suitably qualified male operatives in both the city and the province. Although the first and second urban curia directly elected three deputies each to the State Duma, the method of electing the single workers' representative was indirect. Operatives chose a total of 185 delegates (70 for the city and 102 the province), who in turn selected 6 electors to the provincial electoral assembly. This body, comprising 70 electors (landowners, peasants, workers), then designated the working-class deputy.

3. K. St., 'Itogi vyborov po rabochei kurii v Peterburge', *Pravda*, no. 151 (24 October 1912), p. 1.

4. V. I. Lenin, 'The election campaign and the election platform', *Sotsial-demokrat*, no. 24 (31/18 October 1911); *Resolutions of the Prague Conference*; 'Fundamental problems of the election campaign', *Prosveshchenie*, nos. 1 and 2 (December 1911 and January 1912) – all in *CW*, Vol. 17, pp. 278–86, 414–19, 468–71. G. E. Zinoviev, *The Fourth Duma Elections and Our Tasks* (December 1911); 'The election campaign in the elections to the Fourth Duma', *Rabochaia gazeta*, no. 7 (22 December 1911) both in *Sochineniia* (Moscow, 1923), Vol. 2 (1923), pp. 109–27, 140–4; 'The election campaign in the Fourth Duma', *Zvezda*, no. 6/42 (2 February 1912), p. 3.

5. Lenin; as note 4; Zinoviev, 'Vybory', *Nevskaia zvezda*, no. 20 (5 August 1912), p. 1.

6. F. Dan, 'Burzhuaziia i konstitutsionnyi rezhim', *Golos sotsial-demokrata*,

no. 13 (April 1909), p. 5; 'Politicheskoe obozrenie: posle "Leny"', *Nasha zaria*, no. 5 (1912), pp. 60–9; L. Martov, 'Zametki publitsista', *Zhizn'*, no. 1 (1910), pp. 1–5; 'Nakanune novago desiatiletiia', *Delo zhizni*, no. 1 (1911), pp. 1–10; V. O. Levitskii, 'Probuzhdenie burzhuaznoi oppozitsii', *Nasha zaria*, no. 3 (1911), pp. 54–63.

7. L. Martov, 'Tret'ia duma', *Sovremennyi mir*, no. 8 (1912), p. 248; V. O. Levitskii, 'Chto takoe izbiratel'naia platforma?', *Zhivoe delo*, no. 8 (9 March 1912), p. 1; L. Sedov, 'Lenintsy i izbiratel'naia kampaniia', *Nasha zaria*, no. 6 (1912), pp. 25–30.

8. *Nasha zaria*, nos. 7–8 (1911), pp. 42–53; *Izveshchenie o konferentsii organizatsii RSDRP* (Paris, 1912: repr. New York, 1982), pp. 17–18, 24–8, 45–53. The final version of the election platform, as drafted by a commission at the Vienna conference, in which Martov played the dominant role, bore the marks of a compromise between the majority of delegates who opposed the adoption of very revolutionary slogans as 'unreal' and the minority, including Trotskii, who feared that this decision would alienate Vperedists, Party Mensheviks and Bolshevik Conciliators (G. Uratadze, *Reminiscences of a Georgian Social Democrat*, Stanford, 1968, pp. 249–51).

9. L. Germanov (Frumkin), 'Voprosy o izbiratel'noi platforme', *Zvezda*, no. 3/39 (21 January 1912); two issues later the editorial board endorsed Frumkin's stand.

10. *Iz epokhi 'Zvezdy' i 'Pravdy' (1911–1914)* (Moscow, 1921), Vol. 3, letter from Zinoviev to the editorial board of *Pravda*, 21 July 1912 (p. 188); V. I. Lenin, *Polnoe sobranie sochinenii* (PSS) (Moscow, 1958–65), Vol. 48, pp. 94, 98.

11. *Nevskii golos*, no. 6 (5 July 1912), p. 1; no. 9 (31 August 1912), p. 3; *Nevskaia zvezda*, no. 16 (8 July 1912); *Luch*, no. 1 (16 September 1912), p. 4.

12. G. I. Zaichikov, *Bor'ba rabochikh deputatov Gosudarstvennoi Dumy protiv tsarizma v 1907–1914gg.* (Moscow, 1981), p. 105; E. D. Chermenskii, 'K istorii dumskoi taktiki partii bol'shevikov (1905–1914gg.)', *Voprosy istorii KPSS*, no. 19 (1981), p. 48.

13. *Sotsial-demokrat*, nos. 28–9 (18/5 November 1912); *Luch*, no. 1 (16 September 1912), p. 4; no. 64 (December 1912), p. 2; TsGAOR, f.102, DPOO., 1912g., d.307, 1.221.

14. Two issues alone of *Zvezda* in 1912 published the Bolsheviks' electoral platform [no. 13/49 (1 March 1912) and no. 23/59 (29 March 1912)] and none of *Pravda*: the Mensheviks' appeared only in nos. 7–8 (1911) of *Nasha zaria* and *Zhivoe delo*, no. 8 (9 March 1912). None of these commanded the wide circulation of the new Bolshevik daily newspaper.

15. C. Rice, 'The Socialist Revolutionary Party and the urban working class in Russia, 1902–1914' (Birmingham, Ph.D., 1984), pp. 225–33; M. Melancon, 'The Socialist Revolutionaries from 1901 to 1907: peasant and workers' party', *Russian History/Histoire Russe*, vol. 12, no. 1 (1985), pp. 35–40. At the second stage of the elections Bolsheviks and Mensheviks united to elect solely Social Democratic electors, ignoring their rivals' sizeable vote.

16. N. D. Avksent'ev, 'Boikot ili uchastie v vyborakh?', *Znamia truda*, no. 35 (April 1911), pp. 7–9; *Pochin*, no. 1 (June 1912), pp. 1–2, 8–10; Andrei Ivanovich, 'Boikot ili vybory?', *Izvestiia oblastnogo zagranichnago komiteta*, no. 15 (April 1911), pp. 14–17.

17. N. I. (pseudonym of N. I. Rakitnikov), 'Vybirat'-li v dumu?', *Znamia truda*, no. 36 (June 1911), pp. 14–18; 'O vyborakh v chetvertuiu dumu', ibid., no. 4 (March 1912), pp. 1–2; *Zemlia i volia*, no. 25 (February 1912), pp. 1–3.

18. 'K izbiratel'noi kampanii', *Znamia truda*, no. 44 (June 1912), pp. 1–3; B., 'Vybory v gosudarstvennuiu dumu', ibid., no. 47 (1912), pp. 6–8.

19. *Luch*, no. 6 (22 September 1912), p. 1; no. 24 (13 October 1912), p. 1.

20. *Pravda*, no. 120 (18 September 1912), p. 2; no. 121 (19 September 1912), p. 2; no. 123 (21 September 1912), p. 2; *Luch*, no. 2 (18 September 1912), p. 2; no. 3 (19 September 1912), p. 3; *Rech'*, no. 2209 (17 September 1912), p. 2.

21. B., 'Vybory', op.cit., pp. 6–7; 'Rabochie v vyborakh v chetvertuiu dumu', *Sotsial-demokrat*, nos. 28–9 (18/5 November 1912), pp. 4–5.

22. M. Oskarov (pseudonym of Iu. A. Isuv), 'Itogi vyborov po rabochei kurii', *Nasha zaria*, nos. 9–10 (1912), p. 115. An examination of the socialist press furnished details on 56 delegates,

of whom 44 classed themselves as Social Democrats, seven as 'Left', four as 'non-party' and one as a Narodnik.

23. The sources are as cited in note 20. The complete absence of Vyborg in the socialist press coverage is striking and difficult to explain. The election files of the Ministry of the Interior, which were unavailable to the author, may reveal a rather different view of voting patterns.

24. Rice, 'Socialist Revolutionary Party', op.cit., pp. 229–30.

25. K. St., 'Itogi vyborov', op. cit., p. 1; Oskarov, 'Itogi', op.cit., p. 115; see also sources cited in note 20.

26. *Pravda*, no. 125 (23 September 1912), p. 1; no. 135 (5 October 1912), p. 1; no. 143 (14 October 1912), p. 1; no. 145 (17 October 1912), p. 2; *Sotsial-demokrat*, nos. 28–9 (18/5 November 1912); Chermenskii, 'K istorii', op.cit., p. 50. After 1961 Soviet historians ceased referring to the *nakaz* as Stalin's work, either passing over in silence its authorship or assigning it to the Russian Bureau and Petersburg Committee. The *nakaz* was only published as an illegal leaflet some time after 17 October 1912.

27. *Pravda*, no. 136 (6 October 1912), p. 1; no. 146 (18 October 1912), pp. 1–2; *Luch*, no. 19 (7 October 1912), p. 2; no. 28 (18 October 1912), p. 1; no. 29 (19 October 1912), p. 2. In *Nasha zaria*, M. Oskarov maintained that the Bolshevik *nakaz* was not put to the vote on 17 October ('Itogi', op.cit., p. 116). It is impossible to ascertain which version is the truth. The moderate, conciliatory tone of the *nakaz* may have induced many delegates to vote for it.

28. *Luch*, no. 31 (21 October 1912), p. 1; Chermenskii, 'K istorii', op.cit., pp. 50–1.

29. *Pravda*, no. 153 (20 October 1912), p. 2; *Sotsial-demokrat*, no. 30 (25/12 January 1913); *Luch*, no. 29 (19 October 1912), p. 2; Ia. L., 'Vybory', *Ezhegodnik gazetoi 'Rech'' na 1913 god* (St Petersburg, 1913), p. 230.

30. Beletskii informed the provisional government's Investigation Commission in 1917 that 'the entire aim of my guidance was to avoid any chance of the party uniting'; 'Malinovskii was instructed that he, as far as he could, was to assist the splitting of the party.' (*Padenie tsarskogo rezhima*, Moscow,

1924–7, Vol. 3, pp. 280, 286.)

31. S. M. Gribkova, 'V. I. Lenin i bol'shevistskaia fraktsiia iv gosudarstvennoi dumy (po novym materialam)', *Istoriia SSSR*, no. 2 (1965), p. 116.

32. TsGAOR, f.102, DPOO., 1912g., d.307, l.286; 1913g., d.307, l.179; *Luch*, no. 10 (27 September 1912), p. 4; *Nasha rabochaia gazeta*, no. 50 (2 July 1914), p. 2.

33. *Luch*, no. 78 (18 December 1912), p. 1.

34. Zaichikov, *Bor'ba*, op.cit., p. 111; *Padenie*, op.cit., Vol. 3, pp. 486–8; M. L. Lur'e, *Bol'shevistskaia fraktsiia iv gosudarstvennoi dumy. Sbornik materialov i dokumentov* (Leningrad, 1938), pp. 104–9.

35. Lenin, *CW*, op.cit., Vol. 18, pp. 460–1; *Pravda*, no. 26/230 (1 February 1913), p. 2; M. A. Tsiavlovskii (ed.), *Bol'sheviki: dokumenty po istorii bol'shevizma s 1903 po 1916 god byvsh. Moskovskago okhrannago otdeleniia* (Moscow, 1918), p. 129.

36. *Pravda*, no. 167 (13 November 1912), p. 2; no. 47/251 (26 February 1913), p. 1. M. S. Ol'minskii, the veteran Bolshevik intellectual and one of the paper's editors, made a similar plea in no. 45/249 (23 February 1913), p. 1.

37. The pretexts included the unfounded charges that the Menshevik seven deprived the Bolshevik six of opportunities to address the House and of their due share of seats on parliamentary commissions (*Za pravdu*, no. 13 (18 October 1913), p. 1; *Novaia rabochaia gazeta*, no. 61 (19 October 1913), p. 1).

38. Lenin, *CW*, op.cit., Vol. 20, pp. 508–9.

39. L. Martov, 'Raskol v sotsial-demokraticheskoi fraktsii', *Nasha zaria*, nos. 10–11 (1913), pp. 97–8.

40. As the Malinovskii affair has been thoroughly illuminated by Ralph Carter Elwood, it has not been re-examined in this work: see R. C. Elwood, *Roman Malinovsky. A Life Without a Cause* (Newtonville, Mass., 1977).

41. TsGAOR, f.102, DPOO., 1913g., d.307, prod.III, ll.160, 230; prod.IV., l.39; 1914g., d.307, ll.53, 68, 128, 207; *Novaia rabochaia gazeta*, no. 10/128 (14 January 1914), p. 2.

42. Lenin, *CW*, op.cit., Vol. 20, p. 505.

43. *Luch*, no. 63 (30 November 1912), p. 4; F. Dan (ed.), *Materialy po istorii russkogo revoliutsionnogo dvizheniia. vol.*

II. *Iz arkhiva P. B. Aksel'roda: pis'ma P. B. Aksel'roda i Iu. O. Martova, 1901–1916* (Berlin, 1924), letter of Iu. Martov to P. Garvi, 23 April 1912 (p. 222) and Iu. Martov to P. B. Aksel'rod, 13 May 1912 (p. 231).

44. *Zvezda*, no. 28 (5 November 1911), p. 1; no. 33 (10 December 1911), p. 2; no. 1/37 (6 January 1912), p. 1; no. 20/56 (20 March 1912); Tsiavlovskii, *Bol'sheviki*, op.cit., pp. 102–3; B. I. Nikolaevskii, *Materialy*, (Papers) (Oxford), Vol. 6, item 190, letter of A. N. Potresov to Iu. Martov, 29 January 1912; *Iz epokhi*, op.cit., p. 235–7; Lenin, *PSS*, op.cit., Vol. 48, p. 54.

45. *Zvezda*, no. 2/38 (15 January 1912), p. 4; no. 33/69 (22 April 1912), p. 4; Tsiavlovskii, *Bol'sheviki*, op.cit., p. 103; Nikolaevskii, *Materialy*, op.cit., Vol. 6, f. 84, p. 45. The latter claims in this note that Tikhomirnov donated 100,000 roubles to the new publishing venture, but elsewhere (note 148, p. 85) he states the sum was 30,000 roubles.

46. *Severnaia rabochaia gazeta*, no. 53 (13 April 1914), p. 1; *Put' pravdy*, no. 53 (3 April 1914), p. 2; *Zhivoe delo*, no. 2 (27 January 1912), p. 2. Indirect evidence suggests that two members of the 'Initiative Group' were Kuz'min (the Pipes works) and A. N. Smirnov (vice-chairman of the union of metalworkers); both at this time belonged to the Menshevik St Petersburg Initiative Group (*Pravda*, no. 2 (24 April 1912), p. 2).

47. *Zhivoe delo*, no. 12 (6 April 1912), p. 3; no. 13 (13 April 1912), p. 3; *Metallist*, no. 13 (1912), pp. 12–13; no. 20 (1912), pp. 7–10; *Severnaia rabochaia gazeta*, no. 53 (13 April 1914), p. 1; no. 59 (20 April 1914), p. 1; no. 63 (25 April 1914), p. 2; *Nevskaia zvezda*, no. 8 (27 May 1912).

48. *Zvezda*, no. 31/67 (17 April 1912); *Severnaia rabochaia gazeta*, no. 43 (30 March 1914), p. 3; no. 63 (25 April 1914), p. 2; *Metallist*, no. 15 (1912), pp. 8–10.

49. Dan, *Materialy*, op.cit., letter of Iu. Martov to P. Garvi, 27 July 1912 (p. 243); B. Sapir (ed.), *Theodore Dan. Letters (1899–1916)* (Amsterdam, 1985), letter of F. I. Dan to P. B. Aksel'rod, 14 September 1912 (p. 274); P. A. Garvi, *Zapiski Sotsial-Demokrata (1906–1921)* (Newtonville, Mass., 1982), p. 218–19.

50. *Pravda*, no. 152 (25 October 1912), p. 4; no. 160 (4 November 1912), p. 4; no. 184 (4 December 1912), p. 2; no. 185 (5 December 1912), p. 4; no. 194 (15 December 1912), p. 4; no. 199 (21 December 1912), p. 4; no. 29/233 (5 February 1913), p. 3; *Luch*, no. 6/92 (8 January 1913), p. 3; *Biulleten' kontorshchika*, no. 1 (14 June 1913), p. 8.

51. G. V. Petriakov, 'Deiatel'nost' V. I. Lenina po rukovodstvu "Pravdoi" v 1912–1914gg.', *Voprosy istorii*, no. 1 (November 1956), p. 3. In English this topic has received illuminating treatment by R. C. Elwood in 'Lenin and Pravda, 1912–1914', *Slavic Review*, vol. 31, no. 2 (June 1972), pp. 355–80.

52. M. S. Ol'minskii, 'Obshchii obzor epokhy', *Iz epokhi*, op.cit., Vol. 1, pp. 40–1.

53. Petriakov, 'Deiatel'nost', op.cit., p. 4. In the absence of the publication of and access to the archives of *Pravda*, it is impossible to prove or disprove the argument of V. T. Loginov that the board was split between Bolshevik Conciliators and Leninists. His incorrect description of Poletaev as a 'Leninist' in this matter raises doubts about his case (V. T. Loginov, 'V. I. Lenin i "Pravda" (1912–1914gg.)', *Voprosy istorii*, no. 5 (1962), p. 20).

54. *Pravda*, no. 1 (22 April 1912), p. 1; Lenin, *PSS*, op.cit., Vol. 48, p. 78; *Iz epokhi*, Vol. 2, pp. 240, 243.

55. Lenin, *PSS*, op.cit., Vol. 48, pp. 70–1, 156–8; *CW*, op.cit., Vol. 41, pp. 272–3; *CW*, Vol. 43 pp. 316–17, 318, 335; V. T. Loginov, 'O rukovodstve TsK RSDRP bol'shevistskoi gazetoi "Pravda" v 1912–1914gg.', *Voprosy istorii KPSS*, no. 1 (1957), p. 121.

56. V. T. Loginov, et al., 'Deiatel'nost' TsK RSDRP po rukovodstvu gazetoi "Pravda" (1912–1914gg.)', *Istoricheskii arkhiv*, vol. 5, no. 4 (1959), pp. 45, 51, 52; Lenin, *CW*, op.cit., Vol. 43, p. 394; Lenin, *PSS*, op.cit., Vol. 48, p. 279.

57. Dan, *Materialy*, op.cit., letter of Iu. Martov to P. Garvi, 23 April 1912 (pp. 222–3); *Iz epokhi*, op.cit., Vol. 3, letter of Iu. Martov to Malysheva, 20 March 1913 (pp. 265–6).

58. L. Sedov, 'Mass i podpol'e', *Luch*, no. 15/101 (19 January 1913), p. 1: the *P. Aksel'rod Archives* (Amsterdam), letter of Iu. Martov to P. Aksel'rod, 3 February 1913; Martov to Dan, 11

February 1913; Martov to Aksel'rod, 24 May 1913; 5 June 1913; Sapir, *Theodore Dan*, op.cit., Dan to Martov, 12 February 1913 (p. 294); 2 May 1914 (p. 297); Dan to Aksel'rod, May 1913 (p. 299).

59. Lenin, *PSS*, op.cit., Vol. 48, p. 132; Dan, *Materialy*, op.cit., letter of Iu. Martov to F. Dan, 21 January 1913 (p. 258); Sapir, *Theodore Dan*, op.cit., letter of F. Dan to Iu. Martov, 2 May 1913 (p. 296); Vl. Maksakov (ed.), 'Zhandarmy o "Pravde"', *Proletarskaia revoliutsiia*, vol. 14 (1923), p. 463.

60. *Put'pravdy*, no. 67 (22 April 1914), p. 7; *Severnaia rabochaia gazeta*, no. 51 (11 April 1914), p. 2; V. G. Kikoin, '"Zvezda" i "Pravda". Iz istorii bor'by tsarskogo pravitel'stva s legal'noi rabochei pechati v Peterburge', *Krasnaia letopis'*, no. 2 (1930), p. 99. Because of the cumbersome procedures governing confiscation, police raids normally occurred too late and a mere 10–15 per cent of copies were seized (Maksakov, 'Zhandarmy', op.cit., pp. 461–2).

61. V. T. Loginov and N. A. Kurashova, 'Leninskaia "Pravda" i edinstvo rabochikh Rossii (novye dannye o gruppovykh rabochikh sborakh 1912–1914gg.)', *Istorii SSSR*, no. 3 (1982), pp. 56, 58, 82.

62. Lenin, *CW*, op.cit., Vol. 20, pp. 548–55.

63. *Put'pravdy*, no. 42 (21 March 1914), p. 1.

64. Lenin, *CW*, op.cit., Vol. 43, p. 325; V. T. Loginov et al., 'Deiatel'nost'', op.cit., pp. 41–2; A. M. Volodarskaia, 'Podgotovka s"ezda bol'shevistskoi partii v 1914g.', *Istoricheskii arkhiv*, vol. 4, no. 6 (1958), p. 12; A. N Potresov and B. I. Nikolaevskii (eds), *Sotsial-demokraticheskoe dvizhenie v Rossii: materialy* (Moscow, 1928), p. 233; Dan (ed.), *Materialy*, op.cit., letter of Iu. O. Martov to P. B. Aksel'rod, 1 February 1915 (p. 318).

65. Lenin's contemporary charge (repeated ever since in Soviet publications) that *Pravda* was a workers' newspaper and its Menshevik rival a 'bourgeois' publication on account of their respective sources of funds should be treated as polemic rather than historical fact.

66. The survey covered the months January to May 1912, March and August 1913 and March to May 1914.

67. Lenin, *CW*, op.cit., Vol. 20, p. 552; *Nasha rabochaia gazeta*, no. 33 (12 June 1914), p. 2.

68. *Pravda*, no. 68/272 (22 March 1913), p. 3; *Rabochaia pravda*, no. 16 (31 July 1913), p. 2; *Severnaia rabochaia gazeta*, no. 44 (1 April 1914), p. 1.

69. The contemporary social investigator L. Kleinbort was the first to draw attention to the emergence of the 'worker–intellectual' after 1905; L. Kleinbort, 'Ocherki rabochei demokratii: umstvennyi pod"em', *Sovremennyi mir*, no. 2, 2nd edn (May 1913), pp. 113–34.

70. *Luch*, no. 22/108 (27 January 1913), p. 4; *Novaia rabochaia gazeta*, no. 32 (14 September 1913), p. 4; no. 102 (8 December 1913), p. 4; *Put' pravdy*, no. 17 (20 February 1914), p. 3; no. 18 (21 February 1914), p. 3.

71. In his book, *When Russia Learned to Read. Literacy and Popular Culture, 1861–1917* (Princeton, 1985), Jeffrey Brooks provides a brilliant survey of the evolution of popular urban and rural culture before the revolution.

72. *Pravda*, no. 23/227 (29 January 1913), p. 3; *Pravda truda*, no. 9 (20 September 1913), p. 4; *Proletarskaia pravda*, no. 10/28 (13 January 1914), p. 3; *Severnaia rabochaia gazeta*, no. 44 (1 April 1914), p. 1.

73. *Luch*, no. 89/175 (19 April 1913), p. 3; *Zhivoe delo*, no. 7 (2 March 1912), p. 4; *Pravda*, no. 77 (28 July 1912), p. 2.

74. L. Kleinbort, 'Ocherki rabochei demokratii. Stat'ia tret'ia. Otkrytaia pressa', *Sovremennyi mir*, no. 8 (August 1913), pp. 175–98; *Put'pravdy*, no. 67 (22 April 1914), p. 3.

Chapter 7

1. V. L. Lenin, *Collected Works* (Moscow, 1963–9), Vol. 20, pp. 507–8 (hereafter *CW*); TsGAOR, f.102, DPOO., 1913g., d.5, ch.57, 11.303, 307; G. A. Pochebut in *Ocherki istorii Leningradskoi organizatsii KPSS. Chast' I. 1883–oktiabr' 1917g.* (Leningrad, 1962), p. 360; V. E. Bonnell, *Roots of Rebellion. Workers' Politics and Organizations in St Petersburg and Moscow, 1900–1914* (Berkeley, 1983), p. 441.

2. *Vserossiiskaia konferentsiia Ros. Sots.-Dem. Rab. Partii 1912 goda* (Paris, 1912; repr, New York, 1982), pp. 16, 18.

3. Late in 1912 the union of architectural and construction workers had a Bolshevik chairman, secretary and treasurer (*Pravda*, no. 39/243 (16 February 1913), p. 4) and in the spring of the same year the union of bakers, a Bolshevik secretary and treasurer (*Nevskaia zvezda*, no. 6 (22 May 1912), p. 4).

4. It is possible that oral directives concerning trade-union work were transmitted from the Cracow gathering via the Duma deputies, but no evidence exists to verify this hypothesis.

5. *Put' pravdy*, no. 14 (6 February 1914), p. 3; no. 46 (26 March 1914), p. 3; f.102, DPOO., 4 d-vo., 1913g., d.61, ch.9, l.20.

6. C. Rice, 'The Socialist Revolutionary Party and the urban working class in Russia, 1902–1914' (Birmingham, Ph.D., 1984), p. 256; *Znamia truda*, no. 18 (10 May 1909), pp. 5–8.

7. *Pochin*, no. 1 (June 1912): editorial, (pp. 1–3) and A. Voronov, (pp. 23–6).

8. *Pravda*, no. 83/287 (10 April 1913), p. 4; no. 92/296 (23 April 1913), p. 4; no. 93/297 (24 April 1913), p. 4; *Luch*, no. 92/178 (23 April 1913), p. 2; F. A. Bulkin, 'Departament politsii i soiuz metallistov', *Krasnaia letopis'*, no. 9 (1923), pp. 134–5; A. A. Mitrevich, 'Zametki po rabochemu dvizheniiu ot 1912 goda', *Proletarskaia revoliutsiia*, vol. 4 (1922), p. 225.

9. f.102, DPOO., 4d-vo., d.61, ch.9, 1.46; *Metallist*, no. 8/32 (18 September 1913), pp. 11–12; *Severnaia pravda*, no. 20 (25 August 1913), p. 1; no. 21 (27 August 1913), p. 3; *Novaia rabochaia gazeta*, no. 14 (24 August 1913), p. 1; no. 16 (27 August 1913), p. 3; no. 26 (7 September 1913), p. 4; Bulkin, 'Departament', op.cit., pp. 151, 153–4.

10. The Okhrana was kept well informed of the union's business as at least two officers were its agents – the Bolshevik Sesitstkii and the Menshevik Abrosimov.

11. F. A. Bulkin, 'Rabochaia samodeiatel'nost' i rabochaia demagogiia', *Nasha zaria*, no. 3 (1914), pp. 59–60.

12. *Metallist*, no. 8/32 (18 September 1913), p. 10.

13. 'Za god', *Metallist*, no. 10 (11 February 1912), p. 2; S. P-skii (pseudonym of F. Moravskii), 'K voprosu 'chto delat'?', ibid., no. 11 (23 February 1912), pp. 4–5; *Nash put'*, no. 17 (23 May 1911), p. 11; *Nevskaia zvezda*, no. 9 (29 May 1912), p. 3.

14. Iu. Chatskii, 'Ocherednye zadachi', *Nash put'*, no. 18 (17 June 1911), pp. 3–8; Batrak (pseudonym of M. P. Zatonskii), 'Chto Delat'?', *Metallist*, no. 3 (27 October 1911), pp. 2–5; A. V., 'Chto Delat'?', ibid., no. 5 (26 November 1911), pp. 3–5; Al. Vlas, 'O zavodskikh gruppakh', ibid., no. 3/27 (15 June 1913), pp. 4–5.

15. As note 14; *Metallist*, no. 4 (10 November 1911), pp. 12–13; no. 7 (30 December 1911), p. 8; *Nevskaia zvezda*, no. 9 (29 May 1912), p. 3.

16. As the vice-chairman A. N. Smirnov pointed out to a general meeting in October 1911, broadening the scope of mutual aid entailed raising membership dues, a risky course which could frighten away potential members (*Metallist*, no. 4 (10 November 1911), pp. 12–13).

17. *Novaia rabochaia gazeta*, no. 25 (5 September 1913), p. 1; *Severnaia pravda*, no. 21 (27 August 1913), p. 1.

18. Lenin, *CW*, op.cit., Vol. 19, pp. 426–7.

19. *Derevoobdelochnik*, no. 1 (22 April 1914), p. 1; *Put' pravdy*, no. 23 (27 February 1914), p. 3; *Severnaia rabochaia gazeta*, no. 40 (27 March 1914), p. 4; *Vestnik prikazchika*, no. 13 (1914), pp. 8, 11; *Vestnik portnykh*, no. 8 (1914), pp. 10–11.

20. *Pravda*, no. 190 (11 December 1912), p. 4; *Nashe pechatnoe delo*, no. 2 (November 1913), pp. 8–10; no. 12 (May 1914), pp. 4–7; *Trudovaia pravda*, no. 29 (1 July 1914), p. 2.

21. *Put'pravdy*, no. 14 (6 February 1914), p. 3; *Novaia rabochaia gazeta*, no. 85 (17 November 1913), p. 4; *Severnaia rabochaia gazeta*, no. 58 (9 April 1914), p. 4; *Nasha rabochaia gazeta*, no. 9 (13 May 1914), p. 4; no. 28 (6 June 1914), p. 4.

22. Between 1912 and 1914 Lenin wrote about the strike movement, Taylorism, the concentration of production in Russia, factory owners and labour disputes, but not a single article devoted to trade-union issues as such. At most he drafted the resolutions of the Prague Conference and the Poronin meeting of the Central Committee which touched upon the party's relationship to trade unions.

23. In the general assembly of the *kassa* the ratio of elected representatives to appointed members was 3:2, but in the executive board operatives enjoyed only a majority of one over the employer's nominees. The law allowed, but did not oblige, factory owners to act as chairmen of the board and general assembly.

24. G. Swain, *Russian Social Democracy and the Legal Labour Movement, 1906–1914* (London, 1983), p. 165. The Law on Accident Insurance, passed at the same time, little attracted the attention of the revolutionaries, since the insurance companies, which were to administer the scheme, were completely controlled by the industrialists.

25. The Bolshevik critique was elaborated by N. Aleksandrov (pseudonym of Dr Semashko) in 'Gosudarstvennoe strakhovanie rabochikh', *Sotsial-demokrat*, no. 23 (14/1 September 1911), p. 1 and was repeated by Lenin in his resolution for the Prague Conference (*Vserossiiskaia konferentsiia*, op.cit., pp. 24–6). The Menshevik view was reflected in the comments drafted by the capital's trade unions ('Tezisy po strakhovaniiu rabochikh', *Nash put'*, no. 16 (1911) p. 5). The Socialist Revolutionary attitude was defined by B. Voronov, 'Kto vinovat'?', *Za narod*, no. 41 (July 1911), pp. 3–5 and 'Zakony o strakhovanii rabochikh', *Zavety*, no. 6 (September 1912), pp. 24–34.

26. *Pravda*, no. 107 (2 September 1912), p. 1; no. 203 (29 December 1912), p. 1; *Luch*, no. 80 (20 December 1912), p. 1.

27. *Vserossiiskaia konferentsiia*, op.cit., pp. 24–6; Lenin, *CW*, op.cit., Vol. 18, pp. 461–3; f.102, DPOO., 1913g., d.341, prod.II, l.266 (report of 20 September 1913).

28. G. Baturskii (pseudonym of B. S. Tseitlin). 'Professional'nye soiuzy i strakhovaia kampaniia', *Metallist*, no. 1/25 (19 April 1913), pp. 4–6; M. K. Korbut, 'Strakhovye zakony 1912 goda i ikh provedenie v Peterburge', *Krasnaia letopis'*, no. 1 (1928), pp. 136–71.

29. Voronov, as note 25; *Trudovoi golos*, no. 1 (17 February 1913), p. 4; *Voprosy strakhovaniia*, no. 1 (26 October 1913), p. 3.

30. In addition to the sources cited in note 25, the Bolshevik list was set out by B. G. Danskii (pseudonym of K. A. Komarowski) in *Strakhovaia kampaniia* (St Petersburg, 1913), pp. 76–8. The August Conference of the Mensheviks formulated their identical version. (*Izveshchenie o konferentsii organizatsii RSDRP* (Paris, 1912; repr, New York, 1982), p. 37).

31. f.102, DPOO., 1913g., d.307, l.114.

32. *Pravda*, no. 116 (13 September 1912), p. 1; I. S. Astrov, 'Strakhovanie rabochikh i ocherednyia zadachi', *Nasha zaria*, nos. 7–8 (1912), p. 52. The August Conference endorsed the concept. (*Izveshchenie*, op.cit., p. 39); Iu. Chatskii, 'Strakhovyi s"ezd rabochikh', *Nevskii golos*, no. 5 (28 June 1912), p. 2.

33. B. G. Danskii, 'Strakhovaia kampaniia', *Prosveshchenie*, no. 4 (April 1913), p. 81; *Luch*, no. 79 (19 December 1912), p. 1.

34. *Nevskaia zvezda*, no. 26 (16 September 1912); *Pravda*, no. 116 (13 September 1912), p. 1; no. 177 (25 November 1912), p. 2; no. 184 (4 December 1912), p. 2; *Luch*, no. 64 (1 December 1912), p. 1. *Nevskii golos*, no. 5 (28 June 1912), p. 2.

35. For the Bolsheviks, see B. G. Danskii, 'Strakhovaia kampaniia', *Prosveshchenie*, no. 6 (June 1913), p. 97, and *Voprosy strakhovaniia*, no. 2 (2 November 1913), p. 2; for the Mensheviks, V. E. (Ezhov), 'Ustav bolnichnoi kassy', *Luch*, no. 42 (4 November 1912), p. 1; no. 49 (13 November 1912), p. 1; no. 80 (20 December 1912), p. 1.

36. The letter of V. Ezhov in *Novaia rabochaia gazeta*, no. 57 (15 October 1913), p. 3; f.102, DPOO., 1913g., d.307, ll.301–9.

37. E. E. Kruze in *Istoriia rabochikh Leningrada. tom pervyi. 1703–fevral' 1917* (Leningrad, 1972), p. 441. It is a curious fact that Soviet literature has almost completely neglected the history of the social insurance institutions and the party's activities within them in 1912–17.

38. *Luch*, no. 17/103 (22 January 1913), p. 2; Ch. Gurskii (pseudonym of S. S. Danilov), 'Strakhovaia kampaniia v Peterburge', *Prosveshchenie*, no. 1 (January 1913), p. 76. The eight factories comprised six engineering (Erikson, Lessner, Nobel', Phoenix,

St Petersburg Metals and Semenov), one chemical (Neva Stearine) and one rubber (Russian-American Rubber).

39. f.102, DPOO., 1913g., d.5, ch.57, l.308.

40. Ibid., d.307, ll.301–9; M. A. Tsiavlovskii (ed.), *Bol'sheviki; dokumenty po istorii bol'shevizma s 1903 po 1916 god byvsh. Moskovskago okhrannago otdeleniia* (Moscow, 1918), p. 135.

41. *Severnaia pravda*, no. 17 (22 August 1913), p. 3; B. G. Danskii, 'Strakhovaia kampaniia i metallisty', *Metallist*, no. 8/32 (18 September 1913), p. 9.

42. Lenin, *CW*, op.cit., Vol. 19, pp. 426–7.

43. Danskii, *Strakhovaia kampaniia*, op.cit., p. 75; *Pravda*, no. 68/272 (22 March 1913), p. 3; I. Gladnev (pseudonym of S. M. Zaks), 'Eshche o ocherednikh zadachikh', *Severnaia pravda*, no. 24 (30 August 1913), p. 2; *Pravda truda*, no. 17 (29 September 1913), p. 2; *Voprosy strakhovaniia*, no. 1 (26 October 1913), p. 13; no. 2 (2 November 1913), p. 1.

44. Dr Swain has argued that the differences concerning the general municipal *kassa* should be regarded as a genuine ideological dispute, but the entire tenor of the evidence suggests otherwise (see Swain, *Russian Social Democracy*, op.cit., pp. 167–70).

45. V. Ezhov, 'Bol'nichnye kassy', *Metallist*, no. 24 (14 December 1912), p. 8; *Luch*, no. 33/119 (9 February 1913), p. 3. As both Bolsheviks and Mensheviks frequently referred vaguely to 'general *kassy*', the distinctions between the two slogans can scarcely have been obvious to party militants themselves, let alone ordinary factory hands.

46. *Pravda truda*, no. 11 (22 September 1913), p. 2; *Za pravdu*, no. 6 (10 October 1913), p. 2; *Voprosy strakhovaniia*, no. 2 (2 November 1913), p. 5.

47. *Novoe pechatnoe delo*, no. 2 (1913), pp. 10–11; *Nashe pechatnoe delo*, no. 2 (November 1913), pp. 8–10.

48. *Nasha zaria*, no. 12 (1912), p. 45.

49. *Severnaia pravda*, no. 17 (22 August 1913), p. 3; I. Gladnev, 'Eshche o ocherednikh zadachikh', ibid., no. 21 (27 August 1913), p. 2 and no. 24 (30 August 1913), p. 2. The appeal was repeated twice in *Pravda truda* late in September and twice in *Za pravdu*, early October 1913.

50. f.102, DPOO., 1913g., d.5, ch.57, l.308; M. K. Korbut, 'Strakhovye zakony 1912 goda i ikh provedenie Peterburge', *Krasnaia letopis'*, no. 2 (1928), p. 167.

51. As note 50; *Pravda truda*, no. 19 (8 October 1913), p. 4; *Za pravdu*, no. 23 (30 October 1913), p. 3; *Voprosy strakhovaniia*, no. 3/13 (18 January 1914), p. 1; Iv. Iv., 'O strakhovom tsentre', *Metallist*, no. 10/34 (25 October 1913), p. 10. The Bolshevik press asserted that the all-city central insurance centre was established, but the Okhrana's reports reveal confusion on this point.

52. K. A. Komarovskii, "Pravda' i rabochaia strakhovaia kampaniia', *Proletarskaia revoliutsiia*, vol. 102/3 (1930), pp. 172, 173; *Voprosy strakhovaniia*, no. 21/31 (24 May 1914), p. 1.

53. *Za pravdu*, no. 3 (4 October 1913), p. 2; *Voprosy strakhovaniia*, no. 1 (26 October 1913), p. 2.

54. *Za pravdu*, no. 3 (4 October 1913), p. 2; no. 5 (6 October 1913), p. 3; no. 9 (13 October 1913), p. 2; no. 25 (1 November 1913), p. 3; *Pravda truda*, no. 20 (9 October 1913), p. 2; *Metallist*, no. 8/32 (18 September 1913), p. 10; no. 11/35 (16 November 1913), p. 14.

55. Kruze, *Istoriia*, op.cit., p. 442.

56. *Pravda truda*, no. 17 (29 September 1913), p. 2; *Proletarskaia pravda*, no. 8 (15 December 1913), p. 2; *Voprosy strakhovaniia*, no. 9 (21 December 1913), p. 2; *Novaia rabochaia gazeta*, no. 104 (11 December 1913), p. 3; no. 106 (13 December 1913), p. 3; no. 110 (18 December 1913), p. 3.

57. *Proletarskaia pravda*, no. 12 (20 December 1913), p. 2. *Voprosy strakhovaniia* dismissed the conference as an 'accidental meeting' (ibid., no. 1/11 (4 January 1914), p. 13). It is unfortunate that there exists no evidence as to the composition of the factories which sent delegates.

58. A. K. Tsvetkov-Prosveshchenskii, *Mezhdu dvumia revoliutsiiami (1907–1916gg.)* (Moscow, 1957), p. 90; f.102, DPOO., 1913g., d.341, prod. III, l.104; 1914g., d.341, l.10; *Proletarskaia pravda*, no. 15 (24 December 1913), p. 3; no. 18 (31 December 1913), p. 3.

59. *Voprosy strakhovaniia*, no. 8/18 (22 February 1914), p. 2; *Put' pravdy*, no. 19 (22 February 1914), pp. 1, 2; no.

26 (2 March 1914), p. 2; *Severnaia rabochaia gazeta*, no. 14 (25 February 1914), p. 3; no. 17 (28 February 1914), p. 3.

60. No exact lists of the factories represented on 2 March survive. As state enterprises were excluded from the scope of the insurance law, private works alone were entitled to send delegates. It is known that from the metal-processing sector Erikson, Koppel', Lessner, Neva Shipyards, Putilov, Rozenkrants, the Russian Society, St Petersburg Nails and Struk, sent electors who greatly outnumbered those from other forms of production. There is no direct proof of the factional allegiance of most of those present, but indirect evidence would suggest that at this time at least the *kassy* boards of Erikson, Lessner, Putilov and St Petersburg Metals contained both Bolsheviks and Mensheviks.

61. *Voprosy strakhovaniia*, no. 19/20 (8 March 1914), p. 5; *Put' pravdy*, no. 27 (4 March 1914), pp. 1, 2; no. 31 (8 March 1914), p. 2; G. Baturskii, 'Vybory v sovet po delam strakhovaniia rabochikh', *Strakhovanie rabochikh*, no. 5 (March 1914); *Nasha rabochaia gazeta*, no. 13 (18 May 1914), p. 4.

62. *Put' pravdy*, no. 30 (7 March 1914), p. 2. One of the two was P. I. Sudakov, a member of the *kassa* board at St Petersburg Metals, who had headed the poll in the Fourth Duma elections in the labour curia in St Petersburg on 17 October 1912.

63. *Put' pravdy*, no. 27 (4 March 1914), p. 2; *Severnaia rabochaia gazeta*, no. 21 (5 March 1914). Several of the Bolsheviks elected to the Insurance Council were experienced revolutionaries, such as G. M. Shkapin (a delegate to the Fifth Party Congress and vice-chairman of the Putilov *kassa* board); S. D. Chudin (a contributor to the Bolshevik insurance journal) and N. M. Shvernik (a former Vperedist).

64. *Severnaia rabochaia gazeta*, no. 40 (27 March 1914), p. 2; no. 43 (30 March 1914), p. 4.

65. No source provides a full list of the factories represented on 30 March but at least Erikson, Franco-Russian, Geisler, Neva Shipyards, Putilov, St Petersburg Engineering, St Petersburg Metals, St Petersburg Nails, St Petersburg Wagons, Siemens-Schukkert and United Cables, sent delegates, i.e. the majority came from the electrical, engineering and machine construction sector.

66. *Put' pravdy*, no. 51 (1 April 1914), p. 2; *Strakhovanie rabochikh*, no. 7 (April 1914), p. 22; *Severnaia rabochaia gazeta*, no. 44 (1 April 1914), p. 3; no. 45 (2 April 1914), p. 1. Four of the six members and alternates elected claimed to be Bolsheviks, and all six came from metal-processing establishments. None apparently had a revolutionary past and all were unknown names.

67. *Voprosy strakhovaniia*, no. 16/26 (19 April 1914), p. 3; *Put' pravdy*, no. 65 (19 April 1914), p. 2; *Severnaia rabochaia gazeta*, no. 54 (14 April 1914), p. 3. Those six elected comprised the three Bolsheviks whose names had been published beforehand in *Put' pravdy*, as well as three non-factional Social Democrats chosen at the meeting, one of whom was Rubtsov. Five of the six came from the engineering sector, and two were members of the board of the union of metalworkers, Rubstov and the Bolshevik N. Iv. Iakovlev.

68. V. Sh., 'Vybory v strakhovyia uchrezhdeniia v Peterburge i zadachi edinstva', *Bor'ba*, no. 6 (1914), p. 20.

69. Bonnell, *Roots of Rebellion*, op. cit., p. 355.

70. Bulkin, 'Departament', op. cit., p. 159; *Zhizn' pekarei*, no. 2/5 (10 May 1914); *Trudovaia pravda*, no. 8 (6 June 1914), p. 3; *Nashe pechatnoe delo*, no. 6 (1 February 1914), p. 6.

71. *Metallist*, no. 2/39 (4 February 1914), p. 12. In 1908 the union's strength had lain, in descending order, in the districts of Neva, Vasil'evskii Island, Vyborg, Petersburg Side, Town, Narva, Moscow. (*Materialy ob ekonomicheskom polozhenii i professional'noi organizatsii Peterburgskikh rabochikh po metallu*, St Petersburg, 1909, p. 74).

72. *Za pravdu*, no. 42 (23 November 1913), p. 4; *Metallist*, no. 13/37 (14 December 1913), p. 10; no. 1/38 (January 1914), p. 15.

73. This pattern of recruitment was similar to that in 1908, when 24 per cent of workers involved in electrical-mechanical factories and 26 per cent in machine construction were union members, but only 11 per cent in

shipbuilding, 7 per cent in metal rolling and 3 per cent in nails (*Materialy*, op.cit., p. 75).

74. *Put' pravdy*, no. 50 (30 March 1914), p. 3; *Vestnik portnykh*, no. 5 (13 October 1913), p. 8; *Pravda*, no. 171 (17 November 1912), p. 4; *Metallist*, no. 2/39 (4 February 1914), p. 12; *Rabotnitsa*, no. 6 (1914), p. 10; *Nasha rabochaia gazeta*, no. 13 (1914), p. 9; *Vestnik prikazchika*, no. 13 (1914), p. 9.

75. *Pravda*, no. 158 (2 November 1912), p. 3; *Metallist*, no. 3/27 (15 June 1913), p. 13; *Proletarskaia pravda*, no. 6 (13 December 1913), p. 1. This problem has received illuminating treatment by Rose L. Glickman in *Russian Factory Women. Workplace and Society, 1880–1914* (Berkeley, 1984), pp. 198–207, 216–18.

76. *Pravda truda*, no. 1 (11 September 1913), p. 3; *Novoe pechatnoe delo*, no. 1 (1912), p. 3; *Metallist*, no. 2/39 (4 February 1914), p. 12.

77. *Golos bulochnika i konditera*, no. 1/12 (1912), p. 11; *Pravda truda*, no. 1 (11 September 1912), p. 3; *Luch*, no. 28/114 (3 February 1913), p. 3; *Novaia rabochaia gazeta*, no. 59 (17 October 1913), p. 4; *Bor'ba*, no. 2 (18 March 1914), p. 13.

78. *Pravda*, no. 169 (15 November 1912), p. 4; *Severnaia pravda*, no. 30 (6 September 1913), p. 3; *Put'pravdy*, no. 1 (22 January 1914), p. 4; *Nasha rabochaia gazeta*, no. 16 (22 May 1914), p. 3; *Severnaia rabochaia gazeta*, no. 66 (29 April 1914), p. 4.

79. *Metallist*, no. 13/37 (14 December 1913), p. 10; no. 2/39 (4 February 1914), p. 12.

80. *Zhizn' pekarei*, no. 1/4 (10 March 1914), p. 13; *Luch*, no. 12 (16 November 1912), p. 4; *Put'pravdy*, no. 3 (24 January 1914), p. 3; no. 51 (1 April 1914), p. 4.

81. *Nevskaia zvezda*, no. 7 (24 May 1912), p. 3; *Severnaia pravda*, no. 31 (7 September 1913), p. 3; *Zhizn' pekarei*, no. 1/4 (10 March 1914), p. 14; *Metallist*, no. 2/39 (4 February 1914), p. 12; *Nashe pechatnoe delo*, no. 12 (May 1914), p. 6.

82. *Zhivoe delo*, no. 6 (24 February 1912), p. 3; *Severnaia pravda*, no. 31 (7 September 1913), p. 3; *Zhizn' pekarei*, no. 1/4 (10 March 1914), p. 14.

83. *Luch*, no. 3 (19 September 1912), p. 4; *Biulleten' kontorshchika*, no. 1 (14 June 1913), p. 9; *Vestnik prikazchika*, no. 10 (November 1913), p. 13; *Vestnik portnykh*, no. 5 (3 October 1913), p. 9; *Pravda truda*, no. 1 (11 September 1913), p. 3.

84. *Novaia rabochaia gazeta*, no. 60 (18 October 1913), p. 4; *Nashe pechatnoe delo*, no. 6 (1 February 1914), p. 6.

85. *Luch*, no. 72/158 (27 March 1913), p. 3; *Pravda*, no. 57/261 (9 March 1913), p. 3; *Put' pravdy*, no. 3 (24 January 1914), p. 3; *Novoe pechatnoe delo*, no. 2 (1913), p. 5.

86. *Pravda truda*, no. 1 (11 September 1913), p. 3; *Novaia rabochaia gazeta*, no. 103 (10 December 1913), p. 3; *Put' pravdy*, no. 53 (3 April 1914), p. 3.

87. *Pravda truda*, no. 8 (19 September 1913), p. 3; *Put' pravdy*, no. 1 (22 January 1914), p. 3.

88. *Vestnik portnykh*, no. 5 (13 October 1913), p. 8; nos. 6–7 (2 January 1914), p. 17; no. 8 (31 March 1914), p. 11.

89. *Pravda*, no. 11 (5 May 1912), p. 4.

90. f.102, DP., 4 d-vo., 1913g., d.61, ch.2, t.2, l.29; *Metallist*, no. 7/31 (24 August 1913), p. 11; no. 8/32 (18 September 1913), p. 11; no. 11/35 (16 November 1913), pp. 13, 14; no. 12/36 (5 December 1913), p. 8; no. 2/39 (4 February 1914), p. 11.

91. *Metallist*, no. 11/35 (16 November 1913), p. 14; Swain, *Russian Social Democracy*, op.cit., p. 180.

92. TsGIA, f.23, op.16, d.95, ll.17–19.

93. The list includes New Aivaz, Erikson, New Lessner, Putilov, St Petersburg Metals and St Petersburg Wagons.

94. Kruze, *Istoriia*, op.cit., note 37, p. 442. The seven were Erikson, Geisler, New Lessner, Neva Shipyards, Putilov, St Petersburg Engineering, St Petersburg Metals and St Petersburg Wagons. The two were New Aivaz and Erikson.

95. The evidence for this point rests on a correlation between the profile of Bolshevik PK and district committee members in 1912–14 (as ascertained from the Okhrana archives) and the names of those elected to *kassy* boards (published in the socialist and insurance press).

96. B. G. Danskii, 'Strakhovaia kampaniia v Peterburge', *Prosveshchenie*, no. 1 (January 1914), p. 77; *Voprosy strakhovaniia*, no. 21/31 (24 May

1914), p. 1.

97. *Pravda*, no. 145 (17 October 1912), p. 2; Gurskii, 'Strakhovaia kampaniia' op.cit., pp. 75, 76; Danskii, 'Strakhovaia kampaniia', op. cit., ibid., no. 6 (June 1913), p. 95; S. Shvarts, 'Rabochaia strakhovaia kampaniia v Peterburge', *Nasha zaria*, nos. 7–8 (1913), p. 80; f.102, DP., 4d-vo., 1913g., d.61, ch.2, t.2, l.304.

98. Shvarts 'Rabochaia strakhovaia kampaniia', op.cit., pp. 80–2.

99. *Novaia rabochaia gazeta*, no. 27 (8 September 1913), p. 3; no. 38 (21 September 1913), p. 3; no. 59 (17 October 1913), p. 4; no. 18/136 (23 January 1914), p. 3; *Voprosy strakhovaniia*, no. 5 (23 November 1913), p. 5.

100. *Novaia rabochaia gazeta*, no. 28 (10 September 1913), p. 3; no. 72 (1 November 1913), p. 3; *Za pravdu*, no. 18 (24 October 1913), p. 3.

101. The engineering *kassy* were at New Aivaz, Erikson, Phoenix, St Petersburg Metals and Westinghouse.

102. B. G. Danskii, 'Strakhovaia kampaniia v Petersburge', *Prosveshchenie*, no. 1 (January 1914), p. 77.

103. *Luch*, no. 97/183 (28 April 1913), p. 3; no. 108/194 (12 May 1913), p. 2; *Voprosy strakhovaniia*, no. 1/11 (4 January 1914), pp. 10, 11; no. 10/20 (8 March 1914), p. 15.

104. S. Shvarts, 'Rabochaia strakhovaia kampaniia v Peterburge'', *Nasha zaria*, nos. 4–5 (1913), pp. 28–31; *Luch*, no. 149/235 (2 July 1913), p. 2.

105. N. Asnik (pseudonym of Skrypnik), 'Rabochii strakhovye predstavitely i zadachi edinstva', *Voprosy strakhovaniia*, no. 16/26 (19 April 1914), p. 3; no. 17/27 (26 April 1914), p. 2; no. 19/29 (29 May 1914), p. 6; no. 22/32 (31 May 1914), p. 8.

106. *Trudovaia pravda*, no. 15 (14 June 1914), p. 2; *Nasha rabochaia gazeta*, no. 33 (12 June 1914), p. 3.

107. *Pravda*, no. 175 (23 November 1912), p. 4; *Luch*, no. 54 (18 November 1912), p. 3; no. 80/166 (6 April 1913), p. 4; no. 136/222 (15 June 1913), p. 4.

108. It is a curious fact that Bolshevik littérateurs before 1914 and Soviet historians since the revolution have devoted little attention to this complex problem. Both ascribe the faction's advance (without elaboration) to workers' growing revolutionary consciousness and the correctness of its political line (for an example of such a pre-revolutionary explanation, see G. Zinoviev in *Za pravdu*, no. 34 (13 November 1913), p. 1).

109. G. Rakitin (pseudonym of V. O. Tsederbaum), 'Rabochaia massa i rabochaia intelligentsiia', *Nasha zaria*, no. 9 (1913), pp. 58–9; L. M. (Martov), 'Otvet Bulkinu', ibid., no. 3 (1914), pp. 55–70; F. Bulkin, 'Raskol fraktsii i zadachi rabochikh', ibid., no. 6 (1914), pp. 41–51.

110. Leopold Haimson, 'The problem of social stability in urban Russia, 1905–1917 (part one)', *Slavic Review*, vol. 23, no. 4 (December 1964), pp. 619–42.

111. V. Sher, 'Nashe professional'noe dvizhenie za dva poslednikh goda', *Bor'ba*, no. 4 (28 April 1914), pp. 21–3; V. Torskii, 'Nasha molodezh'', ibid., no. 6 (1914), pp. 41–3.

112. The Mensheviks' second-rank leaders were of a similar age profile. The dates of birth of 18 of 42 members of the Central Initiative Group, 1911–14, could be traced. The median age in 1913 was 32 years: three fell in the age cohort, 21–5 years; six, 26–30 years; five, 31–5 years; four were over 35; none were under 21 years of age.

113. F. Bulkin, 'Rabochaia samodeiatel'nost' i rabochaia demagogiia', *Nasha zaria*, no. 3 (1914), pp. 55–64.

114. L. M. (Martov), 'Otvet Bulkinu', op.cit., pp. 55–70; Bonnell, *Roots of Rebellion*, op.cit., p. 432.

115. Menshevik legal activists, too, were all of working-class birth in the pre-war years. The Central Initiative Group, however, tended to include a higher percentage of intellectuals in its membership – in December 1912, six members were from the intelligentsia and eight were operatives.

116. Haimson, 'Problem of social stability', op.cit., pp. 637–8.

117. Heather Hogan, 'Labour and management in conflict: the St Petersburg metalworking industry, 1900–1914' (Michigan, Ph.D., 1981), pp. 504–6, 509.

118. Torskii, 'Nasha molodezh'', op.cit., p. 43.

Chapter 8

1. Dick Geary, *European Labour Protest, 1848–1939* (London, 1981), pp. 104–

5; S. H. F. Hickey, *Workers in Imperial Germany. The Mines of the Ruhr* (Oxford, 1985), pp. 184–5; E. H. Hunt, *British Labour History 1815–1914* (London, 1981), pp. 318–29; Charles Tilly and Edward Shorter, *Strikes in France, 1830–1968* (Cambridge, 1974), pp. 118–22.

2. *Svod otchetov fabrichnykh inspektorov za 1909 god* (St Petersburg, 1910), pp. 162, 174; ibid., *za 1910 god* (St Petersburg, 1911), pp. LXX–XXI, 294; ibid., *za 1911 god* (St Petersburg, 1912), pp. LXXXIV, LXXXVI, 289; ibid., *za 1912 god* (St Petersburg, 1913), pp. LXXVI–VIII, 291; ibid., *za 1913 god* (St Petersburg, 1914), pp. LXXII–LXXX; ibid., *za 1914 god* (St Petersburg, 1915), pp. XI–XII, LXI–VII; TsGIA, f.23, op.17, d.671, ll.19, 27, 33; ibid., op.16, d.118, ll.1, 11, 26, 54.

3. V. I. Lenin, *Collected Works* (Moscow, 1963–9), Vol. 18, pp. 456–7 (hereafter C. W.); A. Chuzhennikov, 'Russkoe rabochee dvizhenie', *Ezhegodnik gazetoi "Rech" na 1913 god* (St Petersburg 1913), p. 151; TsGIA, f.150, op.1, d.58, l.36.

4. G. Zinoviev, 'Itogi i perspektivy', *Prosveshchenie*, no. 1 (January 1914), pp. 79–85; Chuzhennikov, 'Russkoe rabochee dvizhenie', op.cit., p. 163; TsGIA, f.32, op.1, d.59, l.68; M. L. Lur'e (ed.), 'Tsarizm v bor'be s rabochim dvizheniem v gody pod"ema', *Krasnyi arkhiv*, vol. 1, no. 74 (1936), p. 53.

5. Lenin, *CW*, op.cit., Vol. 16, pp. 395–406 ('Strike statistics in Russia', *Mysl'*, nos. 1 and 2 (December 1910 and January 1911)); *Severnaia pravda*, no. 23 (29 August 1913), p. 1.

6. A. Mikhailov, 'K kharakteristike sovremennago rabochago dvizheniia v Rossii', *Nasha zaria*, nos. 11–12 (1912), pp. 80–9.

7. *Novaia rabochaia gazeta*, no. 1/119 (1 January 1914), p. 2; f.150, op.2, d.72, l.55; f.23, op.17, d.648, l.15.

8. Mikhailov, 'K kharakteristike', op.cit., p. 84; *Luch*, no. 1/87 (1 January 1913), p. 1; L. M. (Lev Martov), 'Bor'ba obshchestvennykh sil v 1913 godu', *Nasha zaria*, no. 1 (1914), pp. 95–100; L. Martov, 'Na pereputi', *Sovremennik*, no. 5 (1914), pp. 63–73; F. Dan, 'Krizis', *Sovremennik*, no. 9 (1914), pp. 59–64.

9. G. A. Arutiunov, *Rabochee dvizhenie v Rossii v period novogo revoliutsionnogo pod"ema 1910–1914gg.* (Moscow, 1975), p. 379.

10. *Istoriia rabochego klassa SSSR. Rabochii klass Rossii. 1907–fevral' 1917 g.* (Moscow, 1982), pp. 201, 227.

11. Arutiunov, *Rabochee dvizhenie*, op.cit., pp. 383–4; *Istoriia*, op.cit., pp. 198, 227.

12. In view of the deficiencies of the factory inspectorate's statistics it is not impossible that there is validity in M. S. Balabanov's claim that in 1910 the actual total of strikers in the Empire was higher than in the previous year (M. S. Balabanov, *Ot 1905 k 1917 godu; massovoe rabochee dvizhenie*, Moscow, 1927, p. 132).

13. Ibid., p. 142.

14. *Svod otchetov fabrichnykh inspektorov za 1911 god* (St Petersburg 1912), p. 318; ibid., *za 1912 god*, p. 324.

15. G. Tsyperovich, 'Ekonomicheskaia zhizn' Rossii v 1911 g.', *Sovremennik*, no. 1 (1912), pp. 205–7.

16. These figures are underestimates as the inspectorate did not include the 13,000 dockers who came out in July 1911, or striking tailors.

17. A. Mikhailov, 'Letnee stachechnoe dvizhenie i ocherednyia zadachi rabochikh organizatsii', *Nasha zaria*, nos. 9–10 (1911), p. 41; N. A. Ivanova, *Struktura rabochego klassa Rossii 1910–1914* (Moscow, 1987), p. 251.

18. *Nash put'*, no. 13 (February 1911), p. 9; no. 14 (4 March 1911), p. 1; *Delo zhizni*, no. 4 (1911), p. 76; *Zvezda*, no. 26 (23 October 1911), p. 4.

19. *Nash put'*, no. 13 (February 1911), p. 9; *Mysl'*, no. 3 (February 1911), p. 90; *Delo zhizni*, no. 3 (1911), p. 88; *Zvezda*, no. 34 (17 December 1911), p. 3.

20. *Svod otchetov fabrichnykh inspektorov za 1910 god* (St Petersburg, 1911), p. 294; ibid., *za 1911 god*, p. 289; Mikhailov, 'Letnee stachechnoe dvizhenie', p. 42.

21. There is a good account of the Lena tragedy in Balabanov, *Ot 1905*, op.cit., pp. 155–71.

22. *Svod otchetov fabrichnykh inspektorov za 1913 god*, p. LXXIII; ibid., *za 1914 god*, p. LXII. The factory inspectorate's estimates of the proportion of the factory labour force of St Petersburg province participating in prewar strikes differs from the calcula-

tions in Table 8.vii. The inspectors recorded that 155 per cent of factory workers downed tools in 1912, 162 per cent in 1913 and 335 per cent in 1914.

23. In view of the deficiencies of the official estimates of the strike movement made by the factory inspectorate, which omitted from its purview state-owned enterprises, the distributive trades and the transport sector, as well as seriously underestimating the number and significance of small enterprises and workshops (see Chapter 1, note 12), the author has compiled his own statistical data on the industrial unrest in St Petersburg between 1912 and 1914. These rest on the unpublished reports of the factory inspectorate in the archives of the Ministry of Trade and Industry, the memoranda of the Okhrana's agents and officers and in particular the notices of disputes published in every issue of *Pravda*, *Luch* and trade-union journals for this period. Information was retrieved on almost 4,000 political and economic strikes. As a comparison of Tables 8.vi. and 8.vii. with the official records (in Table 8.i.) reveals, the reworking of the material produces significantly higher estimates than those of the factory inspectorate. It also differs from the assessment made by the Soviet historian E. E. Kruze, who has inflated even further the dimensions of the strike movement (E. E. Kruze, *Peterburgskie rabochie v 1912–1914 godakh*, Leningrad, 1961, Table 13, p. 316). The statistical tables in this chapter should be regarded as approximate. In the tables, furthermore, in Chapter 8 the data refer to the period 1 January 1912 to 3 July 1914. The latter date has been chosen as the cut-off point for two reasons. Firstly the general strike in the capital between 4 and 19 July 1914 requires a separate detailed analysis (see Chapter 10). Secondly, after the outbreak of war at the close of the month industrial conflict almost completely faded away (see Chapter 14).

24. Henry Reichman, *Railwaymen and Revolution. Russia, 1905* (Berkeley, 1987). Two of the four major railway depots in the capital (the North-Western and the Warsaw) experienced no strikes at all and the Baltic and Nikolaev railways a mere five stoppages.

25. Leopold Haimson and Eric Brian, 'Changements démographiques et grèves ouvrières à Saint-Pétersbourg, 1905–1914', *Annales ESC*, no. 4 (July–August 1985), p. 782; *Zvod otchetov fabrichnykh inspektorov za 1909 god* (St Petersburg, 1910), p. 162; ibid., *za 1910 god*, p. 294; ibid., *za 1911 god*, p. 289.

26. Haimson and Brian, 'Changements', op.cit., p. 783; Kruze, *Peterburgskie rabochie*, op.cit., p. 246; Balabanov, *Ot 1905*, op.cit., p. 285; Ivanova, *Struktura*, op.cit., p. 253.

27. A similar tendency was observable at the national level. According to the factory inspectorate the proportion of strikers deriving from branches of manufacturing other than metal-working and textiles fell from 21 per cent of the total in 1912 to 20 per cent in 1913, but rose in the following year to 23 per cent.

28. Arutiunov, *Rabochee dvizhenie*, op.cit., p. 196.

29. The nine establishments were Erikson, Kreiton Shipyards, Franco-Russian, A. Koppel', Neva Shipyards, San Galli, Siemens and Hal'ske, St Petersburg Iron Rolling, Tiudor and United Cables. Three similar stoppages occurred after May Day 1913 and two a year later.

30. *Pravda*, no. 166 (11 November 1912), p. 3; *Pravda truda*, no. 19 (8 October 1913), p. 4; *Proletarskaia pravda*, no. 21 (4 January 1914), p. 3; *Severnaia rabochaia gazeta*, no. 55 (16 April 1914), p. 3.

31. Haimson and Brian, 'Changements', op.cit., p. 785. It is probable that these figures exaggerate somewhat the proportion of political strikers in St Petersburg province (in particular for 1913) as they are based on the higher estimates contained in Table 8.xi and have been calculated as a percentage of the aggregate of political strikers in the Empire as recorded by the factory inspectorate, which seriously underestimated the number involved.

32. It is instructive to note that during the first twenty years of the Third French Republic, in the absence of strongly developed trade unions or socialist parties, strikes became the major form of expression of the

labour movement (Michelle Perrot, *Workers on Strike. France, 1871–1890*, Leamington Spa, 1987, p. 25).

33. *Svod otchetov fabrichnykh inspektorov za 1912 god*, pp. LXVI–LXVII; ibid., *za 1913 god*, pp. LXII–LXXVII; ibid., *za 1914 god*, pp. LXXII–LXXIII.

34. These estimates of the aggregate of strikers for Lena and May Day 1912 in St Petersburg err on the side of caution, as they are based on the incomplete data of the Okhrana and of *Pravda*, whose initial coverage of disputes was not as thorough as in later issues. Throughout the period the total number of strikers in each political stoppage claimed by the police and the socialist press are guesstimates, which almost always differ from the aggregate arrived at by adding up the reported numbers of strikes and strikers per individual plant or workshop.

35. U. A. Shuster. *Peterburgskie rabochie v 1905–1907gg.* (Leningrad, 1976), p. 267.

36. Lenin, *CW*, op.cit., Vol. 19, pp. 312–22 ('Metalworkers' strikes in 1912', *Metallist*, nos. 7, 8 and 10 (24 August, 18 September and 25 October 1913)).

37. *Svod otchetov fabrichnykh inspektorov za 1912 god*, p. LXXXV; ibid., *za 1913 god*, p. LXIIII.

38. Ibid.

39. Nationally the proportion of political strikers deriving from industries other than engineering and textiles witnessed an increase from 16 per cent to 22 per cent in 1914 (see note 37).

40. Such views for example, have been advanced by Arutiunov (*Rabochee dvizhe nie*, op.cit., pp. 152–3), Haimson and Brian ('Changements', op.cit., p. 783) and David Mandel, *The Petrograd Workers and the Fall of the Old Regime. From the February Revolution to the July Days, 1917* (London, 1983), p. 44.

41. The four were Franco-Russian (12 political strikes), Neva Shipyards (18), Putilov (19) and St Petersburg Metals (19). Among the seven giant plants least affected by political unrest were the Baltic Shipyards (6 political strikes), the Izhora Arms Works (1) and St Petersburg Pipes (3).

42. In this category the worst plagued by political stoppages included New Aivaz (15 political strikes), Baranovskii (19), Erikson (18), Geisler (15), Langenzippen (21), New Lessner (20), Nobel' (18), Rozenkrantz (15), the Russian Society (19 and 15 at its two factories respectively), St Petersburg Engineering (22), St Petersburg Wagons (18), San Galli (17) and Zigel' (16).

43. This group embraced Diuflon (15 political stoppages), Ekval (15), Kravtsovich (16), Odner (15), Phoenix (17), the Russian Society of Wireless Telegraphy (15), the First Society of Aeronautics (16), Semenov (17) and Westinghouse (16).

44. Laura Engelstein, *Moscow 1905: Working-Class Organization and Political Conflict* (Stanford, 1982), pp. 87, 110–11, 168.

45. Mandel, *Petrograd Workers*, op.cit., pp. 23–7.

46. Ibid., p. 29.

47. This pattern was repeated in 1917 when, on an all-Russian scale, only 20 per cent of workers in typography plants participated in strikes in contrast to 75 per cent of the metals labour force (Diane Koenker and W. G. Rosenberg, 'Skilled workers and the strike movement in revolutionary Russia', *Journal of Social History*, vol. 19, no. 4 (1986), pp. 618, 623).

48. Mandel, *Petrograd Workers*, op.cit., p. 35.

49. Ibid., pp. 34, 36; S. A. Smith, *Red Petrograd. Revolution in the Factories 1917–1918* (Cambridge, 1983), p. 33.

50. Lenard R. Berlanstein, *The Working People of Paris, 1871–1914* (Baltimore, 1984), pp. 189–96; Engelstein, *Moscow 1905*, op.cit., Chapters 5–8.

51. Hartmut Kaelble, *Industrialisation and Social Inequality in 19th Century Europe* (Leamington Spa, 1986), pp. 172–84; Jürgen Kocka, 'White-collar employees and industrial society in Imperial Germany', in George Iggers (ed.), *The Social History of Politics. Critical Perspectives in West German Historical Writing since 1945* (Leamington Spa, 1985), pp. 113–32.

52. Reichman, *Railwaymen*, op.cit., pp. 303–5.

53. Kruze, *Peterburgskie rabochie*, op.cit., p. 324. Soviet scholars rest their assertion upon the interpretation of demands in political strikes advanced

54. E. Maevskii, 'Svoboda koalitsii', *Novaia rabochaia gazeta*, no. 8 (17 August 1913), p. 1.

by contemporary Bolshevik commentators (cf. G. Zinoviev, 'Itogi i perspektivy', *Prosveshchenie*, no. 2 (February 1914), p. 77).

55. Great caution has to be exercised in the utilisation of factory resolutions as a historical source. Resolutions were often drafted in advance by party activists; no reliable data are available on the proportion of the labour force of particular plants present at meetings or on the frequency of such gatherings; unanimity of voting was a powerful· tradition at workers' assemblies.

56. It is possible that *Pravda* was reluctant to publish such resolutions on the grounds of censorship. Yet the newspaper never hesitated in its articles to substitute the cryptic phrase 'uncurtailed slogans' for the party's minimum programme or, on occasions, to include resolutions which openly proclaimed the Mensheviks' political demands.

57. Perrot, *Workers on Strike*, op.cit., pp. 153–4.

58. Geary, *European Labour Protest*, op.cit., p. 37; Perrot, *Workers on Strike*, op.cit., p. 107.

59. Kruze, *Peterburgskie rabochie*, op.cit., p. 326. The author cites no reference for her statistics.

60. *Otchet otdela promyshlennosti za 1913 god* (St Petersburg, 1914), p. 193; ibid., *za 1914 god* (St Petersburg, 1915), p. 151.

61. *Pravda truda*, no. 10 (21 September 1913), p. 3; no. 13 (25 September 1913), p. 3; TsGAOR, f.102, DP, 4-dvo., 1913g., d.61, ch.2, t.3, l.20. In the sewage works 100 struck, a handful at the electricity station and 400 walked out at the gasworks.

62. *Trudovaia pravda*, no. 25 (26 June 1914), p. 3; no. 28 (29 June 1914), p. 5.

63. *Otchet otdela promyshlennosti za 1912 god* (St Petersburg, 1913), p. 165; ibid., *za 1913 God* (St Petersburg, 1914), p. 192; ibid., *za 1914 god* (St Petersburg, 1915), p. 150.

64. As note 63.

65. Ibid.

66. Tilly and Shorter, *Strikes in France*, op.cit., p. 10; Perrot, *Workers on Srike*, op.cit., p. 313.

67. *Otchet otdela promyshlennosti za 1912 god* (St Petersburg, 1913), p. 166; ibid., *za 1913 god* (St Petersburg, 1914), p. 192; ibid., *za 1914 god* (St Petersburg, 1915), p. 151.

68. In their analysis of strikes some labour historians, such as Balabanov or Perrot, add the category of 'compromise settlements' to that of workers' successes on the ground that the former represents some measure of gain by the strikers (cf. Perrot, *Workers on Strike*, op.cit., p. 243). But it can equally be argued that it records some degree of success on the part of the employer. Furthermore an examination of the outcome of St Petersburg strikes reveals that in compromise settlements the strikers secured only the most minor or least damaging of their demands.

69. P. Rtishchev, 'Zabastovochnaia volna', *Zavety*, no. 10 (1913), pp. 126–37; Lev Kornev, 'Zabastovochnoe dvizhenie u metallistov', *Metallist*, no. 5/29 (19 July 1913), pp. 6–7.

70. Perrot, *Workers on Strike*, op.cit., p. 244.

71. Whereas in 1913 and 1914 compromises constituted 30 per cent and 20 per cent respectively of the outcome of disputes in the industry nationwide, they formed only 6 per cent and 7 per cent of the outcome of metals' strikes in the city.

72. This categorisation is an amended version of that adopted by the factory inspectorate, which included the category of 'working conditions' within that of 'authority at work'. It should be stressed that a majority of strikers put forth a multiplicity of demands which covered the entire spectrum of categories. Thus the categories in Tables 8.xxiv and 8.xxv refer to strikes where that particular demand was put forward by strikers.

73. *Otchet otdela promyshlennosti za 1912 god* (St Petersburg, 1913), p. 164; ibid., *za 1913 god* (St Petersburg, 1914), p. 191; ibid. *za 1914 god* (St Petersburg, 1915), p. 149.

74. In animal products, construction and miscellaneous, too, wages were the dominant concern in 1912.

75. On the other hand, the changes in systems of payment introduced by cost-conscious employers after 1906 (see Chapter 1) – hourly rates of pay, the 'American method' of calculating

pay, wage cuts and centralised rates bureaux – had been deeply resented and distrusted by working people. Thus the 'offensive' wage strikes from the spring of 1912 onwards were in effect workers' delayed 'defensive' response to previous reductions in pay and the consequent intensification in the pace of work.

76. Apart from the level of earnings, other aspects of wage structure were sometimes involved. In metalworking, for example, in 28 disputes operatives requested the introduction of proper pay books or the hanging up of rates tables on workshop walls. Even this modest plea was rejected in all instances except one. In 16 strikes, workers demanded that they should be paid in working time. On the other hand, demands for paid holidays were rare.

77. *Novoe pechatnoe delo*, no. 7 (18 July 1913), p. 2; f.102, DP., 4d-vo., 1913g., d.61, ch.2, t.2, ll.23–4, 40–6.

78. *Pravda*, no. 87 (10 August 1912), p. 3; *Golos bulochnika i konditera*, no. 2/13 (1912) pp. 10–12.

79. f.102, D.P., 4d.-vo., 1913g., d.61, ch.2, t.1, ll.44–5, 79; *Luch*, no. 55/141 (7 March 1913), p. 1; *Pravda*, no. 50/254 (1 March 1913), p. 3.

80. In 1913 in printing the entire labour force of Soikin, numbering 450 people, struck for a day in December to demand the release of their sickness fund delegate (*Proletarskaia pravda*, no. 12 (20 December 1913), p. 3.)

81. *Trudovoi golos*, no. 10 (28 April 1913), p. 4; f.102, DP., 4d-vo., 1913g., d.61, ch.2, t.1, l.104, l.183.

82. *Pravda*, no. 13 (8 May 1912), p. 4; no. 15 (10 May 1912), p. 3; no. 87 (10 August 1912), p. 3.

83. *Rabochaia pravda*, no. 16 (31 July 1913), p. 3.

84. Victoria E. Bonnell, *Roots of Rebellion. Workers' Politics and Organizations in St Petersburg and Moscow, 1900–1914* (Berkeley, 1983), pp. 288–9.

85. Heather Hogan, 'Labour and management in conflict: the St Petersburg metalworking industry, 1900–1914' (Michigan, Ph.D., 1981), pp. 515–16.

86. L. Kleinbort, 'Ocherki rabochei demokratii; stat'ia pervaia', *Sovremennyi mir*, no. 4 (April 1913), pp. 27–

31; N. Garvi, 'Letopis' rabochago dvizheniia', *Nasha zaria*, nos. 4–5 (1913), p. 23; A. Alekseev, 'Rabochee dvizhenie', *Prosveshchenie*, no. 6 (June 1913), p. 87.

87. f.102, DP., 4d.-vo., 1913g., d.61, ch.2, t.2, l.28.

88. TsGIA, f.1405, op.530, d.824, l.98.

89. *Pravda*, no. 71 (21 July 1912), p. 1; *Rabochaia pravda*, no. 17 (1 August 1913), p. 3.

90. G. Rakitin, 'Rabochaia massa i rabochaia intelligentsiia', *Nasha zaria*, no. 9 (1913), p. 52; Chuzhennikov, 'Russkoe rabochee dvizhenie', op.cit., p. 151.

91. f.102, DP., 4d-vo., 1913g., d.61, ch.2, t.2, l.29.

92. 'Bor'ba za i-e maia na zavodakh Simens i Galske', *Metallist*, no. 17 (6 July 1912), p. 14.

93. *Trudovoi golos*, no. 7 (31 March 1913), p. 4.

94. Michael P. Hanagan, *The Logic of Solidarity. Artisans and Industrial Workers in Three French Towns, 1871–1914* (Urbana, 1980); Berlanstein, *Working People*, op.cit.

95. Hogan, 'Labour and management', op.cit., pp. 4, 7, 513–16.

96. Kerosinich, 'Stachka u 'L. Nobelia'', *Metallist*, no. 13 (7 April 1912), p.16.

97. *Rabochaia pravda*, no. 2 (14 July 1913), p. 3; no. 4 (17 July 1913), p. 3; *Severnaia pravda*, no. 13 (17 August 1913), p. 1; *Pravda truda*, no. 5 (15 September 1913), p. 3; Hogan, 'Labour and management', op.cit., pp. 484–94.

98. M. D. Rozanov, *Obukhovtsy* (Leningrad, 1965), pp. 256–74; E. K. Minina (ed.), *Partiia bol'shevikov v gody novogo revoliutsionnogo pod''ema, 1910–1914; dokumenty i materialy* (Moscow, 1962), pp. 461–2; *Rabochaia pravda*, no. 16 (31 July 1913), p. 3; *Za pravdu*, no. 35 (14 November 1913), p. 3.

99. Haimson and Brian, 'Changements', op.cit., pp. 786–90.

100. N. Gar-vi, 'Nachalo lokautnoi epidemii', *Nasha zaria*, no. 2 (1913), p. 22.

101. f.102, DP., 4d-vo., d.61, ch.2, t.1, l.107; ch.2, t.2, l.17; d.61, ch.9, l.18; *Pravda*, no. 96/300 (27 April 1913), p. 4; *Luch*, no. 102/188 (5 May 1913), p. 2.

102. *Novoe pechatnoe delo*, no. 7 (18 July 1913), p. 2; f.102, DP., 4d-vo.,

1913g., d.61, ch.2, t.2, 1.40, 1.47.

103. f.102, DP., 4d.-vo., 1913g., d.61, ch.2, t.1, 1.45; *Luch*, no. 62/148 (15 March 1913), p. 4; no. 110/196 (15 May 1913), p. 4.

104. f.102, DP., 4d.-vo., 1913g., d.61, ch.2, t.2, 1.28.

105. Ibid.

106. Mikhailov, 'K kharakteristike', op.cit., p. 89; *Novyi professional'nyi listok*, no. 1 (9 May 1914), p. 2.

107. f.102, DPOO., 1913g., d.341, prod.II, 1.104; 1914g., d.5, ch.57, t.1, 1.14.

108. 'Bor'ba za i-e maia', op.cit., p. 14; no. 18 (August 1913), p. 9; *Pravda*, no. 17 (12 May 1912), p. 3; no. 27 (31 May 1912), p. 3; no. 56 (4 July 1912), p. 3; f.102, DP., 4d-vo., 1912g., ch.2, t.2, 1.103.

109. f.102, DP., 4d-vo., d.61, ch.2, t.2, 1.28; *Novyi professional'nyi listok*, no. 1, (9 May 1914), pp. 2–3.

110. *Pravda*, no. 29 (2 June 1912), p. 10.

111. *Rabochaia pravda*, no. 14 (28 July 1913), p. 3.

112. Haimson and Brian, 'Changements', op.cit., p. 789.

Chapter 9

1. The pre-1905 institutional history of the capital's industrial entrepreneurs has been studied by Victoria A. P. King in her doctoral dissertation, 'The emergence of the St Petersburg industrialist community, 1870 to 1905: the origins and early years of the Petersburg Society of Manufacturers ' (Berkeley, Ph.D., 1982).

2. TsGIA, f.150, op.1, d.53, 1.113; d.60, 1.185; *Nevskaia zvezda*, no. 25 (9 September 1912).

3. *Nevskaia zvezda*, no. 25 (9 September 1912).

4. Statutes of the Society, 1907: f.150, op.1, d.53, 1.29; op.2, d.77, 1.35.

5. The eleven dominant personalities within the POZF were: V. V. Diufur, vice-president of the Society from 1912 (Westinghouse, electrical goods, 300 workers, French); M. I. Tripolitov, vice-president from 1907; A. A. Bachmanov, vice-president of the Engineering Section (Lessner, engineering, 1,500 workers, German); M. P. Pankov (St Petersburg Metals, engineering, 3,000 workers, German); B. A. Efron (who represented both St Petersburg Wagons, 1,000 workers, German, and Siemens and Halske, electrical, 800 workers, German); L. I. Schpergaze (Erikson, electrical, 1,000 workers, Swedish); I. K. Kommissarov (lawyer), secretary of the Society; R. R. Liander (United Cables, electrical, 1,200 workers, German); P. A. Bartmer, vice-president of the Engineering Section, and E. L. Nobel, president of the Society, 1912 to 1917 (both represented Nobel', engineering, 1,000 workers, Swedish); N. S. Kalabin (Neva Shipyards, 4,000 workers, bought over by Putilov in 1912).

6. V. Ia. Laverychev, *Tsarizm i rabochii vopros v Rossii (1861–1917gg)* (Moscow, 1972), p. 183.

7. Victoria E. Bonnell, *Roots of Rebellion. Workers' Politics and Organizations in St Petersburg and Moscow, 1900–1914* (Berkeley, 1983), p. 286; *Pravda*, no. 96/300 (27 April 1913), p. 4; no. 81/285 (7 April 1913), p. 4; *Luch*, no. 112/198 (17 May 1913), p. 4.

8. *Metallist*, no. 2/26 (22 May 1913), p. 5; M. Balabanov, *Ot 1905 k 1917 godu; massovoe rabochee dvizhenie* (Moscow, 1927), pp. 194, 217, 230; G. A. Arutiunov, *Rabochee dvizhenie v Rossii v period novogo revoliutsionnogo pod"ema 1910–1914gg* (Moscow, 1975), p. 314.

9. f.150, op.1, d.671, 1.3; d.665, 1.20.

10. Ibid., d.57, ll.35–7. Glezmer resigned as president of the POZF in June 1912 and was replaced by Emmanuel Nobel, the chairman of the engineering firm of the same name and Nobel Brothers Oil Company. Glezmer represented the Society in the State Council from 1906.

11. Balabanov, *ot 1905*, op.cit., p. 204.

12. f.150, op.1, d.57, ll.39–42.

13. The sixteen imposing fines embraced engineering firms (Atlas, Koppel', Northern Engineering, St Petersburg Iron Rolling); electrical companies (Siemens and Halske, Siemens-Schukkert, United Cables); textile mills (Thornton); the leather trade (Russian-American Rubber, Skorokhod); chemicals (Tentelevskii). Yet several engineering and textile companies refused to levy fines (Neva Shipyards, Nobel, K. Ia Pal', Phoenix, St Petersburg Metals). Nor did any correlation exist between the hardliners and the size of enterprises. Many of the staunchest upholders of the convention were companies closely linked to

German capital (E. E. Kruze, *Peterburgskie rabochie v 1912–1914 godakh* (Moscow, 1961), p. 254). But this point should not be overstressed as two of the arch-opponents of fines included St Petersburg Metals, which was closely linked to the German Meier bank, and the K. Ia. Pal' textile company, which was similarly German controlled.

14. f.150, op.1, d.57, ll.45–9, 53–5, 64–6, 68–9; TsGIA, f.23, op.27, d.377, ll.71–2.

15. f.150, op.1, d.505, ll.1–17.

16. Ibid., d.486, l.1. The convention was soon leaked to the socialist press, which published it in full: *Pravda*, no. 90 (14 August 1912), p. 1; *Nevskaia zvezda*, no. 27 (5 October 1912).

17. Heather Hogan, 'Labour and management in conflict: the St Petersburg metalworking industry, 1900–1914' (Michigan, Ph.D., 1981), p. 457.

18. f.150, op.1, d.58, ll.34–42; op.2, d.72, l.55.

19. C. A. Goldberg, 'The Association of Trade and Industry, 1906–1917: the successes and failures of Russia's organized businessmen' (Michigan, Ph.D., 1974), pp. 105–9; f.150, op.1, d.53, ll.12, 81 (council meeting, 13 February 1909).

20. f.150, op.1, d.671, l.2; *Rabochaia pravda*, no. 9 (23 July 1913), p. 2.

21. Goldberg, 'Association', op.cit., p. 90; M. K. Palat, 'Labour legislation and reform in Russia, 1905–1914' (Oxford, Ph.D., 1973), pp. 246–81, 299–305; f.150, op.1, d.53, ll.51g, 54.

22. By July 1914 there were 64 sickness benefit funds functioning in St Petersburg province (covering 87,888 workers) and 112 in the process of formation. Yet at the same date in Moscow province there were 190 in operation (covering 226,822 workers); f.23, op.16, d.95, ll.17–19; d.96, ll.18–68.

23. f.150, op.1, d.58, ll.2–3, 205–6; d.635, l.33.

24. Ibid., d.58, l.102; d.61, ll.1–2; d.60, l.65.

25. Ibid., d.57, ll.144, 147; d.53, l.158.

26. Ibid., op.2, d.74, ll.1–31.

27. Ibid., op.1, d.671, ll.3–4, 51.

28. Ibid., d.58, ll.20, 119, 129, 183; TsGIA, f.1405, op.530, d.859, ll.2–3, 72–5, 84–7; TsGAOR, f.102, DPOO., 1913g., d.341, prod.III, ll.37–8; *Pravda*, no. 8/212 (11 January 1913), p. 2; no. 81/285 (6 April 1913), p. 4; no. 101/305 (4 May 1913), p. 4.

29. f.150, op.1, d.58, l.194; op.2, d.72, l.69; f.1405, op.530, d.883, ll.2–5, 22–4; *Novaia rabochaia gazeta*, no. 8/126 (11 January 1914), p. 3; *Nasha rabochaia gazeta*, no. 1 (3 May 1914), p. 3.

30. TsGAOR, f.102, DP., 4d-vo., 1912g., d.62, ch.2, t.2, ll.15, 34, 72; 1913g., d.61, ch.2, t.1, l.2; *Pravda*, no. 32 (6 June 1912), p. 4; nos.. 195 and 196 (16 and 18 December 1912), p. 4.

31. f.102, DP., 4d-vo., 1913g., d.61, ch.2, t.1, ll.23, 40–6, 95, 105; *Pravda*, no. 18/222 (23 January 1913), p. 3; no. 29/233 (5 February 1913), p. 3; no. 81/285 (7 April 1913), p. 4; no. 98/302 (30 April 1913), p. 3; no. 102/306 (5 May 1913), p. 3; *Luch*, no. 99/185 (1 May 1913), p. 4; no. 103/189 (7 May 1913), p. 3.

32. f.150, op.1, d.57, ll.54, 58.

33. Ibid., op.2, d.75, l.4; op.1, d.58, l.184; Balabanov, *Ot 1905*, op.cit., pp. 212–13.

34. f.150, op.2, d.72, l.29; op.1, d.77, l.19; d.671, l.51.

35. Ibid., op.2, d.72, ll.78–9; op.1, d.671, l.12; TsGAOR, f.102, DPOO., 1914g., d.341, ll.59, 62, 121; d.307, prod.I, ll.88, 98.

36. TsGIA, f.150, op.1, d.72, l.29; d.60, ll.38–44. The fainting fits among the women employees, between 12 and 14 March, were occasioned by the introduction of a new glue, the fumes of which did not disperse as the result of a breakdown in the ventilation system. The workers, believing they had been 'poisoned', went on strike and the owners shut down the factory (f.1405, op.530, d.883, ll.16–18; *Severnaia rabochaia gazeta*, nos. 28 to 30 (13–15 March 1914)).

37. f.150, op.2, d.72, ll.33, 66–8, 69.

38. Ibid., op.1, d.671, l.7.

39. Ibid., d.77, ll.18–25; d.671, ll.7–9, 11–13, 51–3.

40. Ibid., d.671, ll.11–13; d.60, ll.54–8; op.2, d.72, ll.78–80; TsGAOR, f.102, DPOO., 1914g., d.5, ch.57, t.1, ll.245–6.

41. TsGIA, f.1276, op.10, d.127, l.2; M. Lur'e (ed.), 'Tsarizm v bor'be s rabochim dvizheniem v gody pod"ema', *Krasnyi arkhiv*, vol. 1, no. 74 (1936), pp. 40–1.

42. D. C. B. Lieven, 'The Russian civil service under Nicholas II: some variations on a bureaucratic theme', *Jahr-*

bücher für Geschichte Osteuropas, vol. 29 (1981), pp. 366–403; D. K. Rowney, 'Higher civil servants in the Russian Ministry of Internal Affairs: some demographic and career characteristics', *Slavic Review*, vol. 31 (1972), pp. 101–10.

43. f.23, op.17, d.648, l.15; Bonnell, *Roots of Rebellion*, op.cit., pp.372–3.

44. Bonnell, *Roots of Rebellion*, op.cit., p. 376.

45. *Nevskaia zvezda*, no. 25 (9 September 1912), p. 4; *Pravda*, no. 11/215 (15 January 1913), p. 1; *Severnaia rabochaia gazeta*, no. 46 (3 April 1914), p. 1.

46. *Pravda*, no. 119(16 September 1912), p. 2; *Novaia rabochaia gazeta*, no. 89 (23 November 1913), p. 4; *Put' pravdy*, no. 35 (13 March 1914), p. 3.

47. *Pravda*, no. 108 (4 September 1912), p. 2; *Novoe pechatnoe delo*, no. 1 (1912), p. 2. The four unions were accounting clerks in sales and sales manufacturing enterprises; gold, silver and bronze workers; textile workers; wood-workers (*Biulleten' kontorshchika*, no. 1 (17 March 1912), p. 13; *Pravda*, no. 168 (14 November 1912), p. 4; *Zvezda*, no. 17/53 (13 March 1912), p. 4; *Luch*, no. 93/179 (24 April 1913), p. 3).

48. *Pravda*. no. 101/305 (4 May 1913), p. 6; *Put' pravdy*, no. 44 (23 March 1914), p. 3.

49. Laverychev, *Tsarizm*, op.cit., p. 266; Arutiunov, *Rabochee dvizhenie*, op.cit., p.311; Palat, 'Labour legislation', op.cit., pp.325–6.

50. M. K. Korbut, 'Strakhovye zakony 1912 goda i ikh provedenie v Peterburge', *Krasnaia letopis'*, no. 1 (1928), p. 163.

51. Ibid., pp. 148–55.

52. V. Vengerov, 'Pervye itogi deiatel'nosti bol'nichnykh kass', *Sovremennik*, no. 12 (1914), p. 101.

53. Lur'e, 'Tsarizm v bor'be', op.cit., pp. 41, 42, 50; Kruze, *Peterburgskie rabochie*, op.cit., p. 278.

54. Lur'e, 'Tsarizm v bor'be', op.cit., pp. 41, 49, 56; f.23, op.17, d.648, ll.15, 24; f.150, op.1, d.58, l.150.

55. K. Sidorov, 'Bor'ba so stachechnym dvizheniem nakanune mirovoi voiny', *Krasnyi arkhiv*, vol. 3, no. 34 (1929), pp. 102–7.

56. TsGAOR, f.102, DP., 4d-vo., 1913g., d.61, ch.2, t.2, l.30; Lur'e, 'Tsarizm v bor'be' op.cit., p. 48; TsGIA, f.23, op.17, d.648, ll.16–18;

Laverychev, *Tsarizm*, op.cit., p. 261.

57. Lur'e, 'Tsarizm v bor'be', op.cit., p. 44; f.23, op.17, d.648, l.23; op.27, d.377, l.69.

58. TsGIA, f.150, op.1, d.57, ll.47–8, 53; TsGAOR, f.102, DPOO., 1912g., d.61, ch.2, t.1, l.134.

59. M. A. Rubach (ed.), *Rabochee dvizhenie na Ukraine v gody novogo revoliutsionnogo pod"ema, 1910–1914. Sbornik dokumentov i materialov* (Kiev, 1959), p. 469; Korbut, 'Strakhovye zakony', op.cit., and vol. 2 (1928), p. 171.

60. f.150, op.1, d.635, ll.4, 8.

61. Lur'e, 'Tsarizm v bor'be', op.cit., pp. 43–4.

62. f.23, op.17, d.648, ll.20–1; Sidorov, 'Bor'ba', op.cit., pp. 116–24. There were curious omissions from the report. It failed to recommend the methods of the courts' introduction (by legislation or administrative fiat) or to designate which areas of the country or groups of workers should come under the jurisdiction of the new organs. There was also some confusion in the bureaucracy as to the nomenclature of the proposed institution. It was variously referred to as 'arbitration chambers', 'conciliation courts', and 'conciliation chambers'.

63. Sidorov, 'Bor'ba', op.cit., pp. 108–13; f.23, op.17, d.648, l.20; Goldberg, 'Association', op.cit., p. 125.

64. f.23, op.27, d.377, ll.71–2; f.150, op.1, d.60, l.61.

65. f.1276, op.10, d.127, ll.2–3.

Chapter 10

1. When an outbreak of plague occurred in the Baku oilfields, the operatives demanded a sanitary commission (including workers' representatives), the recognition of factory committees and radical improvements in their abysmal housing. By 2 June 1914 30,000 had downed tools. In the face of this second stoppage within a year, the Congress of Oil Owners was determined to break the strike. On 25 June the Council of Ministers ordered the Viceroy of the Caucasus to evict workers from company dwellings (S. Sef, 'Iz istorii Bakinskogo rabochego dvizheniia (1914g.)', *Proletarskaia revoliutsiia*, vol. 54 (1926), pp. 227–56).

2. TsGAOR, f.102, DPOO., 1914g., d.307, prod.II, ll.330–1; *Listovki Peterburgskikh bol'shevikov. 1902–*

1917. Tom vtoroi. 1907–1917 (Leningrad, 1939), pp. 106–7.

3. E. E. Kruze, *Peterburgskie rabochie v 1912–1914 godakh* (Leningrad, 1961), p. 309; *Trudovaia pravda*, no. 30 (2 July 1914), p. 2; no. 31 (3 July 1914), p. 2; f.102, DPOO., 1914g., d.307, prod. II, l.331.

4. f.102, DPOO., 1914g., d.307, prod. II, l.331; DP., 4-dvo., 1914g., d.61, ch.2, t.2, lit.A, l.134; *Trudovaia pravda*, no. 34 (4 July 1914), p. 1; *Rech'*, no. 179/2848 (4 July 1914), p. 2. *Novoe vremia* is the sole source to describe the location of the assembly as the Peterhof highway outside the factory grounds (*Novoe vremia*, no. 13760 (4 July 1912), p. 2).

5. *Rech'*, no. 180/2849 (5 July 1914), p. 4; *Nasha rabochaia gazeta*, no. 52 (4 July 1914), p. 2. The solitary report in one newspaper that the squadron of police had been concealed in the factory yard since the morning seems inherently improbable (*Russkie vedomosty*, no. 153 (4 July 1914)).

6. f.102, DP., 1914g., d.61, ch.2, t.2, lit.A, l.134; ch.2, t.3, l.47; DPOO., 1914g., d.307, prod.II, l.331; *Trudovaia pravda*, no. 32 (4 July 1914), p. 1; no. 33 (5 July 1914), p. 1; no. 34 (6 July 1914), p. 1.

7. M. Mitel'man, B. Glebov, A. Ul'ianskii, *Istoriia putilovskogo zavoda* (Moscow, 1941), pp. 392, 395.

8. *Rech'*, no. 180/2849 (5 July 1914), p. 4. All Soviet historical accounts ignore the complexities and contradictions in the evidence concerning the events at Putilov in the evening of 3 July; they assert without qualification that the police did open fire, killing two and wounding fifty.

9. f.102, DP., 4 d-vo., 1914g., d.61, ch.2, t.3, ll.6, 49, 55, 63; t. 2, lit.A, ll.143, 160, 191; *Trudovaia pravda*, nos. 33–35 (5–8 July 1914); *Rech'*, nos. 185/2854 to 189/2858 (12–16 July 1914).

10. *Trudovaia pravda*, no. 33 (5 July 1914), p. 1; no. 34 (6 July 1914), p. 2; no. 35 (8 July 1914), p. 2.

11. The daily memoranda written by Colonel Popov, the chief of the St Petersburg Okhranda, for his superiors in the Ministry of Internal Affairs constitute a cardinal source on the events of 3 to 15 July. Many have been published in Soviet collections: S. N. Valk and S. E. Livshits (eds), 'Iiul'skie dni v 1914g. v Peterburge (arkhivnye dokumenty)', *Proletarskaia revoliutsiia*, vol. 30 (1924), pp. 181–214 and vols. 31–2 (1924), pp. 306–22; Iu. I. Korablev (ed.), *Rabochee dvizhenie v Peterburge v gody novogo revoliutsionnogo pod''ema, 1912–1914. Dokumenty i materialy* (Leningrad, 1958), pp. 211–41. Throughout this chapter the original documents contained in the police archives have been utilised.

12. A. S. Kiselev, 'V iiule 1914 goda', *Proletarskaia revoliutsiia*, vol. 30 (1924), pp. 37–42.

13. The dating of this gathering and of the leaflet it issued have given rise to much confusion in the literature. In his memoirs A. E. Badaev assigns it to the evening of 4 July (Badaev, *The Bolsheviks in the Tsarist Duma*, London, n.d.) p. 176). The Soviet collection of Petersburg party leaflets gives the appeal the date 5–6 July (*Listovki*, op.cit., p. 108). E. E. Kruze refers the meeting to the evening of 4–5 July (Kruze, *Peterburgskie rabochie*, op.cit., p. 311). The text of the leaflet, however, reads 'on Friday, Saturday and Monday let not a single factory chimney smoke...'. As 4 July was a Friday, the assembly of Bolshevik activists and the drafting of the appeal must have occurred some time on the evening of the third, after the Putilov incident. Kiselev also relates that on his return he was informed about the decision taken by the PK at a session in the evening of the third (Kiselev, 'V iiule', op.cit., p. 47).

14. *Listovki*, op.cit., p. 108; f.102, DP., 4d-vo., 1914g., d.61, ch.2, t.3, l.50. There is no evidence, however, to support the argument of G. A. Arutiunov that the demonstrations were 'also directed against militarism and the threat of a world imperialist war' (Arutiunov, *Rabochee dvizhenie v Rossii v period novogo revoliutsionnogo pod''ema 1910–1914gg.*, Moscow, 1975, p. 366). The Bolshevik appeal of 4 July makes no reference to international events or President Poincaré's state visit. It describes the three-day strike as an expression of 'indignation against the entire regime of the tsarist monarchy' (*Listovki*, op.cit., p. 108).

15. *Nasha rabochaia gazeta*, no. 53 (5 July 1914), p. 1; no. 54 (6 July 1914), p. 2; *Novoe vremia*, no. 13763 (7 July 1914), p. 2.

16. V. Kaiurov, 'Rabochee dvizhenie v Pitere v 1914g.', *Proletarskaia revoliutsiia*, vol. 44 (1925), p. 191; I. Iurenev, 'Mezhraionka (1911–1917gg.) (vospominaniia)', *Proletarskaia revoliutsiia*, vol. 24 (1924), p. 127; *Nasha rabochaia gazeta*, no. 54 (6 July 1914), p. 2.

17. f.102, DP., 4 d-vo., 1914g., d.61, ch.2, tom.3, ll.48–50; Korablev, *Rabochee dvizhenie*, op.cit., pp. 215–16; *Trudovaia pravda*, no. 33 (5 July 1914), p. 2; *Rech'*, no. 180/2849 (5 July 1914), p. 4; *Novoe vremia*, no. 13761 (5 July 1914), p. 4.

18. f.102, DP., 4 d-vo., d.61, ch.2, t.2, lit.A, ll.143–4, 151; *Rech'*, no. 181/2850 (6 July 1914), p. 3.

19. f.102, DP., 4 d-vo., 1914g., d.61, ch.2, t.2, lit.A, ll.160–3; Korablev, *Rabochee dvizhenie*, op.cit., p. 222; *Rech'*, no. 183/2852 (8 July 1914), p. 4; *Trudovaia pravda*, no. 38 (8 July 1914), p. 1; *Nasha rabochaia gazeta*, no. 55 (8 July 1914), p. 1; *Novoe vremia*, no. 13764 (8 July 1914), p. 5.

20. f.102, DP., 4 d-vo., 1914g., d.61, ch.2, tom.2, lit.A, ll.191–3; *Rech'*, no. 185/2854 (12 July 1914), pp. 1, 5.

21. f.102, DP., 4 d-vo., 1914g., d.61, ch.2, tom.3, ll.6, 7, 8; tom.2, lit.A, l.202; Korablev *Rabochee dvizhenie*, op.cit., pp. 230–1; *Novoe vremia*, no. 13766 (10 July 1914), pp. 3, 4; *Rech'*, no. 185/2854 (12 July 1914), p. 5; *Birzhevye vedomosty*, no. 14244 (10 July 1914), p. 2.

22. f.102, DP., 4 d-vo., 1914g., d.61, ch.2, tom.2, lit.A, ll.204–6; *Rech'*, no. 185/2854 (12 July 1914), p. 5; *Novoe vremia*, no. 13767 (11 July 1914), p. 3.

23. f.102, D.P., 4 d-vo., 1914g., d.61, ch.2, tom.3, l.63; *Birzhevye vedomosty*, no. 14246 (12 July 1914), p. 2; *Rech'*, no. 186/2855 (13 July 1913), p. 5.

24. *Trudovaia pravda*, no. 35 (8 July 1914), p. 1; *Nasha rabochaia gazeta*, no. 55 (8 July 1914), p. 2.

25. Kiselev, 'V iiule', op.cit., p. 44; Kaiurov, 'Rabochee dvizhenie', op.cit., pp. 192–3; Alexander Shlyapnikov, *On the Eve of 1917* (trans. Richard Chappell, London, 1982), p. 11.

26. f.102, DP., 1914g., d.61, ch.2, tom.3, ll.9, 63; *Listovki*, op.cit., pp. 109–10; Kiselev, 'V iiule', op.cit., pp. 44–5.

27. f.102, DP., 4 d-vo., 1914g., d.61, ch.2, t.2, lit.A., ll.219–20, 227; ch.2, tom.3, l.158. An analysis of the list of the 29 arrested on the evening of 12 July reveals that the Bolshevik rebels were scarcely 'youths' – rather most were in their twenties. In correspondence with 'Science Life's' largely artisanal membership, at least some of the 'oppositionists' were artisans rather than factory operatives. Two had served on the executive of the union of bakers, whilst two had been elected to the union of printers on a Pravdist ticket in April 1914. Eight were women.

28. N. N. Krestinskii, 'Iz vospominanii o 1914 gode', *Proletarskaia revoliutsiia*, vol. 30 (1924), p. 59.

29. Leopold Haimson, 'The problem of social stability in urban Russia, 1905–1917 (part one)', *Slavic Review*, vol. 23, no. 4 (December 1964), p. 640.

30. *Mezhdunarodnye otnosheniia v epokhu imperializma. seriia III. tom V. 23oe iiulia – 4 avgusta, 1914g.* (Moscow, 1934), p. 5.

31. f.102, DP., 4 d-vo., 1914g., d.61, ch.2, t.3, ll.10, 50; t.2, lit.A, ll.163, 194; Korablev, *Rabochee dvizhenie*, op.cit., p. 221; *Rech'*, no. 181/2850 (5 July 1914), p. 3; no. 185/2854 (12 July 1914), pp. 5, 6; *Novoe vremia*, no. 13764 (8 July 1914), p. 5.

32. *Utro rossii*, no. 154 (5 July 1914); TsGIA, f.150, op.2, d.72, ll.81–4; f.102, DP., 4 d-vo., 1914g., d.61, ch.2, t.2, lit.A, l.215. The eight firms which at once locked out their workers were Baranovskii (1,019 workers), Erikson (1,640), New Lessner (1,722), Nobel (1,150), Phoenix (625), the Russian Society (1,200), St Petersburg Metals (3,500) and Struk (350) – all were engineering works with the exception of Erikson (electrical equipment). The attitudes of many metal-processing companies towards utilisation of a lock-out were inconsistent. For example, seven of the fourteen hostile to Bachmanov's motion on 8 July had participated in the lock-outs of 20–24 March and 22–24 April (Diuflon, Northern Engineering, Siemens and Halske, Siemens-Schukkert, Tiudor, United Cables and Zigel').

33. f.150, op.1, d.60, ll.67–9.

34. Ibid., l.71; *Russkoe slovo*, no. 158 (11 July 1914); *Rech'*, no. 182/2851 (7 July 1914), p. 2.

35. f.102, DP., 4 d-vo., 1914g., d.61, ch.2, t.2, lit.A, ll.217–18; *Rech'*, no. 185/2854 (12 July 1914), p. 6.

36. E. E. Kruze in *Istoriia rabochikh Lening-*

rada. tom pervyi. 1703 – fevral' 1917 (Leningrad, 1972), p. 457; M. S. Balabanov, *Ot 1905 k 1917 godu: massovoe rabochee dvizhenie* (Moscow and Leningrad, 1927), p. 325.

37. *Mezhdunarodnye otnosheniia*, op.cit., tom. I (Moscow, 1935), pp. 436–7; Graf Friedrich Pourtalès, *Mes dernières négociations à Saint Petersbourg en Juillet 1914*, trans. J. Robillet (Paris, 1929), pp. 21, 99; Robert B. McKean, 'Russia on the eve of the Great War. Revolution or evolution?' (East Anglia, Ph.D., 1971), Chapter 11.
38. f.150, op.1, d.60, ll.71–3.
39. Ibid., op.2, d.72, ll.86–7; f.102, DP., 4 d-vo., 1914g., d.61, ch.2, t.2, lit.A, ll.218, 231; ibid., tom.3, l.132.
40. Kruze, *Istoriia*, op.cit., p. 458; Arutiunov, *Rabochee dvizhenie*, op.cit., p. 371; Balabanov, *Ot 1905*, op.cit., p. 326; Haimson, 'Problem of social stability', (Part Two) op.cit., vol. 24, no. 1 (March 1965), p. 2.
41. G. Dobson, *St Petersburg* (London, 1910), p. 144.
42. O. Chaadaeva, 'Iiul'skie stachki i demonstratsii 1914g.', *Krasnyi arkhiv*, vol. 4/95 (1939), pp. 149–55; K. Voinova, 'Iiul'skie dni v Moskve', *Proletarskaia revoliutsiia*, vol. 30 (1924), pp. 215–23; Arutiunov, *Rabochee dvizhenie*, op.cit., pp. 374–7.

Chapter 11

1. At the outbreak of war, the Germanic name of the capital, St Petersburg, was replaced by Petrograd.
2. TsGIA, f.1291, op.1, d.1752, ll.44–8. These are the official figures supplied by the General Staff in response to an enquiry from the Ministry of Internal Affairs in December 1914. In their article, 'K voprosu o sostave Petrogradskikh promyshlennykh rabochikh v 1917 godu', *Voprosy istorii*, no. 1 (1961), I. P. Leiberov and O. I. Shkarantan mention a figure of 115,225 (p. 50).
3. TsGIA, f.150, op.1, d.60, ll.87–9, 112–15, 117–20.
4. f.150, op.1, d.59, ll.16–17; d.60, ll.82–5, 91–3; *Nashe delo*, no. 1 (January 1915), pp. 52–4.
5. *Promyshlennost' i torgovlia*, no. 27/194 (24 October 1915), p. 499; nos. 38–9 (232) (1 October 1916), p. 237.
6. *Rossiia v mirovoi voine 1914–1918gg. (v tsifrakh)*, (Moscow, 1925), p. 17.

7. Leiberov and Shkaratan, 'K voprosu', op.cit., pp. 49–53. Without access to the military archives it has proved impossible to verify the accuracy of their calculation.
8. *Den'*, no. 40 (11 February 1917), p. 3. Caution must be exercised in the use of these statistical data as the services of the Petrograd Labour Exchange came to be used by employers in other provinces.
9. *Materialy k uchetu rabochago sostava i rabochago rynka. Vypusk I* (Petrograd, 1916), pp. 47–51.
10. *Materialy k uchetu*, op.cit., p. 51; *Promyshlennost' i torgovlia*, nos 38–9 (232) (1 October 1916), p. 237; Peter Gattrell, 'Russian heavy industry and state defence, 1908–1918: pre-war experience and wartime mobilization' (Cambridge, Ph.D., 1979), pp. 274–5.
11. f.150, op.1, d.60, ll.43, 146, 202, 230, 280.
12. *Trudy s"ezda predstavitelei voenno-promyshlennykh komitetov, 25–27 iiulia 1915g.* (Petrograd, 1915), pp. 155–9; *Trudy vtorogo s"ezda predstavitelei voenno-promyshlennykh komitetov, 26–29 fevral'ia 1916g.* (Petrograd, 1916), pp. 282–9; *Izvestiia tsentral'nogo voenno-promyshlennogo komiteta*, no. 103 (2 June 1916), p. 3; no. 118 (9 July 1916), p. 3; *Promyshlennost' i torgovlia*, no. 16/183 (8 August 1915), p. 130.
13. *Trudy s"ezda*, op.cit., pp. 185–6; *Promyshlennost' i torgovlia*, no. 16 (8 August 1915), p. 131; TsGIA, f.23, op.27, d.803, l.19.
14. *Trudy vtorogo s"ezda*, op.cit., pp. 564–5.
15. f.150, op.1, d.54, l.201; *Izvestiia tsentral'nogo voenno-promyshlennogo komiteta*, no. 49 (15 January 1916), p. 3; *Den'*, no. 2 (3 January 1917), p. 5.
16. f.150, op.1, d.64, l.112; f.23, op.19, d.38, l.11; *Materialy k uchetu*, op.cit., p. 51.
17. M. D. Rozanov, *Obukhovtsy* (Leningrad, 1965), pp. 298–9.
18. *Nashe delo*, no. 1 (January 1915), pp. 56–7; *Izvestiia tsentral'nogo voenno-promyshlennogo komiteta*, no. 80 (5 April 1916), p. 3; *Promyshlennost' i torgovlia*, no. 19/222 (14 May 1916), pp. 549–50.
19. f.150, op.11, d.64, l.6.
20. *Izvestiia osobogo soveshchaniia po toplivu*, no. 2 (February 1917), p. 105; *Izvestiia vserossiiskogo soiuza gorodov*, nos. 21–2 (15 December, 1915), pp.

3–9. The Special Council for Fuel compromised seven members each from the State Council and State Duma; two from the All-Russian Unions of Towns and Zemstva; three from the Central War-Industries Committee; eleven representatives from government departments.

21. *Zhurnaly osobogo soveshchaniia po oborone gosudarstva. 1915 god. Chast' I* (repr., Moscow, 1975), pp. 140–1; *Gorno-zavodskoe delo*, no. 28 (15 July 1915), pp. 11399–401; f.150, op.1, d.60, ll.82–3.

22. TsGIA, f.1276, op.11, d.888, ll.178–89; *Izvestiia osobogo soveshchaniia po toplivu*, no. 1 (December 1916), p. 37; *Zhurnaly*, op.cit., *1915 god. Chast' II* (repr., Moscow, 1975), pp. 259–61, 475, 504–6.

23. *Materialy k uchetu*, op.cit., p. 49; *Ekonomicheskoe polozhenie Rossii nakanune velikoi oktiabr'skoi sotsialisticheskoi revoliutsii* (Moscow, 1957), Part 2, pp. 20–1; V. P. Semennikov, *Monarkhiia pered krusheniem* (Moscow, 1927), p. 261; *Trudy pervogo s"ezda raionnykh upolnomochennykh po mineral'nomu toplivu predsedatelia osobogo soveshchaniia o toplive. 30 marta – 2 aprelia 1916 godu* (Khar'kov, 1916), p. 91; *Izvestiia osobogo soveshchaniia po toplivu*, no. 1 (December 1916), p. 37.

24. A. L. Sidorov, *Ekonomicheskoe polozhenie Rossii v gody pervoi mirovoi voiny* (Moscow, 1973), pp. 20, 26, 29; Norman Stone, *The Eastern Front, 1914–1917* (London, 1975), pp. 150–1, 160–1.

25. *Zhurnaly* op.cit., *1915 god. Chast' I*, pp. 24, 47–8; *1915 god. Chast' II*, pp. 297, 513; *1916 god. Chast' I* (repr., Moscow, 1977), pp. 70, 77, 114; T. D. Kuprina, 'Politicheskii krizis 1915g. i sozdanie osobogo soveshchanii po oborone', *Istoricheskie zapiski*, vol. 83 (1969), p. 66

26. V. V. Polikarpov, 'Iz istorii voennoi promyshlennosti v Rossii (1906–1916gg.)', *Istoricheskie zapiski*, vol. 104 (1979), p. 152; Ia S. Rozenfel'd and K. I. Klimenko, *Istoriia mashinostroeniia SSSR* (Moscow, 1961), p. 120; Gattrell, 'Russian heavy industry', op.cit., p. 103; Sidorov, *Ekonomicheskoe polozhenie*, op.cit., p. 124.

27. E. Z. Barsukov, *Artilleriia russkoi armii (1900–1917gg). Tom II. Chast' III. Artillerskoe snabzhenie* (Moscow, 1949), pp. 203–4; Gattrell, 'Russian heavy industry', op.cit., pp. 104, 111, 131–2; K. F. Shatsillo, 'Iz istorii ekonomicheskoi praktiki tsarskogo pravitel'stva v gody pervoi mirovoi voiny (o prichinakh sekvestra voenno-promyshlennykh predpriiatii)', in *Ob osobennostiakh imperializma v Rossii* (Moscow, 1963), pp. 221–5.

28. *Zhurnaly*, op.cit., *1915 god. Chast' I*, p. 194; *Chast' II*, p. 267; Sidorov, *Ekonomicheskoe polozhenie*, op.cit., p. 128; Gattrell, 'Russian heavy industry', op.cit., p. 113; V. S. Diakin, *Germanskie kapitaly v Rossii: elektroindustriia i elektricheskii transport* (Leningrad, 1971), pp. 215, 220; f.23, op.19, d.38, l.9

29. I. P. Leiberov, 'Petrogradskii proletariat v gody pervoi mirovoi voiny', in *Istoriia rabochikh Leningrada. Tom Pervyi. 1703 – fevral' 1917* (Leningrad, 1972), p. 464; f.23, op.19, d.38, ll.9–11; *Tekstil'shchik*, no. 1 (December 1915), p. 6; nos. 2–3 (February–March 1916), pp. 8–9.

30. S. G. Strumilin, *Statistiko-ekonomicheskie ocherki* (Moscow, 1957), pp. 46–248; Gattrell, 'Russian heavy industry', op.cit., p. 115; *Den'*, no. 206 (29 July 1915), p. 4; *Novyi ekonomist*, no. 24 (11 June 1916), p. 12.

31. f.23, op.19, d.38, l.9; f.150, op.1, d.64, l.158; *Letopis'*, no. 1 (January 1917), p. 285.

32. Sidorov, *Ekonomicheskoe polozhenie*, op.cit., p. 409.

33. I. F. Gindin and L. E. Shepelev, 'Bankovskie monopolii v Rossii nakanune velikoi oktiabr'skoi sotsialisticheskoi revoliutsii', *Istoricheskie zapiski*, vol. 66 (1960), pp. 24–8.

34. Ibid., pp. 69–72, 77–79, 82.

35. f.23, op.16, d.318, ll.8, 32, 44; *Materialy po statistike truda severnoi oblasti. Vypusk I* (1918), p. 10; Z. V. Stepanov, *Rabochie Petrograda v period podgotovki i provedeniia oktiabr'skogo vooruzhennogo vosstaniia* (Moscow, 1965), p. 25. A slightly different estimate of the total factory labour force in Petrograd on 1 January 1917 is provided by Leiberov in *Istoriia rabochikh Leningrada*, namely 392,800 (op.cit., p. 465).

36. The lower estimate is given in *Materialy po statistike*, op.cit., p. 18; the higher in *Istoriia rabochikh Leningrada*, op.cit., p. 463.

37. *Istoriia rabochikh Leningrada*, op.cit., Table 18, p. 466. Somewhat different

statistics are furnished in A. G. Rashin, *Formirovanie rabochego klassa Rossii* (Moscow, 1958), p. 83. The significant difference concerns textiles, where he records a fall of 9.7 per cent in the labour force.

38. f.23, op.16, d.318, ll.54–5.
39. A. G. Rashin, *Naselenie Rossii za sto let* (Moscow, 1956), p. 90; *Ocherki istorii Leningrada. Tom tretii. Peri'od imperializma i burzhuazno-demokraticheskikh revoliutsii 1895–1917gg.* (Moscow–Leningrad, 1956), p. 105.
40. *Ocherki*, op.cit., p. 105.
41. *Istoriia rabochikh Leningrada*, op.cit., p. 467.
42. Stepanov, *Rabochie Petrograda*, op.cit., p. 40.
43. The lower figure was provided in *Vserossiiskii zemskii' soiuz. Izvestiia glavnogo komiteta*, nos. 30–1 (1–15 January 1916), p. 156; the higher figure derives from Leiberov and Shkaratan, 'K voprosu', op.cit., p. 44. The province of Petrograd, as distinct from the city, came to be home to an additional 75,000 refugees.
44. *Promyshlennost' i torgovlia*, no. 20/187 (5 September 1915), p. 246; no. 27/194 (24 October 1915), p. 500; *Gorodskoe delo*, no. 21 (1 November 1915), p. 1115.
45. *Promyshlennost' i torgovlia*, no. 19/186 (29 August 1915), p. 220; no. 27/194 (24 August 1915), p. 501; *Glavnyi po snabzheniiu armii komitet. Ocherk deiatel'nosti. 10 iuliia 1915g. – 1 fevral'ia 1916g.* (Moscow, 1916), p. 3.
46. V. Z. Drobizhev, A. K. Sokolov, V. A. Ustinov, *Rabochii klass sovetskoi Rossii v pervyi god proletarskoi diktatury* (Moscow, 1975), p. 96. The defects of the census are analysed in note 87 of Chapter 1.
47. *Istoriia rabochikh Leningrada*, op.cit., p. 468.
48. f.150, op.1, d.207, ll.94–6.
49. Stepanov, *Rabochie Petrograda*, op.cit., p. 36; *Istoriia rabochikh Leningrada*, op.cit., pp. 468, 469.
50. David Mandel, *The Petrograd Workers and the Fall of the Old Regime. From the February Revolution to the July Days, 1917* (London, 1983), p. 48.
51. S. A. Smith, *Red Petrograd. Revolution in the Factories 1917–1918* (Cambridge, 1983), p. 23.
52. Stepanov, *Rabochie Petrograda*, op.cit., p. 44; Leiberov and Shkaratan, 'K voprosu', op.cit., pp. 55–6.

53. Stepanov, *Rabochie Petrograda*, op.cit., Table 5, p. 34.
54. f.23, op.16, d.318, ll.72–5; *Materialy po statistike*, op.cit., p. 51; *Tekstil'-shchik*, no. 1 (December 1915), p. 6.
55. f.23, op.19, d.38, p. 12; *Russkie vedomosty*, nos. 2–3 (October–November 1916), p. 6.
56. *Russkie vedomosty*, no. 1 (August 1916), p. 14.
57. Smith, *Red Petrograd*, op.cit., p. 23.
58. The two statistical series available are the 1900 city census, which covered all hired labour, and the 1918 industrial census which sampled only a proportion of factory hands at a time of intense de-industrialisation. There is no data relating to changes in the age balance of the entire labour force or factory hands between 1900 and 1914.
59. Chapter 1 of this study, pp. 19–20; Stepanov, *Rabochie Petrograda*, op.cit., pp. 37–8; Smith, *Red Petrograd*, op.cit., pp. 25–6.
60. Stepanov, *Rabochie Petrograda*, op.cit., p. 38; Smith, *Red Petrograd*, op.cit., pp. 24, 26.
61. Stepanov, *Rabochie Petrograda*, op.cit., pp. 44–5; Smith, *Red Petrograd*, op.cit., p. 34. The 1918 census may well have overestimated the rate of literacy among women: 43 per cent of 272 female metalworkers at Lessner in 1916 were illiterate, but a mere 7 per cent of the 5,302 men (*Voprosy strakhovaniia*, no. 9/58 (8 October 1916), p. 14).
62. C. Goodey, 'Factory committees and the dictatorship of the proletariat, 1918', *Critique* 3 (1974), p. 31; Smith, *Red Petrograd*, op.cit., p. 32.
63. *Russkie vedomosty*, no. 1 (August 1916), p. 14; f.23, op.16, d.318, ll.72–5.
64. Drobizhev et al. *Rabochii klass*, op.cit., pp. 84–7. Studies of the British engineering industry during the First World War have shown that 'dilution' did not in fact irretrievably damage the dominant position of the skilled metalworker (Charles More, *Skill and the English Working Class, 1870–1914*, London, 1980, pp. 28–32).
65. Rashin, *Formirovanie*, op.cit., p. 105; A. I. Davidenko, 'K voprosu o chislennosti i sostave proletariata Peterburga v nachale XX veka', in *Istoriia rabochego klassa Leningrada. Vypusk II* (Leningrad, 1963), pp. 98–9.

66. f.23, op.16, d.318, ll.54, 55.
67. TsGAOR, f.102, DP., 4d-vo., 1915g., d.61, ch.2, tom 1, lit.A, l.26.
68. *Tekstil'shchik*, no. 1 (December 1915), p. 5.
69. *Den'*, no. 175 (28 June 1915), p. 5; *Rabochee utro*, no. 3 (29 October 1915), p. 3; *Izvestiia vserossiiskogo soiuza gorodov*, nos. 31–2 (May 1916), p. 217.
70. *Voprosy strakhovaniia*, no. 7/45 (31 August 1915), p. 10; no. 11/49 (23 December 1915), p. 2; no. 3/52 (16 March 1916), p. 12; f.23, op.19, d.38, ll.15, 16, 17.
71. Ibid., op.16, d.316, ll.4, 9, 39.
72. Ibid., op.19, d.38, l.11; op.20, d.206, ll.58–91; *Den'*, no. 2 (3 January 1917), p. 5.
73. *Zhizn' farmatsevta*, no. 1/33 (January 1917), p. 5.
74. *Materialy po statistike*, op.cit., Tables 16 and 17, pp. 61, 62. Strumilin defined the daily food intake as black and white bread, groats, meat, fat, potatoes and sugar.
75. *Materialy po statistike*, op.cit., Table 17, p. 62.
76. *Istoriia rabochikh Leningrada*, op.cit., Table 19, p. 470.
77. *Tekstil'shchik*, nos. 2–3 (February–March 1916), pp. 4, 8; *Russkie vedomosty*, nos. 2–3 (October–November 1916), p. 6; *Den'*, no. 351 (21 December 1916), p. 4.
78. f.150, op.1, d.21, ll.22, 23, 29; d.61, l.12; op.2, d.74, l.48.
79. *Petrograd po perepisi 15 dekabria 1910 goda* (Petrograd 1914), tom 2, Table 4, pp. 12–13; *Den'*, no. 338 (8 December 1915), p. 3; Mandel, *Petrograd Workers*, op.cit., p. 53.
80. *Petrograd po perepisi*, op.cit., tom 2, Table 4, p. 23; Mandel, *Petrograd Workers*, op.cit.; Stepanov, *Rabochie Petrograda*, op.cit., p. 30.
81. *Rabochee utro*, no. 3 (29 October 1915), p. 3; *Voprosy strakhovaniia*, no. 1/50 (26 January 1916), p. 3; Stepanov, *Rabochie petrograda*, op.cit., p. 59.
82. *Zhurnal soveshchaniia pod predsedatel'stvom glavnogo nachalnika Petrogradskogo voennago okruge po voprosu o merakh bor'by s povysheniiami tsen* (Petrograd, 1915), pp. 8, 34; *Nashe delo*, nos. 3–4 (1915), pp. 31, 35, 38; *Promyshlennost' i torgovlia*, no. 32/199 (28 November 1915), pp. 651–5; *Izvestiia osobogo soveshchaniia po prodovol'stviiu*, no. 27 (1 September 1916), pp. 128–31.
83. *Izvestiia osobogo soveshchaniia po prodovol'stviiu*, no. 1 (26 September 1915), p. 1; *Izvestiia vserossiiskogo soiuza gorodov*, nos. 21–2 (15 December 1915), pp. 3, 13.
84. *Osoboe soveshchanie dlia obsuzhdeniia i ob"edineniia meropriatii po prodovol'stvennomu delu. Vypusk*, 5 (Petrograd, 1916), pp. 77–8.
85. Ibid., pp. 9, 81–3.
86. f.102, DP., 4d-vo., 1916g., d.61, ch.2, lit.A, tom 2, ll.22–3.
87. Ibid., tom 1, ll.57, 59–61; *Bor'ba s dorogoviznoi i gordoskii upravleniia* (Moscow, 1916), p. 5; *Den'*, no. 89 (31 March 1916), p. 5.
88. *Izvestiia osobogo soveshchaniia dlia obsuzhdeniia i ob"edineniia meropriatiia po prodovol'stvennomu delu*, nos. 25–6 (1 August 1916), pp. 88–93; no. 27 (1 September 1916), p. 186; no. 28 (15 October 1916), pp. 134–7; no. 29 (November 1916), pp. 170–7; no. 30 (January 1917), pp. 156–63; no. 31 (February 1917), pp. 106–9.
89. *Zhurnal soveshchaniia*, op.cit., p. 10; *Den'*, no. 318 (18 November 1915), p. 4; no. 89 (31 March 1916), p. 5; *Osoboe soveshchanie*, op.cit., p. 2.
90. *Izvestiia osobogo soveshchaniia dlia obsuzhdeniia i ob"edineniia meropriatiia po prodovol'stvennomu delu*, no. 31 (February 1917), pp. 114–15; Tsuyoshi Hasegawa, *The February Revolution: Petrograd, 1917* (Seattle, 1981), pp. 199–201; *Russkoe slovo*, no. 34 (11 February 1917), p. 3.
91. *Den'*, no. 316 (16 November 1915), p. 4; no. 329 (29 November 1915), p. 5; *Rabochee utro*, no. 3 (29 October 1915), p. 4; Hasegawa, *February Revolution*, op.cit., p. 89.
92. *Den'*, no. 158 (11 June 1915), p. 4; no. 160 (13 June 1915), p. 4; no. 89 (31 March 1916), p. 5.
93. f.150, op.1, d.60, ll.270–1, 283–4, 296–8, 301–2; d.64, ll.10–11, 113, 117, 142.
94. *Den'*, no. 318 (18 November 1915), p. 5; no. 338 (8 December 1915), p. 5; *Rabochee utro*, no. 2 (22 October 1915), p. 2; no. 5 (19 November 1915), p. 4; *Voprosy strakhovaniia*, no. 10/48 (1 December 1915), p. 3.
95. *Den'*, no. 287 (18 October 1916), p. 4; *Gorodskoe delo*, no. 23 (11 December 1916), p. 1121; *Zhurnaly*, op.cit., *1916 god. Chast' IV*, p. 735.
96. Stone, *The Eastern Front* op.cit., Ch. 9.

Chapter 12

1. G. Plekhanov, 'O voine', *Sovremennyi mir*, no. 2 (1915), pp. 185–203; N. Avksent'ev, 'Put' k svobode', *Prizyv*, no. 2 (9 October 1915), pp. 1–2; 'Resolution of a Conference of Social Democratic and Socialist Revolutionary Activists in Geneva, 5–10 September 1915', in *Obzor deiatel'nosti Rossiiskoi sotsialdemokraticheskoi rabochei partii za vremia s nachala voiny Rossii s Avstro-Vengrei i Germaniei po iiul' 1916 goda* (August 1916).

2. Samuel H. Baron, *Plekhanov. The Father of Russian Marxism* (London, 1963), p. 328; *Prizyv*, no. 17 (22 January 1916), p. 2.

3. G. Plekhanov, 'Dve linii', *Prizyv*, no. 3 (17 October 1915), pp. 2–4.

4. B. Voronov, 'Gosudarstvennaia Duma i demokratiia', *Prizyv*, no. 1 (1 October 1915), p. 1; I. Bunakov, 'Oborona strany i revoliutsiia', *Prizyv*, no. 31 (29 April 1916), pp. 2–3.

5. V. I. Lenin, 'Tasks of revolutionary democracy in the European war', (Seven Theses), *Collected Works*, Vol. 21, (Moscow, 1974), pp. 15–19; 'The war and Russian Social Democracy', ibid., pp. 27–34; 'Resolutions of the Berne Conference', ibid., pp. 158–64.

6. Stephen E. Cohen, *Bukharin and the Bolshevik Revolution. A Political Biography, 1888–1938* (New York, 1973), pp. 23–4, 36–7; G. Shklovskii, 'Bernskaia konferentsiia 1915g.', *Proletarskaia revoliutsiia*, vol. 40 (1925), pp. 186–7.

7. Israel Getzler, *Martov. A Political Biography of a Russian Social Democrat* (Cambridge, 1967), pp. 140, 143, 144; *Nashe delo*, no. 2 (1915), pp. 167–8; *Mysl'*, no. 3 (18 November 1914), p. 1; *Nashe slovo*, no. 20 (20 February 1915), p. 1.

8. Oliver H. Radkey, *The Agrarian Foes of Bolshevism* (New York, 1958), p. 112; L. Trotskii, 'Voennyi krizis i politicheskie perspektivy', *Nashe slovo*, no. 179 (1 September 1915), p. 1. In his thesis Michael Melancon has advanced the view that Chernov and the SR-internationalists were in fact defeatists. Further research is required to establish this case beyond doubt. See Michael S. Melancon, 'The Socialist Revolutionaries from 1902 to February 1917: a party of the workers, peasants and soldiers' (Indiana, Ph.D., 1984), pp. 137–8, 152.

9. *Nashe delo*, no. 2 (1915), pp. 107, 109; L. Martov, 'Protiv idealizma i metafiziki (kriticheskie ocherki)', *Nashe slovo*, nos. 16 and 17 (16 and 17 February 1915), p. 1; *Mysl'*, no. 3 (18 November 1915), p. 1.

10. Abraham Ascher, *Pavel Axelrod and the Development of Menshevism* (Cambridge, Mass., 1972), pp. 308, 312, 315; Getzler, *Martov*, op.cit., p. 141.

11. *Mysl'*, no. 87 (26 February 1915), p. 1; *Vpered*, no. 1 (25 August 1915), p. 46; 'Draft Manifesto for the Second Zimmerwald Conference', in Olga Hess Gankin and H. H. Fisher, *The Bolsheviks and the World War. The Origin of the Third International* (Stanford, Calif., 1960), pp. 392–3; Melancon, 'Socialist Revolutionaries', op.cit., p. 140.

12. L. Martov, 'Voina i russkii proletariat', *Internatsional i voina* (Zurich, 1915), pp. 102–25; Ascher, *Pavel Axelrod*, op.cit., p. 317.

13. *Mysl'*, no. 49 (13 January 1915), p. 1; Radkey, *Agrarian Foes*, op.cit., p. 110; Melancon takes the view that from the outset of the war Chernov argued that the party should plan for revolution ('Socialist Revolutionaries', op.cit., pp. 138–40).

14. L. Trotskii, 'Voennyi krizis i politicheskie perspektivy', *Nashe slovo*, nos. 181–2 (3–4 September 1915), p. 1.

15. The reaction of educated society to the outbreak of the war is explored in depth in R. B. McKean, 'Russia on the eve of the Great War. Revolution or evolution?' (East Anglia, Ph.D., 1971), pp. 307–22.

16. TsGAOR, f.102, DPOO., 1915g., d.5, ch.57, tom 1, 1.358.

17. 'Dokumenty biuro TsK RSDRP v Rossii, iiul' 1914 – fevral' 1917gg.', *Voprosy istorii KPSS*, no. 8 (1965), p. 91.

18. M. G. Fleer, *Peterburgskii komitet bol'shevikov v gody voiny, 1914–1917* (Leningrad, 1929), p. 19.

19. I. I. Mints, *Istoriia velikogo oktiabria. Tom I. Sverzhenie samoderzhaviia* (Moscow, 1967), p. 214.

20. D. Baevskii, 'Partiia v gody imperialisticheskoi voiny', in M. N. Pokrovskii (ed.), *Ocherki po istorii*

oktiabr'skoi revoliutsii. Tom I (Moscow, 1927), p. 376.

21. Tsuyoshi Hasegawa, *The February Revolution: Petrograd, 1917* (Seattle, 1981), p. 5.

22. *Istoriia rabochikh Leningrada. Tom pervyi. 1703–fevral' 1917* (Leningrad, 1972), p. 475.

23. The three resolutions are printed in Gankin and Fisher, *Bolsheviks*, op.cit., pp. 57–9, 72–3, 81–4.

24. Alexander Shliapnikov, *On the Eve of 1917*, trans. Richard Chappell (London, 1982), p. 20. (Shliapnikov misdates his drafting of the leaflet, which, on internal evidence, must have been written before the outbreak of war); *Sotsial-demokrat*, no. 33 (1 November 1914), p. 2; Fleer, *Peterburgskii komitet*, op.cit., pp. 152–3; A. F. Bessonova, 'Antivoennaia rabota bol'shevikov v gody pervoi mirovoi voiny', *Istoricheskii arkhiv*, vol. 7, no. 5 (1961), p. 83.

25. f.102, DP., 4 d-vo., 1914g., d.61, ch.2, t.3, l.134; K. Kondrat'ev, 'Vospominaniia o podpol'noi rabote Peterburgskoi organizatsii RSDRP(B) v period 1914–1917gg.', *Krasnaia letopis'*, no. 5 (1923), p. 230.

26. Shliapnikov, *On the Eve*, op.cit., p. 16.

27. Georges Haupt, *Socialism and the Great War. The Collapse of the Second International* (Oxford, 1972), pp. 18–22; David Kirby, *War, Peace and Revolution. International Socialism at the Crossroads 1914–1918* (Aldershot, 1986), pp. 3–4.

28. I. Iurenev, ''Mezhraionka' (1911–1917gg.) (vospominaniia)', *Proletarskaia revoliutsiia*, vol. 24 (1924), p. 127.

29. Shliapnikov, *On the Eve*, op.cit., p. 14. Melancon claims that SR activists arrested at the start of hostilities were opponents of Russia's entry into the war ('Socialist Revolutionaries', op.cit., pp. 204–5).

30. *Sotsial-demokrat*, no. 33 (1 November 1914), p. 2; Iurenev, 'Mezhraionka', op.cit., p. 126.

31. Shliapnikov, *On the Eve*, op.cit., p. 19; Kondrat'ev, 'Vospominaniia', op.cit., p. 228.

32. 'Podpol'naia rabota v Petrograde v gody imperialisticheskoi voiny (1914–1917gg). Rasskazy rabochikh', *Krasnaia letopis'*, nos. 2–3 (1922), p. 130; Iu. Gavrilov, 'Na

Vyborgskoi storone v 1914–1917gg.', *Krasnaia letopis'*, no. 23 (1927), p. 40.

33. f.102, DP., 4d-vo., 1914g., d.61, ch.2, t.2, lit.A, l.231; t.3, l.140.

34. Ibid., l.141.

35. N. N. Krestinskii, 'Iz vospominanii [o 1914 gode]', *Proletarskaia revoliutsiia*, vol. 30 (1924), p. 60; S. V. Tiutiukin, *Voina, mir, revoliutsiia* (Moscow, 1972), p. 21; Mints, *Istoriia*, op.cit., p. 217.

36. D. A. Longley, 'The Russian Social Democrats' statement to the Duma on 26 July (8 August 1914): a new look at the evidence', *English Historical Review*, vol. 102 (July 1987), pp. 599–621.

37. For a translation of the text, see ibid., p. 617.

38. A. F. Kerensky, *The Kerensky Memoirs. Russia and History's Turning Point* (London, 1966), pp. 129–30, 132; McKean, 'Russia', op.cit., pp. 317–8. The socialists' list of demands included a political amnesty, the restoration of the Finnish constitution, the granting of autonomy to Poland and the implementation of the promise of the October Manifesto concerning civil freedoms.

39. A. Rosmer, *Le Mouvement Ouvrier pendant la Guerre. De l'Union Sacrée à Zimmerwald* (Paris, 1936), appendix XI (Vandervelde's telegram), pp. 512–13; Shklovskii, 'Bernskaia konferentsiia 1915g.', op.cit., pp. 137–8.

40. A report of the Moscow Okhrana, dated 10 October, listed those present at the conference as the deputies Badaev, Muranov, Petrovskii and Samoilov, as well as Kamenev and seven or eight local activists (M. A. Tsiavlovskii (ed.), *Bol'sheviki: dokumenty po istorii bol'shevizma s 1903 po 1916 god byvsh. Moskovskogo okhrannogo otdeleniia*, Moscow, 1918, p. 153).

41. The reply was published in *Sotsial-demokrat*, no. 33 (1 November 1914), p. 1; Gankin and Fisher, *Bolsheviks*, op.cit., p. 59. Hasegawa's account is erroneous in that he mistakenly transposes the discussion of the reply to Vandervelde to the second Bolshevik conference of 2–4 November (*February Revolution*, op.cit., p. 108).

42. I. P. Leiberov, 'V. I. Lenin i Petrogradskaia organizatsiia bol'shevikov v period mirovoi voiny (1914–

1916gg.)', *Voprosy istorii KPSS*, no. 5 (1960), p. 67; I. M. Dazhina, 'Russkoe biuro TsK RSDRP v gody pervoi mirovoi voiny', in A. L. Sidorov (ed.), *Pervaia mirovaia voina* (Moscow, 1968), p. 275; Mints, *Istoriia*, op.cit., p. 221; Tiutiukin, *Voina*, op.cit., pp. 28, 45. Tiutiukin in fact is an exception to the rule in that he subjects the reply to an honest critique, but is then forced by convention to the manifestly contradictory and absurd conclusion that in the party there existed no differences of principle with Lenin. (op.cit., p. 50).

43. Iu. Novin, 'Revoliutsionnaia rabota deputatov protiv voiny', *Krasnaia letopis'*, no. 10 (1924), pp. 96–7 (report of the chief of the Petrograd Okhrana to the palace commandant, 4 November 1914); *Nashe delo*, no. 2 (1915), p. 94; Dazhina, 'Russkoe biuro', op.cit., pp. 275–6; Tiutiukin, *Voina*, op.cit., pp. 45–7. By the time of the Bolshevik conference of 2–4 November 1914 Lenin's views were more widely known as copies of issue 33 of *Sotsial-demokrat* containing the 'Manifesto of the Central Committee' had reached the capital. The police found a copy when they arrested Badaev at the gathering.

44. Shliapnikov, *On the Eve*, op.cit., p. 26; *Sotsial-demokrat*, no. 33 (1 November 1914), p. 2; 'Dokumenty biuro', op.cit., p. 92; Tiutiukin, *Voina*, op.cit., pp. 41, 47, 255 (note 70).

45. TsGIA, f.1405, op.530, d.883, ll.179–81; Tiutiukin, *Voina*, op.cit., p. 259 (note 116); Krestinskii, 'Iz vospominanii', op.cit., p. 62.

46. The major documents of the Zimmerwald and Kienthal conferences have been published in English in the work of Gankin and Fisher cited in note 11. The international socialist movement in the war has been studied by Merle Fainsod, *International Socialism and the World War* (Cambridge, Mass., 1935) and more recently by David Kirby (*War, Peace*, op.cit.). The conclusions of the textual survey of Bolshevik propaganda in Petrograd confirm the findings of a similar exercise carried out by B. Dvinov. He discovered that in the first half of 1916 Bolshevik literature contained no mention of 'civil war' or the Third International (B. Dvi-

nov, *Pervaia mirovaia voina i Rossiiskaia sotsial-demokratiia*, New York, 1962, pp. 136–8).

47. f.102, DPOO., 1914g., d.307, prod. III, l.158; O. A. Ermanskii, *Iz perezhitogo (1887–1921gg.)*, (Moscow, 1927), p. 117; Novin, 'Revoliutsionnaia rabota', op.cit., p. 104.

48. *Sotsial-demokrat*, no. 34 (5 December 1914), p. 2.

49. Mints, *Istoriia*, op.cit., pp. 229–30; *Ocherki istorii Leningradskoi organizatsii KPSS. 1883–1917* (Leningrad, 1980), p. 286. In this respect Tiutiukin is an exception, but is compelled by ideological considerations to come to the conclusion, despite his own evidence, that the Liquidators (i.e. Mensheviks) had become social chauvinists (*Voina*, op.cit. p. 57).

50. f.102, DPOO., d.347, 1915g., ll.247, 248.

51. *Izvestiia zagranichnogo sekretariata organizatsionnogo komiteta RSDRP*, no. 1 (22 February 1915), p. 2 (letter of A. N. Potresov to the Copenhagen conference, February 1915); P. Maslov, 'Voina i demokratiia', *Nashe delo*, nos. 3–4 (1915), p. 52; *Nashe delo*, nos. 5–6 (1915), p. 60.

52. 'Otvet Enzisu', *Delo*, nos. 5–6 (1916), p. 95.

53. Potresov's letter to the Copenhagen Conference (see note 51); 'Otvet Enzisu', op.cit., p. 95.

54. Ibid..

55. A. N. Potresov, 'Razdvoennaia Rossiia', *Delo*, no. 3 (1916), pp. 57, 60; E. Maevskii, 'Duma i strana', *Put'*, nos. 2–3 (10 December 1916), pp. 1–3.

56. Potresov's letter to the Copenhagen Conference (see note 51); 'Otvet Enzisu', op.cit., p. 97.

57. Ermanskii, *Iz perezhitogo*, op.cit., pp. 119–21.

58. 'Pism'o t.A. Burianova', *Prizyv*, no. 18 (29 January 1916), p. 1; f.102, DPOO., 1915g., d.307, t.II, l.23.

59. f.102, DPOO., 1914g., d.307, prod.III, l.210; 1916g., d.5, ch.57, l.52; *Obzor*, op.cit. p. 77.

60. f.102, DPOO., d.347, 1915g., l.248.

61. *Obzor*, op.cit., p. 26; f.102, DPOO., 1916g., d.5, ch.57, l.52; Tiutiukin, *Voina*, op.cit., pp. 59–60.

62. f.102, DPOO., 1915g., d.307, t.II, l.109.

63. Ermanskii, *Iz perezhitogo*, op.cit., p. 120.

64. TsGIA, f.1405, op.530, d.883, ll.38–9 (Central Initiative Group Appeal, August 1914); TsGAOR, f.102, DPOO., 1915g., d.5, ch.57, ll.301–10 (Declaration of Menshevik Internationalists, late 1915); 'Fevral'skaia revoliutsiia v dokumentakh', *Proletarskaia revoliutsiia*, vol. 1 (1923), pp. 275–7 (leaflet of the Central Initiative Group); *Letopis'*, no. 1 (January 1917), p. 293.

65. f.102, DPOO., 1915g., d.5, ch.57, ll.28–9 (Iurenev's manuscript entitled 'Causes of the War'); *Vpered*, no. 1 (27 January 1915), and ibid., no. 1 (13 December 1915), as reproduced in L. Leont'eva, 'V riadakh "Mezhraionka" (1914–1917gg.)', *Krasnaia letopis'*, no. 11 (1924), pp. 137–9, 140–5.

66. *Narodnaia mysl'*, no. 1 (November 1915), p. 1; Melancon, 'Socialist Revolutionaries', op.cit., pp. 205–8.

67. f.1405, op.530, d.1058, l.41; L. M. Shalaginova, 'Esery-internatsionalisty v gody pervoi mirovoi voiny', in A. L. Sidorov, *Pervaia mirovaia voina, 1914–1918* (Moscow, 1968), pp. 325–6; Richard Abraham, *Alexander Kerensky. The First Love of the Revolution* (New York, 1987), p. 91.

68. f.102, DPOO., d.347, 1915g., l.248; *Obzor*, op.cit., p. 86.

69. Shliapnikov, *On the Eve*, op.cit., pp. 28, 30, 32; Shklovskii, 'Bernskaia konferentsiia 1915g.', op.cit., pp. 144–5.

70. In a letter to Shliapnikov in October 1914, Lenin hinted at his displeasure. 'Our group,' he remarked, ' . . . should set forth a consistent point of view' (Lenin, *Collected Works,* Vol. 35, Moscow, 1976, p. 165).

71. Shliapnikov, *On the Eve*, op.cit., pp. 38, 47, 51, 61.

72. Lenin, *Collected Works*, Vol. 43 (Moscow, 1969), p. 439; Shliapnikov, *On the Eve*, op.cit., pp. 61–2.

73. A. Badaev, 'Dumskaia fraktsiia bol'shevikov – 'piaterka' – v russko-germanskuiu voinu', *Krasnaia Letopis'*, no. 10 (1924), p. 89; Dazhina, 'Russkoe biuro', op.cit., pp. 271, 275.

74. Fleer, *Peterburgskii komitet*, op.cit., pp. 20–3; *Ocherki istorii*, op.cit., p. 277; f.102, DPOO., 1914g., d.307, prod.III, l.194; 1915g., d.5, ch.57, tom 1, l.359. The confusion is compounded by the fact that Fleer cites as

his sources the very two secret police memoranda which flatly contradict his argument.

75. f.102, DPOO., 1915g., d.5, ch.57, t.1, l.71; ch.57, l.1.

76. Ibid., ch.57, ll.20, 86, 95.

77. Ibid., ch.57, l.150; Kondrat'ev, 'Vospominaniia', op.cit., p. 31.

78. f.1405, op.530, d.1058, l.8; 'Podpol'naia rabota', op.cit., p. 118.

79. f.102, DPOO., 1914g., d.5, ch.57, t.2, l.25.

80. Ibid., d.307, prod.III, l.194; d.5, ch.57, tom.1, l.358; V. Vinogradov, 'Organizatsiia bol'shevikov na Peterburgskom Metallicheskom zavode v 1915g.', *Krasnaia letopis'*, no. 18 (1926), p. 34; F. Lemeshov, 'Na Putilovskom zavode v gody voiny', *Krasnaia letopis'*, no. 23 (1927), p. 5.

81. f.102, DPOO., 1915g., d.5, ch.57, l.95.

82. Kondrat'ev, 'Vospominaniia', op.cit., pp. 230–42; K. Kondrat'ev, 'Vospominaniia o podpol'noi rabote v Petrograde', *Krasnaia letopis'*, no. 7 (1923), p. 30.

83. f.102, DPOO., 1915g., d.5, ch.57, l.86; Vinogradov, 'Organizatsiia', op.cit., pp. 135–6; V. Zalezhskii, *Iz vospominanii podpol'shchika* (Moscow, 1931), p. 118; Gavrilov, 'Na vyborgskoi storone', op.cit., p. 42.

84. f.102, DPOO., 1915g., d.5, ch.57, l.130.

85. f.1405, op.530, d.883, ll.55–9; f.102, DPOO., 1914g., d.5, ch.57, t.2, l.7.

86. f.102, DPOO., 1915g., d.5, ch.57, l.1; Kondrat'ev, 'Vospominaniia', op.cit., *Krasnaia letopis'*, no. 7 (1923), pp. 31–2; Leiberov, 'V. I. Lenin', op.cit., p. 69. The figure of 500 party members is given by Kondrat'ev and repeated in all Soviet books. There is no independent archival evidence to verify it.

87. *Ocherki istorii*, op.cit., p. 285.

88. f.102, DPOO., 1915g., d.5, ch.57, t.1, ll.69–71, 74–6.

89. f.1405, op.530, d.900, l.15; d.1058, l.8.

90. f.102, DP., 4 d-vo., 1915g., d.61, ch.2, lit.A., ll.1, 7; f.102, DPOO., d.5, ch.57, l.1; *Listovki Peterburgskikh bol'shevikov, 1902–1917. Tom vtoroi, 1907–1917* (Leningrad, 1939), pp. 129–31.

91. f.102, DPOO., 1915g., d.5, ch.57, l.86.

92. Ibid., ch.57, ll.96, 108; *Listovki*,

op.cit., pp. 156–8; TsGIA, f.1405, op.530, d.1061, l.68.

93. f.102, DPOO., 1914g., d.5, ch.57, t.2, l.27; 1915g., d.5, ch.57, l.57.
94. f.DPOO., 1914g., d.5, ch.57, t.2, ll.38, 40.
95. Ibid., 1915g., d.5, ch.57, ll.57, 58.
96. F. Dan (ed.), *Materialy po istorii russkogo revoliutsionnogo dvizheniia. vol. II. Iz arkhiva P. B. Aksel'roda; pism'a P. B. Aksel'roda i Iu. O. Martova, 1901–1916* (Berlin, 1924), pp. 299, 306, 311, 320, 323, 335.
97. The Petrograd factory medical funds represented at the conference comprised Aivaz, Erikson, Franco-Russian, Neva Shipyards and Petrograd Metals (*Izvestiia vserossiiskogo soiuza gorodov*, no. 16 (1915), pp. 51–2).
98. f.DPOO., 1915g., d.5, ch.57, ll.144–7; *Trudy soveshchaniia po ekonomicheskim voprosam, sviazannym s. dorogoviznoi i snabzheniem armii (Moskva 11–13 iiulia 1915 goda)*, (Moscow, 1915), pp. 48–56, 61–7, 121–3, 297; *Strakhovanie rabochikh*, no. 7 (July 1915), pp. 4–8.
99. Tiutiukin, *Voina*, op.cit., pp. 72, 74–5; f.DPOO., 1915g., d.5, ch.57, l.2; Melancon, 'Socialist Revolutionaries', op.cit., pp. 207–9.
100. f.DPOO., 1915g., d.5, ch.57, ll.87, 97.
101. Abraham, *Alexander Kerensky*, op.cit., pp. 81–3.
102. f.1405, op.530, d.1058, ll.34, 40–1; Shalaginova, 'Esery-internatsionalisty', op.cit., p. 325.
103. f.102, DPOO., 1915g., d.5, ch.57, ll.3, 8; *Nabat*, nos. 2–3 (May–June 1915), p. 3; P. Gooderham, 'The anarchist movement in Russia, 1905–1907' (Bristol, Ph.D., 1981), pp. 225–7, 229.
104. Iurenev, 'Mezhraionka', op.cit., pp. 128–38.
105. f.102, DPOO., 1915g., d.5, ch.57, ll.22, 29, 106; Leont'eva, 'V riadakh', op.cit., p. 134.
106. Iurenev, 'Mezhraionka', op.cit., p. 136.
107. f.102, DPOO., 1915g., d.5, ch.57, ll.87, 118–19; Hasegawa, *February Revolution*, op.cit., p. 133.
108. Iurenev, 'Mezhraionka (1911–1917gg) (Vospominaniia)', *Proletarskaia revoliutsiia*, vol. 25 (1924), pp. 114–15; Dan, *Materialy*, pp. 318–19.

Chapter 13

1. TsGAOR, f.102, DPOO., 1915g., d.5, ch.57, l.150; 1915g., d.347, l.246; TsGIA, f.1405, op.530, d.1058, l.56; *Internatsional i voina* (Zurich, 1915), pp. 141–3.
2. f.1405, op.530, d.1058, l.56.
3. Ibid., l.40.
4. f.102, DPOO., 1915g., d.5, ch.57, l.166; f.1405, op.530, d.1061, l.138.
5. f.102, DPOO., 1915g., d.341, t.1, l.187; DP., 4 d-vo., 1915g., d.61, ch.2, lit.A, l.137; DPOO., 1915g., d.5, ch.57, l.184; f.1405, op.530, d.1058, l.141.
6. I. P. Leiberov, 'O vozniknovenii revoliutsionnoi situatsii v Rossii v gody pervoi mirovoi voiny (iiul'-sentiarb' 1815g.)', *Istoriia SSSR*, no. 6 (1964), p. 53; *Istoriia rabochikh Leningrada. Tom pervyi. 1703–fevral' 1917* (Leningrad, 1972), p. 485; Michael S. Melancon, 'The Socialist Revolutionaries from 1902 to February 1917: a party of the workers, peasants and soldiers' (Indiana, Ph.D., 1984), p. 236. Leiberov cites party archives as his source. The author could find no corroborative evidence in the police archives. However, in the light of other evidence concerning the importance many activists attached to the concept of the Soviet at this time and the Bolsheviks' endeavours later on in 1915 to set up such a body, it is likely that Leiberov's account contains elements of truth.
7. V. I. Lenin, 'The Defeat of Russia and the Revolutionary Crisis' (second half of September 1915), *Collected Works*, Vol. 21 (Moscow, 1974), pp. 378–82 (hereafter *CW*). Leiberov's article cited in note 6 provides a good example of the Soviet interpretation.
8. The list of strike-bound factories included only two small mills and two leather-working establishments. Putilov apart, none of the gigantic metalworking state-owned plants were involved.
9. This episode is examined in Chapter 15; Melancon, 'Socialist Revolutionaries', op.cit., p. 236.
10. f.102, DP., 4d-vo., 1915g., d.61, ch.2, lit.A, l.139.
11. Richard Abraham, *Alexander Keren-*

sky. The First Love of the Revolution (New York, 1987), p. 96.

12. f.1405, op.530, d.1058, ll.95, 98–9.

13. Ibid., l.76.

14. f.102, DPOO., 1915g., d.5, ch.57, l.268.

15. Letter of Lenin to Shliapnikov, 10 October 1915 (*CW*, Vol. 35, Moscow, 1976, pp. 208–9); 'Several Theses', *Sotsial-demokrat*, no. 47 (13 October 1915) (*CW*, Vol. 21, op.cit., pp. 401–6). The events of the summer of 1915 in Russia reawakened in Lenin messianic hopes of imminent European revolution. 'The victory of the proletariat in Russia', he wrote in 'Several Theses', 'will create extraordinarily favourable conditions for the development of the revolution in both Asia and Europe'.

16. Lenin to Shliapnikov, before 13 September 1915 (*CW*, Vol. 35, op.cit., pp. 206–7).

17. Alexander Shliapnikov, *On the Eve of 1917*, trans. Richard Chappell (London, 1982), pp. 70–1, 98–9, 104–5; f.102, DPOO., 1916g., d.5, ch.57, l.29. In his memoirs Shliapnikov tries to throw all the blame for the PK's attitude upon the ex-editor of *Pravda*, Miron Chernomazov, who was then secretary of the Lessner medical fund and had long been (correctly) suspected of being a police agent. It is not impossible that fear of provocation was one of Shliapnikov's motives in rejecting the PK's demands, but Chernomazov enjoyed the trust of the members of the PK during the war and Lenin had explicitly furnished his agent with a list of names for the proposed Russian Bureau which excluded the leading Petrograd activists.

18. I. M. Dazhina, 'Russkoe biuro TsK RSDRP v gody pervoi mirovoi voiny', in A. L. Sidorov (ed.), *Pervaia mirovaia voina* (Moscow, 1968), pp. 277–9.

19. f.102, DPOO., 1915g., d.5, ch.57, l.197.

20. Ibid., ch.57, ll.200, 211; DP., 4 d-vo., 1915g., d.61, ch.2, t.1, lit.A, ll.36, 43, 38, 51.

21. f.102, DPOO., 1915g., d.5, ch.57, ll.266–8; DP., 4 d-vo., 1915g., d.61, ch.2, t.1, lit.A, ll.81–2.

22. Evan Mawdsley, *The Russian Revolution and the Baltic Fleet. War and Poli-tics, February 1917–April 1918* (London, 1978), pp. 1–7.

23. f.102, DPOO., 1915g., d.5, ch.57, ll.295–6; TsGIA, f.1405, op.530, d.1060, l.2; Report of A. Khvostov to I. L. Goremykin, 17 November 1915 (C. E. Vulliamy (ed.), *The Red Archives*, London, 1929, pp. 61–3); Iv. Egorov, 'Matrosy-bol'sheviki nakanune 1917g. (iz istorii partiinoi organizatsii Baltiiskogo flota)', *Krasnaia letopis'*, no. 18 (1926), pp. 6–8. Egorov claims, without adducing any evidence, that sailors' Germanophobia concealed discontent with the war (ibid., p. 12).

24. D. Zinevich, 'Voenna organizatsiia pri PK RSDRP(B) v 1914–1916gg.', *Krasnaia letopis'*, no. 61 (1934), p. 97.

25. f.1405, op.530, d.1060, l.2.

26. Egorov, 'Matrosy-bol'sheviki', op.cit., pp. 22, 26.

27. Vulliamy, *Red Archives*, op.cit., pp. 66–7.

28. The reasons behind the labour policies of the Central War-Industries Committee and the decision of the Council of Ministers are explored in Chapter 15. In the first instance, the TsVPK leadership had proposed that the sickness insurance funds would serve as the mechanism for the selection of candidates. The Bolshevik-controlled Labour Group on the Insurance Council and *kassy* representatives turned down this suggestion. (V. Skal'tsov, 'K voprosu ob uchastii rabochikh v TsVPKe', *Voprosy strakhovaniia*, no. 7/45 (31 August 1915), p. 3.) Their refusal had compelled the leaders of the TsVPK to seek direct elections from the factories.

29. f.102, DP., 4 d-vo., 1915g., d.61, ch.2, lit.A, l.157; TsGIA, f.1405, op.530, d.1058, l.79.

30. f.1405, op.530, d.1058, l.79; d.1059, ll.3–5; K. Kondrat'ev, 'Vospominaniia o podpol'noi rabote v Petrograde', *Krasnaia letopis'*, no. 7 (1923), pp. 34, 37.

31. 'Dokumenty biuro TsK RSDRP v Rossii, iiul' 1914–fevral' 1917gg.', *Voprosy istorii KPSS*, no. 8 (1965), p. 93.

32. Lenin, 'Several Theses', *CW*, Vol. 21, op.cit., pp. 401–6.

33. *Vpered*, no. 1 (13 December 1915) as reproduced in L. Leont'eva,

'V riadakh 'Mezhraionka' (1914–1917gg.)', *Krasnaia letopis'*, no. 11 (1924), p. 144.

34. B. Voronov, 'Burzhuaznaia oppozitsiia i proletariat', *Prizyv*, no. 11 (11 December 1915), pp. 2–3; B. Voronov, 'Vne zhiznii', ibid., no. 8 (20 November 1915), p. 2.

35. Gr. P., 'Voenno-promyshlennye komitety i rabochie', *Utro*, no. 2 (19 August 1915), p. 3; f.102, DPOO., d.347, 1915g., 1.86 (an article of V. Ezhov for the Samara journal *Nash golos*). According to Martov, the concept of an All-Russian Labour Congress was first advanced by G. O. Baturskii (pseudonym of B. S. Tseitlin), lawyer and editor of the Menshevik insurance journal *Strakhovanie rabochikh* (letter of Iu. Martov to P. Aksel'rod, 25 September 1915 in F. Dan (ed.), *Materialy po istorii russkogo revoliutsionnogo dvizheniia. vol. II. Iz arkhiva P. B. Aksel'roda: pism'a P. B. Aksel'roda i Iu. O. Martova, 1901–1916*, Berlin, 1924, p. 353).

36. f.102, DPOO., 1915g., d.347, 1.34; Shliapnikov, *On the Eve*, op.cit., p. 74; Lewis H. Siegelbaum, *The Politics of Industrial Mobilization in Russia, 1914–1917. A Study of the War-Industries Committees* (London, 1983), p. 165; S. V. Tiutiukin, *Voina, mir, revoliutsiia* (Moscow, 1972), p. 208; f.1405, op.530, d.1058, ll.82–3; *Nashe slovo*, no. 229 (31 October 1915), p. 1.

37. Melancon, 'Socialist Revolutionaries', op.cit., pp. 239–40.

38. TsGIA, f.32, op.1, d.2120, 1.23.

39. Kondrat'ev, 'Vospominaniia', op.cit., p. 34; V. Zalezhskii, *Iz vospominaniia podpol'schchika* (Moscow, 1931), pp. 131–3.

40. f.1405, op.530, d.1058, 1.103; *Den'*, no. 256 (17 September 1915), p. 3.

41. The Mensheviks' newspaper *Utro* lasted a mere two issues in August 1915; its successor *Rabochee utro* appeared only on 15 October with a life span of one month (seven issues).

42. *f.1405*, op.530, d.1059, 1.18; Tiutiukin, *Voina*, op.cit., p. 208.

43. TsGIA, f.32, op.1, d.2020, 1.23. The five included three cotton mills, one tobacco manufactory and one engineering firm. At the Pipe works, 9,000 of the 13,000-strong workforce cast their ballots, but in the railway

shops at Putilov a mere 100 of 2,000 operatives participated (*Nashe slovo*, no. 224 (26 October 1915), p. 2; F. Lemeshov, 'Na Putilovskom zavode v gody voiny', *Krasnaia letopis'*, no. 23 (1927), p. 10).

44. Siegelbaum, *Politics*, op.cit., p. 269 (note 16).

45. f.1405, op.530, d.1059, 11.21–2, 29–30; Zalezhskii, *Iz vospominaniia*, op.cit., pp. 134–8; Melancon, 'Socialist Revolutionaries', op.cit., p. 242.

46. I. I. Mints, *Istoriia velikogo oktiabria. Tom I. Sverzhenie samoderzhaviia* (Moscow, 1967), p. 280.

47. The Okhrana calculated that the Menshevik and SR electors represented 128,000 workers and the Bolsheviks 70,000; the bases of their estimate are unknown (f.1405, op.530, d.1059, 1.29). In view of the contradictory data, Melancon's argument that the electoral struggle 'contributed greatly to turning Russian workers against the war' is unsustainable ('Socialist Revolutionaries', op.cit., p. 248).

48. f.1405, op.530, d.1059, 1.22.

49. *Den'*, no. 274 (5 October 1915), p. 3 (letter of Gvozdev to the editor); f.102, DPOO., 1915g., d.347, 1.120.

50. f.32, op.1, d.2120, 1.24. The figure of 176 is given in the account of the meeting in the TsVPK archives, whilst the Okhrana reported the presence of 153 delegates (f.1405, op.530, d.1059, 1.79).

51. f.32, op.1, d.2120, 11.47–8; f.1405, op.530, d.1059, 11.66–7.

52. f.1405, op.530, d.1059, 11.79, 85.

53. *Istoriia rabochikh Leningrada*, op.cit., p. 489.

54. f.102, DPOO., 1915g., d.5, ch.57, 1.295; M. G. Fleer, *Rabochee dvizhenie v Rossii v gody imperialisticheskoi voiny* (Leningrad, 1926), p. 234.

55. f.102, DPOO., 1915g., d.5, ch.57, ll.295, 322; *Listovki Peterburgskikh bol'shevikov, 1902–1907. Tom vtoroi. 1907–1917* (Leningrad, 1939), pp. 180–1; Melancon, 'Socialist Revolutionaries', op.cit., p. 254. The leaflet's silence on the war throws doubt upon the report in the Bolsheviks' central organ that the slogans for the strike included 'Down with the war!' (*Sotsial-demokrat*, no. 53 (31 March 1916), p. 2).

56. Fleer, *Rabochee dvizhenie*, op.cit., pp.

233–4.

57. M. G. Fleer, *Peterburgskii komitet bol'shevikov v gody voiny, 1914–1917* (Leningrad, 1927), p. 60.

58. Ibid., p. 65; Iu. I. Korablev (ed), *Rabochee dvizhenie v Petrograd v gody novogo revoliutsionnogo pod"ema. 1912–1917gg. Dokumenty i materialy* (Leningrad, 1958), pp. 398, 403, 404; V. Bystrianskii, 'V nachale 1916 goda (iz dokumentov)', *Krasnaia letopis'*, no. 7 (1923), p. 210.

59. Korablev, *Rabochee dvizhenie*, op.cit., p. 437; f.102, DPOO., 1916g., d.5, ch.57, ll.10–11.

60. TsGIA, f.23, op.16, d.209, l.82; f.102, DP., 4 d-vo., 1916g., d.61, ch.2, lit.A, t.1, l.152.

61. f.102, DP., 4 d-vo., 1916g., d.61, ch.2, lit.A, t.1, l.86; Korablev, *Rabochee dvizhenie*, op.cit., pp. 435–6; Fleer, *Rabochee dvizhenie*, op.cit., pp. 256–7. The Stalinist history of the factory claims that the meeting passed a resolution embodying the Bolsheviks' slogans (M. I. Mitel'man, B. Glebov and A. Ulianskii, *Istoriia Putilovskogo zavoda*, Moscow, 1941, p. 446). The police report of the gathering is emphatic in its agent's assertion that no political speeches were made or resolutions passed (Korablev, *Rabochee dvizhenie*, op.cit., p. 436).

62. Korablev, *Rabochee dvizhenie*, op.cit., pp. 436, 439; Fleer, *Rabochee dvizhenie*, op.cit., pp. 263–4; Lemeshov, 'Na putilovskom zavode', op.cit., pp. 12–13.

63. TsGAOR, f.102, DP., 4 d-vo., 1916g., d.61, ch.2, lit.A, t.1, ll.121, 125, 123, 139, 153; TsGIA, f.23, op.16, d.209, l.88.

64. f.102, DPOO., 1916g., d.5, ch.57, ll.18–19; Bystrianskii, 'V nachale', op.cit., p. 209; *Listovki*, op.cit., pp. 202–3; Melancon, 'Socialist Revolutionaries', op.cit., p. 261. The PK leaflet once more made no reference to the war.

65. George Katkov, *Russia 1917. The February Revolution* (London, 1967), p. 96.

66. Z. A. B. Zeman and W. B. Scharlau, *The Merchant of Revolution. The Life of A. I. Helphand (Parvus), 1867–1924* (London, 1965), pp. 181, 188.

67. f.102, DPOO., 1916g., d.5, ch.57, ll.92–3. A judicious survey of the entire issue of the possible rela-

tionship between Russian revolutionaries and the German authorities during the war appears in: Alfred Erich Senn, 'The myth of German money during the First World War', *Soviet Studies*, vol. 28 (January 1976), pp. 83–90.

68. f.102, DPOO., 1916g., d.5, ch.57, ll.57, 91, 99. The close connection of the police agent Chernomazov with the PK facilitated the Okhrana's liquidations.

69. Kondrat'ev, 'Vospominaniia', op.cit., pp. 59–60; Lemeshov, 'Na putilovskom zavode', op.cit., pp. 18–21; Iu. Gavrilov, 'Na Vyborgskoi storone v 1914–1917gg.', *Krasnaia letopis'*, no. 23 (1927), pp. 45–9; *Peterburgskii komitet RSDRP. Protokoly i materialy zasedanii. Iiul' 1902–fevral' 1917* (Leningrad, 1986), pp. 460, 461, 462, 465.

70. f.102, DPOO., 1916g., d.5, ch.57, l.55.

71. Ibid., ch.57, ll.37, 55–6. On 4 April only 8,000 workers downed tools (f.102, DP., 4 d-vo., d.61, ch.2, lit.A, t.2, l.71).

72. S. Bogolepov, 'Zametki o "tekhnike" Peterburgskogo komiteta RSDRP (bol'shevikov) v 1915–1916gg. (po vospominaniiam)', *Krasnaia letopis'*, no. 10 (1924), pp. 143–6. It is an interesting comment on the state of the local party in the spring of 1916 that Chernomazov wrote most of the third issue of *Proletarskii golos*.

73. f.102, DPOO., 1916g. d.5, ch.57, ll.72–5.

74. 'Dokumenty biuro TsK RSDRP v Rossii, iiul' 1914–fevral' 1917gg.', *Voprosy istorii KPSS*, no. 8 (1965), pp. 79–80; Shliapnikov, *On the Eve*, op.cit., pp. 109, 115, 122.

75. Shliapnikov, *On the Eve*, op.cit., pp. 113, 115–16, 120; Olga Hess Gankin and H. H. Fisher, *The Bolsheviks and the World War. The Origin of the Third International* (Stanford, 1960), p. 239, note 156 (letter of Shliapnikov to Lenin, 11 March 1916).

76. N. Krupskaia, *Memories of Lenin* (London, 1970), pp. 275–9, 284.

77. f.102, DPOO., 1915g., d.347, l.44.

78. f.1405, op.530, d.1059, ll.34–8, 50–3.

79. f.102, DPOO., 1916g., d.5, ch.57, l.51.

80. O. A. Ermanskii, *Iz perezhitogo*

(1887--1921gg.) (Moscow, 1927), pp. 123–4.

81. f.102, DPOO., 1916g., d.5, ch.57, ll.28–35, 77, 125; ibid., d.347, t.1, ll.159, 241, 374; Ermanskii, *Iz perezhitogo*, op.cit., p. 134; Tsuyoshi Hasegawa, *The February Revolution: Petrograd, 1917* (Seattle, 1981), p. 133.

82. f.1405, op.530, d.1059, 1.92; f.102, DPOO., 1916g., d.5, ch.57, l.156; Hasegawa, *February Revolution*, op.cit., pp. 136–7; Melancon, 'Socialist Revolutionaries', op.cit., pp. 251, 253, 255, 264.

83. Abraham, *Alexander Kerensky*, op.cit., pp. 101–7; Melancon, 'Socialist Revolutionaries', op.cit., pp. 251–2.

84. f.102, DPOO., 1915g., d.5, ch.57, 1.189; I. Iurenev, '"Mezhraionka" (1911–1917gg.) (vospominaniia)', *Proletarskaia revoliutsiia*, vol. 24 (1924), pp. 116–7.

85. f.102, DPOO., 1916g., d.5, ch.57, 11.25, 35; Iurenev, '"Mezhraionka"' op.cit., vol. 25 (1924), pp. 117–23, 126.

86. Iurenev, '"Mezhraionka"' op.cit., pp. 123–4; Hasegawa, *February Revolution*, op.cit., p. 134.

87. *Istoriia rabochikh Leningrada*, op.cit., pp. 490, 497; Tiutiukin, *Voina*, op.cit., p. 216.

88. The major documents used in the following analysis are: the speeches and resolutions of the electoral assembly of 29 November 1915 (f.1405, op.530, d.1059, ll.80–6); Gvozdev's address to the TsVPK on 3 December 1915 (f.32, op.1, d.2120, ll.27–8); Gvozdev's reply to a letter from Guchkov, March 1916 (f.102, DPOO., 1916g., d.347, t.1, ll.180–1); Gvozdev's draft address, written by Bogdanov, to the visiting French socialist Minister of Munitions, Albert Thomas, April 1916 (f.102, DPOO., 1916g., d.347, t.8, ll.122–4).

89. f.102, DPOO., 1915g., d.347, ll.251, 254.

90. Ibid., ll.185–6; 1916g., d.347, t.1, l.334.

91. Ibid., 1915g., d.347, ll.220, 307.

92. Ibid., l.191; 1916g., d.347, t.1, l.109; V. V. Grave (ed.), *Burzhuaziia nakanune fevral'skoi revoliutsii* (Moscow, 1927), p. 95. Konovalov's role is described in Chapter 15.

93. I. A. Menitskii, 'K istorii "rabochei gruppy" pri tsentral'-nom voenno-promyshlennom komitete', *Krasnyi arkhiv*, vol. 2/57 (1933), p. 50.

94. f.102, DPOO., 1915g., d.347, ll.265, 279.

95. The Second All-Russian Congress of War-Industries Committees is discussed in Chapter 15.

96. Siegelbaum, *Politics*, op.cit., p. 173.

97. The reaction of industrialists and the authorities to the labour reforms of the TsVPK and the Labour Group is analysed in depth in Chapter 15.

98. The Labour Group's attitude towards strikes was set out in an appeal it published during the protest stoppages of 29 February–4 March 1916. (I. A. Menitskii, 'K istorii Gvozdevshchiny', *Krasnyi arkhiv*, vol. 7, no. 67 (1934), p. 53).

99. f.102, DPOO., 1914g., d.347, t.1, ll.240, 468–9.

100. f.1405, op.530, d.1060, l.91.

101. 'V ianvare i fevrale 1917g. Iz donesenii sekretnykh agentov A. D. Protopopova', *Byloe*, vol. 13 (1918), pp. 121–2; Grave, *Burzhuaziia*, op.cit., p. 170. The economic and social situation of the urban working class on the eve of the February revolution is examined in Chapter 11.

102. f.1405, op.530, d.1060, l.91; f.102, DPOO., 1916g., d.5, ch.57, ll.172, 187; Grave, *Burzhuaziia*, op.cit., p. 125. The high politics of 1916 has been well studied by several authors; Hasegawa, *February Revolution*, op.cit., Chapters 3, 9 and 10; Katkov, *Russia 1917*, op.cit.; Raymond Pearson, *The Russian Moderates and the Crisis of Tsarism, 1914–1917* (London, 1977); V. S. Diakin, *Russkaia burzhuaziia i tsarizm v gody pervoi mirovoi voiny* (Leningrad, 1967).

103. TsGAOR, f.102, DP., 4 d-vo., 1916g., d.61, ch.2, lit.A, t.4, 1.60; TsGIA, f.1405, op.530, d.1060, 1.92; *Listovki*, op.cit., p. 227.

104. *Istoriia rabochikh Leningrada*, op.cit., p. 501.

105. f.1405, op.530, d.1060, 1.92; *Listovki*, op.cit., pp. 225–6.

106. Menitskii, 'K istorii Gvozdevshchiny', op.cit., p. 86.

107. Korablev, *Rabochee dvizhenie*, op.cit., pp. 493, 503, 504.

108. TsGIA, f.1405, op.530, d.1060, ll.86, 87; TsGAOR, f.102, DPOO.,

1916g., d.5, ch.57, l.152; *Listovki*, op.cit., pp. 226–7. The Bolshevik leaflet curiously made no mention of the war nor did it advance as the slogan for the stoppage 'Down with the war'.

109. TsGAOR, f.102, DP., 4 d-vo., d.61, ch.2, lit.A, t.4, ll.117, 134, 147; TsGIA, f.1405, op.530, d.1060, l.90. I. P. Leiberov's assertion that the continuation of the strikes after 28 October compelled Khabalov to reopen the plants he had ordered closed is disproved by the sequence of events (*Istoriia rabochikh Leningrada*, op.cit., p. 503).

110. P.F.K., 'Peterburgskii komitet bol'shevikov v kontse 1916g. i v nachale 1917g. v osveshchenii okhranki', *Krasnaia letopis'*, no. 42 (1931), p. 33.

111. James D. White, 'The Sormovo-Nikolaev Zemlyachestvo in the February Revolution', *Soviet Studies*, vol. 31 (October 1979), pp. 475–88; I. Gordienko, *Iz boevogo proshlogo (1914–1918gg.)*, (Moscow, 1957), pp. 44–6. On the eve of the February revolution, two members of the *zemliachestvo* sat on the PK: I. D. Chugurin and A. K. Skorokhodov.

112. Shliapnikov, *On the Eve*, op.cit., pp. 140–1.

113. There are no contemporary estimates, by either the police or party activists, of party membership. The figure of 3,000 appears in Shliapnikov's memoirs (*On the Eve*, op.cit., p. 164). Over the years I. P. Leiberov has provided figures varying from 1,500 to 2,000 to 3,000. As no proper party records could be kept and as the definition of a party member was far from exact, the estimates must be treated with caution.

114. I. P. Leiberov, 'Petrogradskii proletariat v bor'be za pobedu fevral'skoi burzhuazno-demokraticheskoi revoliutsii v Rossii', *Istoriia SSSR*, no. 1 (1957), p. 48; *Ocherki istorii Leningradskoi organizatsii KPSS. 1883–1917* (Leningrad, 1980), p. 303; Kh. M. Astrakhan, 'O taktike "sniatiia s rabote" v Petrograde v pervye dni fevral'skoi revoliutsii 1917g.', in *Sverzhenie samoderzhaviia: sbornik statei* (Moscow, 1970), p. 123; *Peterburgskii komitet*, op.cit., p. 479. Other good examples of the numerical insignificance of Bolshevik party cells are at the Obukhov works (15 members in a labour force of 10,000 in 1917), the Russian-American Rubber plant (10 members out of 15,000), Erikson (14 members out of 2,▪▪nd Nobel' (9 of 1,500).

115. Shliapnikov, *On the Eve*, op.cit., pp. 141, 185, 187, 200; A. Shliapnikov, *Semnadtsatyi god. vol. I* (Moscow, 1923), pp. 50–2; f.102, DPOO., 1916g., d.5, ch.57, l.223.

116. *Ocherkii istorii*, op.cit., p. 309; Shliapnikov, *On the Eve, op.cit.*, pp. 177–8; *Letopis'*, no. 10 (October 1916), pp. 322–32; ibid., no. 1 (January 1917), pp. 286–95.

117. *Ocherki istorii*, op.cit., p. 309; Abraham, *Alexander Kerensky*, op.cit., p. 110; Melancon, 'Socialist Revolutionaries', op.cit., pp. 408–11.

118. P. Gooderham, 'The anarchist movement in Russia, 1905–1907' (Bristol, Ph.D., 1981), p. 230; P.K., 'V Petrograde nakanune fevral'skoi revoliutsii (v osveshchenii Petrogradskogo okhrannogo otdeleniia)', *Krasnaia letopis'*, no. 22 (1927), p. 45.

119. P.K., 'V Petrograde', op.cit., pp. 45–6; Iurenev, 'Mezhraionka', op.cit., *Proletarskaia revoliutsiia*, vol. 25 (1924), pp. 134–5.

120. f.102, DPOO., 1916g., d.5, ch.57, ll.177, 187; P.K., 'V Petrograde', op.cit., p. 46.

121. Shliapnikov, *On the Eve, op.cit.*, pp. 166–7, and *Semnadtsatyi god*, op.cit., pp. 42–4.

122. f.102, DPOO., 1916g., d.5, ch.57, l.177; E. Maevskii, *Kanun revoliutsii* (Petrograd, 1918), pp. 79–92; *Den'*, no. 284 (15 October 1916), p. 5; 'V ianvare', op.cit., p. 94.

123. *Birzhevye vedomosty*, no. 15911 (8 November 1916), p. 5; *Put'*, nos. 2–3 (10 December 1918), pp. 21–2; Grave, *Burzhuaziia*, op.cit., p. 170. 'Assistance groups' were established *inter alia* at Erikson, Petrograd Engineering, Petrograd Metals, Ordnance and San Galli.

124. *Den'*, no. 325 (25 November 1916), p. 6; no. 237 (27 November 1916), p. 6; no. 337 (7 December 1916), p. 3; Menitskii, 'K istorii Gvozdevshchiny', p. 90; *Russkoe slovo*, no. 272 (25 November 1916), p. 4. The factories selecting a delegation to Rodzianko were Erikson, Petrograd Metals, Putilov and Obukhov.

125. Shliapnikov, *Semnadtsatyi god*,

op.cit., pp. 17–18; f.102, DPOO., 1917g., d.5, ch.57, 1.5; 'Fevral'skaia revoliutsiia v dokumentakh', *Proletarskaia revoliutsiia*, vol. 1 (1923), pp. 25■ ■Melancon, 'Socialist Revolution ▼es', op.cit., pp. 412–13. Both the Mezhraionka and the Central Initiative Group leaflets contained the slogan 'Down with the war', The former set the goal of the revolution as a Provisional Revolutionary Government; the latter as a Constituent Assembly.

126. f.102, DPOO., 1917g., d.5, ch.57, 1.18; f.32, op.1, d.1885, 1.1.

127. f.1405, op.530, d.953, ll.30–1; d.1060, 1.20; 'Fevral'skaia revoliutsiia v dokumentakh', op.cit., pp. 269–71; 'V ianvare', op.cit., pp. 103–4, 109.

128. f.1405, op.530, d.1060, ll.20–1; 'Dokumenty biuro', op.cit., p. 81; Shliapnikov, *Semnadtsatyi god*, op.cit., pp. 27, 35–6; Fleer, *Peterburgskii komitet*, op.cit., p. 113. An excellent discussion of the reaction of the Bolsheviks to the Labour Group's initiative provided by D. A. Longley, 'the Mezhraionka, the Bosheviks and International Women's Day: in response to Michael Melancon', *Soviet Studies*, vol. 41 (October 1989), pp. 625–645.

129. PK, 'V Petrograde', op.cit., pp. 42–3; 'Fevral'skaia revoliutsiia v dokumentakh', op.cit., p. 279; f.1405, op.530, d.953, 1.39; Longley, '*the Mezhraionka*', op.cit., p. 630.

130. f.102, DPOO., 1916g., d.347, t.1, ll.242, 244; *Put'*, no. 4 (22 December 1916), p. 6; *Nashe pechatnoe delo*, no. 33 (6 July 1916), p. 7; no. 34 (23 August 1916), p. 11; Menitskii, 'K istorii "rabochei gruppy"', op.cit., p. 63; I. P. Leiberov, *Na shturm samoderzhaviia. Petrogradskii proletariat v gody pervoi mirovoi voiny i fevral'skoi revoliutsii (iiul' 1914–mart1917g.)*, (Moscow, 1979), p. 61.

131. f.23, op.16, d.15, ll.17–19.

132. The Bolshevik journal was managed during the war by Dr A. N. Vinokurov, K. Eremeev (who had edited the workers' chronicle section in *Pravda*), I. P. Sundukov (the secretary of the Putilov *kassa*)and the Poles R. Arskii (pseudonymn of A. T. Radzishevskii) and the engineer E. T. Faberkevich (R. Arskii, 'V Petrograde vo vremia voiny', *Krasnaia leto-*

pis', no. 7 (1923), p. 80). As before the war, Baturskii continued to edit the Menshevik insurance organ.

133. *Strakhovanie rabochikh*, no. 4 (April 1915), pp. 1–2; no. 10 (October 1915), p. 1; nos. 11–12 (November–December 1915), p. 6.

134. The *nakazy* differed only in that the Bolsheviks demanded the responsibility of the new Labour Group on the Insurance Council to 'the organised Marxists' (i.e. the PK), whilst the Mensheviks' formula was 'to the collective of the *kassy*' (*Voprosy strakhovaniia*, no. 1/50 (26 January 1916), p. 2; *Strakhovanie rabochikh*, nos. 1–2 (January–February 1916), pp. 5–7).

135. *Voprosy strakhovaniia*, no. 3/52 (16 March 1916), p. 3; *Strakhovanie rabochikh*, nos. 1–2 (January–February 1916), pp. 7–21; *Den'*, no. 33 (2 February 1916), p. 4; f.102, DPOO., 1916g., d.5, ch.57, ll.3, 28. Among the nine Bolsheviks elected were three members of the PK.

136. *Voprosy strakhovaniia*, no. 11/60 (13 November 1916), p. 2; *Strakhovanie rabochikh*, no. 9 (1916), pp. 3–4, 27.

137. *Strakhovanie rabochikh*, no. 10 (1916), pp. 15–17; *Voprosy strakhovaniia*, no. 12/61 (19 December 1916), p. 13; *Den'*, no. 301 (November 1916), p. 5.

138. S. Milligan, 'The Petrograd Bolsheviks and social insurance, 1914–1917', *Soviet Studies*, vol. 20 (January 1969), pp. 369–74.

139. Arskii, 'V Petrograde', op.cit., p. 80.

140. Shliapnikov, *On the Eve, op.cit.*, pp. 104–8, 220–1; *Peterburgskii komitet*, op.cit., pp. 457–58.

141. f.102, DPOO., 1916g., d.5, ch.57, 1.113. The Putilov *kassa* provided the most spectacular example of this practice; at least thirteen Bolshevik activists were employed by it during the war.

142. It may be significant that nine of the twenty-nine were employed at New Lessner engineering in Vyborg.

Chapter 14

1. M. G. Fleer, *Rabochee dvizhenie v gody voiny* (Moscow, 1925), pp. 66, 76.

2. The figures for the Empire are calculated from the unpublished monthly reports of the factory inspectorate returned to the Ministry of Trade and

Industry (copies held in the archives of the Ministry of Justice, TsGIA, f.1405, op.530, d.1061 and d.1062). During the war, publication of the annual *Svody otchetov fabrichnykh inspektorov* was suspended. In 1925 Fleer published these reports in the book mentioned in note 1, but the versions in his work are significantly curtailed summaries of the originals in the archives.

3. As with Chapter 8, the deficiencies of the official estimates of the strike movement made by the factory inspectorate (see Chapter 8, note 23) have driven the author once more to compile his own statistical data for the period 19 July 1914–22 February 1917. As well as utilising the unpublished reports of the capital's factory inspectors and the agents of the Okhrana, the files of the Petrograd Society of Mill and Factory Owners and the Central War-Industries Committee were consulted. The demise of the socialist and trade-union press during the war has deprived the researcher of much valuable material, in particular with regard to possible disputes in petty factory and artisanal establishments. The author's calculations once more confirm the serious underestimation of the dimensions of unrest on the part of the authorities. On the other hand they differ to some extent from I. P. Leiberov's slightly higher estimates. Of previous investigators I. I. Krylova's statistical conclusions come closest to those set out in this chapter (see note 4).

4. I. I. Krylova, 'K voprosu o statistike stachek Petrogradskikh rabochikh v gody pervoi mirovoi voiny', in *Iz istorii imperializma v Rossii* (Moscow, 1959), p. 414; I. P. Leiberov, 'Stachechnaia bor'ba Petrogradskogo proletariata v period pervoi mirovoi voiny (19 iiulia 1914g.–16 fevralia 1917g.)', in *Istoriia rabochego klassa Leningrada*, vol. 2 (Leningrad, 1963), p. 156.

5. As the factory inspectors and the police ignored most artisanal workshops and petty establishments in compiling their surveys, the researcher must exercise caution in assuming that the incidence of unrest in these sectors was completely minimal. It may have been, but the concrete evidence is lacking.

6. In this chapter the author has again used as the basis for analysis the criteria for political stoppages adopted by the factory inspectorate. A list of all mass demonstrative strikes in Petrograd between 19 July 1914 and 22 February 1917 is contained in Appendix II.

7. The five mass political stoppages lasting 3–4 days were: 17–20 August 1915; 2–6 September 1915; 29 February–4 March 1916; 17–21 October 1916; 26 October–1 November 1916. The three of one day's duration were 9 January 1916; 9 January 1917; 14–15 February 1917.

8. M. S. Balabanov, *Ot 1905 k 1917 godu; massovoe rabochee dvizhenie* (Moscow, 1927), p. 337.

9. In the eight mass political strikes during the war the share contributed by metalworkers never fell below 83 per cent. In the first political walk-out, 17–20 August 1915, only workers in engineering were involved. In the protests of 29 February–4 March 1916, 99 per cent of participants likewise came from this sector.

10. The list included Diuflon (800 operatives in January 1917), Dinamo (2,100), Langenzippen (1,600), Old Lessner (1,100), Nobel' (1,500), Petrograd Engineering (1,000), Petrograd Wagons (2,000), Phoenix (1,900), Russian Renault (1,600), Semenov (705), Siemens-Schukkert (1,000), Stetinin (2,100) and Westing-house (415).

11. The ten comprised: Aivaz (4,000), Baranovskii (3,200), Franco-Russian (6,600), Erikson (2,200), New Lessner (6,500), Neva Shipyards (6,000), Promet (2,900), Putilov Shipyards (4,100), Rosenkrants (3,700) and the Russian Society (4,000).

12. Among the fifteen were: Ekval' (300), Glazunov (100), Ouf (260), Petrograd Armature Electrical (200), Puzyrev (220), Reikhel' (250), Russian Baltic Motor (370), Russian Society of Wireless Telegraphy and Telephones (490) and Vegman (100).

13. f.1405, op.530, d.1061 and d.1062.

14. Balabanov, *Ot 1905*, op.cit., p. 340.

15. In their analysis of wartime disputes Soviet historians such as Leiberov, following Lenin's analytical practice, split the category 'compromise settlements' into two equal halves, redistributing one half to the workers as their

victories and one to the employers (Leiberov, 'Stachechnaia bor'ba',
op.cit., p. 168). This is an illogical
practice as the essence of a compromise
agreement is mutual concessions
on the part of both parties. In the case
of Leiberov it has led him to exaggerate
the extent of strikers' success.

16. For the categories used in this section,
see Chapter 8, note 72.
17. Balabanov, *Ot 1905*, op.cit., p. 339.
18. f.1405, op.530, d.1061, l.48.
19. The same subdivisions of the rubric
'authority strikes' are employed in this
section as in Chapter 8 (see Table
8.xxv).
20. TsGAOR, f.102, DP., 4 d-vo.,
1915g., d.61, ch.2, tom 1, lit.A, l.44;
f.23, op.16, d.209, l.18.
21. Theodore Steffens, *Die Arbeiter von
Petersburg 1907 bis 1917. Soziale Lage,
Organisation und Spontaner Protest zwischen
zwei Revoliutionen* (Freiburg,
1985), p. 517.
22. f.102, DP., 4 d-vo., 1915g., d.61,
ch.2, tom 1, lit.A, l.20; 1916g., d.61,
ch.2, tom 4, lit.A, l.71.
23. According to the author's estimates
the period January 1912 to 3 July 1914
in St Petersburg witnessed 3,912
strikes and 1,746,426 strikers. In contrast
the thirty months after the outbreak
of war in Petrograd recorded
791 strikes and 965,480 strikers.

Chapter 15

1. Several good studies have been devoted
to the Moscow Progressist
bourgeoisie and the Moscow industrial
world in general. These include:
Thomas Owen, *Capitalism and Politics
in Russia. A Social History of the Moscow
Merchants, 1855–1905* (Cambridge,
Mass., 1980); Alfred J. Rieber,
*Merchants and Entrepreneurs in Imperial
Russia* (Chapel Hill, N. Carolina,
1982); J. L. West, 'The Moscow Progressists:
Russian industrialists in liberal
politics, 1905–1914' (Princeton,
Ph.D., 1975); Robert W. Thurston,
*Liberal City, Conservative State. Moscow
and Russia's Urban Crisis, 1906–
1914* (New York, 1987).
2. T. D. Krupina, 'Politicheskii krizis
1915g. i sozdanie osobogo soveshchania
po oborone', *Istoricheskie zapiski*,
vol. 83 (1969), p. 64; S. A. Somov, 'O
"maiskom" osobom soveshchanii',
Istoriia SSSR, vol. 3 (1973), pp. 118–
19.

The representatives of the Petrograd
business world on the Special Council
were the bankers A. I. Putilov (chairman
of the board of the Russo-Asiatic
Bank), A. I. Vyshnegradskii (Petrograd
International Commercial Bank),
Ia. I. Utin (Petrograd Loan and Discount
Bank) and several managing
directors of leading industrial concerns.
Together they constituted the
Putilov and Tsaritsyn armament
groups.

3. *Den'*, no. 143 (27 May 1915), p. 3; no.
144 (28 May 1915), p. 2; no. 145 (29
May 1915), p. 2; *Russkie vedomosty*,
no. 120 (27 May 1915), p. 3; no. 121
(28 May 1915), p. 3; no. 122 (29 May
1915), p. 3; *Gorno-zavodskoe delo*, no.
25 (22 June 1915), pp. 11269–76;
Promyshlennost' i torgovlia, no. 11/179
(1 June 1915), pp. 542–4.
4. TsGIA, f.32, op.1, d.1983, l.7.
5. *Promyshlennaia Rossiia*, nos. 6–7 (31
May 1915), pp. 1–2; Nos. 10–11 (28
June 1915), pp. 1–3.
6. *Trudy s''ezda predstavitelei voenno-
promyshlennykh komitetov, 25–27 iuliia
1915g.* (Petrograd, 1915), pp. 279–88;
Den', no. 203 (26 July 1915), p. 1.
7. f.32, op.1, d.1983, l.23.
8. The earlier career of Guchkov may be
traced in several works in English:
Geoffrey Hosking, *The Russian Constitutional
Experiment, 1907–1914* (Cambridge,
1973); Ben C. Pinchuk, *The
Octobrists in the Third Duma, 1907–
1912* (Seattle, 1974); M. C. Brainerd,
'The Octobrists and the gentry in the
Russian social crisis of 1913–1914',
Russian Review, vol. 38 (April 1979),
pp. 160–79.
9. *Trudy s''ezda*, op.cit., pp. 4–5, 154,
214, 224.
10. Ibid., pp. 32–6, 64–5, 111–51, 231.
11. Ibid., pp. 256–7.
12. This examination of the power structure
of the Bureau of the TsVPK is
based on the protocols of the Bureau
in the archives of the AIT; f.32, op.1,
d.1976 to 1979.
13. As the main focus of attention in this
chapter is on the Petrograd industrialists,
the wartime political activities of
the TsVPK have not been investigated.
Three excellent studies of this
aspect of the TsVPK are: D. S. Diakin,
*Russkaia burzhuaziia i tsarizm v
gody pervoi mirovoi voiny (1914–1917)*
(Leningrad, 1976); Ray Pearson, *The
Russian Moderates and the Crisis of Tsar-*

ism, 1914–1917 (London, 1977); Lewis H. Siegelbaum, *The Politics of Industrial Mobilization in Russia, 1914–1917. A Study of the War-Industries Committees* (London, 1983).

14. TsGIA, f.150, op.1, d.60, ll.245, 249.
15. *Deiatel'nost' oblastnykh i mestnykh voenno-promyshlennikh komitetov na 10oe fevral'ia 1916g. Chast' I* (Petrograd, 1916), p. 105; *Promyshlennost' i torgovlia*, no. 19/186 (29 August 1915), p. 220; no. 29/126 (7 November 1915), p. 572.
16. *Trudy pervogo s"ezda predstavitelei metalloobratyvaiushchei promyshlennosti. 29go fevral'ia–1go marta, 1916 goda* (Petrograd, 1916), pp. 5–10, 20–8, 31–9, 41–2, 85, 103, 110.
17. Siegelbaum, *Politics*, op.cit., pp. 85–120; A. G. Pogrebinskii, 'Voenno-promyshlennye komitety', *Istoricheskie zapiski*, vol. 11 (1941), p. 167.
18. *Promyshlennost' i torgovlia*, nos. 36–7/231 (17 September 1916), pp. 212–13.
19. The origins of the Special Council for Defence are not the concern of this study. The works already cited, by Diakin, Krupina, Pearson, Siegelbaum and Somov all furnish a reliable guide to this topic.
20. *Izvestiia vserossiiskogo soiuza gordov*, no. 21–2 (15 December 1915), pp. 3–4.
21. *Promyshlennost' i torgovlia*, no. 17/84 (15 August 1915), pp. 139–41; S. V. Voronkova, *Materialy osobogo soveshchaniia po oborone gosudarstva. Istochnikovedchesko issledovanie* (Moscow, 1975), pp. 38, 40, 41, 49–50.
22. *Promyshlennost' i torgovlia*, no. 27/194 (24 October 1915), p. 507; Voronkova, *Materialy*, op.cit., pp. 60–2.
23. *Trudy s"ezda*, op.cit., pp. 111–13, 231, 238, 241–2; *Den'*, no. 205 (28 June 1915), p. 3.
24. TsGAOR, f.102, DPOO., 1916g., d.347, tom 1, l.320.
25. Robert B. McKean, 'Russia on the eve of the Great War. Revolution or evolution?' (East Anglia, Ph.D., 1971), p. 141–4.
26. f.32, op.1, d.1983, ll.33, 36; d.1976, l.25; *Utro*, no. 2 (9 August 1915), p. 3. The actual elections to the TsVPK and the Petrograd Regional War-Industries Committee, as well as the response of the revolutionary parties and ordinary workers, are analysed in Chapter 13.
27. f.32, op.1, d.1983, l.83; d.1976, l.279;

d.1977, ll.83, 94, 96; I. A. Menitskii, 'K istorii Gvozdevshchiny', *Krasnyi arkhiv*, vol. 7/67 (1934), pp. 49–50.
28. f.32, op.1, d.1977, ll.140, 156; Menitskii, 'K istorii Gvozdevshchiny', op.cit., p. 62.
29. *Izvestiia Moskovskogo voenno-promyshlennogo komiteta*, no. 13 (January 1916), pp. 47–51; no. 14 (January 1916), pp. 50–5; no. 15–16 (February 1916), p. 103; *Russkoe slovo*, no. 7 (10 January 1916), p. 4.
30. f.32, op.1, d.2124, ll.2; *Izvestiia Moskovskogo voenno-promyshlennogo komiteta*, nos. 6–7 (October 1915), p. 1.
31. The Soviet point of view finds clear expression in Pogrebinskii, 'Voenno-promyshlennye komitety', op.cit., p. 189; S. V. Tiutiukin, *Voina, mir, revoliutsiia: Ideinaia bor'ba v rabochem dvizhenii Rossii, 1914–1917gg.* (Moscow, 1972), p. 205.
32. *Izvestiia Moskovskogo voenno-promyshlennogo komiteta*, nos. 23–4 (June 1916), pp. 4–8; I. A. Menitskii, 'K istorii "rabochei gruppy" pri tsentral'nom voenno-promyshlennom komitete', *Krasnyi arkhiv*, vol. 2/57 (1933), pp. 72–84.
33. V. V. Grave (ed.), *Burzhuaziia nakanune fevral'skoi revoliutsii* (Moscow, 1927), pp. 93–6. None of these grandiose plans were ever successfully implemented, in part due to preventive action by the Okhrana, in part to the hostility of the majority of industrialists and agrarians to the political motives of the initiators of the projects and the opposition of most Kadets themselves.
34. *Strakhovanie rabochikh*, no. 6 (June 1915), p. 1.
35. f.32, op.1, d.1983, ll.89, 101; d.2120, l.52; d.1877, l.46; *Russkoe slovo*, no. 3 (5 January 1916), p. 3.
36. f.32, op.1, d.1977, ll.122, 152; *Den'*, no. 98 (9 April 1916), p. 2; *Izvestiia Moskovskogo voenno-promyshlennogo komiteta*, nos. 19–20 (April 1916), p. 231; *Trudy vtorogo s"ezda predstavitelei voenno-promyshlennikh komitetov, 26–29 fevral'ia 1916g.* (Petrograd, 1916), p. 633.
37. *Izvestiia tsentral'nogo voenno-promyshlennogo komiteta*, no. 52 (23 January 1916), p. 4; *Trudy vtorogo s"ezda*, op.cit., pp. 282–9, 334–47, 363–4, 372, 629.
38. *Russkoe slovo*, no. 179 (3 August 1916), p. 4; *Izvestiia tsentral'nogo voenno-*

promyshlennogo komiteta, no. 136 (23 August 1916), p. 1.

39. *Zhurnaly osobogo soveshchaniia po oborone gosudarstva 1915 god. Chast' II*, (repr., Moscow, 1975), pp. 485–6; f.32, op.1, d.1983, l.156; *Den'*, no. 346 (16 December 1915), p. 5; no. 4 (5 January 1916), p. 5; *Trudy vtorogo s"ezda*, op.cit., pp. 303–8, 538–44, 630.

40. f.32, op.1, d.1983, ll.112, 158; d.1978, ll.36, 61; d.1977, l.108; *Izvestiia tsentral'nogo voenno-promyshlennogo komiteta*, no. 77 (29 March 1916), p. 4; no. 119 (13 July 1916), p. 2–3; no. 136 (23 August 1916), p. 1.

41. *Trudy vtorogo s"ezda*, op.cit., pp. 556, 634; *Den'*, no. 184 (7 July 1916), p. 2; f.32, op.1, d.1978, l.53.

42. *Trudy s"ezda*, op.cit., pp. 192–6, 198; *Trudy vtorogo s"ezda*, op.cit., pp. 287, 633; *Promyshlennost' i torgovlia*, no. 16/183 (8 August 1915), p. 131; *Izvestiia tsentral'nogo voenno-promyshlennogo komiteta*, no. 1 (24 August 1915), p. 5; *Izvestiia Moskovskogo voenno-promyshlennogo komiteta*, nos. 19–20 (April 1916), p. 3; Menitskii, 'K istorii "rabochei gruppy"', op.cit., pp. 78–80; f.102, DPOO., 1916g., d.347, tom 8, l.373.

43. f.150, op.1, d.60, ll.201, 271; d.206, l.45.

44. f.150, op.1, d.64, ll.20, 24–5, 35–6, 40–3; *Trudy vtorogo s"ezda*, op.cit., pp. 312, 314, 322–3.

45. f.150, op.1, d.64, ll.103, 107; *Izvestiia Moskovskogo voenno-promyshlennogo komiteta*, nos. 27–30 (August–September 1916), p. 194; *Russkoe slovo*, no. 183 (9 August 1916), p. 5; no. 212 (4 September 1916), p. 5.

46. f.150, op.1, d.64, ll.16, 45, 97; *Izvestiia Moskovskogo voenno-promyshlennogo komiteta*, nos. 23–4 (June 1916), p. 177; *Izvestiia tsentral'nogo voenno-promyshlennogo komiteta*, no. 161 (25 October 1916), p. 4; *Den'*, no. 54 (25 February 1916), p. 5; *Put'*, no. 1 (10 October 1916), p. 19.

47. f.150, op.2, d.77, ll.77–9.

48. Ibid., op.1, d.60, l.231; d.64, ll.98–9; d.635, l.41.

49. Ibid., op.1, d.635, ll.36^a–36^b, 44; d.64, ll.37–8.

50. TsGIA, f.1278, op.5, d.1042, l.2; TsGAOR, f.102, DP., 4 d-vo., 1916g., d.61, ch.2, lit.A, tom 2, l.122; tom 1, l.162.

51. f.150, op.1, d.673, ll.14, 16, 18–19; op.2, d.77, ll.73–4; TsGAOR, f.102,

DP., 4 d-vo., 1915g., ch.2, lit.A, ll.73, 86.

52. TsGIA, f.1405, op.530, d.1061, l.147; f.150, op.2., d.77, ll.87–90, 96–8; *Zhurnaly*, op.cit., *1915 god. Chast' I*, (Moscow, 1975), p. 205.

53. See Appendix II.

54. f.150, op.1, d.60, ll.265–6; d.671, l.40^B; *Den'*, no. 244 (5 September 1915), p. 4.

55. TsGIA, f.150, op.1, d.64, ll.6, 139–40; TsGAOR, f.102, DP., 4 d-vo., 1916g., d.61, ch.2, lit.A, tom 4, ll.69, 75–6, 82.

56. f.150, op.1, d.206, l.19; op.2, d.77, ll.73–4, 82, 85; *Utro*, no. 2 (19 August 1915), p. 4; V. V. Grave, 'Militarizatsiia promyshlennosti i rossiiskii proletariat v gody pervoi mirovoi voiny', in *Iz istorii rabochego klassa i revoliutsionnogo dvizheniia. Sbornik statei* (Moscow, 1958), p. 420.

57. TsGAOR, f.102, DP., 4 d-vo., 1915g., d.61, ch.2, lit.A, l.101; TsGIA, f.150, op.1, d.60, l.254; *Zhurnaly*, op.cit., *1916 god. Chast'I* (Moscow, 1977), pp. 149–50; V. Ia Laverychev, *Tsarizm i rabochii vopros v Rossii (1861–1917gg.)* (Moscow, 1972), p. 287.

58. The works cited in note 13 by Diakin, Pearson and Siegelbaum offer reliable accounts of the political crisis of the summer of 1915.

59. M. Cherniavsky, *Prologue to Revolution. Notes of A. N. Iakhontov on the Secret Meetings of the Council of Ministers, 1915* (Englewood Cliffs, New Jersey, 1967), pp. 44–5, 89, 173; Prince V. N. Shakhovskoi, 'Sic transit gloria mundi' (*Tak prokhodit mirskaia slava), 1893–1917gg*. (Paris, 1952), pp. 100–2; A. A. Polivanov, *Iz dnevnikov i vospominanii po dolzhnosti voennogo ministra i ego pomoshchnika* (Moscow, 1924), pp. 204, 206.

60. Cherniavsky, *Prologue*, op.cit., pp. 196–7.

61. *Den'*, no. 2 (3 January 1916), p. 5; no. 116 (29 April 1916), p. 4; no. 122 (5 May 1916), p. 4; no. 131 (14 May 1916), p. 4; no. 172 (25 June 1916), p. 3; *Nashe pechatnoe delo*, no. 34 (23 August 1916), p. 1; *Put'*, no. 4 (22 December 1916), p. 6; *Zhizn' farmatsevta*, nos. 7–8 (28–29) (July–September 1916), p. 4.

62. TsGIA, f.1276, op.10, d.131, ll.2–3, 5–6; 'Soveshchanie gubernatorov v 1916 godu', *Krasnyi arkhiv*, no. 2/33 (1929), p. 153.

63. This aspect of the regime's attitude to the TsVPK has not been explored in depth in this chapter. It can be studied with profit in the earlier cited works by Diakin and Siegelbaum.

64. *Den'*, no. 70 (12 March 1916), p. 4; *Izvestiia tsentral'nogo voenno-promyshlennogo komiteta*, no. 77 (29 March 1916), p. 4; *Izvestiia Moskovskogo voenno-promyshlennogo komiteta*, nos. 19–20 (April 1916), p. 234.

65. TsGAOR, f.102, DP., 4 d-vo., 1915g., d.61, ch.2, lit.A, l.78; TsGAOR, f.102, DPOO., 1915g., d.341, l.51; Laverychev, *Tsarizm*, op.cit., pp. 272–3.

66. f.1405, op.530, d.906, l.43; Menitskii, 'K istorii Gvozdevshchiny', op.cit., p. 45; f.102, DP., 4 d-vo., d.61, ch.2, lit.A, tom 4, ll.121, 147.

67. f.DP., 4 d-vo., 1915g., d.61, ch.2, lit.A, ll.156, 158; f.102, DPOO., 1915g., d.347, tom 2, ll.290–1; TsGIA, f.23, op.27, d.377, ll.117–18, Laverychev, *Tsarizm*, op.cit., pp. 279–80, 287, 290–1.

68. *Zhurnaly*, op.cit., *1916 god. Chast' II*, pp. 281–6.

69. Cherniavsky, *Prologue*, op.cit., p. 146.

70. *Izvestiia Moskovskogo voenno-promyshlennogo komiteta*, nos. 25–26 (July 1916), p. 214.

71. f.102, DPOO., 1915g., d.341, 11.51, 163.

72. Cherniavsky, *Prologue*, op.cit., pp. 196, 233; *Izvestiia Moskovskogo voenno-promyshlennogo komiteta*, nos. 19–20 (April 1916), p. 234.

73. *Den'*, no. 193 (16 July 1915), p. 3; no. 221 (13 August 1915), p. 4; *Russkoe slovo*, no. 195 (24 August 1916), p. 3; *Put'*, no. 1 (10 October 1916), pp. 13–14.

74. f.23, op.9, d.317, 1.11; d.320, 11.2–7, 212; Shakhovskoi, 'Sic transit gloria mundi', op.cit., pp. 69–70; Laverychev, *Tsarizm*, op.cit., pp. 295–6.

75. *Den'*, no. 156 (9 June 1916), p. 3; no. 284 (15 October 1916), pp. 4–5; *Izvestiia tsentral'nogo voenno-promyshlennogo komiteta*, no. 141 (6 September 1916); *Put'*, nos. 2–3 (10 December 1916), pp. 9–11; Laverychev, *Tsarizm*, op.cit., p. 308.

76. *Zhurnaly*, op.cit., *1915 god. Chast' I*, pp. 100–2; *Chast' II*, p. 485; *Den'*, no. 53 (24 February 1916), p. 3.

77. M. S. Balabanov, *Ot 1905 k 1917 godu; massovoe rabochee dvizhenie* (Moscow, 1927), p. 395.

Epilogue

1. The five volumes devoted to the February revolution are: E. N. Burdzhalov, *Vtoraia russkaia revoliutsiia: vosstanie v Petrograde* (Moscow, 1967); Tsuyoshi Hasegawa, *The February Revolution: Petrograd, 1917* (Seattle, 1981); George Katkov, *Russia 1917. The February Revolution* (London, 1967); I. P. Leiberov, *Na shturm samoderzhaviia. Petrogradskii proletariat v gody pervoi mirovoi voiny i fevral'skoi revoliutsii (iiul' 1914–mart 1917g.)* (Moscow, 1979); I. I. Mints, *Istoriia velikogo oktiabria. Tom 1. Sverzhenie samoderzhaviia* (Moscow, 1967). This survey of the February revolution and the part played therein by the revolutionary and labour organisations has been restricted to the events of 23–26 February, partly on the grounds that this study is concerned with the labour movement during the last ten years of Tsardom and partly because the creation of the new regime between 27 February and 2 March (the Petrograd Soviet of Workers' and Soldiers' Deputies and the Provisional Government) belongs to the history of the 1917 revolution proper.

2. As in Chapters 8 and 14, the author has calculated his own estimates of the Petrograd strike movement during the February revolution. The main sources were the factory inspectorate reports (TsGIA, f.23, op.16, d.253, ll.1–118) and the memoranda of the police (TsGIA, f.1282, op.1., d.741). Apart from Leiberov, the character of the February stoppages has strangely received minimal attention from researchers.

3. Among the state-owned plants which struck were: Admiralty Shipyards (4,600), the Arsenal (5,000), Baltic Shipyards (8,200), Obukhov (10,600), Okhta Explosives (10,500), Ordnance (3,500), Petrograd Cartridge (8,200), Petrograd Pipes (19,000).

4. f.1282, op.1, d.741, ll.18, 34, 101, 154; Burdzhalov, *Vtoraia russkaia revoliutsiia*, op.cit., pp. 144–6; A. Shliapnikov, *Semnadtsatyi god. Tom I* (Moscow, 1923), p. 101.

5. f.1282, op.1, d.741, ll.134, 136, 137–8, 141.

6. Ibid., ll.23–4, 38–40; 'Fevral'skaia revoliutsiia i okhrannoe otdelenie', *Byloe*, vol. 29, no. 1 (1918), pp. 161, 166.

7. f.1282, op.1, d.741, ll.83, 85, 89, 91; TsGAOR, f.102, DPOO., 1917g., d.5, ch.57, ll.45, 48; Shliapnikov, *Semnadtsatyi god*, op.cit., pp. 105–6. More detailed accounts of working-class demonstrations and the ensuing clashes with the police and troops are provided by Burdzhalov, Hasegawa and Leiberov (see note 1).

8. 'Fevral'skaia revoliutsiia', op.cit., p. 163.

9. All calculations in this paragraph are those of the author, based on the unpublished and published police archives. As the police's information gathering and reporting began to break down from 25 February, the cases recorded are almost certainly underestimates.

10. f.1282, op.1, d.741, ll.24, 34, 58.

11. Leiberov argues that those guilty of plundering stores were 'backward' workers. Whilst it is true that many participants were women and youths, it would be more accurate to say that such events were highly localised phenomena. Shops were ransacked by those living in adjacent flats (I. P. Leiberov 'Vtoroi den' fevral'skoi revoliutsii (sobytiia 24 fevralia 1917g. v Petrograde', in *Sverzhenie samoderzhaviia. Sbornik statei* (Moscow, 1970), p. 108; f.1282, op.1, d.741, l.31).

12. 'Fevral'skaia revoliutsiia', op.cit., p. 174; N. N. Sukhanov, *The Russian Revolution. 1917. A Personal Record*, trans. Joel Carmichael (Princeton, 1983), p. 16; Claude Anet, *Through the Russian Revolution: Notes of an Eyewitness, from 12th March–30th May* (London, 1917), p. 14.

13. It would be wrong to conclude from the various instances of worker resistance to the police, as Leiberov does, that on 25 February an armed uprising had begun (Leiberov, *Na shturm*, op.cit., p. 163). Such events were in fact isolated occurrences; on each occasion only individual pistol shots were heard. The workers were still totally unarmed.

14. f.102, DPOO., 1917g., d.341, ch.57, l.46; Shliapnikov, *Semnadtsatyi god*, op.cit., p. 112.

15. TsGIA., f.1278, op.10, d.1917g., d.10, l.44.

16. Alan K. Wildman, *The End of the Russian Imperial Army. The Old Army and the Soldiers' Revolt (March–April 1917)* (Princeton, 1980), pp. 124–5.

17. Sukhanov, *Russian Revolution*, op.cit., p. 6.

18. Shliapnikov, *Semnadtsatyi god*, op.cit., p. 82; f.1282, op.1, d.741, l.153; "Fevral'skaia revoliutsiia', op.cit., p. 171. All these incidents involved Don Cossack regiments, which had just been transferred to Petrograd from the northern front. (Wildman, *Russian Imperial Army*, op.cit., p. 126).

19. f.1282, op.1, d.741, l.72.

20. Ibid., ll.83, 91.

21. f.102, DPOO., 1917g., d.341, ch.57, l.98; Shliapnikov, *Semnadtsatyi god*, op.cit., pp. 98, 100.

22. The economic situation of Petrograd in 1916–17 is analysed in Chapter 11.

23. V. V. Grave (ed.), *Burzhuaziia nakanune fevral'skoi revoliutsii* (Moscow, 1927), pp. 125–6, 161–3, 169–75.

24. 'Fevral'skaia revoliutsiia v dokumentakh', *Proletarskaia revoliutsiia*, vol. 1 (1923), p. 296; Sir Alfred Knox, *With the Russian Army, 1914–1917: Being Chiefly Extracts from the Diary of a Military Attaché. Volume II* (London, 1921), p. 529. The Kadet newspaper also reported that Petrograd had on hand a million *puds* of flour (*Rech'*, no. 53 (25 February 1917), p. 6).

25. Knox, *With the Russan Army*, op.cit., p. 529; f.1282, op.1, d.741, l.114.

26. 'V ianvare i fevrale 1917g. Iz donesenii sekretnykh agentov A. D. Protopopova', *Byloe*, vol. 13 (1918), pp. 121–2; Anet, *Though the Russian Revolution*, op.cit., p. 9.

27. f.102, DPOO., 1917g., d.341, ch.57, l.99.

28. f.1282, op.1, d.741, l.133.

29. Ibid., ll.38, 83, 126, 134; Shliapnikov, *Semnadtsatyi god*, op.cit., pp. 75, 82, 83, 96.

30. The Soviet researcher Kh. M. Astrakhan furnishes a figure of 37 instances; Kh. M. Astrakhan, 'O taktike "sniatiia c rabote" v Petrograde v pervye dni fevral'skoi revoliutsii 1917g.', in *Sverzhenie samoderzhaviia. Sbornik statei* (Moscow, 1970), p. 121.

31. f.1282, op.1, d.741, ll.52, 105, 111, 121, 137, 162.

32. TsGIA., f.1405, op.530, d.953, l.46.

33. James D. White, 'Early Soviet historical interpretations of the Russian Revolution 1918–1924', *Soviet Studies*, vol. 37 (July 1985), pp. 330–52; Leon Trotsky, *The History of the Russian Revolution. Volume I* (London, 1967), p. 154.

34. William Henry Chamberlin, *The Rus-

sian Revolution 1917–1921. Volume One (New York, 1965), p. 73; Hasegawa, *February Revolution*, op.cit.

35. The surviving Okhrana files, which are available in the archives or have been published, are mostly devoted to the strike movement of 23–26 February. There is little information in them on the revolutionary organisations as such. It is possible that, for political and ideological reasons, archival material has been withheld from scholars.

36. 'Fevral'skaia revoliutsiia', op.cit., p. 173.

37. V. Kaiurov, 'Shest' dnei fevral'skoi revoliutsii', *Proletarskaia revoliutsiia*, vol. 1 (1923), p. 158; Shliapnikov, *Semnadtsatyi god*, op.cit., pp. 60–1.

38. 'Fevral'skaia revoliutsiia', op.cit., p. 162; 'Fevral'skaia revoliutsiia v dokumentakh', op.cit., pp. 283–4. It is not inconceivable that Soviet compilers, embarrassed by the implications of the leaflet's contents, have doctored it. On the other hand the memoirs of the Mezhraionka leader, Iurenev, describe the proclamation as merely calling upon workers and soldiers to struggle against Tsardom. (I. Iurenev, '"Mezhraionka" (1911–1917gg.) (vospominaniia)', *Proletarskaia revoliutsiia*, vol. 24 (1924), p. 139).

39. Michael S. Melancon, 'The Socialist Revolutionaries from 1902 to February 1917: a party of the workers, peasants and soldiers' (Indiana, Ph.D., 1984), p. 467.

40. Sukhanov, *Russian Revolution*, op.cit., p. 11.

41. Kaiurov, 'Shest' dnei', op.cit., p. 158. This account furnishes a classic example of the probable retrospective exaggeration of their role in the reminiscences of Bolshevik activists. Kaiurov claims that the initiative for the Erikson walk-out emanated exclusively from himself.

42. Factories where the left revolutionary collectives co-operated included Aivaz, Erikson, Obukhov, Okhta Explosives, Okhta Gunpowder, Putilov, Siemens and Halske, and Siemens-Schukkert (Leiberov, *Na shturm*, op.cit., pp. 168, 171; Leiberov, 'Vtoroi den'', op.cit., p. 105).

43. 'Fevral'skaia revoliutsiia', op.cit., p. 174; f.1282, op.1, d.741, l.118.

44. Shliapnikov, *Semnadtsatyi god*, op.cit., p. 74.

45. Ibid., p. 83; 'Fevral'skaia revoliutsiia v dokumentakh', op.cit., pp. 284–5.

46. The fate of the 'PK' (Russian Bureau) leaflet is a matter of dispute among historians. Soviet scholars such as Burdzhalov, Leiberov and Mints state that the leaflet was published and distributed. But the Okhrana's report of its raid on the PK meeting, which *inter alia* was discussing the Russian Bureau draft, makes it plain that it captured all the materials before the PK (f.DPOO., 1917g., d.341, ch.57, ll.42, 44), a point corroborated by Shliapnikov (*Semnadtsatyi god*, op.cit., p. 99). There is an illuminating discussion of this episode in Michael Melancon, 'Who wrote what and when? Proclamations of the February revolution in Petrograd, 23 February–1 March 1917', *Soviet Studies*, vol. 40 (July 1988), p. 481.

47. N. F. Sveshnikov, 'Vyborgskii raionnyi komitet RSDRP(B) v 1917g.', in *V ogne revoliutsionnykh boev (raiony Petrograda v dvukh revoliutsiiakh 1917g.)* (Moscow, 1967), p. 83.

48. f.102, DPOO., 1917g., d.341, ch.57, l.42.

49. Shliapnikov, *Semnadtsatyi god*, op.cit., pp. 86–7. The exact truth of the relationship between the Russian Bureau and second-rank leaders, as well as their respective positions, is difficult to establish. The reminiscences of Kaiurov and Sveshnikov were first written at a time when Shliapnikov was in disgrace politically for his part in the Workers' Opposition, whilst Shliapnikov's account of his view on the garrison's role, which foreshadowed what actually happened on 27 February, seems suspiciously like a case of hindsight. James D. White has argued that underlying the differences towards the soldiers lay hostility on the part of members of the Sormovo–Nikolaev *zemliachestvo* (who were well represented on the Vyborg committee) towards the intelligentsia and their fear that the army's participation would dilute the working-class character of the revolution (White, 'The Sormovo–Nikolaev *zemliachestvo* in the February Revolution', *Soviet Studies*, vol. 31 (October 1979), pp. 475–504).

50. Sveshnikov, 'Vyborgskii raionnyi komitet', op.cit., p. 84; Kaiurov, 'Shest' dnei', op.cit., p. 166; 'Fevral'skaia revoliutsiia', op.cit., p. 171.

51. Iurenev, '"Mezhraionka"', op.cit., pp. 140, 141; L. M. Shalaginova,

'Esery-internatsionalisty v gody pervoi mirovoi voiny', in A. L. Sidorov (ed.), *Pervaia mirovaia voina* (Moscow, 1968), p. 333. Political exigencies forbade Iurenev mentioning in his memoirs his faction's co-operation with the Left SRs.

52. Burdzhalov, *Vtoraia russkaia revoliutsiia*, op.cit., p. 155 (the text of the Mezhraionka leaflet of 24 February).

53. Iurenev, '"Mezhraionka"', op.cit., p. 140; V. Zenzinov, 'Fevral'skie dni', *Novyi zhurnal*, vol. 34 (1953), pp. 207–10. It is of course possible that Iurenev altered his stance retrospectively to fit in with the prevailing party view of the spontaneity of the revolution.

54. f.102, DPOO., 1917g., d.341, ch.57, l.42.

55. Leiberov, *Na shturm*, op.cit., p. 122: Melancon, 'Socialist Revolutionaries', op.cit., p. 508.

56. f.102, DPOO., 1917g., d.341, ch.57, l.9^c; Leiberov, 'Vtoroi den'', op.cit., p. 118. (Leiberov's account of the Aivaz meeting omits the point concerning a march to the State Duma.) The authorities expected a mass procession to the Tauride on 24 February (f.1405, op.530, d.953, l.6).

57. Kaiurov, 'Shest dnei', op.cit., p. 161.

58. Hasegawa, *February Revolution*, op.cit., p. 241.

59. Iurenev, '"Mezhraionka"', op.cit., p. 138. The bureau at first comprised Iurenev, P. A. Aleksandrovich (Left SRs), E. Sokolovskii (Central Initiative Group) and V. Pozhello (Bolshevik). After Pozhello's arrest the Bolsheviks never replaced him.

60. Iurenev, '"Mezhraionka"', op.cit., p. 136; Ziva Galili y Garcia, 'The Menshevik Revolutionary Defensists and the workers in the revolution of 1917' (Columbia, Ph.D., 1980), pp. 28, 32, 35.

61. 'Kak obrazovalsia Petrogradskii sovet', *Izvestiia soveta rabochikh i soldatskikh deputatov*, no. 155 (27 August 1917), pp. 6–7.

62. Melancon, 'Socialist Revolutionaries', op.cit., p. 464.

63. Iurenev, '"Mezhraionka"', op.cit., p. 139.

64. f.102, DPOO., 1917g., d.341, ch.57, l.42.

65. Iu. S. Tokarev, *Petrogradskii sovet rabochikh deputatov v marte-aprele 1917g.* (Leningrad, 1976), p. 19; G. I.

Slokazov, 'Sozdanie Petrogradskogo soveta', *Istoriia SSSR*, no. 5 (1964), p. 105.

66. Sveshnikov, 'Vyborgskii raionnyi komitet', op.cit., p. 84.

67. Tokarev, *Petrogradskii sovet*, op.cit., p. 21. He also notes the unreliability of later Bolshevik memoirs on this point. In addition to the fact that these autors may have mistakenly misdated the timing, there is also the possibility that political considerations may have influenced them, namely the imperative need to disprove the Menshevik claim to have been the originators of the Soviet.

68. Iurenev, '"Mezhraionka"', op.cit., p. 137; Zenzinov, 'Fevral'skie dni', op.cit., pp. 208–9.

69. Sukhanov, *Russian Revolution*, op.cit., p. 20.

70. The location and size of revolutionary cells on the eve of the February revolution is discussed in Chapter 13.

71. 'Fevral'skaia revoliutsiia', op.cit., p. 174.

72. The reader is referred to the thorough accounts in Burdzhalov and Hasegawa (op.cit.) of the actions of the authorities between 23 and 26 February.

Conclusion

1. The Mensheviks' views are explored in Ziva Galili y Garcia, 'Workers, industrialists and Mensheviks: labor relations and the question of power in the early stages of the Russian revolution', *Russian Review*, vol. 44 (1985), pp. 239–69.

2. Historians have been divided in their assessment of the POZF's motives in accepting the 10 March agreement with the Petrograd Soviet. Steve Smith and R. J. Devlin take a more charitable interpretation, whilst Ziva Galili y Garcia is more sceptical: S. A. Smith, *Red Petrograd. Revolution in the Factories. 1917–1918* (Cambridge, 1983), p. 76; R. J. Devlin, 'Petrograd workers and workers' factory committees in 1917' (New York, Ph.D., 1976), p. 66; Garcia, 'Workers, Industrialists and Mensheviks', op.cit., pp. 247, 249–50.

3. Workers' demands in March–April 1917 have been fully analysed in Smith, *Red Petrograd*, op.cit., pp. 65–73.

4. Both Smith and Devlin (op.cit.) provide sound guides to the history of the factory committee movement in 1917.

BIBLIOGRAPHY

Primary Sources

ARCHIVES

Great Britain
St Antony's College, Oxford
  Papers of B. I. Nikolaevskii, vols 3 to 6.

The Netherlands
International Institute for Social History, Amsterdam
  P. B. Aksel'rod Archives.
  Archives of the SR Party:
    430. Polozhenie del v Peterburgskoi organizatsii, sentiabr', 1908g.
    757. Peterburg, 25oe avgusta 1909g.
    792. Stenograficheskii otchet piatogo soveta partii S.R.

Soviet Union

Central State	Historical Archives, Leningrad
fond 23	Ministry of Trade and Industry
fond 32	Council of Congresses of the Representatives of Industry and Trade
fond 150	St Petersburg Society of Mill and Factory Owners
fond 1276	Council of Ministers
fond 1278	State Duma
fond 1282	Chancellery of the Ministry of Internal Affairs
fond 1284	Department of General Affairs of the Ministry of Internal Affairs
fond 1292	Administration of Military Service, Ministry of Internal Affairs
fond 1405	Ministry of Justice
Central State	Archives of the October Revolution, Moscow
fond 102	Department of Police
fond 102	Osobyi otdel. Special Section of the Department of Police
fond 102	IVoe Deloproizvodstvo. Fourth Division of the Department of Police

(References to individual opisi and dela of each fond may be found in the appropriate notes.)

Published Primary Sources

DOCUMENTARY MATERIALS

'Arkhivnye dokumenty i biografii V. I. Lenina (1887–1914gg.) Revoliutsiia 1905–1907gg.', *Krasnyi arkhiv*, vol. 2, no. 62 (1934), pp. 178–214.

'Arkhivnye materialy o revoliutsionnoi deiatel'nosti I. V. Stalina, 1908–1913gg.', *Krasnyi arkhiv*, vol. 2, no. 105 (1941), pp. 3–32.

Baedeker, K., *Russia, with Teheran, Port Arthur and Peking*, London, 1914.

Beliakov, S. T., 'Iz perepiski TsK RSDRP s mestnymi partiinymi organizatsiiami (1912–1914gg.)', *Istoricheskii arkhiv*, vol. 6, no. 2 (1960), pp. 12–35.

Bessonova, A. F. 'K istorii izdanii "Rabotnitsy", 1914', *Istoricheskii arkhiv*, vol. 1, no. 4 (1955), pp. 25–53.

Bessonova, A. F., 'Antivoennaia rabota bol'shevikov v gody pervoi mirovoi voiny', *Istoricheskii arkhiv*, vol. 7, no. 5 (1961), pp. 74–107.

Blek, A., 'Usloviia truda rabochikh na Peterburgskikh zavodakh po dannym 1901 goda (Baltiiskii i drugie desiat' zavodov)', *Arkhiv istorii truda v Rossii*, Book 2 (1921), pp. 65–85.

Bor'ba s dorogoviznoi i gorodskii upravlenniia, Moscow, 1916.

Bulkin, F., 'Departament politsii i soiuz metallistov', *Krasnaia letopis'*, no. 8 (1923), pp. 220–33; no. 9 (1923), pp. 125–62.

Bystrianskii, V., 'V nachale 1916 goda (iz dokumentov)', *Krasnaia letopis'*, no. 7 (1923), pp. 208–11.

Chaadaeva, O., "Iul'skie stachki i demonstratsii 1914g.", *Krasnyi arkhiv*, vol. 4, no. 95 (1939), pp. 146–155.

Cherniavsky, M., *Prologue to Revolution. Notes of A. N. Iakhontov on the Secret Meetings of the Council of Ministers, 1915*, Englewood Cliffs, New Jersey, 1967.

Chuzhennikov, A., "Russkoe rabochee dvizhenie", *Ezhegodnik gazetoi 'Rech'' na 1913 god*, St Petersburg, 1913, pp. 151–165.

Dan, F. (ed.), *Materialy po istorii russkogo revoliutsionnogo dvizheniia. Vol. II. Iz arkhiva P. B. Aksel'roda: pis'ma P. B. Aksel'roda i Iu. O. Martova, 1901–1916*, Berlin, 1924.

Danskii, B. G., *Strakhovaia kampaniia*, St Petersburg, 1913.

Davidovich, M., *Peterburgskii tekstil'nyi rabochii v ego biudzhetakh*, St Petersburg, 1912.

Deiatel'nost' oblastnykh i mestnykh voenno-promyshlennikh komitetov na 10oe fevral'ia 1916g. Chast' I, Petrograd, 1916.

Dobson, C., *St Petersburg*, London, 1910.

'Dokumenty biuro TsK RSDRP v Rossii, iiul' 1914g.–fevral' 1917gg.', *Voprosy istorii KPSS*, no. 8 (1965), pp. 79–86.

Ekonomicheskoe polozhenie Rossii nakanune velikoi oktiabr'skoi sotsialisticheskoi revoliutsii, Moscow, 1957.

Elwood, R. C., *Resolutions and Decisions of the Communist Party of the Soviet*

Union. Volume 1. The Russian Social Democratic Labour Party. 1891–October 1917, Toronto, 1974.

Fedorov, M., 'Finansovoe polozhenie Peterburga', *Gorodskoe delo*, no. 1 (1 January 1909), pp. 10–17.

'Fevral'skaia revoliutsiia i okhrannoe otdelenie', *Byloe*, vol. 29, no. 1 (1918), pp. 158–76.

'Fevral'skaia revoliutsiia v dokumentakh', *Proletarskaia revoliutsiia*, vol. 1 (1923), pp. 259–352.

Fleer, M. G., *Rabochee dvizhenie v gody voiny*, Moscow, 1925.

Frenkel, Z., 'Narodnoe zdorov'e v gorodakh Rossii po offitsial'nym dannym', *Gorodskoe delo*, no. 5 (1 March 1910), pp. 275–82.

Frenkel, Z., 'Neskol'ko dannykh o sanitarnom sostaianii Moskvy i Peterburga za 1909g.', *Gorodskoe delo*, no. 20 (15 October 1910), pp. 1402–9.

Gankin, O. H., and Fisher, H. H., *The Bolsheviks and the World War. The Origin of the Third International*, Stanford, California, 1960.

Glavnoe po snabzheniiu armii komitet. Ocherk deiatel'nosti. 10 iiuliia 1915g.–1 fevral'ia 1916g., Moscow, 1916.

Goncharova, S. M., 'Neopublikovannye resheniia Krakovskogo soveshchaniia TsK RSDRP s partiinymi rabotnikami', *Voprosy istorii KPSS*, no. 7 (1967), pp. 81–3.

Grave, V. V. (ed.), *Burzhuaziia nakanune fevral'skoi revoliutsii*, Moscow, 1927.

Gudvan, A. M., 'Essays on the history of the movement of sales-clerical workers in Russia', in V. E. Bonnell (ed.), *The Russian Worker. Life and Labor under the Tsarist Regime*, Berkeley, California, 1983.

Internatsional i voina, Zurich, 1915.

Iz epokhi 'Zvezdy' i 'Pravdy' (1911–1914). Volume 3, Moscow, 1921.

Izveshchenie o konferentsii organizatsii RSDRP, Paris, 1912; repr., New York, 1982.

Kikoin, V. G., '"Zvezda" i "Pravda". Iz istorii bor'by tsarskogo pravitel'stva s legal'noi rabochei pechati v Peterburge', *Krasnaia letopis'*, no. 2 (1930), pp. 67–109.

Kleinbort, 'Ocherki rabochei demokratii', *Sovremennyi mir*, no. 4 (April 1913), pp. 27–31; no. 2 (2nd edn), (May 1913), pp. 113–34; no. 8 (August 1913), pp. 175–98.

Komarovskii, K. A. (Danskii), '"Pravda" i rabochaia strakhovaia kampaniia', *Proletarskaia revoliutsiia*, vol. 102–3 (1930), pp. 171–6.

Korablev, Iu. I. (ed.), *Rabochee dvizhenie v Peterburge v gody novogo revoliutsionnogo pod"ema, 1912–1914. Dokumenty i materialy*, Leningrad, 1958.

Korbut, M. K., 'Strakhovye zakony 1912 goda i ikh provedenie v Peterburge', *Krasnaia letopis'*, no. 1 (1928), pp. 136–71; no. 2, pp. 157–75.

Kuprianova, L., 'Rabochii Peterburg', in *S. Peterburg i ego zhizn'*, St Petersburg, 1914.

L., Ia., 'Vybory', *Ezhegodnik gazetoi 'Rech'' na 1913 god*, St Petersburg, 1913, pp. 198–239.

Lenin, V. I., *Collected Works*, Moscow, 1963–9, vols. 13, 15–21, 35, 41, 43.

Lenin, V. I., *Polnoe sobranie sochinenii*, Moscow, 1958–65, vol. 48.

'Lenin i "Pravda", 1912–1913gg.; perepiska', *Krasnaia letopis'*, no. 10 (1924), pp. 69–80.

Listovki Peterburgskikh bol'shevikov. 1902–1917. Tom vtoroi. 1904–1917, Leningrad, 1939.

Loginov, V. T. et al., 'Perepiska TsK RSDRP s mestnymi partiinymi organizatsiiami v gody novogo revoliutsionnogo pod"ema', *Istoricheskii arkhiv*, vol. 3, no. 1 (1957), pp. 1–45.

Loginov, V. T. et al., 'Deiatel'nost' TsK RSDRP po rukovodstvu gazetoi "Pravda" (1912–1914gg)', *Istoricheskii arkhiv*, vol. 5, no. 4 (1959), pp. 39–56.

Lur'e, M. L. 'Tsarizm v bor'be s rabochim dvizheniem v gody pod"ema', *Krasnyi arkhiv*, vol. 1, no. 74 (1936), pp. 39–60.

Lur'e, M. L., *Bol'shevistskaia fraktsiia iv gosudarstvennoi dumy. Sbornik materialov i dokumentov*, Leningrad, 1938.

Maevskii, E., *Kanun revoliutsii*, Petrograd, 1918.

Magidov, 'Alkogolizm sredi S. Peterburgskikh rabochikh (po dannym ankety)', *Edinstvo*, no. 16 (1 April 1910), p. 9.

Maksakov, VI. (ed.), 'Zhandarmy o "Pravde"', *Proletarskaia revoliutsiia*, vol. 14 (1923), pp. 454–68.

Materialy k uchetu rabochago sostava i rabochago rynka. Vypusk I., Petrograd, 1916.

Materialy ob ekonomicheskom polozhenii i professional'noi organizatsii Peterburgskikh rabochikh po metallu, St Petersburg, 1909.

Materialy po statistike truda severnoi oblasti. Vypusk I., Petrograd, 1918.

Menitskii, I. A., 'K istorii "rabochei gruppy" pri tsentral'nom voenno-promyshlennom komitete', *Krasnyi arkhiv*, vol. 2, no. 57 (1933), pp. 43–84.

Menitskii, I. A., 'K istorii Gvozdevshchiny', *Krasnyi arkhiv*, vol. 7, no. 67 (1934), pp. 28–92.

Mezhdunarodnye otnosheniia v epokhu imperializma. Seriia III. Tom V. 23oe iiulia–4 avgusta, 1914g., Moscow, 1934.

Minina, E. K. (ed.), *Partiia bol'shevikov v gody novogo revoliutsionnogo pod"ema, 1910–1914: dokumenty i materialy*, Moscow, 1962.

Norman, H., *All the Russias*, London, 1902.

Novin, Iu., 'Revoliutsionnaia rabota deputatov protiv voiny', *Krasnaia letopis'*, no. 10 (1924), pp. 91–110.

Obzor deiatel'nosti Rossisskoi sotsial-demokraticheskoi rabochei partii za vremia s nachala voiny Rossii s Avstro-vengrei i Germaniei po iiul' 1916 goda, 1916.

Oliunina, E. A., 'The tailoring trade in Moscow and the villages of Moscow and Riazan provinces', in V. E. Bonnell (ed.), *The Russian Worker. Life and Labor under the Tsarist Regime*, Berkeley, California, 1983.

Osoboe soveshchanie dlia obsuzhdeniia i ob"edineniia meropriatii po prodovol'stvennomu delu. Vyusk. 5, Petrograd, 1916.

Ostroukhova, K., 'Iz perepiski mestnykh organizatsii s zagranichnym bol'shevistskim tsentrom v 1909g.', *Proletarskaia revoliutsiia*, vol. 80 (1928), pp. 152–92.

Otchet otdela promyshlennosti za 1910 god, St Petersburg, 1911.

Otchet otdela promyshlennosti za 1912 god, St Petersburg, 1913.

Otchet otdela promyshlennosti za 1913 god, St Petersburg, 1914.

Otchet otdela promyshlennosti za 1914 god, St Petersburg, 1915.

P.F.K., 'Peterburgskii komitet bol'shevikov v kontse 1916g. i nachale 1917g. v osveshchenii okhranki', *Krasnaia letopis'*, no. 42 (1931), pp. 32–9.

PK, 'V Petrograde nakanune fevral'skoi revoliutsii (v osveshchenii Petrogradskogo okhrannogo otdeleniia)', *Krasnaia letopis'*, no. 22 (1924), pp. 38–47.

Padenie tsarskogo rezhima, Vol. III, Moscow, 1924–7.

Pazhitnov, K., 'Kvartirnyi vopros v Peterburge', *Gorodskoe delo*, no. 20 (15 October 1910), pp. 1371–83.

Pazhitnov, K., 'Zhilishchnaia politika gorodskoi dumy goroda Peterburga', *Izvestiia Moskovskoi gorodskoi dumy*, vol. 37 (10 October 1914), pp. 29–53.

Peterburgskii komitet RSDRP. Protokoly i zasedanii. Jiul' 1902-fevral' 1917, Leningrad, 1986.

Petriakov, G. V., 'Deiatel'nost' V. I. Lenina po rukovodstvu "Pravdoi" v 1912–1914gg.', *Voprosy istorii*, no. 1 (November 1956), pp. 3–16.

Petrograd po perepisi 15 dekabria 1910 goda, 2 vols, Petrograd, 1914.

'Pis'ma N. Krupskoi k G. L. Shklovskomu, 1910–1916gg.', *Proletarskaia revoliutsiia*, vol. 43 (1925), pp. 110–43.

'Polozhenie promyshlennosti v Petrogradskoi gubernii 1913g.', *Vestnik finansov, promyshlennosti i torgovli*, no. 38 (1914), p. 381.

Polupanov, D., 'K kvartirnomu krizisu Peterburga', *Gorodskoe delo*, no. 20 (15 October 1913), pp. 1350–7.

Popov, K., 'K istorii Prazhskoi konferentsii', *Krasnyi arkhiv*, vol. 6, no. 97 (1939), pp. 91–123.

Potresov, A. N. and Nikolaevskii, B. I. (eds), *Sotsial-demokraticheskoe dvizhenie v Rossii: materialy*, Moscow, 1928.

Prokopovich, S. N., *Kooperativnoe dvizhenie v Rossii. Ego teoriia i praktika*, Moscow, 1913.

Protokly soveshchaniia rasshirenoi redaktsii 'Proletariia' iiun' 1909, Moscow 1934; repr. edited by G. Swain, New York, 1982.

Rammul, A. I., 'O vodosnabzhenii S. Peterburga', *Gorodskoe delo*, no. 22 (15 November 1910), pp. 1588–600.

Rossiia v mirovoi voine 1914–1918gg. (v tsifrakh), Moscow, 1925.

Rubach, M. A. (ed.), *Rabochee dvizhenie na Ukraine v gody novogo revoliutsionnogo pod"ema, 1910–1914. Sbornik dokumentov i materialov*, Kiev, 1959.

Sapir, B. (ed.), *Theodore Dan. Letters (1899–1946)*, Amsterdam, 1985.

Semennikov, V. P., *Monarkhiia pered krusheniem*, Moscow, 1927.

Sidorov, K., 'Bor'ba so stachechnym dvizheniem nakanune mirovoi voiny', *Krasnyi arkhiv*, vol. 3, no. 24 (1929), pp. 95–125.

'Soveshchanie gubernatorov v 1916 godu', *Krasnyi arkhiv*, vol. 2, no. 33 (1929), pp. 145–69.

Svod otchetov fabrichnykh inspektorov za 1909 god, St Petersburg, 1910.

Svod otchetov fabrichnykh inspektorov za 1910 god, St Petersburg, 1911.

Svod otchetov fabrichnykh inspektorov za 1911 god, St Petersburg, 1912.

Svod otchetov fabrichnykh inspektorov za 1912 god, St Petersburg, 1913.

Svod otchetov fabrichnykh inspektorov za 1913 god, St Petersburg, 1914.

Svod otchetov fabrichnykh inspektorov za 1914 god, St Petersburg, 1915.

Trudy pervogo s"ezda predstavitelei metalloobratyvaiushchei promyshlennosti. 29go fevral'ia–1go marta, 1916 goda, Petrograd, 1916.

Trudy pervogo s"ezda raionnykh upolnomochennykh po mineral'nomy toplivu predsedatelia osobogo soveshchaniia o toplive. 30 marta–2 aprelia 1916 godu, Kharkov, 1916.

Trudy pervogo vserossiiskogo zhenskago s"ezda, 10–16 dekabria 1908, St Petersburg, 1909.

Trudy s"ezda predstavitelei voenno-promyshlennykh komitetov, 25–27 iiulia 1915g., Petrograd, 1915.

Trudy soveshchaniia po ekonomicheskim voprosam, sviazannym s dorogoviznoi i snabzheniem armii. (Moskva, 11–13 iiulia 1915 goda), Moscow, 1915.

Trudy vtorogo s"ezda predstavitelei voenno-promyshlennykh komitetov, 26–29 fevral'ia 1916g., Petrograd, 1916.

Tsiavlovskii, M. A. (ed.), *Bol'sheviki: dokumenty po istorii bol'shevizma s 1903 po 1916 god byvsh. Moskovskogo okhrannogo otdeleniia*, Moscow, 1918.

Valk, S. N. and Livshits, S. E. 'Iiul'skie dni v 1914g. v Peterburge (arkhivnye dokumenty)', *Proletarskaia revoliutsiia*, vol. 30 (1924), pp. 181–214.

'V ianvare i fevrale 1917g. Iz donesenii sekretnykh agentov A. D. Protopopova', *Byloe*, vol. 13 (1918), pp. 91–123.

'V. I. Lenin v 1912–1914gg.', *Krasnyi arkhiv*, vol. 2, no. 62 (1934), pp. 224–48.

Voinova, K., 'Iiul'skie dni v Moskve', *Proletarskaia revoliutsiia*, vol. 30 (1924), pp. 215–23.

Volodarskaia, A. M., 'Podgotovka s"ezda bol'shevistskoi partii v 1914g.', *Istoricheskii arkhiv*, vol. 4, no. 6 (1958), pp. 1–35.

Volodarskaia, A. M., 'Otvet V. I. Lenina na pis'mo I.I. Skvortsova-Stepanova', *Istoricheskii arkhiv*, vol. 5, no. 2 (1959), pp. 11–18.

Volodarskaia, A. M. and Orlova, N. V., 'Rabochee dvizhenie v 1913–1914gg.', *Istoricheskii arkhiv*, vol. 1, no. 5 (1955), pp. 68–96.

Volodarskaia, A. M. and Shapeleva, T. V., 'Zasedaniia TsK RSDRP 15–17 aprelia 1914 goda.', *Voprosy istorii KPSS*, no. 4 (1957), pp. 112–25.

Vserossiiskaia konferentsiia Ros. Sots-dem. Rab. Partii 1912 goda, Paris, 1912; repr., New York, 1982.

Vulliamy, C. E. (ed.), *The Red Archives*, London, 1929.

Zharov, L. I. and Kuznetsov, N. K., 'O podgotovke Prazhskoi konferentsii RSDRP', *Istoricheskii arkhiv*, vol. 4, no. 5 (1958), pp. 3–22.

Zhurnal soveshchaniia pod predsedatel'stvom glavnogo nachalnika Petrogradskogo voennogo okruga po voprosu o merakh bor'by s povysheniiami tsen, Petrograd, 1915.

Zhurnaly osobogo soveshchaniia po oborone gosudarstva, 1915 god. Chast' I, Chast' II (repr.), Moscow, 1975; *1916 god. Chast' I, Chast' II, Chast' IV* (repr.), Moscow, 1977.

Zinoviev, G. E., *Sochineniia, Volume 2*, Moscow, 1923.

MEMOIRS

Adamovich, E., 'Legal'nye vozmozhnosti i partiinaia rabota v Peterburge v 1908–1909gg.', *Krasnaia letopis'*, no. 4 (1930), pp. 27–73.

Anet, C., *Through the Russian Revolution: Notes of an Eyewitness, from 12th March–30th May*, London, 1917.

Arskii, R., 'V Petrograde vo vremia voiny', *Krasnaia letopis'*, no. 7 (1923), pp. 75–90.

Arskii, R., 'Epokha reaktsii v Petrograde (1907–1910gg.)', *Krasnaia letopis'*, no. 9 (1924), pp. 63–106.

Arskii, R., 'O partiinoi rabote v 1910 godu v Peterburge (iz vospominanii)', *Krasnaia letopis'*, no. 4 (1932), pp. 100–12.

Badaev, A., *The Bolsheviks in the Tsarist Duma*, London, n.d.

Badaev, A., 'Dumskaia fraktsiia bol'shevikov-'piaterka'-v russko-germanskuiu voinu', *Krasnaia letopis'*, no. 10 (1924), pp. 86–91.

Bogolepov, S., 'Zametki o "tekhnike" Peterburgskogo komiteta RSDRP (bol'shevikov) v 1915–1916gg. (po vospominaniiam)', *Krasnaia letopis'*, no. 10 (1924), pp. 118–66.

Ermanskii, O. A., *Iz perezhitogo (1887–1921gg.)*, Moscow, 1927.

Garvi, P., *Zapiski sotsial-demokrata (1906–1921)*, Newtonville, Mass., 1982.

Gavrilov, Iu. 'Na Vyborgskoi storone v 1914–1917gg.', *Krasnaia letopis'*, no. 23 (1927), pp. 38–61.

Golubkov, A., 'Iz epokhi reaktsii (otryvki iz vospominanii)', *Proletarskaia revoliutsiia*, vol. 80 (1928), pp. 121–51.

Gordienko, I., *Iz boevogo proshlogo (1914–1918gg.)*, Moscow, 1957.

Iakovlev, I., 'Aprel'sko–maiskie dni 1912 goda v Peterburge', *Krasnaia letopis'*, no. 3 (1925), pp. 224–39.

Iurenev, I., ' "Mezhraionka" (1911–1917gg.) (vospominaniia)', *Proletarskaia revoliutsiia*, vol. 24 (1924), pp. 109–39; vol. 25 (1924), pp. 114–43.

Kaiurov, V., 'Shest' dnei fevral'skoi revoliutsii', *Proletarskaia revoliutsiia*, vol. 1 (1923), pp. 157–70.

Kaiurov, V., 'Rabochee dvizhenie v Pitere v 1914g.', *Proletarskaia revoliutsiia*, vol. 44 (1925), pp. 185–95.

'Kak obrazovalsia Petrogradskii sovet', *Izvestiia soveta rabochikh i soldatskikh deputatov*, no. 155 (27 August 1917), pp. 6–7.

Kerensky, A. F., *The Kerensky Memoirs. Russia and History's Turning Point*, London, 1966.

Kiselev, A. S., 'V iiule 1914 goda', *Proletarskaia revoliutsiia*, vol. 30 (1924), pp. 36–48.

Knox, Sir A., *With the Russian Army, 1914–1917: Being Chiefly Extracts from the Diary of a Military Attaché. Volume II*, London, 1921.

Kondrat'ev, K., 'Vospominaniia o podpol'noi rabote Peterburgskoi organizatsii RSDRP(B) v period 1914–1917gg.', *Krasnaia letopis'*, no. 5 (1923), pp. 227–43.

Kondrat'ev, K., 'Vospominaniia o podpol'noi rabote v Petrograde', *Krasnaia letopis'*, no. 7 (1923), pp. 30–70.

Krestinskii, N. N., 'Iz vospominanii [o 1914 gode]', *Proletarskaia revoliutsiia*, vol. 30 (1924), pp. 54–64.

Krupskaia, N., *Memories of Lenin*, London, 1970.

Kudelli, P., 'Iz zhizni Peterburgskoi organizatsii RSDRP(B) v period reaktsii', *Krasnaia letopis'*, no. 14 (1925), pp. 220–3.

Lemeshov, F., 'Na Putilovskom zavode v gody voiny', *Krasnaia letopis'*, no. 23 (1927), pp. 5–38.

Leont'eva, L., 'V riadakh "Mezhraionka" (1914–1917gg.)', *Krasnaia letopis'*, no. 11 (1924), pp. 130–57.

Lobov, S. and Gavrilov, I., 'Iz istorii partiinoi organizatsii na "Krasnom Vyborzhitse', *Krasnaia letopis'*, no. 20 (1926), pp. 130–7.

Mitrevich, A. A., 'Zametki po rabochemu dvizheniiu ot 1912 goda', *Proletarskaia revoliutsiia*, vol. 4 (1922), pp. 225–6, 241–4.

Onufriev, E., *Vstrechi s Leninym*, Moscow, 1959.

Piatnitskii, D., *Memoirs of a Bolshevik*, London, 1933.

'Podpol'naia rabota v Petrograde v gody imperialisticheskoi voiny (1914–1917gg.). Rasskazy rabochikh', *Krasnaia letopis'*, nos. 2–3 (1922), pp. 116–43.

Polivanov, A. A. *Iz dnevnikov i vospominanii po dolzhnosti voennogo ministra i ego pomoshchnika*, Moscow, 1924.

Pourtales, F. Graf, *Mes dernières négociations à Saint Petersburg en Juillet 1914* (trans. J. Robillet), Paris, 1929.

Shakhovskoi, Prince V. N., '*Sic transit gloria mundi.' (Tak prokhodit mirskaia slava), 1883–1917gg.*, Paris, 1952.

Shidlovskii, G., 'Peterburgskii komitet bol'shevikov v kontse 1913g. i v nachale 1914g.', *Krasnaia letopis'*, no. 17 (1926), pp. 119–38.

Shidlovskii, G., 'V Peterburgskikh partiinykh riadakh vesnoi i letom 1910 goda (ocherk)', *Krasnaia letopis'*, nos. 5–6 (1931), pp. 167–93.

Shklovskii, G., 'Bernskaia konferentsiia 1915g.', *Proletarskaia revoliutsiia*, vol. 40 (1925), pp. 134–93.

Shliapnikov, A., *Semnadtsatyi god. Volume I*, Moscow, 1923.

Shliapnikov, A., *On the Eve of 1917* (trans. Richard Chappell), London, 1982.

Shukhanov, N. N., *The Russian Revolution 1917. A Personal Record* (trans. Joel Carmichael), Princeton, New Jersey, 1983.

Sveshnikov, N. F., 'Vyborgskii komitet RSDRP(B) v 1917g.', in *V ogne revoliutsionnykh boev (raiony Petrograda v dvukh revoliutsiiakh 1917g.)*, Moscow, 1967, pp. 81–90.

Timofeev, P., 'What the factory worker lives by', in V. E. Bonnell (ed.), *The Russian Worker. Life and Labor under the Tsarist Regime*, Berkeley, California 1983.

Tsvetkov-Prosveshchenskii, A., *Mezhdu dvumia revoliutsiamii (1907–1916gg.)*, Moscow, 1957.

Uratadze, G., *Reminiscences of a Georgian Social Democrat*, Stanford, California, 1968.

Vinogradov, V., 'Organizatsiia bol'shevikov na Peterburgskom Metallicheskom zavode v 1915g.', *Krasnaia letopis'*, no. 18 (1926), pp. 30–40.

Zalezhskii, V., *Iz vospominanii podpol'shchika*, Moscow, 1931.

Zelnik, R. E. (ed.), *A Radical Worker in Tsarist Russia. The Autobiography of Semen Kanatchikov*, Stanford, California 1986.

Zenzinov V., 'Fevral'skie dni', *Novyi zhurnal*, vol. 34 (1953).

PRE-1917 NEWSPAPERS AND PERIODICALS

Birzhevye vedomosty
Biulleten' kontorshchika
Bor'ba (1908)
Bor'ba (1914)
Delo
Delo zhizni
Den'
Derevoobdelochnik
Edinstvo
Golos bulochnika i konditera
Golos portnogo
Golos sotsial-demokrata
Gorno-zavodskoe delo
Gorodskoe delo
Informatsionnyi listok zagranichnoi organizatsii bunda
Izvestiia Moskovskogo voenno-promyshlennogo komiteta
Izvestiia Moskovskoi gorodskoi dumy
Izvestiia oblastnogo zagranichnogo komiteta SR
Izvestiia osobogo soveshchaniia dlia obsuzhdeniia i obed''ineniia meropriatiia po prodovol'stvennomu delu
Izvestiia osobogo soveshchaniia po prodovol'stviiu
Izvestiia osobogo soveshchaniia po toplivu
Izvestiia S. Peterburgskoi dumy
Izvestiia tsentral'nogo voenno-promyshlennogo komiteta
Izvestiia vserossiiskogo soiuza gorodov
Izvestiia zagranichnogo sekretariata organizatsionnogo komiteta RSDRP
Kuznets
Letopis'
Listok golosa sotsial-demokrata
Listok organizatsionnogo komiteta po sozyvu obshchepartiinoi konferentsii
Listok zagranichnogo biuro tsentral'nogo komiteta
Luch (and its continuation as *Novaia rabochaia gazeta, Severnaia rabochaia gazeta, Nasha rabochaia gazeta*)
Metallist
Mysl'

Nabat
Nadezhda
Narodnaia mysl'
Nash put'
Nasha zaria
Nashe delo
Nashe pechatnoe delo
Nashe slovo
Nevskaia zvezda
Nevskii golos
Novoe pechatnoe delo
Novoe vremia
Novyi ekonomist
Novyi professional'nyi listok
Pochin
Pravda (St Petersburg) (and its continuation as *Rabochaia pravda, Severnaia pravda, Pravda truda, Za pravdu, Proletarskaia pravda, Put' pravdy, Trudovaia pravda)*
Pravda (Vienna)
Prizyv
Professional'nyi vestnik
Proletarii
Promyshlennaia Rossiia
Promyshlennost' i torgovlia
Prosveshchenie
Put'
Rabochaia gazeta
Rabochee utro
Rabochii mir
Rabochii po metallu
Rabotnitsa
Rech'
Russkie vedomosty
Russkoe slovo
Sotsial-demokrat
Sovremennik
Sovremennyi mir
Strakhovanie rabochikh
Tekstil'shchik
Trud
Trudovoi golos
Utro
Utro Rossii
Vestnik portnykh
Vestnik prikazchika

Voprosy strakhovaniia
Vozrozhdenie
Vpered
Vserossiiskii zemskii soiuz. Izvestiia glavnogo komiteta
Za narod
Za partiiu
Zaprosy zhizni
Zavety
Zemlia i volia
Zhivoe delo
Zhizn'
Zhizn' farmatsevta
Zhizn' pekarei
Znamia truda
Zvezda

Secondary Sources

BOOKS AND ARTICLES

Abraham, R., *Alexander Kerensky. The First Love of the Revolution*, New York, 1987.

Akhun, M. and Petrov, V., 'Voennaia organizatsiia pri Peterburgskom komitete RSDRP v 1907–1908gg.', *Krasnaia letopis'*, no. 19 (1926), pp. 124–37.

Anderson, B. A., *Internal Migration During Modernization in Late Nineteenth Century Russia*, Princeton, New Jersey, 1980.

Antonova, S. I., 'Statistika fabrichnoi inspektsii kak istochnik po istorii proletariata', in *Rabochii klass i rabochee dvizhenie v Rossii, 1861–1917*, ed., L. M. Ivanov, Moscow, 1966, pp. 314–44.

Arutiunov, G. A., *Rabochee dvizhenie v Rossii v period novogo revoliutsionnogo pod"ema 1910–1914gg.*, Moscow, 1975.

Arutiunov, G. A., 'Rasprostranenie "Sotsial-demokrata" in "Rabochei gazety" v Rossii (1910–1912)', *Voprosy istorii KPSS*, no. 12 (1984), pp. 54–63.

Ascher, A., *Pavel Axelrod and the Development of Menshevism*, Cambridge, Mass., 1972.

Astrakhan, Kh. M., 'O taktike "sniatiia c rabote" v Petrograde v pervye dni fevral'skoi revoliutsii 1917g.', in *Sverzhenie samoderzhaviia. Sbornik statei*, Moscow, 1970, pp. 120–30.

Avrekh, A. Ia., *Stolypin i tret'ia duma*, Moscow, 1968.

Baevskii, D., 'Partiia v gody imperialisticheskoi voiny', in *Ocherki po istorii oktiabr'skoi revoliutsii. Tom I*, ed. M. N. Pokrovskii, Moscow, 1927, pp. 335–505.

Balabanov, M. S., *Ot 1905 k 1917 godu; massovoe rabochee dvizhenie*, Moscow, 1927.

Barchugov, P. B., *Revoliutsionnaia rabota bol'shevikov v legal'nykh rabochikh organizatsiiakh*, Rostov-na-Donu, 1973.

Baron, S., *Plekhanov, The Father of Russian Marxism*, London, 1963.

Barsukov, E. Z., *Artilleriia russkoi armii (1900–1917gg.) Tom II. Chast' III. Artillerskoe snabzhenie*, Moscow, 1949.

Bater, J. H., *St Petersburg. Industrialisation and Change*, London, 1976.

Bater, J. H., 'Transience, residential persistence, and mobility in Moscow and St Petersburg, 1900–1914', *Slavic Review*, vol. 39, no. 2 (June 1980), pp. 239–54.

Berlanstein, L. R., *The Working People of Paris, 1871–1914*, Baltimore, Maryland, 1984.

Biggart, J., '"Anti-Leninist Bolshevism": the forward group of the RSDRP', *Canadian Slavonic Papers*, vol. 23, no. 2 (1981), pp. 134–53.

Bonnell, V. E., 'Urban working-class life in early twentieth century Russia: some problems and patterns', in *Russian History/Histoire Russe*, vol. 8, part 3 (1981), pp. 360–78.

Bonnell, V. E., *Roots of Rebellion. Workers' Politics and Organization in St Petersburg and Moscow, 1900–1914*, Berkeley, California, 1983.

Bovykin, V. I., 'Banki i voennaia promyshlennost' Rossii nakanune pervoi mirovoi voiny', *Istoricheskie zapiski*, vol. 64 (1959), pp. 82–135.

Bradley, J., *Muzhik and Muscovite. Urbanization in Late Imperial Russia*, Berkeley, California, 1985.

Brainerd, M. C., 'The Octobrists and the gentry in the Russian social crisis of 1913–1914', *Russian Review*, vol. 38 (April 1979), pp. 160–79.

Brooks, J., *When Russia Learned to Read. Literacy and Popular Culture, 1861–1917*, Princeton, New Jersey, 1985.

Brüggemeier, F. J. and Niethammer, L., 'Lodgers, schnapps-casinos and working-class colonies in a heavy-industrial region', in *The Social History of Politics. Critical Perspectives in West German Historical Writing since 1945*, ed. G. Iggers, Leamington Spa, 1985, pp. 217–58.

Burdzhalov, E. N., *Vtoraia russkaia revoliutsiia: Vosstanie v Petrograde*, Moscow, 1967.

Chamberlin, W. H., *The Russian Revolution 1917–1921. Volume One*, New York, 1965.

Chermenskii, E. D., 'K istorii dumskoi taktiki partii bol'shevikov (1905–1914gg.)', *Voprosy istorii KPSS*, no. 19 (1981), pp. 42–55.

Cohen, S. E., *Bukharin and the Bolshevik Revolution. A Political Biography, 1888–1938*, New York, 1973.

Conroy, M., *P. A. Stolypin, Practical Politics in Late Tsarist Russia*, Boulder, Colarado, 1976.

Crew, D. F., *Town in the Ruhr. A Social History of Bochum, 1860–1914*, New York, 1979.

Crisp, O., 'Banking in the industrialisation of Tsarist Russia, 1860–1914', in O. Crisp, *Studies in the Russian Economy before 1914*, London, 1978, pp. 111–58.

Crisp, O., 'Labour and industry in Russia', in *Cambridge Economic History of Europe*, vol. 7, Part 2, Cambridge, 1978, pp. 308–415.

Davidenko, A. I., 'K voprosu o chislennosti i sostave proletariata Peterburga v nachale XX veka', in *Istoriia rabochego klassa Leningrada. Vypusk II*, Leningrad, 1963, pp. 92–112.

Dazhina, I. M., 'Russkoe biuro TsK RSDRP v gody pervoi mirovoi voiny', in *Pervaia mirovaia voina*, ed. A. L. Sidorov, Moscow, 1968, pp. 269–82.

Diakin, V. S., *Russkaia burzhuaziia i tsarizm v gody pervoi mirovoi voiny*, Leningrad, 1967.

Diakin, V. S., *Germanskie kapitaly v Rossii: elektroindustriia i elektricheskii transport*, Leningrad, 1971.

Diakin, V. S. *Samoderzhavie, burzhuaziia i dvorianstvo v 1907–1911gg.*, Leningrad, 1978.

Drobizhev, V., Sokolov, A. K. and Ustinov, V. A., *Rabochii klass sovetskoi Rossii v pervyi god proletarskoi diktatury*, Moscow, 1975.

Dvinov, B., *Pervaia Mirovaia voina i rossiiskaia sotsial-demokratiia*, New York, 1962.

Eason, W. E., 'Population changes', in *The Transformation of Russian Society: Aspects of Social Change since 1861*, ed. C. Black, Cambridge, Mass., 1960, pp. 72–90.

Edmondson, L., 'Russian feminists and the First All-Russian Congress of Women', *Russian History/Histoire Russe*, vol. 3, part 2 (1976), pp. 123–49.

Egorov, Iv., 'Matrosy-bol'sheviki nakanune 1917g. (iz istorii partiinoi organizatsii Baltiiskogo flota)', *Krasnaia letopis'*, no. 18 (1926), pp. 5–29.

Elwood, R. C., 'Lenin and the Social Democratic schools for underground party workers, 1909–1911', *Political Science Quarterly*, vol. 81 (September 1966), pp. 371–9.

Elwood, R. C., 'Trotsky's questionnaire', *Slavic Review*, vol. 29, no. 3, (1970), pp. 296–301.

Elwood, R. C., 'Lenin and Pravda, 1912–1914', *Slavic Review*, vol. 31, no. 2 (June 1972), pp. 355–80.

Elwood, R. C., *Roman Malinovsky. A Life Without a Cause*, Newtonville, Mass., 1977.

Elwood, R. C., 'The congress that never was. Lenin's attempt to call a "Sixth" Party Congress in 1914', *Soviet Studies*, vol. 31 (July 1979), pp. 343–63.

Elwood, R. C., 'Lenin and the Brussels "Unity" Conference of July 1914', *Russian Review*, vol. 39 (January 1980), pp. 32–49.

Engelstein, L. *Moscow, 1905. Working-class Organization and Political Conflict*, Standford, California, 1982.

Fainsod, M., *International Socialism and the World War*, Cambridge, Mass., 1935.

Fedor, T. S., *Patterns of Urban Growth in the Russian Empire in the Nineteenth Century*, Chicago, 1975.

Fitzlyon, K., and Browning, T., *Before the Revolution. A View of Russia Under the Last Tsar*, Harmondsworth, England, 1982.

Fleer, M. G. *Peterburgskii komitet bol'shevikov v gody voiny, 1914–1917*, Leningrad, 1927.

Galili y Garcia, Z., 'Workers, industrialists and Mensheviks: labor relations and the question of power in the early stages of the Russian revolution',

Russian Review, vol. 44 (July 1985), pp. 239–69.

Geary, D., *European Labour Protest 1848–1939*, London, 1981.

Getzler, I., *Martov. A Political Biography of a Russian Social Democrat*, Cambridge, 1967.

Geyer, D., *Kautsky's Russisches Dossier (1910–1915)*, Frankfurt-am-Main, 1981.

Gindin, I. F., and Shepelev, L. E., 'Bankovskie monopolii v Rossii nakanune velikoi oktiabr'skoi sotsialisticheskoi revoliutsii', *Istoricheskie zapiski*, vol. 66 (1960), pp. 20–95.

Gindin, I. F. 'Sotsialno-ekonomicheskie itogi razvitii rossiiskogo kapitalizma i predposylki revoliutsii v nashei strane', in *Sverzhenie samoderzhaviia. Sbornik statei*, Moscow, 1970, pp. 39–88.

Glickman, R. L., *Russian Factory Women. Workplace and Society, 1880–1914*, Berkeley, California, 1984.

Goodey, C., 'Factory committees and the dictatorship of the proletariat, 1918', *Critique*, 3 (1974), pp. 27–47.

Gordon, M., 'Iz zhizni rabochikh i sluzhashchikh na gorodskikh zheleznykh dorogakh Petrograda', *Arkhiv istorii truda v Rossii*, vol. 8 (1923), pp. 79–103.

Grave, V. V., 'Militarizatsiia promyshlennosti i rossiiskii proletariat v gody pervoi mirovoi voiny', in *Iz istorii rabochego klassa i revoliutsionnogo dvizheniia. Sbornik statei*, Moscow, 1958, pp. 416–27.

Gribkova, S. M., 'V. I. Lenin i bol'shevistskaia fraktsiia iv gosudarstvennoi dumy (po novym materialiam)', *Istoriia SSSR*, no. 2 (1965), pp. 113–26.

Haimson, L. H., 'The problem of social stability in urban Russia, 1905–1917 (Part One)', *Slavic Review*, vol. 23, no. 4 (December 1964), pp. 619–42; (Part Two), *Slavic Review*, vol. 24, no. 1 (March 1965), pp. 1–22.

Haimson, L. H. and Brian, E., 'Changements démographiques et grèves ouvrières à Saint-Petersbourg, 1905–1914', *Annales ESC*, no. 4 (July–August 1985), pp. 781–803.

Hamm, M. F. (ed.), *The City in Late Imperial Russia*, Bloomington, Indiana, 1986.

Hanagan, M. P., *The Logic of Solidarity. Artisans and Industrial Workers in Three French Towns, 1871–1914*, Urbana, Illinois, 1980.

Hasegawa, T., *The February Revolution: Petrograd, 1917*, Seattle, Washington, 1981.

Haupt, G., *Socialism and the Great War. The Collapse of the Second International*, Oxford, 1971.

Hickey, S. H. F., *Workers in Imperial Germany. The Miners of the Ruhr*, Oxford, 1985.

Hildermeier, M., *Die Sozialrevolutionäre Partei Russlands: Agrarsozialismus und Modernisierung im Zarenreich (1900–1914)*, Cologne, 1978.

Hosking, G., *The Russian Constitutional Experiment*, Cambridge, 1973.

Hunt, E. H., *British Labour History, 1815–1914*, London, 1981.

Istoriia rabochego klassa SSSR. Rabochii klass Rossii. 1907–fevral' 1917g., Moscow, 1982.

Istoriia rabochikh Leningrada. Tom pervyi. 1703–fevral' 1917, Leningrad, 1972.

Ivanov, L. M., 'Preemstvennost' fabrichno-zavodskogo truda i formirovanie proletariata v Rossii', in *Rabochii klass i rabochee dvizhenie v Rossii, 1861–1917*, ed. L. M. Ivanov, Moscow, 1966, pp. 58–140.

Ivanova, N. A., 'Oktiabr'sko-noiabr'skie stachki 1912g. v Rossii', *Istoriia SSSR*, no. 2 (1965), pp. 138–45.

Ivanova, N. A., *Struktura rabochego klassa Rossii 1910–1914*, Moscow, 1987.

Johnson, R. E., *Peasant and Proletarian: the Working Class of Moscow in the Late Nineteenth Century*, Leicester, 1979.

Kaelble, H., *Industrialisation and Social Inequality in Nineteenth Century Europe*, Leamington Spa, 1986.

Katkov, G., *Russia 1917. The February Revolution*, London, 1967.

Kats, N. I., 'Professional'nye soiuzy Peterburga v gody reaktsii (1907–1909gg.)', in *Istoriia rabochego klassa Leningrada. Vypusk II*, Leningrad, 1963, pp. 132–55.

Kirby, D., *War, Peace and Revolution. International Socialism at the Crossroads, 1914–1918*, Aldershot, 1986.

Kirianov, Iu. I., *Zhiznennyi uroven' rabochikh Rossii*, Moscow, 1979.

Knei-Paz, B., *The Social and Political Thought of Leon Trotsky*, Oxford, 1979.

Kocka, J., 'White-collar employees and industrial society in Imperial Germany', in *The Social History of Politics. Critical Perspectives in West German Historical Writing since 1945*, ed. G. Iggers, Leamington Spa, 1985, pp. 113–36.

Koenker, D. G., *Moscow Workers and the 1917 Revolution*, Princeton, New Jersey, 1981.

Koenker, D. G. and Rosenberg, W. G., 'Skilled workers and the strike movement in revolutionary Russia', *Journal of Social History*, vol. 19, no. 4 (1986), pp. 605–29.

Korbut, M. K., 'Rabota N. G. Poletaeva v 3-i Gos. Dume', *Krasnaia letopis'*, no. 2 (1931), pp. 166–91.

Krupina, T. D. 'Politicheskii krizis 1915g. i sozdanie osobogo soveshchaniia po oborone', *Istoricheskie zapiski*, vol. 83 (1969), pp. 58–75.

Kruze, E. E., *Peterburgskie rabochie v 1912–1914 godakh*, Leningrad, 1961.

Kruze, E. E., *Polozhenie rabochego klassa Rossii v 1900–1914gg.*, Leningrad, 1976.

Kruze, E. E., *Usloviia truda i byta rabochego klassa Rossii v 1910–1914 godakh*, Leningrad, 1981.

Krylova, I. I., 'K voprosu o statistike stachek Petrogradskikh rabochikh v gody pervoi mirovoi voiny', in *Iz istorii imperializma v Rossi*, Moscow, 1959, pp. 414–33.

Laverychev, V. Ia., *Tsarizm i rabochii vopros v Rossii (1861–1917gg.)*, Moscow, 1972.

Leiberov, I. P., 'Petrogradskii proletariat v bor'be za pobedu fevral'skoi burzhuazno-demokraticheskoi revoliutsii v Rossii', in *Istoriia SSSR*, no. 1 (1957), pp. 41–73.

Leiberov, I. P., 'V. I. Lenin i Petrogradskaia organizatsiia bol'shevikov v period mirovoi voiny (1914–1916gg.)', *Voprosy istorii KPSS*, no. 5 (1960), pp. 65–79.

Leiberov, I. P., 'Stachechnaia bor'ba Petrogradskogo proletariata v period pervoi mirovoi voiny (19 iiulia 1914g.–16 fevralia 1917g.)', in *Istoriia rabochego klassa Leningrada. Volume II*, Leningrad, 1963, pp. 156–86.

Leiberov, I. P. 'O vozniknovenii revoliutsionnoi situatsii v Rossii v gody pervoi mirovoi voiny (iiul'–sentiabr' 1915g.)', *Istoriia SSSR*, no. 6 (1964), pp. 33–59.

Leiberov, I. P., 'Vtoroi den' fevral'skoi revoliutsii (sobytiia 24 fevralia 1917g. v Petrograde', in *Sverzhenie samoderzhaviia. Sbornik statei*, Moscow, 1970, pp. 100–19.

Leiberov, I. P., 'Petrogradskii proletariat v gody pervoi mirovoi voiny', in *Istoriia rabochikh Leningrada. Tom I. 1703–fevral' 1917*, Leningrad, 1972, pp. 461–511.

Leiberov, I. P., *Na shturm samoderzhaviia. Petrogradskii proletariat v gody pervoi mirovoi voiny i fevral'skoi revoliutsii (iiul' 1914–mart 1917g.)*, Moscow, 1979.

Leiberov, I. P. and Shkaratan, O. I., 'K voprosu o sostave Petrogradskikh promyshlennykh rabochikh v 1917 godu', *Voprosy istorii*, no. 1 (1961), pp. 42–58.

Letunovskii, N. I., *Leninskaia taktika izpol'zovaniia legal'nykh vserossiiskikh s''ezdov v bor'be za massu v 1908–1911 godakh*, Moscow, 1970.

Levin, A., *The Second Duma. A Study of the Russian Social Democratic Party and the Russian Constitutional Experiment*, Hamden, Connecticut, 1966.

Levin, A., *The Third Duma, Election and Profile*, Hamden, Connecticut, 1973.

Lieven, D., 'The Russian civil service under Nicholas II: some variations on a bureaucratic theme', *Jahrbücher für Geschichte Osteuropas*, vol. 29, Part 3 (1981), pp. 366–403.

Loginov, V. T., 'O rukovodstve TsK RSDRP bol'shevistskoi gazetoi "Pravdy" v 1912–1914gg.', *Voprosy istorii KPSS*, no. 1 (1957), pp. 115–27.

Loginov, V. T., 'V. I. Lenin i "Pravda" (1912–1914gg.)', *Voprosy istorii*, no. 5 (1962), pp. 3–24.

Loginov, V. T. and Kurashova, N. A., 'Leninskaia "Pravda" i edinstvo rabochikh Rossii (novye dannye o gruppovykh sborakh 1912–1914gg.)', *Istoriia SSSR*, no. 3 (1982), pp. 51–67.

Longley, D. A., 'The Russian Social Democrats' statement to the Duma on 26 July (8 August 1914): a new look at the evidence', *English Historical Review*, vol. 102 (July 1987), pp. 599–621.

Longley, D. A., 'The Mezhraionka, the Bolsheviks and International Women's Day: in response to Michael Melancon', *Soviet Studies*, vol. 41 (October 1989), pp. 625–45.

Mandel, D., *The Petrograd Workers and the Fall of the Old Regime. From the February Revolution to the July Days*, London, 1983.

Mawdsley, E., *The Russian Revolution and the Baltic Fleet. War and Politics, February 1917–April 1918*, London, 1978.

Melancon, M. S., 'The Socialist Revolutionaries from 1901 to 1907: peasant and workers' party', *Russian History/Histoire Russe*, vol. 12, part 1 (1985), pp. 2–47.

Melancon, M., 'Who wrote what and when? Proclamations of the February revolution in Petrograd, 23 February–1 March 1917', *Soviet Studies*, vol. 40 (July 1988), pp. 479–500.

Milligan, S., 'The Petrograd Bolsheviks and social insurance, 1914–1917', *Soviet Studies*, vol. 20 (January 1969), pp. 369–74.

Mints, I. I., *Istoriia velikogo oktiabria. Tom I. Sverzhenie samoderzhaviia*, Moscow, 1967.

Mitel'man, M., Glebov, V. and Ul'ianskii, A., *Istoriia Putilovskogo zavoda*, Moscow, 1941.

More, C., *Skill and the English Working Class, 1870–1914*, London, 1980.

Nardova, V., 'Proletariat stolitsy v gody reaktsii', in *Istoriia rabochikh Leningrada. Tom pervyi. 1703–fevral' 1917*, Leningrad, 1972.

Nikolaevsky, B., *Azeff the Spy: Russian Terrorist and Police Stool*, New York, 1934.

Ocherki istorii Leningrada. Tom tretii. Period imperializma i burzhuazno-demokraticheskikh revoliutsii 1895–1917gg., Moscow–Leningrad, 1956.

Ocherki istorii Leningradskoi organizatsii KPSS. Chast' 1. 1883–oktiabr' 1917g., Leningrad 1962; new edn, 1980.

Ol'minskii, M. S., 'Obshchii obzor epokhi', in *Iz epokhi 'Zvezdy' i 'Pravdy' (1911–1914). Volume I*, Moscow, 1921.

Oppenheim, S., 'The making of a Right Communist – A. I. Rykov to 1917', *Slavic Review*, vol. 26, no. 3 (1977), pp. 420–40.

Ostroukhova, 'Sotsial-demokratiia v vybory v 3-iu Gosudarstvennuiu Dumu', *Proletarskaia revoliutsiia*, vol. 25 (1924), pp. 85–99.

Owen, T., *Capitalism and Politics in Russia. A Social History of the Moscow Merchants, 1855–1905*, Cambridge, 1980.

Pearson, R., *The Russian Moderates and the Crisis of Tsarism, 1914–1917*, London, 1977.

Perrot, M., *Workers on Strike. France, 1871–1890*, Leamington Spa, 1987.

Pinchuk, B. C., *The Octobrists in the Third Duma, 1907–1912*, Seattle, Washington 1974.

Pogrebinskii, A. G., 'Voenno-promyshlennye komitety', *Istoricheskie zapiski*, vol. 11 (1941), pp. 160–200.

Polikarpov, V. V., 'Iz istorii voennoi promyshlennosti v Rossi (1906–1916gg.)', *Istoricheskie zapiski*, vol. 104 (1979), pp. 123–67.

Price, R., *A Social History of Nineteenth Century France*, London, 1987.

Radkey, O. H., *The Agrarian Foes of Bolshevism*, New York, 1958.

Rashin, A. G., *Naselenie Rossii za sto let*, Moscow, 1956.

Rashin, A. G., *Formirovanie rabochego klassa Rossii. Istoriko-ekonomicheskie ocherki*, Moscow, 1958.

Reichman, H., *Railwaymen and Revolution. Russia, 1905*, Berkeley, California, 1987.

Rieber, A. J., *Merchants and Entrepreneurs in Imperial Russia*, Chapel Hill, N. Carolina, 1982.

Rosmer, A., *Le Mouvement Ouvrier pendant la Guerre. De l'Union Sacrée à Zimmerwald*, Paris, 1936.

Rowney, D. K., 'Higher civil servants in the Russian Ministry of Internal Affairs: some demographic and career characteristics', *Slavic Review*, vol. 31, no. 1 (March 1972), pp. 101–10.

Rozanov, M. D., *Obukhovtsy*, Leningrad, 1965.

Rozenfel'd, Ia. S. and Klimenko, K. I., *Istoriia mashinostroeniia SSSR*, Moscow, 1961.

Schleifman, N., *Undercover Agents in the Russian Revolutionary Movement. The SR Party, 1902–14*, London, 1988.

Semanov, S. N., 'Sostav i polozhenie rabochikh Petrograda po dannym gorodskikh peripisei', in *Rabochii klass i rabochee dvizhenie v Rossii, 1861–1917*, ed. L. M. Ivanov, Moscow, 1966, pp. 394–403.

Semanov, S. N., *Peterburgskie rabochie nakanune pervoi russkoi revoliutsii*, Moscow, 1966.

Senn, A. E., 'The myth of German money during the First World War', *Soviet Studies*, vol. 28 (January 1976), pp. 83–90.

Service, R., *Lenin: A Political Life. Volume I. The Strengths of Contradiction*, London, 1985.

Shalaginova, L. M. 'Esery-internatsionalisty v gody pervoi mirovoi voiny', in *Pervaia mirovaia voina, 1914–1918*, ed. A. L. Sidorov, Moscow, 1968, pp. 323–34.

Shatsillo, K. F., 'Iz istorii ekonomicheskoi praktiki tsarskogo pravitel'stva v gody pervoi mirovoi voiny (o prichinakh sekvestra voenno-promyshlennykh predpriiatii)', in *Ob osobennostiakh imperializma v Rossii*, Moscow, 1963, pp. 215–33.

Shatsillo, K. F., *Russkii imperializm i razvitie flota nakanune pervoi mirovoi voiny (1906–1911gg.)*, Moscow, 1968.

Shuster, U. A., *Peterburgskie rabochie v 1905–1907gg.*, Leningrad, 1976.

Sidorov, A. L., *Istoricheskie predposylki velikoi oktiabr'skoi sotsialisticheskoi revoliutsii*, Moscow, 1970.

Sidorov, A. L., *Ekonomicheskoe polozhenie Rossii v gody pervoi mirovoi voiny*, Moscow, 1973.

Siegelbaum, L. H., *The Politics of Industrial Mobilization in Russia, 1914–1917. A Study of the War-Industries Committees*, London, 1983.

Slokazov, G. I., 'Sozdanie Petrogradskogo soveta', *Istoriia SSSR*, no. 5 (1964), pp. 103–11.

Smith, S. A., 'Craft consciousness, class consciousness: Petrograd 1917', *History Workshop*, vol. 11 (1981), pp. 86–123.

Smith, S. A., *Red Petrograd. Revolution in the Factories, 1917–1918*, Cambridge, 1983.

Somov, S. A., 'O "maiskom" osobom soveshchanii', *Istoriia SSSR*, vol. 3 (1973), pp. 112–23.

Steffens, T., *Die Arbeiter von Petersburg 1907 bis 1917. Soziale Lage, Organisation und Spontaner Protest zwischen zwei Revolutionen*, Freiburg, 1985.

Stepanov, Z. V., *Rabochie Petrograda v period podgotovki i provedeniia oktiabr'-*

skogo vooruzhennogo vosstaniia, Moscow, 1965.

Stites, R., 'Prostitute and society in pre-revolutionary Russia', *Jahrbücher für Geschichte Osteuropas*, vol. 31, part 3 (1983), pp. 348–64.

Stone, N., *The Eastern Front, 1914–1917*, London, 1975.

Strumilin, S. G., *Statistiko-ekonomicheskie ocherki*, Moscow, 1957.

Surh, G. D., *1905 in St Petersburg: Labor, Society and Revolution*, Stanford, California, 1989.

Swain, G., *Russian Social Democracy and the Legal Labour Movement, 1906–1914*, London, 1983.

Thurston, R. W., *Liberal City, Conservative State. Moscow and Russia's Urban Crisis, 1906–1914*, New York, 1987.

Tilly, C. and Shorter, E., *Strikes in France, 1830–1968*, Cambridge, 1974.

Tiutiukin, S. V., *Voina, mir, revoliutsiia. Ideinaia bor'ba v rabochem dvizhenii Rossii, 1914–1917gg.*, Moscow, 1972.

Tokarev, Iu. S., *Petrogradskii sovet rabochikh deputatov v marte–aprele 1917g.*, Leningrad, 1976.

Trotsky, L., *The History of the Russian Revolution. Volume I*, London, 1967.

Voitinskii, I., 'Boikotizm, otzovizm, ul'timatizm', *Proletarskaia revoliutsiia*, vols. 91–2 (1929), pp. 323–66.

Voitinskii, I., 'O gruppe "vpered" (1909–1917)', *Proletarskaia revoliutsiia*, vol. 95 (1929), pp. 59–119.

Volodarskaia, A. M., 'Poroninskoe soveshchanie TsK RSDRP s partiinymi rabotnikami v 1913g.', *Istoricheskie zapiski*, vol. 59 (1957), pp. 125–80.

Volodarskaia, A. M., 'Podgotovka bol'shevikami s"ezda RSDRP v 1914g.', in *Bol'shevistskaia pechat' i rabochii klass Rossii v gody revoliutsion-nogo pod"ema, 1910–1914*, Moscow, 1965, pp. 176–91.

Voronkova, S. V., *Materialy osobogo soveshchaniia po oborone gosudarstva. Istochnikovedchesko issledovanie*, Moscow, 1975.

White, J. D., 'The Sormovo–Nikolaev Zemlyachestvo in the February revolution', *Soviet Studies*, vol. 31 (October 1979), pp. 475–504.

White, J. D., 'Early Soviet historical interpretations of the Russian revolution 1918–1924', *Soviet Studies*, vol. 37 (July 1985), pp. 330–52.

Wildman, A. K., *The End of the Russian Imperial Army. The Old Army and the Soldiers' Revolt (March–April 1917)*, Princeton, New Jersey, 1980.

Williams, R. C., *The Other Bolsheviks. Lenin and His Critics, 1904–1914*, Bloomington, Indiana, 1986.

Zaichikov, G. I., *Dumskaia taktika bol'shevikov (1905–1917gg.)*, Moscow, 1975.

Zaichikov, G. I., *Bor'ba rabochikh deputatov gosudarstvennoi dumy protiv tsarizma v 1907–1914gg.*, Moscow, 1981.

Zelnick, R. E., *Labor and Society in Tsarist Russia. The Factory Workers of St Petersburg, 1855–1870*, Stanford, California, 1971.

Zeman, Z. A. B. and Scharlau, W. B., *The Merchant of Revolution. The Life of A. I. Helphand (Parvus), 1867–1924*, London, 1965.

Zinevich, D., 'Voennaia organizatsiia pri PK RSDRP(B) v 1914–1916gg.', *Krasnaia letopis'*, no. 61 (1934), pp. 96–111.

DOCTORAL DISSERTATIONS

Desjeans, M. F. 'The common experience of the Russian working class: the case of St Petersburg, 1892–1904', Duke, Ph.D., 1978.

Devlin, R. J., 'Petrograd workers and workers' factory committees in 1917', New York, Ph.D., 1976.

Galili y Garcia, Z., 'The Menshevik Revolutionary Defencists and the workers in the revolution of 1917', Columbia, Ph.D., 1980.

Gattrell, P., 'Russian heavy industry and state defence, 1908–1918: pre-war expansion and wartime mobilisation', Cambridge, Ph.D., 1979.

Goldberg, C. A., 'The Association of Trade and Industry, 1906–1917: the successes and failures of Russia's organized businessmen', Michigan, Ph.D., 1974.

Gooderham, P., 'The anarchist movement in Russia, 1905–1917', Bristol, Ph.D., 1981.

Hogan, H., 'Labour and management in conflict: the St Petersburg metalworking industry, 1900–1914', Michigan, Ph.D., 1981.

King, V. A. P., 'The emergence of the St Petersburg industrialist community, 1870 to 1905. The origins and early years of the St Petersburg Society of Manufacturers', Berkeley, Ph.D., 1982.

McKean, R. B., 'Russia on the eve of the Great War. Revolution or evolution?', East Anglia, Ph.D., 1971.

Melancon, M. S., 'The Socialist Revolutionaries from 1901 to February 1917: a party of the workers, peasants and soldiers', Indiana, Ph.D., 1984.

Neuberger, J., 'Crime and culture: hooliganism in St Petersburg, 1900–1914', Stanford, Ph.D., 1985.

Palat, M. K., 'Labour legislation and reform in Russia, 1905–1914', Oxford, Ph.D. 1973.

Rice, C., 'The Socialist Revolutionary Party and the urban working class in Russia, 1902–1914', Birmingham, Ph.D., 1984.

West, J. L., 'The Moscow Progressists: Russian industrialists in liberal politics, 1905–1914', Princeton, Ph.D., 1975.

INDEX

Unless otherwise stated all references are to St Petersburg/Petrograd.